AMERICA'S HISTORY

Since 1865

R. JACKSON WILSON
Smith College
EDITOR

MICHAEL P. CONZEN
University of Chicago
ADVISORY EDITOR FOR CARTOGRAPHY

AMERICA'S HISTORY

Since 1865

JAMES A. HENRETTA
University of Maryland

W. ELLIOT BROWNLEE
University of California, Santa Barbara

DAVID BRODY
University of California, Davis

SUSAN WARE
New York University

THE DORSEY PRESS
Chicago, Illinois 60604

Printing press featured with New Technology essays,
courtesy Les Feller, Printers Row Printing Museum, Chicago

Cartography by Mapping Specialists, Ltd.

Photo research by Carol Parden

ISBN 0-256-03545-8 (pbk.: v. 1)

ISBN 0-256-03547-4 (pbk.: v. 2)

Library of Congress Catalog Card No. 86–71297

Printed in the United States of America

2 3 4 5 6 7 8 9 0 KR 4 3 2 1 0 9 8 7

FOR OUR FAMILIES

PREFACE

History—the way people think about their society's past—comes in many sizes and shapes. It has been carved in hieroglyphs in Egyptian tombs and temples. It has been told in the chants and legends of countless tribal societies. It has been tucked away in meticulous dynastic diaries kept by Chinese court scholars. It has been cynically revised by prudent kings and careless politicians, beautifully written by blind Greek poets and insightful Hebrew scribes.

But however it has been told, history has usually been about the deeds of the great and powerful. The main actors in the story have been gods and prophets, kings and princes, rulers and presidents. Occasionally, something else might intrude, like a flood, earthquake, or famine. Sometimes even the "people" appeared—usually as an invading "horde," or some sort of unruly "mass" at a moment of riot or revolution. But traditional history has treated such natural and human eruptions as temporary distractions from the main stories of wars and marriages, struggles and follies of great men—and, rarely, great women.

In our own time some of this has changed. No notion has more currency in the twentieth-century world than "democracy." No term carries more weight than "the people." In such a world it is inevitable that historians should look a little away from the thrones and offices of the mighty, and pay some attention to "ordinary" people. From the time of the French and American revolutions, scholars in Europe and America began to talk about a new history, one that would be about "simple" men and women. They also began to think of history not as the outcome of the actions of powerful individuals, but as the result of "forces." These social and economic forces were what made history move. Princes and prime ministers were merely swept along in the stream, under the vain illusion that they could steer the boat or even guide the current itself.

The democratic project of writing history about "the people" occurred wherever the idea—if not the fact—of popular government took root. But for a long time the results were disappointing. In most societies, the documentary evidence had been produced and preserved by the rich and the powerful, and most working historians remained tied to those documents. The discussion of forces usually remained abstract or did not really deliver what it promised: an improved understanding of the daily lives of ordinary men and women.

But historians are nothing if not stubborn. And the twentieth century has seen some real progress. Here and there, rich studies began to be produced on this English village or that French town. "Schools" of historians formed, with the definite and committed purpose of doing what came to be called "social history." Scholarly journals were founded. New kinds of evidence were brought into play. Historians began to look into odd places for radically new kinds of "documentation." They studied the records of the Vienna boys' choir, going back centuries, to find out when boys were moved from soprano to tenor, as a way of getting at an obscure but crucial question: how had the age of puberty changed during centuries of time? They compared military muster rolls to find how men's heights changed over time, and were able to infer the impact of urbanization and city work on the health of white laborers. Slave manifests yielded similar insights on the health and living conditions of black slaves. Slowly, but with a growing measure of sureness, the possibility of a genuine social history became real.

In the United States, this kind of change in the discipline of history reached a climax of sorts beginning in the 1960s. A generation of scholars set out to perfect what they called the "new social history." With energy, dedication, and often real brilliance, they tried to reconstruct the lives of the poor, the dispossessed, and the oppressed. They asked questions not about presidents but about shoemakers and butchers. They turned their attention from exclusively male affairs like treaties and wars to the experiences of women and children. They painstakingly tried to find out what slave families were like. They looked away from the literature of "high" culture—from the supposedly great writings of novelists and poets—to folk tales. The stories of "Br'er Rabbit" gained a significance equal to the novels of Henry James or the writings of Thomas Jefferson. Finding out the age at which most women had their first child became as significant as trying to explain a decision of President Andrew Jackson.

And so, in the past quarter of a century, the ways historians do their work have been deeply changed. The change was partly just a continuation of the democratic project that had been under way in the western world for two centuries. But it was hurried along by two other things. First, the historians themselves were different. More and more they were female or they came from families that were either poor or ethnically outside the cultural mainstream that had produced most of the scholars in American universities before World War II. They were interested in those aspects of the American past that had produced their own and their families' lives. Second, the ways many of them thought about history were shaped by the civil rights movement, the effort to stop the war in Vietnam, and the revival of feminism. They learned to regard the political state with greater skepticism. And when they did their work as historians, they turned their search for the real meanings of history away from politics and the state toward things that seemed to them more illuminating and more concrete.

These changes in the practice of history were profound and—we think—splendid. The question we have pondered most is how to take advantage of a generation's worth of such work in an introductory textbook. Some historians have decided to continue to produce textbooks that still focus mainly on presidents, politics, elections, and wars—the traditional subject matter that the "new" social history tried to displace. Social history could wait, they reasoned, until the student took some more "advanced" course. Other textbooks have sought to inject social history into their books, paring down on the space allotted to traditional political subjects. A few historians have even tried to write introductory texts in which political history is largely dismissed and simply replaced by new material on family, work, childhood, and the like.

It has seemed to us—and this is the conclusion that has shaped our work on *America's History* for several years—that all these solutions were wrongheaded. Continuing to present American history to beginning students as though the important changes in the ways historians work had not happened is just as bad as giving engineering or physics students a textbook that ignores three decades of new scientific and technical discoveries. On the other hand, an introductory text solely concerned with social history would leave out central parts of our nation's history. The existence of the state, the story of political parties, and the effects of presidential action or Supreme Court judgments are just as real as and perhaps more important than marriage customs or childrearing practices.

So we decided to look for ways to combine the new social history and the more traditional focus on politics. But this decision was much easier to make than it was to carry out. We hoped to find some guidance in what we thought might be the best of the new textbooks produced in recent years. But what we found in them was mainly an attempt to *insert* social history into an old framework. The traditional ways of dealing with political history were all still in place, unchanged. The social history had been pinned on, like the tail on the donkey in the old children's game. A chapter on the 1890s—mainly about the election of 1896 and the Spanish-American War of 1898—might include a biographical sketch of a coal-miner, say, or a farm wife, but the individual's life remained outside the major events. The effect, in general, was of two parallel histories—one social, the other political—connected to each other only by the accidental fact that they happened at the same time.

What we have attempted, in contrast, is to put social and political history together, and in ways that use each to make better sense of the other. We realized that the history of American life could be understood best if we could lay out the fundamental conditions that controlled *both* the social lives of ordinary people *and* the practice of politics. This meant moving beyond conventional ways of organizing the story around political events that historians like to think of as "turning points" or "watersheds." Social change might have a pace and rhythm of its own. And understanding this pace and rhythm might even enable us to see political changes in a new light.

We searched for a way of understanding American history as a sequence of long phases of development. We finally decided on a unique chronological division of American history into three periods, each with its own defining characteristics. We have called these periods, first, Preindustrial America, running from the beginning of the sixteenth century down into the second or third decade of the nineteenth century; second, Industrializing America, lasting about a century, from the 1820s to the 1920s; and, third, State and Society, running from about 1920 to the present. Each of these periods had its own logic and its own special kinds of human relationships. Each period produced its own distinctive social *and* political history.

In fact, we realized as we worked that the very distinction between social and political history was a bit of an illusion. Every human action, no matter how trivial or how grandiose, has dimensions that have to be recognized as political and social. Political choices always expressed fundamentally *social* choices, shaped by human relationships like family, village, ethnicity, or class. On the other hand, every human experience—like marriage or employment—is also *political*. Every social action assumes that there are certain kinds of legitimate power, and is part of the same web of history that shapes "political" concepts like the idea of kingship, or election, or legislation.

In the end, we reminded ourselves that there is only *history*. Historians may use categories like economic history or diplomatic history as convenient ways of saying what kind of work they do. But such distinctions are only the devices of scholars, not the reality of human experience. And so we decided to drop the subtitle we had chosen earlier: "The Political and Social History of the United States." We believe we have found ways to fuse the best work of political and social historians into one understandable story. *America's History* is the result of our own effort to reach a coherent understanding of the nation's past, an understanding that speaks to us of both social and political facts: farm wives as well as presidents, social customs as well as acts of Congress, the ways people eat and keep warm as well as the ways they make wars or found governments.

Features

Our text contains a variety of special features that highlight and amplify upon key points in each period:

- Over 110 detailed maps in full color provide geographical context for events in the text. These maps illustrate the nation's history in both conventional and unusual ways, showing major territorial conflicts and military campaigns, the changing shapes and political importance of the states, as well as changes in ethnic and religious distribution, cultural patterns, industrial concentration, the shift from rural to urban life, and much more. Explanatory captions tell the story of each map and link it to the text.

- Each chapter includes a Time Line that graphically summarizes the key events in the chapter, giving students a quick reference for review.

- Scores of primary documents, averaging two per chapter, give students a rich and immediate sense of the past.

- Within each period, essays on New Technology describe revolutionary changes in technology that were central to the economic and cultural life of that period.

- Six photo essays explore the visual worlds and cultural milieu of each major period.

- Over 300 photographs in color and black and white provide visual documents of each chapter's main actors and events, as well as showing contemporary life and culture. Like the maps, all photographs have extensive informative captions that tell students the significance of each illustration.

- Forty-five graphs and tables present data that support arguments in the text, covering topics that range from demographic changes to changes in the national economy.

- Each chapter concludes with an extensive annotated bibliography to guide students' further reading and research.

Finally, our text comes with an *Instructors Manual*, student *Study Guide*, and a companion reader entitled *The Course of United States History*. This reader contains outstanding scholarly articles and innovative essays that teach students how to read primary documents.

Acknowledgments

We wish to thank R. Jackson Wilson for conceiving this project and for sharing with us the trials and thrills of bringing it to fruition. His close attention to the manuscript through its many drafts and his collegial support have meant a great deal to us.

We also thank the editors and the production staff of The Dorsey Press for their invaluable assistance; James Shacter and John Sturman for their masterful copy editing; and the following scholars, who read the manuscript with great care, saved us from many mistakes, and helped us develop a coherent and compelling portrait of the history of the American people: John K. Alexander, University of Cincinnati; Genevieve Berkhofer, University of Michigan; John D. Born, Jr., Wichita State University; Anne Boylan, University of Delaware; Jerry M. Cooper, University of Missouri–St. Louis; Alan Dawley, Trenton State; Robert R. Dykstra, SUNY Albany; Thomas R. Frazier, Baruch College, The City University of New York; James Gilbert, University of Maryland; Maurine Greenwald, University of Pittsburgh; Carl V. Harris, University of California, Santa Barbara; Mary Kelley, Dartmouth College; Bruce Laurie, University of Massachusetts; Russell Menard, University of Minnesota; John Murrin, Princeton University; Jerome Mushkat, University of Akron; David Nasaw, The College of Staten Island; John Schneider, University of Nebraska, Lincoln; Herb Shapiro, University of Cincinnati; James E. Sherwood; Kathryn Kish Sklar, University of California, Los Angeles; Judith E. Smith, Boston College; Emory Thomas, University of Georgia; Robert Weir, University of South Carolina; William Bruce Wheeler, University of Tennessee, Knoxville; John Scott Wilson, University of South Carolina; Nancy Woloch; and Virginia Yans, Rutgers University.

We as authors are listed on the title page in the order in which we have contributed to the text. James A. Henretta wrote chapters 1–10, W. Elliot Brownlee chapters 11–16, David Brody chapters 17–21, and Susan Ware chapters 22–31. Each of us, of course, read and criticized the chapters of the others, and we accept joint responsibility for the book as a whole.

JAMES A. HENRETTA
W. ELLIOT BROWNLEE
DAVID BRODY
SUSAN WARE

CONTENTS

18 The City 549

Urbanization   549

Upper Class/Middle Class   560

City People   568

19 Rural America 588

The Great West   588

The South   601

The Agricultural Interest   608

20 The Public World of Late Nineteenth-Century America 619

Domestic Politics   619

An Emerging World Power   634

21 The Progressive Era 645

Reform Impulses   646

Progressivism and National Politics   660

APPENDIXES   *I*

ILLUSTRATIONS

MAPS

FIGURES

TABLES

AMERICA'S HISTORY

Since 1865

PART TWO

Industrializing

1865-1920

In 1820, America was still a predominantly agricultural society. A century later it had become the world's most powerful industrial economy. This profound transformation in American life began slowly in the northeastern states and then, after the Civil War, quickly accelerated and spread across the entire nation. The impact of the Industrial Revolution was not random; rather, it acted in quite distinctive ways to bring about social and political change. Six *structural* features of the industrializing society shaped the character of American life over this period.

First, technological and organizational innovations stood at the heart of the Industrial Revolution. Water- and steam-powered machines and the

AMERICA

new factory system boosted production, while canals and railroads created a vast national market. Industry produced an ever-increasing share of the country's wealth—from a negligible amount in 1820, to a third in 1869, to more than a half in 1899. The nature of business enterprise also changed, as small companies and independent artisans gave way to nationally organized, bureaucratically run corporations.

Second, industrialization produced an ambitious and increasingly powerful business class that sought to assert its leadership over American society. The business class enlisted religion in its efforts, sometimes to bring about reform, and at other times to justify the new economic order. Business leaders also shaped American politics, especially through their dominating role in the antebellum Whig Party and in the Republican Party from the Civil War onward.

Third, rival social groups rose to challenge the power of the business class and its economic and cultural policies. Many workers proposed the reform of industrial society, first in the workingmen's parties of the 1830s, then in the Knights of Labor, and after 1900 in the Socialist party. They also organized collectively through trade unions, under the leadership of the American Federation of Labor. Farmers turned to political action to protect their interests. They supported Andrew Jackson's Democratic party before the Civil War and, during the 1890s, turned briefly to the Populist party to advance their political demands. Throughout this cen-

tury of social transformation, many immigrants—first from Ireland and Germany and later from south and central Europe—espoused social and religious values different from those of the business class.

Fourth, native-born Americans of middle-class status became increasingly powerful. Many shared the values of business leaders and, in effect, joined the business class. Some middle-class Americans joined an abolitionist movement that attacked southern slavery as a sinful expression of arbitrary personal power, and that eventually achieved its overthrow. Middle-class men and women also expressed reservations about the new industrial order. They formed a variety of religious and reform movements that sought to introduce social order into an economic world where change seemed the only rule. Middle-class reformers likewise played an important role in the Progressive movement between 1900 and 1920. The Progressives secured the passage of state and federal legislation that curbed the arbitrary power of the large corporations that now dominated American economic life.

Fifth, industrialization created sharp sectional divisions in American society and politics. During the 1840s and 1850s, both the industrializing North and the slave-holding South tried to impose their distinctive labor systems on the West, a struggle that led eventually to the Civil War. Then, during the 1880s and 1890s, western and southern farmers protested strongly against eastern railroads and market systems that adversely affected their agricultural economy. Sectional interests likewise played a role in foreign policy, most notably in the Mexican War, and in persistent disputes over protectionism and trade policy.

Sixth, and finally, industrialization spurred the creation of an urban society divided by class. Urban growth occurred initially in textile towns and commercial centers and, after the Civil War, in large industrial cities such as Cleveland, Pittsburgh, and Birmingham. Urban neighborhoods reflected the emerging class structure, with the poor concentrated in the factory districts, the middle class in the suburbs, and the rich in exclusive urban neighborhoods or on country estates.

The industrialization of the United States created a new social order and a set of economic, political, and cultural issues that were fundamentally different from those of the preindustrial era. Between 1820 and 1920, American people lived in a distinct universe of values, thought, and action, one from which our own modern age of the twentieth century springs.

16

THE UNION RECONSTRUCTED

*W*hen the armies of the Confederacy surrendered in 1865, the United States still remained deeply divided. A flourishing, triumphant North confronted a beaten, shattered South. While the people in the North had managed to maintain a high degree of unity during the war, the South was now divided between bitter, fearful whites and exultant, hopeful former slaves.

Abraham Lincoln had spoken in his second inaugural address of the need to "bind up the nation's wounds." The necessity of rebuilding the Union was clear, but many questions remained unanswered. Who would control the rebuilding? How long should the rebuilding last? How far should it go?

Three basic viewpoints emerged in answer to these questions. Some people defined the task of rebuilding as *restoration*. They wanted to restore the southern states to what Lincoln called "their proper practical relation with the Union." This would mean getting loyal, pro-Union state governments into place, restoring southern states' representatives in Congress, and freely exercising federal power in the South.

Other people felt that some degree of *reconstruction* of the South was necessary and that the Union should be very different from what it had been before 1860. For those who held this view, the end of slavery should be followed by steps to ensure a measure of political and even economic equality for the ex-slaves. Steps should also be taken to make the Republican party as strong a political force in the South as it was in the North.

Finally, many white southerners and some northern sympathizers maintained that the problem was one of *redemption.* The Union's total victory had temporarily deprived the dominant majority in the South of control over its own economic, social, and political systems. The Union would be rebuilt only when southerners had regained the same degree of power over their own affairs that the citizens of Indiana or Massachusetts had.

The era of Reconstruction—which historians conventionally date as the years from 1865 to 1877—was shaped by continual, often confused struggles among the men and women who held one version or another of these views. In these struggles, every kind of tactic was brought to bear—the assassination of one president and the impeachment of another; three amendments to the Constitution and a welter of new legislation; nighttime terrorism by robed whites in the South; patient work and resistance by southern blacks; and compromise, maneuvering, and deals by politicians on all sides.

The outcome was as mixed and as unclear as the struggles themselves; no single position emerged triumphant. By 1877, political leaders on all sides were ready to say that what Lincoln had called "the work" was complete. But for many Americans, especially the freed slaves, the work clearly had not been completed, but merely abandoned and left to the slow, frustrating, and imperfect processes of history. It became apparent to many Republicans that they had been much less successful in reconstructing the South than they had been at quickening and consolidating the successes of industrial capitalism in the nation as a whole.

Presidential Restoration

At first, the initiative for rebuilding the Union rested with the president. Lincoln and his successor, Andrew Johnson, both believed that the southern states had never legally left the Union, that Reconstruction was simply a process of restoring governments loyal to the Union, and that this process could take place quickly, largely under presidential direction.

Lincoln saw much evidence that a swift reconciliation between North and South could be achieved. Former Confederate soldiers accepted defeat. After Lee's surrender, his Virginia troops heeded his advice to "go home . . . and help build up the shattered fortunes of our old state." Most ex-slaves also hoped to live in peace with whites. They pleaded to acquire the land they tilled, but they did not plot violence against their former masters. Northerners had accomplished their original war aims—the defeat of southern resistance and the crushing of the "Slave Power"—and had even made slavery unconstitutional. Some northerners insisted on making the South pay for the 360,000 Union deaths. But the typical Union soldier viewed the conflict more compassionately, believing that 260,000 Confederate dead, plus surrender, were payment enough. After Lee surrendered at Appomattox, Grant's soldiers willingly shared their ample rations with hungry Confederates.

Lincoln underestimated Republican demands for a thorough Reconstruction of the South. Had he survived, Lincoln might have demanded more of the ex-Confederates. But Andrew Johnson agreed with the racial attitudes and policies of the defeated Confederacy and did not want to advance the fortunes of the Republican party. He refused to adjust his policies to take account

SMOLDERING RESISTANCE IN THE SOUTH
This engraving, subtitled "Verdict, 'Hang the D—— Yankee and Nigger,' " appeared in *Harper's Weekly* in March 1867. It may have led readers to recall the killing of the Republicans who attended the black suffrage convention in New Orleans the previous summer. We have no reliable estimates of the total number of Republicans, white and black, killed in retaliation by ex-Confederates during Reconstruction. (Library of Congress)

of the opinions of Republican leaders in Congress, and his Reconstruction policy was distinctly sympathetic to the ex-Confederates.

Restoration Under Lincoln

Reconstruction actually began during the war. Lincoln sought to subvert the southern war effort by employing a policy of moderation and reconciliation in the large portions of the South occupied by federal troops. He ignored the imprecise constitutional status of the southern states and relied on his military powers as commander-in-chief to justify his actions.

In December 1863, Lincoln offered a general amnesty to all Confederates except the high-ranking officials of the Confederacy. His simple plan called for Confederates to take an oath (1) pledging their future loyalty to the Union and (2) accepting the Union's wartime acts and proclamations concerning slavery. When just 10 percent of the people who had voted in 1860 had taken the loyalty oath, they could reconstitute their state's government.

Lincoln aimed this plan at former southern Whigs, many of whom he knew well. He hoped they would step forward, declare allegiance to the Union, and take charge of southern state governments. Lincoln's constitutional assumption was simple; states could not legally secede and were therefore still in the Union. (In 1869, in *Texas v. White*, the Supreme Court accepted Lincoln's interpretation, ruling that secession was impossible under the Constitution.)

Lincoln's plan was opposed by members of his own party in Congress, including even his fellow moderates. The most strenuous criticism came from a group of radical Republicans, most of whom had abolitionist backgrounds. Led by Senator Charles Sumner of Massachusetts and Congressman Thaddeus Stevens of Pennsylvania, these radical Republicans wanted the federal government to go beyond abolishing slavery and, in Stevens's words, to "revolutionize Southern institutions, habits, and manners." Stevens declared that "The foundations of their institutions . . . must be broken up and relaid, or all our blood and treasure will have been spent in vain." In particular, the radical Republicans wanted the federal government to ensure that blacks would participate in southern society with full equality.

All radicals agreed full equality required a federal guarantee of voting rights for ex-slaves. Without the vote, blacks could not be genuinely independent from their former masters. Some radicals, however, believed that the vote alone was not enough. Thaddeus Stevens, for example, believed that the redistribution of land to the ex-slaves was the solution.

The radicals assumed that the ex-slaves had the capacity to become full citizens if only they were given political participation and economic independence. Most Republicans had a more pessimistic view of what could be accomplished for or by the freed blacks. They believed that blacks were simply not competent to exercise the franchise, much less to take their place as economically independent farmers. The moderates also worried that any effort to make drastic changes in the economic and social relationships between the races would only provoke resistance and violence from southern whites.

Yet the moderates agreed with the radicals that Lincoln's program of restoration was too lenient. In its place, moderates and radicals joined in advancing three propositions. First, the leaders of the Confederacy should not be allowed to return to power in the South. Second, the abolition of slavery should be guaranteed by an amendment to the Constitution, and the former Confederate states should be forced to accept this amendment before they could return to the Union. Third, steps should be taken to establish the Republican party as a major, even dominant, force in southern political life. The moderates and radicals rejected the new governments that Lincoln had established in Louisiana, Arkansas, and Tennessee.

Republicans in Congress set to work on their own theory of Reconstruction. Legally, they argued, the seceded states *had* left the Union and were now the equivalent of conquered provinces. As territories, they were constitutionally subject to congressional rule rather than administration by the executive branch. To translate their theory into practice, Congress passed the Wade-Davis bill in July 1864. This bill prescribed the conditions necessary for former Confederate states to regain membership in the Union. A majority of the state's adult white males would have to swear an oath of allegiance to the Union. Each southern state would have to write a new constitution. These constitutions would have to abolish slavery, disenfranchise Confederate civil and military leaders, and repudiate all state war debts. Finally, to make sure that the new constitutions would be made by the friends of the Union, the Wade-Davis bill required that the constitutions had to be written by men who could swear an oath that they had never carried arms against the Union or aided the Confederacy in any way—a statement that became known as the "ironclad oath."

The Wade-Davis bill went much further than Lincoln's plan, but it did not satisfy most radicals. Like Lincoln's plan, the bill did not propose to establish any federal control over race relations in the South, and it did not guarantee the political participation of blacks in new southern governments. Nevertheless, the basis for a compromise between Lincoln and the congressional Republicans clearly existed. Skillfully, Lincoln kept his options open. He did not openly challenge Congress by vetoing the bill. Instead, he executed a "pocket" veto by not signing it before Congress adjourned. At the same time, he began informal talks with members of Congress clearly aimed at producing a compromise solution when the war finally ended.

Whether Lincoln and his party could have found a unified approach to Reconstruction became one of the great unanswered questions of American history. On April 14, 1865—Good Friday—Lincoln was shot in the head at Ford's Theater in Washington, by a half-crazed actor named John Wilkes Booth. Ironically, Lincoln might have been spared if the war had dragged on longer, for Booth and his associates had originally plotted to kidnap the president to force a negotiated settlement. After Lee's surrender, Booth became desperate for revenge. In the middle of the play, he leapt to Lincoln's box, shot him at close range, stabbed a member of the president's party, and fled the theater. Booth was hunted down and killed by Union troops. Eight people were eventually convicted as accomplices by military courts and four of them were hanged. Abraham Lincoln never regained consciousness. He died on April 15. The Union—and hundreds of thousands of ex-slaves for whom his name had become synonymous with freedom—went into profound mourning. Even Lincoln's critics suddenly conceded his greatness. Millions of Americans waited in silence to watch the train bearing his body back to Illinois for burial.

The presidency now belonged to Andrew Johnson. Even before the last Confederate armies had surrendered in Alabama, a dramatic change in the prospects for Reconstruction had taken place. At one stroke, John Wilkes Booth had accomplished two important things. He sent Lincoln to martyrdom and convinced many northerners that harsher measures against the South were necessary. He also gave the presidency to a Tennessean, a former Democrat, whose plan of restoration was even milder than Lincoln's. Now there would be no compromise between an elected president and his party in Congress. There would be only a deepening contest in the North for control of Reconstruction and an equally deep struggle in the South for control of the economic, social, and political life of the old Confederacy.

Johnson's Plan for Restoration

Andrew Johnson's middle name was Jackson, in honor of the president who had shaped the Democratic party in the 1830s. Johnson had much in common with Andrew Jackson. He had been born poor but had become a man of wealth—including slaves—in Jackson's Tennessee. His political career had led from the Tennessee legislature to the United States Senate. He shared Jackson's commitment to the preservation of the Union. In fact, the Republicans had handed him the vice-presidency in an effort to promote wartime political unity.

Johnson also had some other political attitudes that were closer to Jackson's than to Lincoln's. He opposed the Republican policy of promoting economic development through tariffs or federal subsidies to railroads. He hated what he called the "bloated, corrupt aristocracy" of the Northeast and charged that the Republican economic program reinforced the power of this elite. Johnson also despised blacks. He accepted their legal freedom, but he wanted to maintain white supremacy through the systematic denial of rights to blacks. Johnson's interest in Reconstruction extended no further than punishing the ex-slaveholding elite—another class that he resented. But he did not require revenge on the scale that most Republicans demanded. For Johnson, simply establishing his personal power over the planters was satisfaction enough. Because he opposed the Republican economic and racial plans, Johnson did not want to see the Republican party prevail in either the North or the South.

Despite their differences, Johnson and the Republican Congress could have avoided a deadlock. Northern Democrats and some moderate Republicans were close in their racial attitudes and policies. Most Republicans in Congress favored the moderate approach to Reconstruction outlined by the Wade-Davis bill. Most ex-Confederates, accepting their defeat in total war, were prepared to submit to a somewhat punitive Reconstruction.

But Johnson risked confrontation with Congress when he announced his own lenient plan and proceeded to execute it during the summer of 1865, when Congress was not in session. Johnson was so thoroughly convinced that Reconstruction should be an exclusively executive function that he believed consultation with Congress was unnecessary. In his view, the southern states had retained all their constitutional rights. He insisted on only three conditions—that they revoke ordinances of secession, abolish slavery, and repudiate the debts they had acquired during the rebellion. Johnson's plan offered amnesty and a return of all property, except slaves, to almost all southerners if they took an oath of future allegiance to the Union. He excluded several categories of southerners from his amnesty—high-ranking Confederate officers and civil officials and, revealing his distaste for planter aristocrats, persons with taxable property of more than twenty thousand dollars. (These individuals were invited to petition Johnson personally. He intended to humble them, but then grant most of them pardons.) By December, all of the former Confederate states had functioning governments and were ready to rejoin the Union under Johnson's plan.

Congressional Reconstruction

Most Republicans supported Johnson's program at first, despite his failure to consult with Congress. They hoped to amend his program so that it would achieve the objectives of the Wade-Davis bill. They also hoped that southern governments would respond positively to Johnson's conciliatory attitude and offer the vote to at least those blacks who were literate and owned property—probably no more than 10 percent of adult black men. In fact, Johnson unofficially advised the southern states to undertake limited enfranchisement of blacks.

But the president soon made more political mistakes. He continued to insult Congress and refused to spearhead a Reconstruction policy that would satisfy moderate Republicans. Provoked by Johnson, Congress took control of Reconstruction and in 1866–1867 imposed a more radical program than Republicans had proposed in the Wade-Davis bill.

As a result, Reconstruction was highly erratic. While Johnson's policy of restoration had encouraged the ex-Confederates, congressional Reconstruction punished them. This alternating policy intensified southern resistance to federal power. The peace that seemed so close at hand in 1865 turned out to be long in coming.

Congress Versus Johnson

Johnson's first mistake was a serious blunder in his relations with Congress. In an August 1865 telegram, Johnson told the provisional governor of Mississippi that if he gave the vote to literate blacks, "the radicals, who are wild upon negro franchise, will be completely foiled." When the telegram became public, it not only enraged radical Republicans but embarrassed moderates. To compound Johnson's problem, provisional governments in the South made no effort to enfranchise blacks. Moderate Republicans began to doubt Johnson's leadership on the suffrage issue. More important, they became increasingly sympathetic to the plight of southern blacks.

During the fall of 1865, news reports from the South further undermined the president's leadership. Northerners read of frequent attacks on ex-slaves and Union supporters and of control of southern governments by ex-Confederates. Moreover, southern voters sent to Congress nine prominent individuals who had served in the Confederate Congress, seven officials from Confederate state governments, four generals and four colonels from the Confederate army, and even Alexander Stephens, the vice-president of the Confederacy. Radical Republicans such as Sumner and Stevens began to attack Johnson for his failure to reconstruct the South properly.

Meanwhile, Johnson increasingly viewed himself as the savior of the Democratic party. He believed he could build a coalition of southerners, northern Democrats, and conservative Republicans under the Democratic banner. Democrats in both the North and the South praised Johnson as the leader they needed to restore their party on a national basis. Northern Democrats, who had strong antiblack feelings, wholeheartedly endorsed Johnson's racial policy.

Moderate Republicans watched Johnson with

ANDREW JOHNSON
The president was not an easy man. This photograph of
Andrew Johnson (1808–1875) conveys some of the
personal qualities that contributed so centrally to his
failure to reach agreement with Republicans on a program
of moderate Reconstruction. (Library of Congress)

increasing dismay and agitation. As the president warmed to Democratic applause, he granted more and more pardons to wealthy southerners—to an average of one hundred pardons a day in September. By December, when Congress convened, Republicans had become convinced that they had to do more to protect the rights of the ex-slaves and to establish the Republican party in the South.

The moderate Republicans controlled Congress when it convened in December 1865. They rejected the newly elected southern representatives—some of whom were ex-Confederate officials—until Johnson would agree with Congress on a Reconstruction program. To develop that program, moderates formed a joint House-Senate committee charged to cooperate with the president. When the Joint Committee on Reconstruction conducted hearings on conditions in the former Confederacy, it heard alarming reports from army officers, federal officials, and white and black southerners. The level of violence was rising, and southern legislatures were enacting Black Codes—laws designed to keep blacks in a condition close to slavery. These laws, passed by every state of the former Confederacy, were written to ensure that blacks remained on the land as agricultural laborers, and that they worked there under terms highly favorable to white landowners.

Moderate Republicans drafted two bills to meet these complaints. The first extended the life of the Bureau of Refugees, Freedmen, and Abandoned Lands. Known commonly as the Freedmen's Bureau, this agency had been created in March 1865 to feed and clothe refugees of both races, to rent confiscated land to "loyal refugees and freedmen," and to draft and enforce labor contracts between ex-slaves and planters. The bureau also cooperated with voluntary associations, such as the Freedmen's Aid Societies, which sent missionaries and teachers to the South to establish schools for ex-slaves. The new bill empowered the bureau to establish courts to protect the rights of ex-slaves until the southern states had been restored to the Union. The bill also sought to extend the occupation by ex-slaves of land confiscated from planters by the Union on the Sea Islands, off the coast of South Carolina and Georgia.

Republicans almost unanimously approved the Freedmen's Bureau bill but, in February 1866, Johnson vetoed it. He argued that the bill was unconstitutional because the Constitution did not authorize a "system for the support of indigent persons" and because "there was no Senator or Representatives in Congress from the eleven States which are to be mainly affected by its provisions." The veto enraged moderates. They could not accept Johnson's implication that *any* Reconstruction legislation they passed without southern representation was necessarily unconstitutional. Moderates tried to override the veto but failed, just barely, to collect the two-thirds majority they needed.

Democrats applauded Johnson's firmness. To celebrate, a group of them went to the White House to serenade him. The president emerged to deliver a speech that suggested to many that he was drunk. Johnson went so far as to accuse the radical Republicans of being traitors who were plotting to assassinate him.

Johnson's veto and his unwise address to the Democrats pushed the moderate Republicans close to a complete break with the president. But they still expected his cooperation on their second major piece of legislation, a civil rights bill. This bill defined the citizenship rights of the ex-slaves—such as the rights to own and rent property, to make contracts, and to have access to the courts—and guaranteed that anyone appealing a case involving these rights could take the case to a federal court. Republicans passed it in March 1866, declaring that blacks had the right to enjoy "full and equal benefit of all laws and proceedings for the security of person and property as it is enjoyed by white citizens." Republicans intended the bill to wipe out the Black Codes and thus ensure the eradication of slavery. They did not mean to guarantee that blacks could vote.

Again, however, Johnson vetoed the bill against the advice of his cabinet. He called it unconstitutional and, with the votes of Democratic wards in the large cities in mind, argued that it discriminated against whites by providing citizenship for newly freed slaves while immigrants had to wait five years for the privilege.

Johnson's veto persuaded almost all moderate Republicans that they must take charge of Reconstruction and adopt a completely independent plan. In April, they overrode Johnson's veto and passed the Civil Rights Act of 1866. In July—after amending the Freedmen's Bureau bill to require ex-slaves to buy the confiscated land on the Sea Islands which they occupied—they passed the bill over a second Johnson veto.

The Fourteenth Amendment

At the same time, the Joint Committee on Reconstruction drafted and submitted to Congress its proposal for the Fourteenth Amendment to the Constitution. This amendment went beyond the Civil Rights Act of 1866 by providing blacks a constitutional guarantee of citizenship and encouraging, although not guaranteeing, black suffrage. The resistance of ex-Confederates and President Johnson had persuaded moderates to adopt a more radical position.

Section 1 of the amendment declared that all native-born or naturalized persons—including blacks—were citizens. No state could abridge "the privileges or immunities of citizens of the United States," or deprive "any person of life, liberty, or property, without due process of law," or deny anyone "the equal protection of the laws." The writers of the amendment in-

tended these phrases to be vague. While they did not foresee that "equal protection," for example, might eventually prohibit racial segregation in schools and other public facilities (as the Supreme Court ruled in 1954), they hoped that the scope and force of this amendment would grow over time.

The amendment's key political provision was Section 2, which penalized any state that denied suffrage to a portion of its adult male citizens. The amendment would reduce the state's representation in Congress by the percentage of adult male citizens denied the vote. Republicans hoped this provision would induce southern states to extend the vote to blacks. But the amendment did not force enfranchisement. Radicals criticized this point, arguing that Congress should take steps to guarantee the vote for blacks. Radicals also complained that the amendment would have little effect on northern states that refused to give blacks the vote.

Johnson attacked the Fourteenth Amendment, despite its moderation. Disregarding precedent, he campaigned personally in the 1866 congressional elections to promote candidates who supported his own views on the matter. In August and September, he made a railroad tour from Washington to Chicago and Saint Louis and back, charging that Congress had acted illegally by approving the Fourteenth Amendment without the participation of all the southern states. He declared that southerners were loyal, while the real traitors were the radical Republicans who were stalling restoration of the Union.

Under Johnson's assault, moderate Republicans escalated their attacks on Democrats. They reminded northern voters of vicious race riots over suffrage that had occurred in Memphis and New Orleans during the late spring and early summer of 1866. In New Orleans, a white mob had attacked the delegates to a black suffrage convention and killed forty people, including thirty-seven blacks. In what became known as "waving the bloody shirt," Republicans went so far as to blame the Democrats for the Civil War. Governor Oliver Morton of Indiana described the Democratic party as "a common sewer and loathsome receptacle, into which is emptied every element of treason North and South, every element of inhumanity and barbarism which has dishonored the age."

The 1866 congressional elections brought a

humiliating defeat for the president. The Republicans won a three-to-one majority in Congress and gained control of every northern state, as well as West Virginia, Missouri, and Tennessee. The moderates interpreted the elections as a clear call for Reconstruction, rather than mere restoration, of the South. They finally accepted the radical proposition that the federal government must guarantee black suffrage.

Radical Reconstruction and the Impeachment of Johnson

In the months following the elections of 1866, moderates and radicals together hammered out a more rigorous plan of Reconstruction. By March, Congress had passed, over Johnson's persistent vetoes, the Reconstruction Acts of 1867. These acts divided the South into five military districts and placed each district under a military commander, who had the responsibility for registering voters. The acts ordered the commanders to register all adult black males but allowed them considerable discretion in registering former Confederates. After registering voters, the commander would call on them to elect a convention to write a state constitution that had to include guarantees for black suffrage. Congress would readmit the state to the Union only if its voters ratified the new constitution, if the new constitution proved acceptable to Congress, if the new state legislature approved the Fourteenth Amendment, and if enough states had already ratified the Fourteenth Amendment to make it part of the Constitution.

Some radicals did not believe that even these measures went far enough to guarantee equality for blacks. They advocated distribution of land to ex-slaves, federal support for black schools, and continued disenfranchisement of ex-Confederates. One radical, George W. Julian, a congressman from Indiana, warned that without such measures, "the power of the great landed aristocracy in these regions, if unrestrained by power from without, would inevitably assert itself." Nonetheless, the radicals accepted the new Reconstruction policies as all they could get in 1867.

Republicans also took action to ensure that President Johnson did not thwart Reconstruction by exercising his executive authority. Congress passed the Tenure of Office Act, which required congressional consent for the removal of any government officer whose appointment required congressional approval. Republicans chiefly wanted to protect Secretary of War Stanton, a Lincoln appointee and the only member of Johnson's cabinet to support congressional Reconstruction. As commander of the armed forces in the South, Stanton could do much to prevent Johnson from frustrating congressional Reconstruction. Congress also required the president to issue orders to the army through its general, Ulysses S. Grant, who also supported a more radical Reconstruction. In effect, Congress attempted to reconstruct the presidency as well as the South. A crisis was clearly at hand.

In August 1867, after Congress adjourned, Johnson made his move. He fired Stanton and replaced him with Grant on a temporary basis, hoping Grant would be more cooperative. He next replaced four Republican generals who commanded southern districts, including Philip H. Sheridan, Grant's favorite cavalry general.

Johnson had misjudged Grant. Grant wrote a letter protesting the president's thwarting of Congress and deliberately leaked it to the press. After Congress overruled Stanton's suspension, Grant resigned, allowing Stanton to resume his office. Johnson's public protests against Grant's resignation led Grant to emerge openly as an enemy of the president.

Johnson decided to test, unequivocally, the constitutionality of the power granted to Congress by the Tenure of Office Act. In February 1868, he again dismissed Stanton. Stanton barricaded the door of his office, refusing to admit the replacement whom Johnson had appointed. Republicans in Congress responded by charging the president with criminal misconduct in office. The Constitution gave the House the power to impeach—to charge formally—federal officials for "Treason, Bribery, or other high Crimes and Misdemeanors," and the Senate the power to convict them, with a two-thirds majority needed in each house. But impeachment and conviction were drastic steps; Congress had removed federal judges from office, but never before had it seriously considered removing a president. After a year of political struggle, on February 24, 1868, radicals and moderates in the House joined to impeach the president. A radical-dominated committee was appointed to bring to the Senate charges of "high crimes and misdemeanors" against Johnson; it concentrated on alleged violations of the Tenure of Office Act.

The Senate, acting as a court, failed to convict Johnson. On May 26, after deliberating for eleven weeks, thirty-five senators voted for conviction—one vote short of the two-thirds required. Seven moderate Republicans had broken ranks, voting with twelve Democrats in support of Johnson. These Republicans reached their decision partly because they feared Benjamin Wade, the radical Republican who, as president pro tempore of the Senate, was next in the line of succession. Primarily, they worried about the precedent of Congress deposing a president over an issue of policy. They believed that the Civil War had demonstrated the need for a strong federal government administered by a powerful executive. Without a strong presidency, the moderate Republicans doubted whether the nation could preserve internal unity, advance the Republican economic program, and defend itself against foreign enemies. The Radical Republicans had failed to convict Johnson, but they had defeated him. For the remainder of his term, Johnson let Reconstruction proceed under congressional direction.

In November 1868, the Republicans won a major electoral victory. The impeachment controversy had led Grant, already the North's most popular war hero, to the Republican presidential nomination. He had supported congressional Reconstruction, "waved the bloody shirt," and yet urged peace between the sections. Grant's opponent was Horatio Seymour, a former governor of New York, who almost declined the nomination, certain that Grant would win. In the face of rising violence in the South, Seymour and the Democrats received little support for their claim that the government should let southern state governments reorganize on their own. Grant won about the same share of the northern vote (55 percent) as Lincoln had in 1864, collected a majority of the national popular vote, and received 214 of 294 electoral votes, including those of six of the eight reconstructed states. The Republicans kept majorities of at least two-thirds in both houses of Congress.

With this strong mandate, Republicans added the last major piece of Reconstruction legislation. They drafted the Fifteenth Amendment, which forbade states to deny their citizens the right to vote on the grounds of race, color, or previous condition of servitude. Once again, some radicals would have preferred more. They had wanted the amendment to go farther and to prevent state governments from using property or literacy qualifications that state governments might use to disenfranchise blacks. But moderates had wished to keep these tactics available to northern and western states that wanted to deny immigrants the vote and therefore opposed a more rigorous proposal. Still, the Fifteenth Amendment was much tougher in protecting black suffrage than the Fourteenth. Passing the amendment in February 1869, Congress required the unreconstructed states of Virginia, Mississippi, Texas, and Georgia to ratify it before they could be readmitted to the Union.

The Issue of Women's Suffrage

The constitutional amendments enacted during Reconstruction could have dramatically changed the legal status of women. The Fourteenth Amendment, however, was even more conservative on suffrage for women than on suffrage for blacks. In referring to "adult male citizens," the amendment wrote the term "male" into the Constitution for the first time and, in effect, sanctioned the denial of the vote to women. Abolitionists such as Elizabeth Cady Stanton and Susan B. Anthony were deeply disappointed. They had led the drive to collect almost four hundred thousand signatures in support of the Thirteenth Amendment, which abolished slavery, and had hoped that abolitionists would unite behind universal suffrage. Many male abolitionists supported women's suffrage, but they did not think the public was ready for the idea. As Wendell Phillips told feminists, "One question at a time. This hour belongs to the Negro." Feminists did not oppose the ratification of the Fourteenth Amendment, but, through the American Equal Rights Association—which they formed in 1866, at their first women's rights convention since the Civil War—they sought to win support for their position among male abolitionists and launched a universal suffrage campaign at the state level.

The Fifteenth Amendment, like the Fourteenth, disappointed those who sought the vote for women; it made no reference to sex and thus allowed states to deny suffrage to women. Stanton and Anthony had already concluded that feminists should develop a political position independent of any political party. The two women broke with Republican abolitionists and refused to support the amendment unless it was accompanied by a sixteenth amendment enfranchising women. Stanton argued that ratification of the Fifteenth Amendment alone would create an "aristocracy of sex." She declared, "All manhood will vote not because of intelligence, patriotism, property or white skin, but because it is male, not female." In promoting a sixteenth amendment, she made a special appeal to women of the business class:

> American women of wealth, education, virtue and refinement, if you do not wish the lower orders of Chinese, Africans, Germans and Irish, with the low ideas of womanhood to make laws for you and your daughters . . . to dictate not only the civil, but moral codes by which you shall be governed, awake to the danger of your present position and demand that woman, too, shall be represented in the government!

Not all advocates of women's suffrage agreed with the tactics of Stanton and Anthony. Lucy Stone, Frederick Douglass, and other former abolitionists formed the New England Woman Suffrage Association in 1868 to maintain an alliance with Republicans and to support the Fifteenth Amendment. They believed that this was the best way to enlist the support of the Republican party for women's suffrage after Reconstruction issues had been settled.

These two different strategies came to characterize long-standing differences within the women's rights movement. In 1869, the American Equal Rights Association split into two organizations as a result of the debate over the Fifteenth Amendment. One group was the National Woman Suffrage Association, which elected Stanton as its first president. It relied on local suffrage societies that Stanton and Anthony's efforts had triggered in communities around the country. In response, the women of the New England Woman Suffrage Association, including Lucy Stone, formed the American Woman Suffrage Association. They elected Henry Ward Beecher, a prominent Brooklyn minister, as president and cultivated strong ties with Republicans and male abolitionists. For twenty-one years, these two national organizations competed for the leadership of the women's movement. The American Association tended to focus on suffrage, while the National Association developed a more comprehensive

A CYNIC'S VIEW OF WOMEN'S SUFFRAGE
This antifeminist Currier and Ives lithograph appeared in 1868 and was called "The Age of iron, or Man as He Expects to Be"—after his wife's emancipation. As the quote above by Elizabeth Cady Stanton indicates, the feminists were willing to invoke traditional morality in response to their opponents. (Museum of the City of New York. Harry T. Peters Collection)

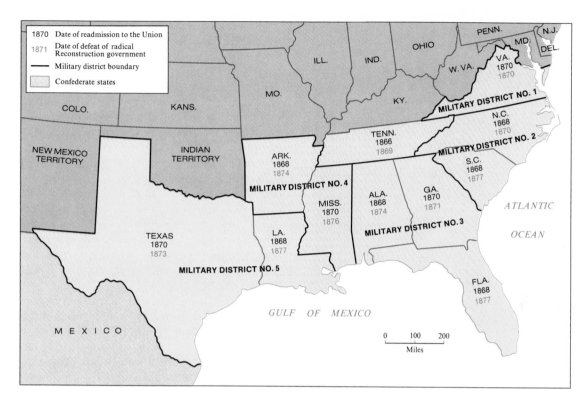

MAP 16.1 RECONSTRUCTION
The federal government grouped states of the ex-Confederacy into military districts during radical
Reconstruction. The two dates in each state indicate when the state was re-admitted to the Union,
and when radical Republicans lost control of the state government. All the ex-Confederate states
rejoined the Union during the period 1868–1870, but the periods of radical rule varied widely. Radicals
lasted only a few months in Virginia; they held until the end of Reconstruction in Louisiana, Florida,
and South Carolina.

feminist position. The contest over the Fifteenth
Amendment had finally disconnected the
women's rights movement from abolitionism,
and women now began to develop political strategies independent of other reform movements.

The South During Reconstruction

Between 1868 and 1871, all the southern states
met the stipulations of Congress and rejoined
the Union. Reconstruction governments under
Republican control remained in power for periods ranging from a few months for Virginia to
nine years for South Carolina, Louisiana, and
Florida. In each government, the Republican
party drew its support from a coalition of blacks,
whites who had not owned slaves, and white
settlers from the North.

Southern Republicans, black and white, did
their best to reconstruct southern society. But
during the 1870s, the ex-Confederates resisted
effectively and exhausted the northern Republicans, who abandoned their southern allies. Even
if the southern Republicans had prevailed, they
would not have produced an economic revolution in the South. Most Republicans, North and
South, remained too steadfastly loyal to established property rights to redistribute wealth on
behalf of ex-slaves or poor whites.

Reconstruction Governments

Blacks played an important role in Reconstruction governments, although they did not dominate in any state. In Alabama, Florida, South
Carolina, Mississippi, and Louisiana, where
blacks constituted a majority of all registered
voters, they contributed heavily to Republican

HIRAM R. REVELS

In 1870 Hiram R. Revels was elected to the U.S. Senate from Mississippi to fill Jefferson Davis's former seat. Revels was a free black from North Carolina who had migrated North and attended Knox College in Illinois. He recruited blacks for the Union army and, as an ordained Methodist minister, served as chaplain of a black regiment in Mississippi, where he settled after the war. (Library of Congress)

victories. In South Carolina, blacks briefly held a majority in one house of the legislature. In other states, they held positions of importance, but never in proportion to their numbers.

Black political leaders came largely from an elite that had been freed before the Civil War. Most of them had been artisans, shopkeepers, teachers, and ministers in southern towns and cities. However, a significant minority had been slaves. An ex-slave named Blanche K. Bruce was one of two black U.S. senators from Mississippi. He had received tutoring on the Virginia plantation of his white father and then escaped during the Civil War to Hannibal, Missouri, where he established a school for blacks. He moved to Mississippi in 1869 and entered politics; he was elected to the Senate in 1874—the only black elected to a full term in the Senate until 1966. All

the black leaders of the Reconstruction South emphasized the need for blacks to vote, and they supported state programs to improve schools and roads.

The Republicans who dominated the reconstructed state governments were satirized and stereotyped by resentful southern whites. Non-slaveholding whites were labeled "scalawags"—worthless, runty animals—by their Democratic opponents. Settlers from the North were called "carpetbaggers"—transient exploiters who carried all their property in cheap suitcases called carpetbags. Carpetbaggers held more than half the Republican governorships in the South and almost half of the South's seats in Congress. Black Republicans were mocked and scorned as ignorant field hands who could only play at politics like children.

Actually, few southern Republicans conformed to these stereotypes. Many carpetbaggers sought personal profit, but they also brought capital and skills to invest in the region's future. Most had been Union army officers who fell in love with the South—its climate, people, and economic opportunities. Many were college graduates and professionals—lawyers, engineers, and teachers. Some scalawags were wealthy ex-Whigs; others were not rich but did often own their own farms. They wished to see a South free of a slaveowning aristocracy and usually had fought against, or at least refused to support, the Confederacy.

The Republican governments in the South were often accused of corruption and incompetence. But corruption and incompetence were common in the northern states and in the federal government during Reconstruction. Southern Republicans modernized state constitutions, extended the right to vote, and made more offices elective than had been traditional in the South. They built roads in areas where roads had never existed. They supervised the rebuilding of the region's blasted railroad network and subsidized investment in manufacturing and transportation. They undertook major public works programs. And they did all this without major federal financing.

Perhaps the main accomplishment of the southern Republicans came in the area of education. They built public schools that served more people, black and white, than free education had ever reached in the prewar South. Blacks of all ages rushed to attend newly established schools, even where they had to pay tuition. An elderly black man in Mississippi explained his desire to go to school: "Ole missus used to read the good book to us . . . on Sunday evenin's, but she mostly read dem places where it says, 'Servants obey your masters.' . . . Now we is free, there's heaps of tings in that old book we is just suffering to learn." By 1877, hundreds of thousands of black children went to school. A child in Augusta, Georgia, explained his presence there in simple terms: "I'm going to school now to try to learn something I hope will enable me to be of some use to my race."

Like politicians everywhere, southern Republicans usually focused on immediate tasks and problems. But beneath their day-to-day efforts— and their mistakes—lay a reasonably coherent idea. The South, they believed, needed to be fundamentally reconstructed. Their goals were to end southern dependence on a cotton agriculture that rested on the unskilled labor of blacks and to create a growing economy based on manufacturing, capital investment, and skilled labor. Southern Republicans fell far short of making this vision a reality. But they accomplished much more of it than their critics, northern or southern, gave them credit for.

The Planters' Reaction

Most ex-slaveowners opposed the Republican program, especially the effort to expand political and economic opportunities for blacks, because it threatened their vested interest in traditional agriculture and their power and status in southern society. A few planters supported subsidized manufacturing, but most wished only to rebuild the transportation system. In any case, the former slaveowners set aside political differences among themselves and united to defeat the Republicans. Their appeals for racial solidarity and southern patriotism focused mass hostility against the Republicans on black suffrage and social status rather than economic issues.

The planters concentrated on recapturing exclusive political control of southern state governments. They used any means, both legitimate and illegitimate, at their disposal. In the eight states where whites formed a majority of the population—all except Louisiana, Mississippi, and South Carolina—planters sought to return ex-Confederates to the rolls of registered voters and unite them under the Democratic banner. Calling themselves the "redeemers," planters and their supporters organized secret societies to frighten blacks and Republican whites from

A FREEDMEN'S SCHOOL
This 1866 sketch from *Harper's Weekly* of a Vicksburg, Mississippi school run by the Freedmen's Bureau illustrates the desire for education by ex-slaves of all ages. Because most southern blacks were farmers, schools commonly offered night classes that left students free for field work during the day. (From *Harper's Weekly*. The Newberry Library, Chicago)

CARPETBAGGER DESCRIBES THE KU KLUX KLAN

Albion W. Tourgée (1838–1905) was a carpetbagger in North Carolina. He described his continual harassment by the Ku Klux Klan in The Invisible Empire *(1880).*

Another thing which shows that . . . [to say the Klan] was merely the work of rough spirits of the lower classes is a libel on the common people of the South, is the fact that the best classes never prosecuted nor denounced these acts, but were always their apologists and defenders. Besides that, they kept the secrets of the Klan better than the Masons have ever kept the mysteries of their craft. It was an open secret in families and neighborhoods. Ladies met together in sewing-circles to make the disguises. Churches were used as places of assembly. Children were intrusted with secrets which will make them shudder in old age. . . . It was a holy trust which the Southern cause had cast upon them, and they would have died rather than betray it.

The fact has been overlooked, too, that whenever positive information has been obtained as to the membership of the Klan, it has been shown to have had its full proportion of the best classes. Two judges, two sheriffs, one State solicitor, one leading editor, four members of the legislature, one Congressman, and numerous lawyers and planters and professional men, are shown by the testimony in *one* State alone, to have been among its members. The confessions of members showed the officers and leading men of the Klans always to have been men of standing and influence in their communities.

There is no sort of doubt that it originated with the best classes of the South, was managed and controlled by them, and was at all times under their direction. It was their creature and their agent to work out their purposes and ends. It was just as much their movement as was the war of rebellion, and animated by similar motives.

---

voting or taking other political action. These societies coerced whites into joining the Democratic party and used intimidation and terror to prevent blacks from supporting the Republicans. The most widespread of these groups, the Ku Klux Klan, was organized in Tennessee in 1865 and quickly spread throughout the South.

The Klan's first leader was Nathan Bedford Forrest, a celebrated Confederate cavalry officer, and its initial organization was based on Confederate army units. Forrest had led the Confederate cavalry that took Fort Pillow in Tennessee in 1864. He had captured the black Union soldiers who held the fort and killed them. In 1868, during an interview in Memphis, Forrest warned Republicans that they would suffer the same fate if they tried to suppress the Klan. "I intend to kill the radicals," Forrest said. He was watching their houses, he added, and "when the fight comes not one of them would ever get out of this town alive."

As Reconstruction advanced, terrorism became more blatant and more elaborate. Paramilitary groups, with names such as Rifle Clubs and Red Shirts, operated openly. They became most visible in Mississippi, where their procedures became known as the Mississippi Plan. In essence, they mobilized and armed whites in virtually every community in order to determine the outcome of elections by force.

The first step in the Mississippi Plan was to compel the state's white Republicans to become Democrats. Overt violence was often used against whites, as it was against blacks, but the tactics also included social ostracism. A white Republican who succumbed explained that the Democrats made it "too damned hot for us to stay out. . . . No white man can live in the South in the future and act with any other than the Democratic party unless he is willing and prepared to live a life of social isolation and remain in political oblivion."

The second step was the relentless intimidation of black voters. In Mississippi's 1875 elec-

INTIMIDATION OF BLACK VOTERS

The following testimony was given by Harriet Hernandes, a black resident of Spartanburg, South Carolina, July 10, 1871, to the Joint Congressional Select Committee investigating conditions in the South.

Question: How old are you?

Answer: Going on thirty-four years. . . .

Q: Are you married or single?

A: Married.

Q: Did the Ku-Klux come to your house at any time?

A: Yes, sir; twice. . . .

Q: Go on to the second time. . . .

A: They came in; I was lying in bed. Says he, "Come out here, sir; come out here, sir!" They took me out of bed; they would not let me get out, but they took me up in their arms and toted me out—me and my daughter Lucy. He struck me on the forehead with a pistol, and here is the scar above my eye now. Says he, "Damn you, fall." I fell. Says he, "Damn you, get up." I got up. Says he, "Damn you, get over this fence!" and he kicked me over when I went to get over; and then he went on to a brush pile, and they laid us right down there, both together. They laid us down twenty yards apart, I reckon. They had dragged and beat us along. They struck me right on the top of my head, and I thought they had killed me; and I said, "Lord o' mercy, don't, don't kill my child!" He gave me a lick on the head, and it liked to have killed me; I saw stars. He threw my arm over my head so I could not do anything with it for three weeks, and there are great knots on my wrist now.

Q: What did they say this was for?

A: They said, "You can tell your husband that when we see him we are going to kill him. . . ."

Q: Did they say why they wanted to kill him?

A: They said, "He voted the radical ticket, didn't he?" I said, "Yes," that very way. . . .

Q: When did [your husband] get back home after this whipping? He was not at home, was he?

A: He was lying out; he couldn't stay at home, bless your soul! . . .

Q: Has he been afraid for any length of time?

A: He has been afraid ever since last October. He has been lying out. He has not laid in the house ten nights since October.

Q: Is that the situation of the colored people down there to any extent?

A: That is the way they all have to do—men and women both.

Q: What are they afraid of?

A: Of being killed or whipped to death.

Q: What has made them afraid?

A: Because men that voted radical tickets they took the spite out on the women when they could get at them.

Q: How many colored people have been whipped in that neighborhood?

A: It is all of them, mighty near. . . .

---

tions, in which the Republican party went down to defeat, local Democratic clubs paraded as full militia companies. They identified black leaders in assassination lists called "dead-books"; broke up Republican meetings; provoked rioting that left hundreds of blacks dead; and threatened voters, who still lacked the protection of the secret ballot. The Republican governor of the state, Adelbert Ames, a Congressional Medal of Honor winner from Maine, appealed for federal troops, but President Grant refused, fearing damage to Republicans in northern elections. Ames contemplated organizing a state militia to resist, but he decided against it, believing that only blacks would join. Rather than escalate the scale of the racial war, he conceded victory to the terrorists.

To defeat the paramilitary forces, southern Republicans needed federal military aid. The Grant administration and moderate Republicans in Congress were unwilling to enlarge what had already become a costly, bloody guerrilla war. In 1870–1871, however, Congress passed the Force Acts, which authorized the president to use military force and martial law to suppress felonies and conspiracies fomented by the Ku Klux Klan. Under these acts, federal agents penetrated the Klan and gathered evidence that provided the basis for thousands of arrests. Federal grand juries indicted more than three thousand Klansmen. The Justice Department, however, lacked the resources necessary to prosecute effectively, especially when Justice Department attorneys faced all-white juries. Only about six hundred offenders received convictions, and only a handful of these served significant prison sentences.

Meanwhile, northern Republicans began to lose heart. They continued to "wave the bloody shirt" but found that it had less effect with each election. Northerners had grown weary over the bloodshed and money needed to support Reconstruction. Most northern Republicans, including even some radicals, concluded that ex-slaves should be able to enjoy their freedom without additional federal assistance. Republicans moved toward a consensus that the federal government had accomplished its Civil War objectives and should end Reconstruction.

Because of the lack of federal help, Republican governments in the South found themselves gradually overwhelmed by ex-Confederate politicians in daylight and by terrorists at night. In 1870, the Democrats, supported by a vigorous Klan, recovered power in Virginia, Georgia, and North Carolina. They overthrew Republicans in Texas in 1873, in Alabama and Arkansas in 1874, and in Mississippi in 1875. By 1877, Republican governments and token U.S. military units remained in only three states—Louisiana, South Carolina, and Florida.

The Plight of the Ex-Slaves

Even at its most effective stage, Reconstruction was as much a scheme to promote the Republican party as to assist the ex-slaves. After receiving their political rights, the blacks were expected to fend for themselves. This meant that the actual outcome of the legal abolition of slavery depended largely on thousands of contests between ex-slaves, acting individually and collectively, and an increasingly unified white South, led by the planter class. Despite the odds against them, the ex-slaves won some modest economic gains. But these gains came only within the restrictions of a form of debt peonage that replaced slavery. Blacks and many whites remained mired in a poverty that both racism and economic forces reinforced powerfully.

Land Reform Fails

To former slaves, freedom had a specific, positive meaning—control over their own lives. But they knew that to have genuine freedom in an agricultural economy, they had to own land.

Emancipation and the advancing Union armies raised black expectations of land ownership. Union officers often left slaves in control of plantations. General Sherman promoted land ownership for blacks by reserving coastal land in Georgia and South Carolina—the Sea Islands and abandoned plantations within thirty miles of the coast—for black refugees and by giving them "possessory titles" to forty-acre tracts. By the end of the war, the Freedmen's Bureau had placed about ten thousand families on half a million acres of this land. Reports of such actions inspired hope among blacks throughout the South. Many continued to work on their old plantations in the hope that they would own some of the land after the war. For example, when planter Thomas Pinckney returned to his South Carolina plantation, his slaves told him, "We ain't going nowhere. We are going to work right here on the land where we were born and what belongs to us." An ex-slave on a Georgia plantation offered to sell to his former master the share of the plantation he expected to receive after the federal redistribution.

Then, in May 1865, Andrew Johnson's amnesty ended all land redistribution. It allowed pardoned Confederates to recover their land if Union troops had confiscated or occupied it. In October, Johnson ordered General Oliver O. Howard, head of the Freedmen's Bureau, to tell blacks on the Sea Islands that they did not hold legal title to the land, and to advise them to come to terms with the legal, white landowners. Howard reluctantly obeyed. The dispossessed blacks replied, "Why do you take away our lands? You take them from us who have always been true, always true to the Government! You give them to our all-time enemies! That is not right!" When some of the Sea Island blacks refused to deal with the restored white owners,

Union soldiers forced them to leave or to work for their old masters. The Freedmen's Bureau did help more than two thousand black families buy their own land in the Sea Islands. But by the end of 1866, the bureau had returned the rest of the land to its white owners.

The only other Reconstruction land-redistribution measure was the Southern Homestead Act of 1866, which designated more than forty million acres of public land in Alabama, Arkansas, Florida, Louisiana, and Mississippi for grants of eighty acres to settlers who cultivated the land for five years. Congress prohibited anyone who had supported the Confederacy from filing a claim until 1867. Yet few ex-slaves or poor white Unionists could exploit this advantage. The cost of equipping new farms was too great. Fewer than seven thousand ex-slaves claimed land and only about a thousand eventually qualified for ownership.

Congressional Republicans never seriously considered a massive redistribution of land in the South. Given their commitment to property rights, such a policy seemed too radical. Most Republicans believed it was unconstitutional as well, for it would deprive landowners of their property without due process of law. Massive redistribution would also endanger, Republicans believed, southern economic recovery. Only Thaddeus Stevens insisted that Reconstruction meant little unless the federal government redistributed land.

The former slaves, however, realized how important land was to freedom. Where they had occupied lands, they resisted removal. Often led by black veterans of the Union army, the ex-slaves fought pitched battles with plantation owners and bands of ex-Confederate soldiers. Whenever possible, the owners attempted to disarm and intimidate the returning black veterans. A black veteran from Maryland wrote, "The returned colard Solgers are in Many cases beten, and their guns taken from them, we darcent walk out of an evening . . . they beat us badly and Sumtime Shoot us."

In this warfare, federal troops often backed the local whites. The necessities of fighting a total war had briefly carried land reform further than even most radical Republicans had wanted to go. Subsequently, the government ensured that land ownership in the South would remain concentrated in the hands of the planters.

Planters Versus Ex-Slaves

Planters now tried to establish a labor system that was as close to slavery as they could make it. High cotton prices provided a powerful inducement for planters to restore the status quo in labor relations. Moreover, on paper, emancipation had cost the slaveowners about $3 billion—the value of their capital investment in former slaves—a sum that equaled nearly three-fourths of the nation's economic production in 1860. In reality, however, their losses depended on the extent to which they lost control over their former slaves. Planters therefore attempted to control the freed blacks and to substitute low wages for the food, clothing, and shelter that the blacks had received as slaves.

WAGE LABOR OF EX-SLAVES
This photograph, taken shortly after the Civil War, shows former slaves being led from the cotton fields. Although they now worked for wages, they were probably organized into a gang not far removed from the earlier slave gangs. Their plug-hatted crew leader is dressed much as his slave-driving predecessor would have been. (The New-York Historical Society)

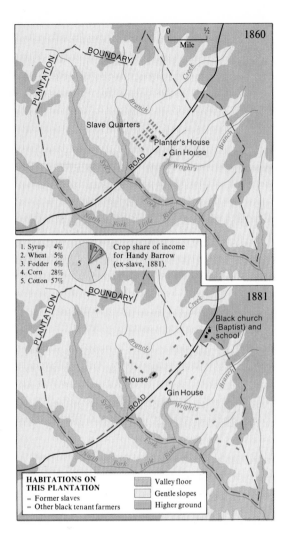

MAP 16.2 THE BARROW PLANTATION
Comparing the maps of this central Georgia plantation reveals the changing patterns of black residence and farming after the Civil War. In 1860, the slave quarters clustered near the planter's house, which sat above them on a small hilltop. The free sharecroppers of 1881 built their cabins along the spurs or ridges of land between the streams, scattering their community over the plantation. A black church and school were built by this date. A typical sharecropper on the plantation earned most of his income from growing cotton.

The ex-slaves resisted, however. During the growing seasons of 1865 and 1866, thousands of former slaves abandoned their old plantations and farms. Many sought better lives in the towns and cities of the South. Others remained in the countryside but either refused to work in the cotton fields or reduced their hours there. They worked instead on their own garden plots, guaranteeing themselves a subsistence level of rations during the postwar disruptions.

Meanwhile, they fortified the institutions that had sustained their spirit during the days of slavery. Black families moved away from the slave quarters, usually building homes scattered around or near their old plantations and farms. Sometimes they established all-black villages. Families strengthened the ties they had long nurtured. Husbands, wives, and children often reunited, sometimes after journeys of hundreds of miles. Couples stepped forward to record their marriages. When they could, mothers rescued their children from the control of planters and overseers. One mother pleaded for the return of her daughter so the girl could go to school and church. She explained that her daughter "never was in a church in her life, and don't know the Lord's prayer." Another mother fought to free her daughter from the ex-master to whom she had become apprenticed after the war. "Our condition is bettered but little," she said, because parents and children were separated. "Give us our children, and don't let them be raised in the ignorance we have."

Blacks moved their religion completely into the open, building their own churches and founding independent organizations within the Baptist and Methodist churches. Many women refused to work in the fields. They insisted on staying at home, where they tended elaborate gardens, managed households, and brought education and religion to their children.

In the fields, ex-slaves refused to submit to the grueling gang labor that had been the major tool for their economic exploitation. Now they wanted a pace of work and independence that reflected their new status. What was freedom all about if not to have a bit more leisure time, to work less intensely than they had as slaves, and to work for themselves and their families?

This modest ambition ran counter to deeply entrenched attitudes among planters and poor whites. Emancipation had not destroyed the racist assumptions and fears that the planters had fostered in order to maintain and defend slavery. One Freedmen's Bureau commissioner in Mississippi wrote that wherever he went, he heard "the people talk in such a way as to indicate that they are yet unable to conceive of the negro as possessing any rights at all." He explained:

> The whites esteem their property by natural right, and however much they may admit that the individual relations of masters and slaves have been destroyed by the war and by the President's emancipation proclamation, they still have an ingrained feeling that the blacks at large belong to the whites at large, and whenever opportunity serves they treat the colored people just as their profit, caprice or passion may dictate.

Thus, former slaveowners and the poorer whites who looked to them for leadership continued to maintain the South's caste system, which rested on racist attitudes that united whites across class lines.

In 1865–1866, planters led the movement to enact the Black Codes, an extract of which appears on page 500. The codes varied from state to state, but almost all of them required the arrest of an ex-slave for vagrancy if he or she were found without employment. In most cases, the vagrant could not pay the fine required to be released from jail, and the county court hired him or her out to an employer. Several courts established specific hours of labor, spelled out the duties expected of laborers, and declared that any laborer who did not meet these standards was a vagrant. The codes usually restricted employment opportunities outside agriculture by establishing licensing procedures for blacks who wished to pursue skills or "irregular job work."

With the sanction of state law, local governments narrowly circumscribed the lives of blacks. They set curfews, required employer-issued passes for black agricultural workers, insisted that blacks who wished to live in town obtain white sponsors, and sharply regulated meetings of blacks, both inside and outside churches. Fines and forced labor were the penalties for violators.

The Black Codes, or similar laws, remained on the books throughout the South even during radical Reconstruction. If challenged by the federal government, state legislatures usually relaxed only marginal provisions. In any case, congressional intervention did not reach the local level. Then, when the "redeemers" came to power, southern states usually established new, even more stringent regulations.

The planters often received support from a source that surprised most of them—the agents of the federal government. Most army officers and federal marshals accepted the basic assumption behind the Black Codes—that ex-slaves were suited only for agricultural labor. In fact, even during the war, Union army officers tended to sympathize with the planters. Officers usually left planters who expressed their loyalty to the Union in control of their plantations and their former slaves.

After Appomattox, representatives of the federal government quickly came to support the economic interests of the planters. As one Louisiana ex-slave described the process, "Whenever a new Provost Marshall comes he gives us justice for a fortnight or so; then he becomes acquainted with planters, takes dinners with them, receives presents; and then we no longer have any rights, or very little." In disputes between employers and laborers, federal marshals generally sided with the planters and sustained their authority. Army commanders complied with the requests of planters for help in forcing blacks to work. The officers expelled former plantation workers from towns and cities and punished blacks for disobedience, theft, vagrancy, and erratic labor.

Even most agents of the Freedmen's Bureau supported the planters. They interpreted their instructions to promote a transition to free labor to mean that they should teach ex-slaves to be reliable agricultural workers. They preached the gospel of work to the blacks. To discourage labor violence, they warned that it was better "to suffer wrong than to do wrong." They urged former slaves to vindicate the cause of abolition by staying at home and working even harder than they had under slavery. One bureau official told ex-slaves that their former master "is not able to do without you, and you will . . . find him as kind, honest, and liberal as other men" and "you can be as free and as happy in your old home, for the present, as anywhere else in the world."

THE MISSISSIPPI BLACK CODE, 1865

. . . All freedmen, free negroes and mulattoes in this State, over the age of eighteen years, found on the second Monday in January, 1866, or thereafter, with no lawful employment or business, or found unlawfully assembling themselves together, either in the day or night time, and all white persons so assembling themselves with freedmen, free negroes or mulattoes, or usually associating with freedmen, free negroes or mulattoes, on terms of equality, or living in adultery or fornication with a freed woman, free negro or mulatto, shall be deemed vagrants, and on conviction thereof shall be fined in a sum not exceeding, in the case of a freedman, free negro, or mulatto, fifty dollars, and a white man two hundred dollars, and imprisoned at the discretion of the court, the free negro not exceeding ten days, and the white man not exceeding six months. . . .

[I]n case any freeman, free negro or mulatto shall fail for five days after the imposition of any fine or forfeiture upon him or her for violation of any of the provisions of this act to pay the same, . . . it shall be, and is hereby, made the duty of the sheriff of the proper county to hire out said freedman, free negro or mulatto, to any person who will, for the shortest period of serve, pay said fine and forfeiture and all costs: *Provided*, A preference shall be given to the employer, if there be one, in which case the employer shall be entitled to deduct and retain the amount so paid from the wages of such freedman, free negro or mulatto, then due or to become due; and in case said freedman, free negro, or mulatto cannot be hired out, he or she may be dealt with as a pauper.

. . . Every freedman, free negro, and mulatto shall, on the second Monday of January, one thousand eight hundred and sixty-six and annually thereafter, have a lawful home or employment, and shall have written evidence thereof as follows, to-wit: if living in any incorporated city, town, or village, a license from the mayor thereof; and if living outside of an incorporated city, town, or village, from the member of the board of police of his beat, authorizing him or her to do irregular and job work; or a written contract, as provided in section six in this act, which licenses may be revoked for cause at any time by the authority granting the same.

All contracts for labor made with freedmen, free negroes, and mulattoes for a longer period than one month shall be in writing, and in duplicate, attested and read to said freedman, free negro, or mulatto by a beat, city or county officer, or two disinterested white persons of the county in which the labor is to be performed, of which each party shall have one; and said contracts shall be taken and held as entire contracts, and if the laborer shall quit the service of the employer before the expiration of his term of service, without good cause, he shall forfeit his wages for that year up to the time of quitting.

. . . If any person shall persuade or attempt to persuade, entice, or cause any freedman, free negro, or mulatto to desert from the legal employment of any person before the expiration of his or her term of service, or shall knowingly employ any such deserting freedman, free negro, or mulatto, or shall knowingly give or sell to any such deserting freedman, free negro, or mulatto, any food, raiment, or other thing, he or she shall be guilty of a misdemeanor, and, upon conviction, shall be fined not less than twenty-five dollars and not more than two hundred dollars and the costs; and if said fine and costs shall not be immediately paid, the court shall sentence said convict to not exceeding two months' imprisonment in the county jail, and he or she shall moreover be liable to the party injured in damages.

The minority of Freedmen's Bureau agents who did side with the blacks were stymied by northern racism, lack of funds, understaffing, lack of coordination within the bureau, and uncooperative military authorities. Overall, the Freedmen's Bureau helped the planters reestablish control over their labor force. It also gave legitimacy in the north to the policies of the planter elite.

Sharecropping and Debt Peonage

The Freedmen's Bureau did, however, change the way planters controlled the labor of their ex-slaves. It established a contract labor system by encouraging, even compelling, planters and ex-slaves to agree on written contracts through a formal bargaining process. The labor contract system was a poor substitute for land ownership. But it helped the freedmen attain something else they badly wanted—the elimination of gang labor.

As early as 1865, the written contracts between ex-slaves and planters provided that the ex-slaves would work for wages. However, the contracts also provided for less supervision, a slower pace, and more free time than under slavery, as well as the elimination of drivers and overseers from the plantations. By 1866, however, bargaining between planters and ex-slaves had become more difficult, partly because a shrinking money supply in the South reduced the cash available to pay wages. To resolve the growing number of conflicts, Freedmen's Bureau agents introduced a form of compensation that was common, though not typical, in northern agriculture. This was the payment of agricultural workers in shares of the crop, rather than in wages.

At first, ex-slaves were enthusiastic about sharecropping, and it swept through the South. Former slaves found that sharecropping in-creased their control over working conditions. It also allowed them to improve their standard of living. Under typical sharecropping contracts, sharecroppers turned over between half and two-thirds of their harvested crops to their landlords. The owner's share was not necessarily excessive, because the landlord commonly provided land, seed, fertilizer, tools, and assistance in marketing. The sharecropping system bound together laborers and owners of land and capital in a common sharing of risks and returns.

Sharecropping did not lead to land ownership for many slaves. Some ex-slaves managed to save enough through sharecropping to rent land. As tenant farmers, they could sell their own crops directly to market. Some of these renters were finally able to purchase their own land; by 1910, black farmers owned nearly a third of all the land they cultivated. But black farm owners usually occupied marginal land—in the coastal swamps of Georgia and South Carolina, for example—and the land often cost more than its productivity warranted. Blacks had to

SHARECROPPING

This sharecropping family seems proud of their new cabin and their crop of cotton, which they planted in every available bit of ground. But the presence of their white landlord in the background suggests the forces that led families like this one into debt peonage. (Brown Brothers)

pay high prices for land throughout the South, especially in the most fertile areas, because they were willing to pay a premium for the badge of freedom and because white planters restricted their access to land ownership. Some planters made agreements among themselves not to sell land to blacks or intimidated blacks who tried to buy land. Others devised a system of debt peonage that tied ex-slaves to the land and enabled planters to depress their earnings.

The financial condition of blacks was extremely difficult. Sharecropping and renting of land enabled ex-slaves to increase their incomes but also broadened their financial needs. They wanted more food and better clothing than they had had under slavery; sharecroppers often needed more supplies than their landlords were willing to provide; and renters had to purchase all their seed, fertilizer, and equipment. The purchase of major farm supplies almost always required borrowing. Southern banks, however, were reluctant to lend money to black farmers, whom they saw as bad risks, and cash was generally in short supply.

The owners of country stores stepped in. Eager to lend money to sharecroppers, they furnished everything the black farmers needed and extended credit for the purchases. The country merchants took advantage of the weak bargaining power of the ex-slaves by charging unusually high prices and interest rates. In effect, they were rural loan sharks.

Once the black sharecroppers fell into debt to the country merchants, high interest rates made it difficult for them to settle their accounts. At best, after paying their debts, the sharecroppers broke even. Most sharecroppers fell deeper and deeper into debt. Most southern states gave this system legal force by allowing a merchant to take a lien on crops. This gave merchants a legal right to take the crops to settle the sharecropper's debts, and to seek criminal prosecution of a sharecropper who could not pay the full amount of interest owed. Indebted black farmers faced imprisonment and forced labor unless they toiled on the land according to the instructions of the merchant-creditor. Increasingly, merchants and landlords cooperated to maintain this lucrative system and many landlords themselves became merchants. The ex-slaves had been trapped in the vicious circle of debt peonage.

The North During Reconstruction

The Republicans failed to break the hold of the planter elite on the South, but they did succeed in completing economic reconstruction of the North. They enacted nearly all their nationalizing economic program—a system of national banking, tariff protection, and subsidies for internal improvements—despite resistance from Democrats. The adoption of the Republican program accompanied and promoted unprecedented economic growth and industrial and territorial expansion.

A Dynamic Economy

The destruction and waste of the Civil War disrupted the nation's economic life, but economic growth—gains in productivity—resumed quickly after the fighting ended. By the 1870s, Americans became more productive and their economy expanded faster than ever before. Northeastern industry led the way, particularly iron and steel and railroad construction. The production of iron more than doubled between the end of the Civil War and 1870; it more than doubled again by 1880. Steel production grew even more rapidly—fivefold between 1865 and 1870 and then nearly twenty times by 1880. The era began the "age of capital," a period that lasted until World War I and that was marked by great increases in investment in factories and railroads. It also began the era of big business, characterized by the rise of giant corporations.

As impressive as America's industrial expansion was its territorial growth. During the 1860s, the United States began to seize its potential as a great continental power, integrating its vast western territory into its economy. Northern capitalists built transcontinental railroads. Settlers poured into the Great Plains region. Beginning in 1859, with the discovery of gold near Pike's Peak, miners rushed to Colorado and then to Nevada and the Black Hills of South Dakota. During the late 1860s, Texas cattlemen started their great drives to northern railheads, beginning the creation of the Cattle Kingdom. And the United States launched its wars against western Indians. By 1870, territorial governments had

EXPANSION IN THE MOUNTAIN STATES
The growth of towns like Virginia City, Nevada, pictured here in 1866, helped transform the United States into a wealthy, transcontinental nation. Virginia City's residents built their town, including five newspapers and a stock exchange, around the gold mines that had been discovered in the surrounding Comstock Lode just before the Civil War began. (Library of Congress)

been formed throughout the West. Nevada became a state in 1864, with Nebraska following in 1867 and Colorado in 1876.

During the Civil War, Republicans implemented the economic program that they had inherited from the Whigs. After the war, northern acceptance of the Republican economic programs grew. Economic expansion seemed to validate the promises of renewed prosperity that Republicans had made in 1860. Also, the North's military victory seemed to prove that its society was stronger than the South's and to justify Republican programs as contributing to that strength. In addition, the successful experience of wartime mobilization encouraged Americans

to relax their traditional hostility to concentration of social power.

Many young soldiers—and women who had served in the Sanitary Commission—now accepted the state as a large, centralized entity. Wartime service had been their first direct experience of participation in a complex organization. For the first time, they had lived and worked within an explicit hierarchy that imposed a high degree of job specialization and rigorous discipline. Their service also had taken them, most for the first time, far from their homes and placed them in intimate contact with people who came from distant places and yet served in the same cause. This collective and disciplined national service predisposed many northerners to accept the Republican party and the federal government as agencies of national economic reorganization and, increasingly, to accept large corporations as instruments necessary for prosperity.

Republicans expanded their economic programs, rather than shrinking the federal government back to its prewar scale. They strengthened government regulation of the banking system, winning praise from investors who appreciated a more predictable economic environment. Republican Congresses continued to promote the development of a national transportation system by expanding railroad subsidies and establishing the Atlantic and Pacific Railroad in 1866 and the Texas Pacific in 1871. Republicans expanded the national postal system, funded major river and harbor development, and established a permanent army and navy. They also provided the cavalry forces required to clear the Indians from the Great Plains; military spending accounted for 60 percent of the federal budget by 1880. The Homestead Act subsidized the settling of the Great Plains. To some extent, all these programs stimulated the growth of a national economy and in turn lubricated the Republican political machine.

Even more central to the popularity of the Republican party was an elaborate system of pensions for Union veterans and their dependents. The Civil War pension program, which the government continually extended and broadened, had a distinct welfare component that became especially important during the severe depressions of the 1870s and 1890s. But the prime purpose of the pensions was to solidify the political loyalty of the families of the men who had served in the Union army.

The government financed its bountiful programs with the revenues raised from the tax system introduced during the Civil War. Postwar Congresses kept in force the high tariffs that had proved surprisingly lucrative. Congress also retained taxes on alcohol and tobacco that the Republican party at first had justified as emergency measures. These taxes not only financed the new Republican programs but also provided the funds for repayment of the Union's wartime debts. Wealthy Americans owned most of the war bonds issued by the government. The government repaid these investors out of the proceeds from the tariffs and sales taxes. Because the taxes increased the cost of everyday items, the mass of the American people were actually paying far more on the war debt in proportion to their income than were wealthy people. Republicans praised this redistribution of wealth, for it transferred significant amounts of money from poorer people to richer people, who were more able and likely to save and invest, and thereby increased the supply of capital, raised the rate of capital formation, and accelerated the rate of economic growth—all changes that benefitted the Republican-dominated business class.

Republican Foreign Policy

Americans were heavily preoccupied during the 1860s and 1870s with the development of their own territory. Nonetheless, some Republican leaders were alert to new possibilities for expansion abroad. Perhaps the most important advocate of expansion was William H. Seward, who had been Lincoln's secretary of state and continued in that post under Johnson. Believing in the importance of foreign commerce to the long-term health of the republic, Seward promoted the acquisition of colonies that could be used as trading bases in the Caribbean and the Pacific.

Johnson and Seward inherited their major foreign policy issues from the Civil War. The most pressing one was Mexico. The French emperor, Napoleon III, had intervened in a civil war there and created a puppet government under Archduke Maximilian, the brother of the emperor of Austria. Johnson and Seward decided not to tolerate this assertion of European power so close to the United States. In 1866, Johnson sent fifty thousand battle-hardened veterans to the Mexican border, while Seward negotiated the withdrawal of French troops. The French troops withdrew in 1867, leaving Maximilian to a Mexican firing squad.

The American government was also annoyed over Great Britain's allowing the *Alabama* and other Confederate cruisers to sail from British shipyards to raid Union commerce. Seward claimed that Britain had violated international laws of neutrality and owed compensation for damages. Britain, fearing that Americans might build ships for British enemies in some future war, accepted Seward's legal point and agreed to submit the "Alabama Claims" to arbitration. However, Charles Sumner, chairman of the Senate Foreign Relations Committee, insisted that the compensation cover "indirect" damages. He included lost shipping revenue and the costs of Britain's prolonging the war. Estimating these costs at more than $2 billion, he hoped to acquire Canada as part of a settlement. Sumner's demands blocked a solution during Johnson's presidency.

Meanwhile, Seward's expansionist ambitions met with only mixed success. Supporting naval demands for a base in the Caribbean, Seward negotiated a treaty with Denmark to purchase the Virgin Islands, but Congress rejected the $7.5 million price tag. Congress also turned down his proposal to annex Santo Domingo (now the Dominican Republic), which had won independence from Spain in 1865. Seward did persuade Congress to purchase the small Midway Islands west of Hawaii, after his effort to acquire the Hawaiian Islands had failed. Most important, Seward convinced the Senate, in 1867, to ratify a treaty to buy Alaska from Russia and to appropriate the $7.2 million for the purchase. Critics referred to Alaska as "Johnson's Polar Bear Garden" and "Seward's Folly," but its acquisition promised to obstruct any further British ambitions in North America. Also, the price was reasonable when weighed against even the low estimates that Congress made of Alaska's fish, fur, lumber, and mineral resources.

When Ulysses S. Grant became president in 1869, he promoted expansion in the Caribbean. He was influenced by American investors and adventurers in Santo Domingo, including Orville E. Babcock, a former military aide of Grant's who had become his personal secretary in the White House. Grant proposed a treaty to annex the country as a colony for American blacks dissatisfied with Reconstruction. The Senate defeated Grant's imperial ambition in 1870. Leading the attack was Charles Sumner, who feared that annexation would threaten the independence of the neighboring black republic of Haiti. "These islands by climate, occupation, and destiny . . . belong to the colored people," he declared.

Grant's secretary of state was genteel Hamilton Fish, a former Whig who had been governor of New York and a U.S. senator. Fish had less interest than Seward in acquiring new territory and concentrated on settling differences with Britain. Part of his goal was to strengthen the ties of capital and commerce between the two nations. Interest in annexing Canada still remained high, but Fish finally persuaded Grant in 1870 that Parliament's passage of the British North America Act of 1867, uniting Canada in a federation (the Dominion of Canada), had removed any serious Canadian interest in annexation. Fish then quickly negotiated the Treaty of Washington, which both the Senate and Parliament ratified in 1871. This treaty submitted for arbitration all the outstanding issues between the two countries, including the "Alabama Claims." In 1873, the British government obeyed the ruling of an international tribunal established under the treaty and presented a $15.5 million check to the United States government. A period of unprecedented good will between America and Britain followed.

The Politics of Corruption

The Republican economic program became the primary target of the Democratic party, which tried to reestablish its national base of power. This was not an easy task, because the key elements of Republican policy had wide support. The Democrats tried to avoid attacking specific Republican programs on narrow economic grounds. Instead, they renewed their traditional assault on "special privilege."

Democrats warned that Republican programs created islands of privilege, enabling wealthy individuals to buy favors from the federal government and the Republicans to buy support from the people whom their programs served. The result, Democrats charged, was an increasing concentration of wealth and power and a corruption of the republic. In stressing corruption, the Democrats aimed to attract members of the business class to their party. They appealed to Americans who valued honesty in their economic and political lives and who believed in the ideal of a society composed of independent and virtuous farmers, artisans, and small entrepreneurs. The Democrats wished to restore a competitive economy, one that they argued had been lost during the Industrial Revolution and the Civil War.

During Grant's first term, some Republicans also criticized the management of Reconstruction and the northern economy. These dissidents included some radicals, such as Charles Sumner, who regarded Grant's Reconstruction policies as too conservative. The most important among them, however, included long-time Republicans like Charles Francis Adams, who were wealthy, well-educated members of established northeastern families. They resented and disapproved of the professional politicians who had become crucial to the party.

The dissident Republicans, like the Democrats, specifically attacked Grant for turning the Republican party into a self-serving bureaucracy. They criticized him for relying too heavily on professional politicians in executive positions, especially cabinet posts. These Republicans faulted their party for requiring government workers to pay a portion of their salaries into the party's treasury. They coined the term "Grantism" to describe this new spoils system of party patronage.

The dissident Republicans developed a unified program and a political strategy. They hoped to convince their party to endorse a program of civil service reform, beginning with a merit system to replace the system of rewarding party workers with public offices. They proposed a civil service commission to administer competitive examinations as the basis for appointments. Having mobilized fellow Republicans around this program, they planned to replace Grant as the party's nominee in 1872.

When the dissidents failed to win control of the Republican party, they set up their own party. They called themselves Liberal Republicans to indicate their commitment to liberty, competition, and limited government. They emphasized civil service reform and—to attract Democratic support—advocated amnesty for all former Confederates and removal of troops from

THE GRANT SCANDALS
This cartoon pointed to Grant's inability or unwillingness to deal with corruption among his friends—like General William W. Belknap, who received a bribe of nearly $25,000 for an appointment he made at an army post (Fort Sills). In 1876 the House impeached Belknap, but Grant allowed him to escape conviction by accepting his resignation before the Senate could put him on trial. (The Bettmann Archive)

the South. For president, the Liberal Republicans nominated Horace Greeley, the influential editor and publisher of the *New York Tribune.*

The Democrats attempted to steal the Liberal's thunder by also nominating Greeley. However, they made their endorsement with no great enthusiasm. Greeley supported reconciliation with ex-Confederates, but he had earlier favored radical Reconstruction, and his support for high tariffs conflicted with those of the Democrats.

In the election of 1872, Grant won an even larger percentage of the popular vote—56 percent—than he had in 1868. He received a higher percentage of the popular vote than any candidate since Andrew Jackson in 1828. Grant carried every northern state. And, because Democrats had not yet established control over presidential voting in the South, he lost only Georgia and Texas in the states of the former Confederacy.

The issue of corruption in the Republican party erupted in 1873 as a series of government scandals came to light. A congressional committee confirmed newspaper reports, first published during the 1872 campaign, of a complicated deal in which high-ranking Republicans appeared to have cheated the taxpayers. The scandal centered on Crédit Mobilier, a construction company that contracted for work on the Union Pacific Railroad. It turned out that key Union Pacific stockholders also controlled Crédit Mobilier and had arranged for enormous purchases, sometimes for services never delivered, paid for in Union Pacific stock and federal subsidies, from Crédit Mobilier. To prevent a congressional investigation, the corporate insiders had sold Crédit Mobilier stock at a discount to several members of Congress. The Republican Congress, however, censured only Oakes Ames, a Massachusetts congressman who had been the agent for Crédit Mobilier.

An even more dramatic scandal involved the "Whiskey Ring," a network of large whiskey distillers and Treasury agents who defrauded the Treasury of excise taxes on liquor. The ring was organized by a mediocre Union general, John A. McDonald, whom Grant had appointed supervisor of internal revenue. It was centered in the major distilling centers of Saint Louis, Milwaukee, Chicago, and Indianapolis. Between 1868 and 1873, it diverted as much as $4 million from the Treasury. The conspirators divided the spoils among the distillers, the McDonald organization, and the campaign chests of the Republican party in the Midwest. The ring reached into the White House, where Grant's private secretary, Orville Babcock, kept a protective eye on McDonald's activities.

Secretary of the Treasury Benjamin Bristow destroyed the ring. Appointed in 1874, after his predecessor had resigned under charges of corruption, Bristow launched an extensive investigation. In 1875, he brought indictments against more than 350 distillers and government officials. More than 100 men went to prison, although the courts acquitted Babcock.

The Whiskey Ring scandal crushed whatever prospects Grant might have had for a third term. Grant was known to be a crony of Babcock's and to have gone to extraordinary lengths to protect him, despite his command to Bristow, "Let no guilty man escape." The scandals stung the public all the more for coming in the midst of a pro-longed depression from 1873–1877. Nearly 15 percent of the labor force was unemployed by 1876, and thousands of farmers went bankrupt. Precipitating the depression was the Panic of 1873, which involved the bankruptcy of the Northern Pacific Railroad and its major investor, Jay Cooke. Cooke's favored role as a financier of the Civil War, and the extensive Republican subsidies to railroads, suggested to many Americans that Republican financial manipulations had caused the depression.

The ongoing depression, and the apparent unresponsiveness of the Grant administration to the widespread economic distress, further wounded Republicans. Especially damaging was the money issue. Rapidly decreasing prices prompted small farmers and other people heavily in debt to call for an inflated money supply that they hoped would stabilize prices. Republicans aggravated such people's distress by insisting that Civil War bondholders be paid back fully in gold, even though they had bought their bonds with devalued greenbacks and had received only the guarantee that the interest on the bonds would be paid in gold. In early 1874, the Democrats responded by pushing through Congress a bill that would have increased the number of greenbacks in circulation and eased the money pinch. But Grant vetoed it, fueling Democratic charges that Republicans served only the special interests of capitalists.

In the election of 1874, the Democrats gained in both houses of Congress and won a majority of the seats in the House of Representatives. For the first time since the war, they would control a branch of the federal government. Before the new Congress met in 1875, however, the lame-duck Republicans passed the Resumption Act of 1875. This act provided that the federal government would exchange gold for greenbacks. The new law not only made federal paper money as "good as gold," but it also added to the deflation.

The Political Crisis of 1877

Republican leaders entered the 1876 campaign in a spirit of foreboding. If they were to stem the Democratic momentum, they had to shake themselves free of the atmosphere of scandal that had grown up around Grant. They turned to a little-known Ohioan, Rutherford B. Hayes. Hayes had been governor of Ohio for three scandal-free terms. He had a good Civil War record, a reputation for honesty, and a record of support for civil service reform. He also was a moderate on Reconstruction and a former Whig whose strategy called for appealing to southern conservatives—especially former southern Whigs—to join the Republican cause.

For their part, the Democrats were determined to make the most of the Grant scandals. They nominated Governor Samuel J. Tilden of New York, who built a political career on his reputation as a fighter of corruption. Tilden had helped break the control of an infamous Democratic machine, the Tweed Ring, over New York City politics. The party wrote a platform that emphasized reform, especially of the civil ser-

vice. They promised to save the nation from "a corrupt centralism which has honeycombed the offices of the Federal government itself with incapacity, waste, and fraud."

On election night, the outcome seemed clear. Headlines announced that Tilden had won. Democrats celebrated, and the Republican party plunged into gloom. In Ohio, Hayes simply went to bed, convinced he had been defeated. A majority of the voters, 52 percent, had supported Tilden. The Democrats had made deep inroads in the North, carrying New York, New Jersey, Connecticut, and Indiana. They apparently had swept every southern state.

But before dawn, at Republican campaign headquarters in New York City, two or three sleepless politicians put together a daring strategy. In three southern states—Louisiana, South

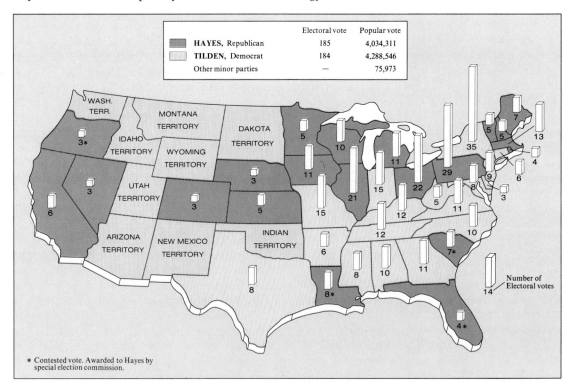

		Electoral vote	Popular vote
▨	**HAYES,** Republican	185	4,034,311
▢	**TILDEN,** Democrat	184	4,288,546
	Other minor parties	—	75,973

* Contested vote. Awarded to Hayes by special election commission.

MAP 16.3 THE ELECTION OF 1876
The Democratic candidate, Tilden, made such inroads in Northern states that Hayes, the Republican candidate, could not win the electoral college without the contested votes of three states in the deep South, despite the fact that he carried most northern and western states.

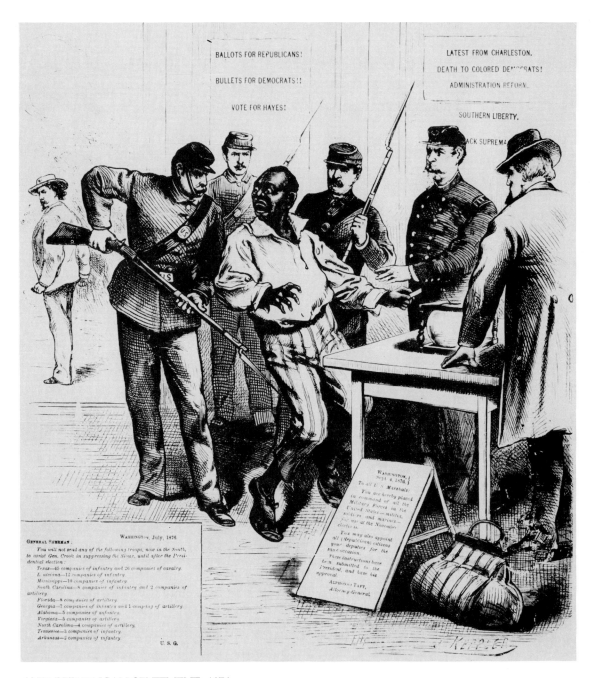

ANTI-REPUBLICAN SENTIMENT, 1876

This Democratic cartoon portrays Union soldiers, with bayonets fixed, coercing blacks to vote
Republican. The carpet bag in the foreground identifies the politics of the civilian at the voting table.
To the far left, the individual casting a watchful eye on the proceedings is probably an ex-planter,
supposedly powerless in the new politics of the South. (Culver)

TIME LINE
THE UNION RECONSTRUCTED

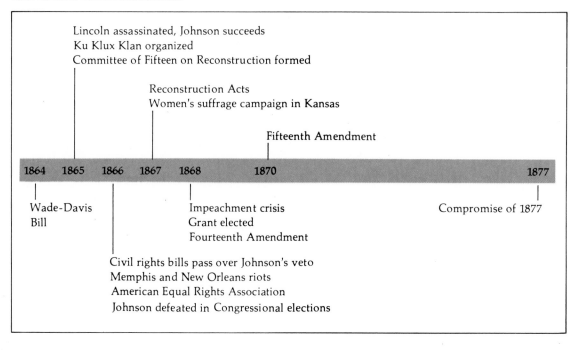

Carolina, and Florida—Republicans still controlled election procedures. If they could argue that Democratic fraud and intimidation had affected the election result in those states, they could certify Republican victories and report Republican electoral votes. Of course, newly elected Democratic officials in the three states would send in electoral votes for Tilden. As a result, there would be two sets of electoral votes from those states when Congress met to count the electoral votes early in 1877. If Congress accepted all the Republican votes, Hayes would have a one-vote electoral majority. The audacious announcement came: Hayes had carried the three southern states and won the election.

The months between the election in November and the inauguration the following March were filled with rumors: There might be a violent coup by Democrats if the Republicans tried to steal the election; President Grant might use the military to prevent Tilden from taking office; there might be a new election, or even be a new civil war. While the rumors flew, various inter-

ests tried to gain some advantage from the situation. Railroad promoters jockeyed for new federal subsidies, promising to deliver blocs of support in Congress to the party that made the best promises. Politicians on all sides flirted with the opposition, hoping for rewards.

In the end, political compromise and accident won out. Congress decided to appoint an Electoral Commission to settle the question. The commission would include seven Republicans and seven Democrats. The fifteenth and deciding vote would go to Justice David Davis of the Supreme Court, a man with a reputation for being free of party loyalty. But Davis resigned from the Court at the crucial moment, and the deciding vote fell to a lifelong Republican. When the commission completed its careful investigation of the election results in Florida, Louisiana, and South Carolina, the decision on each state was made by a straight party vote of eight to seven.

It next remained to be seen whether Congress would accept the result. The Senate was Republican, the House Democratic. Southern Democrats held the balance of power and Hayes's representatives sought their support. Some of these southerners were convinced that Hayes made promises to the "negotiators"—to confine federal troops to their barracks throughout the South, to appoint Democrats to major offices, and to support construction of a railroad across Texas to the West Coast. In any case, enough southerners in the House supported accepting the commission's findings to make Hayes president.

This sequence of events is often referred to as the Compromise of 1877, but historians remain uncertain whether any kind of deal was really struck. Hayes had promised in his campaign to end the military occupation of the South. He had also planned to appoint a few Democrats to his cabinet. And his faction of the Republican party

did not support the Texas railroad scheme. The alleged compromise may have been a fiction created by southern Democrats to justify their votes for Hayes.

The only certainty was that Reconstruction had ended. Those who had wanted *restoration* could be satisfied that the southern states had returned to their "proper practical relation with the Union." Those who had sought *reconstruction* could boast of three amendments to the Constitution, the end of slavery, public schools for black children, and some access to the land for ex-slaves, even if it was mostly as debt-ridden sharecroppers and tenant farmers. Those who had favored *redemption* could point to the fact that all the southern states were now firmly in the control of southern politicians and voters.

---

*A*fter the Civil War ended in 1865, the Thirteenth Amendment made slavery unconstitutional. However, President Abraham Lincoln's plan for quickly restoring the Union encountered opposition from radical Republicans in Congress, who believed that ex-slaves must vote, and moderate Republicans, who wished to punish the South and establish their party in southern states. Lincoln was assassinated before he could negotiate a unified Republican position.

Possibilities for a swift sectional reconciliation continued into the administration of Andrew Johnson, but he could not satisfy both moderate Republicans and the defeated Confederacy. His difficulties in working with Congress resulted in an erratic policy that intensified the South's resistance to federal power.

Congressional Reconstruction extended the civil rights of ex-slaves through the Fourteenth Amendment, protected black suffrage through the Fifteenth Amendment, and encouraged the formation of southern state governments controlled by supporters of the Union. Northern Republicans, however, failed to equip these governments to defeat the old planter elite,

which through appeals to racial solidarity, and by terror and intimidation, overturned all the Reconstruction state governments by 1877. Ex-slaves won some modest economic gains during Reconstruction, but without access to land ownership they became ensnared in a system of debt peonage and once again found themselves dependent on the planters.

In the North, Republicans enacted their entire economic program. Democrats attacked the program with a Jacksonian critique of "special privilege," but most northerners came out of the Civil War more receptive to concentrations of power. Many believed that the Republican program was necessary for sustained prosperity. Scandals during the Grant administration inflamed opposition to the Republicans but Republicans took the election of 1876 by capitalizing on the South's hunger for an end to Reconstruction and for greater influence in national politics. What is sometimes called the Compromise of 1877 kept the Republicans in control of the federal government by cementing an alliance with southern economic elites.

Suggestions for Further Reading

Presidential Restoration, Congressional Reconstruction

The most central studies of Reconstruction politics include Michael Les Benedict, *A Compromise of Principle: Congressional Republicans and Reconstruction* (1974); David Donald, *The Politics of Reconstruction 1863–1867* (1965); W. E. B. Du Bois, *Black Reconstruction* (1935); John Hope Franklin, *Reconstruction* (1965); Eric L. McKitrick, *Andrew Johnson and Reconstruction* (1966); Kenneth M. Stampp, *The Era of Reconstruction* (1965); and Hans L. Trefousse, *Impeachment of a President: Andrew Johnson, the Blacks, and Reconstruction* (1975).

The South During Reconstruction and the Plight of the Ex-Slaves

On conditions in the South during Reconstruction, including the experience of blacks, consult Robert Cruden, *The Negro in Reconstruction* (1969); Richard N. Current, *Three Carpetbag Governors* (1967); Robert Higgs, *Competition and Coercion: Blacks in the American Economy 1865–1914* (1977); Peter Kolchin, *First Freedom: The Responses of Alabama's Blacks to Emancipation and Reconstruction* (1972); Leon F. Litwack, *Been in the Storm So Long, The Aftermath of Slavery* (1979); James M. McPherson, *The Abolitionist Legacy: From Reconstruction to the NAACP* (1975); Howard N. Rabinowitz, *Race Relations in the Urban South 1865–1890* (1977); Roger L. Ransom and Richard Sutch, *One Kind of Freedom, The Economic Consequences of Emancipation* (1977); Willie Lee Rose, *Rehearsal for Reconstruction, The Port Royal Experiment* (1964); Allen W. Trelease, *White Terror: The Ku Klux Klan Conspiracy and Southern Reconstruction* (1972); and Joel Williamson, *After Slavery: The Negro in South Carolina During Reconstruction 1861–1877* (1965).

The North During Reconstruction

On national politics after the Civil War, including the retreat from Reconstruction, see Paul H. Buck, *The Road to Reunion 1865–1900* (1937); Morton Keller, *Affairs of State: Public Life in Late Nineteenth Century America* (1977); Robert Kelley, *The Transatlantic Persuasion, The Liberal–Democratic Mind in the Age of Gladstone* (1968); William S. McFeely, *Grant: A Biography* (1981); K. I. Polakoff, *The Politics of Inertia: The Election of 1876 and the End of Reconstruction* (1973); John G. Sproat, *"The Best Men": Liberal Reformers in the Gilded Age* (1968); and C. Vann Woodward, *Reunion and Reaction* (1956).

17

THE NEW INDUSTRIAL ORDER

*D*uring the last three decades of the nineteenth century, the productive capacity of the United States reached phenomenal levels. The gross national product—that is, the value of goods and services produced—increased six-fold between 1869 and 1899. This productive growth was linked above all to the industrializing sector of the economy. Manufacturing, which had accounted for roughly a third of total commodity output in 1869, accounted for more than half in 1899. By this time, the signs of industrialization could be seen almost everywhere—an industrial labor force of about nine million persons, a landscape of factories and mines, and two hundred thousand miles of railroad tracks.

Fundamentally, however, no break had occurred from the nation's industrial past. The essential characteristic of modern economic development is its capacity for sustained gains in economic efficiency—in obtaining a continually increasing output from a given input of labor and capital. Rising productivity is the basic difference between modern and preindustrial economies. A nation with a preindustrial economy might have a high standard of living, if it has abundant natural resources or a favorable population-to-land ratio. But such societies lack the means to become more efficient. The American colonies, for example, were prosperous at an early point. Only late in the colonial period, however, did the first signs of rising productivity appear. Sustained productivity gains began more than three decades before the Civil War. In the late nineteenth century, the United States maintained and gradually increased the momentum for higher productivity set in motion during the earlier stages of its industrial revolution.

The cumulative impact of industrialization made late nineteenth-century Americans keenly aware that they lived in a new age. What had been partial and limited became general and widespread. America turned into a land of factories, machines, and railroads.

New patterns of business organization were devised. For the first time, enterprise was conducted on a large scale. This, in turn, necessitated new ways of thinking about how to run a business. Methods of modern management emerged.

Working people deeply felt the effects of industrialization. Craft traditions came into sharp conflict with the mechanized factory. The demand for workers stimulated a mass migration of rural people, mainly from European villages, into American industry. After much trial and error, the modern trade-union movement began. Industrialism had become America's way of life.

A Maturing Industrial Economy

Before the Civil War, industrialism in America was overshadowed by a larger agricultural economy. The United States had a national transportation network, but it was based on rivers and canals, not railroads. There was a factory system, but it was limited to producing light consumer goods, such as boots, textiles, and clocks. There also was keen entrepreneurship, but no systematic management or large-scale enterprise. America's industrial revolution had started. It was completed in the late nineteenth century.

The Railroads

The maturing industrial economy required, above all, a transportation system capable of welding the nation into a vast, unified market. Until around 1850, transportation on canals and rivers had kept pace with the interior development of the country. But these waterways did not extend much beyond the Mississippi River. And, while suitable for bulky raw materials, canal barges and riverboats could not provide the year-round, on-time service demanded by the growing industrial and commercial sectors of the economy. Railroads performed this task far better. They had started in the 1830s as feeders for the river and canal traffic but quickly grew into

a system rivaling water transportation. By the 1860s, the dominance of the railroads was assured for both goods and passengers.

Railroad construction burst ahead during the postwar era. In 1870, the nation had about fifty-three thousand miles of track. Most of it lay east of the Mississippi, but it included the first transcontinental railroad linking the Pacific Coast to the rest of the nation. Between 1870 and 1882, the rail network doubled in size, mainly as a result of construction west of the Mississippi and across the continent into southern California and the Pacific Northwest. A final surge of building, which doubled the amount of track again by 1902, filled in the gaps in the South and elsewhere. In 1914, the U.S. railroad network covered over 250,000 miles, more than the rest of the world combined. Virtually every populated area in the country had come within reach of railroad service.

Railroad transportation became highly efficient. The early system, built by competing local companies, had been a jumble of discontinuous segments. Gauges of track varied widely and physical connections were lacking at terminal points between railroads. Many rivers had no railroad bridge. Also, each railroad company reserved the use of its track exclusively for its own equipment. As late as 1880, a shipment of heavy textile machinery had to go through eight transfers en route from Massachusetts to South Carolina.

CENTRAL PACIFIC'S CRACK ENGINE NO. 149
The railroads created a new notion of time. How fast could a person cross the continent? In 1876, a troupe of actors, scheduled to present Shakespeare's *Henry V* in San Francisco, made the trip from New York City in eighty-four hours, a new record. The Central Pacific's engine No. 149 carried them at top speed on the last leg from Ogden, Utah. (Southern Pacific Transportation Company)

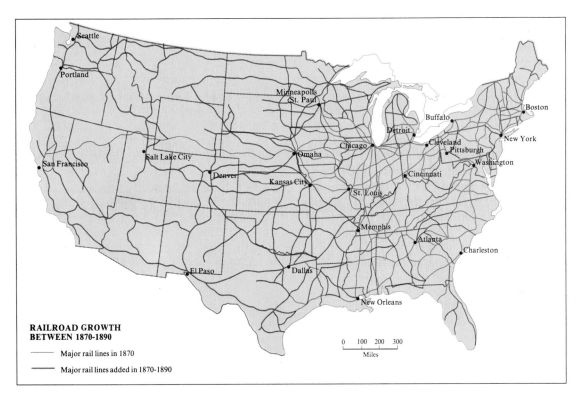

MAP 17.1 EXPANSION OF THE RAILROAD SYSTEM, 1870–1890
In 1870, the nation had 53,000 miles of rail track; in 1890, 167,000 miles. That burst of construction essentially completed the nation's rail network. Statistics confirm what a visual inspection of the map tells us. The main areas of expansion were in the South and west of the Mississippi. The Great Plains and intermountain sectors accounted for over 40 percent of all construction from 1870 onward. By 1890, the West was well served, both in the Pacific northwest and the southwest.

Beginning with the Civil War years, however, pressures increased for integration of the railroads. Track was hastily laid through Philadelphia, Richmond, and other cities in both the North and South to transport huge shipments of troops and equipment. The postwar economy, as it grew more complex and interdependent, demanded a better-organized rail system. Much railroad integration took place through the expansion of the great trunk lines connecting different regions of the country. The Pennsylvania and New York Central railroads pushed west from the East Coast to the Midwest, and the Illinois Central and the Burlington thrust south and west from Chicago. By the end of the 1880s, a standard rail gauge had been adopted across the country. Through the use of fast-freight firms and elaborate accounting procedures among railroads, the network served shippers as if it were a single unit. Breaks in transit, freight transfers between cars, and other causes of delayed rail service became as obsolete by 1900 as handwoven cloth might have seemed back in 1850.

At the same time, railroad technology was advancing. Heavier locomotives with four sets of driving wheels nearly tripled the pulling power of freight trains between 1866 and the turn of the century. To control the great mass and length of the freight trains, George Westinghouse invented the automatic coupler, the air brake, and friction gear for starting and stopping a long line of cars. Beginning in the 1870s, iron rails gave way to steel rails capable of withstanding the tremendous stress and heavy use of the latest freight traffic.

Integrated service and advancing technology increased the efficiency of the railroads. Productivity gains for the carriers advanced more rapidly than for the economy as a whole, averaging 2 percent a year between 1870 and 1910. These increases resulted in a sharp drop in freight rates from 1.12 cents per ton-mile in 1870 to 0.75 cents in 1910.

Considered as a transportation system, the railroads brilliantly met the needs of the maturing industrial economy. However, the dynamism that underlay this achievement did not stem from any orderly plan or design, but from the competitive energy of a free-wheeling market economy. The federal, state, and city governments provided assistance, especially before the 1870s, through extensive land grants and a variety of financial aids. But the actual enterprise of building railroads remained, with a few early exceptions, entirely in private hands.

Railroad construction differed from other kinds of nineteenth-century enterprise because it required, more than anything else, enormous amounts of capital. That was why—long before other businesses did so—the railroads organized themselves as corporations capable of raising funds from the public through the sale of stocks and bonds. Finance became the central arena of entrepreneurial activity in railroading.

The key figures were those with access to capital—their own and/or that of others. For example, John Murray Forbes, a Bostonian who had made his fortune in the China trade, went on to develop the Chicago, Burlington and Quincy Railroad into the preeminent midwestern system by the 1870s. A more aggressive figure was Cornelius Vanderbilt, who left the steamboat business in 1863 to invest his fortune in the New York Central. Vanderbilt and his son William built the Central into an east-west trunk line rivaled only by the Pennsylvania Railroad. They did so primarily through the acquisition of connecting lines and an intensive construction program. Forbes and the Vanderbilts aimed at creating well-constructed, well-financed railroad systems.

Jay Gould, a very different kind of rail entrepreneur, started out as a stock-market speculator. Gould earned early notoriety by his amazing manipulation of Erie Railroad stock in the 1860s and his nearly successful corner of the gold market in 1869. Many people at the time—and historians long after—considered Gould a "robber baron," one who loots commerce and gives nothing in return. But Gould did give something

in return. His great talent lay in gaining control over weak properties—the Erie, the Union Pacific, the Wabash, and the Southwest lines during the 1880s—and making them turn a profit. Some of this success came from stock manipulation, but Gould also earned his money by the kind of management he gave his railroads. He cared little for improving his properties, but he was a fierce competitor—for good reason. Gould's railroads generally had heavy bonded indebtedness, and only a high volume of traffic enabled them to meet the interest charges. His wealthier rivals, such as Forbes and the Vanderbilts, bitterly resented his ruthless rate-cutting tactics, but shippers and consumers benefited from the lower transportation costs that resulted. Gould's stock speculations also had the effect of attracting fresh capital into the railroad industry, money that might not otherwise have gone there. In the free-market economy in which American railroads grew, even a buccaneer like Jay Gould made a positive contribution.

Railroad development in the United States was often sordid, fiercely competitive, and subject to boom and bust. When the panic of 1893 hit, fully a third of the industry (by track mileage) went into receivership. Yet vast sums of capital were raised—$15 billion by 1914—and an integrated, highly advanced transportation system emerged.

Basic Industry

The nation's first manufacturing industries—textiles, boots and shoes, paper, and furniture—had been very much a part of the larger agricultural economy. They processed farm and forest materials and relied on the traditional sources of hand and water power. These industries made primarily consumer goods that substituted for homemade or artisan-made products. In the early industrial economy before 1850, there was not much call for heavy industry. It took increasing demands from such fields as railroad building, urban construction, and metal fabrication to develop a substructure of the mining and metal-processing industry.

Central to this development was iron making, which had become extensive well before the Civil War. The early iron makers engaged in small-batch production of wrought iron, a malleable metal ideal for use on farms and in small shops. In 1856, the English inventor Sir Henry Bessemer perfected a new process for refining iron. Unlike the puddling furnaces that made wrought iron, Bessemer converters produced steel, a harder, more durable metal, and did so in large amounts with little labor. Others took up this invention earlier, but Andrew Carnegie demonstrated its revolutionary importance.

Carnegie, an all-American success story, had arrived from Scotland in 1848 at the age of

TABLE 17.1 INCREASING OUTPUT OF HEAVY INDUSTRY, 1870–1910

	Bituminous Coal (Thousands of tons)	Rolled iron and steel (Thousands of tons)	Copper (tons)	Industrial machinery (in millions of dollars)
1870	20,471	850*	14,112	110.4**
1880	50,757	3,301	30,240	98.6***
1890	111,302	6,746	129,882	185.6
1900	212,318	10,626	303,059	347.6
1910	417,111	24,216	544,119	512.4

*Approximate total.
**Data for 1869.
***Data for 1874.

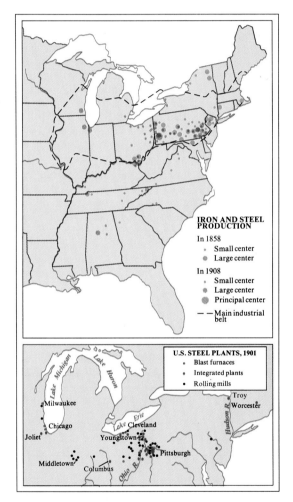

MAP 17.2 CHANGING PATTERN OF IRON AND STEEL PRODUCTION
Before the Civil War, the iron industry was concentrated in eastern Pennsylvania and northern New Jersey. During the late nineteenth century, the rapid development of the railroads and manufacturing spurred growth in steel production. The industry shifted westward, with a new trend toward integrated mills exemplified by the network of U.S. Steel Corporation plants around Pittsburgh.

twelve with his poverty-stricken family. He became a telegraph operator and then went to work for the Pennsylvania Railroad, where he rapidly climbed the managerial ladder. Carnegie resigned in 1865, wealthy from a series of successful speculations, to manufacture iron bridges for the railroads. Keenly aware of the possibilities of the Bessemer converter, Carnegie embarked in 1872 on a project aimed at the fullest exploitation of the new refining process. He built a massive steel-rail mill outside of Pittsburgh that had the most advanced equipment of the day. Equally important, the mill integrated all the stages of production—smelting, refining, and rolling—into a single operation that began with iron ore and ended with finished steel rails. Carnegie's mill, called the Edgar Thompson Works, fully repaid its investment in a few years, and came to be a model for the modern steel industry. Large, integrated steel plants swiftly replaced the older blast furnaces and puddling mills, and steel became a product essential for the further industrial growth of the nation.

The production of copper and other noniron metals went through a similar development. Copper output grew phenomenally, from eight thousand tons in 1860 to eight hundred thousand tons in 1914. Simultaneously, a change occurred in the use of copper. It had been used mainly for household products until the Civil War. Now it became a key ingredient in oil refining, the production of electrical generators and such other new fields as telephone communication.

The growth of the metal industries depended on the intensive exploitation of the country's mineral resources. Major discoveries of rich iron ore deposits occurred from the 1850s onward,

IRON AND STEEL

Iron was not a product new to the nineteenth century in the sense that plastic was new to the twentieth century. Early Europeans made iron tools and weapons at least a thousand years before Christ. Nor did the underlying processes change, for they are dictated by the nature of iron metallurgy. Iron ore must be smelted into metal; the raw metal must be refined to acquire desired properties such as malleability or hardness; and the refined iron must be shaped into useable forms. What did begin to change, slowly at first, were the techniques for carrying out these processes. Only as iron became available in large quantities and at low cost could the Industrial Revolution proceed.

Metallurgical innovation took place in two great waves. The first began in smelting late in the Middle Ages, when blast furnaces appeared in Belgium around 1340. Ore was melted in a charcoal-burning furnace to which limestone had been added. A blast of air then set off a combustion process that combined carbon from the charcoal with the molten iron while its impurities combined with the limestone to form a slag. The slag was drawn off from the top of the furnace while the molten iron was tapped from the bottom into sand forms resembling piglets feeding from a sow—hence the term "pig iron."

By the eighteenth century, the shortage of wood for charcoal had become acute in England. The substitution of coke, made by superheating coal, broke this bottleneck in iron production. An improved refining furnace, with separate chambers for the fuel and iron, was also developing. In 1784, Henry Cort invented the puddling furnace. Molten iron collected in the hollowed-out bottom, where it was worked with a long bar or paddle by hand from the outside. The resulting product was a malleable iron called *wrought iron*. Cort also made a crucial advance in the finishing stage at this time. For the laborious hammering process, he substituted the rolling mill, which shaped iron as it passed through grooved rolls.

This iron technology—blast furnace, puddling furnace, and rolling mill—formed the metallurgical basis for England's industrial revolution in the first half of the nineteenth century. Endowed with ample forests, the United States was slow to adopt the coke-using technology, but by 1860 it had caught up fairly well with England technologically and was producing nearly a million tons of iron annually. The iron industry, as it had developed to this point, met America's needs very well. Wrought iron was admirably suited for farm use because it was malleable and easily worked, and was also suitable for the localized machine- and engine-building characteristic of early industrialism. But wrought iron was too soft for the increasingly heavy service it received as railroad track. The search for a harder, more durable metal resulted in the invention in 1856 of an entirely different refining process by Henry Bessemer, an Englishman.

The Bessemer converter was a pear-shaped, tilting vessel open at the top, with a bottom perforated by many holes. Molten pig iron flowed into the top while the converter was tilted on its side. Air was blasted at great force through the perforated bottom, and the converter then swung back to its upright position. The resulting combustion set off a spectacular display of flame and smoke. Within fifteen minutes, the impurities in the molten iron had burned off and the flames died down. The converter was again tilted on its side and, after manganese and other chemicals had been added, the purified iron was emptied into ingot molds.

The refined metal, called *steel*,

first in upper Michigan and then in the huge Mesabi Range of Minnesota. These ores were readily shipped down the Great Lakes to the great steel-making centers in Illinois, Ohio, and Pennsylvania. Michigan was also the site of the first major copper finds before the Civil War, followed by discoveries in Arizona in the 1870s, and in the more extensive Montana fields during the 1880s. With the invention of the flotation refining process, it became possible to utilize the lower-grade copper ores of these western fields. Coal mining, a minor enterprise before 1850, grew rapidly thereafter, first in the anthracite region of eastern Pennsylvania, and then in the soft-coal Appalachian fields from West Virginia through western Pennsylvania and into Ohio.

had a hardness somewhere between that of wrought iron and the expensive crucible steel that had long been used for fine tools and weapons. The Bessemer process had one significant drawback; it operated successfully only with expensive, low-phosphorous iron. The open-hearth method, developed shortly after the Bessemer process, could handle low-quality iron and was more economical and flexible. By World War I, the open-hearth method was rapidly becoming the dominant refining process. But the Bessemer converter had given life to the modern steel industry.

The device that Bessemer had invented to produce a better metal also proved vastly more efficient than the hand-operated puddling furnace. The Bessemer converter turned out great quantities of steel with virtually no labor. This forced changes up and down the line. To feed the converters' appetite for pig iron, blast furnaces grew ever larger and, with the introduction of the hot blast, much more efficient. To handle the flow of steel from the converters, rolling mills became increasingly mechanized and automatic, so that the steel could move continuously through progressively narrower rolls set in tandem. By means of a variety of metal-handling devices, the stages of production became integrated, enabling the iron to proceed "with perfect regularity" from the blast furnace to the Bessemer converter to its emergence from the rolling mill as a finished rail or girder. The integrated steel plant of 1900, capable of producing twenty-five hundred tons or more a day, was vastly more efficient than the small blast furnaces and iron mills of 1860.

The revolution in steelmaking changed the face of American industrialism. The geographic concentration of industrial activity intensified. The places best located in relation to raw materials, transportation, and markets—Pittsburgh, the steel towns along the Great Lakes, and Birmingham, Alabama—became the great centers of steel production.

A second result involved the scale of business enterprise. The principal steel companies evolved into vertically integrated firms that controlled their own raw materials, some of their transport facilities, and the marketing of their products. For the workers, the effects were no less sweeping. The skills of the puddler, heater, and hand roller became obsolete; gang labor was largely replaced by ore- and metal-handling equipment; and face-to-face relationships with employers disappeared. The typical steelworker of 1900 was a machine-tender in an impersonal, bureaucratic business organization.

Steel made possible dramatic changes in transportation and construction. With steel rails capable of withstanding heavy traffic, and steel locomotives capable of ever greater pulling power, the railroads became the primary carriers of the nation's enormous volume of goods. The efficiency of the railroads rose nearly 70 percent between 1870 and 1900, and freight charges per ton-mile fell by almost the same amount—thanks largely to the use of steel for rails and equipment. In the growth of America's cities, steel played a key role in the construction of skyscrapers, trolley lines, and subways, and the vast underground complexes of pipe that supplied the urban millions with water and gas and carried away their sewage. Steel battleships asserted the nation's new role as a world power. Without steel, the emerging automobile industry would not have grown, nor a host of other American industries. It is no wonder that historians have called the last decades of the nineteenth century America's Age of Steel.

Coal production, scarcely half a million tons in 1860, reached 270 million tons in 1900.

Coal, in turn, was the key to the intensive use of energy in industrial production. The steam engine, limited initially to service as a power source for ships and locomotives, came into increasing use as a driver of machinery during the second half of the century. Steam was as important as water power for industrial purposes by 1870, and six times as important twenty years later. At the Philadelphia Centennial Exhibition of 1876, visitors gazed in wonder at the enormous Corliss reciprocating engine, shown on page 520, with a fly wheel thirty feet in diameter and the capacity to drive all the other exhibits in Machinery Hall.

Steam power became increasingly efficient, first through refinements in the reciprocating engine, then by means of the steam turbine in the 1880s, and finally by coupling the steam turbine to the electric generator in the 1890s. The transformation of coal energy into electric power greatly increased the flexibility of industry. Once electricity could be drawn from distant generating plants, the power needs of factories no longer dictated where they would be located. And, as small electric motors became the power source for machines, factory design no longer was determined by the transmission of power by belts and shafts from the plant's steam engines. These advantages led to the rapid adoption of electric power by manufacturers after 1900.

Following the Civil War, the modern metal-producing industries were established, the nation's mineral resources came under intensive exploitation, and energy was harnessed to the manufacturing system. Production of steel, coal, and horsepower grew after 1870 at rates far exceeding that of manufacturing production. The industrial substructure came into its own during this period, enabling the manufacturing economy to forge ahead rapidly.

Mass Markets and Large-Scale Enterprise

Meanwhile, business organization underwent fundamental change. Until well into the industrial age, economic activity had characteristically been carried on in small units. Now, for the first time, American enterprise became big business.

Early manufacturers had typically produced in limited quantities, mainly for nearby markets. No firm tried to control the flow of its product very far through the industrial process. As distribution widened, producers relied on wholesale merchants and commission agents to market their goods. From the making of raw materials at one end, goods normally passed through numerous hands on their way to the final sale to the customer. Both industry and commerce were carried on by many small, independent entrepreneurs. Shops and factories had an average of about eight employees in 1870.

Then the scale of economic activity began to change markedly. "Combinations of capital on a scale hitherto wholly unprecedented constitute one of the remarkable features of modern business methods," the economist David A. Wells

THE CORLISS ENGINE
The symbol of the Philadelphia Centennial in 1876 was the great Corliss engine, which towered over Machinery Hall and powered all the equipment on exhibit there. Yet, the Corliss engine also signified the incomplete nature of American industrialism at that time; it soon became obsolete. Westinghouse turbines generating electricity would power the nation's next great world's fair, held in Chicago in 1893. (Culver)

wrote in 1889. He already could see "no other way in which the work of production and distribution can be prosecuted." The increasing scale of enterprise seemed "in a certain and large sense, not voluntary on the part of the possessors and controllers of capital, but necessary or even compulsory."

What was there in the nation's economic activity that led to Wells's sense of inevitability? The dynamic features of American growth—availability of capital, receptivity to technology, and the emergence of a heavy industrial base—certainly played a part. They enabled large-scale enterprise to occur. But the key lay in the American market. Immigration and a very high birthrate swelled the population. People flocked into the cities, and the railroads brought these dense consuming markets within the reach of distant producers. The telegraph, which came into widespread use by the Civil War, eliminated communications barriers. Unlike Europe, America was not carved up into many national markets; no political frontiers impeded the flow of goods within the country. Nowhere else did manufacturers have an internal market so vast and accessible for their products.

The impact of the expanding markets on the scale of enterprise can best be seen in the fresh-meat trade. Until the Civil War, this business had hardly changed since the preindustrial era. In every city, butchers purchased livestock directly from nearby farmers and butchered the animals in local slaughterhouses. The diet of city dwellers, especially the poor, depended mostly on salt pork and smoked pork.

With the coming of the railroads, a partial revolution occurred in the fresh-meat business. Cattle raising shifted to the grazing ranges of the Great Plains and to feed lots in the Corn Belt of the prairie states. Chicago, the rail terminal for the upper Midwest, established itself as the hub of the American meat trade. The Union Stock Yards, which opened in Chicago in 1865, immediately became the world's greatest livestock market. Cattle were shipped by railroad from Chicago to eastern cities, where, as before, they were slaughtered in local "butchertowns." By means of regional specialization and an efficient rail network, the meat trade serviced an exploding urban population and, without further development, might have done so indefinitely.

Gustavus F. Swift, a shrewd Massachusetts cattle dealer who settled in Chicago in 1875, saw the future differently. The system of marketing fresh meat seemed inefficient to him. Livestock deteriorated enroute to the East, and local slaughterhouses wasted by-products and labor. Production might be concentrated in Chicago, as it already was for preserved pork products, if dressed beef could be kept fresh in transit. The Chicago pork-packing plants had converted to year-round operation in the 1860s through the development of primitive refrigeration. After Swift's engineers solved the problem of air circulation, he built a fleet of refrigerator cars and established a central beef-packing house at the Chicago stockyards.

This was only the beginning of Swift's activities. No refrigerated warehouses were available in the cities to which he shipped chilled beef, so Swift had to build his own network of branch houses. Then he established a fleet of wagons to distribute his products to retail butcher shops. Swift constructed additional facilities to handle the fertilizer, chemicals, and other usable by-products from his slaughtering operations, and he took on other perishable commodities, including dairy products, to fully utilize his refrigerated cars and branch houses. As the demand grew, he built more packing houses in other stockyards centers, such as Kansas City, Fort Worth, and Omaha.

Step by step, Swift created a new kind of enterprise, the vertically integrated firm—that is, a national company capable of handling within its own structure all the functions of an entire industry. In effect, Swift and Company replaced a large number of small firms that had operated locally. Four other meat packers, which, like Armour and Company, had originated as pork packers, followed Swift's lead. By the end of the 1890s, these firms, all of them nationally organized and vertically integrated, produced nearly 90 percent of all the meat shipped in interstate commerce.

The development of the refrigerator car had made all this possible in the fresh-meat trade. In most other fields, no such single event was so decisive. But other manufacturers did share Swift's perception that the essential step was to identify a mass market. They, like Swift, moved quickly to set up national distribution systems to reach that market. The Singer Sewing Machine Company formed its own sales organization, using both retail stores and door-to-door salesmen. The McCormick Harvesting Machine Company set up a franchise network of dealers. Through such distribution systems, manufacturers provided technical information, credit, and repair facilities for their products. These companies, as did the meat packers, became vertically integrated firms that served a national market.

To gain the benefits of mass distribution, retail business went through a comparable change. Montgomery Ward and Company and Sears, Roebuck and Company developed into national mail-order houses for rural consumers. From Vermont to California, farm families selected identical goods from mail-order catalogues, and became part of the nationwide consumer market. In the cities, mass distribution followed different strategies. Department stores, pioneered by John Wanamaker in Philadelphia, spread to every substantial city in the country. Sometimes this growth occurred through the efforts of a wholesale merchant, but more often—as with R. H. Macy of New York—it came through the addition of departments to a dry goods store. An alternative route to urban distribution was the establishment of extensive chain store systems, in which the Great Atlantic and Pacific Tea Company and the F. W. Woolworth Company were the leaders. Woolworth used the slogan "Large purchases for cash direct from manufacturers explain the high values we offer."

American society prepared citizens to be consumers of standardized goods. The high rate of geographic movement broke down loyalties to local custom and regional distinctiveness that were so strong in Europe. Social class in America, though by no means absent, was blurred at the edges. Equally important, it did not involve special symbols of appearance. Foreign visitors often noted that ready-made clothing made it difficult to tell shop girls from debutantes on the city streets.

The receptivity to standardized goods should not be exaggerated. For example, Gustavus Swift encountered great resistance to his Chicago beef. How could it be wholesome weeks later in Boston or Philadelphia? Cheap prices helped, but advertising perhaps had a greater influence. Modern advertising was born during the late nineteenth century, bringing brand names and

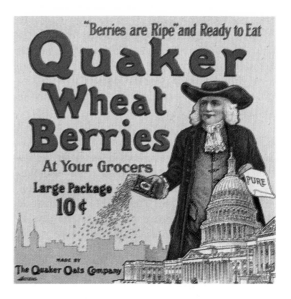

QUAKER OATS

Like crackers, sugar, and other nonperishable foods, oatmeal had traditionally been marketed to consumers in bulk from barrels. In 1882, the grain merchant Henry P. Cowell completed the first continuous-process mill for oatmeal, cutting production costs and greatly increasing output. He also struck on the idea of selling oatmeal in boxes of standard size and weight to a national market. Broadsides showing the Quaker Oats man soon appeared in every American town, advertising a product of reliable quality and uniform price. (Collection of Business Americana, Smithsonian Institution, Courtesy of Quaker Oats Company)

an urban landscape increasingly cluttered by billboards and signs. By 1900, advertisers spent more than $90 million annually for space in newspapers and magazines. Advertisements urged readers to bathe with Pears' soap, to munch Uneeda biscuits, to sew on a Singer machine, and to snap pictures with a Kodak camera. The shaping of these tastes became a major function of American business. An increasing amount of entrepreneurial effort went into the active molding of demand for brand names.

In heavy industry, on the other hand, markets required neither the active shaping, nor the extensive distribution systems called for in selling consumer goods. Steel companies, which sold mostly to such large users as railroads and bridge builders, did not develop extensive marketing organizations. But they did need reliable supplies of raw materials. Andrew Carnegie saw this most clearly. By 1900, he had made his steel company fully self-contained. He had acquired his own coal and iron mines, and built a fleet of ore boats and connecting railroads to carry the raw materials to his western Pennsylvania mills. Other basic steel producers followed this pattern as best they could, and so did the big firms in oil, copper, explosives, and other fields dependent on mined materials. The motive of all these companies was primarily defensive. In a world of limited resources, the big user did well to corner his share before others grabbed it.

Heavy industry thus followed a different pattern of vertical integration—back toward raw materials rather than forward toward the consumer. But in either case, the result was the vertically integrated firm.

Mass Production

Mass marketing, which caused a revolution in American business organization, had an equally decisive effect on production methods. Once products became standardized and production became high-volume, changes in manufacturing processes followed almost inevitably. After the Civil War, as mass marketing expanded, mass production systems came into their own.

For example, great advances accompanied the creation of a national market for dressed beef. The huge packing houses that sprang up in Chicago quickly improved the traditional methods of killing and processing cattle. At the Armour plant in 1907, the work was divided into seventy-eight distinct jobs. Workers performed all these tasks extremely efficiently and at high speed as the carcasses moved along hooked to overhead conveyors. In a ten-hour day, a gang of 157 workers handled 1,050 cattle, many more per employee than if one skilled butcher did everything. Machinery did not replace workers; rather savings resulted from a minute division of labor.

The concept of mass production could be applied even outside factories. The women's clothing industry discovered that the division of tasks might be organized efficiently through a system of subcontracting. Cloth, after being cut in the central shop, was sent out to be sewn and finished in small shops. It often went through further distribution as homework to be done in the shabby tenements of immigrant ghettos in large cities. This was called a "sweated" trade because the low piece rates paid for the work forced people to work extremely long hours and usually involved the labor of wives and children. The production of women's clothing, though performed largely outside of factories, was a genuine mass production industry. It manufactured large volumes of standardized goods at low cost.

The main thrust, however, was toward the large factory, and the central method was mechanization. After work had been subdivided into simple, repetitive tasks, machines generally could be designed to replace hand labor. The main opportunity to do so came with products that could be assembled from standardized, interchangeable parts. These items included agricultural implements, sewing machines, typewriters, and bicycles. The advantages of mass production for such products had been evident to such early inventor-entrepreneurs as Eli Whitney and Simeon North in the manufacture of guns and clocks. But it had taken many years to devise metal-cutting machines—the machine tools—that were speedy, automatic, and, above all, precise. It was essential to eliminate the need for "fitting"—that is, the costly hand-filing of parts before they could be assembled. A separate industry had emerged by the Civil War that specialized in machine tools for new industries making products assembled from interchangeable parts. The machine-tool industry did most of the innovative work, culminating in the turret lathe. This machine made a complex series of cuts automatically and with great speed and accuracy.

The brilliant inventive process that resulted in the turret lathe was directed at the manufacture of high-volume standardized goods. This connection between technology and markets could be seen vividly in the automobile industry. The "horseless carriage," a curiosity when it first appeared in the 1890s, quickly became serious business. By 1900, about eight thousand cars were chugging along the nation's roads. Most of the early buyers were wealthy, but the future of the automobile lay with the development of a mass market.

Of the pioneer car makers, Henry Ford saw this fact most clearly. Ford was the classic tinkerer turned manufacturer. Born on a Michigan farm in 1863, he had moved to Detroit and worked as a machinist at the Edison Illuminating Company. Like many others, Ford became fascinated by automobiles, especially racing cars.

HENRY FORD:
MASS PRODUCING THE MODEL T

During the season 1908–1909 we continued to make Models "R" and "S," four-cylinder runabouts and roadsters, the models that had previously been so successful. . . . But "Model T" swept them right out. We sold 10,607 cars—a larger number than any manufacturer had ever sold. The price for the touring car was $850. . . . This season demonstrated conclusively to me that it was time to put the new policy in force. . . . Therefore in 1909 I announced one morning, without any previous warning, that in the future we were going to build only one model, that the model was going to be "Model T," and that the chassis would be exactly the same for all cars, and I remarked:

"Any customer can have a car painted any color that he wants so long as it is black."

I cannot say that any one agreed with me. The selling people could not of course see the advantages that a single model would bring about in production. . . . They thought that our production was good enough as it was and there was a very decided opinion that lowering the sales price would hurt sales . . . The impression was that a good car could not be built at a low price, and that, anyhow, there was no use in building a low-priced car because only wealthy people were in the market for cars. . . .

We were, almost overnight it seems, in great production. How did all this come about?

Simply through the application of an inevitable principle. By the application of intelligently directed power and machinery. In a little dark shop on a side street an old man had labored for years making axe handles. Out of seasoned hickory he fashioned them, with the help of a draw shave, a chisel, and a supply of sandpaper. Carefully was each handle weighed and balanced. No two of them were alike. . . . His average product was eight handles a week. . . . And often some of these were unsaleable—because the balance was not true.

Today you can buy a better axe handle, made by machinery, for a few cents. And you need not worry about the balance. They are all alike—and every one is perfect. Modern methods applied in a big way have not only brought the cost of axe handles down to a fraction of their former cost—but they have immensely improved the product.

It was the application of these same methods to the making of the Ford car that at the very start lowered the price and heightened the quality. . . .

A Ford car contains about five thousand parts—that is counting screws, nuts, and all. Some of the parts are fairly bulky and others are almost the size of watch parts. In our first assembling we simply started to put a car together at a spot on the floor and workmen brought to it the parts as they were needed in exactly the same way that one builds a house. . . .

The first step forward in assembly came when we began taking the work to the men instead of the men to the work. We now have two general principles . . . a man shall never have to take more than one step . . . [and] no man need ever stoop over.

Along about April 1, 1913, we first tried the experiment of an assembly line. We tried it on assembling the fly-wheel magneto. We try everything in a little way first—we will rip out anything once we discover a better way, but we have to know absolutely that the new way is going to be better than the old before we do anything drastic.

I believe that this was the first moving line ever installed. The idea came in a general way from the overhead trolley that the Chicago packers use in dressing beef. We had previously assembled the fly-wheel magneto in the usual method. With one workman doing a complete job he could turn out from thirty-five to forty pieces in a nine-hour day, or about twenty minutes to an assembly. What he did alone was then spread into twenty-nine operations; that cut down the assembly time to thirteen minutes, ten seconds. Then we raised the height of the line eight inches—this was in 1914—and cut the time to seven minutes. Further experimenting with the speed that the work should move at cut the time down to five minutes. In short, the result is this: by the aid of scientific study one man is now able to do somewhat more than four did only a comparatively few years ago.

MODEL T'S
Henry Ford introduced his Model T in 1908. He became a pioneer in the use of assembly line
techniques, and the Ford Motor Company sold more than fifteen million Model T's during the next
nineteen years. Ford mass-produced his cars by making them all alike, ". . . just like one pin is like
another pin . . ." Here, workers complete final assembly. (The Bettmann Archive)

His interest quickly shifted after he launched his
own company in 1903 with the aid of wealthy
backers. "I will build a motor car for the multitude," Ford declared. This car was the Model T,
which Ford introduced in 1908. It was designed
specifically to match his conception of mass production of automobiles:

> The way to make automobiles is to make one
> automobile just like another automobile, to
> make them all alike, to make them come
> through the factory alike—just like one pin is
> like another pin when it comes from the pin
> factory.

If the pin was the simplest mass-produced
item, the automobile was the most complex. But
volume and standardization made it subject to
the same principles of production.

Assembly was the bottleneck. Even after the
parts of a car had been mass-produced, the vehicle was still assembled individually by skilled
craftsmen. In a stroke of genius, Ford proposed
that the assembly of automobiles also be broken
down into simple, repetitive tasks. This could be
accomplished by moving the unfinished vehicle
past a series of work stations on a continuous

motor-driven chain conveyor. The moving assembly line was limited at first to engines, transmissions, and frames. It began to turn out finished Model T's at Ford's new plant in Highland
Park, Michigan, in 1914. The mass market that
Ford created with his Model T had given rise to
the modern assembly line plant and the first giant automobile company.

The Merger Movement

For a Swift, a Carnegie, or a Ford, growing
larger meant becoming more efficient. These
men saw vertical integration as a form of innovation that, like technology, meant lower operating
costs. For many others, however, big business
provided an answer to entirely different concerns. Economic concentration offered an escape
from the fearsome competition of an uncontrolled marketplace.

After the Civil War, the business cycle became subject to violent fluctuations. From 1873
to 1878 and again from 1893 to 1897, severe depressions gripped the United States. Lesser pan-
ics struck in 1884, 1888, 1903, and 1907. Part of
the problem came from the nation's weak financial structure. The banking system was apt to

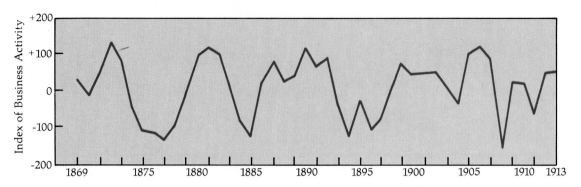

FIGURE 17.1 PERFORMANCE OF THE ECONOMY

collapse under stress, and the money supply was too inflexible for the needs of the growing economy. These weaknesses were compounded by the boom-and-bust character of American investment—feverishly overbuilding capacity in good times and then sharply curtailing activity when demand began to slacken.

Businessmen, even if they could not understand the underlying causes of the volatile economy, knew the consequences—lost earnings for stronger firms and bankruptcy for weaker ones. During the depression of the 1870s, wholesale prices fell about 30 percent. The rate of business failures doubled as forty-seven thousand firms went under. In hard times, the marketplace turned into a jungle.

Despite their lip service to free enterprise, unrestrained competition held few charms for American businessmen. Even before the Civil War, they had sought the shelter of pools—that is, agreements to share the market and to avoid price cutting. Such pacts violated the common-law principle against conspiracies in restraint of trade, however, and therefore, could not legally be enforced. Depressed markets, moreover, almost invariably tempted stronger firms to break away and grab a larger share of the available business. This occurred especially in industries with high fixed costs, such as the railroads and, increasingly, manufacturing as well. Firms were often better off operating at lower prices, or even at a loss, than not operating at all. For a strong competitor like Andrew Carnegie, who could make a profit even on rock-bottom prices, there was "nothing like meeting the market, taking the business and running full." Carnegie said

this when he pulled out of the steel-rail pool in 1894.

If voluntary pools did not work, the only solution was a business strategy that would bring competing firms under a single head. John D. Rockefeller was the pioneering figure in this activity. Rockefeller had been a rising young commission merchant in nearby Cleveland at the time that Colonel E. L. Drake drilled the world's first oil well in western Pennsylvania in 1859. Within a few years, Rockefeller moved into the refining end of the new petroleum industry. His product was kerosene, for which great demand quickly developed for use as an illuminating fuel. Production grew even more rapidly, however. The petroleum industry became intensely competitive and subject to severe booms and busts. Rockefeller's response was two-pronged. He built the Standard Oil Company into a highly efficient and often ruthless competitor. But he also did what he could to reduce the competitive intensity of the oil business, among other ways by buying into rival firms.

Rockefeller's empire building hit a legal snag, however, because his Ohio corporation charter prohibited him from acquiring holdings outside the state. After trying a variety of subterfuges, Rockefeller in 1882 conceived of the *trust* as the answer to his problem. Under this arrangement, participating firms assigned their stock to a board of trustees and in return received certificates entitling them to dividends on the earnings of the trust. The board took full control of all the properties, managing and disposing of them as it saw fit. In this way, Rockefeller hoped to avoid the limitations imposed by his Ohio incorporation and bring his rivals under the control of Standard Oil. Although firms in other industries followed Rockefeller's lead, however, the trust encountered increasing legal problems during the 1880s.

Then a better legal instrument emerged for bringing competing firms under a common management. This was the holding company, a corporation with the power to purchase stock in other corporations. If just one state granted such privileges, the corporation could operate throughout the country. In 1889, the New Jersey legislature provided holding-company privileges in the state's general incorporation law. The promoter of this legislation was James B. Dill, a corporate lawyer. New Jersey was willing because it wanted the revenues expected from the fees and taxes paid by the new corporations. Delaware, West Virginia, and other states soon joined New Jersey in issuing charters to holding companies.

Although a legal, efficient device was now available, a national merger movement did not begin until after the terrible depression of the 1890s. Chastened by the cutthroat competition of that depression, firms rushed to sell out. Bringing them under the control of a holding company was a formidable task. First, a syndicate had to be set up to provide risk capital. Then negotiations were conducted for the purchase—usually through an exchange of stock—of the firms slated to be part of the new combine. Finally, a large volume of holding-company stock had to be marketed in an orderly way. This procedure was primarily a venture in finance, and no one could handle it better than an investment banker.

Investment bankers were financial middlemen who raised capital for American business. After the Civil War, a handful of large investment-banking firms had risen to eminence—J. P. Morgan and Company and the Kuhn, Loeb Company in New York; Lee, Higginson and Company in Boston; and the Drexel Company in Philadelphia. They operated largely to serve the financial needs of the railroads. These firms underwrote—that is, sold at their own risk—issues of railroad stock. They channelled the new securities into allied banks and insurance companies and to large investors in both America and Europe. When a railroad went into receivership, in-

vestment bankers handled the reorganization, a task similar to that of organizing an industrial holding company. The investment bankers, because of their railroad experience and their strategic place in the financial system, played the key role in the merger movement that began in the late 1890s.

When the merger movement began, in 1897, others tried to play the promotional role. The barbed-wire manufacturer John W. ("Bet-A-Million") Gates organized the American Steel and Wire Company, and other promoters launched mergers in tin plate, biscuits, and other fields. But as the financial stakes rose, the professionals

J. PIERPONT MORGAN
J. P. Morgan was the giant among American financiers. He had served an apprenticeship in investment banking under his father, a leading Anglo-American banker in London. A gruff man of few words, Morgan had a genius for instilling trust, and the strength of will to persuade others to follow his lead and do his bidding—qualities the great photographer Edward Steichen captured in this portrait. (The Museum of Modern Art, New York. Gift of A. Conger Goodyear)

entered the picture. In 1898, J. P. Morgan organized the Federal Steel Company, and thereafter investment bankers largely preempted the field. Such new giants as the International Harvester Company, the American Car and Foundry Company, the American Can Company, and United States Steel were the handiwork of Wall Street.

Morgan and his Wall Street compatriots left no doubt about the main purposes of these giant mergers. Their objective, as earlier with the railroads, was to bring order to industries "demoralized" by cutthroat competition. The investment bankers claimed to be marketplace reformers and advocates of "fair" competition, as opposed to "bitter, relentless, overbearing, tyrannical conduct, calculated to drive out the weak." They were interested in changing marketplace behavior, rather than achieving savings and efficiency through mergers.

Once in operation, however, the new combines commonly moved to take advantage of their great size. As the National Biscuit Company reported in 1901, four years after its creation for the admitted purpose of monopolizing the industry:

> We turned our attention and bent our energies to improving the internal management of our own business, to getting the full benefit for purchasing our raw materials in large quantities, to economizing the expense of manufacture, to systematizing and rendering more effective our selling department.

The company shifted from bulk sales for grocery cracker barrels to packaged goods under the brand name Uneeda Biscuit. It embarked on a major advertising campaign, built up global purchasing and marketing systems, and concentrated production in a few giant plants. National Biscuit originally intended "to control competition. We soon satisfied ourselves that within the company itself we must look for success."

Not all mergers ended this way, but those that did not generally failed. The profitable ones rationalized their operations, exploited their advantage of size, and moved in the direction of vertical integration. They thus joined the mainstream of large-scale American enterprise. Whether the starting point had been to benefit from the efficiencies of size, as with Swift, or to control competition, as with National Biscuit, the result was essentially the same. The vertically integrated corporation had come of age.

The Managerial Revolution

At one time, observed the railroad expert Marshall M. Kirkman in 1896, it had been thought "practically impossible to manage a great railway effectively." On the early roads, "management had been personal and autocratic; the superintendent, a man gifted with energy and clearness of perception, moulded the property to his own will. But as the properties grew, he found himself unable to give his personal attention to everything. Undaunted, he sought to do everything and do it well. He ended by doing nothing."

It is not hard to understand the mistake of the early railroad superintendent. How could he know that methods which had worked brilliantly in the past would not work in the future? And where, in a world of small businesses, was there a model for running an enterprise other than by personal and direct control over its activities? How else could a business be run? No problem was harder to see clearly, or, once discovered, more taxing on the business imagination. Nor was any industrial success, once achieved, fated to have more enduring consequences than the mastery of the techniques of modern management.

As trunk lines thrust westward from Baltimore, Philadelphia, and New York before the Civil War, they came up against a managerial crisis that had not troubled shorter roads. In 1856, in a classic statement of the problem, the Erie Railroad official Daniel C. McCallum compared a fifty-mile road and a five hundred-mile road. On the short road, the superintendent could personally attend to every detail, "and any system, however imperfect, may prove comparatively successful." But not on long roads: "I am fully convinced that in the want of a system lies the true secret of their failure." McCallum had crucial insight in realizing the need for a system—a formal administrative structure—in the operation of large-scale, complex enterprises. He knew he was working in the dark: "We have no precedent or experience upon which we can fully rely."

The railroads were the most complex form of nineteenth-century enterprise. They had to raise huge amounts of capital, and their properties stretched over ever greater distances. They employed armies of workers—nearly fifty thousand on the Pennsylvania system by 1890. And, unlike the leisurely traffic on the canals, trains had to be precisely scheduled and closely coordinated. Even after the telegraph became an indispensable operating tool in the 1840s, train accidents took a heavy toll.

Step by step, always under the prod of necessity, the early trunk lines pioneered in the main elements of modern business administration. They separated overall management from day-to-day operations and departmentalized operational activities along functional lines—maintenance of way, rolling stock, and traffic. The Erie Railroad was the first to divide its system into manageable geographic units. Then came the careful definition of the lines of communication upward to the central office. When Albert Fink perfected his cost-accounting system for the Louisville and Nashville Railroad after the Civil War, managers at last had precise data on which to assess the performance of their roads. By the end of the 1870s, the managerial crisis on the railroads had been resolved.

As industrial enterprises became comparably complex, they confronted the same kind of managerial problems. However, industry drew on the experience of the railroads. Sometimes there were direct linkages, as with Andrew Carnegie, who had been a Pennsylvania Railroad executive before going into steel. Starting in 1879, J. P. Morgan attended the monthly directors' meetings of the New York Central and applied what he learned to the manufacturing mergers he later promoted. Whether by trial and error or through the railroad influence, large companies everywhere moved toward a modern management structure. Successful firms, such as Armour and Company, the Singer Sewing Machine Company, and the McCormick Harvesting Machine Company, solved the problems of administering far-flung business empires.

By the beginning of the twentieth century, the main lines of managerial strategy had taken hold throughout large-scale American industry. With few exceptions, vertically integrated firms followed a centralized, functionally departmentalized plan (see Figure 17.2 on page 530). The central office housed a number of departments, each charged with the overall responsibility for a specific area of activity—purchasing, auditing, production, transportation, or sales. These functionally defined departments provided "middle management," and they represented the heart of the managerial revolution in American industry.

Although managers of operating units in the field functioned much like earlier factory owners, middle managers undertook entirely new tasks. They grappled with the complex problems of directing the flow of goods through the integrated enterprise from the purchase of raw materials to the final sale. They were key innovators, equivalent in matters of business practice to engineers in improving technology.

Their superiors, the top executives, could not claim such a complete achievement. The firms that developed through internal growth had been built by individual entrepreneurs. The founding families—the Swifts, Armours, and McCormicks—still largely maintained control into the twentieth century. They were generally reluctant to surrender the tight supervision with which they or their fathers had developed the companies. In 1907, J. Ogden Armour spent his days reading operational reports and issuing orders to his buying, processing, and selling departments. All middle managers reported directly to him. Priding himself on his knowledge of the company and absorbed in the details of its operation, Armour had neither the time, the staff, nor the inclination to engage in long-term, strategic planning or systematic evaluation of his firm's performance. Armour typified an entire generation of owner-managers. Brilliant in creating the subordinate administrative structure, they normally were slow to apply managerial principles to their own tasks.

The large-scale firms formed by mergers had an advantage here. Their top executives were more likely to be salaried officials. They also were inclined to introduce a systematic approach into the central office as well as to the reorganization of the various units of the merged company. Even here, however, absorption in day-to-day activity gave top management little opportunity for long-term planning. It would take further experimentation, prompted by the emergence of the multi-industry firm in the 1920s, for top management to begin to be liberated from the actual direction of industrial activity.

In twenty-five years, the face of American industry had been transformed. By the turn of the century, the hundred largest companies controlled roughly a third of the nation's total productive capacity. The day of the small manufacturer had not passed. He still flourished, or at least survived, in many fields. But he was no longer the dominant figure in American enterprise, and his sphere of activity narrowed every year. The future lay with big business.

The World of Work

In a free-enterprise system, profit drives the entrepreneur. But the industrial order is not populated only by profit makers. It includes—in vastly larger numbers—wage earners. What is done for profit always acts directly and powerfully on those working for wages. Never did those actions have more profound consequences than in the late nineteenth century. During that period, the modern factory system transformed the lives of American workers.

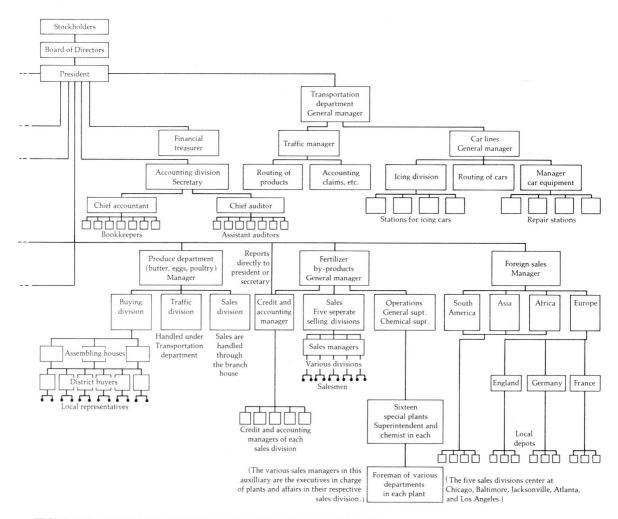

FIGURE 17.2 ORGANIZATION OF ARMOUR & COMPANY, 1907

Autonomous Labor

No one supervised the pick miner. He was a tonnage worker, paid for the amount of coal he produced. He provided his own pick and other tools, worked at his own pace, and knocked off early when he chose. He also used his own judgment in his "room" in the coal mine. Such autonomous craftworkers, almost all of whom were men, flourished in many branches of nineteenth-century industry. They were mule spinners in cotton mills; puddlers and rollers in iron works; molders in stovemaking; and machinists, glass blowers, and many other types of skilled workers.

Within the shop, they abided by the *stint*, a limit placed by the workers themselves on the amount that they should produce each day. This informal system of limitation on output infuriated efficiency-minded engineers. But to the craftworker it signified personal dignity; "unselfish brotherhood" with his fellow employees; and protection against rate cutting, irregular work, and even drunken debauchery. The craftworker took pride in a "manly" bearing, both toward his fellows and toward the boss. One day, a shop in Lowell, Massachusetts, posted regulations requiring all employees to be at their posts in work clothes at the opening bell and remain, with the shop door locked, until the dismissal bell. A machinist promptly packed his tools and quit, declaring that he had not "been brought up under such a system of slavery."

Underlying this ethical code was a keen sense of the craft group, each of which had its own history and customs. Among hat finishers, masters of the art of applying fur felting to hats, an employed man always "asked for" a jobless friend. It would have been unthinkable for the friend himself to request work from a foreman. The hatters had a language of their own. When a hatter was hired, he was "shopped"; if fired, he was "bagged"; when he quit work, he "cried off"; and when he took an apprentice, the boy was "under teach." The hatters, most of whom worked in Danbury, Connecticut, or Orange, New Jersey, formed a distinctive, self-contained community.

The craftworker's skills were crucial to nineteenth-century production. He also was valued for the responsibilities he assumed. He hired his own helpers, supervised their work, and paid them out of his earnings. In an era when the scale of production was expanding, autonomous craftworkers relieved their employers of the mounting burdens of shop-floor management. Many factory managers tried to shift responsibility to employees. A system of inside contracting developed in metal-fabricating firms that did precise machining and complex assemblying. Contractor-employees hired and paid their own men and supervised them completely. They received a contracted rate for the output of their units, in lieu of regular wages as employees. In the New England machine tool industry, which often produced on a to-order basis, inside contractors bid for custom jobs instead of serving as virtual department heads. If a man lost a bid, he sometimes went to work for the winning contractor.

The skilled worker was one central figure of nineteenth-century industry; the common laborer was the other. Great numbers of these laborers had been needed to dig canals, lay railroad tracks, and build cities. They were equally important in heavy industry. Until the last years of the century, virtually all hauling of materials was done by hand. In the steel mills, a third or more of the workers shoveled coal and iron ore from freight cars and wheeled barrows to furnaces. They also handled the tons of metal that passed through the mill daily at every stage of steel production. The steel companies regarded a strong back as the only requirement for all this work. They kept no personnel records on day laborers, considering them to be a floating labor force. The men worked in gangs, and the foreman or gang boss had complete responsibility for them. He hired them, told them what to do, and disciplined and fired them. He was their actual employer.

Dispersal of authority was thus characteristic of nineteenth-century industry. The aristocracy of workers—the craftsmen, the inside contractors, and the foremen—had a high degree of autonomy. However, their subordinates often paid dearly for that independence. The opportunities for abuse were endless. Any worker who paid his helpers from his own pocket might be tempted to exploit them. In the Pittsburgh area, foremen were known as "pushers," notorious for driving their gangs mercilessly. Many foremen also practiced favoritism. For example, they might promote only the sons of craftsmen from the position of helper. On the other hand, industrial labor in the nineteenth century was on a human scale. The crucial relationships were face-to-face, and cohesive ties could develop within a work force. Striking craftworkers commonly received the support of helpers and laborers, and labor gangs sometimes walked out on behalf of a popular foreman.

Systems of Control

As technology advanced and modern management emerged, so did controls over the work process. Workers might have preferred the older system of autonomous work, but they had no choice. They increasingly lost the proud independence that characterized nineteenth-century work.

When undercutting machines appeared in coal mines in the 1880s, they deprived the miner of the pick work that was his most prized skill. "Anyone with a weak head and a strong back can load machine coal," grumbled one Kentucky miner. "But a man has to think and study every day like you was studying a book if he is going to get the best of the coal when he uses only a pick." Similar complaints came throughout the industrialization era from craftworkers whose skills fell victim to machinery—from hand-loom weavers early in the nineteenth century to glassblowers a hundred years later.

The division of labor had the same effect on other skilled workers. "A man never learns the machinist's trade now," a craftworker complained in 1883. In the manufacture of sewing machines, "the trade is so subdivided that a man is not considered a machinist at all. One man may make just a particular part of a machine and may not know anything whatever about another part of the same machine." Such a worker, noted an observer, "cannot be master of a craft, but only master of a fragment."

Although many skilled workers drifted downward into the semiskilled ranks, skilled work itself did not disappear. But its relationship to the production process changed. If weavers, puddlers, and glassblowers became machine tenders, the machines themselves demanded skilled installers and repairers. In the early automobile industry, skilled assemblers soon found themselves replaced by the repetitious, specialized work of the assembly line. But this development led to a new aristocracy of autoworkers, the tool-and-die men and mechanics who prepared and maintained the production lines. It was not so much that mass production eliminated skilled jobs—which actually increased proportionately after 1910—as that it separated them from the production process.

Technology took hold of the pace of operations. The machine, not the worker, determined how fast production would go. In continuous-flow operations, as on an assembly line or in a mechanized rolling mill, the individual worker got caught up in an entire system of externally paced activity. "If you need to turn out a little more," boasted a superintendent at Swift and Company, "you speed up the conveyor a little and the men speed up to keep pace." Complaints about speedups were a sure sign of workers' loss of control over their jobs.

The impact of machinery on workers was essentially unintentional. It amounted to a by-product of decisions made for technological reasons. Employers doubtless recognized that mechanization would better enable them to discipline their workers. But this was only an incidental benefit in addition to the efficiencies that came from the machinery itself. Only slowly, and rarely before 1900, did employers realize that the management of labor might yield the kind of returns that they had gained from technology.

Reform of factory administration began in the 1880s. It aimed at giving managers the means, previously lacking, to control the operations of large industrial plants. As orderly procedures extended down from the central office, workers found themselves subject to general rules and to standard terms of work. Hiring and firing increasingly became the responsibility of the personnel office rather than the foreman. Even so, the actual handling of workers yielded only slowly to central direction. Authority on the shop floor, where the foreman still remained boss, was most resistant of all.

The foreman's traditional rough-and-ready ways always stood as a rebuke to the systematic approach of managerial reformers. Why was it not possible, asked the industrialist Henry R. Towne, to devise "some better method of bringing out of the men the best that is in them in doing their work?" This question applied especially to workers not subject to the discipline of machines or assembly lines.

Among the early management reformers, Frederick W. Taylor took work itself as his special province. Others had experimented with incentive and profit-sharing programs. Taylor, beginning with his landmark essay "A Piece Rate System" (1895), proposed a method for getting the maximum work from the individual worker. He proposed two basic reforms. The first would eliminate the brain work involved in what workers did and give it entirely to managers. The managers would assume "the burden of gathering together all of the traditional knowledge which in the past has been possessed by the workmen and then of classifying, tabulating, and reducing this knowledge to rules, laws, and formulae." The second reform, a logical consequence of the first, would deprive workers of the authority they had normally exercised on the shop floor. Workers would "do what they are told promptly and without asking questions or making suggestions. . . . The duty of enforcing . . . rests with the *management* alone."

Once they had the knowledge and power, according to Taylor, managers would put labor on a "scientific" basis. This meant subjecting each task to a "time-and-motion" study, in which an engineer with a stopwatch tried to measure precisely the steps in each task. A personnel office would hire and train the right person for each job. The worker would be paid at a differential rate—that is, a certain amount if he met the stopwatch standard. He would earn at a higher rate for any greater output. Taylor claimed that his techniques would guarantee the optimum level of worker efficiency.

Taylor called his method "scientific management." It was not, in practice, a roaring success. His reforms called for a total restructuring of factory administration. No company ever adopted Taylor's entire system, and the few that tried to do so paid dearly for the effort. The differential-rate method, which was widely used, met stubborn resistance. "It looks to me like slavery to have a man stand over you with a stopwatch," complained one iron molder. A union leader insisted that "this system is wrong, because we want our heads left on us." Workers deliberately slowed up to fool the time-and-mo-

tion man, and they often prevented the incentive rate from pushing up production.

Yet Taylor, a brilliant publicist, achieved something of fundamental importance. He and his disciples spread his scientific-management teachings throughout American industry. Taylor's successors devised more sophisticated techniques than his simple economic psychology, which assumed an automatic response to the reward of more money. A threshold had been crossed into the modern era of labor management.

So the circle closed in on American workers. With each advance, the quest for efficiency cut deeper into their cherished autonomy. Mechanization, systematic administration, and the growing scale of industrial activity diminished workers and cut them down to fit the productive system. The process occurred unevenly. For textile workers, the loss had come early. Miners and iron workers felt it much more slowly. Others, such as workers in the building trades, escaped the process almost entirely. But increasing numbers of workers found themselves in an environment that crushed any sense of mastery or even understanding.

Industrial Recruits

Wherever industrialism took hold, it set people in motion. Artisans moved into factories. Farm folk migrated to manufacturing centers. An industrial labor force emerged. These events took place in all industrializing nations. But the United States built its work force in a distinctive way. Unlike European countries, it could not rely primarily on its own population.

For one thing, the demand for labor was enormous. American industry required five times as many workers in 1910 as in 1870. No less important, people born in the United States after the 1850s could no longer be attracted into factories. It was not that rural people, who still made up about 75 percent of the population in 1870, refused to leave their farms. Large numbers of them migrated from agricultural areas after 1870. Many went westward and remained farmers. About half did move to cities, but they tended to avoid factory work. The desirable jobs—those of puddlers, rollers, molders, and machinists—required advanced industrial skills not held by rural Americans. They did have a basic education. They could read and calculate, and they understood American institutions and ways of doing things. City-bound white Americans were better qualified for the multiplying white-collar jobs in offices and retail stores than for manual jobs in factories.

As for rural blacks, even the lowest factory job probably seemed better than the debt peonage of southern cotton agriculture. Racial barriers kept them out of factories. In the South, industrial jobs were generally reserved for whites. A trickle of blacks began to migrate northward and westward, roughly eighty thousand between 1870 and 1890, and another two hundred thousand from 1890 to 1910. Most of them settled in cities, but few found factory work. The

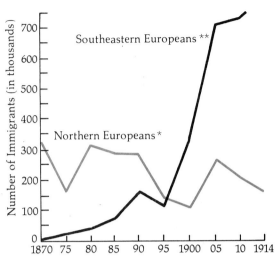

* Includes immigrants from Great Britain, Ireland, Germany, and the Scandinavian countries.
** Includes immigrants from Poland, Russia, Italy, and other Baltic and Eastern European countries.

FIGURE 17.3 AMERICAN IMMIGRATION, 1870–1914

IMMIGRANT WORKERS
Many native-born Americans resented the influx of peasant immigrants from eastern and southern Europe that began in the 1880s. In fact, however, the newcomers, more than any other group, manned the machines, laid the railroad tracks, and did the heavy construction labor in the nation's cities. They were, in truth, Europe's gift—its most vigorous and energetic people. (Lewis Hine. International Museum of Photography at George Eastman House)

great majority of the men ended up as casual laborers and janitors, the women as maids and laundresses. Only 7 percent of all black American males worked in industry in 1890. Industrial employers excluded blacks because of an apparently limitless supply of foreign workers on which they could draw.

The exodus from the Old World had started in the 1840s when the potato famine sent more than a million Irish peasants fleeing to America. During the following years, other traditional rural economies were disrupted by the commercialization of agriculture and an increasing imbalance between population and land. The erosion of peasant agriculture struck first in Germany and Scandinavia. Then it spread east into Austria-Hungary and Russia and south into Italy and the Balkans. In industrial districts of Europe, the force of economic change also cut loose many workers in the declining artisan trades. A total of about 25 million immigrants arrived in America between 1870 and 1914.

Ethnic origin largely determined the kind of work that the immigrants found in their new country. Many western Europeans were seasoned artisans and industrial workers. They generally sought the same types of jobs they had held in the Old World. The nineteenth-century occupational structure took on an ethnic character—the Welsh as tin-plate workers, Germans as machinists and traditional artisans, Belgians as glass workers, and Scandinavians as seamen on Great Lakes boats. For common labor, employers had long counted on the brawn of rural immigrants to dig canals, lay railroad tracks, and provide unskilled labor in factory and construction gangs. These workers included primarily the Irish but also other western European peasants, as well as French Canadians in New England, Mexicans in the Southwest, and Chinese in California.

As industrialization advanced, the demand for unskilled workers increased and the nation's dependence on European craft skills moderated. These developments helped trigger the remarkable shift of immigration away from northern Europe that started in the 1880s. More than nine million people migrated to America from eastern and southern Europe between 1900 and 1914. Italian and Slavic immigrants, almost wholly lacking in industrial skills, flooded into the lowest rungs of American industry. Heavy, low-paid factory labor became essentially the domain of the recent immigrants. Blast-furnace jobs, a

job-seeking investigator heard, was "Hunky work," not suitable for him or any other American.

Other factors beside skill levels determined where immigrants ended up in American industry. Most of the newcomers arrived alone, but they moved within well-defined networks. The immigrants followed relatives or fellow villagers already in America, joined their households as family members or boarders, and relied on them to find a job. A high degree of ethnic clustering resulted, even within one factory. At the Jones and Laughlin steel works in Pittsburgh, the carpentry shop was German, the hammer shop Polish, and the blooming mill Serbian. Sometimes this clustering process led to unlikely ethnic concentrations. Bulgarians made up the unskilled labor force of Granite City, Illinois. Numerous Greeks became coal miners in central Colorado, although few worked in mines elsewhere.

Distinctive ethnic characteristics also determined the jobs that immigrants found. For example, men from Italy sought construction and road work because their village society made them amenable to a gang form of organization

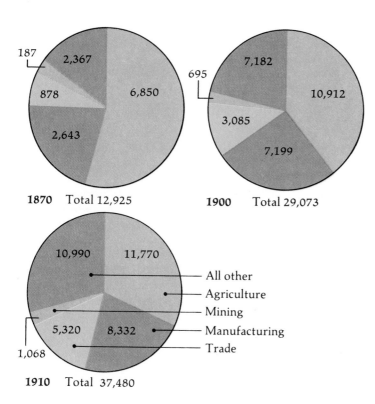

FIGURE 17.4 CHANGES IN THE LABOR FORCE, 1870–1910
The numbers here represent thousands of people employed (i.e., 12,925 = 12,925,000). They reveal both the enormous increase in the total labor force between 1870 and 1910 and the dramatic shift from agriculture in relative terms (the absolute number in the agricultural labor force continued to grow) into industry and other nonagricultural parts of the economy.

1870   Total 12,925
187
2,367
878
6,850
2,643

1900   Total 29,073
7,182
695
10,912
3,085
7,199

1910   Total 37,480
10,990
11,770
5,320
8,332
1,068

- All other
- Agriculture
- Mining
- Manufacturing
- Trade

under a *padrone* (boss). Eastern European Jews flocked into the needle trades because many had tailoring skills. The industry also suited, or could be adopted to, their family and religious needs. The sweating system, which involved the subcontracting of sewing jobs from a central shop, enabled Orthodox Jews to stay in their own neighborhoods. They could observe the Saturday Sabbath, put their wives and daughters to work in the safety of the tenement, and make an easy jump from worker to entrepreneur.

The immigrants entered a modern industrial order, but they saw their surroundings through peasant eyes. With the disruption of the traditional rural economies of eastern and southern Europe, many peasants had begun to lose their land. This meant an intolerable decline into the class of dependent, propertyless servants. Peasants could avoid such a bitter fate only if they had money to buy property. In Europe, job-seeking peasants commonly tried seasonal agricultural labor, or temporary work in nearby cities. America represented merely a larger leap, made possible by the cheap and speedy steamship transportation across the Atlantic. The peasant immigrants, most of them young and male, came with the purpose of earning enough money, and then returning to their native villages.

As long as the work lasted, the peasant worker rarely was inclined to protest against low wages, harsh conditions, or the hardships of his life. When work ran out, as it almost always did, there was a safety valve. In the depression year of 1908, more Italians and Austro-Hungarians returned to Europe than arrived. As many as half of the new immigrants returned to their homelands. No one knows how many saved enough money to fulfill their peasant goals and how many left for lack of work. Clearly, however, the peasants' reasons for coming, and their tendency to leave in bad times, made them an ideal labor supply for the new industrial order.

A few fields, such as railroading, had mostly native-born workers. Southern industry also relied on workers native to the region. Overall, however, immigrants manned American industry. They comprised 60 percent of the labor force of the nation's principal manufacturing and mining industries in 1910.

Working Women

The late nineteenth-century economy also relied on women's labor. Their participation in the work force increased steadily. The female population grew by nearly half between 1870 and 1900, but the number of woman workers jumped by almost two-thirds. They made up more than a fourth of the nonfarm labor force in 1900. Women, like immigrants, entered the industrial economy from another world. The role they found as wage earners was shaped by the fact that they were women. Contemporary beliefs about womanhood largely determined which women entered the work force and how they were treated once they became wage earners.

Wives were not supposed to hold jobs. In 1890, less than 5 percent of all married women worked outside their homes. Employment was acceptable before marriage, at least for young women not in the respectable middle class. For women in America, wage work was typically an adolescent experience that ended when they got married. The majority of all employed women in 1890 were from sixteen to twenty-four years old. When older women worked, remarked one observer, it "was usually a sign that something had gone wrong"—their husbands were gone, jobless, or incapacitated.

Since women were considered inherently different from men, it followed that they should not be permitted to do "men's work." And, regardless of the value of their labor, they could not be paid at men's rates. At the turn of the century, woman workers fell into three roughly equal categories. A third worked as maids or other types of domestic servants. Another third held white-collar jobs also identified as "female" in teaching, nursing, and sales. Sex-typing affected the third of the women in industrial occupations as well. Few worked in the crafts, as supervisors, or as day laborers. Most female industrial workers were classified as "operatives"—machine tenders and hand workers. Women were heavily concentrated in the garment trades and textile mills, but could be found throughout industry in "light" occupations—as packers, inspectors, assemblers, or as sausage stuffers in packing houses.

Sex-typing of work was legitimatized by the

sentimental view of women as the weaker sex. But powerful interests also played a role. Craftworkers protected their male domain, and employers profited from cut-rate work. Wherever they worked, women earned wages below those of the lowest male occupations. In 1914, female industrial workers averaged $7.75 a week, $3 less than unskilled males and $5 less than the average for all industrial employees.

The objection to working wives, also expressed in sentimental and moral terms, was likewise based on solid necessity. From the standpoint of the industrial economy, the basic economic unit consisted of the individual employee. For the worker, however, the family was the real economic unit. In this family economy, the wife contributed crucially. Her household services were not considered as income-producing, nor given a monetary value. But her husband knew that his household could not function without her labor. Therefore, the wife's place was in the home.

Working-class families, especially those below the skilled ranks, required more than one income. Hardly half of these families, one expert estimated in 1912, got along on the husband's earnings alone. Additional funds came mainly from sons and daughters, children as well as

THE MODERN OFFICE

Office work provides a prime example of the process of sex-typing in American employment. During the nineteenth century, most clerks and secretaries were men, and their jobs were regarded as stepping stones to partnerships or senior business positions. As paperwork multiplied in bureaucratic firms, secretarial duties were redefined as women's work, at lower pay relative to men's jobs and with no prospect for advancement. The chap in this office will surely find another line of work . . . or replace the male supervisor standing on the left. (Culver)

adults. In 1890, about 20 percent of the children between the ages of ten and fifteen held jobs.

The immigrants arriving after 1890 relied heavily on the family economy. The high proportion of unmarried males among southern and eastern Europeans put a premium on household labor. As a result, the wife was indispensable in an immigrant family that boarded single workers. Moreover, in an era when people began to value education more highly, many immigrants persisted in treating children as contributors to the family economy. People who placed a high value on education, such as Jewish immigrants, saw their children rise more rapidly into the middle class than did those who preferred the income of their offspring. Finally, some immigrant groups, especially the Italians, objected strongly to the employment of wives outside the home. If the wife was to contribute to the family income, she could do so only within the household, either by doing work at home or keeping boarders.

Despite the immigrant influence, the family economy was changing. Obstacles to child labor appeared. By the 1890s, all the northern industrial states had laws prohibiting the employment of young children and regulating the work hours of teenagers. Most of those states also required children from eight to fourteen years old to go to school for a certain number of weeks each year. At the same time, jobs designated as female were increasing rapidly in teaching, office work, and shops, though not significantly in manufacturing. Finally, the pressure for higher family incomes increased in the twentieth century with the advent of automobiles, appliances, and other durable goods.

Working-class families continued to rely on second incomes, but this money was more likely to come from the wife than the children. By 1920, the proportion of working married women had doubled from what it had been in 1890. For working-class women, entry into the labor market went forward even more rapidly. About a fifth of the wives of unskilled and semiskilled men in Chicago had jobs in 1920. Wage-earning women, including many wives, were on their way to becoming a primary part of America's labor force.

The Labor Movement

Wherever industrialism has taken hold, workers have responded collectively. However, the method they have used to organize themselves has varied from one industrial society to another. In the United States, workers were especially uncertain about the path to take. Only after the 1880s did the American labor movement settle into a fixed course.

Unionists and Reformers

By the late nineteenth century, craftworkers regarded trade unionism as an old story. Unions had long since become central to their working lives. Apprenticeship rules regulated entry into a trade, and the closed shop excluded nonunion and incompetent workers. In the carpenters' unions, the walking delegates—that is, the local union officials—served as employment agents for building contractors and the journeymen workers. Union rules specified the terms of work, sometimes in minute detail. Above all, trade unionism defended the craftworker's traditional skills and rights.

The union also symbolized the social identity of a craft. Hatters took pride in their drinking prowess, an on-the-job privilege jealously guarded, and their unions sometimes resembled drinking clubs. More often, however, the craft union had an uplifting character. A Birmingham iron puddler claimed that his union's "main object was to educate mechanics up to a standard of morality and temperance, and good workmanship." The International Association of Machinists boasted of an elaborate ritual, an expression of fraternalism common to most craft unions. The railroad brotherhoods especially stressed insurance and mutual aid because operating trains was a highly risky occupation. On the job and off, the union played a big part in the lives of craftworkers.

Labor organizations, sometimes sparked by fraternal spirit but more often by the need to defend wage rates, can be traced back to the eighteenth century. The first unions were local groups of workers in the same trade. These organizations grew into national unions. The first to survive, the International Typographical Union, was formed in 1852. By the 1870s, molders, iron and steelworkers, bricklayers, and members of about thirty other trades had formed national unions. Almost invariably, the first order of business was to create a national "traveling card" for wandering journeymen. If work was available in a community, the local union admitted a traveling member and expected him to observe union standards. If there was no work, the local gave him a meal and a bed and then sent him on his way, traveling card in hand. By thus creating a kind of national citizenship, the national union asserted control over the labor market of its trade. As national product markets emerged, a second motivation developed for building national unions. Because goods flowed from different points into a common market, a union had to coordinate bargaining and organize nonunion areas. The union served workers' crucial interests in this effort to standardize labor costs among competing producers.

The protection of job interests was not the only source of collective activity by working people. Distress over the impact of industrialization on their lives had an equally strong effect.

In 1883, a New York wagon driver named Thomas B. McGuire testified before a Senate committee. He had saved three hundred dollars from his wages, "thinking that I might become something of a capitalist eventually." But he soon failed. "A man in the express business today owning one or two horses and a wagon cannot even eke out an existence from the business," McGuire complained. "The competition is too great from the Adams Express Company and all those other monopolies." McGuire's prospects seemed no better in the hack, or taxi business:

> Corporations usually take that business themselves. They can manage to get men, at starvation wages, and put them on a hack, and put a livery on them with a gold band and brass buttons, to show that they are slaves—I beg pardon; I did not intend to use the word slaves; there are no slaves in this country now—to show that they are merely servants.

Slave or liveried servant, the symbolic meaning was the same to McGuire. He was speaking of the crushed aspirations of the independent American workingman.

What would satisfy the Thomas McGuires of the nineteenth century? Only the restoration of a world in which "monopoly" and special privilege did not deprive workers of the chance to rise. In such a world, no distinction would exist between capital and labor. All would be "producers" in what was commonly called the "cooperative commonwealth." This ideal inspired wave after wave of labor-reform movements. They took the form of workingmen's parties in the 1830s, land-reform groups in the 1840s, the National Labor Union after the Civil War, and finally, the Noble Order of the Knights of Labor.

The Knights of Labor started in 1869 as a secret society of Philadelphia garment cutters. The organization gradually spread to other cities and emerged in 1878 as a national movement. Led by Grand Master Workman Terence V. Powderly, the Knights purged themselves of the secrecy and religious verbiage objectionable to the Catholic church. They retained the elaborate ritual and ceremony that appealed so strongly to the fraternal spirit of the nineteenth-century worker. The Knights of Labor typified the American labor-reform tradition. Their goal was to "give voice to that grand undercurrent of mighty thought, which is today [1880] crystallizing in the hearts of men, and urging them on to perfect organization through which to gain the power to make labor emancipation possible."

But how was "emancipation" to be achieved? The Knights tried a number of solutions, including cooperation. Funds would be raised and cooperative enterprises set up, and as these flourished and spread, American society would be transformed into a cooperative commonwealth. But little was actually done. In reality, the Knights concentrated mainly on "education." Powderly regarded the organization as a vast labor lyceum that almost anyone could join. The cooperative commonwealth would arrive in some mysterious way as more and more "producers" became members and learned the group's message in lectures, discussions, and publications. Social evil would not end in a day, but "must await the gradual development of educational enlightenment."

Labor reform might have seemed a far cry from hard-headed, job-conscious unionism. But both were in reality embedded in a single workers' culture. Workers saw no conflict between the two loyalties. Many carried membership cards in both the Knights of Labor and a trade union. The careers of many labor leaders, including Powderly, likewise embraced both kinds of activity. For many years, even the functional lines were indistinct. At the local level, little separated a trade assembly of the Knights from a local trade union; both engaged in fraternal and bargaining activities.

After 1884, the Knights began to act increasingly like a trade union. Boycott campaigns defeated "unfair" employers across the country. With the economy on the upswing, the Knights began to win strikes, including one against Jay Gould's Southwestern railway system in 1885. Workers flocked into the organization, and its membership jumped from a hundred thousand to perhaps seven hundred thousand in less than a year. For a brief time, the Knights stood poised as a potential industrial-union movement capable of bringing all workers within their fold. Craft unions barred women, but the Knights welcomed them and, to a lesser degree, blacks. The Knights could boast that their "great work has been to organize labor which was previously unorganized."

The rapid growth of the Knights of Labor frightened the national craft unions. The unions tried to keep their locals away from the Knights, but without success. The craft unions then began to insist on a clear separation of roles. In May 1886, they offered the Knights a "treaty" that excluded trade-union groups from the organization, leaving to it only its reform functions. When the Knights rejected the treaty, the craft unions formed the American Federation of Labor (AFL) in December.

The AFL embodied the belief of the national unions that they constituted a distinctive movement. The federation, in effect, locked into place the trade-union structure as it had evolved by the 1880s. Underlying this structure was the conviction that workers henceforth had to take the world as it was, not as they dreamed it might be. Their collective strength had to be carefully conserved to improve their lives in the present time. American trade unionism had determined to follow a course of tough-minded realism.

The architect of the AFL, and its president for nearly forty years, was Samuel Gompers. Gompers, a cigar maker from New York City, hammered out the philosophical position that would define American "pure and simple" unionism. First, there would be a steady focus on concrete, short-term gains. Second, unions would rely on economic power rather than politics. Third, they would limit their membership to workers, organized on strictly occupational lines. Finally, the union strongly rejected the theories and grand schemes that had excited the labor reformers. The steady growth of the trade unions after the formation of the AFL seemed to justify Gompers' confidence that he had hit on the correct formula for the American labor movement.

The Knights of Labor faded away. The organization had not been able to sustain its swift growth of 1885–1886 and, after a series of disastrous strikes, had retreated from the trade-union field. Grand Master Workman Powderly turned back to the rhetoric of labor reform. But the appeal to wage earners had disappeared. In its declining years, the Knights survived mainly in small-town America, no longer a workers' movement.

Industrial Battleground

The Noble Order of the Knights of Labor was the last of the nineteenth-century labor reform movements. The difference between the real world of industrial struggle and the idealism of labor reform had become too great. There was no unifying population of "producers," but only employers and workers deeply divided by conflicting interests. Nor was either side responsive to uplifting "education." Labor and management settled their differences by means of strikes, lockouts, boycotts, court-ordered injunctions and even pitched battles. As industrialism advanced in the late nineteenth century, so did the intensity of industrial warfare.

It was not that workers received no share of the returns of industrialism. Real wage rates—that is, the purchasing power of earnings—had advanced at a rate of roughly 1.5 percent a year from the beginning of industrialism. In 1870,

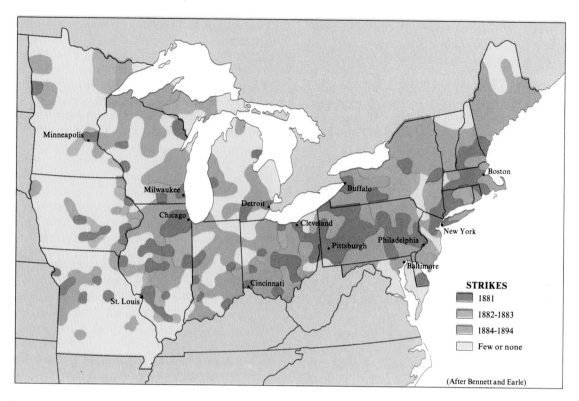

MAP 17.3 THE GEOGRAPHY OF AMERICAN LABOR STRIKES

Labor unrest flared up in the 1880s in patterns that revealed trigger points for strikes and a "ricochet" effect spreading them to neighboring localities. Early strikes blanketed areas of heavy industry, particularly in southern New England, Pennsylvania, and Illinois. By 1894, few parts of the Northeast had remained unaffected. In the Middle West, farming districts inhibited the spread of strikes. In the South, which was thinly industrial and plainly hostile to unions, strikes were rare.

workers earned 50 percent more in real terms than in 1840; the same was true in 1910 compared with 1870. However, the labor system contained a high degree of instability. Employers quickly cut wages when business slackened. Why should they do otherwise? asked a vice-president of the Burlington Railroad. "The labor question is one of supply and demand," he said. "When work is scarce and labor plenty . . . laborers . . . must take what they can get or remain idle." Continual uncertainty about their jobs troubled workers the most. In Massachusetts, they could expect to be unemployed an average of several months a year even during normal periods. The much longer sieges of joblessness that came in hard times caused catastrophe in the lives of workers and their families.

In July 1877, a great wave of strikes hit the nation's railroads. Wage cuts triggered the strikes, but the scope and violence of the conflict stemmed from more deep-seated causes. The United States had been in a severe depression since 1873. Unemployment may have run as high as 25 percent, and suffering was widespread. When the Baltimore and Ohio railroaders walked out on July 16, many idle men and boys joined them. Crowds cheered in railway towns along the B&O tracks as the strikers attacked railroad property and prevented trains from running. The strike spread rapidly across the rail network. In Pittsburgh, the Pennsylvania Railroad roundhouse went up in flames on July 21, followed by the Union Depot the next day. Rioters and looters roamed freely. For nearly a week, riotous strikes swept other cities, including San Francisco, Saint Louis, Omaha, and

Chicago. President Rutherford B. Hayes called up the National Guard, which gradually restored order, and the strikes collapsed. But for a while, the nation had seemed on the edge of revolution.

In 1886, another series of strikes hit the nation. This time the primary issue was the length of the work week, not wages or jobs. The work week had actually been falling, from sixty-six hours in 1860 to sixty hours in 1886, but not fast enough for American workers. As the intensity of work increased, and the value placed on leisure time rose, so did the demand for a shorter work day. "Eight hours for work, eight hours for rest, eight hours for what we will." With this slogan, the national trade unions called for an eight-hour day, effective May 1, 1886. Large numbers of organized and unorganized workers heeded the call, and strikes broke out in cities throughout the country.

The strongest fight for the eight-hour day took place in Chicago. On May 3, a battle erupted between McCormick strikers and strikebreakers. To protest the deaths of four strikers, Chicago anarchists called a meeting for the next evening at Haymarket Square. They used a provocative appeal: "Workingmen, arm yourselves and appear in full force." The meeting went off peacefully, but when police moved in at the end to break it up, someone threw a bomb and several policemen were killed. The anarchist organizers were arrested and, with no evidence against them, found guilty. Four were executed, one committed suicide, and the others received long prison sentences. They were victims of one of the great miscarriages of American justice. And in the wake of nationwide hysteria against the anarchists and strikers, employers largely defeated the campaign for an eight-hour day.

Employers strongly opposed collective dealings with workers. They commonly compiled blacklists of union members. Industrial spies kept tabs on shop sentiment and disrupted unions. Employers required workers to sign yellow-dog contracts, which were guarantees that, as a condition of employment, they would not join a union or engage in a strike. When a union did form, employers fought to deny it recognition and to maintain an open shop. Industrial warfare resulted at least as much from the militancy of antiunion employers as from the determination of workers to improve their lot in life.

LABOR STRIFE, 1912
The grievances voiced by textile workers in Lawrence, Massachusetts, resulted in one of the most dramatic strikes in American history. The companies tried to frighten the strikers into submission. Troops were brought in, picketing was prohibited, and strikers were arrested and, in some cases, given a year or longer in jail. But the men and women held out through the bitter cold of January and February, and won their demands. It was a rare instance in which immigrant workers, striking spontaneously, prevailed against the power of corporate industry. (Library of Congress)

STRIKING AGAINST THE AMERICAN WOOLEN COMPANY

Samuel Lipson gave the following testimony before the U.S. Committee on Rules in 1912.

Mr. Berger: Why did you go on strike?

Mr. Lipson: I went on strike because I was unable to make a living for my family.

Mr. B: How much wages were you receiving?

Mr. L: My average wage . . . is from $9 to $10 a week.

Mr. B: What kind of work do you do?

Mr. L: I am a weaver.

Mr. B: You are a skilled workman?

Mr. L: Yes, sir; for years. . . .

Mr. B: You are a member of the strike committee, are you not?

Mr. L: Yes, sir.

Mr. B: Tell us the immediate cause of the strike.

Mr. L: The workers in the American Wool Co.'s mills had meetings and discussed the question of what we can do to make a living. . . . They tried to speed up the machinery in order to make us do 56 hours work in 54 hours time, and tried to cut off the pay at the same time. . . . It was unbearable. . . .

Mr. B: You were required to do 56 hours work in 54 hours time, because a law has recently passed in Massachusetts cutting down the hours of labor to 54 per week?

Mr. L: Yes, sir. . . .

Mr. B: How many nationalities are there represented among the workers at Lawrence?

Mr. L: Sixteen nationalities.

Mr. B: Mention some of them.

Mr. L: There are Germans, Polish, English, Italians, Armenians, Turks, Syrians, Greeks, Belgians, some from France, Jewish, Lithuanians. . . .

Mr. B: How many of the workers of Lawrence are women and children? How many are men?

Mr. L: I cannot tell you about how many, but I can tell you that the majority of them are women and children, and as we are speeding up, these children are doing more work. . . . If they do not speed up, they are fired out.

Mr. B: If the children do not speed up, they lose their places in the mills?

Mr. L: Yes, sir; and the women who are used in the same place are pushed out sometimes and the children take their places.

Mr. B: Do they have any accidents in the factory?

Mr. L: Yes, sir.

Mr. B: Give a few instances of accidents.

Mr. L: There is a girl over there, Camella Teoli, and everyone present can see her. She is an Italian girl, but also speaks English. She started to work in the spinning department, on a machine that is a long one, with three or four different sides. The machine was speeded up and was running with such speed that her hair was caught and her scalp was cut by the machine. Her scalp was torn down, as you see. . . .

Mr. B: She has not sued the company?

Mr. L: No, sir. That happened two years ago, and she is working to keep up the family. They are poor and she and the father are working to keep up the family. The youngest is a little older than a year.

Mr. B: She would not stand much chance on a lawsuit against the American Woolen Co. The American Woolen Co. is a powerful concern.

Mr. L: Yes, sir; that is true.

Mr. B: What are the demands of the strikers now?

Mr. L: The demands are 15 per cent increase in wages, based on 54 hours work per week, and double pay for overtime. The reason I wish to call your attention to the demand for 15 per cent increase is this: These people work sometimes only two or three days in a week. Her father works only three days in a week, and has $2.88 per week for the family, and they absolutely live on bread and water. If you would look at the other children, you would see that they look like skeletons. . . .

Mr. B: What reception did the strikers get from the mill owners? . . .

Mr. L: They said if we did not like it to get out.

In the steel industry, the decisive attack on trade unionism came with the Homestead lockout of 1892. The Carnegie Steel Company's plant at Homestead, Pennsylvania, had a history of friendly dealings with the Amalgamated Association of Iron and Steel Workers. But by 1892, technological advances had reached the point where the company no longer regarded skilled union men as indispensable. In addition, the accompanying productivity gains created continuing difficulties with the union over the renegotiation of wage rates. The men went on strike on June 29 following a wage cut. Andrew Carnegie and Henry Clay Frick, his second-in-command, had decided to get rid of the union. Frick locked the men out of the plant on July 1, and the strikers decided to prevent strikebreakers from entering. On July 6, when Frick tried to bring in three hundred guards by barge under cover of darkness, the armed strikers were waiting on the shore of the Monongahela River. The strikers won the bloody gun battle that followed, but the Pennsylvania militia arrived a few days later and restored law and order. The company, having broken the strike, reopened the plant.

On the railroads, the battle over trade unionism was renewed on a larger scale two years later. Pullman, Illinois, was a model factory town, built and wholly owned by the sleeping-car magnate George N. Pullman. When the Panic of 1893 hit, Pullman cut wages but kept rents at their high predepression levels. The workers protested in May 1894. The Pullman Company fired their leaders, and the men struck. They belonged to the American Railway Union (ARU), which had recently been formed by the labor leader Eugene V. Debs to represent all railroad workers. In response to the strikers' plea, the ARU directed its members not to handle Pullman sleeping cars, which were attached to trains but were owned and serviced by the Pullman Company. The railroads, although they dealt with the brotherhoods of conductors, locomotive engineers, and firemen, strongly opposed the unionization of their other employees. The Pullman boycott by the ARU gave the railroads their chance to break that union. The General Managers' Association, which represented the railroads serving Chicago, insisted on running the Pullman cars, and a farflung rail strike began.

At this point, the federal government intervened. Attorney General Richard Olney, a former railroad lawyer, had close connections with the General Managers' Association. He sent troops to keep the trains running on the grounds that they carried U.S. mail. When this tactic did not work, Olney got court injunctions prohibiting the ARU leaders from conducting the strike. Debs and the other leaders refused to obey and were held in contempt of court and jailed. The great rail boycott of 1894 had been crushed by this naked use of government power on behalf of the railroad companies.

The American labor movement could make only limited headway against such concentrated resistance. Following the return of prosperity in 1897, unions expanded in some areas, especially in the building trades, transportation, and coal mining. AFL membership climbed from about half a million in 1897 to more than two million in 1904, roughly 10 percent of the nonagricultural work force. Although the number of union members continued to grow slowly, the proportion of organized workers no longer increased. The struggle for recognition went especially badly against unions in such mass-production industries as meat packing, steel, and metal-fabricating. Organized labor settled for the areas of traditional craft strength and gave up on the broad industrial sector characterized by large-scale organization and modern technology. By the second decade of the twentieth century, the AFL had become an arrested movement.

Radicals

Conservatism was the hallmark of Samuel Gompers and his brand of trade unionism. The AFL accepted the economic status quo and sought only to increase labor's share of the economic benefits. It had not been easy for the labor movement to accept such a limited objective. Only after much struggle had pure and simple unionism prevailed against nineteenth-century labor reform. If the Knights of Labor was dead, however, a tougher-minded kind of radicalism—Marxian socialism—took its place in the fight for the loyalty of American workers in the early 1900s.

German refugees had brought the ideas of Karl Marx, a German philosopher and revolu-

THE "RED SPECIAL"
Eugene V. Debs ran for president on the Socialist ticket three times before World War I—in 1904, 1908, and 1912—crisscrossing the country in whistle-stop campaigns in the "Red Special." He had no use for a train in his fourth try, in 1920, because his opposition to the war had landed him in prison. Debs never had a chance of winning, but the campaigns enabled him to spread the gospel of Socialism. (Brown Brothers)

tionary, to America after the revolutions of 1848 in Europe. Marx offered a powerful economic critique of capitalism. His prescription for revolution through class struggle produced the most durable of radical movements throughout the industrial world. Although little noticed in most parts of American society, Marxian socialism struck deep roots in the growing German-American communities of Chicago and New York. There, spilling over from European debates, a bitter dispute flared during the 1870s over a central question of organizational strategy. Should the emphasis be on political action or on the economic organization of workers? The political wing won, and in 1877 it formed the Socialist Labor party.

The overriding problem of the Socialists was how to broaden the popular base of their political movement. This meant, in part, breaking down ethnic barriers and attracting American-born voters. Equally important was gaining the support of the trade unions. These issues came

to a head during the 1890s when Daniel DeLeon began to dominate the Socialist Labor party. A brilliant theorist and inflexible leader, DeLeon preferred a pure party to a popular one. He had little interest in appealing to the American voter, and even less in dealing with what he called the "labor fakers" of the AFL. DeLeon's rigid beliefs prompted a revolt that resulted in the formation of the Socialist Party of America.

The Socialist party dedicated itself to building a broad-based radical movement. The key figure was Eugene Debs. Born in 1855 in Terre Haute, Indiana, Debs served for thirteen years as national secretary and treasurer of the Brotherhood of Locomotive Firemen. Finally repelled by the craft-union exclusiveness he saw on the railroads, Debs began to support industrial unionism. He formed the American Railway Union in 1893 and, in the Pullman boycott the next year, felt the full force of the opponents of organized labor. The union was crushed and Debs was jailed. He came out a radical and, shortly, an

TIME LINE
THE NEW INDUSTRIAL ORDER

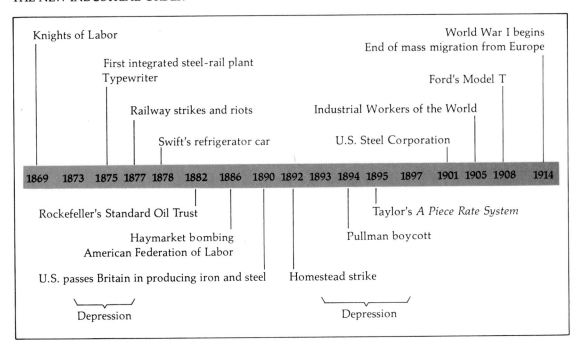

avowed Socialist. Debs, a spellbinding campaigner, was a superb spokesman for the Socialist party. He had the common touch and talked socialism in an American idiom.

The Socialist party grew steadily under Debs. By 1910, it had a national network of branches and state organizations, and numerous elected officials in American cities. The Socialists broke through the ethnic barriers of the past. They won a considerable middle-class following and were highly successful at attracting women activists. Conciliatory toward the AFL, the Socialists developed a large following in the trade unions. They represented as much as 40 percent of the vote at AFL conventions.

Failure to advance beyond that point put a fatal limitation on the prospects of the Socialist party. Without the trade-union base on which European parties relied, American socialism could not hope to prevail. In the West, radical unionism had sprung up among the metal miners. For a decade, beginning with the Cripple Creek strike in Colorado in 1894, they fought a bitter industrial war in western mining areas. As in the Pullman strike, government power sup-

ported the employers. Experience radicalized the metal miners. Their union, the Western Federation of Miners, served as the nucleus for a rival to the AFL. The new labor organization, the Industrial Workers of the World (IWW), was formed in 1905. Its objective was a labor movement suited to the needs of socialism—industrially organized, militant toward employers, and fully supportive of Socialist policies.

The IWW swiftly settled on its own radical course. It turned strongly antipolitical and severed its ties with political socialism. The Wobblies, as IWW members were called, fervently supported the Marxian class struggle, but strictly in the industrial field. By action at the point of production and by an unending struggle against employers—ultimately by a general strike—the workers themselves would bring about a revolution. A workers' society would emerge, run directly by them through their industrial unions. The term *syndicalism* describes this workers' radicalism.

In the East, the Wobblies acted as a shock force, leading strikes of industrial workers, most of them immigrants, but leaving behind no permanent organization. The IWW played this role in a series of strikes at McKees Rocks, Pennsylvania, in 1909; Lawrence, Massachusetts, in 1912; Paterson, New Jersey, in 1913; and Akron, Ohio, in 1913. But its true calling came in the West, where the IWW organized lumberjacks, construction men, miners, and itinerant farm workers following the harvest. To reach these rootless workers the Wobblies engaged in a series of free-speech fights in hostile western towns. In the field, the IWW relied on on-the-job organizers, and pressure tactics against bad bunkhouse conditions. In the West, the IWW became, in effect, a kind of trade union for the dispossessed.

American radicalism flourished during the years after 1900, but only on a limited basis. Socialists and Wobblies lived, in a sense, on the tolerance of society. They later would be crushed without ceremony. Nevertheless, they had served a larger purpose. American radicalism, by its sheer vitality, bore undying witness to what was exploitative and unjust in the new industrial order.

---

*A*merican industrialism took its modern shape during the last decades of the nineteenth century. First an efficient railroad system provided access to national markets. Then a heavy industrial base developed to supply materials, equipment, and energy for manufacturers. The scale of enterprise grew very large, and the vertically integrated firm became the predominant form of business organization. Mass production, the high-volume output of standardized goods, became the prevailing system of manufacturing.

Workers felt these developments most strongly in the loss of control over the labor process. The enormous demand for labor also led to a great influx of immigrants into the industrial economy, making ethnic diversity a distinctive feature of the American working class. After a lengthy period of uncertainty, the labor movement committed itself to pure and simple unionism. The long struggle for organization against the determined opposition of employers had begun.

Suggestions for Further Reading

A Maturing Industrial Economy

The most useful introduction to the economic history of this period is Edward C. Kirkland, *Industry Comes of Age, 1860–1897* (1961). A more sophisticated analysis, but still comprehensible to the attentive student, can be found in W. Elliott Brownlee, *Dynamics of Ascent* (rev. ed., 1979). For up-to-date essays on many of the topics covered by this chapter, the student is advised to consult Glenn Porter, ed., *Encyclopedia of American Economic History* (3 vols: 1980).

On railroads, a convenient introduction is John F. Stover, *American Railroads* (1970). The growth of the railroads as an integrated system has been treated in George R. Taylor and Irene D. Neu, *The American Railway Network, 1861–1890* (1956). Thomas Cochran, *Railroad Leaders, 1845–1890* (1953) is a pioneering study of the industry's entrepreneurs. Julius Grodinsky, *Jay Gould: His Business Career, 1867–1892* (1957) is a complex study demonstrating the contributions this railroad buccaneer made to the transportation system. Books like Cochran's and Grodinsky's have gone a long way to resurrecting Gilded Age businessmen from the debunking tradition first set forth with great power in Matthew Josephson, *Robber Barons: Great American Fortunes* (1934). Peter Temin, *Iron and Steel in the 19th Century* (1964) is the best treatment of that industry. Joseph F. Wall, *Andrew Carnegie* (1970) is the definitive biography of the great steelmaster. Equally definitive on the oil king is Allan Nevins, *A Study in Power: John D. Rockefeller* (2 vols: 1953). Harold C. Passer, *The Electrical Manufacturers, 1875–1900* (1953) treats both the entrepreneurial and technological aspects of this emergent industry. John B. Rae, *American Automobiles* is an excellent introductory account, and James J. Flink, *America Adopts the Automobile, 1895–1910* (1970) is a lively account of the start of the great American love affair. On the presiding genius, the major biography is Allan Nevin and Frank E. Hill, *Ford* (3 vols: 1954–62). A less deferential, but very shrewd, account is Keith T. Sward, *The Legend of Henry Ford* (1948).

On the emergence of modern management, the magisterial work is Aldred D. Chandler, *The Visible Hand: The Managerial Revolution in American Business* (1977), not an easy book, but one that will amply repay the labors of the interested student. Also worth reading is Chandler's earlier *Strategy and Structure: Chapters in the History of Industrial Enterprise* (1962). The standard treatment of industrial combination is Ralph L. Nelson, *Merger Movements in American Industry* (1959), as is Vincent P. Carosso, *Investment Banking in America* (1970) on the related subject of high finance. The kingpin of investment banking received somewhat irreverent treatment in Frederick Lewis Allen, *The Great Pierpont Morgan* (1949). On the money question, the definitive book is Milton Friedman and Anna J. Schwartz, *Monetary History of the United States, 1867–1960* (1963).

The World of Work

To understand the impact of industrialism on American workers, three collections of essays make the best starting points: Herbert G. Gutman, *Work, Culture and Society in Industrializing America* (1976); David Montgomery, *Workers' Control in America* (1979); and Michael S. Frisch and Daniel J. Walkowitz, eds, *Working-Class America: Essays on Labor, Community and American Society* (1983). On the introduction of Taylorism, the most useful book is Daniel Nelson, *Managers and Workers: Origins of the New Factory System* (1975). For a sweeping analysis of long-term change in American labor relations, see David M. Gordon *et al.*, *Segmented Work, Divided Workers: The Historical Transformation of Labor in the U.S.* (1982). There are two valuable recent collections of essays on immigrant workers: Richard Ehrlich, ed., *Immigrants in Industrial America* (1977), and Dirk Hoerder, ed., *American Labor and Immigration History, 1877–1920: Recent European Research* (1983). David Brody, *Steelworkers in America: The Nonunion Era* (1960)

is a study of workers in a single industry. John Bodnar, *Immigration and Industrialization: Ethnicity in an American Mill Town* (1977) is an important case study of a single community. On women workers, the best introduction is Alice Kessler-Harris, *Out To Work* (1982). Leslie Woodcock Tentler, *Wage-Earning Women: Industrial Work and Family Life, 1900–1930* (1979) is a thoughtful treatment of the impact of industrial work on female identity. On black workers, the best introduction is William H. Harris, *The Harder We Run: Black Workers since the Civil War* (1982).

The Labor Movement

The pioneering work on the American labor movement is John R. Commons *et al.*, *History of Labor in the U.S.* (4 vols, 1918–1935), of which vols II and IV cover the period of this chapter. The standard book on the struggle between labor reform and trade unionism is Gerald N. Grob, *Workers and Utopia, 1865–1900* (1961). It should be supplemented by Leon Fink, *Workingmen's Democracy: The Knights of Labor and American Politics* (1983), which captures cultural dimensions of labor reform not seen by earlier historians. The founder of the AFL is the subject of a lively, brief biography by Harold Livesay, *Samuel Gompers and Organized Labor in America* (1978). Among the many books on individual unions, Robert Christie, *Empire in Wood* (1956) best reveals the way pure-and-simple unionism worked out in practice. On industrial conflict, the most vivid book is Robert V. Bruce, *1877: Year of Violence* (1959). Almont Lindsay, *The Pullman Strike* (1943) is definitive on that battle. The best book on the IWW is Melvyn Dubofsky, *We Shall Be All* (1969). On socialism, David Shannon, *The Socialist Party of America* (1955) remains the standard account. There is, however, a fine new biography of that party's leader that supercedes previous studies, Nick Salvatore, *Eugene V. Debs: Citizen and Socialist* (1982). A dimension of American radicalism long neglected has recently received sensitive attention in Mari Jo Buhle, *Women and American Socialism, 1870–1920* (1982).

18

THE CITY

For the first two hundred years of its history, America remained a land of farmers. In 1820, barely 5 percent of the people lived in cities with a population of ten thousand or more. But after that, decade by decade, the urban population swelled, turning into a flood after midcentury. The greatest growth took place in the great metropolitan centers. In 1900, nearly a tenth of the nation—6.5 million persons—lived in cities of over a million. Another tenth made their homes in urban centers of between a hundred thousand and a million. The late nineteenth century, an economist remarked in 1899, was "not only the age of cities, but the age of great cities."

The growth of the cities had enormous implications for American society. The city was the arena of the nation's vibrant economic life. Here the factories went up, and here the multitudes of working people settled. Here, too, lived the millionaires and the new and growing urban middle class of white-collar workers and businessmen. For all these people, the city was more than a place to make a living. It provided the setting for an urban culture unlike anything seen before in the United States. City people, though vastly different among themselves, became distinctively and recognizably urban.

Urbanization

The march to the cities seemed inevitable to nineteenth-century Americans. "The greater part of our population must live in cities—cities much greater than the world has yet known," declared the Congregational minister and social critic Josiah Strong in 1898. "In due time we shall be a nation of cities." There was "no resisting the trend," said another writer. Urbanization became inevitable because of its link to another inevitability that gripped America—industrialization.

Sources of City Growth

During the earlier stages of industrialism, manufacturing had been scattered in the countryside. Mills and factories needed waterpower from the falls of streams, close access to sources of fuel and raw materials, and workers drawn from the surplus farm population. Cities, on the other hand, had engaged primarily in commerce. Located strategically along transportation routes, they were the places where merchants bought and sold goods, distributed them to the interior, or shipped them into the world market. Before

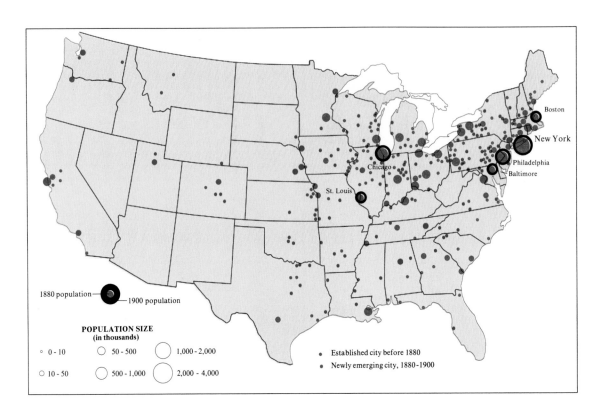

MAP 18.1 THE GROWTH OF AMERICA'S CITIES, 1880–1900
The number of Americans living in urban places more than doubled between 1880 and 1900. The most
dramatic increases occurred in the largest metropolitan centers. New York went from 1.2 million to
3.4 million, Chicago from 0.5 million to 1.7 million. Many small towns also grew rapidly, including
Seattle, Duluth, Sioux City, and Birmingham, which all grew to fifty thousand by 1900.

the Civil War, urban growth resulted primarily
from commerce, not industry. Of the fifteen
largest cities in 1860, only five had as many as 10
percent of the labor force in manufacturing activity.

After midcentury, industrialism began to
abandon the countryside. With the arrival of
steampower, mill operators no longer had to lo-
cate along streams. In the iron industry, coal
replaced charcoal as the primary fuel, so iron
makers did not have to be near forests. Improved transportation, especially on the railroads, gave entrepreneurs a greater choice in selecting the best sites in relation to supplies and
markets. Geographic concentration of industry
resulted. Ironmasters gravitated to Pittsburgh
because of its access not only to coal and iron-
ore sources but also to markets for iron and steel

products. Chicago, ideally located between livestock suppliers and consuming markets, became
a great meat-packing center in the 1870s.

Many smaller industrial cities depended on a
high degree of economic specialization. Youngs-
town, Ohio, and Johnstown, Pennsylvania,
specialized in iron and steel; Brockton and Ha-
verhill, Massachusetts, in boots and shoes; Troy,
New York, in collars and cuffs; and East Liverpool, Ohio, in pottery. Other cities processed the
raw materials of their regions. Sacramento
canned fruits and vegetables, Richmond made
cigarettes, Minneapolis milled grain, and Memphis handled lumber and produced cottonseed
oil.

Geographic concentration was one industrial
source of urban growth in the late nineteenth
century. Another was the increasing scale of

production that became characteristic of modern industry. A factory that employed thousands of workers created a small city in its vicinity. If the plant went up in an outlying area, a company town resulted. For example, Aliquippa, Pennsylvania, became body and soul the property of the Jones and Laughlin Steel Company. More often, firms built near a large city so they could draw on its labor supply and transportation facilities. George Pullman located his sleeping-car works and model town southwest of Chicago, and George Westinghouse put up his electrical plant in East Liberty near Pittsburgh. Sometimes the nearby metropolis spread and absorbed the smaller city, as happened with Pullman, Illinois. Elsewhere, as in northern New Jersey or south of Chicago and across the state line into Indiana, smaller communities merged and formed an extended urban-industrial area.

The established commercial cities also contributed to urban growth. They benefited from the tendency of a maturing industrial economy to create complex marketing and administrative structures. The greatest centers—New York and Chicago—became headquarters for corporations operating across the country. Finance, publishing, distribution, advertising, and fashion were concentrated in the metropolitan centers. Commercial cities attracted certain kinds of industry as well. They had warehouse districts readily convertible to small-scale manufacturing, and they offered ample transportation and service facilities. They also had abundant supplies of cheap labor because they served as gateways for immigrants. Boston, Philadelphia, Baltimore, and San Francisco became hives of small-scale, labor-intensive industrial activity. New York's enormous pool of immigrant workers made it a magnet for men's and women's clothing, cigar making, and diversified light industry. Preeminent as a city of trade and finance, New York also ranked as the nation's largest manufacturing center.

The 1900 census made clear the urban-industrial link. The nation's 209 principal cities, with about a third of the total population, accounted for two-thirds of the nation's industrial activity. The connection also could be seen in the country's regional development. By 1870, a core industrial area had formed from New England down through the Middle Atlantic states to Maryland. This region, with thirty of the fifty-two U.S. cities of more than twenty-five thousand people, had an urban population ratio twice the national average in 1870. Forty years later, the original industrial core was nearly three-quarters urbanized. It had thrust westward to include the Great Lakes states, which became the heartland of America's heavy industry. The centers of this new industrial activity—Pittsburgh, Cleveland, and Detroit—each grew from roughly a hundred thousand to half a million people between 1870 and 1910.

City Building

Cities grew larger under the impact of industrialism. But in so doing, they encountered staggering obstacles. How would so many people move around, communicate, and meet their physical needs? The city demanded innovation no less than did industry itself and, in the end, compiled an equally impressive record of technological achievement.

The preindustrial city had been a compact place, densely settled on a harbor. As late as 1860, Philadelphia covered only six square miles. A person could walk anywhere in the city within forty-five minutes from the foot of Chestnut Street on the Delaware River. Residential and working places remained almost as near each other as they had been in the colonial period. A Philadelphian, whether worker or businessman, normally had only a short distance to go in his everyday affairs.

As cities grew through the years, the need increased for an efficient means of urban transportation. The first step, dating back to the 1820s, was the omnibus, an elongated version of the horse-drawn coach. Once placed on iron tracks, these vehicles could be built to carry up to forty passengers. They were also able to move more rapidly through congested city streets.

Horsecars, as the first streetcars were called, provided the primary means of urban transit from the 1850s to the 1890s. The horse was not an ideal source of locomotion. It moved slowly, had limited pulling power, and left piles of manure behind. Among various early improvements on horsecars, cable cars seemed the most promising. The first ones ran in San Francisco in 1873, and more than twenty other cities used

TRAFFIC JAM IN DOWNTOWN CHICAGO, 1905
The purpose of urban transit systems—streetcars, elevated lines, and subways—was to move masses
of people rapidly and efficiently through the city. Sometimes the results compounded problems that
the transportation networks had been designed to solve. By attracting more people and business
activity, better transportation brought more congestion as well, like this scene of temporary gridlock
at Randolph and Dearborn streets in Chicago. (The Bettmann Archive)

them during the 1880s. Pulled by an endless underground cable, a cable car could run only at a
slow, unvarying speed; systemwide breakdowns
occurred frequently. The electric trolley quickly
replaced it except in hilly San Francisco. This
type of railway was the work primarily of Frank
J. Sprague, an electrical engineer who had
worked with the famous inventor Thomas A.
Edison. In 1887, Sprague designed an electric-
trolley system, utilizing an overhead power line,
for Richmond, Virginia. After Sprague's success,
electric railway construction spread across the
country. The horsecar, which had accounted for
about 70 percent of the surface transit in 1890,
virtually disappeared by 1900.

Meanwhile, congestion led to efforts to move
public transit off the streets. In 1879, the first elevated lines went into operation on Sixth and
Ninth avenues in New York City. Powered at
first by steam engines, the "els" converted to
electricity following Sprague's invention. Chicago developed elevated transit most fully. New
York, because of its crowded downtown area,
next turned to the subway. Although Boston
opened a short underground line in 1897, the
completion in 1904 of a subway running the
length of Manhattan demonstrated the full potential of underground rapid transit. The new subway system (the *New York Times* predicted), "will
open up a region now thinly settled," in which

"a population of ten millions can be, and we believe will be, housed comfortably, healthfully and relatively cheaply." The subway would especially delight "all who travel with the sole purpose of 'getting there' in the least time possible."

Construction techniques also forged ahead. The key breakthroughs occurred in new building materials that made it possible to construct commercial buildings of greater height, interior space, and fire resistance. With the availability by the 1880s of construction steel and mass-produced durable plate glass, a wholly new way of construction opened up. A steel skeleton would support the building, and the walls, hitherto weight-bearing, would serve as curtains enclosing the structure.

In 1885, the architect William Le Baron Jenney designed the ten-story Home Insurance Building in Chicago on this principle. The steel-girdered structure liberated aesthetic perceptions. A Chicago school of architecture sprung up, dedicated to the design of buildings whose form expressed, rather than masked, their structure and function. The masterpiece of the Chicago school was Louis Sullivan's Carson, Pirie, Scott and Company department store (1908). Chicago pioneered in skyscraper construction, but New York, with its unrelenting need for prime downtown space, took the lead after the mid-1890s. The climax of New York's construction surge came with the completion in 1913 of the fifty-five story Woolworth Building. The colossal "Cathedral of Commerce" towered over its neighbors and marked the beginning of the modern Manhattan skyline.

The railroads, which played a vital role in the development of the industrial city, gave rise to the other distinctive forms of urban construction. Rivers, the earlier lifelines of trade, now became barriers that interrupted rail traffic and hindered city expansion. The second half of the nineteenth century became the great age of bridge construction. Hundreds of iron and steel bridges went up during this period. Some, such as the Eads Bridge (1873) spanning the Mississippi River at Saint Louis and the Brooklyn Bridge (1883) over New York's East River, are still in use. The Brooklyn Bridge, a giant suspension structure linking Brooklyn and Manhattan (pictured on page 554), took fifteen years to build. The architectural critic Lewis Mumford called

this engineering marvel "the first product of the age of coal and iron to achieve completeness of expression."

On the other hand, the magnificent rail terminals that graced the great cities tried to mask that modernity. Reflecting the architectural forms of ages past, the terminals were marvels of structural design in their soaring interiors and use of steel, glass, and stone. New York's Grand Central Station (1913), built in the French baroque style, was completely electrified. It made superb use of underground space and had a loop system that enabled trains to turn around without reversing course. New York's other

MANHATTAN'S FIRST SKYSCRAPER
The Tower Building at 50 Broadway was completed in 1889. To the modern eye, the first New York skyscraper seems modest and old fashioned. Compared with its squat neighbors, however, it was a revolutionary building based on new principles of construction and expressing a new form of slender, soaring architecture. (Museum of the City of New York)

THE BROOKLYN BRIDGE
This engraving celebrated the opening of the Brooklyn Bridge, an event of great importance in the city's history. Metropolitan growth in the 1870s made rivers as much barriers to urban development as they were lifelines in the city's economy. Structures like the Brooklyn Bridge were the crucial links in forming unified metropolitan areas. Brooklyn Bridge joined Manhattan and Brooklyn, providing quick transport for land shipment, streetcars, pedestrians, and, later, automobiles. (*Bird's Eye View of the Great New York and Brooklyn Bridge, 1883.* The New-York Historical Society)

great terminal, Pennsylvania Station (1910), was modeled after a Roman bath.

If the railroad was the economic lifeline of the industrial city, electricity was the source of its quickening tempo. The telephone, patented by Alexander Graham Bell in 1876, sped up communication beyond anything imagined previously. By 1900, 1.5 million telephones linked urban decision makers into a network of instant communication. Electricity also lit up the city and extended its activity into the night beyond what had been possible in the gaslight era. Charles F. Brush's electric arc lamps, first installed in the windows of the Wanamaker department store in Philadelphia in 1878, soon illuminated stores, hotel lobbies, and city streets

throughout the country. Meanwhile, Thomas Edison experimented with filaments for his vacuum bulb, which, beginning in 1880, brought electric lighting into homes. Before electricity had any significant effect on industry, it lifted and lowered elevators, powered streetcars and subway trains, and lit up cities. No other invention so transformed America's urban life.

The Private City

City building was very much an exercise in private enterprise. The great innovations—the telephone, the trolley car, electric lighting, the skyscraper, and the elevator—had been spurred by the lure of profit. The investment opportunities looked so tempting that new cities sprang up almost overnight from the ruins of the Chicago fire of 1871 and the San Francisco earthquake of 1906. Likewise, real estate interests, anxious to develop subdivisions, often played an instrumental part in pushing horsecar lines out from the central districts of cities.

When urban transit began to mature, it followed the same consolidation route as in the industrial sector. In the early 1880s, Peter A. B. Widener and William L. Elkins teamed up to unite much of Philadelphia's streetcar system within the Philadelphia Traction Company. They did the same with Charles T. Yerkes in Chicago and with William C. Whitney and Thomas Fortune Ryan in New York. By 1900, their syndicate controlled streetcar systems in more than a hundred cities and had expanded to include gas works and electric lighting as well. The city, like industry, became an arena for enterprise and profit.

There was a difference, however. The city served as a dwelling place for multitudes of people, and what might improve their lives did not necessarily spell profit for entrepreneurs. Moreover, the burden of rights lay on the side of the community. There could be no "complete definition of 'a city purpose,' " the New York state courts ruled in an 1897 case authorizing New York City to build a municipally owned subway. A city had to determine its needs and then carry out those responsibilities as it saw fit. If a city chose to have services provided by others, it did so by, in effect, turning a private corporation into a municipal instrumentality. Even the use of privately owned land was subject to whatever regulations the city might choose to require.

But if municipal powers were thus broadly interpreted by law, cities generally hesitated to use them. America produced what the urban historian Sam Bass Warner has called the "private city," one shaped primarily by the actions of many private individuals. All these persons pursued their own goals and tried to maximize their own profit. Almost everyone believed that the sum of such private activity would far exceed what the community could accomplish through public effort. This meant that the city itself handled only functions, such as police protection, street construction, and sewage disposal, that could not be undertaken efficiently or profitably by private enterprise. The division of responsibility, although varying greatly from city to city, almost always deferred to what favored the interests of private capital. And the functions remaining with the city were to be handled in a way that would encourage private enterprise within its precincts. This system unleashed tremendous energies for city building. But the nation paid an enormous price for such unrestricted development. A century later, we are still adding up the costs in the quality of American urban life.

Some of those costs could be seen right away. In 1879 an English visitor observed the blight that spread along streets on which elevated trains operated:

> The nineteen hours and more of incessant rumbling day and night from the passing trains; the blocking out of a sufficiency of light; the full, close view passengers on the cars can have into rooms on the second and third floors.

Skyscrapers shut out the light and added to downtown congestion. People regarded such conditions as sad but inevitable costs of progress.

Other consequences were more clearly the result of deliberate choice. Priority went to projects considered vital to a city's economic development. Thus, bridge construction flourished. Grand public buildings, which stood as symbols of a city's eminence, enjoyed great popularity. Philadelphia's City Hall, said one critic, had been "projected on a scale of magnificence better suited for the capitol of an empire than the municipal building of a debt-burdened city." On the other hand, the condition of the streets, mainly a matter of convenience for the people, often remained scandalously bad. "Three or four days of warm spring weather," declared a New York journalist in 1893, would turn Manhattan's garbage-strewn, snow-clogged streets into "veritable mud rivers."

The farther from marketplace concerns, the less likely a project was to arouse the interest of city fathers. In 1877, Philadelphia still had about eighty-two thousand privies and cesspools. They gave way only slowly to centralized sewage systems. It took still longer for underground sewage pipes to replace the stinking gutters that connected individual houses to sewer mains.

THE LOWER EAST SIDE, NEW YORK CITY
As cities grew, land values in core areas skyrocketed. For the immigrant poor, with nowhere else to go, the result was incredible crowding in the confined spaces of tenement houses. Life necessarily spilled out into the streets. Much of the neighborhood business was transacted from pushcarts and with peddlers. The streets also offered a bit of fresh air, a chance to socialize with the neighbors, and a playing area for children. Street life was, all things considered, one of the pluses of downtown congestion. (Library of Congress)

Untreated sewage emptied into nearby bodies of water, sometimes poisoning a city's own water supply, as happened with typhoid-ridden Pittsburgh. Or the sewage might pollute the water of users downstream. Coastal cities disposed of garbage in an equally heedless way. They simply towed it out to sea in scows and dumped it in the outgoing tide.

Industrial wastes, accumulated in huge slag heaps, poured into the streams and rivers, and belched from factory stacks. A visitor to Pittsburgh noted "the heavy pall of smoke which constantly overhangs her . . . until the very sun looks coppery through the sooty haze." As for the lovely hills rising from the rivers, "they have been leveled down, cut into, sliced off, and ruthlessly marred and mutilated, until not a trace of their original outlines remain." Pittsburgh presented "all that is unsightly and forbidding in appearance, the original beauties of nature having been ruthlessly sacrificed to utility."

These failures of the industrial city resulted not only from the low value placed on the quality of urban life. The city's dynamism confounded efforts to provide adequate services. New York's Croton aqueduct, when completed in 1842, was hailed as "more akin in magnificence to the ancient and Roman aqueducts [than anything] achieved in our times." Yet, less than a decade later, the growing city's water requirements had outstripped the capacity of the aqueduct. In 1885, New York started to build a second and larger aqueduct. That one also failed to meet the city's needs, and so New York built still another aqueduct a hundred miles away in the Catskill Mountains. Each new facility and innovation seemed to fall short, not merely outstripped by the rising demand, but also contributing to that demand. This occurred with urban transportation, high-rise building, and modern sanitation systems. They attracted more users, created new necessities, and caused additional crowding and shortages.

Dynamic urban growth had the most disastrous impact on the living conditions of the poor. In the preindustrial city, these people had lived on a makeshift basis. They occupied small wooden structures in the alleys and back streets and, increasingly, in the subdivided homes of wealthy families who had fled to other neighborhoods. When rising land values after the Civil War made this practice uneconomical, speculators began to build houses specifically for low-income people. In New York, the dreadful result was the "dumbbell" tenement, so shaped as to be able to utilize nearly all the standard twenty-five by hundred foot lot. A five-story building of this type could house twenty families in cramped, airless apartments. In New York's eleventh ward, an average of 986 persons occupied each acre, a density matched only in Bombay, India. In other cities, the pressure for space was not quite as severe. Chicago, Boston, and Saint Louis housed their poor in two- and three-story buildings, and Philadelphia and Baltimore had dingy row-houses. But people everywhere considered these districts to be blights on the city. A Hull House investigator described Chicago's Halsted Street in 1896:

. . . The filthy and rotten tenements, the dingy courts and tumble-down sheds, the foul stables and dilapidated outhouses, the broken sewer pipes, the piles of garbage fairly alive with diseased odors, and . . . children filling every nook, working and playing in every room, eating and sleeping in every windowsill, pouring in and out of every door, and seeming literally to pave every scrap of "yard."

People recognized the problem but seemed unable to solve it. Reformers favored model tenements financed by public-spirited citizens willing to accept limited dividends on their investments. When such private philanthropy failed, cities tried to impose basic housing codes, a movement that resulted in New York's Tenement Reform Law of 1901. However, it was much easier to set standards than to enforce them. Commercial development had pushed up land values in downtown areas. Only high-density, cheaply built housing could earn a sufficient profit for the landlords of the poor. This basic economic fact defied nineteenth-century solutions. Since housing was not considered a "natural monopoly," it was unthinkable for public money to be spent "competing with private enterprise in housing the masses." It was even less permissible to interfere with the free labor market so that the poor might earn enough to afford better housing.

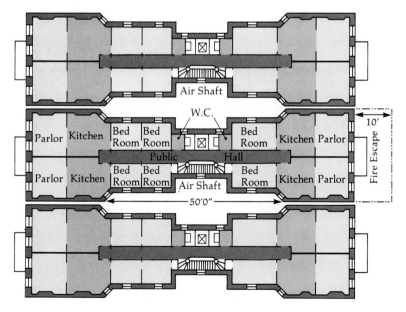

FIGURE 18.1 FLOOR PLAN OF A DUMBBELL TENEMENT

HOW THE OTHER HALF LIVES IN NEW YORK CITY (1890)

The reading public was shocked by the revelations in Jacob Riis's photographs and newspaper articles for the New York Tribune. He later published his collected observations as How the Other Half Lives, *from which this passage is excerpted.*

Down below Chatham Square, in the old Fourth Ward, where the cradle of the tenement stood, we shall find New York's Other Half at home, receiving such as care to call and are not afraid. . . .

Leaving the Elevated Railroad where it dives under the Brooklyn Bridge at Franklin Square, scarce a dozen steps will take us where we wish to go. With its rush and roar echoing yet in our ears, we have turned the corner from prosperity to poverty. We stand upon the domain of the tenement.

Suppose we look into one? No—Cherry Street. Be a little careful, please! The hall is dark and you might stumble over the children pitching pennies back there. Not that it would hurt them; kicks and cuffs are their daily diet. They have little else. Here where the hall turns and dives into utter darkness is a step, and another, another. A flight of stairs. You can feel your way, if you cannot see it. Close? Yes! What would you have? All the fresh air that ever enters these stairs comes from the hall door that is forever slamming, and from the windows of dark bedrooms that in turn receive from the stairs their sole supply of the elements God meant to be free, but man deals out with such niggardly hand. That was a woman filling her pail by the hydrant you just bumped against. The sinks are in the hallway, that all the tenants may have access—and all be poisoned alike by their summer stenches. Hear the pump squeak! It is the lullaby of tenement-house babes. In summer, when a thousand thirsty throats pant for a cooling drink in this block, it is worked in vain. But the saloon, whose open door you passed in the hall, is always there. The smell of it has followed you up. Here is a door. Listen! That short hacking cough, that tiny, helpless wail—what do they mean? They mean that the soiled bow of white you saw on the door downstairs will have another story to tell—Oh! a sadly familiar story—before the day is at an end. The child is dying with measles. With half a chance it might have lived; but it had none. That dark bedroom killed it.

"It was took all of a suddint," says the mother, smoothing the throbbing little body with trembling hands. There is no unkindness in the rough voice of the man in the jumper, who sits by the window grimly smoking a clay pipe, with the little life ebbing out in his sight, bitter as his words sound: "Hush, Mary! If we cannot keep the baby, need we complain—such as we?"

Such as we! . . . What sort of an answer, think you, would come from these tenements to the question "Is life worth living?"

One case that came to my notice some months ago in the Seventh Ward tenement was typical enough . . . There were nine in the family: husband, wife, an aged grandmother, and six children; honest, hard-working Germans, scrupulously neat, but poor. All nine lived in two rooms, one about ten feet square that served as parlor, bedroom, and eating room, the other a small hall room made into a kitchen. The rent was seven dollars and a half a month, more than a week's wages for the husband and father, who was the only breadwinner in the family. That day the mother had thrown herself out of the window, and was carried up from the street dead. She was "discouraged," said some of the other women from the tenement, who had come in to look after the children while a messenger carried the news to the father at the shop.

By relying on entrepreneurial development, the city invoked powerful self-seeking forces within its public life. Americans generally believed that municipal services could be provided most efficiently by private enterprise. Unfortunately, the profit motive operated entirely differently in the public sector than in the marketplace. Transit and utility companies considered it only smart business to keep pliable the city officials who granted them franchises and regulated their operations. "Private ownership of natural monopolies in cities is the chief source of corruption in city government," Mayor Hazen Pingree of Detroit stated in 1891. In city after city for the next twenty years, reform leaders battled the private utilities. The reformers faced a problem that cities had brought upon themselves—the price of making city building a function of entrepreneurial development.

The private city went counter to the creation of a rationally planned environment. America did not lack an urban vision. On the contrary, an abiding rural ideal had exerted a powerful influence on cities for many years. Frederick Law Olmsted, who designed New York's Central Park before the Civil War and many other city parks in later years, wanted cities that exposed people to the beauties of nature. One of Olmsted's projects, the Chicago World's Fair of 1893, gave rise to the influential "City Beautiful" movement. The results included larger park systems, broad boulevards and parkways, zoning laws after the turn of the century, and even planned suburbs.

Cities usually heeded urban planners too little and far too late. "Fifteen or twenty years ago a plan might have been adopted that would have made this one of the most beautiful cities in the world," the Kansas City Park Commissioners reported in 1893. At that time, "such a policy could not be fully appreciated." Nor, even if Kansas City had foreseen its future, would it have shouldered the "heavy burden" of trying to shape its development. The American city had placed its faith in the dynamics of the marketplace, not the restraints of a planned future.

The city symbolized energy and enterprise, with its vaulting skyscrapers, rushing subways and street traffic, and hum of business activity. A British visitor called New York City "colossal, great in height, in spirit, in emotion . . . its great buildings, its spreading luxury, its lights, its air of skeptical pleasure, its moral anaesthesia, its cool ferocity . . . the microcosm of the new civilization of America." But the city also had slums, congestion, suffering, and ugliness. No city reflected the industrial age more than Chicago, a village of four thousand in 1840 and a metropolis of a million in 1890. The famous English author Rudyard Kipling described Chicago in 1899:

> Streets . . . long and flat and without end . . . interminable vistas flanked with nine, ten, and fifteen storied houses . . . no colour in the streets and no beauty—only a maze of wire ropes overhead and dirty stone flagging underfoot. A cab driver . . . said that Chicago was a

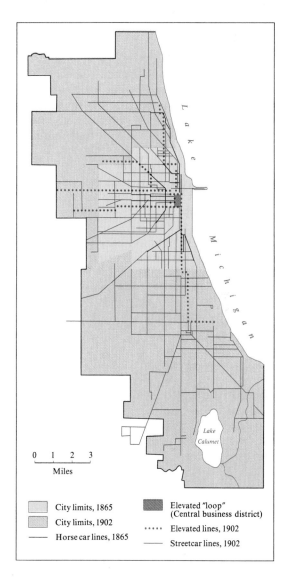

MAP 18.2 THE EXPANSION OF CHICAGO
Chicagoans in 1865 depended on slow horse-car transport to get around town. By 1900 the city limits had expanded enormously, accompanied by equally dramatic extension of streetcar service, by then all electrified. Elevated trains also now helped ease congestion in the urban core. New streetcar lines, some beyond the city limits, were important to suburban development in coming years.

live town, and that all the creatures hurrying by were engaged in business.

Kipling passed judgment on Chicago: "This place is the first American city I have encountered. . . . Having seen it, I urgently desire never to see it again."

Upper Class/Middle Class

Wealth, more than anything else, has determined social class in the United States. By that measure, American society was highly stratified during the nineteenth century. The top 1 percent of Americans held about a fourth of all wealth, and the upper 5 percent owned fully one half. The middle class, made up of the next 30 percent, owned the other half of the nation's wealth. Next to nothing went to the bottom two-thirds of the population. This sharply unequal division of wealth occurred early in America's industrial revolution and continued well into the twentieth century with little change. Late nineteenth-century industrialism apparently did not have much impact on the distribution of wealth in America. However, it did alter greatly the ways in which the resulting distinctions of social class expressed themselves. Such expression was mainly a function of urbanism, because the city became the arena in which social differentiation took place in the industrial age.

In the compact commercial city, the marks of class had depended neither on where people lived nor with whom they rubbed elbows. Class distinctions had been expressed by the way men and women dressed, how they behaved, and the deference they demanded from or granted to others. As the industrial city grew, these interpersonal marks of class began to lose their force. In the anonymity of a large city, recognition and deference no longer served very well as mechanisms for conferring status. Instead, people began to rely on external signs. These included conspicuous consumption of material goods, exclusive associations in clubs and similar social organizations, and, above all, choice of neighborhood.

Residential segregation was hastened by the changing physical layout of the industrial city. A city's economic activities, as they grew more complex, invariably became separated along distinct territorial lines. A downtown area emerged, usually in what had been the original commercial city. Downtown, in turn, broke up into shopping, financial, warehousing, light-manufacturing, hotel and entertainment, and red-light districts. Although somewhat fluid at their edges, all these districts were well-defined areas of specialized activity. Moving out from the center, industrial development tended to follow the arteries of transportation—railroads, canals, and rivers—and, at the city's outskirts, to spread out into complexes of heavy industry. This process acted strongly against the traditional urban living patterns of the commercial city. People wanted to flee at night as far as they could from the places of their employment. Advances in urban transportation gave them a much greater degree of physical mobility.

A person's place of residence had previously depended primarily on the location of his work. Now it became much more a reflection of his personal means and social preference.

The Urban Elite

As early as the 1840s, Boston merchants took advantage of the new railway service to move out of the congested central city. Fine rural estates appeared in Milton, West Roxbury, Newton, and other outlying towns. In 1848, roughly 20 percent of Boston's businessmen made the long trip from countryside to downtown office. They traveled on 118 trains that served stations within fifteen miles of the center of Boston. Ferries that plied between Manhattan and Brooklyn or New Jersey served much the same purpose for New Yorkers. As urban development engulfed downtown residential areas and as transportation services improved, the exodus from cities by the well-to-do spread across America. Wealthy families in Cincinnati settled on the scenic hills rimming the crowded, humid tableland that ran down to the Ohio River. On those hillsides, a traveler noted in 1883, "the homes of Cincinnati's merchant princes and millionaires are found ... elegant cottages, tasteful villas, and substantial mansions, surrounded by a paradise of grass, gardens, lawns, and tree-shaded roads." Residents of the area, called Hilltop, founded five country clubs, the Cincinnati Riding Club, the New England Society, five downtown gentlemen's clubs, and many other institutions that assured an exclusive social life for Cincinnati's elite.

Despite the temptations of suburban life, many of the very richest people preferred the heart of the city. Chicago had its Gold Coast; San Francisco, Nob Hill; Denver, Quality Hill; and Manhattan, Fifth Avenue. The New York novelist Edith Wharton recalled how the comfortable midcentury brownstones—"all so much

THROWING A GREAT PARTY DURING HARD TIMES

Frederick Townsend Martin describes the lavish affair his brother and sister-in-law put on for the crème de la crème of New York society in 1897 during a severe national depression.

Every year my brother Bradley and his wife spent their winters in New York, when they entertained largely. One morning at breakfast my brother remarked—

"I think it would be a good thing if we got up something; there seems to be a great deal of depression in trade; suppose we send out invitations for a concert."

"And pray, what good will that do?" asked my sister-in-law, "the money will only benefit foreigners. No, I've a far better idea; let us give a costume ball at so short notice that our guests won't have time to get their dresses from Paris. That will give an impetus to trade that nothing else will."

Directly Mrs. Martin's plan became known, there was a regular storm of comment. . . .

We were besieged by reporters, but my brother and his wife invariably refused to discuss the matter. Threatening letters arrived by every post, debating societies discussed our extravagance, and last, but not least, we were burlesqued unmercifully on the stage.

I think every one anticipated a disturbance, but nothing of the kind took place, and the evening passed without any untoward incident.

The best way I can describe what is always known as the "Bradley Martin Ball," is to say that it reproduced the splendour of Versailles in New York, and I doubt if even the Roi Soleil himself ever witnessed a more dazzling sight. The interior of the Waldorf-Astoria Hotel was transformed into a replica of Versailles, and rare tapestries, beautiful flowers and countless lights made an effective background for the wonderful gowns and their wearers. I do not think there has ever been a greater display of jewels before or since; in many cases the diamond buttons worn by the men represented thousands of dollars, and the value of the historic gems worn by the ladies baffles description.

My sister-in-law personated Mary Stuart, and her gold embroidered gown was trimmed with pearls and precious stones. Bradley, as Louis XV, wore a Court suit of brocade, and I rep-

resented a gentlemen of the period. The whole thing appealed most strongly to my imagination. . . .

The power of wealth with its refinement and vulgarity was everywhere. It gleamed from countless jewels, and it was proclaimed by the thousands of orchids and roses, whose fragrance that night was like incense burnt on the altar of the Golden Calf.

I cannot conceive why this entertainment should have been condemned. We Americans are so accustomed to display that I should have thought the ball would not have been regarded as anything very unusual. Every one said it was the most brilliant function of the kind ever seen in America, and it certainly was the most talked about.

After the ball the authorities promptly raised my brother's taxes quite out of proportion to those paid by any one else, and the matter was only settled after a very acrimonious dispute. Bradley and his wife resented intensely the annoyance to which they had been subjected, and they decided to sell their house in New York and buy a residence in London.

---

alike that one could understand how easy it would be for a dinner guest to go to the wrong house"—gave way to the " 'new' millionaire houses," which then spread northward beyond Fifty-ninth Street and up Fifth Avenue along Central Park. On the other side of the park, along Central Park West at Seventy-second Street, stood the monumental Dakota Apartment House, completed in 1884. It was furnished so luxuriously, one admiring journalist wrote, as to "guarantee to the tenants comforts which would require unlimited wealth to procure in a private residence." However, most millionaires preferred private homes that reflected wealth. Great mansions, reminiscent of European aristocratic houses and filled with Old World artifacts, lined Fifth Avenue at the turn of the century.

The creation of fashionable areas in the heart of a city showed the ability of the rich to assert their will over the larger society. But great fortunes did not automatically mean high social standing. An established elite stood astride the

561

THE BREAKERS
The favorite summering place of the New York elite was the historic colonial port of Newport, Rhode Island. The opulent mansions there were known as "cottages." Among the grandest was The Breakers, built in 1892 at a cost of $5 million. Richard Morris Hunt, a favorite architect of the Newport set, designed it for Cornelius Vanderbilt II in the style of an Italian palace. The Breakers had seventy rooms, thirty-three of them to house the small army of servants. The ornate dining room is shown in this photograph. (The Preservation Society of Newport County, R.I.)

social heights even in such relatively raw cities as San Francisco and Denver. It had only taken a generation—and sometimes less—for money made in commerce or real estate to shed its tarnish and become "old" and genteel. In more venerable cities, such as Boston, wealth passed intact through several generations. A high degree of intermarriage occurred there among the Brahmin families. By withdrawing from trade, and by asserting a high cultural and moral code, the proper Bostonians kept moneyed newcomers at bay. Elsewhere, urban elites tended to be more open, but only to the socially ambitious who were prepared to make visible and energetic use of their money.

New York's Metropolitan Opera was one of the products of this ongoing struggle among the wealthy. The Academy of Music, home to the city's opera since 1854, was controlled by the Livingstons, the Bayards, the Beekmans, and other old New York families. Frustrated in their efforts to purchase boxes at the academy, the Vanderbilts and their allies determined to sponsor a rival opera house. In 1883, with its

glittering opening to the strains of *Faust*, the Metropolitan asserted its ascendancy over the field and, in due course, won the patronage of even the Beekmans and Bayards. During this battle of the opera houses, the Vanderbilt circle achieved social recognition.

New York became the home of a national elite. The most successful people gravitated from everywhere to this preeminent center of American economic and cultural life. Manhattan's extraordinary vitality, in turn, kept the city's high society fluid and relatively open. The tycoon Frank Cowperwood, in Theodore Dreiser's novel *The Titan* (1914), reassured his unhappy wife that if Chicago society would not accept them, "there are other cities. Money will arrange matters in New York—that I know. We can build a real place there, and go in on equal terms, if we have money enough." New York thus came to be a magnet for millionaires. The city attracted them not only by its importance as a financial center, but also by the opportunities it offered for display and social recognition.

From Manhattan radiated out an extravagant

life of leisure in such resort centers as Saratoga Springs, New York; Palm Beach, Florida; and Newport, Rhode Island. Newport featured a grand array of summer "cottages," crowned by the Vanderbilts' Marble House and The Breakers. To these resorts, and elsewhere, the affluent traveled in great comfort by private railway car. A style of living emerged that was incredible for its lavish excess, ranging from yachting and horseracing to huge feasts at such luxurious restaurants as Sherry's and Delmonico's. "Our forefathers would have been staggered at the cost of hospitality these days," remarked one New Yorker.

This infusion of wealth shattered the older elite society of New York. Seeking to be assimilated into the upper class, the flood of moneyed newcomers simply overwhelmed it. Then followed a curious process of reconstruction, a deliberate effort to define the rules of conduct and identify those who properly belonged in New York society. In 1888, the first *Social Register* appeared. It announced that it would serve as a "record of society, comprising an accurate and careful list of its members, with their addresses, many of the maiden names of the married women, the club addresses of the men, officers of the leading clubs and social organizations, opera box holders, and other social information."

The career of Ward McAllister as arbiter to New York society was even more significant. He instructed the socially ambitious on how to select guests, set a proper table, arrange a ball, and launch a young lady into society. McAllister fostered an ordered social round of assemblies, balls, and dinners that defined the boundaries of an elite society. The key lay in the creation of sponsored associations by social leaders, "organized social powers, capable of giving a passport of society to all worthy of it." McAllister himself played a part in this selective process. He had the idea of the "Four Hundred," the true cream of New York society. His list corresponded to those invited to Mrs. William Astor's great ball of February 1, 1892.

Social registers, junior leagues, and lesser versions of Ward McAllister soon popped up in cities throughout the country. They represented the price paid for the fluidity at the height of the social order.

Americans were adept at making money, noted the journalist E. L. Godkin in 1896, but they lacked the European traditions for spending it. "Great wealth has not yet entered our manners," Godkin remarked. "No rules have yet been drawn to guide wealthy Americans in their manner of life." In their struggle to find the rules and establish the manners, the moneyed elite made an indelible mark on urban life. If there was magnificence in the American city, it was mainly their handiwork. And if there was conspicuous waste and vulgarity, it was likewise their doing. In a democratic society, wealth finds no easier outlet than through public display.

The Middle Class

The middle class left a much smaller imprint on the city. Its members, unlike the rich, preferred privacy and retreated into the domesticity of suburban comfort and family life.

The emerging corporate economy spawned a new salaried middle class. Bureaucratic organizations required managers, accountants, and clerks. Advancing technologies needed engineers, chemists, and designers. The distribution system sought salesmen, advertising men, and buyers. These salaried ranks increased sevenfold between 1870 and 1910, much faster than any other occupational group. The traditional middle class—independent businessmen and professionals—also grew but only at a third of the rate of salaried personnel. Nearly nine million people held white-collar jobs in 1910, more than a fourth of all employed Americans.

The middle class, particularly its salaried portions, was an urban population. Some lived within the city, in the rowhouses of Baltimore or Boston, or in the comfortable apartment houses of New York or other metropolitan centers. But far more preferred to escape from the clamor and congestion of the city. They were attracted by a persisting "rural ideal." They agreed with the landscape architect Andrew Jackson Downing, who thought that "nature and domestic life are better than society and manners of town." With the extension of rapid transit service from the city center, middle-class Americans followed the wealthy into the countryside. All sought what a Chicago developer promised of his North Shore subdivision in 1875—"qualities of which the city is in a large degree bereft, namely its pure air, peacefulness, quietude, and natural scenery."

MIDDLE-CLASS DOMESTICITY

For middle-class Americans of the late nineteenth century, the home was a place of nurture, a refuge from the world of competitive commerce. Perhaps that explained why their residences were so heavily draped and cluttered with bric-a-brac, every space filled with overstuffed furniture. All of it emphasized privacy—and the pride of possession. The young woman shown playing the piano symbolizes another theme of American domesticity—wives and daughters as ornaments, and as bearers of culture and refinement. (Museum of the City of New York)

No major American city escaped rapid suburbanization during the last third of the nineteenth century. City limits everywhere expanded rapidly. By 1900, more than half of Boston's people lived in "streetcar suburbs" outside the original city. When the United States Bureau of the Census began to designate "metropolitan districts" in 1910, it found that about 25 percent of the urban population lived outside the city limits.

The suburbs were middle-class territory. But the middle class was not monolithic. It ranged from prosperous businessmen and lawyers to clerks and traveling salesmen who earned no more than foremen and craftworkers. There was no better map of class standing than the geography of the suburbs, because where a family lived told where it ranked. The farther the distance from the center of the city, the finer the houses and the larger the lots. This arrangement re-

flected the ability to pay, and the work situations that went with varying income levels. The well-to-do had the leisure and flexible schedules to travel the long distance into town. People closer in wanted a direct transit line convenient to home and office. Lower-income suburbanites were likely to have more than one wage earner in the family, less security of employment, and to hold jobs requiring movement around the city. They needed easy access to crosstown transit lines, which ran close to the city center.

Divisions within suburbs, although always a precise measure of economic ranking, never became rigidly fixed. People in the center who wanted to better their lives moved to the cheapest suburbs. Fleeing from these newcomers, those already settled pushed the next higher group farther out in search of space and greenery.

Suburbanization was the sum of countless individual decisions. Each move represented an advance in living standards—not only more light, air, and quiet, but also better housing than the city afforded. The housing had more space and better design, as well as indoor toilets, hot water, central heating, and, by the turn of the century, electricity. Even the inner suburbs came to regard these amenities as standard comforts. The suburbs also restored a basic opportunity that had seemed sacrificed by rural Americans who had moved to the city. In the suburbs, home ownership again became a norm. "A man is not really a true man until he owns his home," propounded the Reverend Russell H. Conwell in his sermon, "Acres of Diamonds."

The small town of the rural past had fostered community life. Not so the suburbs. The grid street pattern, while efficient for laying out lots and providing utilities, offered no natural focus for group life. Nor did stores and services that lay scattered along the trolley-car streets. Not even schools and churches were located to make them the centers of community life. Suburban development conformed to the economics of real estate and transportation, and so did the thinking of middle-class home seekers entering the suburbs. They wanted a house that gave them good value and convenience to the trolley line.

The need for community had lost some of its meaning for middle-class Americans. Two other attachments assumed greater importance. One was work, the other, family.

Families

The family had been the primary productive unit in the preindustrial economy. Farmers, merchants, and artisans had carried on their work within a family setting. The value of family members could be reckoned by their economic contribution. The family circle included not only blood relatives, but all others living and working within the household. With the onset of industrialism, the family gradually lost its function as a productive unit. Throughout the city, members of the household left the home to help earn the family's living. Families also stopped producing for their own consumption. Almost all men's clothing was ready-made by 1900, and so was a growing share of food that came in the form of packaged and canned goods. Urban families reduced the number of their children and excluded all but nuclear members. The typical middle-class family of 1900 consisted of husband, wife, and three children.

Within this small circle, relationships between family members became intense and affectionate. "Home was the most expressive experience in life," recalled the literary critic Henry Seidel Canby of his growing up in the 1890s. "Though the family might quarrel and nag, the home held them all, protecting them against the outside world." In a sense, the family served as a refuge against the competitive, impersonal business world into which its employed members plunged daily. The suburbs provided a fit setting for middle-class families. The quiet, tree-lined streets created a domestic world insulated from the hurly-burly of commerce and enterprise. The symbol of middle-class suburbia was the house, standing on its own lot as an expression of family sanctity.

The burdens of this domesticity fell heavily on the wife. It was nearly unheard of for her to seek an outside career; that was her husband's role. She had the job of managing the household. "The woman who could not make a home, like the man who could not support one, was condemned," Canby remembered. But with better household technology, greater reliance on purchased goods, and fewer children, the wife's workload declined in these years. Moreover, servants still played an important part in middle-class households. The 1910 census reported about two million domestic servants, the largest job category for women.

The easing of household work put greater stress on the need for higher quality homemaking. This was the theme of Catharine Beecher's bestselling book *The American Woman's Home* (1869) and of such magazines as the *Ladies' Home Journal* and *Good Housekeeping*, which first appeared during the 1880s. The wife did more than make sure that food was on the table, that clothes were washed and mended, and that the house was kept clean. She had the higher calling of bringing sensibility, beauty, and love to the household. She made the home a refuge for her husband and a place of nurture for their children.

The wife's role, difficult under the best of circumstances, was made even harder by deep-rooted problems. Foremost was the denial of any sexual basis to the affectionate relationship at the heart of the family. "The majority of women (happily for society) are not very much troubled with sexual feeling of any kind," a popular medical text assured its readers. "What men are habitually women are only exceptionally. . . . Love of home, of children, and of domestic duties are the only passion they feel." Toward their husbands, another manual stated, wives should hold only "motherly tenderness. . . . The higher a woman rises in moral and intellectual culture, the more is the sensual refined away from her nature, and the more pure and perfect and predominating becomes her motherhood." In the face of the male's natural sexual appetites, brides should "struggle as resolutely to secure extreme temperance after marriage as they do to maintain complete abstinence before the ceremony."

Womanly virtue, even if a happy marriage depended on it, by no means put the wife on equal terms with her husband. The law established her subordinate role. It denied political rights to women—in 1890, only four states gave them the right to vote—and subjected them to discriminatory treatment. For example, the husband, but not the wife, could sue for divorce on grounds of adultery. More important, custom dictated the wife's submission to her husband. She relied on his ability as the family breadwinner and, despite her superior virtues and graces, ranked his inferior in vigor and intellect. Her mind could be employed "but little and in trivial matters," wrote one prominent physician, and her proper place was as "the companion or ornamental appendage to man."

Bright, independent-minded women understandably rebelled against marriage. The marriage rate in the United States fell to its lowest point during the last forty years of the nineteenth century. More than 10 percent of the women of marriage age remained single, and the rate was much higher among college graduates and professionals. Only half of the Mount Holyoke College class of 1902 married. When Frances Perkins, a member of the class, married in 1913, she upset her New York social-work colleagues. They thought they had lost her, but her husband's illness forced Perkins to resume her career. She eventually became the first woman cabinet member, serving as secretary of labor under President Franklin D. Roosevelt.

For middle-class women who did marry, the price was often high. A substantial number of families broke apart, but most of these domestic mishaps remained unrecorded because of the stigma attached to divorce. In a Chicago suburb in the 1880s, at a time when divorce was virtually unknown there, about 10 percent of the households had an absent spouse. The national divorce rate increased from 1.2 per thousand marriages in 1860 to 7.7 in 1900. It was more difficult to document the other ways women responded to marriages that denied their autonomy or sexual desires. Middle-class women became the principal victims of neurasthenia, a disorder whose symptoms included depression and general disability. Some unhappy housewives found "silent friends" in opium and alcohol, both often dispensed in well-laced patent medicines.

A happier release came through the companionship of other women. In an age that defined separate men's and women's spheres, close ties commonly formed between schoolmates, cousins, and mothers and daughters. The intimacy and intensity of such attachments can be sensed in surviving letters of separated friends. Such enduring female ties yielded emotional gratification not often found in marriage. Husbands, absorbed in business, frequently played a secondary and remote role in the lives of their wives. The women's own sphere often filled that emotional vacuum.

The middle-class family had long faced a difficult dilemma. Many couples wished to limit the number of their children, but birth control was not an easy matter. Antipornography laws, pushed through by the social-purity campaigner Anthony Comstock during the 1870s, banned distribution of birth control information through the mail. Many states classified such material as obscene literature and prohibited its sale. Abortion became illegal except to save the mother's life. Although the practice of abortion was probably widespread, it was expensive, dangerous, and considered shameful. Family limitation could be best achieved by delaying marriage and then by practicing abstinence. The repressive sexuality within the family resulted from practi-

THE ECONOMY OF THE GHETTO
Downtown immigrant neighborhoods would not have struck the casual observer as industrial districts. But tucked away in the tenements were commercial lofts and small workshops. Sewing machines hummed continually in many apartments. An entire ready-made clothing industry flourished within the tenement sections of large cities, built on the eagerness of immigrants for work and on their reluctance to venture out of the ghetto into the alien world beyond. This Jacob Riis photograph shows a necktie workshop on Division Street in New York City. (Library of Congress)

cal necessities. A fulfilling sexual relationship could not be squared with the desire to limit and space childbearing.

Somewhere around 1890, change set in. Although the birth rate continued to decline, more young people got married and at an earlier age. These developments reflected a sexual revolution within the American middle-class family. With the growing acceptability of contraception, the Comstock laws notwithstanding, people no longer tightly linked sex and procreation. This crucial change initiated the sexual emancipation of women. In succeeding editions of his book *Plain Home Talk on Love, Marriage, and Parentage*, for example, the physician Edward Bliss Foote began to favor a healthy sexuality that gave pleasure to both female and male. During the 1890s, the artist Charles Dana Gibson created the image of the "new woman" in his drawings for *Life* magazine. The Gibson girl was tall, spirited, athletic, and chastely sexual. Such clothing constrictions as bustles, hoop skirts, and hourglass corsets gave way to shirtwaists and other natural styles that did not hide or disguise the female form.

The children of the middle class went through their own revolution. In the past, American children everywhere had been regarded chiefly as economic assets—added hands for the family farm, shop, or counting house. That no longer held true for the urban middle class. Parents stopped treating their children as working members of the family. In the old days, remarked the author Ralph Waldo Emerson in 1880, "children had been repressed and kept in the background; now they were considered, cosseted, and pampered." There was such a thing as "the juvenile mind," lectured Jacob Abbott in his book *Gentle Measures in the Management and Training of the Young* (1871). The family had the responsibility of providing the nurturing environment in which the young personality could grow and mature. Preparation for adulthood became increasingly linked to formal education. School enrollment went up one and a half times between 1870 and 1900. High school attendance, while still covering only a small percentage of teenagers, increased at the fastest rate. The years between childhood and adulthood began to stretch out, and a new stage of life—adolescence—emerged. Rooted in an extended period of family dependency, adolescence at the same time shifted much of the socializing role from parents to peer group. A youth culture started to take shape. It became one of the hallmarks of American life in the twentieth century.

City People

When the budding writer Hamlin Garland and his brother arrived in Chicago from rural Iowa in 1881, they knew immediately that they had entered a new world: "Everything interested us. . . . Nothing was commonplace, nothing was ugly to us." In one way or another, every city-bound migrant, whether from the American countryside or a foreign land, experienced something of this exhilaration and wonder. But with the freedom, opportunity, and boundless variety, there also came profound disorder and uncertainty. The urban world would be utterly unlike the rural communities that the newcomers had left. In the countryside, every person had been known to his or her neighbors. In the city, people were not only strangers but strangers from many lands who spoke many languages. Rural roles and obligations had been well understood, but the only predictable relationships in the city were those dictated by the marketplace.

The newcomers could never recreate in the city the worlds they had left behind. But new ways developed to meet the social needs of urban dwellers—to give them a sense of their place in the community; to teach them how to function in an impersonal, heterogeneous environment; and to make the complex, dynamic city understandable. An urban culture emerged, and through it a new breed of American entirely at home in the modern city.

Immigrants

For immigrants, ethnic identity played the crucial role in forming an urban community. Beginning in the 1880s, observers invariably reported that only foreign-born people lived in the poorer downtown areas. "One may find for the asking an Italian, a German, a French, African, Spanish, Bohemian, Russian, Scandinavian, Jewish, and Chinese colony," remarked the Danish-American journalist Jacob Riis in his study of lower New York in 1890. "The one thing you shall vainly ask for in the chief city of America is a distinctively American community." This foreign-born concentration stemmed partly from

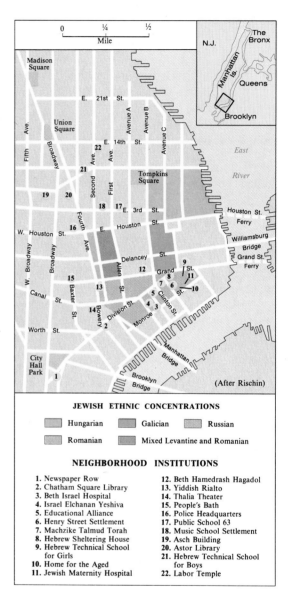

MAP 18.3 THE JEWISH LOWER EAST SIDE, NEW YORK CITY

Jews from Eastern Europe, disembarking in New York City, concentrated in Manhattan's Lower East Side and, within that area, settled among others from their home regions. The same feeling of group identity led to a remarkable flowering of ethnic institutions built by Jewish immigrants to meet their own educational, cultural, and social needs.

economic necessity—the need to live near jobs and the inability to afford better housing. Of all urbanites, immigrant working people had the least freedom to choose where they lived. Their poverty dictated that they be concentrated in the industrial districts and the congested downtown area.

The immigrants did not settle randomly in the tenement districts, however. Even where this seemed to happen, as in Philadelphia, closer study revealed ethnic groups clustering in individual houses and portions of blocks. More commonly, as Riis discovered, an ethnic group took over an entire neighborhood. In New York, Italians crowded into the Irish neighborhoods west of Broadway, and Russian and Polish Jews pushed the Germans out of the lower East Side. A dense colony of Hungarians lived around Houston Street, and Bohemians occupied the upper East Side between Fiftieth and Seventy-sixth streets.

One could also spot a clustering within ethnic groups of people from the same province or even village. Among New York Italians, for example, Neapolitans and Calabrians populated the Mulberry Bend district, and Genoese lived on Baxter Street. Other northern Italians occupied the eighth and fifteenth wards west of Broadway, and southern Italians moved into "Little Italy" far up in Harlem. In 1903, along a short stretch of Elizabeth Street, lived several hundred families from Sciacca, a Sicilian fishing town.

From the feeling of companionship that drew ethnic groups together, a variety of institutions sprung up to meet their needs. Wherever substantial numbers of immigrants lived, newspapers appeared. In 1911, the twenty thousand Poles in Buffalo, New York, supported two daily papers. Immigrants throughout the country avidly read *Il Progresso Italo-Americano* and the Yiddish language *Jewish Daily Forward*, both published in New York City. Conviviality could always be found on street corners, in barbershops and club rooms, and in saloons. A 1905 survey showed that Chicago had as many saloons as grocery stores, meat markets, and dry-goods stores together. Italians marched in saint-day parades, Bohemians gathered in singing socie-

TABLE 18.1 FOREIGN-BORN POPULATION OF PHILADELPHIA, 1870 AND 1910

	1870	1910
Irish	96,698	83,196
German	50,746	61,480
Austrian	519	19,860
Italian	516	45,308
Russian	94	90,697
Hungarian	52	12,495
Foreign-born population	183,624	384,707
Total population	674,022	1,549,008

SOURCE: Allen F. Davis and Mark Haller, *The Peoples of Philadelphia* (Philadelphia: Temple University Press, 1973).P.

ties, and New York Jews patronized a vibrant Yiddish theater. To provide help in times of sickness and death, the immigrants organized mutual-aid societies. The Italians of Chicago had sixty-six of these organizations in 1903, composed mainly of people from particular provinces and towns. Immigrants built a rich and functional institutional life in urban America to an extent unimagined in their native villages.

Most urban blacks, like the immigrants, were newcomers to the cities. Settled black populations in northern cities began to be outnumbered in the late 1800s by migrants from the South. By 1910, New York ranked as the nation's second largest black urban center, after Washington, D.C. New York's ninety-one thousand blacks represented scarcely 3 percent of its 1910 population, but they had a rich community life. They created a flourishing press, fraternal orders, and a middle class that catered to their needs. Newcomers found the black churches particularly important in their lives. Manhattan's Union Baptist Church, housed like many others in a storefront, attracted the "very recent residents of this new, disturbing city" and made Christianity come "alive Sunday mornings."

Religion had an equally important part in the lives of the immigrants. They found greater difficulty, however, establishing churches as they had known them in the old country. These people stubbornly opposed any change from familiar church practice. Also, the ground had been preempted to some degree by others who had already planted their religions in America.

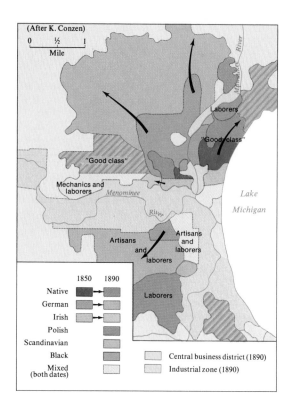

MAP 18.4 THE URBAN ETHNIC MOSAIC:
MILWAUKEE, 1850–1890
Neighborhoods in American cities developed strong class
and ethnic identities in the second half of the nineteenth
century. Core areas near downtown Milwaukee
expanded outward as immigrant populations increased
and new residents arrive. Artisans and laborers tended to
settle near their places of work in and near the industrial
zone. The "good class" (upper and middle classes) and
German residents have remained dominant in certain
areas throughout Milwaukee's history.

By the time the eastern European Jews began
their mass migration in the 1880s, about 250,000
Jews lived in America, mostly of German origin.
The German Jews, well established and increasingly properous, had long since begun to embrace Reform Judaism. Reform Jews abandoned
religious practices "not adapted to the views and
habits of modern civilization." They thus practiced a form of Judaism very remote from the pi-
ous orthodoxy of the Yiddish-speaking Jews.
The eastern Europeans founded their own Orthodox synagogues, often in vacant stores and
ramshackle buildings. The number of synagogues in the United States jumped from 270 in
1880 to 1,901 in 1916.

Many Jews found it difficult to adhere to the
traditional form of their religion. In the insulated
villages of eastern Europe, Judaism comprised
not only worship and belief, but an entire way
of life. Not even the closely confined urban
American ghetto could recreate the communal
environment for strict religious observance. "The
very clothes I wore and the very food I ate had
a fatal effect on my religious habits," confessed
the hero of Abraham Cahan's novel *The Rise of
David Levinsky* (1917). "If you ... attempt to bend
your religion to the spirit of your surroundings,
it breaks. It falls to pieces." Levinsky shaved off
his beard and plunged into the Manhattan clothing business. If Orthodox Judaism survived this
shattering of faith, it did so only by sharply reducing its claims on the lives of the faithful.

The Catholic church faced much the same
problem. The issue, explicitly defined within the
church as "Americanism," turned on how far
Catholicism should respond to American society. Catholics fought out the question on many
fronts, including parochial schooling, education
for the clergy, and relations with non-Catholics.
What was the church's place in a pluralistic society that denied religion any state support or automatic claim to people's allegiance? Bishop John
Ireland of Saint Paul, Minnesota, felt that "the
principles of the Church are in harmony with
the interests of the Republic." But traditionalists,
led by Archbishop Michael A. Corrigan of New
York, denied the possibility of such harmony.
They argued, in effect, for insulating the church
from a hostile environment.

In 1895, Pope Leo XIII announced his support
of the traditionalists. He denied "that in America
is to be sought the type of the most desirable
status of the Church." The pope regretted the
absence of the benefits that came from public
support and urged Catholics "to prefer to asso-
ciate with Catholics, a course which will be very
conducive to the safeguarding of their faith."
Catholicism, because of its hierarchical structure,
had a better chance than Judaism to resist American influences.

The church's traditional wing had the support
of immigrant Catholics, who wanted to preserve
their religion as they had known it in Europe.
But the needs of the immigrants extended beyond purely religious matters. The church also
had to express their ethnic identities. These
Catholics wanted their own parishes, where

they could celebrate their own customs and holidays, speak their own languages, and educate their children in their own parochial schools. When they became numerous enough, they also demanded their own bishops. German Catholics had pressed these ethnic claims for years, and so did the southern and eastern Europeans who flocked to America from the 1890s on.

The church had difficulty responding. Ironically, the institutional strength that preserved Catholicism against "Americanism" made it resistant to the demands of its immigrant congregations. Their claims seemed to challenge the Irish-Catholic hierarchy and, more importantly, the integrity of the church itself. The desire for ethnic parishes did more than divide Catholics; it also led to demands for local control of church property. In addition, to appoint bishops with jurisdiction over specific ethnic groups meant cutting across the diocesan structure of the church.

The severity of the conflict depended partly on the religious traditions of each ethnic group. Italians, for example, had a strong anticlerical feeling, much strengthened by the papacy's opposition to the unification of Italy. Italian men also had a tradition of religious apathy. On the other hand, the church played such an important part in the lives of Polish immigrants that they sometimes tolerated no interference from the Catholic hierarchy. In 1907, fifty parishes formed the Polish National Catholic Church of America, which adhered to Catholic ritual without recognizing the pope's authority.

On the whole, however, the church reconciled its authority with the ethnic needs of the immigrant faithful. It met the demand for representation in the hierarchy by appointing Polish and other immigrant priests as auxiliary bishops within existing dioceses. Before World War I, American Catholics worshiped in more than two thousand foreign-language churches and in many others that were bilingual. The Catholic church became a central institution for the expression of ethnic identity in urban America.

Protestantism and the City

Protestant churches, the products of rural, middle-class America, in some ways encountered even greater challenges in the cities than Judaism or Catholicism. Beginning with the Irish migrations of the 1840s, urban populations fell increasingly outside the Protestant faith. At the same time, Protestant congregations abandoned the older residential neighborhoods. Many formerly prosperous churches found themselves stranded in bleak working-class districts. Seventeen Protestant churches moved out of lower Manhattan during the twenty years after 1868 when the area below Fourteenth Street filled up with immigrants.

Nearly every major city retained great downtown churches where wealthy Protestants worshiped. Some of these churches, richly endowed, took pride in nationally prominent pastors, including Henry Ward Beecher of Plymouth Congregational Church in Brooklyn and

URBAN REVIVALISM
In rural America, the church was as familiar to the community as the schoolhouse, and churchgoing was a normal part of the routine of life. In anonymous city life, faith found fewer established outlets. The revivalist Dwight L. Moody discovered an enormous, pent-up need when he began to preach in American cities in 1875. This crowd of five thousand in Brooklyn at Moody's maiden service prompted the trolley company to lay additional track to accommodate the faithful. (From *Harper's Weekly*. The Newberry Library, Chicago)

Phillips Brooks of Trinity Episcopal Church in Boston. The eminence of these churches, with their fashionable congregations and imposing edifices, emphasized the growing remoteness of Protestantism from mainstream urban life. "Where is the city in which the Sabbath day is not losing ground?" lamented a minister in 1887. The families of businessmen, lawyers, and doctors could be seen in any church on Sunday morning, he noted, "but the workingmen and their families are not there."

To counter this decline, the Protestant churches responded in two ways. They evangelized among the unchurched and indifferent, for example, through the Sunday-school movement that blossomed in these years. Protestants also made their churches instruments of social uplift. Starting in the 1880s, many city churches provided such facilities as reading rooms, day nurseries, clubhouses, and vocational classes. Sometimes the churches linked evangelism and social uplift. The Salvation Army, which arrived from England in 1879, spread the gospel of repentance among the urban poor. A decade later, it added an assistance program that ranged from soup kitchens to homes for fallen women. When all else failed, the down-and-outers of American cities knew they could count on the Salvation Army.

The Young Men's and Women's Christian Associations attracted large numbers of the young single people who flocked into the cities. No other organizations better met the needs of young adults for physical recreation, education, or companionship. Nor did other groups so effectively combine these services with an evangelizing appeal in the form of Bible classes, nondenominational worship, and a strong religious atmosphere.

The need of many people to unite religion with social uplift could be seen in the enormous popularity of a book called *In His Steps* (1896). The author, the Reverend Charles M. Sheldon, told the story of a congregation that resolved to live by Christ's precepts for one year. "If the church members were all doing as Jesus would do," Sheldon asked, "could it remain true that armies of men would walk the streets for jobs, and hundreds of them curse the church, and thousands of them find in the saloon their best friend?"

Yet the most potent form of urban evangelism said little about social uplift. From its beginnings in the eighteenth century, revivalism had steadfastly focused on the individual. It stressed sinfulness and the need for redemption. The solution of earthly problems would follow the conversion of the people to Christ. Beginning in the mid-1870s, revival meetings swept through the cities. The pioneering figure was Dwight L. Moody, a former Chicago shoe salesman and YMCA official. After preaching two years in England, Moody returned to America in 1875. With his talented chorister and hymnwriter, Ira D. Sankey, Moody staged revival meetings that drew thousands of people. He preached an optimistic, uncomplicated, nondenominational message. Eternal life could be had for the asking, Moody shouted as he held up his Bible. His listeners needed only "to come forward and take, TAKE!" Many other preachers followed in Moody's path. The most notable was Billy Sunday, a hard-drinking outfielder for the Chicago White Stockings who mended his ways and found religion. Like Moody and other city revivalists, Sunday was a farm boy. His rip-snorting cries against "Charlotte-russe Christians" and the "booze traffic" carried the ring of rustic America. By realizing that many people remained villagers at heart, revivalists had found the key for bringing city dwellers back into the church fold.

Leisure

City people divided life's activities into separate units, setting workplace apart from home, and working time apart from free time. Leisure became a defined function, marked by the clock and enjoyed in distinctive ways and at designated places. Urban dwellers, in the impersonal, anonymous world they inhabited, increasingly found themselves the paying customers of commercial entertainment.

Amusement parks, such as Elitch's Gardens, which opened in Denver in 1890, went up at the end of trolley lines in cities across the country. Coney Island became immensely popular among New Yorkers. Theatrical entertainment likewise attracted huge audiences. Chicago had six vaudeville houses in 1896, and twenty-two in 1910. Evolving from cheap variety and minstrel

THE SEASHORE
Earlier generations of Americans would have shaken their heads at the sight of swarms of city dwellers heading for the beach on a hot Sunday. Didn't they know about the physical risks of "exposing one's complexion to the harmful rays of the sun" or the moral dangers of mixed bathing in various stages of undress? By 1900, the beach had become one of the great urban institutions of weekend play. (New Haven Colony Historical Society)

shows, vaudeville moved from boisterous beer halls into grand theaters. It cleaned up its routines, making them suitable for the entire family, and turned into thoroughly professional entertainment handled by national booking agencies. With its standard program of nine acts of singing, dancing, and comedy, vaudeville attained the popularity that the movies later achieved.

Of all forms of diversion, none was more specific to the city, nor so spectacularly successful, as professional baseball. The game's promoters decreed that baseball had been created in 1839 by Abner Doubleday in the village of Cooperstown, New York. Actually, baseball was neither of American origin—it developed from the English game of rounders—nor a product of rural life. Organized play began in the early 1840s in New York City, where a group of gentlemen enthusiasts competed among themselves on an empty lot. They wrote the first modern rules in 1845. The next year, as the New York Knickerbockers, they lost to the New York Nine, 23 to 1, in the first game between two organized baseball teams. During the next twenty years, the aristocratic tone of baseball disappeared. Clubs sprang up across the country and intercity competition developed on a scheduled basis. In 1868, baseball became openly professional, following the example of the Cincinnati Red Stockings in sign-

ing players to contracts at a negotiated salary for the season.

Big-time commercial baseball came into its own with the launching of the National League in 1876. The team owners were profit-minded businessmen who ran the sport and carefully shaped it to please the fans. Wooden grandstands gave way to the concrete and steel stadiums of the early twentieth century, such as Fenway Park in Boston, Forbes Field in Pittsburgh, and Shibe Park in Philadelphia.

For the urban multitudes, baseball grew into something more than an occasional afternoon at the ball park. Fans, by rooting for the home team, found a basis for identifying themselves with the city they lived in. Amid the diversity and anonymity of urban life, the common experience and language of baseball acted as a bridge among city people. Students of the game have suggested that baseball was peculiarly attuned to city life. It followed strict, precise rules, which suggested an underlying order to the chaotic city. Far from respecting the rules, however, the players tried to get away with whatever they could in order to win. Did this not match the competitive scramble of urban life? The blue-coated umpires, the symbols of authority, were scorned by players and derided by fans. What better substitutes for the resentment against the

THE NATIONAL PASTIME
This color lithograph commemorates the opening game of the 1889 season, with the Boston Base-Ball Club taking on the New York Base-Ball Club. The National League was then scarcely twelve years old. The fielders played barehanded, but otherwise the game remains today much as the artist pictured it a century ago, even down to the umpire's characteristic stance. What was there about baseball that almost overnight made it the national game and has kept it there virtually unchanged for a century? (Historical Pictures Service)

powers-that-be who ruled the lives of city people? Baseball, like many other emerging urban institutions, served as a mechanism for inducting people into the life of the modern city.

The press undertook this task in a clear-eyed, calculated way. Until Benjamin H. Day founded the *New York Sun* in 1833, American newspapers had limited themselves to a diet of mercantile news and political advocacy. The *Sun* promised "all the news of the day," cost only a penny—hence the term "penny press"—and aimed for a broad audience. When James Gordon Bennett founded the *New York Herald* in 1835, he said he wanted "to record the facts . . . for the great masses of the community." Journalism defined the news to be whatever interested city readers. The *Herald* covered crime, scandal, and sensational events. After the Civil War, *Sun* editor Charles A. Dana added the human-interest story which made news of ordinary, insignificant happenings. Newspapers also targeted specific audiences. A women's page offered recipes and fashion news, separate sections covered sports and high society, and the Sunday supplement helped fill the spare weekend hours.

Newspaper wars erupted periodically, as when Joseph Pulitzer, the owner of the *St. Louis Post-Dispatch* invaded New York in 1883 by buying *The World*. In 1895, William Randolph Hearst, who owned the *San Francisco Examiner*, bought the *New York Journal* and challenged *The World*. Hearst developed a sensational style of newspaper reporting and writing called *yellow journalism*. In his combative zeal, he often abandoned the journalistic canon of telling the truth. The *Journal's* sensational reporting of the civil war in Cuba enabled Hearst's paper to win its circulation battle with *The World*—and helped bring on the Spanish-American War of 1898.

"He who is without a newspaper," said the great showman P. T. Barnum, "is cut off from his species." Barnum was speaking of city people and their hunger for information. By meeting this need, newspapers revealed their sensitivity to the public they served.

The Higher Culture

The great cities implanted the institutions of higher culture into American society. A hunger for the cultivated life did not, of course, originate in cities. Before the Civil War, the lyceum movement had sent lecturers to the remotest of towns bearing messages of culture and learning. The Chautauqua movement, founded in upstate New York in 1874, carried on this work of cultural dissemination in the last decades of the nineteenth century. However, large cultural institutions, such as museums, public libraries, opera companies, and symphony orchestras, could flourish only in metropolitan centers.

The first outstanding art museum, the Corcoran Gallery of Art, opened in Washington, D.C., in 1869. New York's Metropolitan Museum of Art started in rented quarters two years later. In 1880, the museum moved to its permanent site in Central Park and launched an ambitious program of art acquisition. J. P. Morgan became chairman of the board in 1905, thus assuring the Metropolitan's preeminence. The Boston Museum of Fine Arts was founded in 1876, and Chicago's Art Institute in 1879. By 1914, virtually every major city, and about three-fifths of all cities with more than a hundred thousand people, had an art museum.

Top-flight orchestras also appeared, first in New York under the conductors Theodore Thomas and Leopold Damrosch in the 1870s. Symphonies started in Boston and Chicago during the next decade. National tours by these leading orchestras planted the seeds for orchestral societies in many other cities. Public libraries grew from modest collections (in 1870 only seven had as many as fifty thousand books) into major urban institutions. The greatest library benefactor was Andrew Carnegie, who announced in 1881 that he would build a library in any city prepared to maintain it. By 1907, Carnegie had spent more than $32.7 million to establish about a thousand libraries throughout the country.

If the late nineteenth century was the great age of money making, it was also the great age of money giving. Surplus private wealth flowed in many directions, particularly to universities. These schools included Vanderbilt, Tulane, and Stanford universities, all named for their chief benefactors, and the University of Chicago, founded by John D. Rockefeller. Urban cultural institutions also received their share, partly as a matter of civic pride. To some extent, patronage of the arts also served the need of the newly rich to establish themselves in society, as in the founding of the Metropolitan Opera in New York. But the higher culture, beyond being merely a commodity of civic pride and social display, received support out of a sense of cultural deprivation.

"In America there is no culture," pronounced the English critic G. Lowes Dickinson in 1909. Science and the practical arts, yes, "every possible application of life to purposes and ends," but "no life for life's sake." Such condescending remarks received a respectful hearing in the United States because of a deep sense of cultural inferiority to the Old World. In 1873, Mark Twain and Charles Dudley Warner had written a novel, *The Gilded Age*, satirizing America as a land of money grubbers and speculators. This enormously popular book touched a nerve in the American psyche. Its title took root in historical literature as a characterization of late nineteenth-century America, denoting especially the nation's materialism and cultural shallowness. Some members of the upper class, including the novelist Henry James, despaired of the country and moved elsewhere. Others spent their lives in the kind of perpetual alienation that Henry Adams described in his caustic memoir *The Education of Henry Adams* (1907).

The more common response was to try to raise the nation's cultural level. The newly rich had a hard time doing this. They did not have much opportunity to cultivate a taste for art, and a great deal of what they collected was mediocre and garish. On the other hand, George W. Vanderbilt, grandson of the roughhewn Cornelius Vanderbilt, became a patron of the Art Students League in New York and an early champion of French Impressionism. The enthusiasm of moneyed Americans—not always well-directed—largely fueled the great cultural institutions that arose in many cities during the Gilded Age.

A deeply conservative idea of culture sustained this generous patronage. The aim was to embellish urban life, not to probe or reveal its meaning. "Art," says the hero of the Reverend Henry Ward Beecher's sentimental novel *Norwood* (1867), "attempts to work out its end solely by the use of the beautiful, and the artist is to select out only such things as are beautiful."

Culture had also become firmly linked to femininity. In America, remarked one observer, culture was "left entirely to women. . . . It is they, as a general rule, who have opinions about music, or drama, or literature, or philosophy. . . . Husbands or sons rarely share in those interests." Men represented the "force principle," said the clergyman Horace Bushnell, and women symbolized the "beauty principle."

The treatment of life, said one highly successful editor, "must be tinged with sufficient idealism to make it all of a truly uplifting character. . . . We cannot admit stories which deal with false or immoral relations. . . . The finer side of things—the idealistic—is the answer for us." The "genteel tradition," as this literary school came to be called, dominated American cultural agencies, such as universities and publishing companies, from the 1860s on.

Rebellion against the genteel tradition sparked the main creative impulses of late nineteenth century American literature. Realism became the rallying cry of a new generation of writers. Their champion, William Dean Howells, resigned in 1881 as editor of the *Atlantic Monthly* magazine, stronghold of the genteel tradition. He became editor of *Harper's Monthly* magazine and began to call for literature that "wishes to know and to tell the truth" and seeks "to picture the daily life in the most exact terms possible." In a series of realistic novels—*A Modern Instance* (1882), *The Rise of Silas Lapham* (1885), and *A Hazard of New Fortunes* (1890)—Howells captured the world of the urban middle class.

Henry James, a far greater writer, also treated the novel as "a direct impression of life" and aimed above all at achieving "an air of reality." He wrote about the world of leisured Americans, and his central concern was the study of moral decay and regeneration. This concern, often set in motion by the confrontation of American innocence with European corruption, appears in *The American* (1877), *Portrait of a Lady* (1882), and *The Golden Bowl* (1904).

The nostalgia of urbanized Americans helped sustain a vigorous literature of local color and regionalism. These writings included the mining camp stories of Bret Harte, the Uncle Remus tales of Joel Chandler Harris, the Indiana poetry of James Whitcomb Riley, and the New England fiction of Sarah Orne Jewett. Such literature fit comfortably within the genteel tradition, for it was generally sentimental, reassuring, and morally uplifting.

Mark Twain was an entirely different kind of regional writer. Starting as a western journalist and humorist, Twain avoided the influence of the Eastern literary establishment. His greatest novel, *The Adventures of Huckleberry Finn* (1884), violated the custom of keeping "low" characters in their proper place for the amused inspection of the culturally superior reader. Huck, an outcaste boy, seizes control of the story. The words are his, and so is the innocence with which he questions right and wrong in America. No other novel so fully engaged the themes of racism, in-

MARK TWAIN
On steamboats navigating treacherous stretches of the Mississippi River, the leadsman would peer over the bow and call out "mark twain," signifying a depth of two fathoms (twelve feet). Samuel L. Clemens (1835–1910), once a Mississippi pilot, took "Mark Twain" as a pen name when he worked for the Virginia City *Enterprise*. It signified Twain's deep roots in Mississippi country. His best writing, including *Huckleberry Finn*, united the world of the Mississippi with a sharp, perspicacious view of the human condition. (Mark Twain Memorial, Hartford, Ct.)

TIME LINE
THE CITY

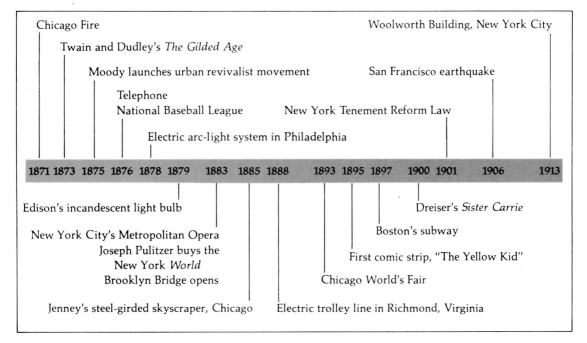

justice, and brutality in nineteenth-century America.

No comparable writing about city life appeared during these years. Realistic novels stopped short of the immigrant slums and working-class neighborhoods or ventured into them hesitantly and without much comprehension. Howells, for example, insisted that the United States was not like Europe: "The sum of cold and hunger is certainly very small, and wrong from class to class is also inappreciable. We invite our novelists, therefore, to concern themselves with the more smiling aspects of life, which are the more American."

Nevertheless, the hard realities of city life crept irresistibly into American fiction. Stephen Crane's *Maggie: A Girl of the Streets* (1893), privately printed because no publisher would touch it, told unflinchingly of the destruction of a slum girl. In another urban novel, Henry Blake Fuller's *The Cliff-Dwellers* (1893), the city itself occupied the center of the author's imagination. This story traces the fortunes of the occupants—"cliff-dwellers"—of a Chicago skyscraper. In *McTeague* (1899), Frank Norris captured the

sights, sounds, and, most acutely, the smells of the city. One reviewer called the story "a study in stinks." Although set in San Francisco, Norris insisted that it "could have happened in any big city, anywhere."

These novels stressed the insignificance of the individual, and his or her helplessness in the face of urban life. This approach, called "naturalism," was inspired by the French novelist Emile Zola, by the contemporary zeal for scientific objectivity, and by the theory of evolution proposed by the British naturalist Charles R. Darwin. Thus, Frank Norris's character McTeague, more animal than man, is the creature of his instincts and his environment, and he cannot escape coming to a bad end. In Norris's *The Octopus* (1901), the implacable force is the Southern Pacific Railroad; in *The Pit* (1903) it is the Chicago grain market. The city itself, however, most powerfully influenced the naturalistic writers.

The best of these authors, Theodore Dreiser, surmounted the crude determinism of Frank Norris. But the city people in his great novels—*Sister Carrie* (1900), *Jenny Gerhardt* (1911), *The Financier* (1912), and *The Titan* (1914)—are no less hostage to an urban world they cannot understand. Dreiser sought to capture this world in all its detail, "to talk about life as it is, the facts as they exist, the game as it is played." Visiting his fiancee's Missouri farm home in 1894, Dreiser had been struck by "the spirit of rural America, its idealism, its dreams." But this was an "American tradition in which I, alas!, could not share."

Said Dreiser, "I had seen Pittsburgh. I had seen Lithuanians and Hungarians in their 'courts' and hovels. I had seen the girls of the city—walking the streets at night." The city had entered the American imagination. By the early 1900s, it had become a main theme of American art and literature.

America, an agrarian society since its birth, became increasingly urbanized after the Civil War. In 1900, about 20 percent of the population lived in cities of a hundred thousand or more. City growth stemmed primarily from industrialization—the concentration of industry at key points, the increasingly large scale of production, and the need for commercial and administrative services best located in urban centers. A burst of innovation, including the telephone, electric lighting, rapid transit systems, and steel frame buildings, solved the problems arising from the concentration of an extremely large population in a confined area.

Within the city, geography defined the social order of the population. The poor were found in the centers and the factory districts, the middle class spread out into the suburbs, and the rich lived insulated either in exclusive central sections or beyond the suburbs. A distinctive urban culture emerged that enabled city dwellers to accommodate themselves to the world of the city.

The great cities of the United States became the sites of a higher culture, including art museums, opera and symphony companies, and libraries. From the late nineteenth century on, American life would increasingly be defined by what happened in the nation's cities.

Suggestions for Further Reading

Urbanization

A useful introduction to urban history is Charles N. Glaab and A. Theodore Brown, *History of Urban America* (1967). The pioneer study for the late nineteenth century is Arthur M. Schlesinger, *The Rise of the City* (1936). Blake McKelvey, *The Urbanization of America, 1860-1915* (1963) provides an account of events that took place within the context of the city. A sampling of innovative scholarship in the field can be found in Stephan Thernstrom and Richard Sennett, eds., *19th Century Cities: Essays in the New Urban History* (1969).

Allan Pred, *Spatial Dynamics of U.S. Urban Growth, 1800-1914* (1971) traces the patterns by which cities utilized the space in which they grew. The impact of trolley-line building is revealed in the pioneering book by Sam B. Warner, *Streetcar Suburbs* (1962). In a subsequent work, *The Private City: Philadelphia in Three Periods* (1968), Warner broadened his analysis to show how private decision-making shaped the character of

the American city. Urban construction is treated in Carl Condit, *American Building Art: Nineteenth Century* (1969), and the emergence of a distinctively American style in his *Chicago School of Architecture* (1964). Another aspect of city building is subtly analyzed in Alan Trachtenberg, *Brooklyn Bridge* (1965). The problems of meeting basic needs can be conveniently studied in Stanley K. Schultz and Clay McShane, "To Engineer the Metropolis: Sewers, Sanitation, and City Planning in Late-Nineteenth-Century America," *Journal of American History* 65 (September 1978): 389-411. Eric H. Monkonnen, *Police in Urban America, 1860-1920* (1981) and David B. Tyack, *The One Best System: A History of American Urban Education* (1974) give accounts of two of the key services demanded by city people. The struggle to reshape the chaotic nineteenth-century city can be explored in Laura Wood Roper, *FLO: A biography of Frederick Law Olmstead* (1973) and William H. Wilson, *The City Beautiful Movement in Kansas City* (1964).

Upper Class/Middle Class

The study of urban classes can properly begin with Stephan Thernstrom's social-mobility analysis, *The Other Bostonians: Poverty and Progress in an American City, 1880-1970* (1973), which contains also a useful summary of mobility research on other cities. Frederic C. Jaher, *The Urban Establishment: Upper Strata in Boston, New York, Charleston, Chicago, and Los Angeles* (1982) is a major comparative study of the elites in America's cities. Dixon Wecter, *The Saga of American Society* (1937) is a lively account of the development of American high society. The flavor of this process can best be captured in Ward McAllister, *Society as I Have Found It* (1890). The tensions of middle-class life in the industrial cities are revealed in Richard Sennett, *Families Against the City: Middle Class Homes of Industrial Chicago, 1872-1890* (1970). Kathryn Kish Sklar, *Catharine Beecher: A Study of American Domesticity* (1973) details the life and influence of the key exponent of the cult of domesticity that ruled middle-class home life in the late nineteenth century. Other aspects of this development emerge from Gwendolyn Wright, *Moralism and the Model Home: Domestic Architecture and Cultural Conflict in Chicago, 1873-1913* (1980), Susan Strasser, *Never Done: A History of American Housework* (1983), and David M. Katzman, *Seven Days A Week: Women and Domestic Service in Industrializing America* (1978). A useful collection on family history is Michael Gordon, ed., *The American Family in Social-Historical Perspective* (1973) Carl N. Degler, *At Odds: Women and the Family in America* (1980) is the leading interpretive survey of the subject. Contemporary notions of male and female are skillfully captured in John S. and Robin M. Haller, *The Physician and Sexuality in Victorian America* (1974).

City People

There is a rich literature on immigrants and the city. Among the leading books are: Moses Rischin, *The Promised City: New York's Jews, 1870–1914* (1962); Josef Barton, *Peasants and Strangers: Italians, Rumanians and Slovaks in an American City, 1890-1950* (1975); Humbert S. Nelli, *The Italians in Chicago, 1860-1920* (1970). On blacks in the city, see Gilbert Osofsky, *Harlem: The Making of a Ghetto, 1890-1930* (1966) and Allan H. Spear, *Black Chicago, 1860-1920* (1966). The problems that Protestantism encountered in the city are treated in Henry F. May, *Protestant Churches and Urban America* (1949) and Aaron I. Abell, *The Urban Impact on American Protestantism* (1943). The starting point on urban revivalism is William G. McLoughlin, *Modern Revivalism* (1959). For the Catholic church, see Robert D. Cross, *The Emergence of Liberal Catholicism in America* (1958) and, ed., *Church and City, 1865-1910* (1967). In *City People: The Rise of Modern City Culture in 19th Century America* (1982), Gunther Barth shows how the department store, baseball, and newspapers helped to shape a distinctive city culture. There is an imaginative accounting of another urban institution in John F. Kasson, *Amusing the Million: Coney Island at the Turn of the Century* (1978). On the fostering of high culture in the American city, see Daniel M. Fox, *Engines of Culture: Philanthropy and Art Museums* (1963). The best introduction to intellectual currents within the emerging urban society is Alan Trachtenberg, *The Incorporation of America: Culture and Society, 1865-1893* (1983). An important case study of working-class leisure is Roy Rosenzweig, *Eight Hours for What We Will: Workers & Leisure in An Industrial City, 1870-1920* (1983).

$\mathcal{S}$EPARATE SPHERES

"The most enlightened of both sexes," a speaker told the graduating class of Mount Holyoke College in 1876, believe "there is a difference of kind in their natural endowments and that there is for each an appropriate field of development and action." The women of Mount Holyoke did not hoot the speaker off the platform, for he was voicing one of the accepted truths of nineteenth-century, middle-class America. Men and women "are different, widely different from each other," asserted the prominent Boston physician Edward Clarke. What was more, "we should cultivate the difference of the sexes, not try to hide it or abolish it."

This was a notion certified by the mightiest scientific authority of the age. In *The Descent of Man* (1871), Charles Darwin proposed that sexual divergence was a consequence of evolution. Motherhood had rendered women dependent on men and thus to some degree removed them from the struggle for survival by which the species evolved. Darwin postulated a hierarchy of mental attributes—climbing from instinct to emotions, intuition, imagination, and, finally, reason. The male brain, as it had evolved, operated best at the higher range, the female brain at the lower range. There was no question, admitted the physiologist Frances Emily White after reading Darwin's book, that men's ancient role as hunters and warriors had resulted in "more robust intellects," while women's family role had produced qualities of "tenderness and love . . . and devotional sentiment."

Physically, too, women were the weaker sex. Medical opinion at the time conceived of the human body as endowed with a finite, nonreplenishable amount of energy. In women's bodies, this energy went primarily to the reproductive organs. It was, said one doctor reverentially, "as if the Almighty, in creating the female sex, had taken the uterus and built a woman around it." Too much mental activity would lead to the atrophy of the female organs and/or to physical breakdown. To conserve their body energy, Dr. Clarke advised women students at Vassar against any studies during menstruation, and a maximum of a third less than male college students at other times. A booming patent medicine industry grew rich catering to, in the words of a Lydia Pinkham advertisement (plate 1), "the peculiar weaknesses of women."

PLATE 1
(Schlesinger Library, Radcliffe College)

Given their profound differences, men and women had to live entirely different kinds of lives. The ideal man had "indomitable energy"; he enjoyed "a *robust health*—full of vigor." He had the will to win, to exert his "force and authority as a man." His field of battle was preeminently the competitive marketplace; "the whirl and contact with the world . . . is the inheritance of our sex." Money-making was strictly a masculine affair, whether it involved the risk-taking of the entrepreneur, the prudence of the banker, the easy fellowship of the salesman, or the brawn of the ironworker (plate 2). So, too, with politics. Politicians dealt in the currency of power, entirely a masculine concern, and party activity was rich with the ritual and camaraderie in which the American male took delight (plate 3, on page 582). No wonder the suffragist demand for the right to vote met ridicule

PLATE 3
The Levi P. Morton Association, the local Republican party, Newport, Rhode Island. (Newport County Historical Society)

PLATE 4
Rudy Sohn's barber shop,
Junction City, Kansas, about
1900. (Kansas Collection,
University of Kansas Libraries,
Joseph J. Pennell Collection)

PLATE 5
In the Maine woods, about 1890. (The Whaling Museum, New Bedford, Mass.)

and disbelief. Equally sacred were such male precincts as the fraternal order, the volunteer fire department, the saloon, and, everywhere, the barbershop. Rudy Sohn's barbershop (plate 4) was surely a mecca for the menfolk of Junction City, Kansas. The regulars deposited their shaving mugs on Rudy's wall racks and came in weekly for a shave and trim, hot towels, and some easy male talk amid the aroma of hazel water and stale cigar smoke.

"There is something enervating in feminine companionship," acknowledged *Cosmopolitan* magazine. "The genuine man feels that he must go off alone or with other men, out in the open air, roughing it among the rough as a mental tonic." A rich young man like Theodore Roosevelt might try his luck in the Wild West or Africa; those of lesser means took their shotguns and fishing gear to woods closer at hand (plate 5). The first college football game took place between Rutgers and Princeton in 1869. In the organized mayhem of football (plate

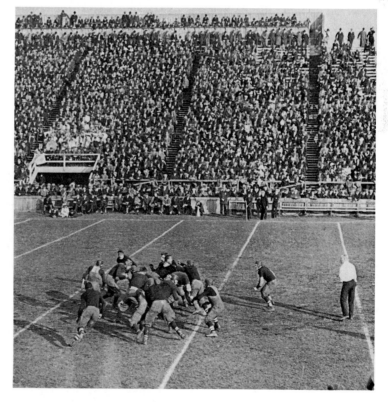

PLATE 6
The Yale Game, about 1900. (New Haven Colony Historical Society. The T. S. Bronson Collection)

583

PLATE 7
Mrs. Glessner's reading group met weekly to discuss fine literature. The ladies in attendance represented many of the ''best'' families in Chicago. (Chicago Historical Society)

PLATE 8
A Portland, Oregon, family, about 1895. (Martin W. Sandler Collection)

6), the young American male could show the stuff he was made of.

Woman's place, on the other hand, was in the home. "Real womanhood" consisted above all of the nurturing qualities that made for a good wife and mother. "We owe to women the charm and beauty of life," said one educator. "For purity of thought and heart, for patient courage, for recklessly unselfish devotion, for the love that rests, strengthens and inspires, we look to women." Theirs was the nurturing function in life. Within the family, gender roles were sharply differentiated. In an 1895 portrait of a family in Portland, Oregon, the husband sits in dignity, his eye on some serious piece of business, while his wife plays lovingly on the floor with the children (plate 8). In such families, husbands remained in some ways strangers to their wives. The women's emotional world, recaptured from surviving correspondence, revolved much more around other women—sisters and cousins, and old school chums who became lifelong, intimate friends. A special feminine sphere—as closed to men as the barbershop world was closed to women—grew from such attachments. Leisure time, a precious commodity to nineteenth-century homemakers, found only a limited compass of social and cultural activity among other women, as in the Methodist–Episcopal church picnic in Junction City, Kansas in 1896 (plate 9).

Women's sphere, though deeply enshrined in American life, did not remain unchanged. Some degree of liberation from the endless drudgery of housework came in the late nineteenth century with the advent of central heating, inside plumbing and hot water, electricity, kitchen appliances, store-bought bread, and mass-produced clothing. In the city, women's sphere began to take on a more public character. Of the new urban institutions catering to women, the most important was the department store, which became a temple for their emerging role as consumers. Similarly, seeking to attract the trade of women, the New Amsterdam National Bank of New York set aside a special section decorated to suit the tastes of their new customers (plate 10, on page 586).

For the daughters of the middle class, higher education became available through limited access to state universities, as well as through the new women's colleges, led by Vassar in 1865. In most of these institutions, academic excellence distinctly took a back seat. Women's colleges, said Dean Briggs of Smith, "exist not for the competition of women with men, but for the ennobling of women as women. They do not, or should not exist primarily for higher learning." Ironically, anxiety about women's frailty led to a strong emphasis on physical fitness in the women's colleges (plate 11, on page 586).

The process of modified liberation went steadily forward.

PLATE 9
Church picnic, Junction City, Kansas, 1906. (Kansas Collection, University of Kansas Libraries. Joseph J. Pennell Collection)

During the 1890s, there was much talk of the "new woman" (plate 12). As she became better educated, more robustly active, and an increasingly public presence in reform movements and at the workplace, the rigidities of separate sphere began to break down. In the twentieth century, more and more of life's activities came to be shared by men and women.

Today, the vast majority of people rejects, both in law and by belief, the notion of female inferiority—which is why nineteenth-century views on sexual divergence sound so quaint. But stereotyping by sex still lives. Consider the masculine appeal of a 1915 tobacco ad (plate 13), with its "live-wire" men enjoying their whiskey and the ladies tucked away in the music room. The modern reader may smile at "Bull" Durham's blatant sexism, but is the message of Virginia Slims—"You've Come a Long Way, Baby"—any less rooted in sex stereotyping? The more things change. . . .

PLATE 10
Special Ladies' Section, New Amsterdam National Bank, 1906. (Museum of the City of New York. The Byron Collection)

PLATE 11
Gymnasium, Wellesley College, 1893. (Photo by Seaver. Wellesley College Archives)

586

PLATE 13
(The Newberry Library, Chicago)

PLATE 12
John Singer Sargent's painting, *Mr. and Mrs. Isaac Newton Phelps Stokes* (1897), captures on canvas the essence of the "new woman" of the 1890s. Nothing about Mrs. Stokes, neither in how she is dressed nor in how she presents herself, suggests physical weakness or demure passivity. She confidently occupies center stage, a fit partner for her husband, who, indeed, is relegated to the shadows of the picture. (The Metropolitan Museum of Art. Bequest of Edith Minturn Stokes)

587

19

RURAL AMERICA

During the last third of the nineteenth century, American society seemed to be at odds with itself. From one angle, the nation looked like an advanced industrial society, with great factories and mills and enormous, crowded cities. But from another angle, America looked like a nation still absorbed in conquering a continent, with settlers streaming toward lonely farms and ranches in the open spaces of the West, and Americans repeating the old dramas of "settlement" they had been performing over and over since 1607. Not until 1890 did the Census Bureau declare that the frontier no longer existed: the country's "unsettled area has been so broken into . . . that there can hardly be said to be a frontier line."

That same year, 1890, the country surpassed Great Britain in the production of iron and steel. Newspapers told about Indian wars and labor strikes in the same edition. The army's massacre of Indians at Wounded Knee, South Dakota, the final tragedy in the suppression of the Plains tribes, occurred only eighteen months before the great Homestead strike of July 1892.

This conjunction of events, unrelated though they might seem, did not occur entirely by accident. The final surge of westward development across the Great Plains was powered primarily by the dynamism of American industrialism. Much the same could be said for the history of rural America in those years. The South rebuilt its plantation agriculture on the basis of a sharecropping tenant system after the Civil War. But though the South remained rooted in its historic cotton culture, it also entered the industrial age.

Its future, for better or worse, was locked into the industrial revolution going on in the North. The nation's farmers, too, had one foot in the Jeffersonian past and the other in the industrial age. The distress they experienced during this period resulted basically from their imperfect integration into the world of the corporation and the international market. Rural America could no longer be understood on its own terms. Its history had become linked ever more tightly to the larger industrial society.

The Great West

Before the Civil War, the vast lands west of the Mississippi Valley—people called it the Great West—had seemed of little importance. Until the 1840s, Americans assumed the Great West would always remain beyond the frontier of white settlement. Accustomed to woodlands and ample rainfall, farmers hung back from the dry country that began several hundred miles west of the Mississippi River.

The Great West consisted of two parts. At roughly the ninety-eighth meridian, running from what are now North and South Dakota down through central Texas, the tall grass of the prairies gave way to the short buffalo grass of semiarid country. This region, the Great Plains, extended to the Rocky Mountains. Beyond the mountains lay a high, arid plateau that spread to the Sierra and Cascade ranges. Schoolbooks referred to the Great Plains as the Great American Desert. Major Stephen H. Long, after exploring the region west of the ninety-eighth meridian in

1820, declared it "almost wholly unfit for cultivation, and of course uninhabitable by a people depending upon agriculture for their subsistence."

Whites generally considered the Great Plains best left to the native American inhabitants—the Apache and Comanche in the Southwest; Arapaho and Pawnee on the central plains; and Crow, Cheyenne, and Sioux to the north. During the eighteenth century, as horses spread northward after being brought to Mexico by Spanish explorers, the Plains Indians had become horsemen. Superb hunters and fierce warriors, they created an essentially new culture that centered on the horse, the buffalo, and the open land. To their hunting grounds now came the woodland Indians as well. After the War of 1812, the nation pursued a relentless policy of removing the eastern tribes beyond the Mississippi to the prairie lands bordering the Great Plains.

In 1834, Congress formally created a permanent Indian country in the Great West. The army built border forts from Lake Superior to the Red

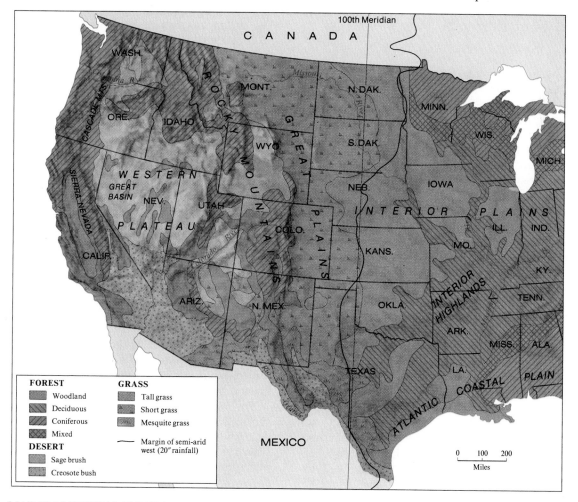

MAP 19.1 NATURAL ENVIRONMENT OF THE WEST

As settlers crossed the Mississippi River, and especially as they pushed into the Great Plains beyond the line of semi-aridity, they sensed the overwhelming power of the environment to determine their fate. In a landscape without trees for fences and barns, without adequate rainfall, farmers had to relearn their business. The West lacked the navigable rivers that had earlier eased pioneer travel, and placed nearly impenetrable barriers of mountains and desert between settlers and the beckoning West Coast. Nowhere did environment so impress itself on settlers—and on the historians who wrote about them—than in the West.

River to keep the Indians in and the whites out. In 1838, the commanding general of the area, Edmund Gaines, recommended that the forts be constructed of stone because they would be there forever. The creation of an Indian country supported the contemporary belief that the Great American Desert could serve only as home, in the words of the explorer Zebulon M. Pike, "to the wandering and uncivilized aborigines of the country."

First Intruders: Wagon Trains, Railroaders, Miners

Solemnly committed to the Indians, the Great West was put to new, more profitable uses almost immediately. The first break came with the acquisition and settlement of the Oregon and California regions during the 1840s. Instead of serving as a buffer against the British and the Mexicans, the Indian country became a bridge to the Pacific. The first wagon train headed west from Missouri for Oregon in 1842. Thousands then traveled the Oregon Trail to the Willamette Valley or, cutting south beyond Fort Hall, down into California. These migrants had no interest in the land they crossed; they considered it barren ground. But their journey marked the intrusion of the modernizing world on the Indian's last remaining habitat.

The rapid white settlement of the Pacific region raised a demand almost at once for a transportation system across the continent. As early as 1853, the federal government began surveying railway routes to the Pacific. A sectional stalemate over the proposed transcontinental route delayed railroad construction for a decade. Wagon freight lines, stagecoaches, and the horseback riders of the Pony Express furnished the first regular links westward. A telegraph line reached San Francisco in 1861. The tracks of the Union Pacific and Central Pacific railroads finally converged at Promontory, Utah, in 1869, uniting the continent by rail. An orgy of western railway building followed, stimulated partly by the availability until 1871 of generous government subsidies. By 1883, after being interrupted by the Panic of 1873, three more continental routes had

been completed—the Southern Pacific line to New Orleans; the Santa Fe to Kansas City; and the Northern Pacific from Portland, Oregon, to Saint Paul, Minnesota.

On the heels of this traffic across the plains and mountains, and generally in advance of the railroads, came the exploitation of the mineral wealth of the Great West. The rush to California had been triggered in 1848 by the discovery of gold in the foothills of the Sierras. By the mid-1850s, disappointed forty-niners, as the prospectors were called, had spread throughout the West in hope of striking it rich elsewhere.

Beginning in 1858, gold was discovered on the Nevada side of the Sierras, in the Colorado Rockies, and along the Fraser River in British Columbia. New strikes occurred in Montana and Wyoming during the 1860s, in the Black Hills of South Dakota in the 1870s, in the Coeur d'Alene region of Idaho during the 1880s, and in the Yukon area of Alaska in 1896.

As the news spread of each gold strike, a wild, remote area turned almost overnight into a mob scene of prospectors, traders, gamblers, prostitutes, and saloonkeepers. At least a hundred thousand fortune seekers flocked to the Pikes Peak area of Colorado in the spring of 1859. Always trespassers on government or Indian land, the prospectors made their own law. The mining codes, devised at community meetings, limited the size of claims to what a man could reasonably work. This kind of popular lawmaking also became an instrument for excluding or discriminating against the Mexicans, Chinese, and blacks in the gold fields. And it turned into hangman's justice for the many lawless men who infested the mining camps.

The heyday of the prospector was always very brief. He was equipped only to skim gold from the surface of the earth and from streambeds. To extract the metal locked in the underground lodes required mine shafts and crushing mills, and these took capital, technology, and business organization. The original claim holders quickly sold out after taking the surface gold or when a generous bidder came along. At every gold-rush site, the prospector soon gave way to entrepreneurial development and large-scale mining.

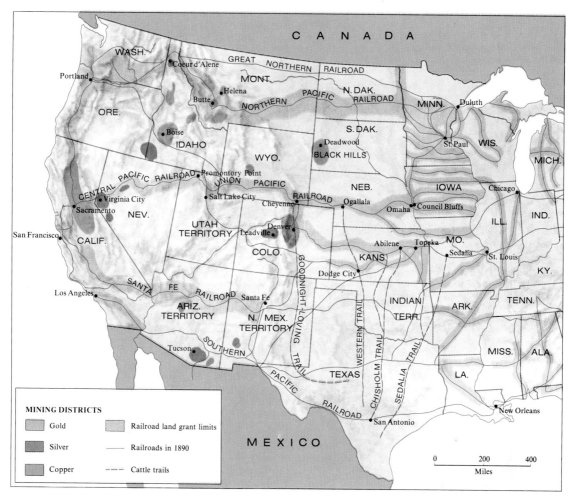

MAP 19.2 DEVELOPMENT OF THE WEST, 1860–1890

Development in the West followed an uneven pattern. The first organized settlements—Mormons around Salt Lake, miners and farmers in California and Oregon—were far from other populated areas. Mining sprang up in isolated spots on the broad terrain of wilderness. The transportation routes of wagon trains, cattle trails, and railroads crossed wide expanses of unpopulated land. The land itself was valued so little that the federal government granted over 180 million acres free to railroads as an inducement to build across unsettled territory.

Orderly law and government followed at this stage. The mining country was organized into territories and then into states of the Union. Rough mining camps turned into cities. Nevada's Virginia City, once a baudy, ramshackle mining camp, boasted a stock exchange and five newspapers a few years after the Comstock lode opened in 1859. By 1875, Virginia City's population had reached twenty thousand. The great fortunes of the mining kings brought restaurants, hotels, opera, Shakespearean theater, and similar amenities to communities that had been wilderness a decade earlier.

In its final stage, the mining frontier passed into the industrial world. At some sites, gold and silver proved less important than the commoner metals with which they had been intermixed. Beginning in the mid-1870s, copper

HYDRAULIC MINING IN
THE BOISE BASIN, IDAHO
Hydraulic mining, invented in the
California gold fields in 1853, was
a highly efficient method that
yielded profits even with low-
grade concentrations of gold. The
technology was simple—it used
high-pressure water under
gravity feed to wash away
hillsides of gold-bearing soil.
Although building the necessary
reservoirs, piping systems, and
sluices required heavy
investment, the profits from
hydraulic mining helped
transform western mining into
big business. But, as Mary
Brown's painting from 1875
suggests, hydraulic mining
destroyed the natural landscape.
(Idaho State Historical Museum)

mining thrived in the Butte district of Montana, especially after the opening of the fabulous Anaconda mine, and also flourished in the Globe and Copper Queen fields of Arizona. In the 1890s, the Coeur d'Alene silver district, following earlier finds at Leadville, Colorado, became the nation's main source of lead and zinc.

In short order, industrialism established itself at these remote places in the Great West. Entrepreneurs raised capital, built rail connections, devised advanced technology to treat the lower-grade copper deposits, constructed smelting facilities, and recruited a labor force. As elsewhere on the industrial scene, trade-union organization appeared among the miners. And, as elsewhere, the western metal industries joined enthusiastically in the merger movement that took place at the end of the century. The Anaconda Copper Mining Company and other Montana mining firms came under the control of the Amalgamated Copper Company in 1899. That same year, the American Smelting and Refining Company brought together the bulk of the nation's lead-mining and copper-refining properties. Still Blackfeet and Crow country in the 1860s, the Butte copper district was a center of industrial capitalism barely thirty years later.

The Cattle Frontier

As with copper and lead mining in the mountain country, market demand pushed the relentless exploitation of the Great Plains. This vast grass region supported enormous herds of buffalo. Some trade in buffalo hides had gone on for years between the Indians and the white trading posts that first began to dot the Great Plains in the 1820s. In the early 1870s, eastern tanneries conducted successful experiments in curing buffalo hides, and a ready market developed among shoe and harness manufacturers. Parties of professional hunters, armed with high-powered rifles, swept across the plains and began a systematic slaughter of the buffalo. The great herds almost vanished within ten years. Many people spoke out against this mass killing, but no method existed here, any more than in gold-rush country, to curb men bent on making a quick dollar. Besides, as General Philip H. Sheridan assured the Texas legislature, the extermination of the buffalo brought benefits. The Indians would be starved into submission, he noted, and feeding grounds would open up for a more valuable commodity, the Texas longhorn.

Since the eighteenth century, these tough Spanish cattle had spread westward across Texas from the grasslands between the Rio Grande and the Nueces River. About five million longhorns roamed the region in 1865, largely untended and unclaimed, and hardly worth bothering about because they could not be marketed. That year, however, the Missouri and Pacific Railroad reached Sedalia, Missouri. At that terminal, connecting as it did to hungry eastern markets, the three-dollar longhorn might command forty dollars. This realization set off the famous Long Drive. Cowboys herded Texas cattle a thousand miles or more north to the railroads as the lines pushed west into Kansas.

At Abilene, Ellsworth, and, beginning in 1875, Dodge City, stockmen sold the cattle and the trail-weary cowboys went on a binge. The wide-open cow towns, like the mining camps, captured the nation's imagination as symbols of the Wild West. But the Long Drive, colorful though it seemed, was actually a makeshift

method of bridging a gap in the developing transportation system. As soon as railroads reached the Texas range country in the 1870s, stockmen abandoned the hazardous and wasteful Long Drive for a more settled kind of ranching.

Meanwhile, longhorns had been introduced to the upper Great Plains and demonstrated their ability to survive the harsh winter climate. In hardly a decade, starting in the late 1860s, the Great Plains changed into ranching country. The land itself was treated as a free commodity, available to anyone who seized it and put it to use. A hopeful rancher would spot a likely area along a creek, and claim 160 acres under the Pre-emption Act of 1841. By a common usage that quickly began among cattlemen, the rancher had a "range right" to all the adjacent land rising up to the "divide," where the land sloped down to the next creek. As herds multiplied, and as they improved through crossbreeding with Hereford and Angus cattle, the stockman quickly became a substantial rancher. But he remained very much a pioneer in relying on himself and, through stockmen's associations, on his fellow ranchers to protect his rights.

A boom during the early 1880s hastened the end of open-range ranching. Eastern and British investors rushed in to capitalize on the high profits. Overgrazing depleted the grasslands. Cattle prices slumped at the Chicago stockyards beginning in 1882, and collapsed as stockmen

THE COWBOY AT WORK
Open-range ranching, where cattle from different ranches grazed together, gave rise to distinctive traditions. At the roundup, cowboys separated the cattle by owner and branded the calves. The cowboy, traditionally a colorful figure, was really a kind of farmhand on horseback, with the skills to work on the range. He earned twenty-five dollars a month, plus his food and a bed in the bunkhouse, for long hours of grueling, lonesome work. (Culver)

dumped stricken cattle during the cold weather and drought of 1885–86. The winter that followed, the most terrible in memory, wiped out vast herds. Open-range ranching came to an end. Cattlemen built fences around their land and laid in hay crops for winter feed. No longer would cattle be left to fend for themselves on the open range. The Great Plains turned into ordinary ranch country. Sheep raising, previously scorned as unmanly work and resisted as a threat to the grass, now became respectable. Some cattlemen even sold out to the despised "nesters," who wanted to try farming the Great Plains.

The Farmers' Frontier

Powerful forces had been pushing against the mental barrier of a Great American Desert ever since the Civil War. As the midwestern states filled up, farmers began to look hungrily farther west. Farmers in Europe, especially in Scandinavia, also were eager to find a place in America. Land speculators, steamship lines, and the western states and territories all encouraged settlement of the Great Plains. Railroads, anxious to sell their huge land holdings and develop traffic for their routes, became especially active sponsors of settlement programs.

Federal land policy also offered a strong attraction. The Homestead Act of 1862 enabled settlers to obtain up to 160 acres of public land free, except for a filing fee, if they lived on it for five years. This law included aliens who had filed their first naturalization papers. Beginning in 1873, settlers could claim an additional 160 acres if they planted trees on at least a fourth of the land.

None of these forces, however, could have pushed the agricultural frontier far out on to the plains without the intervention of a highly inventive society. The notion of a Great American Desert, illusion though it was, did point to a plain truth: the grasslands could not be worked by the known methods of American farmers.

Consider the absence of woodland. Determined pioneers could manage the problem of shelter by cutting dugouts in the side of a hill. Then they built sod houses, using strips of turf cut from the ground. These crude homes served—often for years—until the settler had

earned enough money to buy the lumber for a proper house and barn. But what about fencing to protect the crops? A furious patent race developed to meet this crucial need. In 1874 Joseph F. Glidden, an Illinois farmer, invented barbed wire, which provided a cheap, effective barrier against roaming cattle.

The arid climate presented a tougher problem. The eastern, high-grass prairie received enough rain for grain crops. But the annual rainfall averaged below twenty inches west of ninety-eighth meridian. The Mormons who lived in the area near Great Salt Lake had demonstrated how irrigation could turn a wasteland into a garden. But the Great Plains lacked the surface water needed for irrigation. The answer lay in dry-farming methods, which involved

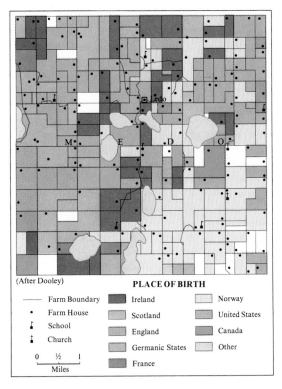

(After Dooley)

PLACE OF BIRTH

— Farm Boundary
• Farm House
School
Church

0   ½   1
Miles

Ireland
Scotland
England
Germanic States
France
Norway
United States
Canada
Other

MAP 19.3 THE RURAL ETHNIC MOSAIC: BLUE EARTH COUNTY, MINNESOTA, 1880
What could have been more natural for emigrants like Ida Lindgren, especially given the isolation and hardship she describes (see document at right), than to settle next to others sharing common ties to a homeland? This map of Medo township reveals that in rural America, no less than in the cities, ethnicity determined spatial patterns of living.

SWEDISH EMIGRANT IN FRONTIER KANSAS

Like many emigrants, Ida Lindgren did not find it easy to adjust to the harsh new life on the frontier. Her diary entries and letters home show that the adjustment for the first generation was never complete.

Diary entry: 15 May 1870, Lake Sibley, Nebraska

What shall I say? Why has the Lord brought us here? Oh, I feel so oppressed, so unhappy! Two whole days it took us to get here and they were not the least trying part of our travels. We sat on boards in the work-wagon packed in so tightly that we could not move a foot, and we drove across endless, endless prairies, on narrow roads; no, not roads, tracks like those in the fields at home when they harvested grain. No forest but only a few trees which grow along the rivers and creeks. And then here and there you see a homestead and pass a little settlement. The Indians are not so far away from here, I can understand, and all the men you see coming by, riding or driving wagons, are armed with revolvers and long carbines, and look like highway robbers.

Diary entry: No date. Probably written in July 1870.

Claus and his wife lost their youngest child at Lake Sibley and it was very sad in many ways. There was no real cemetery but out on the prairie stood a large, solitary tree, and around it they bury their dead, without tolling of bells, without a pastor, and sometimes without any coffin. A coffin was made here for their child, it was not painted black, but we lined it with flowers and one of the men read the funeral service, and then there was a hymn, and that was all.

Manhattan, Kansas, 25 August 1874

Beloved Mamma,

It has been a long time since I have written, hasn't it? . . . when one never has anything fun to write about, it is no fun to write. . . . We have not had rain since the beginning of June, and then with this heat and often strong winds as well, you can imagine how everything has dried out. There has also been a general lamentation and fear for the coming year. We are glad we have the oats (for many don't have any and must feed wheat to the stock) and had hoped to have the corn leaves to add to the fodder. But then one fine day there came millions, trillions of grasshoppers in great clouds, hiding the sun, and coming down onto the fields, eating up *everything* that was still there, the leaves on the trees, peaches, grapes, cucumbers, onions, cabbage, everything, everything. Only the peach stones still hung on the trees, showing what had once been there.

Manhattan, Kansas, 1 July 1877

. . . It seems so strange to me when I think that more than seven years have passed since I have seen you all . . . I can see so clearly that last glimpse I had of Mamma, standing alone amid all the tracks of Eslöv station. Oliva I last saw sitting on her sofa in her red and black dress, holding little Brita, one month old, on her lap. And Wilhelm I last saw in Lund at the station, as he rolled away with the train, waving his last farewell to me. . . .

Source: H. Arnold Barton, ed. *Letters from the Promised Land.* Minneapolis: University of Minnesota Press, 1975. 143–145, 150–156.

---

deep planting to stimulate the capillary action of ground moisture to roots and quick harrowing after rainfalls to turn over a dry mulch that slowed evaporation.

Dry farming produced a low yield per acre. To be economical, a semiarid farm had to operate on a scale much larger than an eastern farm. Therefore, it had to rely much more on machinery. The epitome of western mechanized farming took place on the corporate farms that covered up to a hundred thousand acres in the Red River Valley in the Dakota Territory. But family farms, which remained the norm elsewhere, could not operate with less than three hundred acres of cereal crops and so required machinery for plowing, planting, and harvesting. Such basic inventions as the McCormick reaper came before the Civil War, but the swift growth of the farm-equipment industry occurred later in response to the western demand.

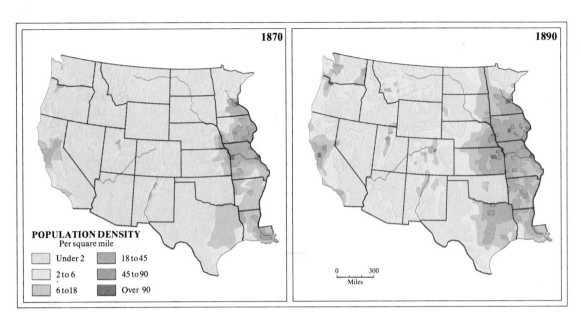

MAP 19.4 GROWING POPULATION IN THE WEST
Western population more than tripled between 1870 and 1890, from 1 million to 3.2 million. In 1890, the superintendent of the Census reported that for the first time in the country's history "there can hardly be said to be a frontier line"; that is, an unbroken line beyond which lay land with fewer than two people per square mile. However, the western population was still scattered amidst vacant land rather than spread in the continuous settlement to be found farther east. Except for a few urban centers, it remained sparsely populated by the standard of the rest of the country.

The push into semiarid lands, despite barbed wire, dry-farming methods, and harvesting machines, involved a great deal of wish fulfillment. The Great Plains happened to experience a wet cycle between 1878 and 1886. "As the plains are settled up we hear less and less of drouth, hot winds, alkali and other bugbears that used to hold back the adventurous," remarked one Nebraska man. Some settlers attributed the increased rainfall to soil cultivation and tree plantings, which somehow generated air moisture and caused more rain. Others credited God. As one settler on the southern plains remarked, "The Lord just knowed we needed more land an' He's gone and changed the climate." No matter how they explained it—and no matter how much scientists warned otherwise—settlers moved westward convinced that the land would receive permanently increased rainfall.

The last frontier thrust across the continental United States was on. More land came under cultivation between 1870 and 1900 than in the previous 250 years. More than a million people went west from the settled Midwest during the 1880s. Northern Europe contributed its share, too. At the peak of the "American fever" in 1882, over 105,000 Scandinavians emigrated to the United States. Swedish and Norwegian became the primary languages of entire areas of Minnesota and Dakota. By 1880, Kansas had 850,000 people. Dakota, which had been very thinly settled when it became a territory in 1861, had twenty thousand inhabitants in 1873. Its population jumped to 135,000 in 1880 and all the way to 550,000 in 1885. The dry years that followed pushed Dakota's population back to 500,000 by 1890, and a comparable departure of drought-stricken farmers occurred up and down the Great Plains. But that vast region, where buffalo herds had thrived a few decades earlier, had been conquered. About half the nation's cattle and sheep, a third of its cereal crops, and nearly three-fifths of its wheat came from the newly settled lands in 1900.

The Indians

And what of the Indians who had inhabited the Great West? Basically, their fate has been told in the foregoing account of western settlement. "The white children have surrounded me and have left me nothing but an island," lamented the great Sioux chief Red Cloud in 1870, the year after the completion of the transcontinental railroad. "When we first had all this land we were strong; now we are all melting like snow on a hillside, while you are grown like spring grass." Every advance of the whites—the Oregon-bound wagon train, the railroad, the buffalo hunter, the miner, the cattleman, the farmer—intruded on the Indians' world. The whites took away the tribes' sustenance, decimated their ranks, and shoved the remnants into remote and barren corners of their former domain. No historical equation could have been more precise or implacable: The progress of the white settlers meant the death of the Indian.

The provision for a permanent Indian country, written into federal law and into treaties with various tribes, was swept away in the westward march of the settler. As early as 1854, upon creating the Kansas and Nebraska territories, the United States formally canceled the Indian policy of 1834. By 1860, all the resettled eastern tribes, treaties notwithstanding, had been forced to cede their lands in Kansas and Nebraska and move farther west. The Plains Indians presented a more formidable barrier. As miners and other pioneers thrust into Indian lands from the late 1850s on, war broke out all along the frontier from the Apache in the Southwest, the Cheyenne and Arapaho in Colorado, to Sioux in the Dakota Territory.

The fierce resistance led to the formulation in 1867 of a new policy for dealing with the Plains Indians. The necessity of moving them out of the path of western development caused hardly any discussion. Neither did the idea that the Indians should be placed on reservations. Efforts to do this had already helped stir up the tribes' anger. What was new was a planned approach to wean the Indians from their nomadic way of life. Under the guidance of the Indian Office, they would be wards of the government until they learned "to walk on the white man's road."

The government set aside two extensive areas for the Indians. It designated the southern quarter of the Dakota Territory—two-thirds of present-day South Dakota—for the northern Plains Indians. The government assigned what is now Oklahoma to the southern Plains Indians, as well as to the five Civilized Tribes—the Choctaw, Cherokee, Chickasaw, Creek, and Seminole—and other eastern Indians already there. Scattered reservations went to the Navaho and Apache in the Southwest and the mountain Indians in the Rockies and beyond. As in the past, the transfer of land went through the legal process of treatymaking. And, as in the past, the whites bribed and tricked the Indian chiefs and in the end forced them to accept what they could not prevent. The Indians had now been provided with homes off "the great road" of the white man. "All who cling to their old hunting-grounds are hostile and will remain so till killed off," stated the western commanding general of the army in 1868.

The Plains Indians inevitably tried to hold on to their way of life. Their subjection was equally inevitable. The native Americans had long been weakened by the white man's whiskey and his diseases. Smallpox had first struck the Indians in the Southwest as early as 1801. It took its heaviest toll in the late 1830s, when a terrible epidemic ravaged the tribes from the upper Missouri River to northern Texas. The Indians never recovered from these losses. They suffered equally from the erosion of their means of subsistence. As the buffalo disappeared, so did the Indian's ability to fight. Hunger and exposure defeated him just as often as did the federal troops.

The wars went on for nearly a decade—in Kansas in 1868–69, in the Texas Red River Valley in 1874, and finally in the climactic Sioux War of 1875–76. Indians occasionally won a victory. In 1876, they wiped out the troops under the immediate command of General George A. Custer on the Little Bighorn River in the Montana Territory. However, the day of reckoning was merely postponed. The Indians had no chance against the overwhelming strength of the soldiers and the relentless white settlement of the land.

Homesick bands of southern Cheyenne learned this bitter truth in 1878 when they

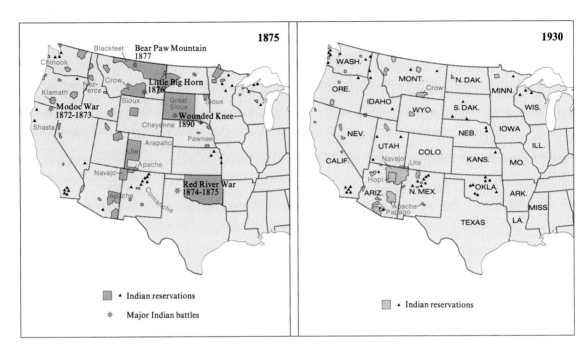

MAP 19.5 THE WESTERN INDIANS
The Plains Indians, who considered the lands they hunted as rightfully theirs, resisted in a series of
sporadic wars the federal government's plan of 1867 to confine them to reservations. Even so, the
reservations provided extensive land and enabled the Indians to live as tribal peoples. But from 1875
on, as whites discovered the reservations' mineral wealth and fertile lands, the Indians lost the land
granted to them in 1867. By 1930, little but barren and arid lands remained in their hands.

escaped from their reservation in the Indian Territory of Oklahoma. Along the route to the Indians' hunting grounds in the Wyoming Territory,
lay three railroads, numerous telegraph lines,
and ranchers and homesteaders eager to report
the Cheyennes' movements. The Indians made
their way through Kansas and Nebraska, but the
army eventually brought them to bay. The government permitted the surviving remnants, who
preferred death to returning to the reservation,
to stay on their native land.

Not the Indian, but the white man wrecked
the reservation policies of 1867. Prospectors discovered gold in 1874 in the Black Hills, part of
the Sioux reservation in Dakota. Unable to hold
back the prospectors or to buy out the Indians,
the government opened up the Black Hills to
gold seekers at their own risk. The Sioux War,
touched off chiefly by this influx, gave the government the excuse to force the cession of the
western third of the Sioux reservation.

The Indian Territory of Oklahoma met the
same fate. Two million acres in the heart of the
territory had not been assigned to any tribe.
White homesteaders coveted the fertile land of
this area. The "Boomer" movement, stirred up
initially by railroads running across the Indian
Territory during the 1880s, agitated ceaselessly
to open this so-called Oklahoma District to
whites. In 1889, the government gave in and
opened the Oklahoma District to the Homestead
Law. On April 22, 1889, a horde of homesteaders rushed in and staked out the entire
district within a few hours. Two tent cities—
Guthrie with fifteen thousand people and Oklahoma City with ten thousand—were in full
swing by nightfall.

The completion of the land-grabbing process
came, ironically, at the hands of the Indians'
avowed friends. The native Americans never
lacked sympathizers, especially in the East. Their
mistreatment after the Civil War resulted in a re-

form movement led by the Indian Rights Association. The movement got a big push from the writer Helen Hunt Jackson, whose powerful book *A Century of Dishonor* (1881) told the story of the unjust treatment of the Indians. The reformers, unfortunately, had little sympathy for the tribal way of life. They could think of no better solution to the Indian problem than assimilation into white society.

From 1871, when Congress had prohibited any more Indian treaties, the government moved consistently to undermine tribal authority. An education program began in 1879. The Indians would be trained for farming and manual work, as well as for citizenship, at boarding schools and at day schools on the reservations. The goal was *severalty*, the individual, rather than tribal ownership of land. However, the Indians found this idea alien and repugnant. It had failed dismally in earlier experiments with land allotments distributed to about 1,750 Chippewa in 1871.

The reformers remained unshaken in their conviction that land ownership would transform the Indians into prudent, hard-working members of white society. With their blessing, the Dawes Severalty Act of 1887 authorized the president to divide tribal lands, giving 160 acres to each family head and smaller plots to other individuals. The land would be held in trust by the

THE CHEROKEE STRIP
This photograph captures the wild race into the Cherokee Strip in the northern part of the Oklahoma Territory on September 16, 1893, the second such "run" that opened the region to white settlement. The winners staked out their claims under the Homestead Act, and looked forward to a prosperous future on the richest farmland in America. Those who lost out hoped for better luck as other parts of the territory opened up. The Indians who had owned the land had nothing to hope for, because this process spelled the end of their way of life. (Oklahoma Historical Society)

BLACK ELK: A HOLY MAN'S MEMORY OF WOUNDED KNEE

We heard that Big Foot was coming down from the Badlands with nearly four hundred people. Some of these were from Sitting Bull's band. They had run away when Sitting Bull was killed, and joined Big Foot on Good River. There were only about a hundred warriors in this band, and all the others were women and children and some old men. They were all starving and freezing, and Big Foot was so sick that they had to bring him along in a pony drag. They had all run away to hide in the Badlands, and they were coming in now because they were starving and freezing. . . .

It was in the evening when we heard that the Big Foots were camped over there with the soldiers, . . . In the morning [December 29, 1890] I went out after my horses, and while I was out I heard shooting off toward the east, and I knew from the sound that it must be wagon guns [cannon] going off. The sounds went right through my body, and I felt that something terrible would happen. . . .

A little way ahead of us, just below the head of the dry gulch, there were some women and children who were huddled under a clay bank, and some cavalrymen were there pointing guns at them. . . .

I had no gun, and when we were charging, I just held the sacred bow out in front of me with my right hand. The bullets did not hit us at all.

When we drove the soldiers back, they dug themselves in, and we were not enough people to drive them out from there. In the evening they marched off up Wounded Knee Creek and then we saw all that they had done there.

Men and women and children were heaped and scattered all over the flat at the bottom of the little hill where the soldiers had their wagon-guns, and westward up the dry gulch all the way to the high ridge, the dead women and children and babies were scattered. . . .

After the soldiers marched away, I heard from my friend, Dog Chief, how the trouble started, and he was right there by Yellow Bird when it happened. This is the way it was:

In the morning the soldiers began to take all the guns away from the Big Foots, who were camped in the flat below the little hill where the monument and burying ground are now. The people had stacked most of their guns, and even their knives, by the tepee where Big Foot was lying sick. Soldiers were on the little hill and all around, and there were soldiers across the dry gulch to the south and over east along Wounded Knee Creek too. The people were nearly surrounded, and the wagon-guns were pointing at them.

Some had not yet given up their guns, and so the soldiers were searching all the tepees, throwing things around and poking into everything. There was a man called Yellow Bird, and he and another man were standing in front of the tepee where Big Foot was lying sick. They had white sheets around and over them, with eyeholes to look through, and they had guns under these. An officer came to search them. He took the other man's gun, and then started to take Yellow Bird's. But Yellow Bird would not let go. He wrestled with the officer, and while they were wrestling, the gun went off and killed the officer. As soon as the gun went off, Dog Chief told me, an officer shot and killed Big Foot who was lying sick inside the tepee.

Then suddenly nobody knew what was happening, except that the soldiers were all shooting and the wagon-guns began going off right in among the people.

Many were shot down right there. The women and children ran into the gulch and up west, dropping all the time, for the soldiers shot them as they ran. There were only about a hundred warriors and there were nearly five hundred soldiers. The warriors rushed to where they had piled their guns and knives. They fought soldiers with only their hands until they got their guns.

Dog Chief saw Yellow Bird run into a tepee with his gun, and from there he killed soldiers until the tepee caught fire. Then he died full of bullets.

It was a good winter day when all this happened. The sun was shining. But after the soldiers marched away from their dirty work, a heavy snow began to fall. The wind came up in the night. There was a big blizzard, and it grew very cold. The snow drifted deep in the crooked gulch, and it was one long grave of butchered women and children and babies, who had never done any harm and were only trying to run away.

Source: Black Elk Speaks: Being the Life Story of a Holy Man of the Ogalala Sioux, John G. Niehardt, ed. New York: William Morrow, 1932. 257–268.

WOUNDED KNEE
In December 1890, U.S. soldiers massacred about two hundred Sioux men, women, and children in the Battle of Wounded Knee in South Dakota. It was the last big fight on the northern plains between the Indians and the whites. Black Elk, a Sioux chief, related that ". . . After the soldiers marched away from their dirty work, a heavy snow began to fall . . . and it grew very cold." The body of Yellow Bird lay frozen where the medicine man had fallen. (Smithsonian Institution, National Anthropological Archives)

government for twenty-five years, and the recipients would be made citizens. Remaining reservation lands would be sold off, the proceeds to be placed in an Indian education fund.

Disaster for the Indians followed. As the law was applied in stages in the coveted Indian Territory, white settlers moved into reservation after reservation. When Oklahoma became a state in 1907, Indians made up a scattered minority among half a million whites. They received little profit from their own land holdings. Their vulnerability spawned an industry of fraud and a flood of leasing scams, and then seizure once the land could be sold. The government invoked severalty even against tribes that resisted strongly. Only land too barren to evoke white greed was spared.

Of the 138 million acres of land owned by Indians in 1887, less than two-fifths, mainly desert, remained theirs in 1934. That year, the government moved to repair the damage caused by the misguided assimilation policy of nineteenth-century reformers. But what had been taken from the Indians could not be restored. "Sympathy and sentiment never stand in the way of the onward march of empire," an Oklahoma editor commented in 1907, the year that his state, Indian land twenty years earlier, joined the Union.

The South

"The South is the Bonanza of the future," the railway magnate Chauncey Depew declared in 1890. He added that "great and sudden opportunities for wealth" no longer existed in the West. So his message was: "Go South, Young Man." Northern investors and promoters did indeed find rich pickings in Louisiana timberlands and Alabama iron fields. But as a region, the South was not the West. The onrush of the western movement had simply swept away the Indian and Mexican civilizations. The social order of the Old South, changed but not crushed by the Civil War and Reconstruction, acted as a brake on the forces transforming the rest of the United States.

The Southern Economy

Long after the Civil War, the South lagged behind. In 1912, southerners had half the per capita wealth and less than two-thirds the per capita income of other Americans. Despite some growth of cities and industries, they remained a rural people. From 1850 into the twentieth century, two out of three southerners east of the Mississippi made a living from the land.

Farming and poverty are not, of course,

necessarily linked. But in the South, they were. Plantation agriculture ended after the Civil War, but not large land-holding. The freed slaves resisted the gang labor their former owners would have preferred and became tenant farmers instead. They worked on a crop-sharing basis, exchanging their labor for the use of land, house, implements, and sometimes seed and fertilizer. Lack of capital prevented them from renting on a cash basis and thrust them into debt to carry their families through the season. The local storekeeper "furnished" the sharecropper and took as collateral a lien on his growing crop. A crop lien, in effect, transferred the crop to the storekeeper, leaving the sharecropper only the proceeds that remained—if any—after his debts had been paid. Nor, once he had established credit with one store, was the sharecropper free to shop around. As a result, merchants imposed terribly high prices on farmers seeking credit. The price of corn in Georgia during the 1880s ran 35 percent higher on credit than for cash. The sharecropper whose account exceeded the value of his crop fell into permanent debt to the merchant. Their bargaining relationship, already unequal, now became wholly one-sided. And if the storekeeper was also the landowner, or was conspiring with the landowner, the debt became a pretext for forced labor. Many indebted sharecroppers found themselves in virtual peonage.

It would be hard to imagine a less progressive system of commercial agriculture. Sharecropping committed the South inflexibly to cotton, despite soil depletion and unprofitable prices. Crop diversification declined after the Civil War, and sharecroppers raised less grain and fewer animals than had the earlier plantations. With leases on a year-to-year basis, neither tenant nor owner had any incentive to invest in long-term improvements. The results included ramshackle buildings; implements in disrepair; and scrawny, untended livestock. At a time of rapid advances in agriculture and farm mechanization, cotton growing remained tied to the mule, the plow, and the hoe. The crop-lien system lined merchants' pockets with earnings—economists estimate the expropriation rate at 13.5 percent—that might otherwise have helped improve agricultural production.

An appalling waste of human resources also held back the South. A freed slave, previously deprived of managerial experience and basic education, had neither the opportunity nor much incentive for self-improvement as a sharecropper. In 1880, more than 75 percent of the black sharecroppers remained illiterate.

All these impediments combined to produce a stagnant agricultural system. Cotton production per capita recovered very slowly from the wreckage of the Civil War. In 1900, it stood at only 75 percent of the level of 1860.

Despite its lagging agriculture, the South had high hopes of a new start after Reconstruction. A highly influential group of young publicists, including Henry W. Grady, editor of the *Atlanta Constitution*, put forth the credo of a "New South." Henry Watterson, editor of the *Louisville Courier-Journal*, declared that "the ambition of the South is to out-Yankee the Yankee." Throughout this New South, imbued with the spirit of industrial capitalism, people shared Watterson's conviction that "the easygoing days . . . have passed away . . . never to return. . . . The South has learned that 'time is money.'"

The small industrial sector of the South, unlike agriculture, recovered rapidly from the devastation of the Civil War. By 1870, the railway system had been rebuilt and manufacturing output exceeded prewar levels. In 1879, with both Reconstruction and the economic depression ended, a railroad boom developed. Track mileage doubled in the next decade. The timber industry expanded greatly in the Gulf states, along with an even more dramatic surge of coal and iron production in Alabama. Northern and English capital played the key role in all these advances. Only the southern textile industry did not depend on outside investors. In the towns of the Piedmont region of North Carolina and Georgia intense public spirit generated enough local capital to build about four hundred cotton mills by 1900.

In other respects, however, the Piedmont mills typified the southern approach to industrial development. Their competitive edge over the older New England mills stemmed partly from more modern machinery but far more from cheap labor. Recruiting exclusively from among poor whites in the surrounding hill country, the industry featured paternalism, long hours, and low wages. An 1897 report estimated the cost of cotton labor as 40 percent lower in the South than in New England. Southern chambers of

A Model Mill

THE INDUSTRIAL SOUTH
No development so buoyed the hopes of New South proponents as the success of the region's textile industry. After 1877, new mills sprung up in South Carolina, North Carolina, and Georgia. Investors received a high return—average profits ran at 22 percent in 1882. Cotton mill employment, boasted the Charleston *News & Courier*, creates new jobs for "the necessitous masses of poor whites" and exposes them "to elevated influences, encourages them to seek education, and improves them in every conceivable respect." This 1887 engraving conveys the South's sense of pride in its new industrial prowess. (The Newberry Library, Chicago)

commerce pushed this kind of advantage to the limit. As one publicist wrote in 1897, "We must induce capital for manufacture to come here by offering cheaper money, cheaper taxation, cheaper labor, cheaper coal, and cheaper power, and much more public spirit."

The burst of industrial development did not liberate the South from its long-resented status as a colonial economy controlled by the North. The southern economy, always reliant on outside financing and distribution, fell even further under northern domination as a result of the merger movement that occurred in the 1890s. The region's railroads were reorganized and consolidated into a few large, cooperating systems, including J. P. Morgan's Southern Railway, controlled by investment bankers on Wall Street. The United States Steel Corporation acquired much of the southern iron industry. By monopolizing pipelines and refining facilities, Standard Oil and its allies exerted a stranglehold on the booming Texas oil fields that went into production starting in 1901.

Southerners headed many regional operations, but basic policy flowed from the controlling interests in the North. These interests aimed at maintaining the interregional status quo. Freight rate differentials encouraged the flow of raw materials but severely handicapped southern manufactured goods in competitive markets. In iron and steel, U.S. Steel created a price structure that protected its capital investment in Pittsburgh. Purchasers of Alabama steel had to pay Pittsburgh prices—despite the lower southern production costs—plus freight charges from Pittsburgh, even though the shipment originated in Birmingham. Southern users of steel were thus severely penalized, the Alabama steel industry lagged in spite of its natural advantages, and Pittsburgh retained its dominant position.

Contrary to the hopes of proponents of the New South, industrialism did not lift the region out of its rural poverty. Industrial output increased, but not enough to have much effect on the dominance of the agricultural sector. The industry that did develop was characteristically extractive, such as forestry and mining. In 1910, nearly two-thirds of the South's labor force worked in the production of raw materials, compared with hardly an eighth in the Middle Atlantic and New England states. Processing rarely went beyond coarse, semifinished goods, even in the textile industry. Relying on cheap, low-skill labor, southern industry fed on the region's poverty and backwardness. Long after Reconstruction, the South remained a tributary economy, a supplier on unequal terms to the advanced industrial heartland of the North.

Race, Class, and Politics

The commercial ambitions of the New South made a deep mark on southern politics. The dominant group was a business elite of new entrepreneurs and older plantation owners committed to southern economic development. Their method of exerting power, however, was strongly influenced by the political inheritance of Reconstruction. With the Republicans wholly discredited, the South became a one-party region. Whoever controlled the Democratic party controlled southern politics.

Because the Reconstruction struggle had been about home rule, the Democrats could portray themselves as the party of southern patriotism. In seizing control of the Democratic party, the economic elite thus had enormous advantages. Not only was there no effective opposition party. Members of the economic elite could cloak themselves in the mantle of the lost cause of the Civil War, and as the champions of southern *redemption* from black Republican rule. The conservative Democrats indeed called themselves the Redeemers.

The test of the Redeemers was their ability to exclude competing interests from the public arena. Class antagonism played a part in southern society. There had been long-smoldering differences between upland farmers and the planters. Fresh sources of conflict now arose in the tenant-farmer system—which increasingly included whites as well as blacks—and in an emerging industrial working class. Under the Redeemers, the South adopted highly conservative state policies. These included less public spending, the defense of property rights, and all possible encouragement of enterprise and investment.

Among the resulting disagreements, the most explosive was the question of heavy state debts incurred during Reconstruction. Failing to pay these obligations in full, conservatives argued, would undermine the public credit and frighten away outside capital. But the cost of such financial integrity would be borne by the people. In states such as Virginia, the burden of Reconstruction debt meant the virtual termination of all social services, including education. Where creditor interests refused to compromise, Readjuster movements sprang up in the poorer farming areas, committed to a reduction of Reconstruction debts.

The Readjusters won some victories. Under the leadership of General William H. Mahone, they controlled Virginia from 1879 to 1883. But the Readjusters could not capture the Democratic machinery. When they allied themselves with the Republicans or appealed to black voters, they became vulnerable to Democratic charges of treason. The Democrats did not hesitate to resort to the rough tactics of Reconstruction days. In Mississippi, South Carolina, and Virginia, the Readjuster movements were defeated in an outbreak of bloodshed and stuffed ballot boxes. These ruthless actions reflected the confidence of a ruling class exercising its claim to political dominance.

The foundation of that claim lay in the white-supremacist order that rose from the ashes of slavery. "The white laboring classes here," wrote an Alabamian in 1886,

> are separated from the Negroes, working all day side by side with them, by an innate consciousness of race superiority. This . . . excites a sentiment of sympathy and equality on their part with the classes above them, and in this way becomes a healthy social leaven.

White workers expressed this "innate consciousness of race superiority" by claiming privileged rights above the blacks. Blacks were systematically driven from the many skilled jobs they had held since the Civil War. Blacks also found themselves entirely excluded, except as janitors, from textile work and tobacco processing.

The social marks of inferiority—segregation and deference—had equally great psychological importance because they asserted that "the lowest white man counts for more than the highest Negro." The pressure for a rigid system of social segregation came primarily from poor whites. "The best people of the South do not demand this separate [railroad] car business," wrote a North Carolina black man. By accepting segregation, he declared, they were "pandering to the lower instincts of the worst class of whites in the South."

In times of economic distress, the logic of class solidarity strongly challenged the doctrine of white supremacy. Blacks and whites worked together in many places, such as coal mines and timber camps and on the waterfronts of southern seaports. There, they sometimes organized together into trade unions and even went on strike side by side. During the mid-1880s, the Knights of Labor preached the message of interracial unionism with considerable effect.

In this predominantly agricultural region, it meant more that distressed white farmers showed some willingness to work with black farmers to achieve their common goals. "They are in the ditch just like we are," asserted a white Texan. Beginning in 1886, white dirt farmers began to agitate for agrarian reform through the Southern Farmers' Alliance. Black farmers formed a separate organization, the Colored Farmers' Alliance, but the two bodies worked together. Once the farmers' movement entered politics in 1890, this formal racial division began to be overcome.

Unable to capture the Democratic party, the Southern Farmers' Alliance formed independent parties in a number of states. It joined with western movements to form the People's party, commonly called the Populist party, in 1891. The southern Populists needed the black vote. "The accident of color can make no difference in the interest of farmers, croppers, and laborers," stated the Populist leader Thomas E. Watson of Georgia. "You are kept apart that you may be separately fleeced of your earnings." By organizing interracially as a third party representing southern dirt farmers, the Populists endangered the structure of conservative southern politics.

The one-party system survived, but at a terrible cost to racial justice in the South. In the contest for the black vote, the conservative Democrats had the advantages of money, power, and paternalistic ties. They also attacked the Populists at their most vulnerable point—that they were courting "Negro domination." When all this did not suffice, fraud at the polls enabled the Democrats to defeat the opposition in Alabama, Georgia, and elsewhere. The race issue, instrumental in bringing down the Populists, also reconciled them to defeat. The embittered poor whites, deeply ambivalent all along about interracial cooperation, turned their fury on the blacks. Southern conservatives, chastened by the Populist show of strength, encouraged this anger.

The Populist struggle tragically produced a brand of white supremacy more virulent and impenetrable than anything the blacks had faced since emancipation. The color line, hitherto incomplete, became rigid and comprehensive. Starting in Florida in 1887, state after state in the South passed laws requiring segregated seating in trains. Such racial legislation, known as Jim Crow laws, soon spread to every type of public facility, even cemeteries. Southern schools had been segregated since the Civil War and social custom had dictated considerable racial separation. But in the 1890s, the South became for the first time a fully segregated society by law as well as fact. The Supreme Court of the United States soon ratified the South's decision. In the case of *Plessy v. Ferguson* (1896), the Court ruled that segregation was not discriminatory—that is, it did not violate black civil rights under the Fourteenth Amendment—if blacks had accommodations equal to those of whites. The "separate but equal" doctrine held for nearly half a century.

The pressure for Jim Crow laws came from poor whites, but Southern conservatives generally took the lead in depriving blacks of their right to vote. Black disfranchisement came through the constitutional adoption, beginning with Mississippi in 1890, of literacy tests, property requirements, and poll taxes. The conservatives called such actions "reforms" because without black voters, they argued, politics would be cleansed of electoral corruption.

The poor whites favored disfranchisement as another expression of militant white supremacy. Their own voting rights were only partially protected from the literacy tests by special exemptions and lenient enforcement, and not at all from the property and poll-tax requirements. They might have objected more had they not been given a voice within the Democratic party. From the 1890s on, a new brand of Southern politician spoke for the poor whites. He no longer appealed to their class interests, but to their racial prejudices. Tom Watson, the fiery Georgia Populist, rebuilt his political career as a brilliant practitioner of race baiting. Starting in the early 1900s, he and other racial demagogues thrived throughout the Deep South.

Race hatred became an accepted part of southern life, manifested in a wave of lynchings and race riots and in the public vilification of blacks. For example, Benjamin R. Tillman, a leading South Carolina Democrat, described them as "an ignorant and debased and debauched race." This ugly racism came from several sources, including intensified competition between white and black workers during the depression of the 1890s and the reaction against a less submissive black generation born after slavery. The nationwide spread of a pseudoscientific theory of racial inferiority also played a part, as did American imperialism and its subjugation of Filipinos, Hawaiians, and Hispanics.

But what had triggered the anti-black offensive was the crisis over Populism. Thereafter, white supremacy propped up the one-party system that had emerged from Reconstruction. If political power had to be shared, it would be on terms agreeable to the southern elite—the exclusion from the political process of any challenge to the economic status quo.

The Black Response

Where did this leave the blacks? In 1890, blacks comprised more than half the population of Grimes County, a cotton-growing area of east Texas. They had managed to keep the local Republican organization going after Reconstruction and regularly sent black representatives to the Texas legislature during the 1870s and 1880s. Also remarkably, the local Populist party that appeared in 1892 among white farmers proved immune to the Democrats' charges of "black rule." A Populist-Republican coalition swept the county elections in 1896 and 1898, surviving well after the collapse of the national Populist movement.

In 1899, defeated Democratic office seekers and prominent citizens of Grimes County organized the secret White Man's Union. Armed men prevented blacks from voting in town elections that year. The two most important black county leaders were shot down in cold blood. Night riders terrorized both white Populists and black Republicans. When the Populist sheriff proved incapable of enforcing the law, the game was up. The White Man's Union, now out in the open, became the county Democratic party in a new guise. The Democrats won Grimes County by an overwhelming vote in the 1900 election. The day after the election, members of the Union laid siege to the Populist sheriff's office. They killed his brother and a friend and drove the sheriff, badly wounded, out of the county forever.

The White Man's Union ruled Grimes County for the next fifty years. The whole episode was the handiwork of the county's "best citizens," suggesting how respectable the naked use of force had become in the service of white supremacy. The Union intended, as one of its leaders said, to "force the African to keep his place." After 1900, blacks could survive in Grimes County only if they tended to their own business and stayed out of trouble with whites.

Booker T. Washington, the top black leader of

BOOKER T. WASHINGTON
In an age of severe racial oppression, Booker T. Washington (1856–1915) emerged as the acknowledged leader of black people in the United States. He was remarkable both for his ability as a spokesman to white Americans and his deep understanding of the aspirations of black Americans. Born a slave, Washington suffered the oppression common to all blacks after emancipation. But, having been befriended by several whites as he grew to manhood, he also understood what it took to gain white support in the black struggle for equality. (Library of Congress)

his day, responded to that grim reality in a famous speech in Atlanta in 1895. Washington marked out a line of retreat from the defiant stand of older black abolitionists. (Frederick Douglass, the greatest of that group, died the same year that the Atlanta speech launched Washington into national prominence.) Washington was conciliatory toward the South; it was a society that blacks understood and loved. He considered "the agitation of the question of social equality the extremest folly." Washington accepted segregation, provided that blacks had equal facilities. He accepted educational and property qualifications for the vote, provided that they applied equally to blacks and whites.

Washington's doctrine came to be known as the Atlanta Compromise. His approach was "accommodationist" in the sense that it avoided any direct assault on white supremacy. Despite the humble face he put on before white audiences, Washington did not concede the struggle, any more than did the Grimes County blacks, who, many decades later, still talked about the battles they had fought and lost during the Populist years. Behind the scenes, Washington fought skillfully against Jim Crow laws and disfranchisement. More important, his Atlanta Compromise, while abandoning the field of political protest, opened up a second front of economic struggle.

Washington sought to capitalize on a southern dilemma about the economic role of the black population. Racist dogma dictated that blacks be kept down and that they conform to their image as lazy, shiftless workers. But for the South to prosper, it needed an efficient labor force. Washington made this need the target of his efforts. Founder of Tuskegee Institute in Alabama in 1881, Washington advocated industrial education—that is, manual and agricultural training. He preached the virtues of thrift, hard work, and property ownership. His industrial-education program won generous support from northern philanthropists and businessmen and, following his Atlanta speech, applause from progressive supporters of the New South.

Washington assumed that black economic progress would be the key to winning black political and civil rights. He regarded members of the white southern elite as his crucial allies because ultimately only they had the power to act.

More importantly, they could "see the close connection between labor, industry, education, and political institutions." When it was in their economic interest, and when they had grown dependent on black labor and black enterprise, white men of business and property would recognize the justice of black rights. As Washington put it, "There is little race prejudice in the American dollar."

For twenty years after his Atlanta address, Washington dominated organized black life in America. He was the authentic voice of black opinion in an age of severe racial oppression. No black dealt more skillfully with the leaders of white America. Washington wielded more political influence than any other black of his generation. The black community knew him as a hard taskmaster. Intensely jealous of his authority, he did not regard opposition kindly. Black politicians, educators, and editors stood up to him at their peril.

Even so, a rift began after 1900, especially among younger, educated blacks. They thought Washington was conceding too much. He instilled black pride, but of a narrowly middle-class and utilitarian kind. What about the special genius of blacks that W. E. B. DuBois celebrated in his collection of essays called *The Souls of Black Folk* (1903)? And what of the "talented tenth" of the black population whose promise could only be stifled by industrial education? At the same time, blacks became increasingly impatient with Washington's silence over segregation and lynchings. The key critic was DuBois, a Harvard-educated sociologist and educator. In 1905, demanding "aggressive action," DuBois helped found the Niagara Movement. The reform atmosphere of the Progressive era also brought a new, though small, group of white allies on the scene. The National Association for the Advancement of Colored People (NAACP), organized by blacks and whites in 1909, absorbed the Niagara Movement and became a biracial vehicle in the fight for black rights. By the time of Washington's death in 1915, his approach had been superseded by a strategy that relied on the courts and political leverage, not on black self-help and accommodation.

History has proved Washington's Atlanta Compromise wrong in contending that only economic strength would give civil rights to blacks.

These rights have been gained without prior achievement of economic equality. But in taking the route of legal protest, the NAACP largely overlooked the bedrock plight of the mass of black people. Washington wisely emphasized the attack on black poverty and ignorance, each of which feeds the other. He also realized shrewdly that the evil race relations of the post-Reconstruction South was rooted in its backward economic order. As long as share-cropping cotton agriculture prevailed, and as long as the southern economy remained subservient to the industrial North, the South would not abandon the oppressive racial system that had been forged out of slavery.

Before Washington died, two events produced changes that would have far-reaching consequences for the economic future of poor blacks. In 1892, the boll weevil moved from Mexico into Texas. During the next thirty years, this small beetle spread throughout the South, attacking the cotton fields and forcing farmers to grow other crops. The second event, World War I, created a sudden demand for black labor and set off a massive, long-term migration to the North. The blacks who left the South found opportunity in northern industry, while those who remained had a stronger bargaining position.

Progress came slowly for the regional economy as a whole. It took much longer than nineteenth-century optimists had expected for the New South to come fully into its own. Now that the South has reached that goal, Booker T. Washington's expectations seem at least partly fulfilled. In the enterprising atmosphere of the modern South, the heart seems to have gone out of racial oppression.

The Agricultural Interest

In the South, the typical farmer was a sharecropper. Elsewhere in the country, he was an independent freeholder. The freeholder tradition was deeply rooted in the Jeffersonian ideal of a nation of virtuous yeoman farmers and was enshrined in the policy of free land for the settler. Family farms predominated throughout rural America in the late nineteenth century. The average farm comprised about 150 acres and employed an average of fewer than one hired hand. Farm ownership also was widespread. In 1880, owners occupied 75 percent of Iowa's farms. In an age of trusts and corporations, the farmer succeeded as did no other group in retaining the *forms* of economic individualism. But his *functions* took him far from the self-sufficient yeoman farmers of Jeffersonian America. He had been fully inducted into the modern economic order.

The Farming Business

American farmers of 1880 stood at the center of a vast and complex system of trade. They depended on the railroads to carry their crops to market. A highly sophisticated network of commodity exchanges determined prices and found buyers throughout the country and beyond. Great processing industries turned wheat into flour, livestock into dressed meat, and fruit and vegetables into canned goods. Only through this modern commercial system could farmers gain access to the expanding urban markets in the United States and overseas. About 20 percent of American agricultural production went abroad during the late nineteenth century.

TABLE 19.1 FREIGHT RATES FOR TRANSPORTING CROPS

Grand Island to Omaha (150 miles)			
Date effective	Corn	Wheat	Oats
	(In cents per hundredweight)		
January 1, 1883	18	19½	18
April 16, 1883	15	16½	15
January 10, 1884	18	19½	18
March 1, 1884	17	19½	17
August 25, 1884	20	20	20
April 5, 1887	10	16	10
November 1, 1887	10	12	10

Grand Island to Chicago (650 miles)			
Date effective	Corn	Wheat	Oats
	(In cents per hundredweight)		
January 7, 1880	32	45	32
September 15, 1882	38	43	38
April 5, 1887	34	39	34
November 1, 1887	25	30	25
March 21, 1890	22½	30	25
October 22, 1890	22	26	22
January 15, 1891	23	28	25

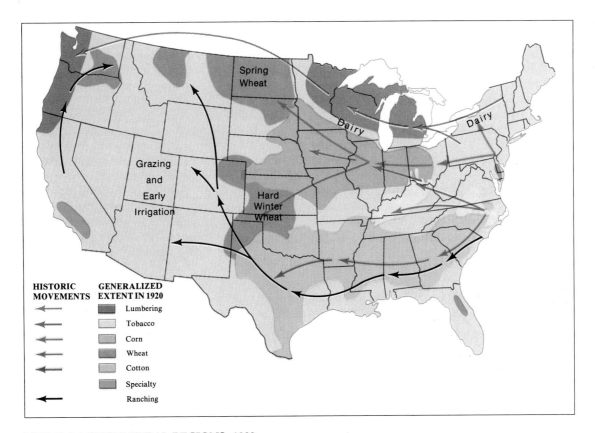

MAP 19.6 AGRICULTURAL REGIONS, 1900

The development of agricultural regions reflected the commercial bent of American agriculture—that is, growing crops for market rather than home consumption. Regional specialization matched climate and soil to the most suitable crops. Many crops moved west along with settlers. For some commodities, such as dairy products, the crop region simply expanded. Wheat, which was usually replaced by other crops after early years of settlement, concentrated finally on the Great Plains and the northwest. Agricultural regions continue to shift somewhat, as in the recent decline of cotton in the South and its growth in California.

American farmers were likewise well supplied with modern goods and services. They met their credit needs through mortgage companies that drew on eastern and European capital. The McCormick Reaper Company, John Deere and Company, and other manufacturers sold them labor-saving farm machinery. Other industries supplied an increasing share of household and farming needs. "The old rule that a farmer should produce all he required is part of the past," noted a farm journal. "Agriculture, like all other business, is better for its subdivisions, each one growing that which is best suited for his soil, skill, climate and market, and with its proceeds purchasing his other needs."

Farmers eagerly followed this advice. Subsis-

tence farming persisted in infertile, hilly areas, and general farming, in which no crop represented as much as 40 percent of a farm's total production, went on throughout rural America. But farmers everywhere tended to concentrate on a cash crop, though not, as in the cotton South, to the exclusion of some gardening and small-stock raising. As a result, a high degree of regional specialization developed by the end of the century.

Distinct crop regions emerged. The wheat belt lay on the western edge of the Midwest from North Dakota down to Kansas and into northern Texas. Wheat had long been a virgin crop, the first to be planted when new land opened up. As the frontier moved on, wheat growing moved steadily westward. Wheat settled on the Great Plains, partly because of the suitability of the land and partly because of the arrival of hardy Russian varieties. Russian wheat prospered in the harsh plains climate and produced a bread flour superior to the soft wheat of milder regions. From Iowa eastward ran the corn belt, which devoted most of its product directly to livestock raising. The dairy belt, north of the corn belt, stretched from Minnesota as far east as New York and New England. It produced the nation's milk, butter, and cheese. In California, wheat raising gave way to orange groves and a wide variety of fruits and vegetables.

This agricultural specialization served as the best indicator of the commercial path taken by American farmers. But there were many other signs as well, such as the attitude toward land. Americans had little of the passionate identification with the soil that held European peasants to their inherited plots. In 1910, more than half the farmers lived on different land than they had inhabited five years earlier. The farmer saw his acreage as a commodity to be bought and sold, and to be valued for the price it could bring on the market. Most farmers believed they could earn as much profit, if not more, from the appreciation of the land's value as from the crops it produced. This attitude fostered the willingness to operate on borrowed capital. In boom times, farmers rushed into debt to extend their land holdings.

The commercial spirit also made farmers enthusiastic about the innovations of the industrial age. Farm machinery cut production costs for the leading crops by about half between 1850 and 1900. The railroad, especially the prospect of local rail service, delighted the western pioneers. They happily supported whatever inducements might be necessary, such as the public purchase of railway bonds, to lure the line to their towns.

Agrarian Distress

Farmers participated eagerly in the new industrial order. They embraced its entrepreneurial spirit, yet found themselves more victims than beneficiaries of the modern economy. The late nineteenth century was a time of deep agricul-

A WISCONSIN FARM FAMILY
On the frontier, pioneers struggled to tame the land and bring in the first cash crop. But as the frontier receded, as it had in Wisconsin by the late nineteenth century, farming settled down into a seasonal routine of plowing, planting, and harvesting. In this portrait, the young farmers proudly display their corn (the cash crop), ample produce, good health, and, in the woman's starched apron and the infant's white smock, their respectability. (State Historical Society of Wisconsin)

tural discontent. For thirty years, protest movements swept across the farm belt.

Part of the farmers' anger stemmed from the harshness of rural life. No one labored longer or harder. The farmer worked an average of sixty-eight hours a week in 1900, twelve hours longer than industrial workers; he had worked only six hours longer in 1850. Mechanization had not actually reduced work loads on farms as it had in factories. Crop acreage tended to increase with the availability of planting and harvesting machinery. Most other chores remained on the farmer's shoulders.

For the farm wife, the burdens increased. Larger harvests meant more field hands for whom to cook and clean up. At the same time, her own work in the kitchen remained almost unaffected by the conveniences and appliances that were becoming common in many urban homes. She and the children, as soon as they were old enough, also pitched in with the farm chores and field work. "Many a time a shudder has passed through the mother heart of me," said a Missouri woman in 1909, "at the sight of some little fellow struggling with the handles of a plow, jerking and stumbling over cloddy ground from daylight till dark. Boys 'making a full hand,' 'helping Pa.' " Farm children in 1900 attended school only two-thirds as many days as did city children, and they left school at an earlier age.

The farmer may have accepted how hard he labored, and how he wore out his wife and sacrificed his children, for the living he wrested from the soil. He found it harder to swallow the widening discrepancy in the quality of life between farm and city. In an age of rapidly advancing urban education, his children still attended gloomy, ungraded one-room schools—hardly the little red schoolhouses of popular mythology. Electricity, indoor plumbing, and paved roads had not yet come to the farm. The rural diet consisted of salt pork, bread, and potatoes for much of the year. A nationwide survey in 1918 by the U. S. Public Health Service showed that farm sanitation remained primitive. On two-thirds of all farms the water supply was threatened by "potentially dangerous contamination from privy contents."

Hardest of all was the sense of isolation from the variety and pleasures that farm people associated with urban life. Isolation was worst on the Great Plains, with its cruel winters and the long, empty distances. But farm life everywhere tended to be lonely and circumscribed. Rural neighborhoods, even in long-settled areas, amounted to three or four square miles where perhaps a dozen families lived. As one writer remarked, "the end of the neighborhood was almost the end of the world." Hamlin Garland and other authors of the late nineteenth century wrote powerfully about the dreariness of the countryside and the lure of the city. "I hate farm life," grumbled one of Garland's heroines. "It's nothing but fret, fret and work the whole time, never going any place, never seeing anybody but a lot of neighbors just as big fools as you are. I spend my time fighting flies and washing dishes and churning. I'm sick of it all."

Understandably, when farmers formed organizations, they provided for social activity first of all. The Patrons of Husbandry, familiarly known as the Grange because its branches were called granges, became a rural social center through its dances, picnics, and lectures. It encouraged women as well as men to join. Oliver H. Kelley, the government clerk who founded the Grange in 1867, hoped that participation by "the young folks of both sexes . . . will have a tendency to instill in their minds a fondness of rural life, and prevent in great measure so many of them flocking to the cities."

The hunger for social activity cemented organizational ties, but the dynamism of farmers' movements came from economic grievances. The farmers' basic problem was their imperfect participation in the economic transformation of the late nineteenth century. They embraced the era's commercialism, welcomed its technology and products, and sent their crops into a network of national and international markets. In one way, however, farmers did not change. They remained individual operators in a world of business consolidation and large-scale enterprise. In certain ways, they were acutely aware of their predicament.

One solution for farmers might have been to create their own versions of large-scale enterprise. Cooperative activity, especially through stores and creameries, had started before the Civil War. The Grange took up the cooperative idea in a big way by organizing bulk purchasing

A PIONEER COUPLE TWENTY YEARS LATER

Life on the frontier was harsh, but things improved through the years. The first photograph shows Mr. and Mrs. Ephraim Finch in front of their log-and-mud hut in Nebraska during the 1880s. This bleakness, common on the frontier, fed the agrarian discontent of those years. Twenty years later, the Finches posed again to record their prosperity. Their hut has given way to a handsome frame house, and the trees they may have planted as a wind break have grown into tall shade trees. (Nebraska State Historical Society)

from manufacturers, along with scattered cooperative banks, insurance companies, grain elevators, and processing plants. In Iowa, the state Grange started to manufacture farm implements in 1873. The Southern Farmers' Alliance, which became active in the middle 1880s, likewise strongly encouraged cooperation, especially for marketing cotton and operating cotton gins. The ambitious Texas Exchange began as a statewide cotton marketer in 1887. In an attempt to break the oppressive crop-lien system, it quickly evolved into a comprehensive marketing and purchasing exchange. However, banks and suppliers refused to do business with it, and the organization collapsed, as did most cooperative ventures of this era. The opposition by private business was too unrelenting, cooperative managers too unskilled, and the farmers themselves too individualistic.

Residual benefits did remain, among them an efficient mail-order business that emerged from farmers' hostility to middlemen. In 1872, Montgomery Ward and Company was founded specifically to "meet the wants" of the Grange. The early cooperative activity also led to more permanent institutions after the turn of the century, especially for dairy farmers and fruit growers.

Cooperative stores, grain elevators, and telephone exchanges became familiar parts of the countryside throughout rural America. As a solution to the organizational weakness of the late nineteenth-century farmer, however, cooperative movements had to be accounted a failure.

Another alternative for the farmers would have been to enlist the power of government against economic monopoly. Western farmers, generally served by only one grain elevator or railroad, felt continually cheated on storage charges and wheat grading. They also complained about paying freight rates higher than those farther east. The Grange, itself strictly a social-education organization, gave rise to independent political parties during the early 1870s that captured a number of state legislatures on antimonopoly platforms. The resulting Granger laws regulated grain elevators, fixed maximum railroad rates, and prohibited discriminatory practices against small and short-haul shippers. In *Munn v. Illinois* (1876), the Supreme Court upheld these laws on the ground that such enterprises involved the public interest. Reversing that decision in *Wabash v. Illinois* (1886), a more conservative Court ruled that the states lacked the power to regulate interstate commerce. By then, however, a movement had started for federal regulation of the railroads. The passage of the Interstate Commerce Act (1887), partly as a result of the Wabash case, made railroad regulation a permanent part of American public policy.

Farmers turned to cooperatives and government regulation out of a deep sense of economic disadvantage. But their difficulties did not actually stem from the monopoly power of the suppliers of goods and services. Manufacturers, railroads, and banks lacked the degree of market control ascribed to them by angry farmers. From 1865 to 1890, manufacturers could not establish a relative price advantage over agriculture. In fact, the wholesale price of all commodities fell at a slightly faster rate than did farm product prices during those years. Nor did the heavy transportation costs for grain shipments result primarily from the monopoly power of the railroads. More important factors were the increasing distance from farms to Chicago, the principal grain market; the thin settlement on the Great Plains; and the seasonality of grain shipments.

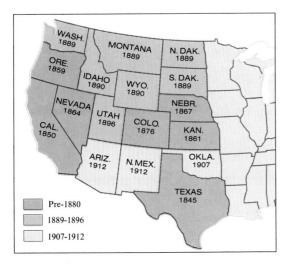

MAP 19.7 STATEHOOD FOR WESTERN STATES
In the Northwest Ordinance of 1787, the United States made a crucial political decision: the western territories, when sufficiently populated, would be admitted to the union as states "on an equal footing with the original states in all respects whatsoever." The entry of the western states had considerable political consequences. They were the seat of the Populist protest of the 1890s. And because each new state gained two votes in the Senate, the 4.4 million western citizens (scarcely 6 percent of the nation's total) had a disproportionate voice in national policy.

After the 1870s, as railroad technology improved and the volume of western traffic increased, freight rates fell steadily and east-west differentials narrowed. Even the much-maligned mortgage companies could not rig credit markets in the western states. Their interest rates matched those in the rest of the country. Farmers sometimes fell victim to suppliers, railroads, and moneylenders. But the impact of such abuses was not great enough to account for unprofitable farming.

Agrarian discontent centered on the Great Plains. This was the grain belt of the 1880s. Ten years earlier, when the grain belt lay farther east, Iowa, Illinois, and Wisconsin had been the scene of the Granger agitation. The special militancy of grain growers resulted partly from the nature of their market, which was international, highly volatile, and unpredictable. Grain prices, depressed in the late 1870s, surged in 1880. Chicago prices for a bushel of No. 2 corn went from 37.7 cents to 67.5 cents in 1882, and No. 2 wheat rose from $1.05 to $1.16.

Such price increases triggered a second weakness. A speculative climate tended to prevail in freshly settled areas. With grain prices on the rise, the price of land was rapidly bid up. In Harrison Township, Nebraska, first settled in 1872, land that sold for eight dollars an acre in 1880 sold for twenty-five dollars and up a few years later. At that price, the purchaser in effect gambled that grain prices—and land prices— would continue to rise. But grain prices collapsed in 1883–84. Anyone who had taken out a mortgage and bought land at twenty-five dollars an acre in Harrison Township could not hope to meet his payments, at 6 percent interest, at the prevailing price for wheat. "One is almost tempted to draw the moral that the would-be purchaser . . . had almost better throw his money away than invest it in farming operations in Nebraska," an investigator concluded in 1892.

Such advice came too late—and, in any case, it would not likely have been taken by the western farmer. His predicament seemed fundamental to him and to stem not from individual errors of judgment but from deep-rooted inequities in the economic system. As grain prices sank after 1884 and foreclosures swept across the grain belt, the western farmer turned to the one course of action that seemed able to rescue him—politics.

Populism and After

A second cycle of agrarian organization began in the 1880s. In the South, the leading groups were the Southern Farmers' Alliance and the Colored Farmers' Alliance; in the western states, most important was the National Farmers' Alliance of the North West. Originally intended as social and mutual-aid societies, these organizations increasingly began to take up the economic grievances of sharecroppers and grain farmers. In both the South and West, they tried to gain a hearing from the major political parties. When this did not succeed, the farmers turned to independent politics. In 1890, they won control of the Nebraska and Kansas legislatures, and captured several governorships as well as eight state legislatures in the South. Two years later, the southern and western organizations joined together in Saint Louis to form the Populist party. In the 1892 elections, the Populists, with James B. Weaver, an Iowa congressman, as their presidential candidate, won a million votes—9 percent of the total—and carried four states. For the first time, agrarian protest showed potential as a national political movement.

Populism contained a strong radical bent. Severe economic distress, Populists felt, could stem only from some basic evil. They identified this evil as the control of the "money power" over the levers of the economic system. "There are but two sides," proclaimed a Populist manifesto. "On the one side are the allied hosts of monopolies, the money power, great trusts and railroad corporations. . . . On the other are the farmers, laborers, merchants and all the people who produce wealth. . . . Between these two there is no middle ground." This reasoning allied agriculture with labor and identified farmers and workers as a single producer class. In 1887, the Southern Farmers' Alliance changed its name to the Farmers' and Laborers' Union of America, and the Populists sought to ally themselves with the labor movement.

The Populist platform of 1892 revealed the scope of the party's program. It called for nationalization of the railroads; protection of the land, including natural resources, from monopoly and alien ownership; a graduated income tax; and postal savings banks. The Populist platform also included the Southern Alliance's sub-treasury plan, by which farmers could borrow money at a nominal 2 percent interest with their crops serving as collateral. In addition, the Populists adopted resolutions supporting organized labor, veterans' pensions, and such political reforms as the secret ballot and direct election of senators. Finally, the Populists called for the unlimited coinage of silver. From a comprehensive program, this currency question became the overriding issue of the Populist party.

Until 1873, the nation had operated on the bimetallic standard, by which silver and gold had served as legal tender at a ratio of sixteen to one. At a given unit of monetary value, sixteen parts of silver equaled one part of gold. Because of the scarce supply of silver, its market price rose above its official value. Hence, silver disappeared from currency circulation and in 1873 was officially dropped as a medium of exchange, putting the nation on a gold standard. Soon thereafter, great silver discoveries occurred in Nevada, Arizona, and elsewhere in the West. With this new supply, silver prices dropped swiftly in relation to gold. If the government returned to the bimetallic standard, at the ratio of

MARY ELIZABETH LEASE
As members of a political movement, the Populists were short on cash and organization, but long on rank-and-file zeal and tub-thumping oratory. No one was more rousing on the stump than Mary Elizabeth Lease, who came from a Kansas homestead and pulled no punches. "What you farmers need to do," she urged in her speeches, "is to raise less corn and more *Hell!*" (Brown Brothers)

sixteen to one silver would flow into the Treasury and greatly expand the volume of currency. Although the Sherman Silver Purchase Act of 1890 permitted limited Treasury purchases, the Populists began to demand free silver.

The reasons were in part narrowly economic. Farmers would benefit from free silver because it was inflationary. A larger money supply would raise farm prices and reduce the burden of farm debt; farmers would be paying back cheaper dollars than they had borrowed. But free silver was also defended in radical terms, based on a conspiracy theory about eastern bankers and "goldbugs." Their stranglehold on the money supply, according to this theory, was the central evil of the capitalist system and the primary means of exploiting the producing classes. *Coin's Financial School* (1894), a powerful pamphlet by William H. Harvey, trumpeted this message at the height of the free-silver agitation.

However, the Chicago Socialist Henry Demarest Lloyd, Georgia's Tom Watson, and other left-wing Populists clearly saw the conservative logic behind free silver. It meant money in the pockets of western farmers and hefty party contributions from silver-mining interests. These mine operators, scornful though they might be of the Populist program, yearned for the day when the government would buy all the silver they could produce—at a premium price.

On the other hand, free silver had no appeal for city workers. Any chance of a farmer-labor alliance that might transform Populism into an American version of a social-democratic party would be doomed. As Lloyd complained, free silver was "the cowbird of reform," stealing in and taking over the nest that others had built.

Events soon proved the truth of Lloyd's jibe. When the Democratic party came out for free silver in the 1896 presidential election, the Populists could not prevent themselves from being absorbed into the Democratic campaign and from losing their independent identity. With the victory of William McKinley, a Republican, Populism died.

Populism did not disappear because farmers had changed their minds about the need for a larger money supply. They had made the right economic analysis, only it was not free silver that came to their rescue. During the 1890s, gold was discovered in South Africa, Colorado, and Alaska. New refining techniques, especially the cyanide method, greatly increased ore yields. The gold discoveries did for the embattled farmers just what they had hoped to accomplish through free silver. Prices rose nearly 50 percent between 1897 and 1914, and their debt burdens eased.

Moreover, the growing urban population increased the demand for farm products. As domestic markets began to absorb the farm surplus, farm exports dropped sharply after 1900. Wheat went from 72 cents a bushel in 1896 to 98 cents in 1909, corn from 27 cents to 57 cents, and cotton from 6 cents to 14 cents a pound. Farm prices rose faster than those of other products, and, as a result, so did the real income of farmers. A new spirit of prosperity and optimism took hold in the "golden age" of American agriculture before World War I.

Farmers abandoned Populism because rising prices eased their economic distress shortly after the 1896 election. More deep-seated changes, already underway, would ensure that, even in the harshest times, they would not express their discontent through a twentieth-century version of Populism. The farmers' sense of deprivation and inferiority—that they were "rubes" and "hicks," and that life was inherently better in the city—began to subside after 1900. The new prosperity helped bring about this significant change in their feelings. More farmers could afford to expand and modernize their houses. They purchased labor-saving home appliances and farm machinery to lighten field work.

New inventions helped ease the isolation and monotony of rural life. The telephone became commonplace, not so much because of the spread of commercial service, but through the determined efforts of farmers themselves. Telephone cooperatives became the most numerous type of farm cooperatives in the early twentieth century. The automobile, especially after the Ford Model T came on the market in 1908, spread across rural America. President Theodore Roosevelt's Country Life Commission, formed in 1908, took a sunny view of farm society: "There has never been a time when the American farmer was as well off as he is today, when we consider not only his earning power, but the comforts and advantages he may secure."

The farmer's self-conception also underwent an irreversible transformation. As long as farmers remained in the majority, they naturally

TIME LINE
RURAL AMERICA

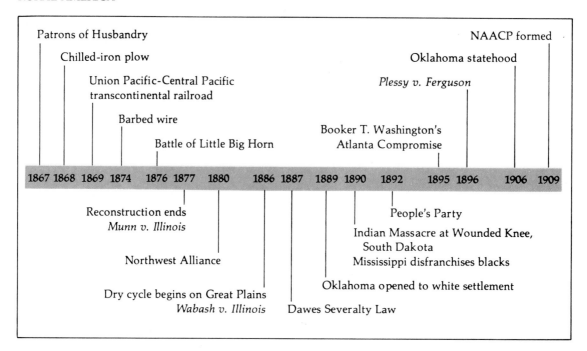

considered themselves as representative of the American norm. They could readily regard their own economic distress as a general disorder of the entire nation. Pushed far enough, they might seek to mobilize their fellow producers—farmers and workers—to seize political power. In short, they could become Populists. But by the opening of the twentieth century, farmers no longer composed the majority of the population. In 1910, only about a third of the labor force earned a living from the soil. The farmers' realization that their number could only decrease with each census persuaded them to abandon the Jeffersonian illusion of a rural yeomanry.

"Now the object of farming is not primarily to make a living, but it is to make money," stated an agricultural writer in 1904. "To this end it is to be conducted on the same business basis as any other producing industry." This commercial spirit expressed itself in a fresh interest in improved farming methods and marketing techniques and, above all, in the recognition of

supply and demand as the farmers' central concern. Federal assistance, which went back to the Morrill College Land Grant Act of 1862, expanded to provide many new marketing and educational services for farmers. The budget of the Department of Agriculture increased thirty-fold between 1890 and 1920. New farm organizations sprang up, such as the Farmers' Educational and Cooperative Union, the American Society of Equity, and, strongest of all, the American Farm Bureau Federation. These groups cultivated a strong service orientation and concerned themselves chiefly with the profitable marketing of agricultural commodities. They avoided politics except to advance farmers' practical needs, and they acted in these cases as interest groups, not as a political movement.

All these developments reflected the new reality facing the farmer. Agriculture had been at the heart of American life. In the twentieth century, it was but one more economic interest—an important one, but now subordinate in the larger scheme of the modern industrial order.

*I*n the late nineteenth century, rural America was drawn increasingly into the orbit of the new industrial way of life. The surge across the Great Plains and the Rockies, the final phase of the westward movement, was strongly linked with the nation's economic development. Industry needed mineral resources; the cities demanded agricultural products; and the railroad, barbed wire, and other products of an industrial age made the conquest of the West relatively easy. Doomed by the swift penetration of their lands, the western Indians were largely the victims of events that occurred far off in the nation's industries and cities.

The South, emerging from the ravages of the Civil War and Reconstruction, tried to follow the example of the industrial North, but with only mixed success. Southern politics were strongly influenced by entrepreneurial values, and southerners made strenuous efforts to encourage industrial development. However, the South remained locked into its deep-rooted heritage of staple-crop agriculture and racial division. As the nation's underdeveloped region, it remained subordinate to the more advanced economy of the North.

Western farmers also stood in an uncomfortable relationship to the industrial sector. Operating as family farmers in an age of increasing organization and complexity, they found farming persistently unprofitable. The causes of their difficulty baffled them, which led to the rise of Populism, a protest movement that briefly challenged the two party system during the 1890s. After 1897, farm prices rose and a new age of prosperity began for farmers. The flow of the new products of industrialism—telephones, household appliances, and automobiles—began to relieve the isolation and hardship of farm life.

Suggestions for Further Reading

The Great West

The liveliest and most sensitive introduction to western history is Robert V. Hine, *The American West* (2nd ed. 1984). The seminal statement on the significance of the frontier is in Frederick Jackson Turner, *The Frontier in American History* (1920). Another highly influential work is Walter P. Webb, *The Great Plains* (1931), which stresses man's adaptation to the western climate and environment. A good regional survey is Robert G. Athearn, *High Country Empire: High Plains and Rockies* (1960). The best book on western mining is Rodman Paul, *Mining Frontiers of the Far West: 1848–1880s* (1963). For the farming pioneers, see Everett Dick, *Sod-House Frontier* (1954), and on the cattlemen, Lewis Atherton, *The Cattle Kings* (1961) and Robert R. Dykstra, *Cattle Towns* (1968). Cowboys receive full treatment in Joe B. Frantz and Julian E. Choate, *American Cowboy: Myth and Reality* (1955).

Native Americans

A useful introduction to Native American history is William T. Hagan, *American Indians* (1961). Two valuable collections by deans of the subject are Wilcomb E. Washburn, ed., *Indian and White Man* (1964) and Francis Paul Prucha, *Indian Policy in the United States: Historical Essays* (1981). Ralph K. Andrist, *Long Death: Last Days of the Plains Indians* (1964) tells that tragic story eloquently. The most recent study of white attitudes is Richard Drinnon, *Facing West: The Metaphysics of Indian-Hating and Empire-Building* (1980).

The South

On the South, the seminal book for the post-Reconstruction period is C. Vann Woodward, *Origins of the New South, 1877–1913* (1951), which still defines the terms of discussion among historians. Two recent books stress the continuities between the Old South planters and the post Civil War economic development: Dwight B. Billings, *Planters and the Making of "New South": North Carolina, 1865–1900* (1979) and Jonathan M. Wiener, *Social Origins of the New South: Alabama, 1860–1885* (1978). The standard book on New South thought is Paul M. Gaston, *The New South Creed: A Study of Southern Myth-making* (1973). Gaston's book can profitably be read in conjunction with a much older study, Paul M. Buck, *The Road to Reunion, 1865–1900* (1937).

The economic aftermath of slavery and the plantation system is treated with great insight by two economists, Roger Ransom and Richard Sutch, *One Kind of Freedom* (1977). Pete Daniel, *Shadow of Slavery* (1972) gives a vivid account of peonage. The classic book on segregation is C. Vann Woodward, *The Strange Career of Jim Crow* (2nd rev. ed. 1968), but it should be supplemented by Howard N. Rabinowitz, *Race Relations in the Urban South, 1865–1890* (1978). Disfranchisement is treated with great analytic sophistication in

J. Morgan Kousser, *The Shaping of Southern Politics: Suffrage Restriction and the Establishment of the One-Party South, 1880–1910,* and as an aspect of progressivism in Jack Temple Kirby, *Darkness at the Dawning: Race and Reform in the Progressive South* (1972). Rayford W. Logan, *The Betrayal of the Negro* (new ed. 1965) is the standard history of blacks after Reconstruction. August Meier, *Negro Thought in America, 1880–1915* (1963) is a key analysis of black accommodation and protest. The pre-eminent exponent of accommodation has been the subject of a superb two-volume biography by Louis B. Harlan, *Booker T. Washington: The Making of a Black Leader* (1973) and *Wizard of Tuskegee* (1983).

The Agricultural Interest

On agriculture, the standard works are Fred A. Shannon, *The Farmer's Last Frontier, 1860–1897* (1945) and Gilbert C. Fite, *The Farmer's Frontier, 1865–1900* (1966). Women's role on the frontier is now beginning to receive its due. See especially Julie Roy Jeffrey, *Frontier Women: The Trans-Mississippi West* (1979). The flavor of farm life can best be captured in fiction: Hamlin Garland, *Main-Travelled Roads* (1891), Willa Cather, *My Antonia* (1918), and O. E. Rolvag, *Giants in the Earth* (1927).

Populism

The standard work on Populism is John D. Hicks, *The Populist Revolt* (1931). Richard D. Hofstadter, *Age of Reform* (1955) advanced an interpretation that stressed the darker side of Populism, in which intolerance and paranoia figured heavily. Hofstadter's thesis, which dominated debate among historians for some years, has now given way to a much more positive assessment of Populism. The key book here is Lawrence Goodwyn, *Democratic Promise: The Populist Moment in America* (1976), which argues that it was the last broadly-based, radical response to industrial capitalism. Goodwyn stresses the Southern roots of Populism, and has consequently stimulated other work studying this aspect of subject—for example, Steven Hahn, *The Roots of Southern Populism: Yeoman Farmers and the Transformation of the Georgia Upcountry, 1850–1890* (1983). The carry-over of southern Populism into twentieth-century agrarian socialism has received detailed study in James R. Green, *Grass-Roots Socialism: Radical Movements in the Southwest* (1978). A highly stimulating book that traces the evolution of other strands of Populism into twentieth-century agrarian conservatism is Grant McConnell, *The Decline of Agrarian Democracy* (1953).

20

THE PUBLIC WORLD OF LATE NINETEENTH-CENTURY AMERICA

In times of national ferment, as a rule, public life becomes magnified. Leaders emerge. Electoral campaigns debate great issues. The powers of government expand. That had certainly been true of the Civil War era. The crises of Union and Reconstruction had tested to the utmost the nation's public institutions and resources. The transforming economic changes that followed Reconstruction did not bring a comparably large political response. As the sectional crisis lost its force during the 1870s, so did the nation's commitment to activist government. Political life went on, but was drained of its earlier potency. In the 1880s there were no Lincolns, no great national debates, and little exercise of state power. Public life was vigorous in other ways—highly organized and rife with cultural conflict—but not through the formal, governmental processes by which a nation confronts its central concerns.

The rule enunciated above—that great events call forth great politics—applied to the new industrial age, but with a lag in the political response. Eventually, enough social pressure built up to require government action. Equally important, industrialism made the United States—

whether or not the nation desired it—a world power. That change in itself was a political event. Both truths came home to the country during the 1890s. By the end of that decade, public life had taken on new meaning in America.

Domestic Politics

Late nineteenth-century America was richly endowed with brilliant political observers—James Bryce of Great Britain, Moisei Ostrogorski of Russia, and a young American political scientist named Woodrow Wilson. Unanimously, they deplored the politics they saw in post-Reconstruction America. "The conditions of public life in this country," wrote Wilson in his *Congressional Government* (1885), "are not what they were in the early years of the federal government; they are not what they were even twenty years ago. . . . Since [the Civil War] we . . . are perplexed at finding ourselves denied a new order of statesmanship to suit the altered conditions."

National Politics

The presidents of the period from 1877 to 1897 were estimable men. Rutherford B. Hayes (1877–1881), James A Garfield (1881), and Benjamin Harrison (1889–1893) all had distinguished war records. Hayes had served well as governor of Ohio for three terms, and Garfield as a congressional leader for many years. Chester A. Arthur (1881–1885), despite his cloudy reputation as a machine politician, had demonstrated fine administrative skills in heading the New York Custom House. Grover Cleveland (1885–1889 and 1893–1897), the only Democratic president of these years, had made his mark as reform mayor of Buffalo and governor of New York. None of these men was a strong or charismatic leader. Cleveland, the most aggressive and high principled, asserted himself in a largely negative way; he vetoed a record number of bills. But circumstances, more than their personal qualities, explain why these presidents did not make a larger mark on history.

The executive functions of the presidency did not amount to much in those days. As late as 1901, the White House staff consisted of three secretaries and half a dozen clerks, doorkeepers, and messengers. During the 1880s, the government departments were sleepy places carrying on largely routine duties. The civil service had mostly low-quality employees, and the diplomatic service received little attention. The army and navy handled mainly frontier duty and coastal patrol. The government was not responsible for social welfare, education, or economic regulation. So modest were its functions, in fact, that the government continually wound up with a financial surplus in the 1880s. The problem of how to reduce federal revenues ranked as one of the most troublesome issues of the decade.

The presidents spent much time dispensing political patronage through the spoils system, which gave public offices as rewards for party services. Civil service reform became a national issue after Charles Guiteau, a disappointed office seeker, assassinated President Garfield in 1881. The Pendleton Act of 1883 created a civil service list of jobs to be filled through examination by the new Civil Service Commission. The list originally included only 10 percent of all federal jobs. Each president added to it, generally at the close of his term in order to safeguard some of his appointees. But patronage remained a preoccupation in the White House. Cleveland groaned over the "damned, everlasting clatter for office." Benjamin Harrison spent four to six hours a day dealing with office seekers during the first eighteen months of his term.

The presidents took a back seat to Congress on national policy making. But they consistently defended the integrity of the presidency against congressional encroachment. This matter primarily involved appointments, over which Congress had asserted broad jurisdiction in the Tenure of Office Act of 1867 during the battle with President Johnson over Reconstruction policy. From

GROVER CLEVELAND

In the years after Reconstruction, Americans did not look for charismatic personalities or dramatic leadership in their presidents. They preferred men who accepted the limits of executive power, men of "sound conservatism." Grover Cleveland fitted this bill to perfection. For political reformers, Cleveland had the additional virtues of independence and personal integrity. Cleveland best represented the late nineteenth-century ideal of the American president. (Culver)

Rutherford B. Hayes on, each president of this era stubbornly held on to his appointive powers. Many fierce scraps developed with such congressional leaders as Senator Roscoe Conkling of New York until the Tenure Act was repealed in 1887. Nevertheless, the presidents had no thought of leading Congress on policy matters. The presidency, insisted Cleveland, was "essentially executive in nature." A good president ought to give efficient, honest service and veto measures that he considered ill advised or extravagant, as Cleveland regularly did with veterans' pension bills. Otherwise, policy making should be left to Congress. Scarcely any important legislation originated in the White House during these years.

American government, complained Professor Woodrow Wilson of Princeton University in 1885, was congressional government. But Congress was not well set up to do its work. In the House of Representatives, the rules had grown so complicated and numerous that they frequently brought business to a standstill. In neither the House nor the Senate could the party leadership exert discipline over the members. Nor did either party ever stay in power long enough to design or push through a legislative program. From 1877 to 1893, neither Democrats nor Republicans controlled both houses for more than a single congressional term. Most of the time, the Democrats controlled the House, the Republicans the Senate. Consequently, the ability of Congress to take forceful action was extremely limited.

The major parties, for their part, had little stomach for strong programmatic positions. Historically, they represented somewhat different traditions—the Democrats favoring states' rights and limited government, the Republicans supporting government encouragement of economic development. But after Reconstruction, neither party was eager to translate these differences into well-defined positions. On most leading national issues of the day—civil service reform, the currency, and regulation of the railroads and trusts—the divisions occurred within the parties, not between them. The laws that resulted could not be clearly identified as either Democratic or Republican legislation.

The tariff was something of an exception. After the Republicans came to power in 1861, they had increased tariffs, and the protective walls remained high for the next half century. It was an article of Republican faith, as President Harrison said in 1892, that "the protective system . . . has been a mighty instrument for the development of the national wealth and for protecting the home of the workingman from the invasion of want." The Democrats, free traders by tradition, regularly attacked Republican protectionism.

Actually, however, the parties disagreed only about the degree of protection. More important, congressmen voted their own local interests on tariffs, regardless of party rhetoric. All tariff bills consisted of patchworks of many bargains among special interests. In 1887, President Cleveland made a mighty effort to sharpen the battle. He devoted his entire annual message to Congress to tariff reform. Then he made tariffs the issue of his 1888 campaign for reelection. His narrow defeat seemed to confirm the political wisdom of evading big issues. "They told me it would hurt the party," he later wrote. "Perhaps I made a mistake from the party standpoint; but damn it, it was right. I had at least that satisfaction."

The major parties treated issues gingerly partly because they feared each other. The Democrats, in retreat immediately after the Civil War, quickly regrouped and, by the end of Reconstruction, stood on virtually equal terms with the Republicans. Every presidential election from 1876 to 1892 was decided by a thin margin, and neither party gained commanding control over Congress. Political caution seemed wise; any false move on national issues might tip the balance to the other side.

James Bryce, accustomed to philosophical divisions between English Tories and Liberals, grumbled about the indistinctness of American politics. "Neither party has any principles, any distinctive tenets," he wrote in his classic *American Commonwealth* (1888). Perhaps Lord Bryce exaggerated when he added, "All has been lost, except office or the hope of it." But electoral success had unquestionably taken precedence over party principle. This was evident particularly in the way the Republican party treated its Civil

War legacy. The major unfinished business was black rights in the South. Republicans gave lip service to the Blair Education Bill, appropriating federal funds to combat illiteracy, and the Lodge Election Bill, providing federal supervision for southern congressional elections, but let both pro-black measures die in 1890. The Republican administrations, more interested in building white support in the South, backpedaled on the race issue and gradually abandoned the blacks to their fate.

The Republicans were not so willing to abandon their identification with the Civil War itself. In every election campaign until the 1890s, Republican orators "waved the bloody shirt" against the "treasonous" Democrats. People considered service in the Union army to be the best claim for public office. One third of the Republican congressmen of the 1880s had a war record, and veterans' benefits always stood high on the Republican agenda. The Democrats played the same game in the South as the defenders of the Lost Cause. Bryce criticized American politicians for "clinging too long to outworn issues and . . . neglecting . . . the problems which now perplex the country."

The campaigns were not, in fact, intended to address those problems. The main thing was to avoid making too clear a statement on any issue of real controversy. After speaking in the 1880 campaign, James Garfield often confided in his diary, "I think no harm has been done." The personal reputations of the candidates overshadowed everything else in the hard-fought election of 1884. Was it more important that Grover Cleveland, a man of impeccable public honor, had years earlier fathered an illegitimate child? Or that James G. Blaine, perhaps the most gifted Republican of his generation, had taken favors from the railroads? In the midst of all the mudslinging, the issues got lost.

The issues did not, on the whole, absorb the politicians of the 1880s. The Republicans fought bitterly among themselves after President Grant left the White House in 1877. For the next six years, the party was divided into two clashing factions—the Stalwarts, who followed Senator Roscoe Conkling of New York, and the Halfbreeds, led by Representative Blaine of Maine. The split resulted from a personal feud between Conkling and Blaine, and it lasted because of a furious struggle over patronage. The Halfbreeds represented a newer Republican generation, more inclined to give lip service to political reform and less committed to the old Civil War issues. But principle actually had litle to do with the war between Stalwarts and Halfbreeds.

Although standards of conduct rose after the Grant years, a backroom atmosphere continued to pervade Gilded-Age politics. Congressmen

THE REPUBLICAN CONVENTION IN UPROAR
At the 1880 Republican convention in Chicago, the Stalwarts blocked Blaine, the Halfbreeds blocked Grant, and Garfield carried off the nomination. To placate the Stalwarts, one of their own—Chester A. Arthur of New York—was nominated as vice president. Garfield won the election but was shot on July 2, 1881 by a demented office-seeker, Charles Guiteau, who shouted: "I am a Stalwart and Arthur is President!" Guiteau was a madman, but he was prompted by the same emotions that had excited the convention—not over policy, but over control of the party, and the spoils that came with it. (From *Harper's Weekly*. The Newberry Library, Chicago)

still openly accepted railroad passes, took gifts and favors from the lobbyists swarming around Capitol Hill, and engaged routinely in private business activities that conflicted with their legislative responsibilities. "A remarkable nonchalance underlies the sound and fury of partisan politics," observed Henry Jones Ford the journalist.

The characteristics of public life in the 1880s—the inactivity of the federal government, the evasiveness of both political parties, and the absorption in politics for its own sake—came from the conviction that little was at stake in public affairs. Both parties shared a deep suspicion of activist government. In 1887, President Cleveland vetoed a small appropriation for drought-stricken Texas farmers with the remark that "though the people support the Government, the Government should not support the people." Government activity was in itself considered a bad thing. All that the state can do, said Senator Conkling, "is to clear the way of impediments and dangers, and leave every class and every individual free and safe in the exertions and pursuits of life. . . . Wealth can never be conjured out of the crucible of politics." Conkling was expressing the doctrine of laissez faire, which reigned supreme in late nineetenth-century America.

The Ideology of Individualism

In 1885, the cotton manufacturer Edward Atkinson gave a talk to the restless textile workers of Providence, Rhode Island. They had, he told them, no cause for discontent. "There is always plenty of room on the front seats in every profession, every trade, every art, every industry," Atkinson declared. "There are men in this audience who will fill some of those seats, but they won't be boosted into them from behind." Every man, he added, gets what he deserves. For example, Cornelius Vanderbilt had amassed a fortune of $200 million by building the New York Central Railroad. Atkinson went through some rapid calculations. Every person in the audience consumed about a barrel of flour a year. In 1865, it had cost $3.45 to ship that barrel from Chicago to Providence. In 1885, the New York Central carried it for 68 cents, taking 14 cents as profit,

while the workingman saved nearly $3. "Wasn't Vanderbilt a cheap man for you to employ as a teamster?" Atkinson asked. "Do you grudge him the fourteen cents?"

Atkinson's homely talk went to the roots of conservative American thought—that any man, however humble, could rise as far as his talents would carry him; that everyone received his just reward, great or small; and that the success of the individual contributed to the progress of the whole. This message appeared in a wide variety of writings, from the rags-to-riches tales of Horatio Alger to the stream of success manuals with such titles as *Thoughts for the Young Men of America, or a Few Practical Words of Advice to those Born in Poverty and Destined to be Reared in Orphanages* (1871). It was a lesson celebrated in the lives of such self-made men as Andrew Carnegie, whose book *Triumphant Democracy* (1886) paid homage to a nation in which a penniless Scottish child could rise from bobbin boy to steel magnate.

From the pulpit came the assurances of Bishop William Lawrence of Massachusetts that "Godliness is in league with riches." American Protestantism closely linked one's earthly calling and eternal salvation. This link enabled a conservative ministry to make morally reassuring the furious acquisitiveness of industrial America. "To secure wealth is an honorable ambition," intoned the Baptist minister Russell H. Conwell in his lecture "Acres of Diamonds," which became phenomenally popular. "Money is power. Every good man and woman ought to strive for power, to do good with it when obtained." Carnegie elevated this notion of stewardship into a formal doctrine that he called "the gospel of wealth," the responsibility of the rich to put their wealth to good social use. This should be done not by coddling the less privileged, Carnegie noted, but by providing the libraries, education, and cultural and scientific institutions by which they might prepare themselves for life's challenges.

The intellectual base of American individualism had long rested on classical economics. This economic theory, launched by the British economist Adam Smith in *The Wealth of Nations* (1776), postulated a self-regulating, competitive economy. Classical economics was fading as an intellectual formulation though it was still preached in classrooms, on editorial pages, and from lecture platforms. Relying on unproven principles, it seemed increasingly sterile and more a dogma than a theory that invited research.

The defense of individualism fell increasingly to a sociological theory more in keeping with the scientific spirit of the age. In his great book *The Origin of Species* (1859), the English naturalist Charles R. Darwin presented a theory to explain the evolution of plants and animals. In nature, Darwin wrote, all living things struggle and compete. Individual members of a species are born with certain characteristics that better enable them to survive. Future generations inherit these characteristics, and the species evolves.

This process, which Darwin called natural selection, created a revolution in biological science. It also had profound social implications. The British philosopher Herbert Spencer proposed the theory of Social Darwinism. He developed an elaborate analysis of how society evolves through constant competition among its members. In America, William Graham Sumner, a Yale sociology professor, became the leading exponent of Social Darwinism. Competition, said Sumner, is a law of nature that "can no more be done away with than gravitation." Furthermore, "if we do not like the survival of the fittest, we have only one possible alternative, and that is the survival of the unfittest. The former is the law of civilization; the latter is the law of anti-civilization." Who are the fittest? "The millionaires. . . . They may fairly be regarded as the naturally selected agents of society. They get high wages and live in luxury, but the bargain is a good one for society."

The political meaning of Social Darwinism was clear and convincing. As Sumner put it, "Minimize to the utmost the relations of the state and industry." Social Darwinism also inculcated deep belief in social determinism. "The great stream of time and earthly things will sweep on just the same in spite of us," Sumner wrote in his famous essay "The Absurd Attempt to Make the World Over" (1894). "That is why it is the greatest folly of which a man can be capable to sit down with a slate and pencil to plan out a new social world." As for the government, it had "at bottom . . . two chief things . . . with which to deal. They are the property of men and the honor of women. These it has to defend against crime."

This antigovernment appeal not only paralyzed political initiative. It also shifted the governmental balance away from the executive and legislative branches. "The task of constitutional government," declared Sumner, "is to devise institutions which shall come into play at critical periods to prevent the abusive control of the powers of a state by the controlling classes in it." Sumner meant the judiciary. From the 1870s on, the courts increasingly took the role that he assigned to them. During this period, judicial attack was directed mainly against legislative activism by the states. The number of decisions striking down state social welfare and regulatory laws rose markedly in the 1880s and after. The Supreme Court's crucial weapon in this campaign was the Fourteenth Amendment (1868), which prohibited the states from depriving "any person of life, liberty, or property, without due process of law." This due-process clause, intended to protect the civil rights of the freed slaves, gradually became a tight restraint against state interference with economic and business activity. The Supreme Court erected similar barriers against the federal government through narrow interpretations of the Constitution. It ruled in 1895 that the power to regulate interstate commerce did not cover manufacturing and that the power to tax did not extend to personal incomes.

Judicial supremacy went far beyond these negative functions. At a time when electoral politics were hesitant and disreputable, the legal system filled the void in effective governance. When Congress took up the issue of economic regulation in the 1880s, it passed laws designed to let the courts define their precise meaning as well as enforce them. The Interstate Commerce Act of 1887 and the Sherman Antitrust Act of 1890 were little more than the shells of effective legislation. With increasing aggressiveness, the courts took over the shaping of public policy on economic affairs.

Power conferred status. The legal profession and the courts, not politics, attracted the ablest men and held the public's esteem. A Wisconsin judge boasted: "The bench symbolizes on earth the throne of divine justice. . . . Law in its highest sense is the will of God." Judicial supremacy reflected the low esteem to which American politics sank after Reconstruction.

Cultural Politics

Yet, for all its formal weakness, politics figured centrally in the nation's life. Proportionately more voters turned out in presidential elections from 1876 to 1896 than at any other time in American history. Party loyalty ran high, and voting swings rarely occurred from one election to the next. This loyalty extended to party membership. In 1880, a fourth of the Republican voters in New York City were dues-paying party members. National conventions attracted huge crowds. "The excitement, the mental and physical strains," remarked an Indiana Republican after the 1888 convention, "are surpassed only by prolonged battle in actual warfare, as I have been told by officers of the Civil War who later engaged in convention struggles." The convention he described had nominated the colorless Benjamin Harrison on a routine platform. What was all the excitement about? Why did politics mean so much to late nineteenth-century Americans?

For one thing, politics had a vibrant part in the nation's culture. American journalist George M. Towle told an English audience that America "is a land of conventions and assemblies, where it is the most natural thing in the world for people to get together in meetings, where almost every event is the occasion for speechmaking." Such orators as Robert G. Ingersoll, who delivered the soaring Republican nominating speech of 1876 in which James G. Blaine became the "Plumed Knight," drew enormous crowds at campaign meetings. During the election season, party paraphernalia flooded the country—handkerchiefs, mugs, posters, and buttons emblazoned with the Democratic donkey or the Republican elephant, symbols that had been adopted in the 1870s. In 1888, pictures of the twenty-five presidential hopefuls appeared on cards, like baseball players, packed into Honest Long Cut tobacco. The campaigns had the suspense of baseball pennant races, plus the excitement of the circus coming to town. In an age before movies and radio, politics ranked as one of the great American forms of mass entertainment.

Party loyalty was a deadly serious matter, however. The emotions of the Civil War lasted a long time in both North and South. The Ohio Republican party, recalled the urban reformer Brand Whitlock of his youth, was "a synonym for patriotism, another name for the nation. . . . It was inconceivable that any self-respecting person should be a Democrat." The two parties did, in fact, represent different sorts of people. Republicans prided themselves on being the respectable elements of northern society. Senator George F. Hoar of Massachusetts described Republicans as "the men who do the work of piety and charity in our churches . . . administer the school systems, own and till their own farms . . . perform the skilled labor in the shops." Class played a role, too. The more money a man had, the more likely he would vote Republican.

More important, however, were religion and ethnic background. The two parties drew on different ethnocultural sections of northern society. Statistically, Democrats tended to be foreign born and Catholic, Republicans native-born and Protestant. Among Protestants, the more pietistic the theology—that is, the more personal and direct the person's relationship to God—the more likely the Republican identification. In political terms, this translated into a party policy favorable to using the powers of the state to legislate public morality and regulate individual behavior. On the other hand, the Democrats favored "the largest individual liberty consistent with public order," as the state platform in Ohio put it.

During the 1880s, ethnocultural tensions began to build up in many cities. Education became an arena of bitter conflict. One issue concerned the place of foreign languages in schools. Immigrant groups, especially the Germans, wanted their children taught in their own language. However, native-born Americans pushed through laws making English the language of instruction. In Saint Louis, a heavily German city, a fight developed over whether the teaching of German should continue to be compulsory for all students.

Religion was an even more divisive school issue. Reading from the Protestant Bible in school angered Catholics. They also fought a losing battle over public aid for parochial schools. By 1900, such aid had been prohibited by twenty-three states. In Boston, a furious controversy broke out in 1888 over the use of an anti-Catholic history text. After the school board withdrew the offending book, angry Protestants mounted a

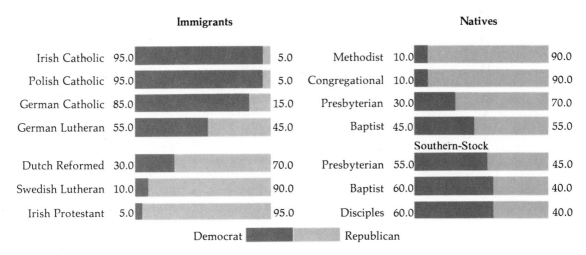

Immigrants			Natives		
Irish Catholic	95.0	5.0	Methodist	10.0	90.0
Polish Catholic	95.0	5.0	Congregational	10.0	90.0
German Catholic	85.0	15.0	Presbyterian	30.0	70.0
German Lutheran	55.0	45.0	Baptist	45.0	55.0

Southern-Stock

Immigrants			Southern-Stock		
Dutch Reformed	30.0	70.0	Presbyterian	55.0	45.0
Swedish Lutheran	10.0	90.0	Baptist	60.0	40.0
Irish Protestant	5.0	95.0	Disciples	60.0	40.0

Democrat   Republican

FIGURE 20.1 MIDWESTERN ETHNOCULTURAL VOTING PATTERNS, 1870–1892

drive, threw the moderates off the board, and put the text back into the curriculum.

Similar tensions developed over the regulation of public morals. Evangelical Protestants renewed their efforts to enact and enforce Sunday blue laws. The Nebraska Supreme Court approved a ban on Sunday baseball as a blow struck in "the contest between Christianity and wrong." But German and Irish Catholics, who saw nothing evil in a glass of beer and a ball game on Sunday considered the ruling a blow against their personal freedom. The same kind of ethnocultural conflict flared in the liquor question. Upon introducing the first national prohibition amendment in 1876, Senator Henry W. Blair of New Hampshire declared: "Upon discussion of this issue Irishman and German will in due time demonstrate that they are Americans." Although the Blair amendment languished, the antiliquor movement intensified. The Women's Christian Temperance Union, formed in 1874, became a powerful force throughout the country. Many states adopted strict licensing and local option laws governing the sale and consumption of alcoholic beverages. Indiana permitted drinking, but only joylessly in rooms containing "no devices for amusement or music . . . of any kind."

All these issues—education, temperance, and observance of the Sabbath—were contested along ethnic and religious lines. Because they were also party issues—more so than tariffs,

CARRY NATION UNDER ARREST
Opponents of alcohol had traditionally advocated temperance; that is, self restraint. The Women's Christian Temperance Union took a more coercive approach. It demanded legal prohibition of alcohol. Some prohibitionists turned to direct action. Carry Nation became famous for her ax-wielding attacks on saloons. She meant to draw attention to the struggle, and so gladly went to jail—where she is headed in this photograph, taken in Enterprise, Kansas in 1901. (Kansas State Historical Society)

currency, or civil service reform—they gave deep significance to party affiliation. Crusading Methodists thought of Republicans as the party of morality. For embattled Irish or German Catholics, the Democratic party was the defender of their freedom. Fought out mostly at the state and local levels, such ethnocultural issues as public education and the liquor question gave an importance to party politics that would have been scarcely apparent to anyone focusing exclusively on national elections.

Organizational Politics

Political life also was important because of the remarkable organizational activity that it generated. By this time each of the major parties had evolved a formal, well-articulated structure. At the base lay the precinct or ward, whose meetings could be attended by all party members. County, state, and national committees ran the ongoing business of the parties. Nominating conventions, corresponding to the electoral units of the state and federal systems, determined party rules, adopted platforms, and selected the party's candidates for public office.

At election time, the party functioned mainly to get out the vote. In the South, where a Democratic nomination was equivalent to election, little organized effort went into election day. As a result, fewer people voted than anywhere else in the country. In states or communities with hard-fought elections, however, the parties put on intensive efforts organized down to the individual voter. In Indiana, for example, the Republicans appointed ten thousand "district men" in 1884, each responsible for turning out a designated group of voters. The Pennsylvania Republican party maintained a list of eight hundred thousand voters, each classified according to his degree of voting reliability.

Only professionals could manage such a highly organized political system. The German sociologist Max Weber remarked that Americans regarded "politics as a vocation." This factor, above all else, gave American politics its special character. The distinguishing trait of American politicians, James Bryce observed, was "that their whole time is more frequently given to political work, that most of them draw an income from politics . . . that they . . . are proficient in the arts of popular oratory, of electioneering, and of party management." The party system required professionals, and professionalism created careers. Politics, like professional sports and trade unionism, served as an avenue of upward mobility for many who, because of ethnic or class background, had been barred from the more conventional opportunities of industrial America.

Party administration was, on the face of it, highly democratic. Representation emanated either directly, as in county committees and district conventions, or indirectly, as at the state and national levels, from the membership in wards and precincts. In practice, however, the professionals ran the parties. They did this through unofficial, internal organizations called machines, which consisted of insiders willing to accept discipline and do work in exchange for the rewards of patronage and/or graft. The machines tended toward one-man rule, though more of a consensual than of a dictatorial nature. Each state party had a "boss," such as, in New York during the 1890s, the Republican Thomas C. Platt and the Democrat David B. Hill. Sometimes the state leader held public office—the U.S. Senate was preferred because senators were selected by the state legislature. Therefore, the office lay directly in the hands of the parties. But public office was not necessary for the boss to do his job.

The organizational development of political parties had started in the 1820s with the first mass parties and had grown more refined through the years. Now the machine began to play a central role in city politics. It did so primarily in response to a crisis in city governance at a time of explosive urban growth. City governments, which had taken shape in a simpler age, consisted of an accumulation of unplanned, overlapping, highly decentralized jurisdictions. In some cities, each ward had its own school board and ran its own schools. Administration was a largely unknown art. At the same time, enormous responsibilities for services and construction passed to the cities. In an age of laissez faire, the city stood as a great exception; the importance of the public sector in the urban economy could not be denied. Also, the older governing elites—the merchants in most cases— lost their capacity to run things. Rapid urban growth multiplied the number and complexity of interest groups, ranging from businessmen to labor unions to a variety of ethnic and reform movements. These groups often found it impossible to agree on matters of urgent city business.

Into the breach stepped the party machines. They alone seemed capable of getting things done. In Cincinnati, George B. Cox's Republican machine was widely greeted as an answer to the problems of an increasingly ungovernable city. In New York City, the Tammany Hall machine came to life after many years of weakness following the Tweed Ring scandals of 1871. A party machine had two great strengths, its highly developed organization and its strategic location between the public and private sectors.

For immigrants and tenement dwellers, the machine acted as a rough-and-ready social service agency. It provided work for the jobless, a helping hand for a bereaved family, and intercession against an unfeeling city bureaucracy. As a Boston ward boss remarked, "There's got to be in every ward somebody that any bloke can come to—no matter what he's done—and get help. *Help, you understand; none of your law and justice, but help.*" The machine also served a similar function for a different clientele. Entrepreneurs of many kinds wanted something from the city. Contractors sought city business; gas companies and traction firms wanted licenses and privileges; manufacturers needed services and not-too-nosy inspectors; and the liquor trade and numbers racket relied on a tolerant police force. All of them went to the machine boss and his lieutenants. In addition to these daily functions, the machine continually mediated among conflicting interests and oiled the wheels of city government. It became an integral part of the urban order.

Of course, all these services of the machine exacted a price. The tenement dweller gave his vote. The businessman wrote a check. Those who became the machine's beneficiaries enabled it to function. There were additional costs as well, including corruption. The Tammany ward boss George Washington Plunkitt often insisted that he had no need for kickbacks and bribes. He favored what he called "honest graft," the easy profits that came to political insiders from sure-fire investments—for example, the purchase of a vacant lot soon to be needed for a city

project—and easy-term partnerships. One way or another, legal or otherwise, most machine politicians died fairly well off.

The machine's operations also affected the tone of party politics. Absorbed in the tasks of power brokerage, the machine boss tended to see issues as somewhat irrelevant. The influence of the machine system had a lot to do with the absence of strong programs in electoral politics.

And yet, the record was by no means wholly negative. For one thing, the machine system contained some means for its own reform. From an organizational perspective, corruption amounted to a form of inefficiency. As fund-raising operations became better regulated, the diversion of funds into private pockets largely ceased. Charles F. Murphy, the dour Tammany leader of the early twentieth century, was a far cry from Boss William M. Tweed, who ended his days in jail. The machine influence also raised the standards of government in certain ways. As seasoned machine politicians rose to higher office, their professionalism and party discipline measurably improved the performance of state legislatures and Congress. Above all, the party machines filled a void in the nation's public life. They did informally much of what the governmental system left undone. "Nowhere else in the world," observed Henry Jones Ford, "has party organization had to cope with such enormous tasks, . . . and its efficiency in dealing with them is the true glory of our political system."

For all its effectiveness, machine politics never managed to win public legitimacy. The social elite of the cities—professionals, intellectuals, well-to-do businessmen, and old-line families—deeply resented politics that left little room for public service by the "best men." There was, too, a genuine clash of values. For political reformers the operative terms were "disinterestedness" and "independence"—the opposite of the self-serving careerism and the party regularity fostered by the machine system.

In 1884, this public-spirited elite split from the Republican party because they could not stomach its presidential candidate, James G. Blaine, whom they associated with corrupt party politics. Spurred by their efforts for Grover Cleveland, the Mugwumps, as they became known, grew into something of a national movement,

ROBERT A. WOODS: A BOSTONIAN'S VIEW OF WARD POLITICS, 1898

There are usually in the tenement-house sections several distinctly political clubs. Standing at the head of these clubs is the "machine club." It is now quite the custom of those in control of the party, and known as the "machine," to have such an organization. All the men in the ward having good political jobs are members. It is a question of bread and butter with them. In addition to City employees the various machine workers are enrolled. The room of the club is ordinarily very pleasant. There are, of course, in these clubs the usual social attractions, among other things poker and drinking. At the head of the club stands the boss of the ward.

One of the bosses whom the writer knows is fairly typical. He is considered the "prince of jolliers," on account of his alluring ways. He has for many years been in public office of one kind or another. His early opportunities were small. His native abilities, however, enable him to fulfill his official duties with real effectiveness—when political business does not interfere. The politician must provide something with which to feed his hungry followers. The jobs that he tries to get for his followers, however, are not secured as the private employer seeks men—for efficiency. The motive of the boss in seeking favors from the City government is to satisfy claims against him and to maintain himself.

On the whole, partly for the love of position and power, and partly from a good heart, the boss enjoys doing good turns for men. Stories are told by his admirers of his generous deeds. For instance, he has been known to pay the funeral expenses of poor people who have no insurance. At Christmas time and Thanksgiving he gives turkeys to certain needy families. This all sounds very generous; but the chief admirers of the boss cannot deny that when the supremacy in the ward is at all endangered, he makes capital of all his good deeds. In other words, every man to whom he has granted a favor is made to feel that the boss expects a vote.

Votes are his business—they mean money, power. The boss can never be a disinterested member of society. He is forced to make men act and vote with him,—the weaker their wills, the fewer their convictions, the better for him. He gives another drink to the drunkard: he has a vote. The only morality he seeks in men is loyalty to him. The merit system he regards always with a horror and indignation which would be amusing if it were not so serious. . . .

There are certain lesser figures characteristic of ward politics known as "heelers." They do the dirty work. As a rule, they prefer to serve the well-established boss, as he can best protect them if they are found out and prosecuted in the execution of their villainy. As a rule, a "heeler" is a broken-down "bum," afraid of work, fond of his cups, in touch with loafers and the semi-criminal class, more of a fox than they, energetic enough in a campaign, possessed of a strong dramatic sense, loving the excitement of ward politics with its dark plots and wire pulling, glad to be lifted into temporary importance by having money to spend on the "boys."

In analyzing ward politics, it is necessary to understand something of the morale of the various groups of voters. As to race complexion, in the local wards the Irish voters prevail. Next in number are the Jews. There is a good sprinkling of "Yankees," a term which for political purposes includes the British element. Foreigners other than those mentioned do not cut much of a figure in politics. It goes without saying that the greatest degree of political activity is found among the Irish. The Jews, however, are commencing to take considerable interest in politics. There seems to be a special antipathy ordinarily on the part of the Irish for the Jews. Not so with the Irish politician. He solves the race problem in short order. He fraternizes with the Jew, eats with the Jew, drinks with the Jew, and dickers with him in politics. . . .

In noting the various classes of voters in these wards, it is also necessary to keep steadily in mind the large number of unemployed men. The few secure a job; the many get promises. Those who get jobs are the slaves of the boss. According to the ethics of the district, a man who receives a job is under the most sacred obligations to the politician who bestowed it. The lack of employment, therefore, is one of the most important factors working in the interest of the boss and boss rule.

spawning good-government campaigns across the country. Although they scored some municipal victories, the Mugwumps achieved greater importance as the nation's opinion molders. They controlled the respectable newspapers and journals and occupied a strategic place in the urban world.

Most of all, the Mugwumps defined the terms of political debate. They stressed not the usefulness of the machine system, but its violation of American political values. The potency of their attack helped win their campaign for the Australian secret ballot. This reform, adopted throughout the United States in the early 1890s, eliminated the means by which the parties kept tabs on voters. Instead of submitting a party-supplied ticket at the polling place, citizens now chose candidates on an official ballot in the privacy of a voting booth.

The Mugwumps injected an elitist bias into respectable political thinking. Mark Twain was not alone in proclaiming "an honest and saving loathing for universal suffrage." Corrupt politics, remarked another writer in 1897, seemed to arise from "the ignorance and corruption of the people, and therefore . . . a growing class in America desires to restrict the suffrage, to have less frequent elections to take power from the people." In the South, such reform thinking rationalized the disfranchisement of blacks. Elsewhere, antidemocratic sentiment had a less decisive though widely felt impact. The expansion of suffrage, which had been going on for half a century, went into reverse after the 1870s as northern states began to impose literacy tests and restrict alien voting rights.

The Republican Ascendancy

The Mugwump bible was *The American Commonwealth*. In that book, Lord Bryce deplored the absence of serious debate in American national life. A basic political fact that inhibited debate between the parties was their evenly balanced strength. In the late 1880s, that stalemate began to break down, at first in favor of the Democrats. Their support within the immigrant populations of key northern states strengthened as ethnocultural tensions intensified, especially over the liquor question. This issue also drew Republican votes into the Prohibition party and forced the Republicans to compete by taking a harder line on liquor and other ethnocultural issues.

In the 1890 elections, the number of Democrats in the House of Representatives jumped from 159 to 235. Democrats also won state offices in Pennsylvania, Massachusetts, and other normally Republican states. Two years later, Grover Cleveland, who had lost his bid for reelection in 1888, regained the presidency.

But then the Panic of 1893 hit, and the pendulum swung toward the Republicans. The party in power usually gets blamed if the economy falters, but Cleveland compounded the costs to the Democratic party. Although farmers were suffering terribly from deflated prices, Cleveland adhered to his defense of the gold standard. The Republicans had passed the highly protectionist McKinley tariff in 1890. But Cleveland could not deliver on his campaign promise of tariff reduction. The Wilson-Gorman Tariff of 1894, which he let go into law without his signature, caved in to special interests and cut average tariff rates only slightly.

The president had no answer for the jobless except a call for law and order. His response to the unemployed who came to Washington pleading for federal relief under the leadership of Jacob S. Coxey was to arrest Coxey and to disperse his followers. In July, when the Pullman strike turned into a national railway walkout, Cleveland called out federal troops to crush the strikers. His record did little to reassure a nation in the throes of a terrible depression.

The result was a Democratic disaster in the 1894 elections. The party lost nearly a third of its congressional seats and suffered severe setbacks in the states. A sweeping political realignment was in the making.

The catalyst was the money question, by far the most explosive economic issue of the late nineteenth century. The economy had suffered from deflationary pressures ever since the Civil War. The wholesale price index went steadily downward. It was 30 percent lower in 1880 than in 1870, nearly 20 percent lower in 1890 than in 1880. The favored solution by those who felt injured by this persistent deflation of prices—especially debtors, users of imported goods, those generally lacking in market power—was to increase the money supply. But many Americans considered it unwise, even immoral, to tamper

COXEY'S ARMY
During the winter of 1893–1894, with unemployment at more than 18 percent, desperate workers began to demand public relief. An Ohio labor reformer, Jacob S. Coxey, called them to march on Washington to present their grievances to Congress. When "Coxey's Army" reached Washington in April 1894, police dispersed the few hundred demonstrators and arrested Coxey for trespassing on the Capitol lawn. (The Bettmann Archive)

with the currency. The stability of the economic order, they thought, depended on "sound" money.

The battle was fought first, in the decade after the Civil War, over the greenback issue. The Lincoln administration had helped finance the war by printing paper notes, or greenbacks. After the war, sound money men, dominant in both parties, moved to retire some of the greenbacks and back the rest with specie, that is, to make the paper money exchangeable for gold from the U.S. Treasury. Despite strong opposition, this policy prevailed, and went fully into effect in 1879. The money fight then shifted to the free coinage of silver. If the United States would return to the bimetallic standard (which it had abandoned in 1873), and if the Treasury would accept all silver offered at the old ratio of sixteen to one with gold, the volume of currency would balloon overnight, and the nation's deflation would be reversed.

Until the 1890s, the battle between inflationists and sound money men had cut across party lines. Under the pressure of the economic depression, the money question became a more clear-cut partisan issue.

Within the Democratic party, the silver wing gained strength. President Cleveland, though a determined sound-money advocate, had difficulty maintaining the gold standard in the face of mounting pressures on U.S. gold reserves. In 1893, at Cleveland's urgent behest, Congress repealed the Sherman Silver Purchase Act of 1890. This action canceled a hard-won concession to the silver interests for monthly public purchases of a limited amount of silver at prevailing market rates. In 1895, as his administration's difficulties deepened, Cleveland turned to a syndicate of private bankers led by J. P. Morgan to finance gold purchases needed to replenish the Treasury's depleted gold reserves. The administration's secret negotiations with Wall Street, once discovered, raised a furor among Democrats.

Free silver also attracted the Democrats because of the challenge posed by the Populist party. Normally, third parties serve to define issues, not to contend seriously for political power. But as the 1896 elections approached, the Populists appeared to be making a real challenge. They had taken up the free-silver issue in hope of broadening their appeal beyond the limited areas of their strength among the distressed farmers of the South and West. With the growing popular support for free silver, they had a chance; but the silver Democrats intended to beat them to the punch.

In 1896, at their national convention in Chicago, the Democrats repudiated Cleveland and the gold standard. The leader of the triumphant silver Democrats was William Jennings Bryan, a

LAWYERS MARCH FOR THE GOLD STANDARD
Presidential campaigns of the late nineteenth century
were always hard-fought. In 1896, big issues were at
stake. Would the country stay on the gold standard, or
dramatically increase the money supply through the free
coinage of silver? Lawyers paraded in the streets of New
York City to demonstrate their conviction that the
nation's fate hung on "sound money" and on the election
of the Republican William McKinley. (The New-York
Historical Society)

Nebraska congressman. Only thirty-six years old
and not yet a national figure, Bryan was already
a consummate politician. He had quietly been
building up delegate support while keeping a
distance between himself and convention poli-
ticking. Bryan probably had the presidential
nomination locked up even before he electrified
the convention with his stirring attack on the
gold standard: "You shall not press down upon
the brow of labor this crown of thorns, you shall
not crucify mankind upon a cross of gold."
Bryan's nomination meant that the Democrats
had identified themselves as the party of free silver; his "cross of gold" speech meant he would
turn the money question into a national crusade.

The Republicans took up the challenge. Their
key party figure was Mark Hanna, a wealthy

Cleveland ironmaker, a brilliant political manager, and an exponent of the new industrial capitalism. Hanna's candidate, Ohio congressman
William McKinley, personified the virtues of Republicanism, standing solidly for prosperity,
protection, and honest money. While Bryan
broke with tradition and criss-crossed the country in a furious whistle-stop campaign, the dignified McKinley received delegations at his home
in Canton, Ohio. As Bryan orated with passionate moral fervor, McKinley talked of industrial
progress and a full dinner pail.

The Republicans, beating a strategic retreat
from the politics of morality, aimed to escape the
ethnocultural issues that had hurt their popularity just before the depression. McKinley himself
represented a mixed district in northeastern
Ohio. In appealing to his immigrant and working-class constituents, he had learned the art of
easy tolerance, as expressed in his phrase, "live
and let live." Of the two candidates, the prairie
orator Bryan, with his Christian rhetoric and
moral righteousness, presented a more alien image to traditional Democratic voters in the big
cities.

No election since Reconstruction had evoked

WILLIAM JENNINGS BRYAN
Already a polished campaigner at 36, William Jennings
Bryan (1860–1925) took his free silver crusade across the
country, speaking at every whistlestop to crowds of
voters. Bryan's campaign style was exuberant and
forceful. Here he strides, beaming confidently, to the
speaker's platform at a Democratic rally in California.
(American Heritage)

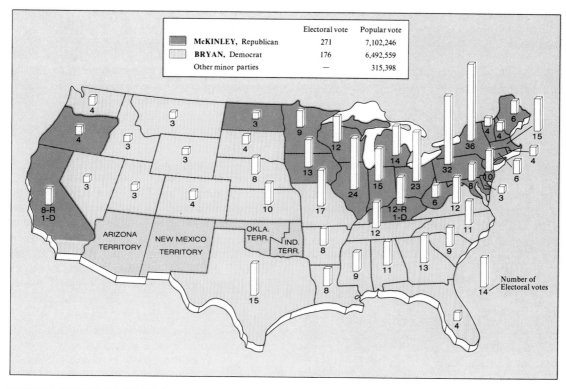

	Electoral vote	Popular vote
McKINLEY, Republican	271	7,102,246
BRYAN, Democrat	176	6,492,559
Other minor parties	—	315,398

MAP 20.1 ELECTION OF 1896

The 1896 election was one of the decisive elections in American political history. Not only did the Republican party win by its largest popular margin since 1872, but it also established a firm grip on the key midwestern and middle Atlantic states—especially New York, Indiana, Ohio and Illinois—the decisive states for all the elections since Reconstruction. The 1896 election broke a party stalemate of twenty years duration, and began a period of Republican dominance that lasted until 1932.

such a sharp division over issues. The gold Democrats bolted to a splinter Democratic ticket or supported McKinley; silver Republicans went over to the Democrats. The Populists, meeting after the Democratic convention, accepted Bryan as their candidate. The free-silver issue had become so vital that they could not do otherwise. For all practical purposes, despite their best efforts, the Populists found themselves absorbed into the Democratic silver crusade.

Not since 1860 did the United States have such a hard-fought election, and over stakes that loomed so high. The nation's currency had exceptional social significance in American life. For the middle class, sound money meant the soundness of the social order. Now, with workers tramping the streets and farmers up in arms, Bryan's fervent assault on the gold standard struck fear in many hearts. Republicans de-

nounced the Democratic platform as "revolutionary and anarchistic." They called Bryan's supporters "social misfits who have almost nothing in common but opposition to the existing order and institutions." The formidable party machinery was pumped up to the limit. Contributions flowed from businessmen in record amounts. Hanna's network kept close tabs on the race in every state; and about fourteen hundred Republican orators went out on the hustings. The political debate reached a level of intensity and significance unequaled since the days of the Lincoln-Douglas debates.

McKinley won handily with 271 electoral votes to 176 for Bryan. He kept the Republican ground that had been won in 1894 and also pushed into Democratic strongholds, especially in the cities. Boston, New York, Chicago, and Minneapolis, all taken by Cleveland in 1892, went for McKinley in 1896. Bryan ran strongly only in the South, in silver-mining states, and in the Populist West. The gains his evangelical style brought him in some Republican rural areas fell far short of what he lost in traditionally Democratic urban districts.

The paralyzing equilibrium of American politics ended in 1896, and the Republicans emerged as the majority party. They accomplished the victory by exploiting both the economic and cultural aspects of party allegiance. The Republicans persuaded the nation that they were the party of prosperity and they reduced their burden of being the party of morality. In 1896, too, electoral politics regained its place as an arena for national debate. The silver question quickly subsided; other issues such as social reform and the trusts lay ahead.

An Emerging World Power

"A policy of isolation did well enough when we were an embryo nation," remarked Senator Orville Platt of Connecticut at the beginning of the 1890s. "But today things are different. . . . We are 65 million people, the most advanced and powerful on earth, and regard to our future welfare demands an abandonment of the doctrines of isolation." Platt had his facts right. The United States had become the equal, by any population or economic measure, of the greatest world powers of the late nineteenth century. He also concluded correctly that the nation would move into the world arena. Equally significant, however, was the senator's need to make the case for a more vigorous international role. Americans were slow to shed their identity as an "embryo nation." Not many of them agreed with Platt's call for "an abandonment of the doctrines of isolation."

The Roots of Expansionism

For almost a century after George Washington's farewell address, the United States followed his advice against involvement in permanent alliances with foreign powers. The westward push of Americans across the continent had brought the nation into periodic conflict with other powers, and so did the Civil War. But to a remarkable degree, the development of the United States went ahead in isolation. Geography helped. Wide oceans kept the world at a distance. Relying on British naval supremacy to maintain freedom of the seas, the United States let its navy rot away after the Civil War. Nor did any European conflicts entangle the United States as had happened during the Napoleonic era. The balance of power, erected at the Congress of Vienna in 1815, held firm for almost a hundred years.

The European powers of the nineteenth century expressed their national prowess primarily through empire building. This activity did not tempt the United States. Even so ardent an American nationalist as the young Theodore Roosevelt saw the folly of overseas expansion. "We want no unwilling citizens to enter our Union," he wrote in 1886. "European nations war for the possession of thickly settled districts which, if conquered, will for centuries remain alien and hostile to the conquerers; we, wiser in our generation, have seized the waste solitudes that lay near us."

Some Americans, few in number but well placed, took the opposite view. William H. Seward, secretary of state under Presidents Lincoln and Johnson, dreamed of an American empire, perhaps with a capital in Mexico, that extended into South America and across the Pacific to Asia. President Grant had been an eager, if less grandiose, expansionist. His successors lacked Grant's enthusiasm, but some kind of scheming was always afoot, especially in the State Department, for overseas projects.

Little came of it, however. Seward's only notable success was the purchase from Russia of Alaska in 1867. Grant's strongest efforts could not persuade the Senate to purchase Santo Domingo in 1870, and later moves to acquire bases in Haiti, Cuba, and Venezuela were also blocked. So were repeated efforts to gain approval for construction of a canal across Central America to link the Atlantic and Pacific oceans. However, the United States strongly opposed any foreign undertaking of such a project; no canal would be tolerated unless under American control. The Monroe Doctrine, which declared the Western Hemisphere off limits to European expansionism, played a big role in the thinking of James G. Blaine, secretary of state briefly in 1881 and later under President Benjamin Harrison from 1889 to 1892. Blaine was an avid Pan-

Americanist, a believer in closer ties among the nations of the Western Hemisphere. The Washington Conference of 1889, held at his instigation, called for economic cooperation and reciprocal trade and set up an agency that became the Pan-American Union.

In the Pacific, American interest centered on Hawaii. American missionaries had long been active among the natives on the islands. With a climate ideal for raising sugar cane, Hawaii also attracted many American planters and investors. Nominally an independent nation, Hawaii fell increasingly within the American orbit. In 1875, a treaty of commercial reciprocity declared that no Hawaiian territory could be ceded to a third power. A second treaty in 1887 added U.S. naval rights at Pearl Harbor.

Having encouraged the sugar economy in Hawaii, the United States withdrew Hawaii's trading advantages in the McKinley Tariff of 1890. All foreign sugar could now enter the United States duty free, while domestic producers received a special subsidy to compensate for the drop in sugar prices. Anxious to gain that benefit, American planters in Hawaii began to plot for annexation to the United States. Aided by the U.S. minister to Hawaii, they revolted in January 1893 against Queen Liliuokalani, who had begun to reassert native control over the islands. Before annexation could be approved by the Senate, Grover Cleveland returned to the presidency. Following an investigation of the Hawaiian episode, he withdrew the treaty. To annex Hawaii, he declared, would violate both America's "honor and morality" and its "unbroken tradition" against acquiring territory far from the nation's shores.

By the 1890s, however, the anticolonial tradition encountered powerful crosscurrents. One source of expansionist thinking was Social Darwinism. If animals and plants evolved through the survival of the fittest, so did nations. "Nothing under the sun is stationary," warned the American historian Brooks Adams in *The Law of Civilization and Decay* (1895). "Not to advance is to recede." By this criterion, the United States had no choice; if it wanted to survive, it had to expand.

Linked to Social Darwinism was a spreading belief in racial inequality. On both sides of the Atlantic, Anglo-Saxonism had come into great vogue, proclaiming the English-speaking "race"

inherently superior. John Fiske, an American philosopher and historian, popularized Social Darwinism and Anglo-Saxonism by lecturing the nation on its future responsibilities. "The work which the English race began when it colonized North America," Fiske declared, "is destined to go on until every land on the earth's surface that is not already the seat of an old civilization shall become English in its language, in its religion, in its political habits, and to a predominant extent in the blood of its people."

Fiske entitled his famous lecture "Manifest Destiny." He revived the notion that had justified the nation's thrust across the continent half a century earlier. Now, in the 1890s, with the frontier officially declared at an end, Manifest Destiny turned outward. The young historian Frederick Jackson Turner suggested as much in his landmark essay "The Significance of the Frontier in American History" (1893). "He would be a rash prophet who should assert that the expansive character of American life has now entirely ceased," Turner wrote. "Movement has been its dominant fact, and, unless this training has no effect upon a people, the American energy will continually demand a wider field for its exercise." A strong current of ideas, deep-rooted in American experience and ideology, had set the nation on a course of overseas expansion.

Economic forces did the same thing. The gross national product quadrupled between 1870 and 1900, and industrial output quintupled. As the economy burst ahead, so did American exports. In 1876, for the first time, the United States became a net exporter, initially because of the agricultural trade, but increasingly in manufacturing as well. Industrial exports exceeded industrial imports by 70 percent in 1900. Only about 7 percent of the national output left the country. Even so, the development of foreign markets loomed large in business thinking and became urgent once the panic of 1893 struck. Unlike farmers, who blamed the scarce money supply, industry attributed the depression to overproduction. Foreign markets seemed the only likely outlets for the American surplus.

In Europe, however, protectionist sentiment was rising. Even worse, markets elsewhere in the world were being closed off. European imperialism, which had slackened in the middle of the century, suddenly revived after 1880. The European powers carved up Africa and, along

FIGURE 20.2 BALANCE OF U.S. IMPORTS AND EXPORTS, 1870–1914

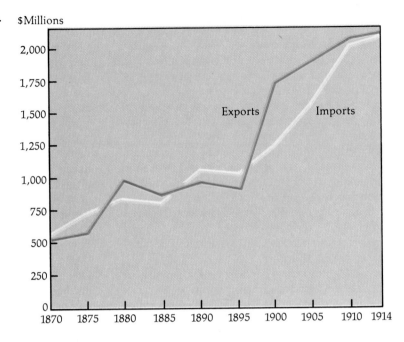

with Russia and Japan, pressed into China during the 1890s. As their navies grew, they posed a challenge to U.S. interests even in Latin America. These underdeveloped parts of the world seemed crucially important because they, not Europe, constituted the future consumers of American goods. The China market, above all, exerted a powerful hold on the American mercantile imagination. Many felt that the China trade, although actually negligible, would one day be the key to American prosperity. Therefore, the underdeveloped world must not be closed to the United States—and this, in turn, spelled overseas expansion.

"Whether they will or not, Americans must now begin to look outward. The growing production of the country requires it." So wrote Captain Alfred T. Mahan, America's leading naval strategist, in his book *The Influence of Seapower upon History* (1890). The United States should no longer regard the oceans as barriers, but as "a great highway . . . over which men pass in all directions." To traverse that highway required a merchant marine, which had fallen on hard times since its heyday in the 1850s, and a powerful navy to protect American commerce. "When a question arises of control over distant regions . . . it must ultimately be decided by naval power," Mahan advised. To sustain that navy and commerce, the United States needed strate-

gic overseas bases. Here technology played a part because, having converted to steam, navies required coaling stations distant from home. Otherwise, Mahan warned, warships were "like land birds, unable to fly far from their own shores."

Mahan called first of all for a canal across Central America to connect the Atlantic and Pacific oceans. Such a canal would enable the eastern United States to "compete with Europe, on equal terms as to distance, for the markets of East Asia." Guarding its approaches would require bases in the Caribbean Sea. It also would be necessary to annex Hawaii in order to extend American power into the Pacific, a step that Mahan called "natural, necessary, irrepressible." Mahan discriminated carefully between colonies as potential markets, and colonies as strategic bases necessary to gain access to markets. His interest lay strictly in the second kind, as did that of nearly all the economic expansionists of the 1890s. They sought strategic territory by which American power could be asserted where Americans wanted to trade rather than extensive colonies of the European type.

Mahan's thinking struck a resonant chord among other great-power exponents. They included navy men, diplomats, publishers like Whitelaw Reid of the *New York Tribune,* and such young politicians as Theodore Roosevelt of New

York and Senator Henry Cabot Lodge of Massachusetts. The influence of these men, few in number but strategically placed, increased during the 1890s. They pushed steadily for what Lodge called a "large policy." One result was the rebuilding of the U.S. Navy. Begun in the mid-1880s, the naval program shifted after 1890 from shore defense to an offensive strategy, which meant the construction of a battleship fleet. This "large policy," warned Carl Schurz, the antiexpansionist editor of the *New York Evening Post*, aimed at acquiring "such territory, far and near, as may be useful in enlarging our commercial advantages, and in securing to our navy facilities desirable for the operations of a great naval power."

A growing nationalism attended the great-power sentiment. It infected even the antiexpansionist Cleveland administration. For years, a border dispute had simmered between Venezuela and British Guiana. On July 20, 1895, Secretary of State Richard Olney sent a bristling note to London; Cleveland called it Olney's "twenty-inch gun." Invoking the Monroe Doctrine, Olney accused Britain of aggressive actions against Venezuela. He warned that the United States could not tolerate any European attempt to overthrow an American state. "Today the United States is practically sovereign upon this continent, and its fiat is law upon the subjects to which it confines its interposition," Olney asserted. In support of that bombastic claim, the United States said it was prepared to take on all comers. The British agreed in 1896 to the American demand for arbitration, and the crisis passed.

No series of events better caught the American mood—the nation's growing sense of power and nationalism. People called it "jingoism." The United States, eager to step onto the world stage, needed only the right occasion.

The Spanish-American War

In February 1895, Cuba rebelled against Spanish rule. A bloody standoff developed; the Spaniards controlled the towns, the insurgents the countryside. During the fall of 1897, the brutal Spanish commander, General Valeriano Weyler, adopted a policy of "reconcentration." The Spaniards forced the entire population into armed camps and treated any Cuban on the out-side as a rebel. The strategy, while militarily effective, took a dreadful toll among the Cubans. Thousands died of starvation, exposure, and dysentery.

Cuban rebellions had occurred since the 1820s and were always troublesome to the United States. The last uprising, which lasted from 1868 to 1878, had raised serious tensions with Spain. These tensions now became intolerable.

A wave of sympathy for the Cuban rebels swept across the United States. As in the past, Cuban exiles skillfully played on public opinion. But now they got help from a yellow press eager to capitalize on the situation. Locked in a circulation war, William Randolph Hearst's *New York Journal* and Joseph Pulitzer's *New York World* elevated the atrocities and skirmishes into front-page news. However, more than sentiment brought the United States into conflict with Spain. The Cuban troubles involved American interests, especially large investments in Cuban sugar. As in past rebellions, the Spaniards arrested American citizens and destroyed American property. The United States considered its new strategic plans even more important. If a canal across Central America were to be built and Caribbean bases acquired, the United States could not tolerate a chronically unstable Cuba.

On September 18, 1897, the American minister asked the government in Madrid "whether the time has not arrived when Spain . . . will put a stop to this destructive war." If Spain could not give assurances of an "early and certain peace," he warned, the United States would take whatever steps it "should deem necessary to procure this result."

At first, the Spanish response sparked some hope. The conservative regime fell, and a liberal government, upon taking office in October 1897, moderated the Cuban policy. Spain recalled Weyler, eased reconcentration, and adopted an autonomy plan. But Madrid's incapacity soon became clear. In January 1898, Spanish loyalists in Havana rioted against the grant of autonomy. The Cuban rebels, encouraged by the prospect of American intervention, then demanded full independence.

Relations between the United States and Spain worsened. On February 9, the *New York Journal* published a private letter of Dupuy de Lôme, the Spanish minister to the United States. He insulted President McKinley and suggested

"REMEMBER THE MAINE!"
The U.S.S. *Maine* enters Havana harbor on a courtesy call in late January 1898, en route to disaster.
On the evening of February 15, a mysterious blast sent the battleship to the bottom. Although no
evidence ever linked the Spanish authorities to the explosion, the event fed the emotional fires
preparing the nation for war with Spain. (National Archives)

that the American government was not acting in good faith. A week later, the U.S. battleship *Maine* blew up and sank in Havana harbor, with the loss of 260 men. The findings of a naval board of inquiry, issued on March 21, proved highly damaging to the Spanish position. The explosion, the board reported, had been caused by a mine, not, as experts had widely suspected, by an internal malfunction, on the *Maine*. No evidence linked the Spaniards to the explosion, but they had failed to meet their responsibility of protecting the American vessel from such an attack.

Spanish sovereignty had broken down. This was the theme of a memorable speech by Senator Redfield Proctor of Vermont after a visit to Cuba. His account of the conditions there led to the conclusion that Spain had lost its claim to rule Cuba.

President McKinley did not seek war. He had no stomach for the martial spirit sweeping the country. His supporters in the business world likewise preferred peace. With the economy finally coming out of depression, they strongly wanted to avoid any disturbances. But, in the end, McKinley had no choice. Whipped up by the lurid journalism of the Hearst newspapers, angered by the awful spectacle of the sunken Maine, the American people were calling for blood.

In late March, Spain made a series of desperate concessions, climaxed by an offer on April 5 to suspend hostilities in Cuba for six months. However, not even this proposal guaranteed the restoration of order as demanded by Washington. In any case, the public pressure on McKinley could no longer be resisted. The president's message to Congress on April 11 was remarkably restrained. McKinley did not ask for war, but for authorization to intervene at his discretion. He identified the United States as an "impartial neutral" between Spain and Cuba, withheld recognition of the rebels, and remained silent on Cuban independence.

McKinley did not come close to satisfying the war hawks in the Senate. They pushed through a joint congressional resolution that asserted Cuban independence, required Spanish evacuation of the island, and directed the president to use force to achieve those goals. McKinley signed the resolution. Spain broke off diplomatic relations with the United States, and Congress declared war on April 25, 1898.

The United States did not go to war with the intention of seizing Spanish territory. The most avid interventionists in the Senate were western Democrats and Populists. They were eager for an independent, republican Cuba as a matter of principle, but they were also strongly antiexpansionist. As part of the war resolution following McKinley's message of April 11, they sponsored the Teller amendment in which the United States disclaimed any intention of taking Cuba. The amendment also pledged "to leave the government and control of the island to its people." Nor did conventional expansionist projects make much headway at that time. During the spring of 1898, neither a canal bill nor a Hawaiian annexation measure got through the Senate. Yet the Spanish-American War, once it started, quickly set the United States on an imperial course.

The crucial event occurred not in Cuba but far off in another Spanish colony, the Philippines. Acting on standing orders in the event of war, Commodore George Dewey's small fleet set sail immediately from Hong Kong. The Americans cornered the Spanish fleet in Manila harbor on May 1 and destroyed it. The victory produced euphoria in the United States. Immediately, part of the army being trained on the Gulf of Mexico for the Cuban campaign was diverted to the Philippines. Manila, the Philippine capital, fell on August 13, 1898.

Dewey's victory meant that Manila Bay, the western Pacific base long coveted by naval strategists, would not be returned to Spain. At this time, too, the great powers were carving up China. If American commerce wanted a place in that glittering market, the power of the United States would have to be projected into Asia.

American businessmen, foot draggers in the race to war, now rushed to the flag. "With a strong foothold in the Philippine Islands, we can and will take a large slice of the commerce of Asia," asserted Mark Hanna, now an Ohio senator. "That is what we want . . . and it is better to strike while the iron is hot." The logjam on Hawaii also broke, and annexation won approval in July 1898. The capture of Manila had enhanced the strategic importance of Hawaii as a half-way station in the mid-Pacific. Overnight, expansionism had been legitimized.

The campaign in Cuba, the main theater of operations, was something of an anticlimax. The

FIGHTING THE FILIPINOS
The United States went to war against Spain in 1898 partly out of sympathy with the Cuban struggle for independence. Yet the United States found it necessary to use very much the same brutal tactics to put down the Filipino struggle for independence as the Spaniards had used against the Cubans. Here the Twentieth Kansas Volunteers march through the burning village of Caloocan. The regiment's commander, Colonel Frederick Funston, vowed to "rawhide these bullet-headed Asians until they yell for mercy." (From *Harper's Weekly*. The Newberry Library, Chicago)

U.S. forces made short work of the demoralized, outgunned Spaniards. Their fleet was bottled up in Santiago harbor. The ill-prepared U.S. army, greatly augmented by volunteers, landed east of Santiago late in June. On July 1, American troops assaulted San Juan Hill; Colonel Theodore Roosevelt's dismounted Rough Riders led the attack on nearby Kettle Hill. Despite heavy casualties, the Americans took the heights commanding Santiago and its harbor. They sank the Spanish fleet on July 3 when it made a suicidal daylight attempt to run the American blockade.

Three weeks later, Spain sued for peace. The two nations signed an armistice in which Spain agreed to give up Cuba and cede Puerto Rico and Guam, one of the Mariana Islands in the Pacific, to the United States. American forces would occupy Manila pending a peace treaty that would decide the fate of the Philippines.

The Imperial Experiment

"Without any original thought of complete or even partial acquisition," admitted President McKinley, "the presence and success of our arms at Manila imposes upon us obligations which we cannot disregard." Thus the imperial entanglements began. McKinley's few advisers who knew anything about the Philippines assured him that Manila could not be held without taking the entire archipelago of over 7,000 islands. The defeat of Spain had created a power vacuum. Germany and Japan were on the prowl and were interested in the Philippines. The Americans considered the Filipinos incapable of immediate self-rule. By taking the Philippines, the United States would assume "the white man's burden" and bring the blessings of western civilization to "our little brown brothers."

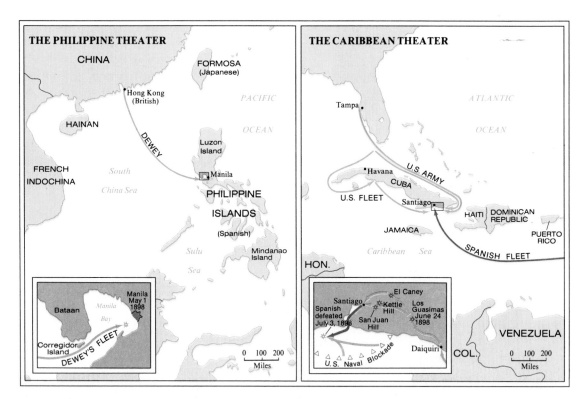

MAP 20.2 SPANISH-AMERICAN WAR
The swift American victory in the Spanish-American War derived from overwhelming U.S. naval superiority. Dewey's destruction of the Spanish fleet in Manila harbor doomed the Spaniards in the Philippines. In Cuba, American ground forces won a hard victory on San Juan Hill, but they were ill-equipped and poorly supplied. With the United States in control of the seas, however, the Spaniards saw no choice but to give up the battle for Cuba. Had they chosen to fight on, it would not have seemed the "splendid little war" of which McKinley's next secretary of state, John Hay, boasted.

THE IDEALS AND REALITIES OF SUBDUING THE FILIPINOS

Major General Arthur MacArthur, Commanding General, U.S. Forces in the Philippines, to the Senate Committee on the Philippines, 1902.

From the beginning of civilization man has tried to mitigate and escape as far as possible from the consequences of his own barbarous environment. In pursuance of these laudable efforts, the human race, from time immemorial, has been propagating its higher ideals by a succession of intellectual waves, one of which is now passing through our mediumship, beyond the Pacific, and carrying therewith everything that is implied by the beautiful flag which is a symbol of our nationality.

At the time I returned to Manila [May 1900] to assume the supreme command it seemed to me that we had been committed to a position by process of spontaneous evolution. . . . [O]ur permanent occupation of the islands was simply one of the necessary consequences in logical sequence of our great prosperity, and to doubt the wisdom of [occupation] was simply to doubt the stability of our own institutions and in effect to declare that a self-governing nation was incapable of successfully resisting strains arising naturally from its own productive energy. . . . [O]ur conception of right, justice, freedom, and personal liberty was the precious fruit of centuries of strife; that we had inherited much in these respects from our ancestors, and in our own behalf have added much to the happiness of the world, and as beneficiaries of the past and as the instruments of future progressive social development we must regard ourselves simply as the custodians of imperishable ideas held in trust for the general benefit of mankind. In other words, I felt that we had attained a moral and intellectual height from which we were bound to proclaim to all as the occasion arose the true message of humanity as embodied in the principles of our own institutions.

All other governments that have gone to the East have simply planted trading establishments; they have not materially affected the conditions of the people. They have perfected organizations which have systematized living conditions, but have not planted an idea that would be self-sustaining. There is not a single establishment, in my judgment, in Asia to-day that would survive five years if the original power which planted it was withdrawn therefrom.

The contrasting idea with our occupation is this: In planting our ideas we plant something that can not be destroyed. To my mind the archipelago is a fertile soil upon which to plant republicanism. . . . We are planting the best traditions, the best characteristics of Americanism in such a way that they never can be removed from that soil. That in itself seems to me a most inspiring thought. It encouraged me during all my efforts in those islands, even when conditions seemed most disappointing, when the people themselves, not appreciating precisely what the remote consequences of our efforts were going to be, mistrusted us; but that fact was always before me—that going down deep into that fertile soil were the imperishable ideas of Americanism.

F. A. Blake, Red Cross worker, quoted in the San Francisco Call, *March 30, 1899.*

I never saw such execution in my life and hope never to see such sights as met on all sides as our little corps passed over the field, dressing wounded legs and arms nearly demolished, total decapitation, horrible wounds in chest and abdomen, showing the determination of our soldiers to kill every native in sight.

Richard T. O'Brien, M Company, 26th Infantry Volunteers, U.S. Army, to the Senate Committee on the Philippines, 1902.

[H]ow the order started and who gave it I don't know, but the town was fired on. I saw an old fellow come to the door, and he looked out: he got a shot in the abdomen and fell to his knees and turned around and died. . . .

After that two old men came out, hand in hand. I should think they were over 50 years old, probably between 50 and 70 years old. They had a white flag. They were shot down. At the other end of the town we heard screams, and there was a woman there; she was burned up, and in her arms was a baby, and on the floor was another child. The baby was at her breast, the one in her arms, and this child on the floor was, I should judge, about 3 years of age. They were burned. Whether she was demoralized or driven insane I don't know. She stayed in the house.

The Spaniards had little choice. They ceded the Philippines to the United States and received a payment of $20 million in return. The Treaty of Paris, signed in December 1898, encountered harder going at home. Events in the Philippines reawakened traditional antiexpansionism. An organized movement formed in many cities, starting with Boston, and grew into the formidable Anti-Imperialist League in October 1899. The Philippine issue delayed the treaty in the Senate for weeks. Senator George Hoar of Massachusetts protested that annexation violated the Constitution. "The power to conquer alien people and hold them in subjugation is nowhere expressly granted [and] nowhere implied," he protested. With only a vote to spare, the Senate approved the treaty on February 6, 1899.

Two days earlier, on February 4, fighting had broken out between American and Filipino patrols on the edge of Manila. Shortly after the destruction of the Spanish fleet, the United States Navy had brought the Filipino leader Emilio Aguinaldo back from exile to help organize local resistance to the Spaniards. Aguinaldo quickly asserted his nation's independence and, confronted by American annexation, turned his guns on the U.S. forces.

The ensuing conflict far exceeded the ferocity of the war just concluded with Spain. Fighting tenacious guerillas, the United States Army resorted to the same tactics used by the Spaniards in Cuba, moving the people into the towns, carrying out indiscriminate attacks beyond the perimeters, and burning crops and villages.

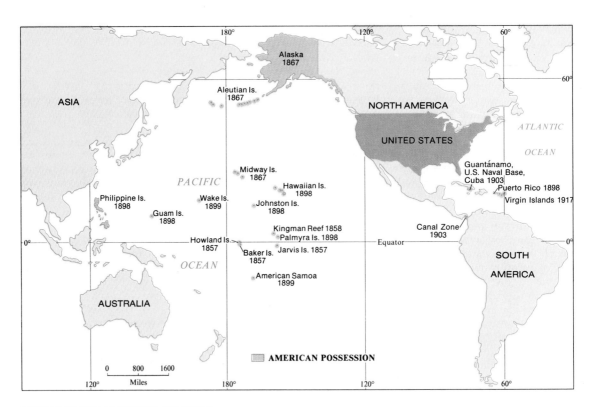

MAP 20.3 THE AMERICAN EMPIRE

In 1890, the great strategist Captain Alfred T. Mahan wrote that the United States should regard oceans no longer as protective barriers but rather as "a great highway" across which America would carry on world trade and exert its naval power. That was precisely what resulted from the empire the United States acquired in the wake of the Spanish-American War. The Caribbean possessions, the Panama Canal, and strategically located holdings that spanned the Pacific gave the United States commercial and naval access to a new, wider world.

TIME LINE
THE PUBLIC WORLD OF LATE NINETEENTH-CENTURY AMERICA

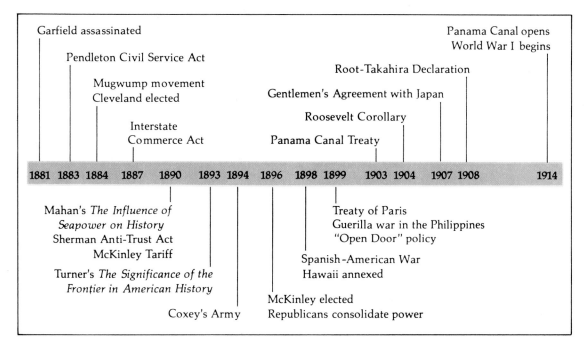

Garfield assassinated

Pendleton Civil Service Act

Mugwump movement
Cleveland elected

Interstate
Commerce Act

Panama Canal opens
World War I begins

Root-Takahira Declaration

Gentlemen's Agreement with Japan

Roosevelt Corollary

Panama Canal Treaty

| 1881 | 1883 | 1884 | 1887 | 1890 | 1893 | 1894 | 1896 | 1898 | 1899 | 1903 | 1904 | 1907 | 1908 | 1914 |

Mahan's *The Influence of
Seapower on History*
Sherman Anti-Trust Act
McKinley Tariff

Turner's *The Significance of the
Frontier in American History*

Coxey's Army

Treaty of Paris
Guerilla war in the Philippines
"Open Door" policy

Spanish-American War
Hawaii annexed

McKinley elected
Republicans consolidate power

Atrocities became commonplace. The U.S. forces specialized in the "water cure"—forcing water into a person's stomach and then pounding it out—to force captured guerillas to talk. In more than three years of warfare, forty-two hundred Americans and thousands of Filipinos died. The fighting ended in 1902, and Judge William Howard Taft, appointed governor by President McKinley, set up a civilian government. He intended to make the Philippines a model of American road building and sanitary engineering.

In a few years, the United States had acquired a modest overseas empire—Hawaii, Puerto Rico, Guam, and the Philippines. In 1900, this overseas expansion concluded with the acquisition in the South Pacific of several islands of Samoa, over which the United States, Germany, and Great Britain had established a joint protectorate in 1889.

In the 1900 election, the Democrats nominated William Jennings Bryan for a second try against McKinley. An avid antiexpansionist, Bryan declared imperialism the "paramount is-

sue" in the campaign. But, sensing his opposition to imperialism to be a losing cause, he backed away from it by election day. McKinley's convincing victory nevertheless suggested popular satisfaction with America's overseas adventure.

Yet a strong sense of misgiving also was evident. Americans had not anticipated the brutal methods needed to subdue the Filipino guerillas. In addition, there were disturbing political issues to be resolved. Did the Constitution extend to the acquired territories? Did their inhabitants automatically become citizens? In 1901, the Supreme Court ruled negatively on both questions; these were matters for Congress to decide. In its report on administration for the Philippines, the special commission appointed by McKinley recommended ultimate independence after an indefinite period of U.S. rule, during which the Filipinos would prepare for self-government.

The colonial adventure had clearly ended. But this did not mean any renunciation of America's pursuit of global power. The United States had stepped permanently onto the world stage.

After Reconstruction ended in 1877, national politics became less issue-oriented and, as a formal process, less important in American life. This situation resulted from weaknesses in governmental institutions, from the prevailing philosophy of laissez faire, and from the paralysis of evenly matched political parties. Yet the politics of the period from 1877 to 1893 had great vigor. For one thing, politics provided the arena in which the nation's ethnocultural conflicts could be fought out. Equally important, the party machines performed crucial functions that properly belonged to, but were still beyond the capacity of, government institutions.

During the 1890s, national politics again became an important arena. Threatened by the rise of Populism, the Democratic party committed itself to free silver and made the 1896 election a contest over issues of great significance. The Republicans won decisively, ending the paralyzing party stalemate that had lasted twenty years and assuring themselves of political dominance for the next thirty years.

At the same time, the nation's growing population and industrial strength gave the United States the potential to be a world power. After a century of self-absorption and relative isolation, Americans began to push into the international arena after 1890. In 1898, the United States won the Spanish-American War and, as a result of the victory, acquired an overseas empire. The nation clearly had joined the great powers of the world.

Suggestions for Further Reading

Domestic Politics

The best introduction to the politics of the late nineteenth century is John A. Garraty, *The New Commonwealth, 1877–1890* (1968). Much more detailed is Morton Keller, *Affairs of State: Public Life in late 19th Century America* (1977). Among other books that deal with aspects of national politics are: Ari Hoogenboom, *Outlawing the Spoils: The Civil Service Reform Movement, 1865–1883* (1961); Robert D. Marcus, *Grand Old Party: Political Structure in the Gilded Age* (1971); H. Wayne Morgan, *From Hayes to McKinley: National Party Politics, 1877–1896* (1969); and David J. Rothman, *Politics and Power: The Senate, 1869–1901* (1966). On the development of public administration, see Leonard D. White, *The Republican Era, 1869–1901* (1958) and Stephen Skowronek, *Building a New American State: The Expansion of National Administrative Capacities* (1982).

The ideological basis for conservative national politics is fully treated in Robert L. Bannister, *Social Darwinism: Science and Myth* (1979); Sidney Fine, *Laissez Faire and the General Welfare State, 1865–1901* (1956); Richard Hofstadter, *Social Darwinism in American Thought* (rev. ed., 1955); and Robert G. McCloskey *American Conservatism in the Age of Enterprise* (1951).

The ethnocultural dimensions of party politics have been studied in Paul Kleppner, *The Cross of Culture: A Social Analysis of Midwestern Politics* (1970) and in Richard Jensen, *The Winning of the Midwest, 1888–1896* (1971). A sophisticated reinterpretation of urban machine politics is to be found in David C. Hammack, *Power and Society: Greater New York at the Turn of the Century* (1982). See also John M. Allswang, *Bosses, Machines and Urban Voters: An American Symbiosis* (1977), and Zane Miller, *Boss Cox's Cincinnati* (1968). Among the many books on the liberal reformers, the most useful are Geoffrey T. Blodgett, *Gentle Reformers: Massachusetts Democrats in the Cleveland Era* (1966) and John G. Sproat, *The Best Men: Liberal Reformers in the Gilded Age* (1965).

The money question is elucidated in Walter Nugent, *Money and American Society, 1865–1880* (1968) and Allan Weinstein, *Prelude to Populism: Origins of the Silver Issue* (1970). On the crisis of the 1890s, see especially Peter H. Argersinger, *Populism and Politics: William Alfred Peffer and the People's Party* (1974); Robert F. Durden, *Climax of Populism: The Election of 1896* (1965); and Paul W. Glad, *McKinley, Bryan and the People* (1964).

An Emerging World Power

Good introductions to the diplomatic history of this period are Foster R. Dulles, *Prelude to World Power, 1865–1900* (1965) and Robert L. Beisner, *From the Old Diplomacy to the New, 1865–1900* (1975). A highly influential interpretation of American expansionism is Walter LaFeber, *The New Empire, 1860–1898* (1963). Other important books dealing with aspects of American expansionism are David Healy, *U.S. Expansionism: Imperialist Urge in the 1890s* (1970); Thomas McCormick, *China Market* (1967); Robert Seager, *Alfred T. Mahan* (1977); William C. Widenor, *Henry Cabot Lodge and the Search for an American Foreign Policy* (1980). Frank Freidel, *Splendid Little War* (1958), is lively, but David F. Trask's, *The War With Spain* (1981) provides a fuller account. Robert L. Beisner, *Twelve Against Empire* (1968) treats the anti-imperialist response in the United States. On the occupation of the Philippines, see Leon Wolff, *Little Brown Brother* (1961), and for the subsequent history, Peter Stanley, *A Nation in the Making: The Philippines and the U.S., 1899–1921* (1974).

21

THE PROGRESSIVE ERA

*O*n the face of it, the political ferment of the 1890s ended after the 1896 election. The bitter struggle over free silver left the victorious Republicans no stomach for political crusades. The McKinley administration devoted itself to maintaining business confidence: sound money and high tariffs were the order of the day. The main thing, as party chief Mark Hanna said, was to "stand pat and continue Republican prosperity." Insofar as the Republicans felt a need to express crusading zeal, they channeled it into the public's absorption with overseas expansion.

Yet surface appearances were deceiving. The depression of the 1890s had unveiled harsh truths not acknowledged in better days. One such discovery was the power of vested economic interests. In Wisconsin, for example, utility and transit companies had raised fares, reduced services, and demanded and received special tax relief—all at the expense of the public. This discovery of corporate arrogance launched movements in Wisconsin for tax reform, municipal ownership of utilities, and progressive politics. The labor unrest of the 1890s produced a similar response. When the American Railway Union went on strike in 1894, the Cleveland administration plotted with the railroad operators, issued injunctions against the strikers, and sent in troops to restore railroad service. The architect of this policy, Attorney General Richard Olney, took little satisfaction from his success. He asked himself what might

be done in the future to avoid the need for such one-sided intervention. Olney began to advocate labor legislation, first expressed in the Erdman Mediation Act of 1898, that would regulate labor relations on the railroads and prevent crippling rail strikes. In such ways did the crisis of the 1890s turn the nation's thinking toward reform.

The problems themselves, however, went back much further in U.S. history. For more than half a century, Americans had been absorbed in the furious development of their country. Now, at the beginning of the twentieth century, they paused, looked around, and began to add up the costs. Industrialization had led to a frightening concentration of economic power in corporate hands, and an equally troubling growth of a large and restless working class. The great cities spawned widespread misery and corrupt machine politics. The heritage of an earlier America seemed to be succumbing to the demands of the new industrial order.

These problems had concerned reformers in the past, and many of the progressive generation had become active long before 1900. Nor were most reform prescriptions freshly minted. What made the progressive years distinctive was primarily a matter of emphasis. Reform, earlier a marginal activity, became a central and absorbing concern. It was as if social awareness had reached a critical mass around 1900 that set reform activity going as a major, self-sustaining phenomenon of early twentieth-century America.

Reform Impulses

Historians have sometimes spoken of a progressive "movement." But, except as this term refers to Theodore Roosevelt's Progressive party of 1912, progressivism was not a movement in any meaningful sense. There was no single progressive constituency, no agreed-upon agenda, and no unifying organization or leadership. At different times and places, different social groups became active. The arena might be private, as with settlement-house work, or on any of several public levels. People who were reformers on one issue might be conservative on another. The term *progressivism* refers not to a single movement but to a widespread, many-sided effort after 1900 to build a better society in the United States. Progressive reformers shared only this objective, plus an intellectual style that can be called "progressive."

The Progressive Mind

Intellectual climates change. It is usually hard to explain *why* they change but not so difficult to tell *when* new ideas take hold. Such a change of ideas clearly seemed to be in the wind as the twentieth century began.

The new age stressed realism. Americans wanted the facts; they wanted to confront reality. John Sloan, George Luks, William Glackens, and other young artists, many of them trained as newspaper illustrators, began to paint city streets and factory life. The art of this "Ashcan School" portrayed the ugly, commonplace world of the tenement, the rush hour, and the prize fight. The social counterpart of realistic painting was the scientific investigation. The federal government launched massive statistical studies of immigration, of women's and children's labor, and of working conditions in many industries. Vice commissions studied the morals of a number of cities. Among private investigative efforts, the classic was the multivolume *Pittsburgh Survey* (1911–1914). Financed by Margaret Olivia Sage and other New York City philanthropists, it described living and working conditions of the steel district in great detail.

The facts were important because they formed the basis for corrective action. When the young journalist Walter Lippmann wrote *Drift and Mastery* (1914), he asserted the Progressive's confidence in people's ability to act purposefully and constructively. This sense of mastery expressed itself in many ways. For example, people had great faith in the capacity of experts. When Robert M. La Follette became governor of Wisconsin in 1900, he relied heavily on the University of Wisconsin for advice and personnel. "The close intimacy of the university with public affairs explains the democracy, the thoroughness, and the scientific accuracy of the state in its legislation," boasted one La Follette supporter in 1912. "It, as much as any other influence, kept Wisconsin true to the progressive movement during these years."

One of the most admired experts was Frederick W. Taylor, who had devised scientific management as a technique for cutting labor costs in factories. Scientific management also seemed to offer solutions to waste and inefficiency in municipal government, in schools and hospitals, and even in homes and churches. "The fundamental principles of scientific management are applicable to all kinds of human activities," Taylor stressed, and could solve all the social ills that arise "through such of our acts as are blundering, ill-directed, or inefficient." Nothing, Taylor suggested, lay beyond the human capacity to improve through "scientific," purposeful action.

The essential thing was to resist intellectual formulations that denied people this sense of mastery. Such had been the effect of Herbert Spencer's Social Darwinism, with its elaborate laws for the automatic development of society. Spencer now came under severe attack from scholars who, while accepting social evolution, denied that it could not be made subject to human direction. Man could "shape environmental forces to his own advantage," argued the sociologist Lester F. Ward. Society could advance through "rational planning" and "social engineering."

A comparable struggle went on in many academic disciplines. This involved an attack on what has been termed nineteenth-century "formalism," in which abstract theory, not empirical inquiry, formed the heart of the scientific method. In economics, for example, the market

REALISM OF THE ASHCAN SCHOOL

Newspapers still relied on drawings to illustrate the news before the turn of the century. John Sloan, for example, came of age as an artist doing on-the-spot drawings of tenement fires, mine explosions, and political campaigns for the Philadelphia *Press*. The apprenticeship shaped the way he, and others of the "ashcan" school, saw the urban world. His *Wake of the Ferry* (left) captured the somber mood, *Shop Window* (right) something of the joys of city life. (Left, The Phillips Collection, Washington; Right, The Newark Museum. Gift of Mrs. Felix Fuld)

was presumed to be perfectly competitive, and hence always subject to the laws of supply and demand. Such a perfect system had no room for reform, which would only disrupt what could not be improved.

Critics of classical economics—they called themselves "institutional economists"—denied that the market ever operated this perfectly. They conducted field research to determine how institutions and power relationships actually controlled the operation of the marketplace. In his *The Theory of the Leisure Class* (1899) and *The Instinct of Workmanship* (1914), the economist Thorstein Veblen lampooned the classical economists' abstract image of the economic man. In the real world, he noted, people acted not out of pure economic calculation, but from complex human motives ranging from vanity to pride in their work.

No field was more a victim of nineteenth-century formalism than the law. After Recon-

struction, the courts had elevated the Fourteenth Amendment into a set of eternal principles in defense of the rights of property. The key clause denied to the states the power to "deprive any person of life, liberty, or property, without due process of law." Intended to protect the civil rights of the freed slaves, the due-process clause gradually became a bar against state regulation of the economy. Any such interference violated the property rights of persons—who were defined to include corporations—under the due-process clause. The Supreme Court, in *Lochner v. New York* (1905), invalidated a maximum-hours law for bakers in New York on the grounds that it violated the contractual rights of both employers and workers. Dissenting, Justice Oliver Wendell Holmes saw this interpretation as a fictional equality outside the real world of labor-management relations. Holmes had earlier asserted the essence of progressive jurisprudence in *The Common Law* (1881): "The life of the law has not been logic; it has been experience. The felt necessities of the time, even the prejudices which judges share with their fellow-men, have had a good deal more to do than the syllogism in determining the rules by which men shall be governed."

The lawyer Louis D. Brandeis acted successfully on Holmes's dictum in *Muller v. Oregon* (1908), a case that involved a ten-hour law for women working in Oregon laundries. Brandeis set aside the usual legal arguments about constitutional meaning. Instead, he drew upon social research that showed how long hours damaged women's health. "Sociological jurisprudence," as Dean Roscoe Pound of the Harvard Law School termed it, called for "the adjustment of principles and doctrines to the human conditions they are to govern rather than assumed first principles." Only as the courts came to accept this legal view—as they did in *Muller v. Oregon*—could progressive legislation move forward.

The philosopher William James took up the task of attacking the core ideas of formalism. James denied the existence of absolute truths. His philosophy of "pragmatism" judged ideas by their consequences and used ideas as guides to action that produced desired results. Philosophy should concern itself with solving problems, said James, not with contemplating ultimate ends. James's most important disciple was John Dewey. Like James, Dewey had a great interest in psychology, and even more in applying psychological insights to education. In his Laboratory School at the University of Chicago, Dewey broke from the rigid curriculum of traditional education and instead stressed problem solving and practical activity as the keys to children's educational growth. Nowhere could the intellectual bent of progressivism in action be seen better than in Dewey's experiments. Fittingly, they came to be known as progressive education.

Progressive reformers prided themselves on being tough minded. They wanted to confront and know social reality. They had confidence in people's capacity to take purposeful action. But there was another side to the progressive mind. It was deeply infused with idealism. Progressives framed their intentions in terms of high principle. The progressive cause, pronounced Theodore Roosevelt, "is based on the eternal principles of righteousness."

Much progressive idealism came from the past, from a refurbishing and sharpening of American values. Abraham Lincoln loomed large in the minds of Progressives. For many, the Great Emancipator had been a guide from childhood, and they identified their own efforts with the early Republican party and with the abolitionist struggle. Past values found clearest expression in the battle for political reform. "Go back to the first principles of democracy; go back to the people," Robert La Follette told his audience when he first launched his attack on Wisconsin machine politics in 1897. Political reformers typically described theirs as a work of political restoration. They frequently said they had converted to reform after discovering how far the actual practice of party politics had drifted from their inherited ideals of representative government.

Progressive idealism also derived from American radical traditions. Many Progressives traced their conversion to reform to Henry George's *Progress and Poverty* (1879), with its plea for the single tax to crush the evils of land monopoly. George, a social reformer, believed that the government should get all its funds from a tax on land. Other Progressives found inspiration in the journalist Edward Bellamy's *Looking Backward* (1888), with its utopian vision of an ordered, affluent American socialism; or in the writer Henry Demarest Lloyd's *Wealth Against Commonwealth* (1894), with its powerful indictment of a predatory Standard Oil Company. In later years, this radical tradition came to be transmitted mainly through the Socialist party. It was no coincidence that socialism and progressivism flourished during the same period. Both drew, to some degree, on the same sources of discontent. Walter Lippmann and many other young reformers passed through socialism on their way to progressivism.

The boundaries between progressivism and socialism were often clouded, especially at the municipal level. In about 350 cities where Socialists won public office between 1910 and 1919, they could hardly be distinguished from other reform administrators. On the other hand, strong tensions arose between socialism and progressivism. The more militant Socialists, such as Eugene V. Debs, had little but contempt for moderate reform; they called for Marxian class struggle and revolution. Nevertheless, they had a stimulating effect on progressivism. In the business sector, corporate reformers acted partly out of fear of the socialist appeal among workers. And, despite the discomfort it caused, socialism asserted ideals that served as a beacon for more moderate reformers.

The most important source of progressive idealism, especially among social reformers, was religion. Within the Protestant churches, confrontation with cities had given rise to the new doctrine of the Social Gospel. For the Reverend Walter Rauschenbusch, the shaping experience was his ministry at a German Baptist congregation near the squalid Hell's Kitchen area of New York City. Shocked by the conditions he found there, Rauschenbusch fought for more playgrounds and better housing in slum neighborhoods. The churches had to reassert the "social aims of Jesus," Rauschenbusch argued. The "Kingdom of God on Earth" would be achieved, he said, not by striving only for personal salvation, but by struggling for social justice. Many clergymen agreed with Rauschenbusch that unrestrained American capitalism was only "semi-Christian." The Social Gospel, increasingly heard from urban Protestant pulpits after the turn of the century, led to the formation of the Federal Council of Churches in 1908. The council aimed at "promoting the application of the law of Christ in every relation to human life."

The Social Gospel addressed the concerns of the Protestant ministry, but the underlying religious sentiment extended far beyond formal church boundaries. Progressive leaders characteristically grew up in families imbued with evangelical piety. Many went through a religious crisis, having sought and failed to experience a conversion, and ultimately settled on a career in social work, education, journalism, or politics. There they could translate inherited religious belief into modern secular action. Jane Addams, for example, had taken up settlement-house work with this intent. By uplifting the poor in tenement districts, settlement workers would themselves be uplifted. They would experience "the joy of finding the Christ which lieth in man, but which no man can unfold save in fellowship."

As a result, progressive thought contained a pervading Christian undercurrent. The phil-osopher John Dewey thus called democracy "a spiritual fact" and the "means by which the revelation of truth is carried on." Only in democracy, "through community of action, did the incarnation of God in man (man, that is to say, as organ of universal truth) become a living present thing." Theodore Roosevelt launched his Progressive party with the battle cry, "We stand at Armageddon and we battle for the Lord." His supporters at the party's national convention of 1912 marched around the hall singing "Onward Christian Soldiers."

The progressive mode of thought—idealistic in intent and tough minded in approach—nurtured a new kind of reform journalism. A growing urban audience had already given rise to a rash of popular magazines, including *Munsey's*, *McClure's*, and *Collier's*. Unlike the highbrow *Atlantic Monthly* or *Harper's*, these journals sold for only ten cents and catered to a broad audience. They attracted people, publisher Frank A. Munsey remarked, by low prices, attractive formats, and "good cheer and human interest throughout." After the magazines discovered a popular appetite for the exposure of evil, investigative journalism became their hallmark. Lincoln Steffens wrote about the corrupt ties between business and political machines in the cities. Ida M. Tarbell (pictured on page 650) attacked Standard Oil, and David Graham Phillips told how money controlled the Senate. William Hard exposed industrial accidents in "Making Steel and Killing Men" (1907) and child labor in "De Kid Wot Works at Night" (1908). Others described prostitution, Wall Street abuses, and adulterated food. Hardly a sordid corner of American life escaped the scrutiny of these brilliant and tireless reporters. They were moralists as well. They made their writing powerful not only by uncovering facts, but also by telling the facts with great indignation.

President Roosevelt, among many others, thought they went too far. In a 1906 speech, he compared them to the man with the muckrake in *The Pilgrim's Progress,* by the seventeenth-century English preacher John Bunyan. The man was too absorbed with raking the filth on the floor to look up and accept a celestial crown. Thus, the term "muckrakers" became attached to journalists who exposed the underside of American life. Their efforts were, in fact, health-

IDA TARBELL TAKES ON ROCKEFELLER

A popular biographer of Napoleon and Lincoln in the 1890s, Ida Tarbell turned her formidable journalistic talents to muckraking. Her first installment of "History of the Standard Oil Company" appeared in *McClure's Magazine* in November 1902. John D. Rockefeller, she wrote, "was willing to strain every nerve to obtain for himself special and illegal privileges from the railroads which were bound to ruin every man in the oil business not sharing them with him." As Tarbell built her case, a crescendo of criticism rained down on Rockefeller. A more sympathetic cartoon in the magazine *Judge* pleads with Rockefeller's critics: "Boys, don't you think you have bothered the old man just about enough?" (Ida M. Tarbell Collection, Allegheny College; Culver)

giving. More than any other group, the muckrakers called the people to arms.

Political Reformers

Progressives wanted to know and confront social reality. They infused their efforts with a deep sense of ideals. They were confident of the human capacity to take purposeful action. This much Progressives had in common. But, once in action, they revealed more complicated characteristics. Different groups took up different reforms, and, to a greater or lesser degree, they did so for reasons of self-interest. Nowhere were these cross-currents stronger than among political reformers.

In many cities, the demand for better government came from local businessmen. They complained that the economic burdens of old-fashioned party rule had become too heavy. Taxes went up while services fell short of the businessmen's growing needs. There had to be a stop, as one manufacturer said, to "the inefficiency, the sloth, the carelessness, the injustice and the graft of city administrations." The solution, argued John Patterson of the National Cash Register Company as early as 1896, lay in putting "municipal affairs on a strict business basis." Cities should be run "not by partisans, either Republican or Democratic, but by men who are skilled in business management and social service."

In 1900, a hurricane devastated Galveston, Texas. Local businessmen took over and, during the course of rebuilding the city, replaced the mayor and board of aldermen with a five-man commission. The Galveston plan, although widely copied, had a serious flaw. It gave too much power to the individual commissioners. Dayton, Ohio, resolved this problem in 1912 by giving the legislative duties to a nonpartisan commission and the administrative functions to an appointed city manager. The commission-manager system soon became the preferred way to run an American city "in exactly the same way as a private business corporation." Municipal political reform was preeminently the work of the business community, and overtly a matter of the balance sheet. Efficient government amounted to good business.

It was also a species of power-grab. Municipal reformers favored city-wide elections, nonpartisanship, and professional city administration. All these reforms attacked means by which ethnic and working-class groups gained access to political power and influence. As a result, municipal control moved into the hands of the urban middle class. In fact, municipal reform contained a decidedly antidemocratic bias. "Ignorance should be excluded from control," said former Mayor Abram Hewitt of New York in 1901. "City business should be carried on by trained experts selected upon some other principle than popular suffrage."

A different kind of political progressivism opposed such elitist reform. Mayor Brand Whitlock of Toledo, Ohio, believed "that the cure for the ills of democracy was not less democracy, as so many people were always preaching, but more democracy." Shoe manufacturer Hazen S. Pingree, an early example of this breed of urban politician, led the Republicans to victory against the Democratic machine in Detroit in 1889. Although drafted by a business coalition, Pingree skillfully appealed for support from trade unions and ethnic groups. His administration not only attacked municipal corruption and inefficiency, but also concerned itself with the needs of Detroit's working people. They swept him back into office by a large majority in 1893. A number of other cities likewise came under the leadership of such progressive mayors, including Samuel M. "Golden Rule" Jones in Toledo, Tom Johnson in Cleveland, and Mark Fagan in Jersey City. By combining popular programs and campaign magic, they won over the urban masses and challenged the rule of the entrenched machines.

The democratic Progressives found their major battleground at the state level. Robert La Follette in Wisconsin, Harold U'Ren in Oregon, Hiram Johnson in California, and Woodrow Wilson in New Jersey profoundly altered state government in America. They did so, like business reformers in cities, by means of structural reforms. However, the state Progressives did not aim at restricting popular representation. They worked to expand it. The most important reform was the direct primary election, by which candidates were nominated by popular vote rather than by party conventions and caucuses. The direct election of senators, enacted into law in 1913 by the Seventeenth Amendment, deprived the party-dominated state legislatures of that power. Other democratizing reforms included the initiative, the referendum, and the recall.

In city halls and state houses, political Progressives pictured themselves as democratic idealists. They wanted to return to "the people" what had been stolen by corrupt bosses and the vested interests. La Follette vowed "never to abandon the fight until we have made government truly representative of the people." This rhetoric was sincere but it did not tell the whole

ROBERT M. LAFOLLETTE
LaFollette was transformed into a political reformer when a Wisconsin Republican boss attempted to bribe him in 1891 to influence a judge in a railway case. As he described it in his *Autobiography*, "Out of this awful ordeal came understanding; and out of understanding came resolution. I determined that the power of this corrupt influence . . . should be broken." As Wisconsin governor in 1901, he rooted out the old machine politics and made Wisconsin a "laboratory for democracy." (State Historical Society of Wisconsin)

story. For political reform aimed as much at winning office as it did at purifying politics.

The progressive generation of political reformers did not consist of refurbished Mugwumps of the 1880s. Many Progressives were seasoned politicians. La Follette, for example, had followed a conventional party career—lawyer, district attorney, and then a congressman for three terms—before breaking with the Wisconsin Republican machine after 1890 and turning to reform politics. If they were newcomers—as was Woodrow Wilson, the president of Princeton University, when he won election as governor of New Jersey on the Democratic ticket—they showed a quick aptitude for politics and gained a solid mastery of the trade.

The Progressives had little sympathy for the disinterested amateurism of the Mugwumps. They accepted the party system but operated within it entirely differently than did the party regulars. George Washington Plunkitt of Tammany Hall had scorned the value of rhetoric and speechmaking in politics. But not the Progressives. They used the skills of the political campaigner to dramatize issues and generate grass-roots support, often as a way of seizing control from machine politicians.

The welling up of reform sentiment gave such politicians their chance, and they seized it. "I was merely expressing a common and widespread, though largely unconscious, spirit of revolt among the people," La Follette said of his fight against the Wisconsin Republican machine. After three defeats, he finally gained the Republican nomination for governor in 1900 by his skillful, persistent appeal to rank-and-file voters. Once in office, he immediately pushed through a direct primary law. This democratic reform expressed his political ideals; it also suited his particular political talents perfectly. The direct primary gave La Follette the means to maintain his control over the Republican party in Wisconsin. Through good times and bad, he kept it until his death twenty-five years later.

What was true of La Follette was more or less true of all successful progressive politicians. They supported democratic ideals and made skillful use of the reforms that expressed those ideals. Once in office, they asserted control over their parties. From Golden Rule Jones and Tom Johnson in city halls, to Hiram Johnson in the California governorship, to Roosevelt and Wil-

son in the White House, the progressive politicians beat the party bosses at their own game. They practiced a new kind of politics. In a reform age, it could be a more effective way to power than the backroom techniques of the old-fashioned machine politicians.

Social Feminism

Among the groups activated by the reform ferment, none played a more crucial role than American women. For half a century after the Seneca Falls convention of 1848, the women's rights movement had concentrated mainly on gaining the vote. By 1900, this effort had fully succeeded in only four states—Wyoming, Colorado, Idaho, and Utah. The rival campaign for a women suffrage amendment to the Constitution, once promising, also failed. The formation of the National American Women Suffrage Association in 1890 restored unity to the movement, but the old momentum had been lost. The pioneering generation of Elizabeth Cady Stanton, Lucy Stone, and Susan B. Anthony was passing from the scene, to be replaced by less visionary and skillful leaders. The women's rights movement went through the "doldrums," as suffragists called it, from the mid-1890s to 1910.

During those years, reform energies drifted from the voting issue. Women turned instead toward social uplift—protecting working women and children, improving the lives of immigrants and slum dwellers, and assisting destitute families. These social-reform causes, although taken up by men as well, came to be identified especially with woman progressives.

Middle-class women had long borne much of the burden for humanitarian work in American cities. During the Civil War, ladies' aid societies sprang up almost everywhere to assist soldiers and their families. Afterward, vocational schools, orphan asylums, and "homes for the friendless" assisted war widows and orphans. As their number multiplied in the cities, working women became the principal concern of organized charity, especially through social clubs and job exchanges.

After the depression of the 1870s, the need to coordinate various relief agencies led to the creation of charity-organization societies. Voluntary investigators visited needy families, assessed their problems, and certified them to the appropriate agencies. Women did most of this work, in keeping with the traditional concept of the woman as a nurturer. She appropriately filled this role for society as well as within her own family and continued to do so as the nation entered the progressive era.

Social uplift, the special province of American women, now showed a new brand of aggressiveness. After many years of dedicated charity work, Mrs. Josephine Shaw Lowell of New York City concluded that it was not enough to give assistance to the poor. "If the working people had all they ought to have, we should not have the paupers and criminals," she declared. "It is better to save them before they go under, than to spend your life fishing them out afterward." Mrs. Lowell founded the New York Consumers League in 1890. Her goal was to improve the wages and working conditions of the female clerks in the city's stores. To help bring pressure on reluctant merchants, the league issued a "White List"—a very short one at first—of shops that met its standards. The league then expanded its interest beyond retail stores and spread to other cities. The National Consumers League was founded in 1899. Under the crusading leadership of Florence Kelley, formerly a chief factory inspector in Illinois, it became a powerful lobby for protective legislation for women and children.

Among its achievements, none was more important than the *Muller v. Oregon* decision (1908), which validated the Oregon Ten-Hour Law for woman laundry workers. The Consumers League had pushed that law through the state legislature and successfully defended it before the Supreme Court. The Muller case opened the way for protective legislation throughout the country. Women's organizations became a mighty force in state legislatures and Congress on behalf of women and children. Their victories included the first law providing public assistance for mothers with dependent children, in Illinois in 1911; the first minimum wage law for women and children, in Massachusetts in 1912; and the creation of the children's and women's bureaus in the U.S. Labor Department, in 1912 and 1920, respectively. In 1916, Congress passed a national child labor law banning the products of child labor from interstate commerce. Two years later, however, the Supreme Court declared this law unconstitutional.

A second thrust of social feminism, equally as strong as public advocacy, aimed at direct engagement with the underprivileged of industrial America. The settlement-house movement

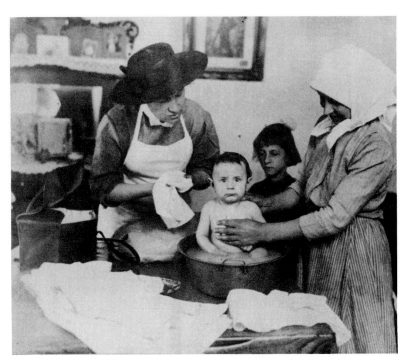

SAVING THE CHILDREN
In the early years at Hull House, toddlers sometimes arrived for kindergarten tipsy from breakfasts of bread soaked in wine. To settlement-house workers, education in childcare seemed the obvious answer to such ignorance, and so began the program to send visiting nurses into immigrant homes. They taught mothers the proper methods of caring for children—including, as this photograph shows, the daily infant bath, in a dishpan if necessary. (Chicago Historical Society)

THE MAKING OF A SOCIAL FEMINIST

Jane Addams's autobiography Twenty Years at Hull House *(1910) is as good an account as we have of the motives that led to social feminism.*

The winter after I left school was spent in the Woman's Medical College of Philadelphia, but the development of the spinal difficulty which had shadowed me from childhood . . . inevitably put aside the immediate prosecution of a medical course, and although I had passed my examinations . . . I was very glad to have a physician's sanction for giving up clinics and dissecting rooms and to follow his prescription for spending the next two years in Europe. . . .

The long illness left me in a state of nervous exhaustion with which I struggled for years, traces of it remaining long after Hull-House was opened in 1889. At the best it allowed me but a limited amount of energy, so that doubtless there was much nervous depression at the foundation of the spiritual struggles which this chapter is forced to record. . . .

One of the most poignant of these experiences, which occurred during the first few months after our landing upon the other side of the Atlantic, was on a Saturday night, when I received an ineradicable impression of the wretchedness of East London, and also saw for the first time the overcrowded quarters of a great city at midnight. A small party of tourists were taken to the East End by a city missionary to witness the Saturday night sale of decaying vegetables and fruit. . . . On Mile End Road, from the top of an omnibus which paused at the end of a dingy street lighted by only occasional flares of gas, we saw two huge masses of ill-clad people clamoring around two hucksters' carts. . . . They were huddled into ill-fitting, cast-off clothing, the ragged finery which one sees only in East London. . . . Yet the final impression was not of ragged, tawdry clothing nor of pinched and sallow faces, but of myriads of hands, empty, pathetic, nerveless and work-worn, showing white in the uncertain light of the street, and clutching forward for food which was already unfit to eat. . . .

For two years in the midst of my distress over the poverty . . . thus suddenly driven into my consciousness . . . there was mingled a sense of futility, of misdirected energy, the belief that the pursuit of cultivation would not in the end bring either solace or relief. I gradually reached a conviction that the first generation of college women had taken their learning too quickly, had departed too suddenly from the active, emotional life led by their grandmothers and great-grandmothers. . . .

This, then, was the difficulty, the assumption that the sheltered, educated girl has nothing to do with the bitter poverty and the social maladjustment which is all about her, and which, after all, cannot be concealed, for it breaks through poetry and literature in a burning tide which overwhelms her; it peers at her in the form of heavy-laden market women and underpaid street laborers, gibing her with a sense of her uselessness. . . .

It is hard to tell just when the very simple plan which afterward developed into the Settlement began to form itself in my mind. It may have been even before I went to Europe for the second time, but I gradually became convinced that it would be a good thing to rent a house in a part of the city where many primitive and actual needs are found, in which young women who had been given over too exclusively to study, might restore a balance of activity along traditional lines and learn of life from life itself. . . .

In those early days we were often asked why we had come to live on Halsted Street when we could afford to live somewhere else. . . . In time it came to seem natural to all of us that the Settlement should be there. If it is natural to feed the hungry and care for the sick, it is certainly natural to give pleasure to the young, comfort to the aged, and to minister to the deep-seated craving for social intercourse that all men feel.

In addition to the neighbors who responded to the receptions and classes, we found those who were too battered and oppressed to care for them. To these, however, was left that susceptibility to the bare offices of humanity which raises such offices into a bond of fellowship.

From the first it seemed understood that we were ready to perform the humblest neighborhood services. We were asked to wash the new-born babies, and to prepare the dead for burial, to nurse the sick, and to "mind the children."

Perhaps even in those first days we made a beginning toward that object which was afterwards stated in our charter: "To provide a center for a higher civic and social life; to institute and maintain educational and philanthropic enterprises, and to investigate and improve the conditions in the industrial districts of Chicago."

began in London in 1884, when Oxford University students founded Toynbee Hall. Inspired by that example, two young women, Jane Addams and Ellen Gates Starr established Hull House on Chicago's West Side in 1889. During the next fifteen years, scores of settlement houses sprang up in the slum neighborhoods of the nation's cities. The houses served as community centers run by middle-class settlement residents. Hull House had meeting rooms, an art gallery, clubs for children and adults, and a kindergarten. Jane Addams herself led battles for garbage removal, playgrounds, better street lighting, and police protection. At the Henry Street Settlement in New York, Lillian D. Wald made visiting nursing a major service. Mary McDowell, head of the University of Chicago Settlement, installed a bathhouse, a children's playground, and a citizenship school for immigrants.

Beyond the modest good they did in slum neighborhoods, settlement houses served as a breeding ground for social feminism. The residents were expected to work full-time, and so the settlement house helped break the convention of social uplift as a female avocation. At least half the female residents went on to lifelong careers in some branch of social service. The settlement houses thus contributed strongly to the emerging profession of social work. To a remarkable degree, too, the leaders of social reform—both men and women—served settlement-house apprenticeships. The settlement houses became "spearheads of reform," as one historian called them.

On the surface, social feminism seemed to divert energy from the struggle for women's suffrage. But it was a diversion richly repaid. In a famous essay, Jane Addams spoke of the "subjective necessity" of the settlement house. She meant that it was as much a response to the middle-class women eager to serve as it was to the needs of city slum dwellers. Addams herself was a case in point. She had grown up in a comfortable Illinois family and graduated from Rockford College. Then she faced an empty future—an ornamental wife if she married, a sheltered spinster if she did not. Hull House became her salvation. It gave her contact with what she thought was the real world plus a useful career and a sense of purpose and personal worth.

Hundreds of other college-educated women who found their calling in social reform shared

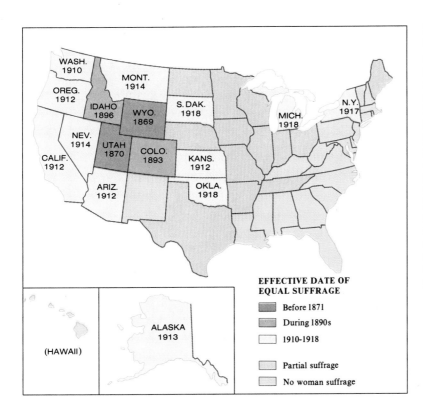

MAP 21.1 WOMAN SUFFRAGE BEFORE 1920
As a reform movement, the fight for woman suffrage was remarkable for the persistent resistance it encountered. By 1910, after more than sixty years of agitation, only four lightly populated western states had granted women full voting rights. A number of other states granted partial suffrage, limited mostly to voting for school boards and such issues as taxes. After 1910, as the effort shifted to a national struggle for a constitutional amendment, ten states were added to the short list of full suffrage. The most stubborn resistance was in the South.

EFFECTIVE DATE OF EQUAL SUFFRAGE

- Before 1871
- During 1890s
- 1910-1918

- Partial suffrage
- No woman suffrage

Addams's experience. Almost inevitably, they became suffragists. Why should a woman capable of running a settlement house or lobbying a bill be denied the right to vote? Suffrage, moreover, became linked to social feminism. If women had the right to vote, they and their male supporters argued, more enlightened legislation and better government would certainly result. Social feminism thus broadened the base of the suffrage movement. Some social reformers, believing that working women should be enabled to help themselves, founded the National Women's Trade Union League in 1903. Financed and led by wealthy supporters, the league organized women workers, played a considerable role in their strikes, and, perhaps most importantly, developed working-class leaders. Rose Schneiderman, for example, became a union organizer among the garment workers in New York City; Agnes Nestor led the woman glove workers in Illinois; and both were lobbyists for women's protective legislation. Such trade-union women identified their cause with the broader struggle for women's rights.

A genuine sense of sisterhood developed that cut across class lines. Well-to-do women rallied to the side of immigrant girls in the great shirtwaist-makers' strike of 1909 in New York City. Socialites and sweatshop girls marched side by side in the city's suffrage parades. When the state of New York held referenda on women's suffrage in 1915 and 1917, strong support came from the Jewish and Italian precincts inhabited by unionized garment workers. The women's rights movement thus expanded beyond its original base in the middle class.

Meanwhile, suffrage activity was reviving nationwide. Women won the right to vote in the state of Washington in 1910, in California in 1911, and in four more western states during the next three years. Women also started to shift their tactics. Beginning in 1903, suffragists in England had picketed, assaulted politicians, and gone on hunger strikes in jail. The effectiveness of this disruptive strategy impressed suffragists in the United States.

The most important of the new militants was Alice Paul, a young Quaker. Rejecting the slower route of enfranchisement by the states, Paul took aim at a constitutional amendment that would give women across the country the

SUFFRAGISTS ON PARADE, 1913
After 1910, the suffrage movement went into high gear. Suffragist leaders decided to demand a constitutional amendment rather than battle for the vote state by state, and to adopt the direct-action methods pioneered by English suffragists. The great parade of women—and near riot—in Washington, D.C. at Woodrow Wilson's inauguration served notice on the new president that the suffragists meant business. (The Bettmann Archive)

right to vote. In 1914, Paul organized the militant National Women's party. The National American Woman Suffrage Association (NAWSA), from which Paul had split off, was also rejuvenated. Carrie Chapman Catt, a skilled political organizer from the New York movement, took over as national leader in 1915. Under her guidance, the NAWSA brought a broad-based organization to the campaign for a federal amendment.

Urban Liberalism

At first, progressivism was a product of middle-class America. In almost every case, the initiative for reform came from the educated, the native born, and the economically comfortable. But progressivism changed over time, and its constituency shifted.

When Hiram Johnson ran for governor of California in 1910, he was the candidate of the middle class and the countryside. Johnson had first attracted attention as the successful prosecutor of the San Francisco political boss Abe Ruef. In his platform, Johnson pledged to purify California politics and to curb the Southern Pacific Railroad, the dominating power in the state's economic and political life. By his second term, Johnson was championing social and labor legislation. His original base of support had strongly eroded and had been replaced by the immigrant, working-class vote that kept him in power for years.

These events illustrated the most enduring achievement of progressivism—the activation of America's working people as a force in reform politics. The cities served as the main arena for this development. Historians have called the result *urban liberalism*—that is, a reform movement by city people for social protection attained by state intervention.

Thirty minutes before quitting time on Saturday afternoon, March 25, 1911, fire broke out at the Triangle Shirtwaist Company in downtown New York. The flames trapped the workers, mostly young immigrant girls. Forty-seven leaped to their deaths; another hundred never made it to the windows. The tragedy caused a national furor and led, two months later, to the creation of the New York State Factory Commission. During four years of work, the commission developed a remarkable program of labor reform, totalling fifty-six laws that dealt with such matters as fire hazards, unsafe machines, home work, and wages and hours for women and children. The chairman of the commission was Robert F. Wagner; the vice-chairman, Alfred E. Smith. Both were Tammany Hall politicians and Democratic party leaders in the state legislature. Wagner and Smith sponsored the resolution establishing the commission, participated fully in its work and, most important, marshalled the party regulars to pass the proposals into law. All this the two men did with the approval of the Tammany machine. The labor code that resulted was the most advanced in the United States.

Tammany's reform role reflected a trend in American cities. Urban political machines increasingly saw their limits as social agencies in the modern industrial age. Only the state could prevent future Triangle fires or cope with the evils of factory work and city life. Also, a new generation had entered machine politics. Al Smith and Robert Wagner, men of social vision, absorbed the lessons of the Triangle investigation. They formed durable ties with such middle-class progressives as the social worker

THE TRIANGLE SHIRTWAIST FIRE
The doors were the problem. Most were locked (to keep the working girls from leaving early); the few that were open became jammed by bodies trying to escape the flames. When the fire trucks finally came, the ladders were too short. Compared to those caught inside, the girls who leaped to their deaths were the lucky ones. "As I looked up I saw a love affair in the midst of all the horror," a reporter wrote. A young man was helping girls leap from a window. The fourth "put her arms about him and kiss[ed] him. Then he held her out into space and dropped her." He immediately followed. "Thud—dead, Thud—dead . . . I saw his face before they covered it. . . . he was a real man. He had done his best." (Brown Brothers)

Frances Perkins, who came to the commission as representative of the New York Consumers League.

For all their organizational strength, moreover, the urban machines could not ignore the voters' sentiments. In the successes of such middle-class reform politicians as Toledo's Sam Jones and Cleveland's Tom Johnson, the urban machines saw the appeal of progressive programs in working-class wards. The political universe of the machines had changed. In the age of the direct primary, more attention had to be paid to opinion in the precincts.

Political reform was, of course, hailed as an assault on the machine system, and some measures did threaten the machine. City-wide elections diluted the vote of the working-class wards, nonpartisan ballots undercut party loyalty, and commission government threatened the spoils system. The machines strongly resisted these reforms. The commission-manager system was confined largely to middle-sized cities where machine politics had not been so well entrenched.

Reforms aimed at broadening popular participation in politics were far less threatening. Democratization actually put a premium on the organizational resources of the urban machines. This was clearly the case, for example, with the direct primary. The machines, while forced to work harder, generally succeeded as well at bringing out the vote in party primaries as at manipulating conventions and caucuses. Moreover, democratizing reforms had a highly favorable effect on the urban-rural balance in state politics. Cities in industrial states had invariably been underrepresented in the state legislatures. In Connecticut, an extreme case, rural towns of a few hundred people had as much representation as did Hartford and New Haven. Any shift to a popular vote, such as primary elections and the direct election of senators, benefited the populous cities, and hence the urban machines.

Always highly pragmatic in their operations, the city machines adopted urban liberalism without much ideological struggle. The same could not be said of the trade unions, the other important institution that represented American workers. During its early years, the American Federation of Labor (AFL) had strongly opposed state interference in labor's affairs. Samuel Gom-

pers preached that workers should not seek "at the hands of government what they could accomplish by their own initiative and activities." Economic power and self-help, not the state, would be the workingman's salvation. Voluntarism, as trade unionists called this antistate doctrine, did not die out, but it weakened substantially during the progressive years.

Organized labor enlisted, although reluctantly, in the cause of urban liberalism—partly for defensive reasons. In the early twentieth century, the labor movement came under severe attack by open-shop employers, who had powerful legal weapons. For one thing, they could sue unions under the Sherman Antitrust Act. In the Danbury Hatters (*Loewe v. Lawler*) case (1908), the Supreme Court found a union boycott to be a conspiracy in restraint of trade. The Court awarded triple damages to the company. More injurious was the routine use of injunctions against unions during labor disputes. Upon an employer's plea of irreparable damages, a sympathetic judge would, without evidence or testimony, prohibit the union from carrying on a strike or boycott.

Only a political response might blunt this assault on labor's crucial economic weapons. In its Bill of Grievances of 1906, the AFL demanded immunity from court attack. The labor organization then campaigned to "reward our friends and punish our enemies" in congressional elections. Getting a cold reception from the Republicans, organized labor moved into closer alliance with the Democratic party, notwithstanding an official AFL policy of nonpartisanship.

Having breached the political barriers for defensive reasons, the labor movement had difficulty denying the case for social legislation. The AFL, after all, claimed to speak for the entire working class. When muckrakers exposed exploitation, and middle-class Progressives came forward with solutions, how could the labor movement fail to respond? Gompers served on the Triangle factory commission, and if—according to Frances Perkins—he was a less eager student than the Tammanyite members, learn he did. In state after state, organized labor joined the battle for progressive legislation and increasingly became its strongest advocate. Conservative labor leaders found some consolation by making a careful distinction: protective laws were for women and children, who lacked the ability to defend themselves.

But the lure of beneficial legislation proved too strong. Accident rates took an appallingly high toll in American mills and mines. Liability laws were archaic and heavily favored the employer. Under the common law, which still governed in this field, an injured worker could sue for damages, but he or she had little hope of succeeding. Nothing cried out more for reform than the plight of maimed workers and penniless widows. In Germany and England, accident-insurance systems guaranteed compensation regardless of fault. Efforts to adopt similar insurance laws in America quickly received the support of the trade unions. Between 1910 and 1917, workmen's compensation for industrial accidents and illnesses went into effect in all the industrial states.

If for factory illness and injury, why not state-mandated insurance for unemployment, old age, and the other hazards of industrial life? Conservative unionists argued that workmen's compensation should be considered a special case. They insisted that labor was better off gaining protection through collective bargaining, rather than through the enactment of laws. But the logic of social insurance could not be resisted for long. Because the needs of working people for security could be met only through state action, the labor movement eventually supported social insurance.

Not only social-welfare goals shaped urban liberal politics. It was also influenced by the sharpening attack on the ethnocultural claims of city voters. Old-stock, evangelical Protestants had long agitated for the political imposition on society of their moral and cultural norms. During the progressive period, these activities took a new lease on life. The Anti-Saloon League, which called itself "the Protestant church in action," became a formidable force in many states. Prohibition linked up with other reform concerns: the saloon made for dirty politics, poverty, and bad labor conditions. Old battles heated up again over the social purposes of education. The schools ought not to perpetuate foreigners' ways, but "to civilize, to Christianize, and to Americanize them."

The moral-reform agenda expanded to include a new objective, immigration restriction.

Large numbers of southern and eastern Europeans had entered the United States since the 1890s. Many Americans, including respected social scientists, believed these new immigrants threatened American society. Its Anglo-Saxon population would be "mongrelized" and its Puritan heritage swamped by "inferior" Mediterranean and Slavic cultures. This ethnic argument, though misconceived, appealed strongly to a wide spectrum of middle-class, native-born Americans. The Immigration Restriction League spearheaded a movement to end America's historic open-door policy.

These moral-cultural issues, expressed in reform terms, were as much a part of the progressive spirit as were the social-reform concerns of the settlement houses and the National Consumers' League. But urban liberals bitterly resented the demands for prohibition and immigration restriction. They considered such "reforms" to be attacks on the personal liberty and worthiness of urban immigrants. Prohibition, protested a Catholic economist, was "despotic and hypocritical domination." The Tammany politician Martin McCue accused the Protestant ministry of "seeking to substitute the policeman's nightstick for the Bible."

A hard-fought but unequal battle resulted. The first federal immigration-restriction law, setting up a literacy test, went into effect in 1917. In 1921, the Dillingham Act imposed a quota system that discriminated flagrantly against southern and eastern Europeans. In 1920, the Eighteenth Amendment made prohibition the law of the land.

By fighting these measures, urban liberalism gained an ethnocultural identity. Urban-liberal leaders championed both the economic needs of city dwellers and their right to follow their religious and cultural preferences. In many ways, certainly until the Great Depression of the 1930s, ethnocultural issues provided a stronger basis for urban-liberal politics. And because the Democrats were the party identified with tolerance and diversity, they became the beneficiaries of the rise of urban liberalism. The growing size of the city vote destined the Democrats to become the majority party. The shift from Republican domination, although not completed until the New Deal came to power in the 1930s, began during the progressive era.

Progressivism and National Politics

The gathering forces of progressivism reached the national scene only slowly. Reformers had been activated by immediate concerns, by problems that affected them directly, and by evils visible and tangible to them. Washington seemed remote from the battles they were waging in their cities and states. But progressivism was bound to come to the capital. In 1906, Robert La Follette went from the governor's office in Wisconsin to the United States Senate. Other seasoned Progressives, also ambitious for a wider stage, made the same move. By 1910, a highly vocal progressive bloc was making itself heard in both houses of Congress.

Problems of a nationwide character had begun to emerge, most of them stemming from the country's economic growth. As the economy had become more industrialized, it had also become more national in scope. At the same time, the economy began to function in ways that made Americans increasingly uneasy. At the national level, progressivism concerned itself mainly with reform of the economic system—the railroads, consumer protection, exploitation of natural resources, finance, and, above all, corporate power. Such reform demanded a great expansion of government power, which had resided mostly at the state and local levels in the nineteenth century.

During the progressive era, the center of power shifted decisively to Washington. There it remained, continually becoming stronger, during the twentieth century. The modern American state had its origins in national, progressivism.

The Square Deal

Theodore Roosevelt brought progressivism into national politics. Sheer accident set him on that course. Roosevelt had not wanted the Republican nomination for vice-president under William McKinley in 1900. Then, soon after the inauguration, an anarchist named Leon F. Czolgosz assassinated President McKinley. By this twist of fate, Roosevelt became president on September 14, 1901.

Roosevelt was cut from much the same cloth as other progressive politicians, except for his rather aristocratic background. He came from a wealthy, old-line New York family, attended Harvard, and might well have chosen the life of a leisured, literary gentleman. Instead, scarcely out of college, he plunged into Republican politics and in 1882 entered the New York state legislature. His reasons matched the high-minded motives of other budding Progressives. Like most of them, Roosevelt had received a moralistic, Christian upbringing. A political career would enable him to act constructively on those beliefs. Roosevelt always identified himself—loudly—with the side of righteousness. On the other hand, he did not scorn power and its uses. He showed contempt for the amateurism of the Mugwumps, whom he called "those political and literary hermaphrodites," and much preferred the professionalism of party politics. Roosevelt rose in the New York party because he skillfully translated his moral fervor into broad popular support and thus forced himself on reluctant state Republican bosses. Other emerging progressive politicians followed the same route of party advancement.

After returning from the Spanish-American War as the hero of San Juan Hill, Roosevelt won the New York governorship in 1898. During his single term, he clearly indicated his inclinations toward reform. Roosevelt pushed through civil-service reform and a tax on corporate franchises. He discharged the corrupt superintendent of insurance over the Republican party's objections and asserted his confidence in the government's capacity to improve the life of the people. Ironically, in an attempt to neutralize him, the party bosses promoted Roosevelt to what normally would have been a dead-end job as vice-president. Mark Hanna, hearing of McKinley's assassination, knew "that damn cowboy" would make trouble in the White House.

Roosevelt moved cautiously at the outset. In his first official statement, he reassured the nation that he would "continue absolutely unbroken" McKinley's policies. The conservative Republican bloc in Congress greatly limited his freedom of action. He treated the Senate leader, Nelson W. Aldrich of Rhode Island, with kid gloves. Roosevelt spent much of his energy, through the skillful use of the patronage powers of his office, gaining control of the Republican

JOHN MUIR AND PRESIDENT ROOSEVELT IN YOSEMITE
John Muir, one of America's great naturalists, considered the defense of the nation's forests against commercial exploitation a battle "between landscape righteousness and the devil." Yosemite became a national park in 1890, largely through Muir's crusading efforts. He accompanied Roosevelt on a camping trip through the park in 1903, when this photograph was taken, and helped persuade the president to create sixteen national monuments and double the number of national parks. (Library of Congress)

party. He had fully accomplished this task by the time Senator Hanna died in 1904. But Roosevelt was also restrained by uncertainty about what reform role the federal government ought to play. At first, the new president might have been described as a Progressive without a cause.

Even so, Roosevelt gave early evidence of his activist bent. He devoted part of his first annual message to conservation. Roosevelt, an ardent outdoorsman, loved the West and had invested—unprofitably—in Dakota cattle ranching in the 1880s. A national movement began in the late nineteenth century to conserve the country's natural resources and scenic wonders against reckless exploitation. Yellowstone National Park, the first national park, had been established in 1872, and the withdrawal of timberlands from development had begun under the Forest Re-

serve Act of 1891. Roosevelt added more than 125 million acres to the national forest reserve and brought mineral lands and waterpower sites into the reserve system. In 1902, he backed the Newlands Reclamation Act, which designated the proceeds from public land sales for irrigation development in arid regions. His administration strongly upgraded the management of public lands and, to the chagrin of some Republicans, energetically prosecuted violators of federal land laws. In the cause of conservation, Roosevelt demonstrated his enthusiasm for exercising executive authority and his disdain for those who sought profit "by betraying the public service."

The same inclinations influenced Roosevelt's handling of the national anthracite coal strike of 1902. Hard coal was the main fuel for home heating. As cold weather approached with no settlement in sight, the government faced a national emergency. The United Mine Workers, led by John Mitchell, were willing to submit to arbitration, but the coal operators adamantly opposed any recognition of the union. Roosevelt's advisers told him there was no legal basis for federal intervention. Nevertheless, the president took the unprecedented step of calling both sides to a conference at the White House on October 1, 1902. When the conference failed, Roosevelt threatened the operators with a government take-over of the mines. He also persuaded the financier J. P. Morgan to use his considerable influence with them. At this point, the coal operators caved in. The strike ended with the appointment by Roosevelt of an arbitration commission to rule on the issues, another unprecedented step. Roosevelt did not especially support organized labor, but he became infuriated by what he labeled the "arrogant stupidity" of the mine employers.

"Of all the forms of tyranny the least attractive and the most vulgar is the tyranny of mere wealth," Roosevelt wrote in his autobiography. He was prepared to deploy all his presidential authority against the "tyranny" of irresponsible business.

The growing concentration of corporate power brought the issue to a head. For more than thirty years, the structure of business enterprise had been evolving into the modern form of the large-scale, vertically integrated corporation. Following the depression of the 1890s, this process of business concentration suddenly accelerated. Earlier, companies had grown mainly through internal expansion, but now corporate growth occurred through an astonishing scramble to merge rival firms. The resulting trusts greatly increased the degree of concentration in the economy. The term *trust,* which had applied to a specific legal form of business control introduced by Standard Oil in the 1880s, was used more broadly after 1900 to describe all business combinations. Of the seventy-three largest industrial companies in 1900, fifty-three had not existed three years earlier. By 1910, 1 percent of the nation's manufacturers accounted for 44 percent of the total industrial output.

The sheer power of the new combines was not the only disturbing factor. Most of them were heavily "watered"—that is, capitalized in excess of their real value. Financiers had taken huge fees for their underwriting services and, even worse, had not relinquished control over the trusts they had fathered. Almost overnight, a "money power" seemed to have gained a stranglehold on the American economy. Roosevelt's sense of the nation's uneasiness became evident as early as his first annual message, in which he referred to the "real and grave evils" of economic concentration. But what weapons could the president use?

Economic concentration threatened the free competition of the marketplace. Under the common law, which America had inherited from England, any person could sue for damages against injury caused by conspiring competitors or by a monopolistic firm. These common-law rights had been enacted into statute law in many states during the 1880s, and then, because the magnitude of the problem exceeded state jurisdictions, were incorporated into the Sherman Antitrust Act of 1890. Free competition was more vigorously defended in two ways under this federal law. First, the law considered an action in restraint of trade as a crime and hence subject to more severe punishment than liability for damages to an injured party. Second, the law enabled the government, as well as injured parties, to bring suit in the federal courts against violators.

Neither the Cleveland nor the McKinley administrations had been much inclined to enforce the Sherman Act, except against organized labor. Of the eighteen suits brought before 1901,

half were against trade unions. Court rulings were equally negative. In *United States v. E. C. Knight* (1895), the Supreme Court ruled that manufacturing was not covered by the Constitution's commerce clause and hence lay beyond the reach of federal regulation. This ruling crippled the Sherman Act but did not kill it. The potential of the act rested, above all, in the fact that it incorporated common-law principles of unimpeachable validity. In the right hands, the Sherman Act could be a strong weapon against the abuse of economic power.

Roosevelt made his opening move when he strengthened the government's capacity to enforce the law. In 1903, despite considerable opposition, Congress established the Bureau of Corporations within the newly created Department of Commerce and Labor. Empowered to investigate business practices, the bureau provided the factual record on which the Justice Department could mount antitrust suits. The first suit had already been filed in 1902 against the Northern Securities Company, a combination of the railroad systems of the Northwest. In 1904, the Supreme Court ordered Northern Securities dissolved, the first such action against a holding company. The next year, in an antitrust case against the major meat packers, the Court reversed the Knight doctrine excluding manufacturing from federal antitrust law.

In 1904, Roosevelt handily defeated a weak Democratic candidate, Judge Alton B. Parker, for a second term. President in his own right, Roosevelt stepped up the attack on the trusts. He took on forty-five of the nation's giant firms, including Standard Oil, American Tobacco, and DuPont. The president accompanied these actions with a rising crescendo of rhetoric. He became the nation's trustbuster, a crusader against "predatory wealth."

Actually, Roosevelt's bark was worse than his bite. He was not antibusiness, and he regarded large-scale enterprise as a natural result of modern industrialism. Only firms that abused their power deserved punishment. But how would those companies be identified? Under the common law, and under the Sherman Act as originally intended, it had been up to the courts to decide whether a given restraint of trade was "unreasonable." The Supreme Court unexpectedly rejected this "rule of reason" in *United States v. Trans-Missouri* (1897). The very fact of conspiracy or monopoly, irrespective of the impact on the market, was sufficient under the Sherman Act. So, if the rule of reason were to survive, it would have to be exercised by those who initiated prosecutions. Roosevelt welcomed the responsibility of making his own distinctions between "good" and "bad" trusts.

In November 1904, shortly after the Bureau of Corporations began to investigate the United States Steel Corporation, the company chairman, Elbert H. Gary, met with Roosevelt. Gary proposed an arrangement: cooperation in exchange for preferential treatment. The company would open its books to the Bureau of Corporations. If the bureau found evidence of wrongdoing, the company would be advised privately and given a chance to set matters right. Roosevelt accepted this "gentlemen's agreement," which was followed by one with International Harvester the next year. J. P. Morgan controlled both firms. From the financier's standpoint, the arrangement seemed entirely sensible. Two great powers, one political and the other economic, met as equals and settled matters between them. For Roosevelt, the gentlemen's agreements eased a serious dilemma. He could accommodate the realities of the modern industrial order while maintaining his public image as the champion against the trusts.

Roosevelt turned his attention to the railroads as well. The main lines of national policy, as with the trusts, had already been laid down. Under the Interstate Commerce Act of 1887, the government established the nation's first regulatory agency, the Interstate Commerce Commission (ICC), to oversee the railroads. But, as with the Sherman Act, railroad regulation remained pretty much a dead letter in its early years. Stymied by a hostile Supreme Court, the ICC lapsed into a mere collector of statistics. Roosevelt was determined to put teeth into the law. The Elkins Act of 1903 empowered the ICC to act against discriminatory rebates—that is, reductions on published rates for preferred or powerful customers. Then, with the 1904 election behind him, Roosevelt pushed for firmer regulation of the railroads.

The central issue was the setting of rates. This power had been denied the ICC, but Roosevelt considered it essential. Senator Nelson Aldrich

and his conservative bloc opposed it just as firmly. In 1906, after nearly two years of wrangling, Congress passed the Hepburn Railway Act. This law gave the ICC the power to set and put into effect maximum rates upon complaint of a shipper, and also the authority to examine railroad books and prescribe uniform bookkeeping. But Roosevelt gave up his demand for limited court review of ICC rate decisions. He also failed to get physical valuation—that is, an inventory of railroad property and equipment—as the basis for fixing fair rates.

The Hepburn Act stood as a testament to Roosevelt's skills as a political operator. He had maneuvered brilliantly against determined opposition and come away with the essentials of what he wanted. Despite grumbling by Senate progressives, Roosevelt was satisfied. He had achieved a landmark expansion of the government's regulatory powers over business.

These powers then began to extend to consumer protection, an area where the muckrakers

CAMPAIGNING FOR THE SQUARE DEAL
When William McKinley ran for president in 1896, he sat on his front porch in Canton, Ohio, and received delegations of voters. That was not Theodore Roosevelt's way. He considered the presidency a "bully pulpit," and he used the office brilliantly to mobilize public opinion and to assert his leadership. The pre-eminence of the presidency in American public life begins with Roosevelt's administration. Here, at the height of his crusading powers, he stumps for the Square Deal in the 1904 election. (Library of Congress)

FILTH AND CHICANERY
IN CHICAGO MEAT-PACKING, 1906

Novelist Upton Sinclair is best remembered for his virulent attack on the meat-packing industry, The Jungle. *This brief excerpt indicates why his novel prompted a wave of investigations and regulatory legislation.*

When Jurgis had first inspected the packing plants with Szedvilas, he had marveled while he listened to the tale of all the things that were made out of the carcasses of animals, and of all the lesser industries that were maintained there; now he found that each one of these lesser industries was a separate little inferno, in its way as horrible as the killing-beds, the source and fountain of them all. The workers in each of them had their own peculiar diseases. . . .

There were the "hoisters," as they were called, whose task it was to press the lever which lifted the dead cattle off the floor. They ran along upon a rafter, peering down through the damp and the steam, and as old Durham's architects had not built the killing room for the convenience of the hoisters, at every few feet they would have to stoop under a beam, say four feet above the one they ran on, which got them into the habit of stooping, so that in a few years they would be walking like chimpanzees. Worst of any, however, were the fertilizer men, and those who served in the cooking rooms. These people could not be shown to the visitor—for the odor of a fertilizer man would scare any ordinary visitor at a hundred yards, and as for the other men, who worked in tank rooms full of steam, and in some of which there were open vats near the level of the floor, their peculiar trouble was that they fell into the vats; and when they were fished out, there was never enough of them left to be worth exhibiting—sometimes they would be overlooked for days, till all but the bones of them had gone out of the world as Durham's Pure Leaf Lard! . . .

There was never the least attention paid to what was cut up for sausage; there would come all the way back from Europe old sausage that had been rejected, and that was mouldy and white—it would be dosed with borax and glycerine, and dumped into the hoppers, and made over again for home consumption. There would be meat that had tumbled out on the floor, in the dirt and sawdust, where the workers had tramped and spit uncounted billions of consumption germs. There would be meat stored in great piles in rooms; and the water from leaky roofs would drip over it, and thousands of rats would race about on it. It was too dark in these storage places to see well, but a man could run his hand over these piles of meat and sweep off handfuls of the dried dung of rats. These rats were nuisances, and the packers would put poisoned bread out for them, they would die, and then rats, bread, and meat would go into the hoppers together. . . . All of their sausage came out of the same bowl, but when they came to wrap it they would stamp some of it "special," and for this they would charge two cents more a pound.

---

truly made their mark. In 1905, Samuel Hopkins Adams published a series of articles on the patent-medicine business in *Collier's Weekly*. The first paragraph opened with these riveting words:

> Gullible America will spend this year some seventy-five millions of dollars in the purchase of patent medicines. In consideration of this sum it will swallow huge quantities of alcohol, an appalling amount of opiates and narcotics, a wide assortment of varied drugs ranging from powerful and dangerous heart depressants to insidious liver stimulants; and, far in excess of all other ingredients, undiluted fraud. For fraud, exploited by the skillfullest of advertising bunco men, is the basis of the trade.

In the Agriculture Department, the chemist Harvey W. Wiley had long been analyzing the chemical adulteration of food products. He began to test the additives on twelve healthy, young male volunteers who had agreed to serve as guinea pigs in the public interest. Wiley's

"Poison Squad" captured national attention. Numerous pure food and drug bills, introduced in Congress in 1905, had been stymied by industry lobbies. Then, in 1906, Upton Sinclair's novel *The Jungle* appeared. Sinclair had aimed at exposing labor exploitation in the Chicago meat-packing houses, but his graphic descriptions of rotten meat and filthy conditions excited—and sickened—the nation. President Roosevelt, hitherto not greatly concerned about consumer issues, now threw his weight into the legislative battle. Congress passed the Pure Food and Drug and Meat Inspection acts within months.

During the 1904 presidential campaign, Roosevelt had taken to calling his program the "Square Deal." This kind of labeling was new to American politics. It introduced a political style that dramatized issues, mobilized public opinion, and asserted leadership. But the Square Deal meant something of substance as well. After many years of passivity and weakness, the federal government had reclaimed the large role it had abandoned after the Civil War. Now, however, the target became the new economic order. When companies misused corporate power, the government had the responsibility of correcting matters and assuring Americans of a "square deal." Under Roosevelt's leadership, progressivism had come to national politics.

The Aftermath of Colonial Expansion

Theodore Roosevelt left a similar imprint of vigorous action—laced with prudence—on the conduct of the nation's foreign affairs. He had been thrust into the presidency in 1901 just as the United States was concluding its brief burst of overseas expansion by subduing the Filipino independence movement. The next step was to exploit the resulting strategic opportunities in the Caribbean and the Pacific. This was Roosevelt's main foreign policy task, and he welcomed it.

In the 1890s, Roosevelt had been an exuberant expansionist and an admirer of the geopolitics of Captain Alfred T. Mahan. "All the great masterful races have been fighting races," Roosevelt declared. Nothing would be worse for the United States, already too commercial for his aristocratic taste, than "slothful and ignoble

peace." But a nation's power had to be used only for good ends and, in particular, to keep the world from sliding into anarchy. Roosevelt stated his foreign policy in a colorful phrase, "Speak softly and carry a big stick." The international forces for disorder were such, he maintained, as to "render it incumbent on all civilized and orderly powers to insist on the proper policing of the world." This view licensed the United States to exert power as needed in regions that, because of the country's overseas expansion, had fallen under its direct influence.

A canal across Central America headed Roosevelt's agenda. After persuading Britain in 1901 to give up its treaty right to a joint canal enterprise, Roosevelt proceeded to more troublesome matters. During the 1880s, a company headed by Ferdinand M. de Lesseps, a French engineer, had started to build a canal across the isthmus of Panama, a province of Colombia. De Lesseps had previously directed the construction of the Suez Canal. The United States agreed to pay $40 million for the company that owned the de Lesseps assets. The Roosevelt administration then entered into negotiations with Colombia to lease the strip of land through which the canal would run. The Colombian legislature voted down the proposed treaty, partly because the company's rights would soon expire and the sale to the United States could then be renegotiated to Colombia's benefit. Furious over what seemed to him a breach of faith, Roosevelt contemplated outright seizure of Panama but settled on a more devious solution.

The key intermediary in the sale of the de Lesseps assets, an engineer named Philippe Bunau-Varilla, let Roosevelt know that an independence movement was brewing in Panama. The United States in turn informed Bunau-Varilla that American naval ships were steaming toward Panama. When the U.S.S. *Nashville* dropped anchor at Colon on November 3, 1903, the revolution against Colombian rule went off on schedule. The United States recognized Panama the next day. Less than two weeks later, with Bunau-Varilla serving as representative of the new republic, Panama signed a treaty with the United States. The agreement granted the United States a perpetually renewable lease on a canal zone. The Panama Canal, completed in 1914, gave the United States a commanding

THE PANAMA CANAL

The Canal Zone was acquired through devious means in which Americans could take no pride (and which led in 1978 to the Senate's decision to restore the property to Panama). But the building of the Panama Canal itself was a triumph of American ingenuity and drive. Dr. William C. Gorgas cleaned out the malarial mosquitoes that had earlier stymied the French. Under Col. George W. Goethals, the U.S. army overcame formidable obstacles of terrain and construction in a mighty feat of engineering. This photograph shows the lower main gates of the Miroflores Locks on July 5, 1913 as the canal nears completion. (Historical Pictures Service)

commercial and strategic position in the Western hemisphere.

Next came the task of making the Caribbean Basin secure. The countries there, said Secretary of State Elihu Root, had been placed "in the front yard of the United States" by the Panama Canal. Therefore, as Roosevelt put it, they had to "behave themselves." In the case of Cuba, this was readily managed in the settlement following the Spanish-American War. Before the United States withdrew from Cuba in 1902, it reorganized Cuban finances and concluded a sanitation program that eliminated yellow fever from the island. This disease had ravaged Cuba for many years. As a condition for gaining independence, Cuba was required to include in its constitution a proviso called the Platt Amendment. The amendment gave the United States the right to intervene if Cuban independence were threatened or if Cuba failed to maintain internal order. Cuba also granted the United States a permanent lease on Guantanamo Bay, where the U.S. Navy built a large base.

Roosevelt believed that instability in the Caribbean invited the intervention of European powers. For example, Britain and Germany blockaded Venezuela in 1902–1903 for failing to meet its debt payments. In 1904, Roosevelt announced that the United States would act as

"policeman" of the region, stepping in "however reluctantly, in flagrant cases . . . of wrongdoing or impotence." This policy became known as the Roosevelt Corollary to the Monroe Doctrine. Under its cloak, the United States intervened regularly in the internal affairs of Caribbean states. In 1905, the United States took over the custom and debt management of the Dominican Republic. When similar financial intervention by the United States touched off a rebellion in Nicaragua in 1912, American marines landed and occupied the country.

Roosevelt's thinking was primarily strategic; his successor, William Howard Taft, took a more commercial view. American investments in the Caribbean region grew dramatically during the Taft administration, from 1909 to 1913. The United Fruit Company owned about 160,000 acres in Central American countries by 1913, and U.S. investments in Cuban sugar plantations quadrupled in fifteen years. Taft quickly intervened when disorder threatened American property. But he also regarded business investment as a force for stability in underdeveloped areas. Taft spoke for "dollar diplomacy," the aggressive coupling of American diplomatic and economic interests abroad.

In the Far East, commercial interests had always stood at the forefront. In 1899, with China carved up into spheres of influence, Secretary of State John Hay sent an "Open Door" note to the occupying powers seeking assurances of equal trading opportunities for all nations. The replies were noncommittal or ambiguous, but Hay chose to interpret them as accepting the American position. When a secret society of Chinese nationalists launched the Boxer Rebellion in 1900, the United States joined the campaign to raise the siege of the foreign legations in Peking. America took the opportunity to assert a second principle to the Open Door, the preservation of China as a "territorial and administrative entity." As long as the legal fiction of an independent China survived, so would American claims to equal access to the China market.

In the wake of the Spanish-American War, the United States had quickly consolidated its strategic position in the Pacific. The partition of the Samoan Islands in 1900 with Germany secured America's South Pacific anchor and completed the network of U.S. island bases. The naval strength of the United States could now be projected across the Pacific, where the nation faced strong rivals in Asia. The European powers had acceded to American claims to preeminence in the Caribbean, including the Roosevelt Corollary. But Britain, Germany, France, and Russia were strongly entrenched in the Far East, with no inclination to defer to American interests. The United States also confronted a strategically placed Asian nation—Japan—that had vital interests at stake.

Japan was a rising world power. It had unveiled its military strength in the Sino-Japanese War of 1894–1895, which began the dismemberment of China. The Anglo-Japanese Alliance of 1902 removed the English naval challenge to Japan in the Far East. In 1904, provoked by Russian assaults on Manchuria, Japan suddenly attacked the czar's fleet at Port Arthur, Russia's leased port in China. In a series of brilliant victories, the Japanese demolished the Russian military forces in Asia. Roosevelt, anxious to restore some semblance of a power balance, mediated a settlement of the Russo-Japanese War at Portsmouth, New Hampshire, in 1905. Japan emerged as the predominant power in North Asia.

Despite his bombastic rhetoric, Roosevelt took an accommodating stance toward Japanese ex-

pansionism. However, a surge of anti-Oriental feeling in California complicated his efforts. In 1906, the San Francisco school board placed all Asian students in a segregated school, infuriating Japan. The "gentlemen's agreement" of 1907, in which Japan agreed to restrict immigration to the United States, smoothed matters, but the periodic resurgence of racism in California led to continuing tensions with the proud Japanese. Roosevelt meanwhile moved to balance Japan's military power by increasing American naval strength in the Pacific. American battleships visited Japan in 1908 and then made a global tour in an impressive display of sea power. Late that year, near the end of his administration, Roosevelt achieved his accommodation with Japan. The Root-Takahira Agreement between the two nations confirmed the status quo in the Pacific, as well as the principles of free oceanic commerce and equal trade opportunity in China.

However, William Howard Taft entered the White House in 1909 convinced that the United States had been shortchanged. Throughout his administration, Taft pressed for a larger role in the Far East for American bankers and investors, especially in the railroad construction going on in China. Taft hoped that American capital could serve as a counterbalance against Japanese power and as a lever for increased commercial opportunities. When the Chinese Revolution of 1911 toppled the ruling Manchu dynasty, Taft supported the Chinese Nationalists as a new counterforce to the Japanese. The United States thus entered a long-term conflict with Japan that ended in war thirty years later.

The triumphant thrust across the Pacific lost its luster. The United States had become embroiled in a distant struggle that promised many future liabilities but little of the fabulous profits that had lured Americans to Asia. It was a chastening experience for an emerging world power.

The New Nationalism

During his two terms as president, Theodore Roosevelt struggled to bring a modern corporate economy under control. He was well aware that his Square Deal had built on nineteenth-century foundations. In his final presidential speeches, Roosevelt dwelt on the need for a reform agenda for the twentieth century. When he left office in

1909, he thought he had arranged matters so there would be steady movement in that direction. He was mistaken. By the time Roosevelt returned in 1910 from a year-long safari in Africa, turmoil reigned in Washington. Modern progressive reform would come, not from thoughtful debate or careful planning, but in political battle.

The agencies of historical change sometimes take strange forms. A person out of tune with the times can, by the sheer friction he or she generates, serve as the catalyst for great events. Such became the fate of William Howard Taft, Roosevelt's handpicked successor. Taft was an estimable man in many ways. He had been an able jurist and a superb administrator. He had served Roosevelt loyally and well as governor general of the Philippines and as secretary of war. But he was not by nature a progressive politician. Taft was incapable of dramatizing issues or of stirring the people. He disliked the give-and-take of politics, he distrusted power, and he generally deferred to Congress. Moreover, Taft was, in different ways than Roosevelt, deeply conservative. He sanctified property rights, he revered the processes of the law, and, unlike Roosevelt, he found it hard to trim his means to fit his ends.

By 1909, the reform ferment had unsettled the Republican party. On the right, the conservatives were girding themselves against further losses. Under Senator Aldrich, they still dominated on Capitol Hill and had strong influence in the party. On the other hand, progressive Republicans were rebellious. They had broad popular support, especially in the Midwest, and, in Robert La Follette, a fiery leader. And they were not about to be pawned off. The resourceful Roosevelt had somehow stymied them. No more compromise for them. To reconcile these conflicting forces within the Republican party would have been a daunting task for the most accomplished politician. For Taft, it spelled disaster.

First there was the tariff. Taft had campaigned for "a sizable reduction." Senator Aldrich won him over during the lengthy drafting process and he came out for the protectionist Payne-Aldrich Tariff Act of 1909, which especially favored eastern industry. Then Taft infuriated his former tariff-cutting allies by touring the country and touting the new tariff legislation as the "best" ever passed.

Next came the battle over "Uncle Joe" Cannon, the Speaker of the House of Representatives. Joseph G. Cannon of Illinois, a died-in-the-wool conservative, virtually controlled the flow of legislation in the House. Progressives were determined to depose him. Taft abandoned them in exchange for Cannon's help on administration legislation. A House revolt broke the Speaker's power in 1910. Cannon's defeat was regarded as a defeat for the president as well.

Most damaging to Taft was the Pinchot-Ballinger affair. U.S. Chief Forester Gifford Pinchot, an ardent conservationist and chum of Roosevelt's, accused Taft's Secretary of the Interior, Richard A. Ballinger, of involvement in a scheme to transfer public coal lands in Alaska to a private syndicate. When Pinchot went public with the charges in January 1910, Taft fired him for insubordination. A true conservationist, Taft compiled a stronger record of protecting the wilderness than had Roosevelt. Somehow it did not matter. In the eyes of the Progressives, the Pinchot-Ballinger affair marked Taft for life as a friend of the "interests."

Solemnly pledged to carrying on in Roosevelt's tradition, Taft managed to work his way into the conservative Republican camp in less than two years. While doing so, he helped transform the reformers into a distinct faction of the party. By 1910, they were calling themselves "Progressives" or, in more belligerent moments, "insurgents." Taft responded by trying to purge them in the Republican primaries that year. This vendetta climaxed Taft's record of disastrous leadership.

The Progressives emerged much stronger and angrier than before. They formed the National Progressive Republican League in January 1911 and began a drive to take control of the Republican party. La Follette was the Progressives' leader and their designated presidential candidate, but they knew their best hope would be Theodore Roosevelt.

Roosevelt, home from Africa, yearned to reenter the political fray. He was not easily reconciled to the absence of power and would have been troublesome for Taft under any circumstances. As it was, the president's handling of the Progressives fed Roosevelt's mounting sense of outrage. But Roosevelt was too loyal a party man to defy the Republican establishment, and too astute a politician not to recognize that a party split would benefit the Democrats. He could be spurred into rebellion only by the discovery of a true clash of philosophies.

Taft again proved obliging. He attacked the problem of economic concentration—the overriding issue of the day—in a way that crystallized Roosevelt's thinking and led him to formulate a policy called the New Nationalism.

From the first, Roosevelt had been troubled by the Sherman Antitrust Act. To enforce competition seemed to him to fly in the face of the inevitable modern tendency toward economic concentration. By distinguishing betwen good and bad trusts, Roosevelt had managed to reconcile public policy and economic reality. But this was a makeshift solution, depending as it did on a president inclined to stretch his powers to the limit. Taft had no such inclination. His legalistic mind rebelled at the discretionary use of presidential authority. The Sherman Act was on the books. "We are going to enforce that law or die in the attempt," Taft promised grimly. Attorney General George W. Wickersham stepped up the pace of antitrust actions, taking no notice of the "gentlemen's agreements."

Giant business firms found themselves caught in a legal dilemma. If they competed freely, they would drive out weaker companies and be guilty of monopoly. But if they tried to share the market with these companies, they would be guilty of conspiracy in restraint of trade. Taft's blindness to this dilemma forced some big-business leaders, especially those active in the National Civic Federation, to advocate a basic shift of public policy away from the Sherman Act.

This conclusion was driven home to Roosevelt in a peculiarly painful way. A government suit against the United States Steel Corporation in 1911 charged that the firm had violated the antimonopoly clause of the Sherman Act by acquiring the Tennessee Coal and Iron Company in 1907. That acquisition had been personally approved by Roosevelt as a necessary step—so U.S. Steel representatives explained it to him— to prevent a financial collapse on Wall Street. The suit thus amounted to a humiliating attack on Roosevelt. Either he had conspired to circum-

vent the Sherman Act or he had been tricked by U.S. Steel. Nothing was better calculated to propel Roosevelt into action than an issue that was both an affair of personal honor and a question of broad principle.

The country did not have to choose between breaking up big business and submitting to corporate rule, Roosevelt argued. There was a third way. The federal government could be empowered to oversee big business to make sure it acted in the public interest. In a speech in Osawatomie, Kansas, in August 1910, Roosevelt discussed what he termed the New Nationalism. The central issue, he said, was human welfare versus property rights. In modern society, property had to be controlled "to whatever degree the public welfare may require it." The government would become "the steward of the public welfare."

This formulation removed the restraints from Roosevelt's thinking. Ultimately, he did not stop short of advocating government price fixing for corporate industry. He took up the cause of social justice, adding to his program a federal child labor law, federal workmen's compensation, regulation of labor relations, and a minimum wage for women. Then, recognizing the courts as a bastion of conservatism, Roosevelt took them on by proposing sharp curbs on their powers and even popular recall of court decisions.

Beyond these specifics, the New Nationalism presented a new political philosophy. As propounded in Herbert Croly's *The Promise of American Life* (1909), the New Nationalism called for uniting rival strains in the American political tradition. From Hamilton's federalism, it took reliance on strong national government; from Jefferson's republicanism, regard for the interests of the common man. The New Nationalism marked a genuine break from America's political past.

Early in 1912, Roosevelt announced his candidacy for the presidency and immediately swept the progressive Republicans into his camp. A bitter and divisive battle ensued. Taft proved a tenacious opponent. Roosevelt virtually swept the field in states that held primary elections. But Taft controlled the party organizations elsewhere. The party regulars dominated the national convention, and they threw the nomination to Taft.

Roosevelt, considering himself cheated out of the nomination, led his followers into a new Progressive party. In a crusading campaign, he offered New Nationalism to the people.

The New Freedom

A rival reform philosophy was emerging within the Democratic party. Demoralized since the free-silver campaign of 1896, the Democrats had come to life in the 1910 elections. They won a number of traditionally Republican governorships and gained a solid majority in the House of Representatives for the first time since 1892. William Jennings Bryan, after fourteen years as party leader and three tries at the presidency, reluctantly made way for a new generation of leaders who had been swept into office by the reform wave.

The ablest, by all odds, was Woodrow Wilson of New Jersey. A noted political scientist, he had served for eight years as president of Princeton University. Then, defeated in a controversy over graduate-school education at Princeton, he resigned to accept the Democratic nomination for governor of New Jersey in 1910. Wilson compiled a brilliant record as governor and won the Democratic presidential nomination in 1912. He could identify himself as a reformer by his achievements in New Jersey—defeat of the boss system and passage of a direct primary law, workmen's compensation, and regulation of railroads and utilities.

Wilson had, to a fault, the qualities of moral certainty that characterized the progressive politician. A brilliant speaker, he almost instinctively assumed the mantle of righteousness—and, by the same token, had little tolerance for the views of his critics. At the time of his presidential nomination, Wilson had no national reform program. Only during the election campaign did he hammer out a coherent program to oppose Roosevelt's New Nationalism.

The New Freedom, as Wilson called his program, had its roots in old-fashioned Jeffersonian ideas. Born and bred in Virginia, Wilson was by tradition a states-rights Democrat. He supported low tariffs and disliked big government and special privilege. He believed in an independent, self-reliant citizenry. Wilson fashioned these traditional notions into a modern reform agenda.

July 13 1912   THE NEW RIDER   Price 10 Cents

ON TO THE WHITE HOUSE
At the Democratic convention, Woodrow Wilson only narrowly defeated the front-runner, Champ Clark of Missouri. *Harper's Weekly* triumphantly depicted Wilson immediately after his nomination—the scholar-turned politician riding off on the Democratic donkey, his running mate, Thomas R. Marshall, hanging on behind. *Harper's* editor, George Harvey, had identified Wilson as of presidential timber as early as 1906, long before the Princeton president had thought of politics, and worked on his behalf ever since. (The Newberry Library, Chicago)

Louis D. Brandeis, known as the "people's lawyer," gave Wilson a sophisticated critique of economic concentration. Bigness did not mean efficiency, Brandeis argued. On the contrary, the trusts were inherently wasteful compared to firms vigorously competing in a free market. Nor would the public interest be served by governmental oversight of big business. The more likely result would be a comfortable alliance between regulators and regulated. The country needed not a powerful trade commission, Brandeis concluded, but a better Sherman Antitrust

Act that would "so restrict the wrong use of competition that the right use of competition will destroy monopoly."

As he warmed to the debate, Wilson drew the issue in the fundamental terms of slavery and freedom. "This is a struggle for emancipation," he proclaimed in October 1912. "If America is not to have free enterprise, then she can have freedom of no sort whatever." Wilson also scorned Roosevelt's social-welfare program. It might be benevolent, he declared, but it also would be paternalistic and contrary to the traditions of a free people. The New Nationalism represented a future of collectivism, Wilson warned, whereas the New Freedom would conserve the political and economic liberties of the individual.

Wilson won the 1912 election. But did Americans prefer the New Freedom to the New Nationalism? One cannot judge by the outcome of the election. The Republican vote was divided.

Taft ran a poor third, but he kept Roosevelt from winning. Wilson received 42 percent of the popular vote—fewer votes than Bryan got against Taft in 1908—but won by a landslide in electoral votes. One sign of the reform-minded nature of the 1912 electorate was a record nine hundred thousand votes for the Socialist candidate, Eugene V. Debs. But because of the party splits, the 1912 election could not be considered a national referendum between the New Nationalism and the New Freedom.

Likewise on the matter of implementation. Would a victorious Roosevelt have put the New Nationalism into effect? This question also remains unanswerable. Roosevelt would certainly have had a hard time of it. Since the Progressive party had fielded only a presidential ticket, with no congressional candidates, Congress probably would have posed tremendous obstacles. Not only did Wilson win the presidency, but his

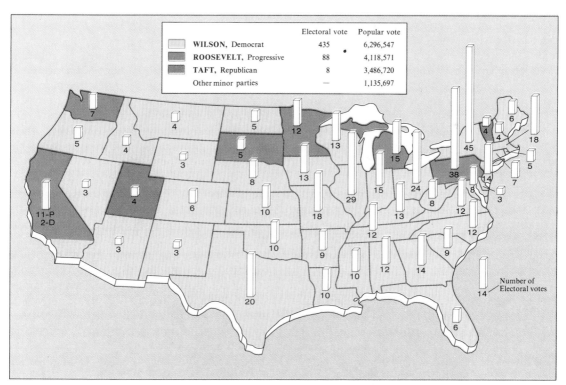

	Electoral vote	Popular vote
WILSON, Democrat	435	6,296,547
ROOSEVELT, Progressive	88	4,118,571
TAFT, Republican	8	3,486,720
Other minor parties	—	1,135,697

MAP 21.2 ELECTION OF 1912

The 1912 election reveals why the two-party system is so strongly rooted in American politics. The Democrats, although a minority party, won an electoral landslide because the Republicans became, in effect, two parties for the election. The disastrous result indicated the enormous incentive for major parties against splintering. The Socialists, despite a record vote of 900,000, got no electoral votes at all, suggesting the fatal weakness of third parties in the American political system. To vote Socialist in 1912 meant, in effect, to throw away one's vote.

party, for the first time since the 1850s, gained control of both houses of Congress. Yet the Democratic program eventually enacted was a far cry from Wilson's campaign pronouncement of the New Freedom.

Upon entering the White House, Wilson chose a flank attack on the problem of economic power. So long out of office, the Democrats were hungry for tariff reform. From the prevailing average of 40 percent, the Underwood Tariff Act of 1913 pared rates down to an average of 25 percent and applied the sharpest cuts to the trust-dominated industries. Democrats confidently expected the Underwood Tariff to spur competition and reduce prices in American markets.

The administration then turned to the nation's banking system, whose key weakness was the absence of a central reserve bank. In practice, this role had been assumed by the major New York banks, which accepted the deposits of lesser banks and assisted them if they came under pressure. However, if the New York institutions themselves weakened, the entire system could totter and even collapse. This had nearly happened during the Panic of 1907. The need for a reserve system became widely accepted, but the form it should take was hotly debated. Wall Street wanted a centralized system, controlled by the bankers. Rural Democrats and their spokesman, Senator Carter Glass of Virginia, preferred a decentralized network of reserve banks. Progressives of both parties agreed that the essential factor should be public control over the reserve system. The bankers, who had come under severe criticism from a congressional investigation of the "money trust" early in 1913, were on the defensive in this contest.

President Wilson, no expert to begin with, learned quickly and reconciled the reformers and bankers. The monumental Federal Reserve Act of 1913 gave the nation a banking system resistant to financial panic. The act delegated reserve functions to twelve district reserve banks, which would be controlled by the member banks. The Federal Reserve Board imposed public regulation on this regional structure. In one stroke, the act strengthened the banking system considerably and placed a measure of restraint on the "money trust."

Having dealt with tariff and banking reform, Wilson turned at last to the central issue of the New Freedom. The issue of economic concentration had seemed straightforward enough during the 1912 campaign. Roosevelt wanted to abandon the antitrust approach, while Wilson wished to make the existing Sherman Act airtight. Wilson's thinking had been crystallized by the recent Supreme Court decision in *Standard Oil v. United States* (1911), which ordered the dissolution of the oil trust. In this case the Court reasserted the "rule of reason"—that is, judicial discretion over what constituted illegal restraints of trade. At another time, this restoration to the Sherman Act of an ancient rule of the common law might have caused little controversy. But in 1911, the Standard Oil ruling seemed intended to weaken the antitrust act. In response, Wilson proposed revisions to the Sherman Act so tightly drawn as to nullify the rule of reason, including explicitly prohibiting such practices as price discrimination and interlocking directorates. Precise prohibitions, vigorously enforced by the government, made up the New Freedom approach to the problem of monopoly.

In midcourse, Wilson changed his mind. In its final version, the Clayton Antitrust Act of 1914 added the following phrase to the prohibited business practices: "where the effect may be to substantially lessen competition or tend to create a monopoly in any line of commerce." These words, in effect, amounted to a return to the rule of reason. The motive for Wilson's retreat was partly practical. He had lost confidence in the effectiveness of rigid legal prohibitions, and his adviser, Louis Brandeis, now advocated a regulatory approach. The idea of a powerful trade commission came from Roosevelt, but he had intended it to replace the antitrust law. Brandeis proposed that the trade commission enforce competition. The Federal Trade Commission Act of 1914 gave the FTC broad powers to investigate companies and to issue "cease and desist" orders against unfair trade practices that violated antitrust law.

However, the Clayton and FTC acts involved more than a tactical shift. By the spring of 1914, Wilson was actively mending his fences with big business. "The antagonism between business and Government is over," he proclaimed. To the chagrin of Brandeis, Wilson's appointees to the FTC were probusiness and disinclined to act as watchdogs over industrial activity. Cooperation, not prosecution, became the commission's watchword. Wilson himself showed little enthusiasm for trust busting—far less, certainly, than had Taft.

In the end, Wilson came close to the position Roosevelt had held under the Square Deal. Wilson welcomed business leaders, including J. P. Morgan, to the White House. In addition, the Justice Department announced its willingness to advise corporations about how to avoid antitrust actions. The Wilson administration thus raised the "gentlemen's agreements" pioneered by Roosevelt to the status of official national policy.

On social policy, too, Wilson drifted from the principles of the New Freedom. During the campaign, he had denounced the social program of the New Nationalism as paternalistic. Compared to his dealings with big business, Wilson proved resistant to "class" legislation for labor and agriculture. He accepted cosmetic language in the Clayton Act stating that labor and farm organizations were not illegal combinations. But he rejected the exemptions they wanted for immunity from antitrust prosecution.

The labor vote had grown increasingly important to the Democratic party, however. As the prospect of a second presidential campaign loomed larger, Wilson lost some of his scruples about prolabor legislation and championed a host of landmark bills beneficial to American workers. These included the Seamen's Act of 1915 and a model federal workmen's compensation law, a federal child labor law, and the Adamson eight-hour law for railroad workers, all in 1916. Likewise, after stubbornly resisting earlier farm-credit measures, Wilson approved in 1916 the Federal Farm Loan Act, providing the low-interest rural-credit system long demanded by farmers.

Four years in the White House carried Woodrow Wilson far from his Jeffersonian principles. In the end, he presided over a major intrusion of the federal government into people's lives. Wilson encountered the same kind of dilemmas that confronted all successful Progressives—the claims of moral principle versus the unyielding realities of political and economic life. Progressives were high minded but not radical. They saw evils in the system, but they did not consider the system itself evil. They also prided themselves on being realists as well as moralists. So it stood to reason that Wilson, like other Progressives who achieved power, would drift to the center.

Progressivism and the Mexican Intervention

Foreign affairs offered a better chance for holding to the moral ground of progressive idealism. So it seemed, at any rate, to Woodrow Wilson. For one thing, foreign matters did not involve the exasperating complexity of domestic America—those stubborn interests and demands that required constant trimming of Wilson's high-minded policy. The world stage seemed a simpler place for progressive reform, because the objective was to bring other nations into conformity with American ideals. Moreover, the power equation appeared more favorable beyond the nation's borders. The United States was a great power, overwhelmingly so in relation to its neighbors to the south. Mexico seemed less formidable in world affairs than, for example, the House of Morgan in domestic politics.

To think in this vein, of course, betrayed Wilson's inexperience in world politics. He had far less knowledge about international affairs than had Theodore Roosevelt a decade earlier. Wilson's choice for secretary of state, William Jennings Bryan, knew more about diplomacy. But he, like Wilson, had a strong missionary and moralistic approach. Both of them deplored William Howard Taft's "dollar diplomacy" as the extension abroad of the business influence they were trying to curb at home. It seemed to Wilson "a very perilous thing to determine the foreign policy of a nation in terms of material interest."

Wilson aimed to foster the "development of constitutional liberty in the world" and, above all, to extend it to the nation's neighbors in Latin America. In a major policy speech in October 1913, he vowed to them that the United States would "never again seek one additional foot of territory by conquest." The president said he would strive to advance "human rights, national integrity, and opportunity" in Latin America. To do otherwise would make "ourselves untrue to our own traditions." Guided by such a moral policy, future generations would arrive at "those great heights where there shines unobstructed the light of the justice of God."

Mexico became the first object of Wilson's ministrations. A cycle of revolutions had begun there in 1911. The long dictatorship of Porfirio Diaz was overthrown by Francisco Madero, who

TIME LINE
THE PROGRESSIVE ERA

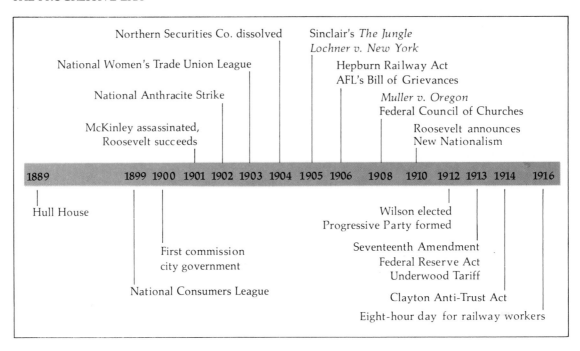

Northern Securities Co. dissolved

National Women's Trade Union League

National Anthracite Strike

McKinley assassinated,
Roosevelt succeeds

Sinclair's *The Jungle*
Lochner v. New York

Hepburn Railway Act
AFL's Bill of Grievances

Muller v. Oregon
Federal Council of Churches

Roosevelt announces
New Nationalism

| 1889 | 1899 | 1900 | 1901 | 1902 | 1903 | 1904 | 1905 | 1906 | 1908 | 1910 | 1912 | 1913 | 1914 | 1916 |

Hull House

First commission
city government

National Consumers League

Wilson elected
Progressive Party formed

Seventeenth Amendment
Federal Reserve Act
Underwood Tariff

Clayton Anti-Trust Act

Eight-hour day for railway workers

spoke much as Wilson did about liberty and constitutionalism. But before Madero could get very far with his reforms, he was deposed and murdered in February 1913 by his chief lieutenant, Victoriano Huerta. Other powers quickly recognized Huerta's provisional government, but the United States had not yet acted when Wilson entered the White House the next month.

Wilson abhorred Huerta and called his coup a "usurpation" and Huerta himself a murderer. Wilson pledged "to force him out." The United States denied recognition to Huerta's government, although this policy opposed America's long-standing tradition of recognizing new governments. Wilson also subjected Mexico to other pressures, including the threatened use of force. By intervening in this way, Wilson insisted, "we act in the interest of Mexico alone. ... We are seeking to counsel Mexico for its own good." Wilson meant he intended to put the Mexican revolution back on the constitutional path started by Madero.

Wilson's determination was strengthened by the emergence of armed opposition to Huerta in northern Mexico under Venustiano Carranza.

This constitutionalist movement, as it became known, gave Wilson some grounds for denying recognition to Huerta—his government did not fully control the country. More important, it signified to Wilson the vitality of the reformist politics that he wanted to foster in Mexico.

The Constitutionalists were ardent nationalists. They had no desire for American intervention in Mexican affairs. Moreover, they wanted a complete revolution. Carranza angrily rebuffed Wilson's efforts to bring about elections through a compromise between the rebels and the Mexican government. He also vowed to resist by force any intrusion of U.S. troops in his country. All he wanted from Wilson, Carranza asserted, was recognition of the Constitutionalists' belligerent status so they could purchase arms in the United States. In exchange for vague promises to respect property rights and "fair" foreign concessions, Carranza finally got his way in 1914. American weapons began to flow to his troops.

The American contribution to the Constitutionalists' cause went much further than selling them arms. For one thing, Wilson isolated Huerta diplomatically. Huerta's crucial support came from the British, who wanted to ensure a steady flow of Mexican oil for their fleet. Under intense pressure from Washington, the British withdrew recognition from Huerta in late 1913—in return for making the United States the guarantor of British property interests in Mexico. When it became clear that neither the loss of British support nor the supplying of Carranza would turn the trick against Huerta, the United States threw its own forces into the game.

Using the pretext of a minor insult to the U.S. Navy at Tampico, Wilson ordered the occupation of the major port of Vera Cruz on April 21, 1914. This action cost 19 American and 126 Mexican lives. With Wilson preparing for a thrust at Mexico City, the Huerta regime began to crumble. Carranza nevertheless condemned the United States for intervening, and his own forces came close to engaging the Americans. When he entered Mexico City in triumph in August 1914, Carranza had some cause to thank the United States. But if any sense of gratitude existed, it was overshadowed by the anti-Americanism inspired by Wilson's insensitivity to Mexican pride and revolutionary zeal.

The later phases of the Mexican revolution dragged the United States ever more deeply into the unprofitable morass of interventionism. No sooner had the Constitutionalists triumphed than Carranza was challenged by his northern general, Pancho Villa. This illiterate but shrewd former bandit had carefully cultivated American representatives in Mexico and won their support in his bid for power against Carranza. But Carranza defeated Villa and drove him northward.

Meanwhile, World War I had broken out, and the United States became entangled with Germany over submarine attacks on civilian ships. The stakes of continued friction with Mexico began to rise. The Wilson administration granted *de facto* recognition to the Carranza government on October 9, 1915.

Pancho Villa was not finished, however. Reduced to the status of a bandit leader, he began to attack U.S. citizens. He killed sixteen Americans after taking them from a train in Chihuahua in January 1916, and then crossed the border and razed the town of Columbus, New Mexico, in March. If Villa wanted to stir up trouble between Washington and Mexico City, he succeeded thoroughly. Wilson sent troops led by General John J. Pershing into Mexico after the elusive Villa. Carranza accepted this action at first, but he grew alarmed as the Americans penetrated deeply into his country. Pershing's force continually increased in size so that it resembled an army of occupation more than a punitive expedition. Mexican public opinion demanded that

IN PURSUIT OF PANCHO VILLA
Pancho Villa's attacks on American citizens were an early example of the terrorism that bedevils American foreign policy in the 1980s. Similarly, Pershing's punitive expedition into Mexico in response was an early demonstration of the difficulties great powers encounter in trying to seize terrorists able to melt away into a larger civilian society. The invading U.S. troops captured some of Pancho Villa's followers, but the wily Villa (center) and his main force got away. (The Bettmann Archive)

Pershing withdraw immediately. But Americans insisted that the threat to U.S. security be stamped out first. Armed clashes with Mexican troops began.

At the brink of war, the two governments backed off. Tempers cooled during a period of inconclusive negotiation, and the U.S. troops began to withdraw early in 1917. With its new constitution ratified and elections completed, the Carranza government received official recogni-

tion from Washington on March 13, 1917, less than a month before the United States entered World War I.

This sad chapter in Mexican-American relations might have been worthwhile if it had taught Woodrow Wilson a lesson, but it did not. The same mixture of high principle, bullying methods, and masked national interest played itself out on a grander stage at Versailles in 1919—with far more tragic results.

A new chapter in American reform began at the start of the twentieth century. For decades, the problems resulting from industrialization and city growth had been mounting. Now, after 1900, a broad progressive movement sprang up that dominated the nation's public life until World War I intervened. The unifying element in the reform activity was a common intellectual outlook, highly principled and idealistic as to goals, and confident of the human capacity to find the means.

Beyond this shared outlook, progressivism broke up into diverse, often conflicting, groups. Political reformers, for example, included business groups concerned chiefly with improving the efficiency of city government. There also were state reformers, such as Robert La Follette, who opposed privilege and wanted to democratize the political process. Both groups worked—in different ways—to enhance their power against entrenched party machines.

Progressivism also drew new groups into reform activity. Social welfare became very much

the province of American women, and the social feminism that resulted had a strong influence on the struggle for women's rights. In the cities, working people and immigrants also became reform minded and thereby set in motion a new political force, urban liberalism.

At the national level, attention focused primarily on controlling the economic power that had become concentrated in corporate business. This overriding problem led to Theodore Roosevelt's Square Deal, then his New Nationalism, and finally to Woodrow Wilson's New Freedom. During the course of these developments, a troubling weakness of progressivism became apparent: righteous idealism could not be easily accommodated to the need for compromise in the real world of power and diversity. Wilson managed well enough on the domestic front, but not when he encountered the outside world. This problem became apparent in the American involvement in the Mexican revolution. The stakes grew vastly higher after the United States entered World War I.

Suggestions for Further Reading

Reform Impulses

The best narrative treatments of the Progressive era are two volumes in the New American Nation Series: George E. Mowry, *The Era of Theodore Roosevelt: 1900–1912* (1958) and Arthur S. Link, *Woodrow Wilson and the Progressive Era: 1900–1917* (1954). Harold U. Faulkner, *The Quest for Social Justice, 1898–1914* (1931) is a useful portrait of the social setting within which progressivism developed. The most influential interpretation of

progressive reform, although its arguments have been effectively disputed, is Richard Hofstadter's *Age of Reform* (1955). A radical critique that stresses the reforming role of big business is James Weinstein, *The Corporate Ideal in the Liberal State, 1900–1918* (1968). Robert H. Wiebe, *The Search for Order, 1877–1920* (1967) places progressive reform in a broader context of organizational development.

The progressive mind has been studied from many different angles. The religious underpinnings are stressed in Robert M. Crunden, *Ministers of Reform: The Progressives' Achievement in American Civilization, 1889–1920* (1982). In *The New Radicalism in America, 1889–1963* (1965), Christopher Lasch sees progressivism as a form of cultural revolt. Samuel Haber traces the influence of Frederick W. Taylor in *Efficiency and Uplift: Scientific Management in the Progressive Era* (1964). On the intellectual basis for progressivism, the key book is Morton White, *Social Thought in America: The Revolt Against Formalism* (1975). For leading figures in this anti-formalist tradition, see Samuel Konefsky, *The Legacy of Holmes and Brandeis* (1956) and David Riesman, *Thorstein Veblen* (1963). On political thinkers, the most useful book is Charles Forcey, *The Crossroads of Liberalism: Croly, Weyl, Lippmann and the Progressive Era* (1961). Clarke A. Chambers, *Paul U. Kellog and the Survey* (1971) treats one of the key social investigators. For the muckrakers, see Louis Filler, *Crusaders for American Liberalism* (1938); Harold S. Wilson, *McClure's Magazine and the Muckrakers* (1970); and, for documents, Arthur and Lila Weinberg, eds., *The Muckrakers* (1961). To savor fully this brand of journalism, the reader should turn to Lincoln Steffens, *The Shame of the Cities* (1904) and, for one career, *The Autobiography of Lincoln Steffens* (1931).

Political Reform

Political reform has been the subject of a voluminous literature. Wisconsin progressivism can be studied in David P. Thelen, *The New Citizenship: Origins of Progressivism in Wisconsin, 1885–1900* (1972); Thelen, *Robert LaFollette and the Insurgent Spirit* (1976); and Robert S. Maxwell, *LaFollette and the Rise of Progressivism in Wisconsin* (1956). Other important state progressives are treated in Spencer C. Olin, *California's Prodigal Son: Hiram Johnson and the Progressive Movement* (1968); Robert F. Wesser, *Charles Evans Hughes: Politics and Reform in New York State, 1905–1910* (1967); and Richard Lowitt, *George W. Norris: The Making of a Progressive* (1963). On city reform, see Bradley R. Rice, *Progressive Cities: The Commission Government Movement* (1972); Jack Tager, *The Intellectual as Urban Reformer: Brand Whitlock and the Progressive Movement* (1968); and Melvin G. Holli, *Reform in Detroit: Hazen S. Pingree and Urban Politics* (1969).

Social Reform

On social feminism, the reader should begin with Allen F. Davis, *American Heroine: Jane Addams* (1973) and George Martin, *Madame Secretary: Frances Perkins* (1976). The connection to working women is effectively treated in Nancy S. Dye, *As Equals and Sisters, Feminism, the Labor Movement, and the Women's Trade Union League of New York* (1980). On the ideology of women's suffrage, see Aileen Kraditor, *Ideas of the Women's Suffrage Movement, 1890–1920* (1965). The best treatment of the settlement-house movement is Allen F. Davis, *Spearheads of Reform* (1967). The struggle for tenement-house reform is ably covered in Roy Lubove, *The Progressives and the Slums, 1890–1917* (1962). The seminal essay on urban liberalism is J. Joseph Huthmacher, "Urban Liberalism and the Age of Reform," *Mississippi Valley Historical Review* 44 (September 1962): 231–241. Huthmacher's ideas have been fully developed in John D. Buenker, *Urban Liberalism and Progressive Reform* (1973). The relationship to organized labor can be followed in Irwin Yellowitz, *Labor and the Progressive Movement in New York City* (1965). The rise of American nativism has received authoritative treatment in John Higham, *Strangers in the Land* (1955). James H. Timberlake, *Prohibition and the Progressive Crusade* (1963) covers another important aspect of progressive moralism.

Progressivism and National Politics

National progressivism is best approached through its leading figures. Good biographies include: William Harbaugh, *Power and Responsibility: The Life and Times of Theodore Roosevelt* (1961); G. Wallace Chessman, *Theodore Roosevelt and the Politics of Power* (1969); John Morton Blum, *The Republican Roosevelt* (1954); Donald E. Anderson, *William Howard Taft* (1973); Arthur S. Link, *Woodrow Wilson* (5 vols., 1947–65); John Morton Blum, *Woodrow Wilson and the Politics of Morality* (1956). Aspects of national progressive politics can be followed in James Penick, *Progressive Politics and Conservation: The Ballinger-Pinchot Affair* (1968); Robert Wiebe, *Businessmen and Reform* (1962); Gabriel Kolko, *The Triumph of Conservatism* (1963); James Holt, *Congressional Insurgents and the Party System* (1969). On the South, a comprehensive treatment is provided by Jack Temple Kirby, *Darkness at the Dawning: Race and Reform in the Progressive South* (1972).

On progressive diplomacy, the starting point remains Howard K. Beale, *Theodore Roosevelt and the Rise of America to World Power* (1956). On the thrust into the Caribbean, see Walter LaFeber, *The Panama Canal* (1979); Dana G. Munroe, *Intervention and Dollar Diplomacy in the Caribbean, 1900–1921* (1964); and David Healy, *The United States in Cuba, 1898–1902* (1963). Akira Iriye, *Pacific Estrangement: Japanese and American Expansion, 1897–1911* (1972) covers the Pacific theatre effectively. The Mexican involvement is treated in P. Edward Haley, *Revolution and Intervention: The Diplomacy of Taft and Wilson with Mexico, 1910–1917* (1917). There is a lively and critical analysis of Wilson's misguided policies in Robert E. Quirk, *An Affair of Honor: Woodrow Wilson and the Occupation of Vera Cruz* (1962). The revolution as experienced by the Mexicans is brilliantly depicted in John Womack, *Zapata and the Mexican Revolution* (1968).

22

PROGRESSIVISM GOES TO WAR

*T*he course of American participation in World War I was fundamentally shaped by the progressive period that preceded it. The connections between progressivism and the war may not be immediately obvious. What greater contrast could there be to agitating for domestic reform than fighting a foreign war?

In fact, many Americans saw close links between the two experiences. Reformers eagerly embraced wartime America as an opportunity to put progressive ideals into practice. Educator and philosopher John Dewey argued that wars represented a "plastic juncture" when societies became more open to reason and new ideas. Business could be rationalized, class unity promoted, and scientific efficiency strengthened. In the collective effort of fighting and winning a war, society could be improved. Dewey's optimistic view matched the spirit of the times. Unfortunately, a dissenting observation by Randolph Bourne, an outspoken pacifist and intellectual who had once been a pupil of Dewey's, came closer to reality. "If the war is too strong for you to prevent," Bourne asked, "how is it going to be weak enough for you to control and mold to your liberal purposes?"

Progressivism also influenced the wartime roles of business and government. Mobilization encouraged large-scale industrial organization and set in motion an unparalleled expansion of the national administrative structure. The war experience completed the process of industrial development begun during the nineteenth century and accelerated the centralizing tendencies prominent in economic and political life since the late nineteenth century. As a result of World War I, the United States moved closer to the model of a corporate bureaucratic state that would prevail in the modern era, where the lines between the public and private sectors became increasingly blurred. However, older patterns of informal, localized power coexisted with the new bureaucratic order well into the twentieth century.

Foreign policy showed the link between progressivism and World War I most clearly. The crusading spirit of progressivism spilled over into world affairs, as it had during the Mexican crisis. President Woodrow Wilson declared that American participation would "make the world safe for democracy," "end all wars," and "bring peace and safety to all nations." Imperialism and power politics would give way to morality and good deeds. By pegging American involvement to such lofty goals, Wilson virtually guaranteed disappointment. Even if America won the war, his ideals for world reformation were too far-reaching for practical attainment.

Fighting the War

"It would be the irony of fate if my administration had to deal chiefly with foreign affairs," Woodrow Wilson confided to a friend early in his first term. His remark proved prophetic when Archduke Francis Ferdinand of Austria was assassinated in the Bosnian town of Sarajevo on June 28, 1914. The Great War—few anticipated a second world war just a generation later—erupted in August. Initially it pitted the Allies (Great Britain, France, Japan, Russia, and, in 1915, Italy) against the Central Powers (Germany, Austria-Hungary, Bulgaria, Romania, and Turkey). Early in the war, most Americans saw no reason to get involved in a war among Europe's imperialistic powers. So firmly did they support nonintervention that Wilson won reelection in 1916 with the slogan "He kept us out of war." But several months later, in April 1917, the president stood before Congress and asked for a declaration of war.

The Perils of Neutrality

The entry of the United States into World War I has often been portrayed as a sharp break from the nation's traditional isolation from world affairs. This view is only partly correct. The war did represent America's first sustained participation in European political affairs; after the conflict ended, the United States attained what seems a permanent place as a great world power. Yet the country had hardly been uninvolved in world affairs before 1917. America's dramatic industrial growth and increasing agricultural production during the nineteenth century had led to a search for new and wider markets. The United States found them not only in Europe or Africa, where Great Britain and Germany dominated, but also in Mexico, Canada, South America, and the Far East.

To accompany this economic expansion, American leaders developed a philosophy that provided the ideological basis for U.S. diplomacy.

MAP 22.1 EUROPE AT THE START OF WORLD WAR I
By early August 1914, a complex set of interlocking alliances had drawn the major European powers into war. At first, the United States held aloof from the conflict. The *Plain Dealer*, a Wabash, Indiana, newspaper, captured the prevailing isolationist sentiment when it noted, "We never appreciated so keenly as now the foresight of our fathers in emigrating from Europe." Not until April 1917 did the United States enter the war on the Allied side.

LOVE AND CRISIS IN THE PRESIDENT'S LIFE

The White House
13 September 1915

Monday morning, 9:50

My precious Darling,

The weight of public matters rests rather grievously upon me this morning and I have been obliged to fill the morning with many important engagements, beginning with the Secretary of State in half an hour, but there is one resource for me always: I can turn to you (what would it not be worth to me if I could *go* to you) and all the burden will fall away with the realization of your love and vital, comprehending sympathy.

The Secretary and I will be obliged this morning, I fear, to make some decisions that *may* affect the history of the country more than any decisions a President and Secretary of State ever made before and it gives me such a steadiness and added *balance* in my thinking that you have come to my side and put your hand in mine and given your splendid life to sustain mine. . . .

Your own
Woodrow

Source: Edwin Tribble, *A President in Love: The Courtship Letters of Woodrow Wilson and Edith Bolling Galt.* Boston: Houghton Mifflin, 1981. 178.

Expansion depended on a peaceful world order based on principles of international law and harmony. Specifically, capitalism flourished in an atmosphere of low national trade barriers, freedom of the seas, and strong support for neutrality rights. The Open Door policy in China, stressing free trade rather than spheres of influence, represented a commitment to such liberal capitalist expansion. The United States has followed this path throughout the world ever since.

Of course, commitments to free trade and peaceful economic expansion in the world marketplace served America's own national interests. For example, a strong belief in neutrality rights—the freedom to trade with nations on both sides of a conflict—suited the country's expansive trade policies. Similarly, persistent calls for national self-determination and the dismantling of European colonial empires opened new areas to American trade.

The economic expansion of the United States in the late nineteenth and early twentieth centuries raised the nation's stature as a world power. A combination of provincialism and arrogance made it feel superior to the great European powers. America had remained free of large standing armies, entangling alliances, and, excepting the Caribbean and Pacific acquisitions in the wake of the Spanish-American War, overseas imperial expansion. The prevailing American belief that the United States was different and better than the rest of the world played an important role in the national identity. It eventually compelled Woodrow Wilson to commit the United States to war.

Before the outbreak of war in 1914, Europe had enjoyed more than four decades of peace following the Franco-Prussian War of 1870. This peace was at best fragile. Chancellor Otto von Bismarck's unification of the German empire in 1871, coupled with Germany's dramatic industrial development, introduced a new force into world affairs, both diplomatically and economically. The rush of imperialism in the late nineteenth century represented another potentially divisive factor. Between 1880 and 1895, the major European powers acquired extensive colonial empires throughout the world. Africa, carved up among Britain, France, Germany, Italy, Belgium, and Portugal, became the main target for European imperialism, but domination extended to the Far East as well.

With the heyday of imperialist expansion in the late nineteenth century came increasing friction and rivalry among the great powers. In

1879, Bismarck proposed a military alliance that linked Germany with Austria-Hungary; the inclusion of Italy in 1882 completed the Triple Alliance. In response, France initiated the Franco-Russian alliance in 1894. Britain, with the oldest and most extensive colonial empire, initially stayed free of such entangling alliances. Then, in 1904, the British and French became allies through the *Entente Cordiale* (cordial understanding). In 1907, an alliance called the Triple Entente linked Britain, France, and Russia.

Skillful diplomacy and an unwillingness to resort to war kept minor disturbances from escalating into major conflicts throughout most of the late nineteenth and early twentieth centuries. The complex alliance system, however, had the potential for bringing a host of countries into war over a comparatively minor incident. Following the assassination of Archduke Francis Ferdinand in 1914, Austria declared war on Serbia. The assassin was a Bosnian student who lived in Serbia, and Austria-Hungary suspected that Serbia had been involved in the murder of the heir to the Austrian throne. The alliance system that had kept Europe out of war since 1870 now quickly pulled all the major powers into the conflict.

President Wilson called on the United States to remain neutral in thought and action. Two factors—economic and political ties with the Allies, and a commitment to neutrality rights and freedom of the seas—eventually undermined the nation's determination to steer clear of the European war. The United States enjoyed strong cultural and historic bonds with England and France, and its economic ties across the Atlantic were even stronger. Supplying the needs of the Allies had started an economic boom in the United States, and Wilson did not want to deflate the prosperity. American trade with England and France grew from $825 million in 1914 to $3.2 billion in 1916. By the time America officially entered the war in 1917, U.S. bankers had loaned the Allies $2.5 billion. In contrast, American trade with and loans to Germany in that year totaled only $29 million and $27 million, respectively.

Despite these American ties to the Allied cause, many British policies strained relations with the United States. Most troublesome was disagreement over neutrality rights. British naval policy conflicted with America's long-standing commitment to freedom of the seas. The British based their strategy against Germany on a blockade of continental Europe. They aimed to cripple the enemy's war effort by cutting off military supplies and starving the German people into submission. Such a blockade violated international law, which differentiated between "contraband," mainly munitions, and "non-contraband,"

THE PRESIDENT AND MRS. EDITH GALT
For Woodrow Wilson, love and war were interwoven. Wilson's first wife, Ellen, died in August 1914, just as war was breaking out in Europe. The next year the president carried on an intense courtship of Washington widow Edith Galt at the height of the submarine crisis. Here they attend a World Series game in Philadelphia shortly after their engagement. They were married in December 1915. (Library of Congress)

items such as foodstuffs or raw cotton. Although Germany legally was supposed to be able to import non-contraband items during wartime, Britain's blockade honored no such distinction. Neutral nations such as the United States were effectively prevented from trading at all with Germany and its allies. The United States chafed at the British infringement of the trading rights of neutral nations, but could do little else because of Britain's domination of the seas.

Meanwhile, Germany developed its own response to the British blockade. The Germans could not match the British in sea power, so they turned to a devastating weapon, a submarine called the U-boat, short for *Unterseeboot* (undersea boat). In 1915, Germany announced that its submarines would attack enemy ships caught transporting military supplies in the war zone between the European continent and the British Isles. Traditional rules of naval warfare required that the crew and passengers be allowed to leave their ship before an attacking vessel sank it. If a submarine surfaced to carry out this requirement, however, it lost its greatest advantage—surprise—and left itself vulnerable to attack. The Germans began sinking enemy ships without warning.

What if a U-boat attacked a neutral trading vessel or an unarmed passenger ship by mistake? This situation occurred when the Germans sank a British passenger liner, the *Lusitania*, off the Irish coast on May 7, 1915. Almost 1,200 people died when the *Lusitania* went down, including 128 Americans. The fact that the passenger ship carried military contraband came to light only later.

Woodrow Wilson sent a strong letter to Germany protesting this assault on the freedom of nonbelligerents to travel on the high seas. However, the president would not ban Americans from traveling on the ships of Germany's enemies to avoid such incidents in the future. The *Lusitania* episode divided Wilson's government into pro- and anti-British factions. Secretary of State William Jennings Bryan resigned in protest. Bryan could not support Wilson's harsh criticism of Germany's violation of neutrality rights, which he also feared might risk war, while at the same time the president remained silent about Britain violating American rights with its blockade.

Throughout 1915 and 1916, Wilson had tried at several points to mediate an end to the European conflict through his aide Colonel Edward House. However, House concluded that neither side was interested in serious peace negotiations. In the meantime, Wilson tried to remain flexible yet firm in his response to the German submarine attacks. His policy paid off, at least temporarily, when Germany agreed in May 1916 to end the unrestricted assaults. For the Germans, the danger of drawing the United States into the war over neutrality rights and freedom of the seas far offset the benefits of attacking British ships. A temporary lull set into the naval war. On land, the Allies and the Central Powers continued to grind each other down in the bloody stalemate of trench warfare that characterized the fighting during World War I. Between February and June 1916, for example, 350,000 French soldiers and 330,000 Germans died as Germany tried to break through the French lines at Verdun. The front did not move.

After the sinking of the *Lusitania*, Wilson had confided to a cabinet member, "I wish with all my heart I saw a way to carry out the double wish of our people, to maintain a firm front in respect of what we demand of Germany and yet do nothing that might by any possibility involve us in war." The events of early 1917 diminished whatever hope Wilson had of staying out of the conflict. On January 31, Germany announced the resumption of unrestricted submarine attacks, a decision dictated by the impasse of the ground war. Germany planned boldly to sever the trade links between America and the Allies. Even if submarine attacks brought the United States into the war, the Germans hoped to destroy Allied shipping and defeat the Allied armies before the Americans could join the fighting. In response, Wilson broke off diplomatic relations with Germany on February 3.

In March, U-boats started to attack American ships without warning, sinking three U.S. ships on March 18 alone. While these attacks continued to push the United States toward war, another event jolted American public opinion. The State Department released evidence of German interference in Mexican affairs—the so-called Zimmerman telegram, a communication from Germany's state secretary for foreign affairs to the German minister in Mexico City. In a direct snub to the Monroe Doctrine's warning to European powers not to interfere with nations of the Western Hemisphere, Germany urged Mexico, which American policymakers still considered a revolutionary trouble spot, to enter the war against the United States. In return, Germany promised to help Mexico recover its "lost provinces" of Texas, New Mexico, and Arizona. This threat to the territorial integrity of the United States brought the war even closer to home.

On April 2, 1917, President Wilson went before a special session of Congress and asked for a declaration of war. He had concluded that in order to influence the shape of the postwar peace, America would have to enter the fighting. The United States declared war on April 6, but six senators and fifty members of the House voted against the action. They included Representative Jeannette Rankin of Montana, the first woman elected to Congress. "I want to stand by my country," she declared, "but I cannot vote for war."

Setting War Aims

Woodrow Wilson linked American participation in the war with lofty ideals. "It is a fearful thing to lead this great peaceful people into war, into the most terrible and disastrous of all wars, civilization itself seeming to be in the balance," he stated when calling for a declaration of war.

> But the right is more precious than peace, and we shall fight for the things which we have always carried nearest our hearts—for democracy, for the right of those who submit to authority to have a voice in their own Government, for the rights and liberties of small nations, for a universal dominion of right by such a concert of free peoples as shall bring peace and safety to all nations and make the world itself at last free.

Several factors led Wilson to justify the war in ideologically charged terms. In the first place, as reflected by the lack of unanimity in Congress, the nation remained deeply divided about the war. From 1886 to 1916, almost twenty million immigrants had come to the United States. The 1910 census estimated that a third of the population was foreign born, or had at least one parent born abroad. While the sympathies of these new Americans gravitated towards the Allies, such loyalty was potentially unstable. Irish-Americans felt anger at the harsh British suppression of Ireland's Easter Rebellion in 1916. Many recent immigrants traced their heritage to one of the Central Powers. German-Americans made up the largest, best-established ethnic group in the United States. Many aspects of German culture, including music and Germany's university system, were widely admired. Such factors limited support for American involvement on the Allied side.

A strong antiwar movement also limited the support for American participation in the war. Pacifist sentiment was broad but diffuse. Progressive Republican senators, such as Robert La Follette of Wisconsin and George Norris of Nebraska, opposed Wilson's call for armaments. Practically the entire political left, led principally by Eugene Debs and the Socialist party, spoke out forcefully against the war. Strong pacifist groups, among them the American Union Against Militarism and the Women's Peace party, also mobilized popular opposition. Feminists Jane Addams and Crystal Eastman were especially outspoken against war as an instrument of national policy. So were the prominent industrialists Andrew Carnegie and Henry Ford, who bankrolled antiwar activities. Ford spent half a million dollars in December 1915 to send more than a hundred men and women on a "peace ship" to Europe in the hope of hastening a negotiated end to the war.

Ironically, the 1916 election had not served as an American referendum on European affairs. The Republicans passed over Theodore Roosevelt and his prowar belligerence in favor of Justice Charles Evans Hughes of the Supreme Court, a former reform governor of New York. The Democrats renominated Wilson. Many observers saw little difference between the foreign policies of the two candidates, although the Democrats picked up votes with their widely circulated campaign slogan about keeping the United States out of war. They won a narrow victory over a Republican party reunited after its 1912 split. Despite polling three million more votes than he had received in 1912, Wilson defeated Hughes by only about six hundred thousand popular votes and a twenty-three-vote majority in the electoral college. This slender

JEANNETTE RANKIN
Jeannette Rankin, a former suffrage organizer, was the
first woman elected to Congress, in 1916. She actively
supported protective legislation, prohibition, and
"preparedness that will make for peace." Her vote against
U.S. entry into World War I in 1917 cost her the chance
for election to the Senate in 1918. In 1940, Rankin once
again won election to Congress from Montana. True to
her lifelong commitment to pacifism, she cast the only
vote against U.S. entry into World War II. (The Bettmann
Archive)

margin limited Wilson's options both in mobilizing the nation for war and planning the postwar
peace.

The president's personality also played a
prominent role in his decision to justify the war
in sweeping terms. Wilson, the child of a Pres-
byterian minister, approached foreign affairs
with missionary zeal. He never doubted the superiority of the Christian values he had learned
as a boy. In his mind, private morality and public policy were two sides of the same coin. Such

an orientation had guided his response to the
Mexican situation several years earlier.

Throughout his terms as president, Woodrow
Wilson eloquently articulated a vision of a new
international order based on American ideals. In
January 1917, he proposed a "peace without victory," reminding his audience that only "a peace
among equals" would last. At other times, he
called for security against aggression; an end to
secret diplomacy; and the right of nations, large
and small, to choose their own sovereignty. He
envisioned a permanent international tribunal to
settle disputes and uphold national rights of self-
determination and freedom. His goal, Wilson
stated, was "not a balance of power, but a community of power; not organized rivalries, but an
organized common peace."

Wilson declared his highest ideals in January
1918, when he announced his Fourteen Points in
a speech to Congress. Although the outcome of
the war was still in doubt in early 1918, the Fourteen Points represented Wilson's blueprint for
the peace to follow. The president called for
open diplomacy, "absolute freedom of naviga-
tion upon the seas," removal of economic barriers to trade, an international commitment to
territorial integrity, and arms reduction.

More specifically, the fifth point reaffirmed
Wilson's long-standing commitment to national self-determination and an end to colonial
empires. He proposed redrawing national
boundaries following the breakup of the
Austrian-Hungarian, Russian, and German empires, including the creation of an independent
Polish state. The highlight of Wilson's vision
was the last point, the creation of a multinational
organization "for the purpose of affording
mutual guarantees of political independence and
territorial integrity to great and small States
alike." This League of Nations became Wilson's
obsession.

The Fourteen Points matched the spirit of
progressivism. Widely distributed as propaganda during the final months of the war, they
proposed to extend the benefits of the American
way of life—democracy, freedom, and peaceful
economic expansion—to the rest of the world.
The League of Nations would serve as a kind of
Federal Trade Commission for the world.

Unfortunately, Wilson's lofty pronouncements did not sit well with America's allies.

Britain, for example, had much to lose from open diplomacy and freedom of the seas. Wilson's call for self-determination of colonial peoples clashed with Allied plans for the acquisition of Germany's colonies at the end of the war. Furthermore, his humanitarian vision of a world made safe for democracy and peaceful economic expansion struck many European leaders as a self-centered view. They thought Wilson had conveniently defined the interests of the world as synonymous with those of the United States. The Fourteen Points produced the first of many misunderstandings that doomed both the Treaty of Versailles and the League of Nations.

Over There

After the declaration of war, many Americans were surprised to learn that their country planned to send troops to Europe. They had naively assumed that the nation's participation could be limited to military and economic aid. The United States had always avoided having a large standing army in peacetime; it had only 175,000 soldiers, mostly life-time volunteers, on active duty in 1915. The government turned to conscription to field a substantial fighting force.

On June 5, 1917, more than 9.5 million young men registered for military service. By the end of the war, almost 4 million men, plus a few thousand female navy clerks and army nurses, were in uniform. Nearly 3 million men were inducted by a draft lottery; the rest volunteered. Over 300,000 men evaded the draft, and another 4,000 were classified as conscientious objectors. During the eighteen months that the United States fought in the war, 50,000 American servicemen were killed in action. Another 60,000 died from other causes, mainly the influenza epidemic that swept the world in 1918–1919. The nation suffered minimal casualties compared with the 8 million soldiers lost by the Allies and the Central Powers. The French lost far more soldiers in the siege of Verdun than the United States did in the entire war.

American troops were eager to serve. As the novelist John Dos Passos recalled, "We had spent our boyhood in the afterglow of the peaceful nineteenth century. . . . What was war like? We wanted to see with our own eyes." Yet the Americans were slow to have an impact on the

European fighting. By June 1917, only 15,000 American troops had landed in France; the number reached 87,000 by the fall. Allied commanders pleaded for American reinforcements to be assigned to their units to replace men lost in battle, but American leaders were unwilling to put their soldiers under the command of the British and the French. Instead, the United States created an independent fighting unit, the American Expeditionary Force (AEF). General John J. Pershing, who had recently returned from pursuing Pancho Villa and his bandits in Mexico, led the AEF.

At first, the United States contributed more at sea than on land. German submarines were sinking Allied ships at the alarming rate of about nine hundred thousand tons a month when the

THE CALL TO ARMS
To build popular support for the war effort, the government called on the services of such artists as Howard Chandler Christy, Charles Dana Gibson, and James Montgomery Flagg. This 1917 recruiting poster by Flagg was adapted from a June, 1916 cover of *Leslie's Illustrated Weekly Newspaper*. The model was the artist. Four million copies of this poster were printed during World War I. (Library of Congress)

THE FLYING ACES
Although airplanes were not yet the decisive factor they would become in World War II, the exploits of American flyers captivated the popular imagination. Tales of such daredevil pilots fighting it out in the skies like medieval knights in combat provided more thrills than reports of monotonous trench warfare. One of America's best known aces was former professional race car driver Eddie Rickenbacker (right), who was credited with twenty-six "victories" over enemy aircraft. (The Bettmann Archive)

ness of the government headed by Czar Nicholas II, and a revolution overthrew his repressive regime in March 1917. The new government headed by Alexander Kerensky pledged to press for victory against Germany. Russian peasants, however, were sick of suffering deprivation and heavy casualties because of a war that seemed distant and unrelated to their lives. A new leader, Vladimir Ilych Lenin, rapidly gained power by promising "peace, land, and bread" for all Russians. Lenin, who had been living in exile in Switzerland when the March revolution took place, followed the teachings of German revolutionary theorist Karl Marx, especially Marx's emphasis on the inevitability of class struggle between the ruling class and the workers. The Germans arranged Lenin's safe passage home, hoping to promote internal strife in Russia. Lenin and a group of Bolshevik revolutionaries arrived in Petrograd (now Leningrad) in

United States entered the war in mid-April. The U-boats had seriously crippled the attempt to send supplies and munitions to the Allies and threatened the transport of American troops to the European front. Adopting a plan that aimed for safety in numbers, the government immediately began sending armed convoys across the ocean. The plan worked. No American soldiers were killed on their way to Europe. A stepped-up American naval campaign cut the Allied shipping losses to four hundred thousand tons a month by late 1917 and two hundred thousand tons by April 1918.

Meanwhile, revolutionary changes in Russia were affecting the course of the war. The strain of fighting the Germans had exposed the weak-

THE MEUSE-ARGONNE CAMPAIGN
The Meuse-Argonne produced its share of heroes. Corporal Alvin York, a conscientious objector from Tennessee, singlehandedly killed twenty-eight Germans and took one hundred twenty-three prisoners during this offensive. The popular fascination with York suggested a deep-seated need to anoint individual heroes in what was becoming an increasingly depersonalized and mechanized war. (The Bettmann Archive)

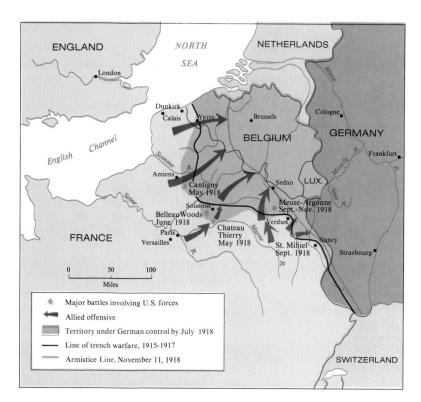

MAP 22.2 U.S. PARTICIPATION ON THE WESTERN FRONT, 1918 When American troops finally reached the European front in significant numbers in 1918, the Allied and Central powers had been grinding each other down in a war of attrition for almost four years. New, long-range artillery and the concentrated fire of machine guns gave a tremendous advantage to defensive positions. Huge massed armies faced each other across a front that contained more than 25,000 miles of trenches. The influx of American troops and supplies broke the stalemate. Successful offensive maneuvers by the American Expeditionary Force included Belleau Wood, Château Thierry, and the Meuse-Argonne campaign.

April. In November, Lenin led the Bolshevik seizure of power, completing the Russian Revolution.

The new Bolshevik government quickly sued for peace with the Germans to end the unpopular war and consolidate its position at home. Peace talks opened at Brest-Litovsk in December 1917, and the Bolsheviks signed a treaty with Germany in March 1918 in which they surrendered to German control the territory of Poland, the Baltic provinces, and the Ukraine. With Russia knocked out of the war, Germany could turn its full force to the stalemate on the western front. On March 21, 1918, the Germans launched a major offensive that advanced within fifty miles of Paris. Allied leaders intensified their calls for fresh American troops. About seventy thousand American soldiers helped the French repel the Germans in the battles of Château-Thierry and Belleau Wood. The German offensive ground to a halt after a summer of fighting.

American reinforcements now began to arrive in force. Fresh troops flooded the ports of Liverpool in England and Brest and Saint Nazaire in France—245,000 in May, 278,000 in June, and 306,000 in July. In September 1918, General Pershing launched a major assault that pitted a million American soldiers against vastly outnumbered and exhausted German troops. The successful forty-seven-day Meuse-Argonne campaign near Verdun pushed the enemy back across the Somme River and broke the German defenses.

World War I ended on November 11, 1918, with the signing of an armistice. The flood of American troops and supplies during the last six months of fighting provided the Allied margin of victory.

"You're In the Army Now"

About two million American soldiers were in France when the war ended. Two-thirds of them had seen at least brief action on the western front. However, most American doughboys escaped the horrors of sustained trench warfare that had sapped the morale of Allied and German troops. The war in France became a great adventure for many young Americans because they experienced the war more as tourists than as soldiers. Large numbers of recruits had barely traveled beyond their hometowns before joining the army, and the journey across the ocean to Europe was a monumental event in their lives. In France, the young men were struck by how old everything seemed, compared to an America just one generation removed from the closing of the frontier.

High progressive ideals set the tone for military service. One reform instituted by the army was the Stanford-Binet intelligence test. Army psychologists, who administered the test to all recruits, expressed shock at the level of illiteracy among draftees—as high as 25 percent. Racial and ethnic variations also turned up in the test scores. But these lower scores stemmed from the cultural biases of the tests rather than innate differences in intelligence among ethnic groups. How many recent immigrants or rural blacks could be expected to know who wrote "The Raven"; the city in which the Overland car was manufactured; or the importance of the painter Rosa Bonheur? The army dropped the test in 1919, but revised versions of intelligence tests soon became a standard part of the American educational system.

The military forces also adopted progressive solutions to the vices of alcohol and sex. Reflecting the anti-liquor fever taking hold in America, the army banned drinking by soldiers in uniform and declared army bases and the surrounding localities officially dry. This experiment in imposed temperance added momentum to the adoption of national prohibition in 1920.

The army mounted an ambitious program of sex education. In an era when people rarely discussed sex in public, the army program represented an attempt to bring the subject into the open. Concerned that venereal disease might sap the strength of the fighting men (antibiotics had not yet been developed), the army launched an anti-VD campaign. As soldiers ate dinner in their mess halls, they looked up at posters that proclaimed "A German Bullet is Cleaner than a Whore" or "How could you look the flag in the face if you were dirty with gonorrhea?" In France, the army continued its campaign against venereal disease, although it never totally stopped American soldiers from patronizing French prostitutes. Army-issue condoms and safety razors (a novelty that changed the shaving habits of an entire generation of men) were two of the souvenirs that American soldiers brought home from France.

Reformers had expressed high hopes for the democratization and educational potential of military service. Theodore Roosevelt, whose offer to raise an independent regiment was politely but firmly refused by President Wilson, hoped that army duty would foster class unity. "The military tent where they all sleep side by side will rank next to the public school among the great agents of democratization," Roosevelt predicted. Yet the army reflected the same problems that afflicted American society at large. About a fifth of the American soldiers had been born in another country, leading some people to call the

A BLACK VETERAN RETURNS HOME
Black soldiers received segregated and unequal treatment at every stage of their military service. When the war ended, black veterans faced hostility from many whites alarmed that blacks no longer "knew their place." (Amistad Research Center)

AEF the American Foreign Legion. At a camp in Georgia, the army assigned Italians and Slavs to ethnically segregated units. These men were commanded by officers who spoke their language, and the troops were even serviced by cooks trained in the respective culinary traditions.

Black soldiers received the worst treatment, a reflection of their subordinate position in American society. White Southerners became especially alarmed at training blacks to bear arms, and few whites from any part of the country would have consented to serve under a black officer. As a result of such prejudice, blacks were organized into rigidly segregated units, in all but a few cases under the control of white officers. In addition, blacks were always assigned to the most menial tasks. Despite the official policy of segregation designed to minimize contact between black and white recruits, racial violence erupted at several camps. The worst incident occurred in Houston, where black members of the Twenty-fourth Infantry's Third Battalion killed seventeen white soldiers who had goaded them. The army immediately tried more than a hundred black soldiers in military courts. Thirteen were executed within days, and six more were later hanged.

Despite such incidents, over four hundred thousand black men volunteered or were drafted for military service. Blacks made up 13 percent of the armed forces. In France, black soldiers found the French far more willing to socialize with them on an equal basis than were many white American soldiers. Despite documented cases of extreme heroism, no black received the Congressional Medal of Honor, the nation's highest military award. As with President Wilson's lofty ideals and the actual course of the war, the black experience in World War I reflected the persistent gap between progressive rhetoric and reality.

Mobilizing the Home Front

Fighting World War I required extraordinary economic mobilization on the home front. Business, the work force, and the public all cooperated to win the war. At the height of mobilization, a fourth of the gross national product went for war production. Business and government proved especially congenial partners. Their cooperation put into action the New Nationalism urged by Theodore Roosevelt during the 1912 presidential campaign.

Financial and Economic Mobilization

The war forced government and business to organize and perform on an unprecedented scale. This process had begun even before the formal declaration of war, as the United States geared up as the arsenal for Allied supplies and financing. Almost overnight, America reversed its historic debtor position to that of creditor toward other nations as the Allies bought more U.S. exports and paid for them in gold. In addition, U.S. financial institutions increasingly provided capital for foreign investment on the world market now that the British pound sterling was diverted to the Allied war effort. This American export capital guaranteed the nation a major role in international financial affairs from then on.

The monetary cost of World War I reached $32 billion, a huge sum for a government unaccustomed to large expenditures. The United States raised about a third of this amount from taxes; the rest came from loans, especially the popular Liberty Loans that encouraged public support for the war effort. The government also helped pay for the war by using the Federal Reserve System to expand the money supply, which made it easier to borrow money. Even so, the federal debt increased from $1 billion in 1915 to $20 billion in 1920. Federal expenditures never again dropped to their prewar levels.

The debt obligations and money expansion fueled inflation, and the consumer price index doubled during the war. Inflation, however, proved a more politically acceptable way of paying for the war than increasing income taxes or imposing a federal sales tax. The Sixteenth Amendment to the Constitution, which allowed a federal income tax, had been in effect only since 1913. Few Americans except those in the top income brackets had to file federal returns. Because inflation raised incomes and thus brought more households into the tax system, the war emergency accustomed a broader cross section of the population to paying higher taxes to support the expanded functions of the government.

In addition to raising money, mobilization required coordination of economic production. The government never seriously considered exercising total control over the economy. But the war hastened the creation of a national administrative structure to match the consolidated power of the business and banking communities. For the most part, the government turned to those who knew the capacities of the economy best—the nation's business leaders. These executives flocked to Washington, regarding war work as both a duty and an opportunity for professional advancement.

Economic mobilization operated within a series of boards and agencies that tried to rationalize and coordinate the national economic structure. A network of industrial committees linked war agencies to organizations in private industry. Government leaders utilized a combination of public and private power to enforce their decisions.

The Fuel Administration, directed by President Harry Garfield of Williams College, allocated coal resources. Its task became more difficult during the especially severe winter of 1917–1918, when coal shortages occurred in major northeastern cities and industries. At one point, Garfield ordered all factories east of the Mississippi River to shut down for four days. By raising the price of coal to artificially high levels, the Fuel Administration eventually stimulated production of coal from previously unprofitable mines to meet the nation's energy needs.

The Railroad War Board, under Secretary of the Treasury William G. McAdoo, brought order to the nation's sprawling transportation system by nationalizing the railroads in December 1917. The government guaranteed railroad owners a "standard return" equal to average earnings between 1915 and 1917. It also promised that the carriers would be returned to private control no later than twenty-one months after the war. Railroad workers received wage hikes totaling $300 million, which were financed by rate increases passed on directly to shippers and the public. The government quickly returned the railroads to private ownership after the armistice.

Perhaps the most successful government agency was the Food Administration, led by Herbert Hoover, a Stanford-trained engineer.

Using the slogan "Food will win the war," Hoover expanded domestic production of wheat and other grains from forty-five million acres in 1917 to seventy-five million in 1919. This increased production not only fed the large domestic market, but also allowed a threefold rise in food exports to war-torn Europe. At no time did the government contemplate domestic food rationing. Much of Hoover's success resulted from the voluntary cooperation of consumers who patriotically followed government reminders to "Serve Just Enough" and "Use All Left-Overs." Wheatless Mondays, Meatless Tuesdays, and Porkless Thursdays and Saturdays enabled substantial conservation of food resources. Hoover emerged from the war as one of the nation's most admired public figures.

The central agency for wartime mobilization was the War Industries Board (WIB), established in July 1917. After a fumbling start, the Wilson administration reorganized the board under the direction of Bernard Baruch, a Wall Street financier, in March 1918. Baruch's financial experience and his ability to cajole American business to cooperate with the government contributed significantly to the success of the WIB.

The WIB reflected the ambiguities that characterized business–government cooperation during the early twentieth century. While it emphasized cooperation over competition, it left patterns of private power undisturbed. Baruch organized the WIB around specific commodities and industries, whose administrators then negotiated such issues as market allocation with their equivalents in private industry. This frequent consultation blurred the lines between the needs of business and government.

Bernard Baruch was no economic dictator, but the WIB produced an unparalleled expansion of the federal government. The board allocated scarce resources, gathered economic data and statistics, controlled the flow of raw materials, ordered conversion of factories to war production, set prices, imposed efficiency and standardization procedures, and coordinated purchasing. The board had the authority to compel compliance, but Baruch preferred to win voluntary acceptance from business. He saw himself as a partner of business, not its enemy. To a large degree, business supported this government expansion because federal growth coincided with its interests so well.

The fundamental reason for America's successful economic mobilization lay less in administrative theory than in hard cash. Corporate profits soared, aided by the suspension of antitrust laws and competitive bidding during wartime. Profits on war work were further guaranteed through "cost-plus" contracts—that is, industries' profits came on top of their actual production costs. War profits created about forty-two thousand new millionaires, and produced an economic boom that continued uninterrupted until 1920.

With the signing of the armistice in November 1918, the United States scrambled to dismantle its wartime apparatus. The government had no comprehensive plans to guide the economy through postwar reconversion. Concentrated power in the hands of business and government could be tolerated by business executives and the general public in an emergency, but not yet as a permanent feature of the American economy.

Although U.S. participation in the war lasted only eighteen months, it left an important legacy for the modern bureaucratic state. Entire industries had been organized as never before, linked to a maze of government agencies, congressional committees, and executive departments. These changes had been under way before 1917, but the war accelerated them. The partnership between business and government had been mutually beneficial, a lesson that both partners would put to use well in the modern era.

Manpower and Womanpower

Wars cannot be won just by a nation's armed forces and its business and government executives. Such crises demand the participation and cooperation not only of the work force but of the entire civilian population. However, World War I produced fewer rewards for the workers who produced the war products than for their managers in Washington.

Labor's position improved during the war, although it remained a junior partner to business and government. Samuel Gompers, leader of the American Federation of Labor (AFL), traded labor's support of the war for a voice in government policy. This bargain proved acceptable to government and business leaders concerned with averting strikes that could cripple war production. Gompers represented labor's interests on both the National Defense Advisory Commission and the National War Labor Board (NWLB). In addition, the War Labor Policies Board, headed by Felix Frankfurter, a Harvard law professor, coordinated labor and welfare programs in government and industry. This board established the United States Employment Service, which placed four million workers in war jobs.

Far more important to workers themselves were the actions of the National War Labor Board. The NWLB functioned more as a judicial than an administrative body; labor leaders often called it "labor's Supreme Court." Comprised of representatives of labor, management, and the public, the NWLB was co-chaired by former President William Howard Taft, representing management, and Frank P. Walsh, a labor lawyer. During the eighteen months of the NWLB's existence, it arbitrated about 1,250 cases. The board's decisions favored labor more often than management, giving important federal support to the goals of the labor movement.

The board stipulated that workers not disrupt war production through strikes or other disturbances. In return, it supported the right of workers to organize unions and required employers to deal with shop committees. The board established an eight-hour day for war workers, with time-and-a-half pay for overtime; it also endorsed equal pay for woman workers. The NWLB had ample power to enforce its decisions and intervene in unresolved disputes. For example, NWLB examiners supervised elections for shop committees in the steel industry. When the Smith and Wesson arms plant in Springfield, Massachusetts, flouted NWLB rules by discriminating against union employees, the federal government took over the firm.

Following years of hostility toward labor by management and the federal government, such actions by the National War Labor Board improved labor's status and power. From 1916 to 1919, AFL membership grew by almost a million workers, reaching nearly three million by the end of the war. Few of these wartime gains lasted, however. Wartime inflation ate up most of the wage hikes, and a virulent postwar anti-union movement drove union membership into a rapid decline that lasted until the 1930s. The labor movement did not yet have enough power to bargain on an equal basis with business and government.

Small gains also occurred for certain groups of workers. When men go to war, the resulting labor shortage usually makes jobs available to workers normally excluded from them. Blacks, for example, found jobs in northern defense industries that never would have accepted them in peacetime. The magnet of industrial jobs and an escape from the southern agricultural system lured between 400,000 and 450,000 blacks to northern and western cities during the war. Henry Ford sent agents to the South to recruit black workers for his automobile plants and even provided special trains to bring them north. In Detroit, blacks shared in the unprecedented five-dollar daily wage that Ford had instituted in 1914. This migration of blacks from the South represented one of the most fundamental population shifts of the twentieth century.

Mexican-Americans in California, Texas, New Mexico, and Arizona also found their lives improved by wartime labor needs. Many left their segregated *barrios* (neighborhoods) for industrial opportunities in northern cities. Some Mexican-Americans, however, fearing they would be drafted into the army, had returned to Mexico. The exodus of all these workers increased the labor shortage in agriculture. The government quickly exempted agricultural workers from the draft, whereupon the migration resumed. At least a hundred thousand Mexican-Americans entered the United States between 1917 and 1920.

Women made up the largest group that took advantage of new opportunities in wartime. White women and, to a lesser degree, black women, like black and Mexican-American men, found jobs open to them in factories and war industries as never before. About four hundred thousand women joined the labor force for the first time. In addition, many of the nation's eight million women who already held jobs switched from low-paying fields, such as domestic service, to higher-paying industrial work. Americans soon got used to the novel sight of woman

WARTIME OPPORTUNITIES
Women took on new jobs during the wartime emergency, working as mail carriers, police officers, drill-press operators, and farm laborers attached to the Women's Land Army. These three women clearly enjoyed the camaraderie of working in a railroad yard in 1918. When the war ended, women usually lost such employment. (National Archives)

streetcar conductors, train engineers, and defense workers. But everyone—including the women themselves—believed that these jobs would return to men after the war.

World War I proved even more liberating for middle-class women outside the work force. Women's clubs and groups had grown steadily since the nineteenth century, and they turned much of their organizational energy to the war effort. Suffragist leaders such as Carrie Chapman Catt and Anna Howard Shaw mobilized women's support for the war through the Women's Committee of the Council of National Defense. Housewives played a crucial role in the success of Herbert Hoover's Food Administration. Other groups, including the American Red Cross and the Young Women's Christian Association (YWCA), sent volunteers to the front lines in France.

Professional women also found opportunities in government service. Mary Van Kleeck, an industrial sociologist and expert on the problems of woman wage earners, joined the Army Ordnance Department and the Department of Labor to lobby for equal pay and better working conditions for woman workers. Pauline Goldmark, a social reformer from the National Consumers' League, acted as a women's rights advocate at the Railroad Administration. Mary Anderson, a trade unionist who had been Van Kleeck's assistant, became the first director of the Women's Bureau, established by the Labor Department in 1920. Women's groups failed, however, to get a woman named to the National War Labor Board.

The war had an important impact on the battle for woman suffrage as well. A small minority of radical feminists, led by Alice Paul and her Congressional Union, opposed the war. But the main suffrage organization, the National American Woman Suffrage Association (NAWSA), threw the support of its two million members solidly behind the Wilson administration. Carrie Chapman Catt, president of the organization, realized that women had to prove their patriotism in order not to jeopardize the suffrage movement.

Women's wartime contributions helped push their campaign for suffrage to its successful conclusion. Especially effective was a simple moral question. How could the United States fight to make the world safe for democracy while denying half its citizens their democratic right to vote? Woodrow Wilson, who had converted to woman suffrage in 1916 but preferred to leave the matter to the states, withdrew his opposition to a federal woman suffrage amendment in January 1918. The constitutional amendment quickly passed the House but took eighteen months to get through the Senate. Then came another year of hard work for ratification by the states. Finally, on August 26, 1920, Tennessee gave the Nineteenth Amendment the last vote it needed. The goal that had first been declared at the Seneca Falls convention in 1848 won approval seventy-two years later, partly because of women's contributions to the war effort.

Promoting National Unity

Whereas the successful climax of woman suffrage confirmed John Dewey's prediction that social progress could occur in a war context, the excesses committed in the name of building national unity corroborated Randolph Bourne's warnings about the passions that could get out of control during wartime. Widespread support for the war was never a foregone conclusion. Many citizens felt far removed from the conflict. Why should they sacrifice their sons and their taxes in a European imperialist conflict far across

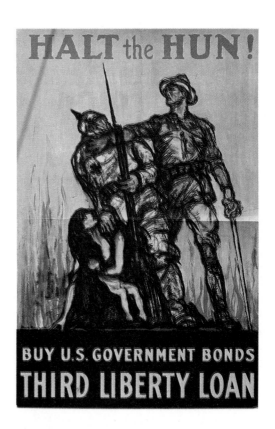

DRUMMING UP PATRIOTIC DOLLARS
This poster made it clear who the enemy was, and what was the proper patriotic American response. Treasury Secretary William McAdoo reinforced the point when he said in 1917, "Every person who refuses to subscribe or who takes the attitude of let the other fellow do it, is a friend of Germany and I would like nothing better than to tell it to him to his face. A man who can't lend his government $1.25 per week at the rate of 4 percent interest is not entitled to be an American citizen." (Historical Pictures Service)

the Atlantic Ocean? Support for the war remained tentative from immigrants who had ties to the Central Powers. Pacifist sentiment continued strong even after the United States declared war. Because of such domestic opposition, the Wilson administration recognized the need to manufacture support for the war. "It is not an army we must shape and train for war, it is a nation," the president said.

Wilson chose the Committee on Public Information (CPI) to promote public backing for the war. This government propaganda agency, headed by the reform journalist George Creel, acted as a magnet for reformers and muckraking journalists, such as Ida Tarbell and Ray Stannard Baker. The CPI professed high goals, such as educating citizens about democracy, promoting national unity, Americanizing immigrant groups, and breaking down the isolation of rural life. Indirectly, it acted as a nationalizing force by promoting the development of a common national ideology.

The CPI touched the lives of practically every American during World War I. In these days before radio and television, the CPI depended heavily on the printed word. It distributed seventy-five million pieces of literature during the war. At local movie theaters before the feature presentation (which might be a CPI-supported film, such as *The Prussian Cur* or *The Kaiser, Beast of Berlin*), a volunteer called a "four-minute man" made a short speech supporting the war. About seventy-five thousand volunteers delivered more than 755,000 speeches during the war. They reached an audience estimated at more than three hundred million, three times the population of the United States at the time. Yet the tactics of the CPI often went too far, overriding the right of individual expression in favor of national conformity in wartime. By early 1918, for example, the CPI was encouraging the four-minute men to use inflammatory stories of alleged German atrocities in their speeches to build support for the war effort.

As a spirit of total conformity pervaded the home front, many Americans found themselves the targets of suspicion. Local businesses donated ads to newspapers and magazines which asked citizens to report to the Justice Department "the man who spreads pessimistic stories, cries for peace, or belittles our efforts to win the war." Posters encouraged Americans to join the army or be on the lookout for German spies. One of the most popular posters, called "Spies and Lies," began by warning that "German agents are everywhere." An unintended by-product of this wartime propaganda was the stimulation of the advertising industry, which became a major force in shaping patterns of consumption in the 1920s. More aggressive were quasi-vigilante groups, such as the American Protective League. This organization mobilized about 250,000 self-appointed "agents" to spy on their neighbors, fellow workers, and innocent bystanders. The American Protective League (whose members were furnished with badges issued by the Justice Department) and groups including the Sedition Slammers and the Boy Spies of America staged violent raids against draft evaders and other war opponents in 1918.

German-Americans bore the brunt of the Americanization campaign. The CPI urged ethnic groups to give up their old-world customs and become "Unhyphenated Americans." In an orgy of hatred generated by propaganda about German militarism and war atrocities, everything German became suspect. German music, especially opera, was banished from the concert repertoire. Publishers removed pro-German references from textbooks, and many communities banned the teaching of the German language. Sauerkraut became "liberty cabbage," and hamburgers were called "liberty sandwiches" or Salisbury steaks. Even the German measles got a new name, "liberty measles."

In this campaign for total conformity, the government tolerated little criticism of American values and institutions. Militant suffragists became early targets of repression. When women chained themselves to the White House fence and burned copies of President Wilson's speeches on democracy to protest female disenfranchisement, the government swiftly retaliated. The suffragists, charged with obstructing traffic and blocking sidewalks, were sentenced to seven months in jail. To protest these stiff sentences as well as the terrible conditions in prison, the women prisoners went on hunger strikes and were forcibly fed. Public shock at their treatment made them martyrs and ultimately aided the suffrage cause. But the suffragists' status as white middle-class women

LETTERS FROM PRISON

Suffragist Rose Winslow smuggled out descriptions of the treatment she and militant feminist Alice Paul, founder of the National Woman's Party, endured in Occoquan prison.

The women are all so magnificent, so beautiful. Alice Paul is as thin as ever, pale and large-eyed. We have been in solitary for five weeks. There is nothing to tell but that the days go by somehow. I have felt quite feeble the last few days—faint, so that I could hardly get my hair brushed, my arms ached so. But to-day I am well again. Alice Paul and I talk back and forth though we are at opposite ends of the building and a hall door also shuts us apart. But occasionally—thrills—we escape from behind our iron-barred doors and visit. Great laughter and rejoicing!

Alice Paul is in the psychopathic ward. She dreaded forcible feeding frightfully, and I hate to think how she must be feeling. I had a nervous time of it, gasping a long time afterward, and my stomach rejecting during the process. I spent a bad, restless night, but otherwise I am all right. The poor soul who fed me got liberally besprinkled during the process. I heard myself making the most hideous sounds. . . . One feels so forsaken when one lies prone and people shove a pipe down one's stomach.

We still get no mail; we are "insubordinate." It's strange, isn't it; if you ask for food fit to eat, as we did, you are "insubordinate"; and if you refuse food you are "insubordinate." Amusing. I am really all right. If this continues very long I perhaps won't be. I am interested to see how long our so-called "splendid American men" will stand for this form of discipline.

All news cheers one marvelously because it is hard to feel anything but a bit desolate and forgotten here in this place.

All the officers here know we are making this hunger strike that women fighting for liberty may be considered political prisoners; we have told them. God knows we don't want other women ever to have to do this over again.

Source: Doris Stevens, *Jailed for Freedom.* New York: Schocken Books, 1976; originally published 1920. 188–191.

---

protected them from some of the harsher reprisals meted out to others who dared to criticize the government during wartime.

The main legal tools for curbing dissent were the Espionage Act of 1917 and the Sedition Act of 1918. The espionage law set stiff penalties for antimilitary actions and empowered the federal government to ban treasonous material from the mails. The definition of treason was left to the discretion of the postmaster general. The sedition law went further, punishing anyone who might "utter, print, write or publish any disloyal, profane, scurrilous, or abusive language about the form of government in the United States, or the uniform of the Army or the Navy." More than a thousand persons were convicted under these broad restrictions on freedom of speech in wartime.

One tempting target for repression was the Industrial Workers of the World, the labor organization whose members were known as Wobblies. IWW organizers spoke out against militarism and threatened to disrupt war production in the western lumber and copper industries. In September 1917, the Justice Department arrested 113 top IWW leaders for interfering with the war effort. Vigilante groups contributed their own reprisals. A mob in Butte, Montana, dragged IWW organizer Frank Little through the streets and hanged him from a railroad trestle. By the end of the war, the Wobblies were decimated.

Socialists, who also criticized the war and the draft, encountered similar attacks. The postmaster general banned their publications from the mails. Party leader Eugene Debs drew ten years in jail for stating that the master classes caused wars while the subject classes fought them. Victor Berger, a Milwaukee socialist, was twice prevented from taking his seat in the United States House of Representatives. Berger had served in the House from 1911 to 1913. He was reelected in 1918 and 1919, but the House refused to seat him because he had been jailed under the Espionage Act for his antiwar views. The Supreme Court reversed Berger's sentence in 1921, and he served in the House again from 1923 to 1929.

Rarely did the Supreme Court overturn the wartime excesses. In *Schenck v. United States* (1919), Justice Oliver Wendell Holmes ruled in a unanimous decision that if an act of speech constituted a "clear and present danger to the safety of the country," Congress could constitutionally restrict it. The defendant, an official of the Socialist party, had been convicted for mailing pamphlets that urged army recruits to resist induction. In *Abrams v. United States* (1919), the Court upheld the conviction of Jacob Abrams, an immigrant printer who had distributed pamphlets denouncing American military intervention in Russia to destroy the Bolshevik regime. Holmes dissented in this case, seeing no clear threat to the conduct of the war. He and Justice Louis Brandeis made up the minority in the 7 to 2 decision. During a national war emergency, limits on freedom of speech were tolerated that would not have been acceptable in peacetime.

An Unsettled Peace

The mobilization of the home front and the defeat of Germany were major accomplishments, but they came at a price. Following the armistice, dormant problems rose to the surface. Woodrow Wilson confronted the task of making the Allies live up to the high ideals he had put forward as the basis for peace. He then faced a Senate hostile to the treaty he brought home. At the same time, ethnocultural and racial tensions that had smoldered during the war erupted in violence and strife. And fears of domestic radicalism boiled over in the Red Scare.

Versailles and the League of Nations

President Wilson scored an early victory when the Allies accepted his Fourteen Points as the basis for the peace negotiations that began in January 1919. But other factors limited Wilson's ability to enforce his views of a just peace. Despite the president's plea to make the November 1918 elections a referendum on the peace settlement, American voters returned a Republican majority

to Congress. Nevertheless, Wilson failed to appoint even one Republican senator to the United States delegation to the peace conference. His shortsightedness later helped doom the treaty's chances for approval in the Senate.

The peace delegation sailed for Europe in December 1918. Wilson toured the major European capitals and received a tumultuous welcome. To Europeans, the American president represented the hope for national self-determination that had become a major justification for the war. In Paris, two million people lined the Champs-Elysees to pay tribute to "Wilson the Just." This lofty reception encouraged Wilson to press ahead with his plans to dominate the peace conference.

Twenty-seven countries sent representatives to the peace conference in Versailles, near Paris. The victorious Allies did not invite either Germany or Russia. Wilson firmly opposed the

TRIUMPHANT WOODROW WILSON
After the armistice, Woodrow Wilson toured Europe to popular acclaim. His heady reception from millions of adoring Europeans, who saw him as the embodiment of the long-sought goal of national self-determination, contrasted sharply with the cool reception he received from leaders of the European powers. When the Versailles treaty was in trouble with the U.S. Senate, Wilson pursued the same tactic of taking his case directly to the people, this time with disastrous results. (Library of Congress)

WILSON'S DIPLOMACY AT PARIS

Journalist Walter Lippmann reflects on the Peace Conference at Paris, 1919.

Five great powers sent plenipotentiaries to Paris and with them came delegates from a host of small nations, provisional governments, and classes. Together they constituted the representatives of a coalition that had won at terrible cost a complete mastery of the organized military and economic power of the world. The process of victory had entailed the destruction of established authority in four of the great empires, and out of their ruin had issued angry, frightened, resentful, and wildly hopeful masses of men. It was by flashes black night and golden morning, the new day and the end of the world.

At Paris men looked out upon two continents in revolt, upon conflicts and aspirations more intricate and more obscure than any they had ever been called to resolve. . . . Through it all the primary problem of the conference was to find men who had sufficient authority to negotiate a peace. Soon there was discovered a truth, which political science seemed to have ignored: that you cannot wage war with or dictate peace to an unorganized people. . . .

For an understanding of what has happened at Paris these last six or seven months, it is necessary to study the peculiar technique of the Wilson diplomacy as it operated in contact with these imponderables. . . . The facts are, I believe, about as follows. Throughout the war he was increasingly convinced that the masses in Europe were passionately determined upon the kind of peace which he himself desired. When he "clarified" this common thought he found himself the acknowledged spokesman of the populations of Europe, and gradually he came to believe that no power on earth could successfully resist this democratic insistence. "Statesmen must follow the common clarified thought or be broken." Therefore, why become involved in the complications of governmental diplomacy when all that will be swept aside by popular demand? Why commit the governments (who, by the way, could have been committed to anything while they needed American military assistance) when the people accept the President's leadership? All the rest can be ignored so long as the heart of the people is expressed. . . .

Source: Walter Lippmann, *The Peace Conference. The Yale Review*, July 1919. 710–711, 716, 719.

Bolshevik regime. The outcome of the Russian Revolution troubled him so greatly that he approved the landing of American troops in Siberia in 1918, supposedly to aid thousands of trapped Czechoslovakian soldiers. Actually, Wilson wanted to topple the new Soviet state. He continued to be deeply disturbed by Lenin's calls for a proletarian revolution to liberate the world from capitalism and imperialism. Even though Lenin did not attend the peace conference, leaders of many nations began to see that the new Soviet state was changing the complexion of power in Eastern Europe—and the world.

The Big Four—Wilson, Prime Minister David Lloyd George of Great Britain, Premier Georges Clemenceau of France, and Prime Minister Vittorio Orlando of Italy—did most of the negotiating at Versailles. The three European leaders sought a peace that differed radically from Wilson's plan. They put a high priority on punishing Germany through heavy reparations. They also planned to treat themselves to the spoils of war. In fact, secret treaties among Britain, France, and Italy had already divided up territory of the defeated German empire. Issues of self-interest separated the three nations, but they agreed that they did not want Wilson to write the peace settlement unilaterally.

It is a tribute to Woodrow Wilson that he managed to influence the peace agreement as much as he did. His presence at Versailles softened some of the harshest demands for reprisals against Germany. National self-determination, a fundamental American principle enunciated in Wilson's Fourteen Points, found fulfillment in the creation of the independent states of Austria, Hungary, Poland, Yugoslavia, and Czechoslovakia from the defeated empires of the Central

Powers. The establishment of a *cordon sanitaire* (sanitary zone) of the new nations of Finland, Estonia, Lithuania, and Latvia further served Wilson's determination to isolate the new Bolshevik state from the rest of Europe.

The president also won limited concessions regarding the colonial empires of the defeated powers. Wilson had favored complete independence for the colonies involved; the Allies did not favor such a challenge to the system of prewar imperialism which they hoped to maintain. The resulting compromise put the colonies under a mandate system of protectorates. France and England received parts of the old Turkish and German empires in the Middle East and Africa, and Japan assumed responsibility for the former German colonies in the Far East.

However, Wilson had to back down from his goals on many other issues in the Fourteen Points. Certain topics, such as freedom of the seas and free trade, never even made the agenda because of Allied resistance. Wilson's call for "open covenants of peace openly arrived at" was mocked by the secret negotiating sessions held by the Big Four at Versailles. Wilson yielded to French and British demands for a guilt clause, which provided the justification for the heavy restitution demanded from Germany. Wilson agreed to reparations of $33 billion, even though he realized that this staggering amount could cripple the Germans' ability to rebuild their devastated economy.

In the face of his many disappointments, Wilson consoled himself with the peace conference's commitment to his proposed League of Nations. He acknowledged that the treaty had defects. But he expressed confidence that they could be resolved by a permanent international organization that brought nations together for the peaceful resolution of disputes.

German leaders reacted with dismay at the severity of the treaty, but they had no choice but to accept it. On June 28, 1919, representatives of the participating nations gathered in the Hall of Mirrors in the Palace of Versailles to sign the treaty. Wilson sailed home immediately after the ceremony and presented the treaty to the Senate on July 10. To reject it, he piously declared, "would break the heart of the world." The treaty was already in trouble, however, with support in the Senate far short of the two-thirds vote

necessary for ratification. Would Wilson compromise? "I shall consent to nothing," he told the French ambassador. "The Senate must take its medicine."

Opposition to the Versailles treaty came from several sources. One group, called the "irreconcilables," consisted of such Western progressives as William E. Borah of Idaho, Hiram W. Johnson of California, and Robert M. La Follette of Wisconsin. They disagreed fundamentally with the premise of permanent U.S. participation in European affairs. Moreover, they were horrified at the severity of the treaty's sanctions against Germany.

Less dogmatic, but more influential, were a group of Republicans led by Senator Henry Cabot Lodge of Massachusetts. By raising objections to the peace settlement Wilson had negotiated, Republicans sought to capitalize politically on the controversy with an eye toward the 1920 election. They expressed strong reservations about the break with American isolationism represented by membership in the League of Nations. Lodge's Republicans proposed a list of amendments that, scholars now agree, would not have seriously weakened the peace treaty. Most of these changes centered around Article X, the section of the League of Nations covenant calling for collective security measures if a member nation were attacked. Lodge correctly argued that this provision restricted Congress's constitutional authority to declare war. More importantly, Lodge and many other senators felt that the treaty imposed unacceptable restrictions on the freedom of the United States to pursue a unilateral foreign policy.

Wilson still refused to budge, especially to placate Lodge, his hated political rival. Sensing widespread popular support for the treaty, the president launched an extensive speaking tour to take his case to the American people. He brought large audiences to tears with his impassioned defense of the treaty. But the strain proved too much for the ailing sixty-three-year-old president, and he collapsed in Pueblo, Colorado, in late September. Two weeks later in Washington, Wilson suffered a severe stroke that left him paralyzed on one side of his body.

While his wife, Edith Galt Wilson, and his physician oversaw the routine business of government, Wilson slowly recovered. But he was never the same again. He had delusions of making the 1920 election campaign "a great and solemn referendum" on the League of Nations, and even hoped to run for a third term as president. Neither dream ever became a serious possibility. Woodrow Wilson died in 1924, "as much a victim of the war," David Lloyd George noted, "as any soldier who died in the trenches."

We will never know whether a healthy Wilson could have mobilized public support for the League of Nations and gained Senate ratification. If he had allowed the Democrats to compromise, the treaty might have been saved. From his sickbed, however, Wilson ordered the Democratic senators to vote against all Republican amendments. The treaty came up for a vote in November 1919 and failed to be ratified. Another attempt several months later fell seven votes short of approval, and the issue was dead.

The United States never signed the Versailles treaty nor joined the League of Nations. Many wartime issues remained only partially resolved, notably the future of Germany, the fate of colonial empires, and rising nationalist demands for self-determination. These unsolved problems played a major role in the coming of World War II and its aftermath.

Racial Strife and Labor Unrest

Woodrow Wilson spent only ten days in the United States between December 1918 and June 1919. This remarkable fact illustrates his total preoccupation with the peacemaking process at Versailles. For more than six months, Wilson was practically an absentee president. Unfortunately, many urgent domestic problems demanded his attention.

The immediate postwar period brought a severe decline in race relations throughout the country. In the South, the number of lynchings rose from forty-eight in 1917 to seventy-eight in 1919. Southern whites lynched several blacks who were still wearing their military uniforms. Northern blacks also faced hostility. Serious racial violence broke out in more than twenty-five northern cities, and the resulting death toll for the summer of 1919 reached 120.

The riots in northern cities resulted from the northward migration set in motion by World War I. Superficially at least, northern cities promised new freedoms. But southern blacks faced a difficult readjustment to the diverse urban environment from life in the rural South, with its traditional patterns of deference to whites. In turn, white northerners had never seen so many blacks before; ethnic groups such as Italians and Poles were especially hostile. Violence between blacks and whites erupted as early as 1917 in East Saint Louis, Illinois. Nine whites and more than forty blacks died in a riot sparked by competition over jobs at a defense plant.

One of the worst race riots took place in Chicago in July 1919. It began at a Lake Michigan beach when a black teenager named Eugene Williams swam into the area of water customarily reserved for whites. Someone threw a rock that hit him on the head, and he drowned. The incident touched off five days of rioting in which twenty-three blacks and fifteen whites died. Extensive property damage also occurred.

Chicago on the eve of the riot was a tinderbox waiting to ignite. The arrival of fifty thousand black newcomers during the war years had strained the city's social fabric. In politics, black male voters often provided the balance of power in close elections. Blacks and whites competed for jobs, and the more heavily unionized white population deeply resented blacks who became strikebreakers. White stockyard workers considered the words "Negro" and "scab" synonymous. Blacks and whites competed for scarce housing as well. Blacks soon overflowed the racially segregated South Side into Chicago's intensely ethnic neighborhoods. Even before that sultry July afternoon at the beach, tensions had erupted in bombings of black homes and other forms of harrassment.

Chicago blacks did not sit meekly by as whites destroyed their neighborhoods. They fought back, both in self-defense and for their rights as citizens. World War I had an indirect effect on their actions. Many blacks had served in the armed forces. The rhetoric about democracy and self-determination raised their expectations, too.

Workers had similar hopes as a result of the war. The war years had provided important breakthroughs for many industrial employees, including higher pay, shorter hours, and better working conditions. Relations between labor and

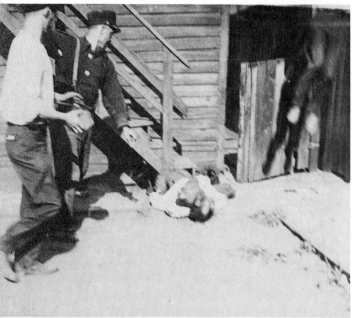

RACIAL VIOLENCE IN CHICAGO

Much of the violence perpetrated against blacks during the 1919 Chicago race riot was perpetrated by white teenagers and young men, many of Irish descent, who belonged to gangs such as the "Dirty Dozen" and "Our Flag." A city commission later concluded that without the gang activities, "it is doubtful if the riot would have gone beyond the first clash." (Chicago Historical Society)

management had also improved. Soon after the armistice, however, many employers returned to older patterns of hostility toward union activity. Many consumers blamed workers for the rising cost of living, and some people continued to identify unions with radicalism and foreigners. Nevertheless, workers hoped to expand their wartime gains. The worst problem was rapidly rising inflation, which threatened to wipe out their wage increases.

More than four million workers went on strike in 1919. The year began with a walkout by shipyard workers in Seattle. Their action spread into a general strike that crippled the city. In the fall, the Boston police force struck. The idea of public employees trying to unionize shocked many Americans. Governor Calvin Coolidge of Massachusetts propelled himself into the political spotlight by declaring, "There is no right to strike against the public safety by anybody, anywhere, any time." Harvard undergraduates acted as strikebreakers after university president A. Lawrence Lowell promised that their grades would not suffer. The strike failed, and the entire police force was fired. The public supported this harsh reprisal, and Coolidge received the Republican vice-presidential nomination in 1920 largely because of his stand against the striking police officers.

The most extensive labor disruption in 1919 was the great steel strike. More than 350,000 steelworkers walked off the job in late September. The main issue was union recognition, but strikers were also protesting such conditions as twelve-hour shifts and seven-day weeks. Elbert H. Gary, chairman of the United States Steel Corporation, refused to meet with representatives of the steelworkers' union to discuss their demands. The company hired Mexican and black strikebreakers and maintained steel production at about 60 percent of the normal level.

The continued high production rate doomed the strike. Striker solidarity began to slacken as winter approached; by January, the strike had collapsed. The union charged that U.S. Steel's "arbitrary and ruthless misuse of power" had crushed the strike. Just as important to the union's defeat was the lack of public support for the goals of organized labor. Unions had made important gains during the war, but they were unable to hold on to them.

The Red Scare

In addition to postwar racial violence and labor unrest, another cause for concern soon arose—fear of radicalism. Wartime hatred of the German Hun was quickly replaced by postwar hostility toward the Bolshevik Red. The Russian Revolution of 1917 set these fears in motion. The call of the Communist International, an organization established in the Soviet Union in 1919 to export revolution globally, threatened the American vision of a world order based on democracy, capitalism, and international harmony. Americans suddenly began seeing radicals everywhere.

Ironically, as the public became increasingly concerned about domestic Bolshevism, American radicalism rapidly lost members and political power. No more than seventy thousand Americans belonged to the fledgling U.S. Communist party or the Communist Labor party in 1919. The IWW and the Socialist party had been broken by wartime repression and internal dissension. Yet the public and the press continued to blame almost any disturbance on radicals. "REDS DIRECTING SEATTLE STRIKE—TO TEST CHANCE FOR REVOLUTION," warned a typical newspaper headline in January 1919.

Then a series of bombings shocked the nation in early spring. "The word 'radical' in 1919," one historian observed, "automatically carried with it the implication of dynamite." Thirty-six mail bombs addressed to prominent government officials were discovered by an alert postal worker before they exploded. Many people immediately suspected that the intended bombings had been timed to coincide with the communist celebration of International Labor Day on May 1. In June, a bomb exploded outside the Washington townhouse of the recently appointed attorney general, A. Mitchell Palmer. His family escaped unharmed, but the bomber was blown to bits. One of Palmer's neighbors, Assistant Secretary of the Navy Franklin D. Roosevelt, called the police. Despite intensive efforts, law enforcement agencies never traced the origin of a single bomb.

As hysteria mounted in the fall, the federal government became involved. President Wilson's debilitating stroke prevented him from providing decisive leadership. Attorney General

Palmer, a former Democratic member of Congress from Pennsylvania who had been a strong supporter of Woodrow Wilson's in 1912, assumed leadership. Angling for the presidential nomination, Palmer rode the crest of public hysteria about domestic radicalism into 1920.

Palmer set up an antiradicalism division in the Justice Department and appointed a young government attorney named J. Edgar Hoover to direct it. Hoover's division shortly became the Federal Bureau of Intelligence. In November 1919, on the second anniversary of the Russian Revolution, the attorney general staged the first of what became known as "Palmer raids." These attacks on the headquarters of radical organizations captured such supposedly revolutionary booty as a set of drawings that turned out to be blueprints for an improved phonograph, not sketches for a bomb. The dragnet netted thousands of aliens who had committed no

crime, but were suspect for their anarchist or revolutionary beliefs or merely their immigrant backgrounds. Lacking the protection of U.S. citizenship, they faced deportation without formal trial or indictment. In December 1919, the *U.S.S. Buford*, nicknamed the "Soviet Ark," embarked for Finland and the Soviet state with a cargo of 294 deported radicals. Its passengers included two famous anarchists, Emma Goldman and Alexander Berkman.

The peak of Palmer's power came with his New Year's raids in January 1920. In one night, with the greatest possible newspaper publicity, Palmer rounded up six thousand radicals. Agents invaded private homes, union headquarters, and meeting halls. The government held both citizens and aliens without specific charges and denied them legal counsel, a violation of their civil liberties. Some prisoners were even forced to march through the streets handcuffed

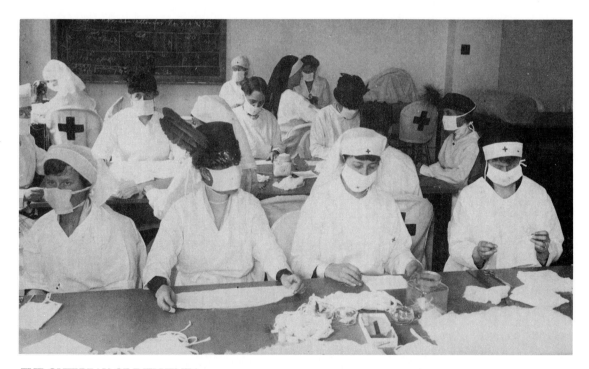

THE OUTBREAK OF INFLUENZA
The influenza epidemic of 1918–1919 strained the resources of a public health system already fully mobilized for the war effort. Novelist Mary McCarthy recalled in *Memories of a Catholic Girlhood* how "no hospital beds were to be had and people went about with masks or stayed shut up in their houses, and the awful fear of contagion paralyzed all services and made each man an enemy to his neighbor." McCarthy lost both her parents to influenza that terrible winter. (Chicago Historical Society)

TIME LINE
PROGRESSIVISM GOES TO WAR

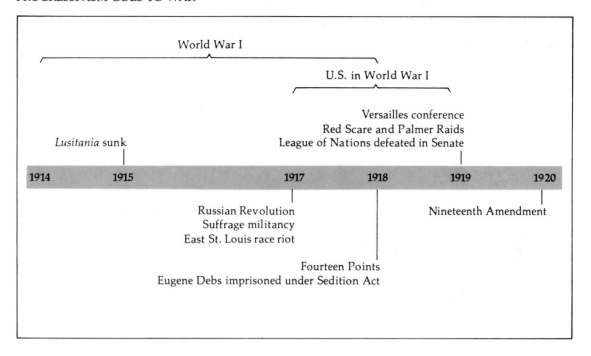

and chained to one another. One of the few moments of comic relief came when "patriotic" prisoners in a Chicago jail rioted when they were ordered to share cells with arrested radicals. "There are some things at which even a Chicago crook draws the line," a local newspaper reported.

Palmer was riding high, and his ambitions for the presidency swelled. But then he overstepped himself. Palmer predicted that May Day 1920 would bring a major plot to overthrow the United States government. Buildings were put under protection, state militia called up, and police put on twenty-four-hour alert to defend the nation against revolutionary violence. Not a single incident occurred. The hysteria of the Red Scare began to abate as the summer of 1920 passed without major labor strikes or renewed bombings.

One dramatic episode kept the wartime legacy of antiradicalism alive well into the next decade. In May 1920, at the height of the Red Scare, Nicola Sacco, a shoemaker, and Bartolomeo Vanzetti, a fish peddler, were arrested for the robbery and murder of a shoe company paymaster in South Braintree, Massachusetts. Sacco and Vanzetti were self-proclaimed anarchists and Italian aliens who had evaded the draft; both were armed at the time of their arrest. Regardless of their guilt or innocence, serious doubts still remain about whether they received a fair trial from the American judicial system.

Sacco and Vanzetti were convicted in 1921 and sat on death row for six years. Shortly before his death in the electric chair on August 23, 1927, Vanzetti claimed triumph.

> If it had not been for these thing, I might have live out my life among scorning men. I might have die, unmarked, unknown, a failure. Now we are not a failure. This is our career and our triumph. Never in our full life can we hope to do such work for tolerance, for justice, for man's understanding of man, as now we do by an accident.

World War I had caught the United States at a crossroads. The triumphs and tragedies between 1917 and 1920 were as much a response to the forces of industrialization, immigration, and urbanization as they were to the demands of a people at war. Over the past half century, the country had completed a fundamental transformation from a predominantly agricultural economy to an industrial one. Its population, which had been swelled by millions of immigrants from Europe and Russia, had become increasingly concentrated in urban areas. At the same time, the United States had broken from its former isolationist stance to take on a more active role in world affairs. By 1920,. the United States stood on the threshold of the modern era.

---

*D*uring World War I, the United States confronted international challenges caused by the outbreak of hostilities in 1914 and domestic tensions related to the nation's emergence as a modern industrial society. America entered the war in 1917 because of violations of its neutrality rights at sea, but, more broadly, because the country's foreign policy reflected the same moral concerns that animated the domestic reform movement. After the war ended in 1918, the Versailles treaty only partially reflected the hopes of President Woodrow Wilson for such international goals as freedom of the seas, peaceful economic expansion, and national self-determination. His postwar plans suffered a worse blow when the Senate refused to ratify the treaty, which included U.S. participation in the League of Nations.

On the home front, the conduct of the war was also shaped by the progressive period which preceded it. The war called for a mobilization of economic resources that accelerated the concentration of power in the federal government and large corporations. The government tried to mobilize the minds of the American people as well but succeeded mainly in inflaming passions. Certain groups, such as woman suffragists, found new opportunities during the war. But others became targets of repression, including blacks who migrated to northern cities, labor activists who called widespread strikes, and Socialists and other radicals who criticized the government. Domestic tensions erupted in race riots in many northern cities, and in the Red Scare of 1919–1920.

Suggestions for Further Reading

David M. Kennedy, *Over Here: The First World War and American Society* (1980), provides a comprehensive overview. For the links between the progressive era and the war, see Robert M. Crunden, *Ministers of Reform: The Progressives' Achievement in American Civilization, 1889–1920* (1982). Ellis W. Hawley, *The Great War and the Search for a Modern Order, 1917–1933* (1979), stresses the continuities between the war years and the 1920s.

Fighting the War

On American entry into World War I, see Ernest May, *The World War and American Isolationism* (1959); Ross Gregory, *The Origins of American Intervention in the First World War* (1971); and Daniel Smith, *The Great Departure: The United States and World War I, 1914–1920* (1965). There is a large body of material on the policies and personality of Woodrow Wilson, beginning with Arthur Link's five-volume biography (1947–1965), as well as his *Wilson the Diplomatist* (1957). See also Alexander L. George and Juliette L. George, *Woodrow Wilson and Colonel House: A Personality Study* (1956), and John M. Blum, *Woodrow Wilson and the Politics of Morality* (1956). Later studies of Wilson include Edwin Weinstein, *Woodrow Wilson: A Medical and Psychological Biography* (1981), and John Milton Cooper, Jr., *The Warrior and the Priest: Woodrow Wilson and Theodore Roosevelt* (1983).

For American military participation in the war, Russell Weigley, *The American Way of War* (1973); Edward M. Coffman, *The War to End All Wars* (1968); and Harvey deWeerd, *President Wilson Fights His War* (1968), provide useful introductions. They can be supplemented by Laurence Stallings, *The Doughboys: the Story of the AEF, 1917–1918* (1963), and A. E. Barbeau and Florette Henri, *The Unknown Soldiers: Black Troops in World War I* (1974).

Over Here: Mobilizing the Home Front

Robert D. Cuff, *The War Industries Board: Business-Government Relations During World War I* (1973), provides an excellent case study of war mobilization. See also Stephen Skowronek, *Building a New American State: The Expansion of National Administrative Capacities, 1877–1920* (1982); Charles Gilbert, *American Financing of World War I* (1970); David F. Noble, *America by Design* (1977); and Paul A. C. Koistinen, "The 'Industrial-Military Complex' in Historical Perspective: World War I," *Business History Review*, 41 (1967), 378–403. Valerie Jean Conner, *The National War Labor Board* (1983), covers federal policies toward labor.

Maurine Greenwald, *Women, War, and Work* (1980), provides a good overview of women's wartime experiences. Anne F. Scott and Andrew Scott, *One Half the People* (1975), and Eleanor Flexner, *Century of Struggle* (1959), cover the final stages of the woman suffrage campaign. For the experiences of Mexican-Americans, see Rodolfo Acuna, *Occupied America* (1980), and Wayne Cornelius, *Building the Cactus Curtain: Mexican Migration and U.S. Responses from Wilson to Carter* (1980). Efforts to promote national unity are covered in Stephen Vaughn, *Holding Fast the Inner Lines: Democracy, Nationalism, and the CPI* (1980); Paul L. Murphy, *World War I and the Origin of Civil Liberties* (1979); George Blakey, *Historians on the Homefront* (1970); and

Frederick Luebke, *Bonds of Loyalty: German-Americans and World War I* (1974).

An Unsettled Peace

N. Gordon Levin, Jr., *Woodrow Wilson and World Politics* (1968), offers a stimulating interpretation of Wilson's diplomacy. For more on Versailles and the League of Nations, see Thomas Bailey, *Woodrow Wilson and the Great Betrayal* (1945); Ralph A. Stone, *The Irreconcilables: The Fight Against the League of Nations* (1970); John A. Garraty, *Henry Cabot Lodge* (1953); and Arno J. Mayer, *Politics and Diplomacy of Peacemaking: Containment and Counter Revolution at Versailles* (1967). On American intervention in Russia, see George F. Kennan, *The Decision to Intervene* (1958); John L. Gaddis, *Russia, the Soviet Union, and the United States* (1978); and Peter Filene, *Americans and the Soviet Experiment, 1917–1933* (1967). Ronald Steel's fine biography *Walter Lippmann and the American Century* (1980) offers another view of the Versailles conference.

Robert K. Murray, *The Red Scare* (1955), summarizes the antiradicalism of the immediate postwar period. See also James Weinstein, *The Decline of Socialism in America, 1912–1923* (1967); John Higham, *Strangers in the Land* (1955); and Burl Noggle, *Into the Twenties* (1974). David Brody, *Labor in Crisis* (1965), describes the steel strike of 1919, while William M. Tuttle, Jr., covers racial strife in *Race Riot: Chicago in the Red Summer of 1919* (1970). For an introduction to the complicated Sacco and Vanzetti case, see Louis Joughin and Edmund Morgan, *The Legacy of Sacco and Vanzetti* (1948), and Roberta Strauss Feuerlicht, *Justice Crucified* (1977).

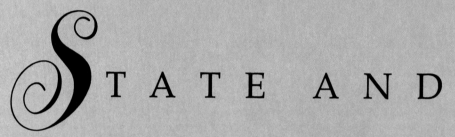

PART THREE

STATE AND

1920 TO

THE PRESENT

Just as no single turning point indicates the onset of industrialization in early nineteenth century America, no event or date marks the emergence of the United States as a mature industrial society. By the early twentieth century, however, a different mode of organization shaped American economic, political, and social life than had prevailed in industrializing America. Many of the outlines of modern America were firmly in place by the 1920s. The period following World War II produced a noticeable quickening in the pace of change.

One of the most dramatic changes of the twentieth century has been the growth of a postindustrial state with a significant impact on all aspects of soci-

SOCIETY

ety, especially economic life. Two world wars greatly increased the concentration of political and economic power in the federal government and the presidency, as did the Great Depression. By the 1960s, the United States had erected an extensive federal apparatus that accepted responsibility for the basic social well-being of its citizens. It also intervened in the economy when private initiatives could not maintain steady economic growth.

The United States also assumed a dramatically different stance in foreign affairs than the position it had held through most of the nineteenth century. The critical turning point occurred after 1945, when the United States emerged from World War II committed to a foreign policy that included a wide-ranging involvement in international affairs. The most consistent thrust of American foreign policy ever since has been the tendency to interpret international events in terms of a deep-rooted conflict between Communism and the Free World. The Korean and Vietnam wars were a direct outgrowth of this Cold War mentality.

A third theme characterizing present-day America is that its citizens are increasingly drawn into a web of interlocking national experience, fostered by the development of a mass culture based on technological innovations such as radio, movies, and television as well as the widespread dissemination

of the values of consumerism. In addition, the growth of metropolitan areas has given the nation an increasingly urban tone while geographic mobility has broken down old regional differences.

A fourth theme of twentieth-century life has been its growing social and political diversity. The political domination by elite white males has been undercut by the broader participation in public life of labor, women, and blacks, and other ethnic and racial minorities. During the period after World War II, and especially in the 1960s, many groups challenged American society to make good on its promise of liberty and equality for all. The resulting hard-won reforms dramatically expanded the democratic system, although the promise of full equality remains unfulfilled. The saga of civil rights and the fight against discrimination, like so many other stories in modern America, does not yet have an ending.

The final section of this book continues our attempt to relate the contours of ordinary lives and individual decisions to broader historical forces and patterns. Yet the focus shifts somewhat as we enter the twentieth century. To a remarkable extent, outside events now impinge directly on individual lives. The actions of an expanding federal bureaucracy, the tensions of international relations, the complexity of sprawling metropolitan areas, and the economic impact of giant multinational corporations have broken down older patterns of local autonomy and isolation. Because state and society have become inextricably entwined in the modern era, the structures of a complex bureaucratic society increasingly circumscribe and control the conditions under which Americans live.

Despite the nationalizing trends so evident in twentieth-century economic, political, and cultural life, however, the collective American experience continues to be defined as much by diversity as by uniformity or consensus. There is not one American story, but many. How we live is still fundamentally shaped by age, gender, religion, ethnic or racial background, and socioeconomic class. Describing the ongoing diversity of American social history, while at the same time connecting it to the centralizing tendencies in a mass bureaucratic society, offers clues to the complexity of American history from the 1920s to the present.

23

THE 1920s:
TOWARD A CORPORATE
ECONOMY
AND MASS CULTURE

*M*odern America began in the 1920s. In economic organization, political outlook, and cultural values, the 1920s have more in common with the United States of the 1980s than with the industrializing America of the late nineteenth century. Although this transformation did not occur overnight, by the 1920s there was little doubt that the United States had entered a new age.

By the 1920s, the process of industrialization was complete and the foundations of the modern corporate economy were firmly in place. Large-scale bureaucracies run by sophisticated tools of modern management, planning, and production strategies dominated the economy. The business–government partnership accelerated by World War I expanded on an informal basis throughout the "New Era" of the 1920s, and the successful performance of the economy seemed to confirm the efficacy of these capitalist choices. Even though the prosperity of the 1920s could not be sustained on a permanent basis, the economic reverses of the Great Depression in the

1930s did not wipe out the corporate organizational structure of the previous decade. This bureaucratic order reached its height in the postwar prosperity of the 1940s and 1950s.

The 1920s also represented an important watershed in the development of a mass national culture. The invention of the radio, the growing popularity of movies, and the spread of mass circulation magazines fostered a sense of shared national experience that broke down older patterns of isolation and provincialism. Advertising glorified new values of consumption and spending, although only the more prosperous members of the middle class could afford this expensive lifestyle. Meanwhile, the automobile had a revolutionary impact on both the nation's values and its landscape, signaling, among other things, a new emphasis on leisure and amusement that has come to characterize the modern era.

Such changes were troubling to many Americans. The 1920s were marked by deep controversy over the extent to which modern secular

Corporatism, the Mesh of Public and Private Power

The booming economic prosperity of the 1920s provided the backdrop for the business and government initiatives during that decade. After a brief but sharp downturn in 1921 and 1922, the economy took off. Between 1922 and 1929, the gross national product, which is the total value of the nation's output of goods and services, grew by 40 percent, from $74.1 billion to $103.1 billion. Per capita income rose from $641 in 1921 to $847 in 1929. After 1922, unemployment hovered around 3 or 4 percent and inflation was negligible. Behind this economic growth lay new management and production techniques, especially the wide-spread introduction of electricity into factories and a strong increase in worker productivity. The automobile industry became the symbol of mass production and mass consumption. The world admired the extraordinary economic accomplishments of the United States.

Corporate Capitalism

The 1920s brought the triumph of the managerial revolution that had been reshaping the structure of the American economy since the late nineteenth century. Large-scale corporate organizations with bureaucratic structures of authority replaced older, family-run businesses. Ownership was divorced from control, and the visible hand of management replaced what the eighteenth-century economist Adam Smith had called the invisible hand of market forces.

A wave of mergers took place, surpassed in intensity only by the heyday of combinations in the 1880s and 1890s. There were 368 mergers in 1924 and 1,245 in 1929. The largest numbers of mergers occurred in rapidly growing industries such as chemicals (led by Du Pont), electric power (Westinghouse and General Electric), and automobiles (General Motors). By 1930, the two hundred largest corporations controlled just under half the nonbanking corporate wealth in the United States and received 43 percent of the corporate income. This concentration of economic power did not produce monopolies; rarely did

ONE SIDE OF THE TWENTIES
Rarely has a decade been defined so predominantly in cultural cliches as the 1920s—flappers, bathtub gin, speakeasies, the Charleston, and gangsters shooting it out on the streets of Chicago. John Held, Jr.'s cover for *McClure's* magazine suggests why one historian satirized the decade as "one long party" where "everyone had a hangover (known as the depression) in the morning." This version of the 1920s tells only part of the story. Most Americans were too concerned with earning a living and raising a family to learn the latest dance craze. (Culver)

values should prevail. Cultural and political conflict broke out over such issues as immigration restriction, prohibition, and race relations. Rural Americans, now a minority, felt threatened by the country's increasingly urban tone. Despite such ambivalence about the transformations under way in American culture, the 1920s stand as a major turning point in the shift from older values characterized by self-denial and the Protestant work ethic to a fascination with consumption, leisure, and self-realization that is the essence of modern times.

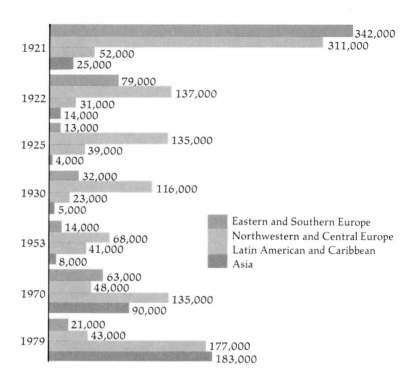

FIGURE 23.1 AMERICAN
IMMIGRATION SINCE
WORLD WAR I

any corporation control an entire industry. Rather, oligopolies, in which a few large producers controlled the market of an industry, became the norm.

By 1920, techniques of modern business enterprise dominated many industries, especially in manufacturing. The multi-unit enterprise coordinated production and distribution through divisions organized by functions, such as sales, operations, and investment. Alfred P. Sloan, Jr., an engineer and mid-level manager at General Motors in the 1920s, further refined the structure when he devised a bureaucratic strategy that relieved top management of all day-to-day control of production. The managers in the central office concentrated solely on long-range planning, while a series of autonomous, integrated divisions met short-range production goals. General Motors' innovative structure set the pattern for large companies in the 1920s and 1930s.

Perhaps the most important management change of the 1920s came with a greatly increased commitment to research and development within the corporate framework. This decision involved using current earnings to finance future profits. The increase in resources generated by the merger movement provided an

important source of capital for this purpose. By 1927, more than a thousand corporations had set up independent research programs to improve products or services, reduce production costs, or develop new products. The formal incorporation in 1925 of Bell Laboratories, the research arm of the American Telephone and Telegraph Company, reflected this trend.

Running these huge modern corporate structures called for a new breed of men. (Women found few opportunities in the corporate hierarchy until the 1960s and 1970s.) Professionalization of management became the watchword, especially emphasis on knowledge of management theory and techniques. Professionalization entailed a growing reliance on graduate training at business schools, such as Wharton and Harvard; the organization of professional societies and journals; and the growth of management consultants. Many of these new managers had engineering training. The chief executives in the 1920s at General Motors, General Electric, Singer, Du Pont, and Goodyear had been engineering classmates at the Massachusetts Institute of Technology.

The expansion and consolidation of the nation's financial resources paralleled its corporate growth. Total bank assets rose from almost $48 billion in 1919 to $72 billion in 1929. Rising deposits in savings accounts and business and loan associations, along with life insurance accounts and policies, accounted for much of the gain. Mergers between Wall Street banking establishments enhanced New York's role as the financial center of the United States. About 250 banks, 1 percent of the nation's total, controlled almost half its banking resources in 1929.

Business leaders enjoyed enormous popularity and respect in the 1920s. Their reputations often surpassed those of the rather lackluster politicians of the day. Styling themselves as trustees of the public interest, they promoted service and social responsibility through business. Many drew parallels between religious activity and business leadership. As President Calvin Coolidge solemnly declared, "The man who

HENRY FORD AND THOMAS EDISON

Henry Ford (1863–1947) and Thomas Alva Edison (1847–1931), two of the decade's most widely respected (and richest) business leaders, were also good friends. Edison (right), inventor of the phonograph, electric lighting, and motion pictures, was a founder of the company that eventually became General Electric. Henry Ford (left) revolutionized the auto industry with the introduction of the Model T in 1908 and was one of the most influential industrialists of the twentieth century. (Library of Congress)

builds a factory builds a temple. The man who works there worships there." The secularization of religion, and the glorification of business, reached its height in *The Man Nobody Knows* (1925), a book by advertising executive Bruce Barton. The man was Jesus Christ, whom Barton portrayed as the founder of modern business. Christ, he wrote, "picked up twelve men from the bottom ranks of business and forged them into an organization that conquered the world." Americans made Barton's parable an instant bestseller.

Henry Ford ranked as the most respected business leader of the decade, and a genuine folk hero as well. His background as a poor farm boy who made good symbolized the values of rural society and American individualism in a rapidly changing world. Ford was widely revered as a pioneer in labor relations for introducing the five-dollar-a-day wage in 1914. His factories, especially the Rouge plant in suburban Detroit, represented the triumph of mass production. Ironically, this American capitalist hero achieved great popularity in the Soviet Union, where he won respect as an economic innovator. At a time when the United States and the Soviet Union did not have formal diplomatic relations, Ford sold the Russians twenty-five thousand tractors between 1920 and 1926.

Although labor lagged behind business in reaping the benefits of technological advance, workers shared in the prosperity of the 1920s. Business supported higher wages as a deliberate strategy to increase consumer buying power. Shorter work weeks, down to five and a half days, including a half day on Saturday, gave workers more leisure time.

The 1920s also were the heyday of a system of labor relations that stressed management's obligation for the well-being of employees. Corporations provided their own programs—called "welfare capitalism"—as a calculated substitute for unions. Paternalism tinged such systems, but they provided benefits to workers at a time when federally guaranteed unemployment compensation and old age pensions did not exist. The corporate programs were not, however, primarily concerned with workers' security. Management's long-term goals included control over the workplace; the open, or nonunion, shop; and worker loyalty.

Welfare capitalism took several forms. For example, workers could increase their stake in a company's success by purchasing the firm's stock below the stock market price. By 1927, about eight hundred thousand workers had invested more than $1 billion in 315 companies. Some firms subsidized mortgages or contributed to employee savings funds; others set up insurance and pension plans. Many voluntarily adopted programs for consultation between management and the elected representatives of the workers. These employee representation plans, actually a device to avert unionization, were called the American Plan so as to establish the idea that unions were un-American.

Welfare capitalism represented a form of labor relations squarely in keeping with the values of the 1920s. It provided freedom from government interference to both workers and managers, placing the responsibility for economic welfare on the private rather than the public sector. The system had serious gaps, however. It offered no protection against unemployment. Only a minority of companies provided pension plans and stock-purchase programs. Most welfare capitalism programs appeared in the largest, most prosperous firms, such as General Electric and U.S. Steel. Furthermore, corporate profits dictated the nature of the programs. The Proctor & Gamble Company guaranteed its soap-manufacturing workers forty-eight weeks of employment a year because of the steady public demand for soap. The firm did not extend a similar pledge to workers who processed vegetable oils, which were subject to severe sales fluctuations.

In general, welfare capitalism satisfied management's main objective: it reversed the advance of unionization. Union membership dropped from 5.1 million in 1920 to 3.6 million in 1929. At the same time, the number of strikes fell dramatically from the 1919 level. Welfare capitalism seemed to represent the wave of the future in industrial relations.

The Economy

America's transition from a wartime to peacetime economy hardly foreshadowed the strong economic record of the 1920s. Runaway inflation was the worst problem during the immediate postwar period. Prices jumped by a third in 1919 and tripled their 1914 level by 1920. Feverish economic activity accompanied the inflation. However, the postwar boom was more a reflection of consumers' desire to buy goods before prices rose even higher than of solid economic growth.

The inflationary bubble burst in 1920 when the Wilson administration sharply reduced federal expenditures in an attempt to balance the budget. The national deficit had risen to the unprecedented level of $13 billion. In contrast, the largest deficit during the period between the Civil War and World War I was about $89 million, recorded in 1899 and 1909. The Federal Reserve System also tightened credit in 1920 because its previous expansive money polices had encouraged people to borrow and spend, thereby pushing prices even higher. The resulting recession demonstrated that the government still had much to learn about protecting the stability of economic life.

The recession of 1920–1921 was the sharpest short-term downturn the United States had ever faced. Production fell, unemployment reached 10 percent, and the demand for goods and services slackened. Nearly five million Americans were out of work. Foreign trade dropped by almost half, from $13.5 billion in 1920 to less than $7 billion in 1921. Prices fell so dramatically—more than 20 percent—that the contraction wiped out much of the inflation of World War I. Fortunately, the recession lasted only a short time. Recovery started by 1922 and continued until 1929, broken only by brief, mild downturns.

One sector of the economy, agriculture, never fully recovered from the 1920 recession. During the inflationary period from 1914 to 1920, farmers had piled up large debts for mortgages and farm equipment as they expanded production in response to government incentives, increased demand, and rising prices. When the war ended, a glut of agricultural products hit the world market. Furthermore, the government withdrew price supports for wheat on May 31, 1920. Farm income plunged as the price of wheat dropped 40 percent, corn 32 percent, and hogs 50 percent. Total net farm income, which peaked at more than $10 billion in 1919, barely reached $4.1 billion in 1921.

Each year brought larger agricultural surpluses, which depressed farm prices even further. Farmers turned to the political system for help. The McNary-Haugen bill, a far-reaching attempt to create federal price supports for agricultural products, used the idea of a "fair exchange

SIGNS OF PROSPERITY
The success of the automobile industry provided a major component of the prosperity of the 1920s. With the introduction of the moving assembly line in 1914, the time it took Ford workers to assemble an auto dropped from fourteen hours to ninety-three minutes. By 1929, there were more than twenty-three million cars on the road, many of them caught up in traffic jams like the one pictured above. Billboards advertising brand-name products were another manifestation of the growth of a mass national culture. (Museum of Science & Industry, Chicago)

value" to guarantee that farmers earn at least their production costs, no matter what price prevailed on the world market. A 1924 bill applying this principle only to grain failed in Congress. When cotton, rice, and tobacco were added to win southern farm support, the measure twice passed, only to draw presidential vetoes in 1927 and 1928. Coolidge opposed the measure as an unhealthy government intrusion into the economy, a view seconded by the eastern business interests that controlled the Republican party. By the end of the decade, farmers had seen their share of the national income plunge from 16 percent in 1919 to 8.8 percent just ten years later.

Most other sectors of the economy fared considerably better during the 1920s. The value of total new construction increased from $6 billion in 1921 to $12 billion in 1927. Manufacturing output expanded 64 percent during the decade, fueled by a 40 percent increase in worker productivity. New industries turning out automobiles, chemicals, electric power, radios, aircraft, and movies stimulated economic growth. The demand for goods and services kept unemploy-

ment low throughout the 1920s, but the expanded demand was not so strong that it produced inflation.

This record of low unemployment and low inflation represented a significant accomplishment, but the economy contained several soft spots. In addition to agriculture, certain "sick industries," including coal and textiles, did not share in the prosperity of the 1920s. Unemployment remained far higher than the national average for workers in those industries. Moreover, seasonal or part-time work often cut workers' income, a fact not adequately reflected in the rather primitive economic statistics of that time. This underside of economic life foreshadowed the Great Depression of the 1930s.

As the economy expanded, its international dimensions enlarged correspondingly. America's emergence as the world's largest creditor nation, a reversal of its pre–World War I debtor status, represented a dramatic shift of power in the world capital markets. During the 1920s, the United States had the world's most productive economy, with great capacity to compete in markets abroad. The most visible aspect of this outward thrust was the dramatic extension of private investment, which more than doubled between 1919 and 1930. By the end of the 1920s, foreign investment stood at $15.2 billion.

Manufacturers led the way in foreign investment. Automobile companies found it cheaper to ship car parts to assembly plants outside the country and build the vehicles there than to export the finished products. Ford had major facilities in England, Canada, and throughout the British Empire; General Motors took control of such established firms as Vauxhall in England and Opel in Germany. Electric companies, including General Electric, built new plants in Latin America, China, Japan, and Australia. The International Telephone and Telegraph Corporation, founded in 1920, owned twenty-four factories in Europe by 1929. It employed ninety-five thousand workers outside the country, more than any other U.S. company. Underlying this increase of multinational economic activity was a growing foreign demand for the fruits of American mass production, such as radios, telephones, automobiles, and sewing machines.

Other U.S. companies invested internationally during the 1920s not so much to increase their foreign markets as to obtain supplies or take advantage of lower production costs. They concentrated their investments mainly in Latin America and Canada. The three major American meat packers—Swift, Armour, and Wilson—built packing plants in Argentina to capitalize on lower livestock prices. Fruit growers such as the United Fruit Company, searching for tropical products unavailable in the United States, developed vast tracts of land in Costa Rica, Honduras, and Guatemala. American capital dominated sugar plantations in Cuba and rubber plantations in the Phillipines, Sumatra, and Malaya.

American companies also made massive investments in mining and oil, concentrating on South American and Canadian sources. Chile attracted the greatest U.S. investment in mining; the Anaconda Copper Corporation owned Chile's largest copper mine. Led by Standard Oil of New Jersey, American oil companies put new emphasis on acquiring foreign oil. These firms retained extensive investments in Mexico but, discouraged by the tough bargaining of the Mexican government, turned to Venezuela as well.

By 1929, Venezuela ranked second only to the United States in oil production. American companies did not begin to pump oil from the Persian Gulf area of the Middle East until the 1930s.

American banks supported U.S. enterprises abroad. The banks not only facilitated direct corporate investments, but also made extensive loans of their own. Lending by American banks, particularly to foreign governments, became especially active after 1925.

The strong European demand for American private capital resulted primarily from the need to finance economic recovery after World War I, especially in Germany. The Allies' need for dollars to pay off wartime loans also contributed to the demand. As late as 1930, the Allies still owed the United States $4.3 billion. American political leaders, responding to the disenchantment with the nation's costly participation in the war, rigidly demanded payment. "They hired the money, didn't they?" scoffed President Calvin Coolidge.

The United States made repayment more difficult because of its high protective tariffs. The Fordney-McCumber Tariff of 1922 raised protectionism to an all-time high. Such tariffs, desired by American manufacturers who feared that foreign competition would reduce their high profits, limited the volume of European imports allowed into the United States. In turn, the difficulty in selling goods in the United States made it more difficult for European nations to use dollars to pay off their debts.

American business was concerned about debt repayment. The American banking community, and many U.S. corporations with European investments, opposed excessively high tariffs and urged modification of the debt structure. They recognized that a rapidly recovering Europe and a free-trade environment would help American business. Conversely, banks feared that a weak European economy might undermine their long-term loans and investments.

In 1924, the United States, France, Great Britain, and Germany, at the prodding of the United States, jointly agreed to a plan to promote European financial stability. The Dawes plan, named for Charles G. Dawes, a Chicago banker who negotiated the agreement, involved substantial American loans to Germany and a reduction in the amount of reparations owed the Allies. But the Dawes plan hardly provided a permanent solution. The international economic system was inherently unstable. It depended on the flow of American capital to Germany, reparations payments from Germany to the Allies, and the repayment of debts to the United States. If the outward flow of capital from the United States slowed or stopped, the whole international financial structure could collapse. This economic instability helped turn the recession that began in 1929 into a depression of worldwide proportions by the 1930s.

The Republican Ascendancy

The 1920 election returned the Republicans to power. Their domination of national politics in the 1920s stemmed from a reorientation in the national party system during the 1890s. Between 1894 and 1896, the Republican party broke the stalemate that had characterized national politics since the 1870s. William McKinley's presidential victory in 1896 marked the beginning of Republican control of the national government that lasted, with the exception of Woodrow Wilson's two terms, until 1932.

The Republicans built their party around various blocs of voters, drawn chiefly from the native-born Protestant middle class. This group included owners of small businesses, white collar workers, and farmers. To this solid base the Republicans added skilled workers who approved the party's promises of protection of home industries through high tariffs. They also relied on the black vote, traditionally Republican since Lincoln had freed the slaves and the Democratic party had fallen under the domination of southern politicians. In addition, wealthy industrialists supported Republican policies that encouraged business and economic development. These corporate leaders supplied the substantial cash resources that formed the party's stable financial base. Geographically, Republican strength was concentrated in the Northeast and West.

Throughout the first third of the twentieth century, the Democratic party had difficulty competing with its more popular and better-financed rival. Democrats had two main bases of support, the Solid South, consisting of the former Confederate states, and northern urban political machines, such as Tammany Hall in New

WARREN HARDING AND CALVIN COOLIDGE
The political careers of New Era political leaders Warren G. Harding (1865–1923) and Calvin Coolidge (1872–1933) present a study in contrasts. Harding (left), a small-town politician from Marion, Ohio, was prone to cronyism and mediocrity. Calvin Coolidge (right), of Vermont, was cut from a different cloth: taciturn, upright, stern, and capable. In the wake of the Harding scandals, Coolidge reassured citizens' faith in Republican government by his unimpeachable ethics. (Culver)

York. Until they could broaden their support and build an effective national organization to rival the Republican party, the Democrats would remain a minority party.

Woodrow Wilson had temporarily overcome the Democrats' weakness by exploiting the split in the Republican party in 1912 and by capturing electoral support from reform-minded progressives and western farmers. By 1918, Wilson's progressive coalition was floundering. In 1920, the Democrats passed over the ailing Wilson in favor of Governor James M. Cox of Ohio. Assistant Secretary of the Navy Franklin D. Roosevelt received the vice-presidential nomination. The Democratic platform urged ratification of U.S. participation in the League of Nations and a continuation of Wilsonian progressivism. Cox and Roosevelt lost in a landslide to Warren G. Harding and Calvin Coolidge.

President Harding was hardly a towering national figure. He had built an uninspiring record in Ohio state politics before winning election to the United States Senate in 1914. With a

Republican victory almost a certainty in 1920, party leaders wanted a presidential candidate they could dominate after he had taken office. Genial, loyal, and mediocre, "Uncle Warren" fit the bill.

Harding realized his limitations and assembled a strong cabinet to help him guide the government. Charles Evans Hughes, former presidential candidate and Supreme Court justice, headed the State Department. Secretary of Agriculture Henry C. Wallace set up conferences that brought farmers together with government agencies such as the Bureau of Agricultural Economics. Financier Andrew W. Mellon ran the Treasury Department, where he engineered a massive tax cut to reduce the federal surplus. Most of the benefits went to the wealthy, fulfilling Mellon's goal of releasing money for private investment.

By far the most active member of the Harding administration was Secretary of Commerce Herbert Hoover. Hoover made Commerce the most important cabinet position in both the Harding and Coolidge administrations. Cynics grumbled that he not only ran his own department, but also acted as undersecretary for all the others.

Hoover embodied the business–government cooperation that dominated the 1920s. Unlike Secretary of the Treasury Mellon, who sought the least amount of federal activity possible, Hoover supported expansion of the federal government in what he called the spirit of "associationalism." He developed his ideas to meet the needs of highly competitive, disorganized industries such as agriculture, construction, and mining. Hoover sought to eliminate waste, stabilize prices, and assure general economic stability in these volatile sectors of the economy through voluntary cooperation in the public interest. He used persuasion, educational conferences, and fact-finding commissions to accomplish his broad goals.

The key to Hoover's vision of "associated individualism" was his promotion of trade associations. These groups, which numbered about two thousand by 1929, represented almost every major industry and commodity. Serving as instruments of voluntary cooperation, they proved especially important in industries where excessive competition hampered productivity. Trade associations attempted to bring stability to modern economic life through conferences, conventions, publicity, lobbying, and trade practice controls. Statistics gathered by the Commerce Department and private groups, such as the National Bureau of Economic Research, aided corporate planning and the allocation of investments and markets. The Commerce Department's trade conferences provided a supportive climate for this exchange of information. The Republican-dominated Federal Trade Commission, conveniently ignoring antitrust laws that forbade such arrangements in restraint of trade, then approved the resulting agreements.

Unfortunately, many of Harding's lesser appointments fell far short of Hoover. The president was personally an honest man, but several of his appointees, often his cronies from his days in Ohio politics, lacked ethical standards. "My God, this is a hell of a job," Harding told journalist William Allen White in 1923. "I have no trouble with my enemies. . . . But my damned friends, my God-damn friends, White, they're the ones that keep me walking the floor nights!" Alice Roosevelt Longworth, Theodore Roosevelt's sharp-tongued and witty daughter, described Harding as a "slob" and characterized the mood at the White House as "a general atmosphere of waistcoat unbuttoned, feet on desk, and spittoons alongside."

Harding died unexpectedly in San Francisco in August 1923 after making the first presidential trip to Canada and Alaska. Evidence of widespread fraud and corruption in his administration had just started coming to light. The worst scandal concerned the government's leasing of oil reserves in Teapot Dome, Wyoming, and Elk Hills, California, to private companies. Secretary of the Interior Albert Fall eventually was convicted of taking almost half a million dollars in bribes. He became the first cabinet officer in American history to serve a prison sentence.

Harding's death catapulted Vice-President Calvin Coolidge into the White House. In contrast to Harding's political cronyism, Coolidge represented Vermont rectitude. He believed in limited government and performed all his presidential duties in four hours a day. As vice-president, "Silent Cal" often sat through entire dinner parties without uttering a word. His dinner partner once challenged him by saying, "Mr. Coolidge, I've made a rather sizable bet with my friends that I can get you to speak three words this evening." Replied Coolidge, "You lose." Alice Longworth quipped that Coolidge had been weaned on a pickle, but his unimpeachable morality reassured voters in the wake of the Harding scandals. Coolidge soon announced he would run for president in 1924.

The 1924 campaign featured a third-party challenge by Senator Robert M. La Follette of Wisconsin, who ran on the Progressive ticket. His candidacy mobilized progressive reformers and labor leaders, as well as farmers discontented over plunging farm prices. The Progressive party platform called for nationalization of the railroads, public ownership of utilities, and the right of Congress to overrule Supreme Court decisions. The platform also favored election of the president directly by the voters, rather than by the electoral college.

The Democrats were even more divided than usual when they gathered in the sweltering July heat of New York City to nominate a candidate for president in 1924. Their convention, the first to be broadcast live on national radio, lasted seventeen days, prompting humorist Will Rogers to joke, "This thing has got to come to an end. New York invited you people here as guests, not to live." The convention became hopelessly deadlocked between Governor Alfred E. Smith of New York, who had the support of northern urban politicians, and William G. McAdoo of California, Wilson's secretary of the treasury (and son-in-law), the western and southern choice. McAdoo also had the backing of a large faction of the Ku Klux Klan. The delegates needed 103 ballots to agree on compromise candidate John W. Davis, a Wall Street lawyer who had served as a West Virginia congressman and ambassador to Great Britain. To attract rural voters, Democrats chose Governor Charles W. Bryan of Nebraska, brother of William Jennings Bryan, for vice-president.

The Republicans won impressively. Coolidge received 15.7 million popular votes to 8.4 million for Davis and scored a decisive victory in the electoral college. Despite La Follette's vigorous campaign, he could not draw many midwestern farm leaders away from the Republican party; his labor support also proved soft. La Follette got almost 5 million popular votes but won only the support of Wisconsin in the electoral college.

Perhaps the most significant fact about the 1924 election was voter apathy. Only 52 percent of the electorate bothered to take part. Although voter participation had been declining since its nineteenth-century high, the turnout in 1924 was low partly because so few of the nation's newly enfranchised women voted. In 1920, the first presidential election since passage of the Nineteenth Amendment, barely a third of the women eligible to vote did so. Most people still considered politics a male preserve. Putting polling places in schools and churches, rather than their former location in saloons, helped women feel more comfortable with their new political role. By the end of the decade, women's voting turnout was on the rise, encouraged by the extensive education campaigns undertaken by the recently founded League of Women Voters.

Rather than forming their own party, women sought integration into the traditional political system. The two major parties only grudgingly granted women token positions. In 1920, Harriet Taylor Upton of Ohio, a former officer of the National American Woman Suffrage Association, became a vice-chairman of the Republican National Committee. In 1924, Emily Newell Blair, a former Missouri suffragist, took over the same position for the Democrats. In most cases, however, political officeholding for women remained a "widow's game." Both Miriam ("Ma") Ferguson of Texas and Nellie Tayloe Ross of Wyoming won election as their states' governors in 1924, but only after their husbands, because of impeachment or death, respectively, could not run. About two-thirds of the women in Congress were named to fill their late husbands' unexpired terms.

Women played more influential roles as lobbyists. The Women's Joint Congressional Committee, a Washington coalition of ten major women's organizations, lobbied for reform legislation of interest to women. Its major accomplishment was winning the passage in 1921 of the Sheppard-Towner Federal Maternity and Infancy Act, one of the nation's first federally funded health care programs. In an attempt to reduce the high rates of maternal and infant mortality, Congress appropriated $1.25 million for medical clinics, educational programs, and visiting-nurse projects. The Sheppard-Towner law passed because politicians feared that women would vote them out of office otherwise.

As one supporter noted, "If the members could have voted in the cloak room, it would have been killed." Once politicians realized that women did not vote as a bloc, they cut off appropriations for the program after 1929.

A New National Culture

In millions of homes during the 1920s, Americans sat down to a breakfast of Kellogg's corn flakes and toast prepared in a General Electric toaster. After breakfast, they got into their Ford Model T to go about the day's business, perhaps shopping at one of the new chain stores that had spread across the country. In the evening, the family gathered to listen to favorite radio programs such as "Great Moments in History" and "True Story." Or they read the latest issue of the *Saturday Evening Post* or *American Mercury*. On Friday or Saturday night, the family might hop into the car to see the latest Charlie Chaplin film at the local movie theater. Similar scenes took place throughout the United States. Millions of Americans shared the same daily experiences, signaling the development of a national culture.

Not every family participated in this new way of life, however. Urban blacks, rural farmers, and recent immigrants could rarely afford it. Other Americans found that the new values conflicted with religious and cultural mandates to work hard and live frugal lives. But, the patterns of consumption and leisure that appeared during the prosperous 1920s quickly became entrenched in American culture.

Toward a Mass National Culture

Nineteenth-century America was dominated by small towns and rural settlements where people felt in control of their own destinies and had little contact with outside forces. Even in the nineteenth century, however, community self-reliance and isolation were breaking down rapidly. The railroads, symbols of the new industrial order, threatened the older settled ways. Railroads brought in outside goods and ideas, and they took away products and people. By the 1920s, the isolation of most rural communities had been permanently shattered by forces even more powerful than the railroads. Automobiles, paved roads, parcel post service, movies, radios,

THE MAGIC OF THE MOVIES
Moving picture theaters were primarily located in working-class neighborhoods around the turn of the century. In order to lure the more prosperous middle class to this new form of mass entertainment, movie theaters in the 1920s featured lavish interiors decorated to mimic European palaces. The recently restored Chicago Theatre shows the architectural grandeur of the vintage picture palaces of the era. (© Don DuBroff and Russell B. Phillips)

THE GREAT HEART-THROB, RUDOLPH VALENTINO
In *The Shiek* (1921), Rudolph Valentino portrayed a British aristocrat disguised as an Arab chieftain who seduces a liberated Englishwoman, played by Agnes Ayres. When Valentino suddenly died in 1926 at the age of thirty-one, the lines of loyal fans at his funeral stretched for eleven blocks. (MOMA/Film Stills Archive)

telephones, mass circulation magazines, brand names, and chain stores—all lessened geographical isolation. Americans became linked by an ever-expanding web of national experience.

The movie industry probably did more than anything else to promote the diffusion of common values and attitudes throughout the United States. Its growth coincided with America's transformation into a predominantly urban, industrial society. Movies were the most popular, and probably the most influential, element of the new urban-based mass media. By the end of the 1920s, the nation had almost twenty-three thousand movie theaters. In Muncie, Indiana, a city of thirty-five thousand people, nine theaters operated seven days a week, with a rotating schedule of films. Muncie became famous as the typical American city, "Middletown," of Robert and Helen Lynd's 1929 sociological study.

National weekly movie attendance grew dramatically from 40 million in 1922 to 95 million in 1929, and reached 115 million in 1930. The introduction in 1927 of "talkies," movies with sound,

contributed to this growth. *The Jazz Singer* (1927), starring Al Jolson, was the first feature-length talking picture. Silent films soon became obsolete.

Movies began in working-class nickleodeons around the turn of the century, but by the 1920s they had reached into middle-class neighborhoods. The major film studios built elaborate movie palaces in most large cities. A doorman in a frock coat opened the car door at the curb and directed moviegoers to the ticket booth. Then a white-gloved usher showed the patrons to their seats. People joked that they would pay their way into these lavish theaters just to see the rest rooms. "Mama, does God live here?" asked a small moviegoing child in a *New Yorker* cartoon of the period.

Movies became big business, one of the main growth industries of the decade. During the first years of the twentieth century, most films had been made in New York City or in Fort Lee, New Jersey. After 1910, moviemakers started flocking to southern California, which had cheap land, plentiful sunshine, and mountains, deserts, cities, and the Pacific Ocean within easy access for use as scenery. Los Angeles was also a notoriously anti-union town, another attraction. Also flocking to California were the new movie stars. Actors such as Buster Keaton, Charlie Chaplin, Harold Lloyd, Mary Pickford, Douglas Fairbanks, and Clara Bow (the "It" girl), became national idols. Foreign distribution of films made Lloyd, Chaplin, and other stars familiar to European audiences as well. It also stimulated the market for the American material culture so lavishly documented on movie screens.

Movies fed the materialistic desires of a mass consumption economy. They stimulated fantasy and encouraged new patterns of leisure and recreation. They established national trends in clothing and hairstyles. Movies also served as a form of sex education. Though not salacious, they thrived on themes of romance and desire. Rudolph Valentino, best known as the hero of *The Sheik* (1921), symbolized passion on the screen. The message was not wasted on the nation's youth. "It was directly through the movies that I learned to kiss a girl on her ears, neck, and cheeks, as well as on the mouth," confessed one boy. Many girls noticed that actresses kissed with their eyes closed, and so they did, too. A sociologist concluded that movies made young people more "sex-wise, sex-excited, and sex-absorbed" than any previous generation. The links between movies and changing patterns of morality and sexuality have remained strong ever since.

Other instruments of mass culture also helped establish national standards of taste and behavior. In 1922, ten magazines claimed a circulation of at least 2.5 million; twelve others sold a million copies of each issue. The *Saturday Evening Post*, the *Ladies' Home Journal*, *American Mercury*, *Collier's Weekly*, and *Good Housekeeping* could be found in homes throughout the country. *Reader's Digest*, *Time*, and *The New Yorker* all began publication in the 1920s, with *The New Yorker* snidely boasting that it was "not for the old lady in Dubuque." People in all parts of the United States read the same articles, thanks to syndicated columns and features in newspapers. They also read the same best-selling books, partly as the result of the founding of the Book of the Month Club in 1926.

The newest instrument of mass culture truly was a child of the 1920s. Professional radio broadcasting began on November 2, 1920, when station KDKA in Pittsburgh carried the presidential election returns. By 1929, about 40 percent of the nation's households had a radio. (Map 25.2 on page 784 shows how far radio had spread by 1938). More than eight hundred stations were broadcasting, most of them loosely grouped in two major networks, the Columbia Broadcasting Service and the National Broadcasting Company. American radio stations, unlike those in Europe, operated for profit, not as government monopolies. The U.S. government licensed the stations, however.

Americans loved radio. They listened avidly to the World Series and other sports events, as well as to variety entertainment shows featuring the Cliquot Club Eskimos, the Lucky Strike Orchestra, and the A & P Gypsies, all sponsored by advertisers of major brand name products. One of the most popular radio shows of all time, "Amos 'n' Andy," premiered on the NBC network in 1929. This comedy series featured black characters played by white actors. Soon fractured phrases from "Amos n' Andy" like "I'se regusted" and "Check and double check" became part of everyday speech. So many people

"tuned in" (another new phrase in the 1920s) that the country almost seemed to come to a halt at the time of favorite programs.

New Patterns of Leisure

The 1920s sometimes seem to have consisted of one fad after another—crossword puzzles, miniature golf, contract bridge, flagpole sitting, and Mah-Jongg (a Chinese game played with small tiles). Crazes reflected the diffusion of popular culture by the media and the increased leisure time Americans enjoyed. One of the most significant developments in modern life has been the growing freedom of many workers from constant physical toil on the job. The work week shrank an average of four hours per decade from 1900 to 1950, and some workers even won the right to paid vacations. As a result, Americans had more time to spend in leisure activities.

Public recreation flourished during the 1920s. Urban communities opened baseball diamonds, tennis courts, swimming pools, and golf courses, many built by state or municipal governments. In the New York metropolitan area, city planner Robert Moses masterminded the creation of a vast system of parks, playgrounds, and picnic areas. His greatest achievement was Jones Beach on Long Island. Moses created not only the beach; he also built limited-access highways from Manhattan to the Long Island shore. Any New Yorker with a car (an important limit on the democratic impulse of consumption) could escape to a free public beach in less than forty minutes.

As recreational facilities grew, so did professional sports, reflecting a trend toward the commercialization of leisure. People could watch a sports event in a comfortable stadium or listen to it on the radio. Millions followed boxing. The rematch between Jack Dempsey and Gene Tunney in 1927 featured the famous "long count" that enabled Tunney to recover from a knockdown and win the bout. This fight was one of the most talked about events of the year, probably surpassed only by Charles A. Lindbergh's solo flight across the Atlantic Ocean.

Baseball drew between nine and ten million fans each year. The sport was tarnished by the "Black Sox" scandal of 1919, when some Chicago White Sox players accepted gamblers'

CHARLES A. LINDBERGH
In 1928, *Time* magazine chose Charles A. Lindbergh (1902-1974) as its first Man of the Year. Lindbergh had successfully made the first solo nonstop flight between New York and Paris the year before in *The Spirit of St. Louis.* For the 3,610 mile, 33½-hour flight, Lindbergh took only five sandwiches and one day's worth of tinned rations. "If I get to Paris," he later explained, "I won't need any more, and if I don't get to Paris, I won't need any more either." Lindbergh captivated America because he personified the mastery of new technology (the airplane) in combination with the traditional American virtues of individualism, self-reliance, and hard work. His charm and boyish good looks didn't hurt, either. At the time of his record-breaking flight, he was twenty-five years old. (Missouri Historical Society)

bribes to throw the World Series. But baseball bounced back into popular favor with the rise of new heroes, most notably Babe Ruth of the New York Yankees. Nicknamed the "Sultan of Swat," Ruth electrified crowds by hitting more home runs—and hitting them farther—than any other player up to that time. Ruth's record of 714 career homers stood until Henry Aaron of the Atlanta Braves surpassed it in 1974. Yankee Stadium became known as the "house that Ruth built."

Newspapers heightened popular interest in sports. Their coverage of games and fights proved especially well suited to the tabloid, a small-sized newspaper featuring sensational stories and photojournalism. One of the chief beneficiaries of the heightened journalistic enthusiasm for sports was college football. The annual Harvard-Yale and Rose Bowl games received national coverage. Football fans could not read enough about the Four Horsemen of Notre Dame, the most famous backfield in college football history. In 1924, Red Grange of the University of Illinois became known throughout the country for scoring five touchdowns the first five times he carried the ball against the University of Michigan.

Other sports also gave the public numerous heroes to follow and admire. Bobby Jones ranked as the decade's best golfer. Bill Tilden dominated men's tennis, while Helen Wills and Suzanne Lenglen reigned in the women's game. The decade's best-known swimmer, male or female, was Gertrude Ederle, who shattered all records in 1927 by swimming the English Channel in just over fourteen hours. The muscle-bound bodybuilder Charles Atlas made his weight-lifting program nationally famous with the testimonial "I was a 97-pound weakling." Thanks to the attention of the media, the popularity of sports figures rivalled the fame of movie stars.

A musical innovation called jazz provided a different kind of entertainment. Jazz originated in the South but achieved nationwide prominence after black musicians brought its new rhythms to Chicago, New York, and other northern cities. Phonograph records spread the appeal of jazz by capturing its spontaneous improvisational excitement. All the early jazz musicians were black, including Ferdinand ("Jelly Roll") Morton and Louis Armstrong, who got his start with Joseph ("King") Oliver's Creole Jazz Band. White musicians such as Benny Goodman and Bix Beiderbecke later took up jazz, which became so popular that the 1920s are often called "the Jazz Age."

Consumption and Advertising

The 1920s were a critical decade in the development of the American consumer society. Consumption became a dominant cultural ideal among the middle class, often providing the criterion for self-worth that character, religious affiliation, and social standing formerly supplied. Americans were encouraged to believe that they could not live without the abundance of products and styles that appeared during the decade. Spending money became a form of self-fulfillment and gratification of personal needs.

The unequal distribution of income, however, limited the adoption of these new patterns of consumption to the more prosperous members of the middle class. About 65 percent of America's families had an income of less than $2,000 a year at the height of prosperity in the 1920s. The average family income for the bottom 40 percent of the population was $725. With that amount, a family would spend an average of about $290 a year for food, $190 for housing, and $110 for clothing. These expenditures left only $135 for everything else.

A dramatic increase in installment buying partially overcame this problem. With easier credit and buying on time, families could spend on the basis of future, as well as current, income. It is difficult to realize how revolutionary the philosophy of "buy now, pay later" was to consumers. Before World War I, most urban families paid cash for everything except the major purchase of a home. Then, during the 1920s, the automobile overcame people's fears of buying on time. Probably two-thirds of the cars in the United States in the 1920s were bought on the installment plan. Once consumers saw how easily they could finance the purchase of a car, they moved on to radios, refrigerators, and sewing machines. "A dollar down and a dollar forever," a cynic remarked. By 1929, the provision of consumer credit by banks, finance companies, credit unions, and other institutions exceeded $7 billion a year. It had become the tenth largest business in the United States.

Many of the new products were electric appliances, for which consumers spent about $667 million in 1927. By 1930, 85 percent of the nation's nonfarm households had the electricity necessary to run such gadgets. The most popular appliances were irons and vacuum cleaners, followed by phonographs, sewing machines, and washing machines. Radios, whose production increased twenty-five-fold in the 1920s, sold for around $75. One of the most expensive items was a refrigerator, which at the beginning of the

Proud that it is a Frigidaire

THE hostess whose home is equipped with Frigidaire Electric Refrigeration takes real pride in showing it to her guests—in serving delicious, wholesome desserts, taken from Frigidaire's freezing compartment—in telling them how it keeps all foods fresh and delicious for surprising lengths of time.

She takes pride in the fact that it is a genuine Frigidaire—the finest electric refrigerator built—with its beautiful exterior finish of lustrous white Duco, its clean, smooth, gleaming porcelain.

enamel lining, its quiet, dependable, automatic operation. And she does not hesitate to say that the cost of operation is surprisingly little.

The new low-priced metal cabinet Frigidaires offer outstanding values and can be bought on deferred payments.

We should like you to have copies of two Frigidaire books: recipes for delightful frozen desserts, and a book of prize-winning kitchens equipped with Frigidaire. Send to us, or ask for them at any Frigidaire display room.

DELCO-LIGHT COMPANY, Dept. Y-42, DAYTON, OHIO
Subsidiary of General Motors Corporation
The World's Largest Builder of Electric Refrigerators

Frigidaire
ELECTRIC ❄ REFRIGERATION

ADVERTISING ON A NATIONAL SCALE
Refrigerators did not save as much time or labor as other appliances such as irons and vacuum cleaners, but they did have advantages. For example, food stayed fresh longer, which reduced the need to shop every day. In the 1920s, refrigerator manufacturers launched major advertising campaigns to promote the advantages of their product over the old-fashioned icebox. Their advertising budgets peaked at $20 million in 1931, approximately $7 for every refrigerator sold. (The Newberry Library, Chicago)

decade cost $900. Technology quickly brought the price down, but even a $180 refrigerator remained beyond the reach of many families, who continued to use iceboxes.

This new technology, much of it concentrated in the home, had dramatic implications for women. The appliances promised liberation from the drudgery of domestic chores. An electric iron was easier to use than an iron heated on the stove, and a vacuum cleaner worked quicker and more efficiently than a broom. A washing machine saved hours of toil over a washboard, and clothes came out much cleaner. Paradoxically, however, the time that women spent on housework did not decline. Since fewer poor women were entering domestic service, more middle-class women began to do their own housework; electric servants replaced human ones. Technology often raised standards of cleanliness as well. A man could wear a clean shirt every day, not just on Sunday, and a house could be vacuumed daily rather than weekly. All this made more work for women.

Advertising became big business in the 1920s. By 1929, advertisers spent an average of $15 annually for every man, woman, and child in the United States, a total of $3.4 billion. That year, advertising comprised 3 percent of the gross national product, comparable to its share in the post–World War II period. Many major advertising firms were founded, some with direct or indirect links to the expanding field of psychology. The advertising pioneer Edward Bernays was the nephew of the controversial Austrian psychoanalyst Sigmund Freud. The prominent psychologist John B. Watson left Johns Hopkins University in 1922 to become vice-president of the J. Walter Thompson advertising agency.

Psychology played an important role in advertising. Since few of the new products could be considered basic necessities, ads had to create a desire to buy. Advertisers often used the implied approval of science, represented by the white-coated doctor who appeared in many advertisements, to sell their products. Ad writers also sold products by calling attention to people's insecurities. They came up with a variety of socially unacceptable diseases, including "sneaker smell," "paralyzed pores," "vacation knees," "ashtray breath," and the dreaded "B.O." (body odor). After the term *halitosis* was discovered in an obscure British medical journal, the ugly-sounding word made many consumers buy Listerine mouth wash to prevent bad breath.

Advertising claims soared higher and higher. Not only would a toothpaste prevent "pink toothbrush" (bleeding gums), it would also assure a dazzling smile and improve the buyer's love life. Zelda Fitzgerald, the wife of novelist F. Scott Fitzgerald and herself a novelist, reflected this faith in advertising when she confessed, "I still believe that one can learn to play

the piano by mail and that mud will give you a perfect complexion." Yet American consumers were not passive victims of evil "captains of consciousness" who manipulated their every whim and desire. America gloried in its role as the world's first mass consumption economy.

The Automobile Culture

The automobile, the predominant symbol of the 1920s, typified the new consumer-based economy. "Why on earth do you need to study what's changing this country?" a Middletown (Muncie, Indiana) resident challenged the sociologists. "I can tell you what's happening in just four letters: A-U-T-O!" Showpiece of modern capitalism and the ultimate consumer toy, the automobile revolutionized patterns of leisure and consumption. Cars changed the nation's vernacular with such phrases as "filling station," first recorded in 1921. They even affected patterns of crime, providing gangsters with a "getaway car" and the option of "taking someone for a ride." Cars touched so many aspects of American life that the word *automobility* was coined to describe their revolutionary impact on production methods, the nation's landscape, and even American values.

The automobile stimulated the prosperity of the 1920s. Car sales climbed from 1.5 million in 1921 to 5 million in 1929, when Americans spent $2.58 billion on new and used autos. By the late 1920s, a new Ford Model T cost only $295. Decreasing cost, combined with installment buying, increased yearly car registrations from 8 million in 1920 to 23 million in 1929. By the end of the decade, Americans owned about 80 percent of the world's automobiles, with an average of one car for every five people.

The growth of the auto industry had a multiplier effect on the American economy. In 1929, 3.7 million workers directly or indirectly owed their jobs to the automobile. Auto production stimulated basic industries, such as steel, petroleum, chemicals, rubber, and glass. The advertising industry also grew hand in hand with the automobile, which was one of the most heavily marketed products of the decade. Highway construction became a billion-dollar-a-year activity, financed by federal subsidies and state gasoline taxes. Because everyone wanted more roads, gas taxes were probably the most popular taxes ever proposed. Car ownership also spurred the suburban boom and contributed to real estate speculation. It spawned the first shopping center, Country Club Plaza, in Kansas City in 1922. Not even the twenty-five thousand people killed each year in traffic accidents, 70 percent of them pedestrians, could diminish America's love affair with the automobile.

Nowhere was this infatuation more evident than in the changing patterns of leisure. Americans took to the roads and became a nation of tourists. The American Automobile Association reported that about forty-five million people took vacations by automobile in 1929. Of the $10 billion spent on recreation in 1930, two-thirds went for cars and related expenses. People regarded automobiles as instruments of personal freedom far preferable to trains, with their predetermined tracks and timetables. Only twelve motorists had driven across the United States in 1912, but twenty thousand made the trip in 1921. With improved roads, motorists could average more

than forty-five miles per hour. By the 1930s, they drove three hundred to four hundred miles a day. Autocamps and tourist cabins, the forerunners of motels, began to offer services for traveling motorists.

People did not have to travel such long distances to experience the impact of the automobile. Will Kennicott, the main character of Sinclair Lewis's popular novel *Main Street* (1920), confessed to four loves, in no particular order—his wife, his automobile, his medical practice, and hunting. City dwellers could escape from urban crowding for a day in a rural area, in the mountains, or at the seashore. Cars broke down the isolation of rural and farm life.

Young people loved cars because they made possible a social life independent of parental supervision. Contrary to many parents' views, sex was not invented in the back seat of a Ford. But a Model T offered more privacy and comfort than the family living room or front porch. City elders in Muncie, Indiana, overreacted by calling automobiles "prostitution on wheels." Cars, like

THE AUTOMOBILE VACATION

This contented couple was autocamping in Yellowstone Park in 1923. Autocamping was portrayed as a great liberation from seedy hotels and rigid railroad timetables. When farmers complained about auto tourists' tendency to camp right in their fields, towns instituted auto camps. When auto camps became associated with transients and hobos in the depression, tourist cabins (with a spot to park your car next to the cabin) became the vogue. By the 1940s, it was just a short step to the modern motel chain. (Library of Congress)

*M*IDDLETOWN RESIDENTS TALK ABOUT THEIR AUTOMOBILES

In 1925, Robert and Helen Lynd conducted a pioneering sociological study of community life in Muncie, Indiana. In their book on the findings, they named the location "Middletown."

"We'd rather do without clothes than give up the car. We used to go to his sister's to visit, but by the time we'd get the children shoed and dressed there wasn't any money left for carfare. Now no matter how they look, we just poke 'em in the car and take 'em along."

———————

"We don't spend anything on recreation except for the car. We save every place we can and put the money into the car. It keeps the family together."

———————

"No, sir, we've *not* got a car. *That's* why we've got a home."

———————

"The Ford car has done an awful lot of harm to the unions here and everywhere else. As long as men have enough money to buy a second-hand Ford and tires and gasoline, they'll be out on the road and paying no attention to union meetings."

———————

"We don't have no fancy clothes when we have the car to pay for. The car is the only pleasure we have."

———————

"He don't like to go to church Sunday night. We've been away from church this summer more'n ever since we got our car."

———————

"I'll go without food before I'll see us give up the car."

———————

"An automobile is a luxury, and no one has a right to one if he can't afford it. I haven't the slightest sympathy for any one who is out of work if he owns a car."

Source: Robert S. Lynd and Helen Merrell Lynd, *Middletown: A Study in Modern American Culture.* New York: Harcourt, Brace, 1929. 254–257, 362.

———————————————————————

movies, changed the ways that American youth discovered sex.

The Model T was the most popular car of the decade. The Ford Motor Company manufactured fifteen million Model Ts between 1908 and 1927. Charles Lindbergh drove one when he was not flying, and Buffalo Bill Cody used one to promote his traveling Wild West show. Even the Mexican bandit chief Pancho Villa retreated to the mountains in a Model T. The "Tin Lizzies," as the dependable Model T's were affectionately nicknamed, came in one color. "Any customer can have a car painted any color he wants so long as it is black," said Henry Ford, keeping a close eye on costs. A Model T required a mechanically inclined driver. The motorist had to hand-crank the car to start it and then keep one hand on the accelerator and the other on the wheel while driving. The only way to check how much gas remained was to remove the front seat and peer into the tank. As late as 1919, only about 10 percent of the nation's cars had a roof.

People eventually became discontented with the plain Model T's. Ford faced stiff competition from General Motors, whose five automobile divisions produced products for specialized markets. The luxury Cadillac featured the highest prices and lowest volume of sales; the Chevrolet boasted the cheapest price tag and highest sales; Oldsmobile, Pontiac, and Buick were geared to incomes in between. GM cars also offered such conveniences as self-starters and foot accelerators. Henry Ford finally bowed to consumer demands for yearly style changes, optional colors, and greater comfort when he introduced the Model A in 1927. Consumers trusted Ford so completely that four hundred thousand of them made a down payment on the Model A before even seeing its design or knowing its cost. (The price ranged from $495 to $570.) More than a million New Yorkers visited the Ford showroom during the five days after the new model was unveiled. The Model A lived up to consumers' high expectations, and helped make the automobile a permanent part of American culture.

Another Part of the Twenties

Not all Americans accepted the secular values that characterized the mass consumption society of the 1920s. In addition to the families who could not afford such a life-style, others opposed the new values as an affront to a more traditional way of life rooted in small towns and farming communities. In Dearborn, Michigan, a suburb of Detroit, Henry Ford created Greenfield Village, a nostalgic memorial to the world of his youth, just as his automobiles were transforming the rural countryside. Many Americans shared Ford's ambivalence about the dramatic changes in society. Their conservative outlook represented another part of the Twenties.

Urban Majority/Rural Minority

One of the most conspicuous features of modern America has been the rapid growth of cities. In 1920, 52 percent of the population lived in urban areas, compared with 28 percent in 1870, only fifty years earlier. When the 1920 census revealed that city people outnumbered rural dwellers for the first time, Americans realized that a dramatic transition had taken place. It produced feelings as intense as those that had greeted the 1890 announcement of the end of the frontier.

Actually, the 1920 report did not represent as great a turning point as it seemed. The census bureau had distinguished between urban and rural populations for the first time in 1870, setting the dividing line at a population of 8,000. In 1900, it lowered the number to 2,500, which would hardly fill more than a village. If urban areas had been defined as population centers of more than 10,000, a more realistic standard, as late as 1930 only 47.6 percent of the population would have been classified as urban.

Yet there was no mistaking the trend. Americans were moving to the cities in ever-increasing numbers. By 1929, ninety-three cities had a population of over 100,000. In the 1920s, New York City exceeded 7 million and the population of Los Angeles doubled to more than 1.2 million. The growth outside the major cities was even more impressive. Extended metropolitan areas and suburbs sprang up, encouraged by cheap land and better highway transportation. This trend started long before the post-World War II suburban boom.

As rural dwellers felt mounting threats to their cultural and economic superiority, they often lashed out at the most convenient symbol, the city. The essential rootlessness of urban life offended traditional community standards, and the frantic emphasis on consumption mocked values of thrift and character. Automobiles, radios, and mass circulation magazines brought these unwelcome facts of life into previously isolated rural areas.

The conflict between cultures that had been building since the late nineteenth century took on special force in the 1920s. Farmers continued to struggle after the recession of 1920–1921, and rural communities lost people to urban areas at an alarming rate. During the 1920s, about six million Americans left the farms for the cities, including many blacks who abandoned the South altogether for the greater freedom of northern society. The boundaries of political districts did not reflect this population shift, however, and rural areas still controlled most state legislatures. Battles over the equitable use of tax dollars, especially for city services, intensified the rural–urban political conflict.

Yet it would be wrong to describe this conflict as just a futile last-ditch effort on the part of rural America to hold onto political and cultural dominance. The lives of many rural people had changed in response to the same forces that influenced urban life. The old ideal of the self-reliant yeoman farmer was giving way to a new model of the farmer as entrepreneur. Much of the new technology enhanced rural life, especially electricity and automobiles. Rural people were tempted by the new values trumpeted by radio programs, magazines, and movies. Even though they tried to resist, many Americans found more to attract than to repel them in the new ways. The cultural conflict in the 1920s may have been so heated because both rural and urban dwellers realized how far they had already strayed from older values.

Dissenters to the New Values

The 1920s brought an upsurge in political mobilization centering around cultural issues. This political action included a willingness to use coercion or legislation to enforce a specific point of view. Americans troubled by the growing number of immigrants turned to national legis-

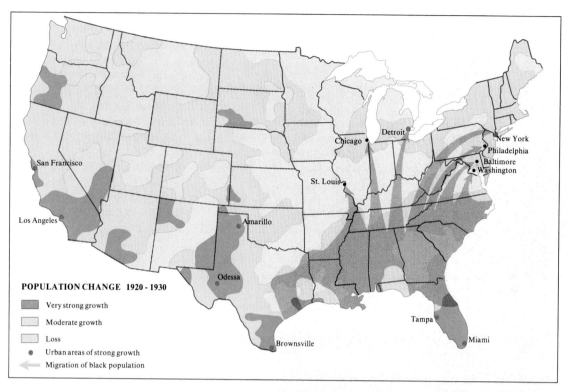

MAP 23.1 THE SHIFT FROM RURAL TO URBAN POPULATION, 1920–1930
Despite the increasingly urban tone of modern America after 1920, regional patterns of population
growth and decline were far from uniform. Cities in the South and West grew most dramatically, as
southern farmers moved to more promising areas in familiar climates. One important component of
the growth of northern cities, such as New York and Chicago, was the migration of southern blacks
set in motion by World War I.

lation to restrict the flow. The Ku Klux Klan rose
again to defend white Anglo-Saxon Protestantism against the intrusion of blacks, Catholics,
Jews, and immigrants. Fundamentalist religious
leaders fought what they considered the inroads
of science in the nation's classrooms. And prohibition imposed the views of the nondrinking
majority on a vocal and thirsty minority.

Tension between city and country played a
part in all these conflicts, but it was not the sole
cause. Resistance to change and a desire to stop
the clock of progress, feelings that transcended
the urban–rural polarity, probably had a greater
influence. Many city dwellers had been born
and raised in rural areas or small towns, and
memories of the nineteenth century still had a
strong hold on their lives. In many ways, these
cultural conflicts resembled those of the 1970s,
when conservative groups proposed constitutional amendments on abortion, school prayer,

and school busing in an effort to legislate social
values.

The successful drive against immigration in
the 1920s tapped deep feelings of nativism in the
United States. Native-born white Americans
doubted the nation's ability to absorb the growing number of newcomers who brought different values and customs with them. Many of the
new immigrants were Catholics or Jews, whose
religion clashed with the country's dominant
Protestant tone. Large numbers came from peasant backgrounds, which gave them little preparation for participation in democratic forms of
government. Senator William Bruce of Maryland
called such immigrants "indigestible lumps" in
the "national stomach."

Prejudice against Orientals had already closed
off immigration from Japan and China. In 1917
the United States established a literacy test for all
immigrants. This requirement proved to be only

a slight deterrent, however. If immigrants were determined to find a new life in America, they also were prepared to learn enough reading and writing skills to pass a simple test. Demands for stricter limits intensified.

In 1921, Congress passed a bill limiting the number of immigrants to 3 percent of each national group, based on the 1910 census. President Wilson refused to sign the bill, but it was reintroduced after Warren Harding took office in 1921. The new law produced results that same year. During the fiscal year ending in June 1921, 805,228 immigrants entered the United States; the number dropped to 309,556 in fiscal 1922.

For many citizens, a quota system that admitted 300,000 immigrants a year was a sieve with too many holes. As a result, the National Origins Act of 1924 limited immigration to 2 percent of each nationality as reflected in the 1890 census. Congressional leaders chose the 1890 cutoff because at that time, few immigrants had arrived from the "undesirable" areas of southeastern Europe and Russia. The 1924 quotas cut the total annual immigration to 164,000 persons, with national origins heavily favoring Great Britain, Ireland, and Germany. The law admitted only 4,000 Italians. It excluded Japanese and Chinese immigrants entirely.

An even more restrictive system took force in 1929. A ceiling of 150,000 persons annually was placed on incoming immigration, to be apportioned on the basis of the national origins revealed in the 1920 census. President Herbert Hoover lowered the quota even further in 1931. The next year, during the depth of the Great Depression, more foreigners left the United States

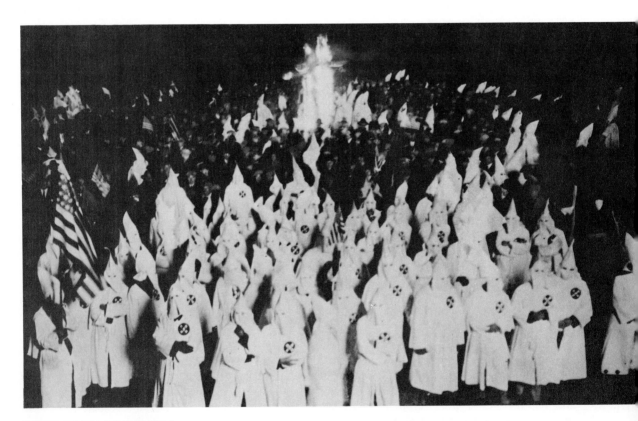

RESURGENCE OF THE KKK
The Ku Klux Klan was not limited to the South. Here a group of Klansmen conduct an initiation rite outside of Milwaukee, Wisconsin. Note the juxtaposition of the symbols of the Ku Klux Klan—white robes and burning crosses—with the traditional symbol of patriotism, the American flag. (FPG)

THE KLAN COMES TO KOKOMO, INDIANA

The Konklave was an important day in my life. I was nine years old, with a small boy's interest in masquerades and brass bands. But I was also a Catholic, the son of a Catholic who taught in the public schools and who consequently was the object of a good deal of Klan agitation. If anything worse was to come, the Konklave probably would bring it. Every week or so the papers had been reporting Klan atrocities in other parts of the country—whippings, lynchings, tar-and-feather parties—and my father and my family were logical game in our locality. . . .

As we sat on our front porch after watching the parade, we could see the Klansmen of our neighborhood trickling home. Some still wore their regalia, too tired to bother with taking it off before they came into sight. Others carried little bundles of white: they were the ones who still made some pretense of secrecy about being members. One of the last to come down the street was old Mrs. Crousore, who lived a few doors away. Her white robe clung damply, and

her hood was pushed back. As she climbed her steps and sank solidly into a rocking chair on her porch, we could hear her groan, "Oh, my God, my feet hurt!"

Mrs. Crousore spoke with such feeling that her words seemed to summarize the whole day. My parents adopted her comment as a family joke. July 4, 1923, became for us the day when Mrs. Crousore's feet hurt. But it was clear to me when I grew a little older that my parents needed that joke as much as Mrs. Crousore needed her rocking chair. There were wild rumors in the town in the months that followed: Father Pratt, the pastor at St. Patrick's Church, was on the list for tar-and-feathering; the church was going to be burned; the Klan was going to "call" on the Jewish merchants; it was going to "get" my father and Miss Kinney, another Catholic who taught in the public schools. Considering all the violent acts committed by the Klan elsewhere in the country, it seemed quite possible that any or all of these notions might mature into action.

As it turned out none of them

did. . . . Perhaps the answer lay in the dead level typicalness of the town: a population overwhelmingly white Protestant, with small, well-assimilated numbers of Catholics, Jews, foreigners, and Negroes, and an economy nicely balanced between farming and industry. There were few genuine tensions in Kokomo in 1923, and hence little occasion for misdirected hate to flame into personal violence.

It may be asked why, then, did the town take so wholeheartedly to the Klan, which made a program of misdirected hate? And the answer to that may be, paradoxically enough, that the Klan supplied artificial tensions. Though artificial, and perhaps never quite really believed in, they were satisfying. They filled a need—a need for Kokomo and all the big and little towns that resembled it during the early 1920s.

Source: Robert Coughlan, "Konklave in Kokomo," in Isabel Leighton, ed., *The Aspirin Age, 1919–1941.* New York: Simon & Schuster, 1949, 1976. 107, 110–111.

---

than entered. In contrast, 1,285,000 immigrants had entered the country in 1907, the peak year of immigration.

America had always been a nation of immigrants. Whoever could afford the passage to the United States was free to seek a new life there. But now the gates were closing tight. The sole loophole, which grew in significance through the years, permitted unrestricted immigration from countries in the Western Hemisphere. Central and Latin Americans crossed the border in increasing numbers, filling the places vacated by the cutoff of immigration from Europe and the Far East.

The National Origins Act was just one example of the rise of nativism during the 1920s. Colleges instituted quotas to limit the enrollment of Jewish students, and many law firms refused to hire Jewish lawyers at all. Henry Ford spoke for many Americans when he warned of the menace of the "International Jew." Ford became so closely identified with anti-Semitism that decades passed before some Jewish families could bring themselves to buy one of his cars.

The most striking example of nativism in the 1920s was the revival of the Ku Klux Klan. Confirming the power of the media, the Klan found encouragement in D. W. Griffith's epic film *Birth of a Nation* (1915), a glorification of white southerners fighting to overturn the social and political changes introduced by the Civil War and Reconstruction. Racism pervaded the movie, and its plot pandered to fears of sexual relations between whites and blacks. White audiences everywhere cheered the famous scene in which the Klan rode to the rescue of endangered white southern womanhood.

Unlike its earlier version in the post-Civil War era, the Ku Klux Klan did not limit its activities to harassment of blacks. Its targets were just as likely to be immigrants, especially Catholics and Jews. Nor did the Klan have only rural supporters. The modern Klan was organized in Atlanta and appealed to both city and rural people. It had long outgrown its southern base, finding significant support in the far West, Southwest, and Midwest, especially in Indiana. At the height of its power in 1925, the Klan had almost four million members.

The Ku Klux Klan appealed to Americans who believed in its slogan, "native, white, Protestant supremacy." Hiram Wesley Evans, an "Imperial Wizard" or boss of the Klan, claimed the Klan spoke for "the great mass of Americans of the old pioneer stock" who were deeply distressed by the moral breakdown in society:

> One by one all our traditional moral standards went by the boards, or were so disregarded that they ceased to be binding. The sacredness of our Sabbath, of our homes, of chastity, and finally even of our right to teach our own children in our own schools fundamental facts and truths were torn away from us. . . . We found our great cities and the control of much of our industry and commerce taken over by strangers, who stacked the cards of success and prosperity against us. . . . So the Nordic American today is a stranger in large parts of the land his fathers gave him.

Members of the Klan, who wore white hoods and robes at Klan gatherings, developed an elaborate hierarchy of leaders and passwords that filled the emotional needs of its members. But the Klan did not merely practice harmless rituals. Its standard activities included nightriding, arson, tarring and feathering, and other forms of physical intimidation.

After 1925, the Klan declined rapidly, the victim of internal scandals and a changing national climate. Especially damaging was the revelation that Grand Dragon David Stephenson, the Klan's national leader, had kidnapped and sexually assaulted his former secretary, driving her to suicide. The passage of the 1924 immigration act also contributed to the Klan's eclipse.

The religious debate between modernists and fundamentalists represented another example of the cultural conflict that raged in the 1920s. Modernists, or liberal Protestants, attempted to bring religion more in line with modern secular values, especially to reconcile the often contradictory views of religion and science. Fundamentalists believed in a literal interpretation of the Bible. Popular speakers, among them Billy Sunday and Aimee Semple McPherson, promoted their versions of fundamentalist evangelicalism throughout the 1920s.

The modernist-fundamentalist controversy soon entered the political arena, especially in legislation designed to prevent the teaching of evolution in schools. The scientific theories in Charles Darwin's *On the Origin of the Species* (1859) conflicted with the Biblical account of creation in the book of Genesis, which claimed that God created the world in six days. In 1925, Tennessee passed a law providing that "it shall be unlawful . . . to teach any theory that denies the story of the Divine creation of man as taught in the Bible, and to teach instead that man has descended from a lower order of animals."

The newly formed American Civil Liberties Union (ACLU) decided to challenge the constitutionality of the Tennessee law. Its test case involved a teacher named John T. Scopes, who had taught evolution in his high school biology class in Dayton, Tennessee. The famous criminal lawyer Clarence Darrow defended Scopes. The prosecuting attorney was William Jennings Bryan, three-time presidential candidate, spellbinding orator, and a fundamentalist.

The Scopes trial in July 1925 became known as the "monkey trial." That nickname had a double meaning, referring both to Darwin's theory that human beings descended from other primates, and the circus atmosphere that surrounded the trial. Darrow ridiculed Bryan's "fool religion," and Bryan called Darrow "the greatest atheist and agnostic in the United States." More than a hundred journalists crowded into the sweltering Dayton courthouse, and Chicago radio station WGN broadcast the trial live.

Scopes, who readily admitted that he had broken the Tennessee law, played only a minor role as the trial quickly turned to volatile questions of faith and scientific theory. The judge rebuffed defense efforts to call expert scientific witnesses on evolution. He considered such testimony as hearsay because the experts had not been present when lower forms of life evolved. Darrow countered by calling Bryan to the stand as an expert on the Bible. Under oath, Bryan asserted his belief that Jonah had been swallowed by a "big fish," Eve created from Adam's rib, and the world created by God in six days. He hedged, however, about whether the days were literally twenty-four hours long, an inconsistency which Darrow ruthlessly exploited.

Even so, the jury took only eight minutes to find Scopes guilty. The Tennessee Supreme Court upheld the controversial law on appeal, and the statute remained technically in force until the state legislature repealed it more than thirty years later. However, the Tennessee Supreme Court overturned Scopes's sentence on the technicality that his hundred-dollar fine had been incorrectly set by the trial judge rather than the jury. The reversal of Scopes's conviction prevented further appeal of the case. As the 1920s

ended, science and religion faced each other in an uneasy standoff.

The longest-running cultural debate of the 1920s involved prohibition. The Eighteenth Amendment to the Constitution prohibited the manufacture, transport, or sale of intoxicating liquors in the United States after January 16, 1920. The law did not forbid people to drink liquor, however.

Prohibition is often described as a repressive denial of individual freedom. Yet it was viewed by many people at the time as a progressive reform. The twentieth-century crusade for prohibition had roots in Protestant urban areas, where it drew support from reformers concerned about good government and public morality. It also picked up substantial backing in rural communities. Liquor was equated with all the sins of the city, including prostitution, crime, machine politics, and public disorder. In addition, religious groups such as the Methodists and Baptists who counted their greatest strength in rural areas, condemned drinking.

On the other hand, alcoholic beverages, especially beer and whiskey, played an important role in certain ethnic cultures, especially those of German and Irish immigrants. Most saloons were in working-class neighborhoods and

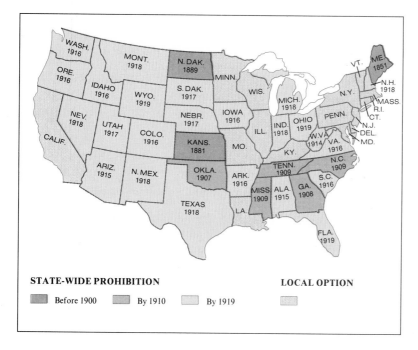

MAP 23.2 PROHIBITION ON THE EVE OF THE EIGHTEENTH AMENDMENT
Prohibition had already made strong headway in the states before the adoption of the Eighteenth Amendment in 1919. States such as Maine, North Dakota, and Kansas had been dry since the nineteenth century; by 1919, two-thirds of the states had already passed laws banning liquor. Most states that resisted the trend were industrial centers or had large immigrant populations. In the intense anti-German hysteria of World War I, the fact that many major U.S. breweries—such as Pabst and Busch—had German names made beer drinking unpatriotic in many people's minds.

THE ADVENTURES OF IZZY AND MOE, PROHIBITION AGENTS

Government agents Isadore (Izzy) Einstein and Moe Smith carried out many raids on illegal liquor stills and speakeasies. Their exploits gained the air of legend as the Prohibition dragged on.

What the newspapers enjoyed most about Izzy and Moe was their ingenuity. Once they went after a speakeasy where half a dozen dry agents had tried without success to buy a drink. The bartender positively wouldn't sell to anyone he didn't know. So on a cold winter night Izzy stood in front of the gin-mill, in his shirt sleeves, until he was red and shivering and his teeth were chattering. Then Moe half-carried him into the speakeasy, shouting excitedly:

"Give this man a drink! He's just been bitten by a frost!"

The kindhearted bartender, startled by Moe's excitement and upset by Izzy's miserable appearance, rushed forward with a bottle of whiskey. Moe promptly snatched the bottle and put him under arrest.

On one of his swings around the so-called enforcement circuit, Izzy made up a sort of schedule showing the length of time it took him to get a drink in various cities. New Orleans won first prize, a four-star hiss from the Anti-Saloon League. When Izzy arrived in the Crescent City he climbed into an ancient taxicab, and as the machine got under way he asked the driver where he could get a drink.

"Right here, suh," said the driver, and pulled out a bottle. "Fo' bits."

Time—thirty-five seconds.

Source: Herbert Asbury, "The Noble Experiment of Izzie and Moe," in Isabel Leighton, *The Aspirin Age, 1919–1941*. New York: Simon & Schuster, 1949, 1976. 40–41, 47.

---

served as gathering places for workers at the end of the day. Members of political machines conducted much of their business in bars. Urban dwellers who regarded liquor and saloons as an important part of their heritage therefore opposed prohibition.

Prohibition caused a temporary decline in drinking in the early 1920s, but several factors undermined its long-term success. America's coastlines and borders enabled liquor smugglers to operate with ease, and organized crime, already a factor in major cities, supplied a ready-made distribution network for bootleg liquor. Government appropriations for enforcement of prohibition were woefully inadequate. In addition, many people abused its exemptions. For example, doctors could prescribe alcohol for medicinal reasons, and churches could use wine for sacramental purposes. Sacramental consumption soon rose to a hefty eight hundred thousand gallons a year. People even learned to make alcoholic beverages at home, hence the term "bathtub gin." However, beer proved more difficult to manufacture and distribute illegally than hard liquor, and beer consumption dropped considerably after 1920. Working-class people had to turn to hard liquor if they wanted to drink.

Once people showed their willingness to flout the law, prohibition had little chance of success. In a typical incident off Coney Island, people on the beach cheered a rum runner who eluded a Coast Guard boat. Illegal saloons called speakeasies flourished openly in all major cities; New York had more than thirty thousand of them. Attorney General William D. Mitchell conceded in 1929 that liquor could be bought "at almost any hour of the day or night, either in rural districts, the smaller towns, or the cities." More than any other issue, prohibition gave the decade its reputation as the Roaring Twenties.

Just before prohibition took effect in 1920, the Yale Club of New York bought a fourteen-year supply of wine and hard liquor. That hoard lasted comfortably throughout the prohibition era. By the middle of the decade, prohibition was clearly failing. The "wets" (those who supported repeal) gained over the "drys." Organizations such as the Women's Organization for National Prohibition Repeal, headed by Pauline Sabin, a wealthy New York Republican, mobilized extensive support among national leaders and organizations. Even a committee appointed by President Hoover in 1931 to study prohibition could not agree on a final report endorsing the law.

The onset of the Great Depression hastened repeal. People argued that liquor production would pump up the faltering economy and provide jobs. On December 5, 1933, the Eighteenth Amendment was repealed. Ironically, drinking had become more socially accepted than it had been before the prohibition experiment began its rocky course.

The 1928 Election

Emotionally charged issues such as prohibition eventually spilled over into national politics. The Democratic party, which drew on Protestant rural supporters in the South and West as well as voters from northern city political machines, was especially susceptible to the urban–rural cultural conflicts of the 1920s. The 1924 Democratic national convention had already revealed intense polarization between the party's urban forces and its rural wing.

The Democrats approached the 1928 campaign in somewhat stronger shape. Senator Robert La Follette had died in 1925, ending the threat of another challenge by the Progressive party. William Jennings Bryan's collapse and death just a week after his impassioned defense of fundamentalism in the Scopes trial removed another potential spoiler. Former contender William McAdoo, well into his sixties, was considered too old for the nomination. As a result, Al Smith, just elected to his fourth term as governor of New York, stood in a commanding position to win the Democratic nomination. In 1924, the Democrats had needed more than a hundred ballots to select a candidate. In 1928, they nominated Smith on the first try.

Alfred E. Smith brought strengths and weaknesses to the Democratic ticket. He was the first national presidential candidate to reflect the aspirations of city dwellers, especially the urban working classes. The grandson of Irish immigrants, Smith had worked his way up in politics from Tammany Hall to the governor's chair in Albany. He was proud of his urban background and adopted "The Sidewalks of New York" as his campaign song. Democrats hoped Smith would attract recent immigrants and working people who traditionally voted Republican. The prominent role of Belle Moskowitz, a New York social worker who served as Smith's political adviser, enhanced his attraction to woman voters and liberal urban Jews.

But Smith had several liabilities that offset his appeal to urban voters. He did not speak well on the radio, and sprinkled his speeches with "ain't" and "he don't" in a heavy New York accent. At times, he seemed to flaunt his eastern manners. Joking with reporters who inquired about the needs of states west of the Mississippi River, Smith asked in reply, "What states *are* west of the Mississippi?" His early career in Tammany Hall troubled many voters, suggesting, unfairly, that he was little more than a typical machine politician. Smith's stand on prohibition presented an even bigger problem. Although committed to enforcing prohibition if elected president, he made no secret of his opposition to the law. Smith drank openly during the 1920s. And he chose John J. Raskob, a wealthy business entrepreneur and one of the nation's most ardent "wets," as head of the Democratic National Committee.

Smith's Catholicism proved by far the most damaging handicap to his campaign. In 1928, Protestant Americans were not ready to elect a Roman Catholic president. Although Smith staunchly insisted that his religion would not interfere with his performance as president, his Catholic faith cost him support from Democrats and Republicans alike. Members of the Protestant clergy, who already opposed Smith because he had flouted prohibition, led the drive against him. "No Governor can kiss the papal ring and get within gunshot of the White House," declared a Methodist bishop from Buffalo. A Baptist minister warned, "If you vote for Al Smith, you're voting against Christ and you'll all be damned."

Smith marked a new kind of presidential candidate for the Democrats, and so did the Republican nominee, Herbert Hoover. In 1927, President Coolidge issued a ten-word announcement: "I do not choose to run for President in 1928." His unexpected declaration opened the field. Hoover led from the start. His popularity and power as secretary of commerce under Harding and Coolidge left no room for contenders such as Vice-President Charles G. Dawes and former Governor Frank O. Lowden of Illinois.

As a professional administrator and engineer, Hoover symbolized the new managerial and technological elite that was restructuring the modern economic order. He had never been elected to any political office. During his campaign, in which he gave only seven speeches, Hoover promised that his vision of individualism and cooperative endeavor would banish poverty from the United States. Many people considered Hoover more progressive than Smith.

Hoover won a stunning victory. He received 58 percent of the popular vote to Smith's 41 percent, and 444 electoral votes to 87 for Smith. For the first time since Reconstruction, a Republican candidate carried Virginia, Texas, and North Carolina, largely because many Democratic voters refused to vote for a Catholic. The participation of eligible voters in the election rose from 52 percent in 1924 to 56.9 percent in 1928, with women accounting for a large share of the increase. Many Catholic and immigrant women cast their ballots for Smith, but native-born Republican women supported Herbert Hoover in even greater numbers.

The 1928 election reflected important underlying political changes. The Democratic turnout, despite the party's overwhelming loss, increased substantially in the big cities. Smith won the heavily industrialized states of Massachusetts and Rhode Island. The Democrats were on their way to a new identity as the party of the urban masses and ethnic voters, a reorientation completed by the New Deal.

In 1928, no Democratic candidate, let alone a Catholic, could have won the presidency. With a prosperous economy, a stable international situation, strong support from the business commu-

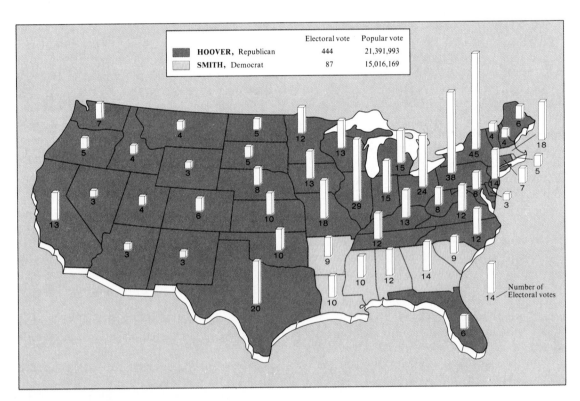

MAP 23.3 ELECTION OF 1928
Historians still debate the extent to which 1928 was a critical election—that is, one that produced a significant realignment in voting behavior. Although Republican candidate Herbert Hoover swept the electoral college, Democrats were heartened that Alfred E. Smith won the heavily industrialized states of Rhode Island and Massachusetts. For the first time, the Democratic ticket carried the nation's twelve largest cities, indicating strong support from immigrants and urban dwellers.

TIME LINE
THE 1920s: TOWARD A CORPORATE ECONOMY AND MASS CULTURE

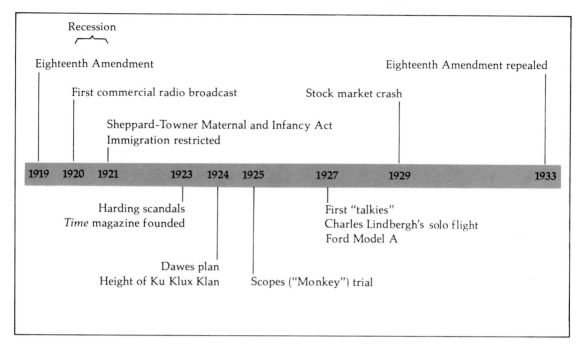

nity, and their status as the majority party, the Republicans were unbeatable. Ironically, Herbert Hoover's victory gave him the unenviable task of leading the United States when the Great Depression struck in 1929. Having claimed credit for the prosperity of the 1920s, the Republicans found it difficult to disassociate themselves from blame for the depression. Twenty-four years passed before a Republican won the presidency again.

*T*he 1920s cemented the partnership between business and government that had been accelerated by World War I. The Republican party controlled the national government and, with the exception of the 1920–1921 recession, the economy performed well. The automobile industry symbolized the new mass production techniques that dominated economic life in the United States.

During the 1920s, a national culture began to develop. It was characterized by the wide diffusion of ideas and values through movies, radio, and other mass media; new patterns of leisure and amusement; and a heightened emphasis on consumption and advertising. These new lifestyles captured the popular imagination, but they were limited to a minority of the population. Only families with at least a middle-class income had enough money to afford cars, radios, vacuum cleaners, and toasters. Credit and installment buying stretched family incomes.

Not everyone welcomed the new secular values of the 1920s. Conflicts arose over prohibition, fundamentalist religion, the Ku Klux Klan, and immigration restriction. These cultural disputes spilled over into politics, especially affecting the already fractured Democratic party. The 1928 election showed that the nation could not yet accept a Catholic presidential candidate. The Republican ascendancy continued under Herbert Hoover, who looked forward to a term filled with even greater prosperity and progress.

Suggestions for Further Reading

General overviews of the 1920s are provided by Ellis Hawley, *The Great War and the Search for a Modern Order, 1917–1933* (1979); William Leuchtenberg, *The Perils of Prosperity* (1958); George Soule, *Prosperity Decade* (1947); Frederick Lewis Allen, *Only Yesterday* (1931); and Geoffrey Perrett, *America in the Twenties* (1982). Robert S. Lynd and Helen Merrell Lynd, *Middletown: A Study in Modern American Culture* (1929), remains a superb sociological study of American life and values in the 1920s. John Braeman, Robert H. Bremner, and David Brody, eds., *Change and Continuity in 20th Century America: The Twenties* (1968), offers interpretations of the decade's major trends.

Corporatism, the Mesh of Public and Private Power

Alfred Chandler provides a stimulating introduction to business life in *Strategy and Structure* (1962) and *The Visible Hand* (1977). Further discussion of corporate developments can be found in Louis Galambos, *Competition and Cooperation* (1966); Robert Himmelberg, *The Origins of the National Recovery Administration: Business, Government, and the Trade Association Ideal, 1921–1933* (1976); James Gilbert, *Designing the Industrial State* (1972), and J. W. Prothro, *The Dollar Decade: Business Ideas in the 1920s* (1954). Irving Bernstein, *The Lean Years* (1960), and David Brody, *Steelworkers in America* (1960) and *Workers in Industrial America* (1980), cover labor developments.

The domestic and international aspects of the economy are treated in Jim Potter, *The American Economy Between the World Wars* (1974), and Joan Hoff Wilson, *American Business and Foreign Policy, 1920–1933* (1968) and *Ideology and Economics: U.S. Relations with the Soviet Union, 1918–1933* (1974). L. Ethan Ellis, *Republican Foreign Policy, 1921–1933* (1968), and William Appleman Williams, *The Tragedy of American Diplomacy* (1962), offer interpretations of foreign policy.

General introductions to politics in the 1920s are found in John D. Hicks, *Republican Ascendancy* (1960); Arthur M. Schlesinger, Jr., *The Crisis of the Old Order* (1957); and Robert Murray, *The Politics of Normalcy* (1973). Biographies of the decade's major political figures include Donald McCoy, *Calvin Coolidge* (1967); David Burner, *Herbert Hoover* (1979); and Joan Hoff Wilson, *Herbert Hoover: Forgotten Progressive* (1975). On women in politics in the 1920s, see J. Stanley Lemons, *The Woman Citizen* (1973); William H. Chafe, *The American Woman* (1972); and Clarke A. Chambers, *Seedtime of Reform* (1963).

A New National Culture

Daniel Boorstin, *The Americans: The Democratic Experience* (1973), provides an excellent introduction to the emerging mass culture. On movies, see Robert Sklar, *Movie Made America* (1975), and Larry May, *Screening Out the Past* (1980). Erik Barnouw, *A Tower in Babel: A History of American Broadcasting in the United States to 1933* (1966), discusses radio. Stewart Ewen, *Captains of Consciousness* (1976), and Daniel Pope, *The Making of Modern Advertising* (1983), cover the new patterns of consumption and advertising, while Paula Fass, *The Damned and the Beautiful* (1977), treats American youth in the 1920s. The impact of the automobile on modern American life is amply documented by James Flink, *The Car Culture* (1975); John Rae, *The American Automobile* (1965); Ed Cray, *Chrome Colossus: General Motors and Its Times* (1980); Bernard A. Weisberger, *The Dream Maker* (1979); and Reynold Wik, *Henry Ford and Grass Roots America* (1972). Good sources for Charles Lindbergh are his two accounts, *"We"* (1927) and *The Spirit of St. Louis* (1953). See also Leonard Mosley, *Lindbergh: A Biography* (1976), and Walter S. Ross, *The Last Hero: Charles A. Lindbergh* (1968).

Another Part of the Twenties

Paul Carter, *Another Part of the Twenties* (1977), outlines the decade's deeply felt cultural controversies. Background on rural and urban life is provided by Don Kirschner, *City and Country: Rural Responses to Urbanization in the 1920s* (1970); Zane Miller, *The Urbanization of America* (1973); and William Wilson, *Coming of Age: Urban America, 1915–1945* (1974). John Higham, *Strangers in the Land* (1955), and Maldwyn A. Jones, *American Immigration* (1960), describe immigration restriction. Kenneth Jackson, *The Ku Klux Klan in the City, 1915–1930* (1965), and David Chalmers, *Hooded Americanism* (1965), cover the KKK's rise and fall. Ray Ginger, *Six Days or Forever?* (1958), and Norman F. Furniss, *The Fundamentalist Controversy, 1918–1933* (1954), cover religion. On prohibition, see Andrew Sinclair, *Prohibition: The Era of Excess* (1962); Joseph R. Gusfield, *Symbolic Crusade* (1963); and Norman Clark, *Deliver Us from Evil* (1976). The treatment of the 1928 election found in David Burner, *The Politics of Provincialism* (1967), and Oscar Handlin, *Al Smith and His America* (1958), should be supplemented by Allan J. Lichtman's quantitative study, *Prejudice and the Old Politics* (1979).

24

THE NEW DEAL: TOWARD THE MODERN WELFARE STATE

For most Americans, the year 1929 means only one thing—the stock market crash that touched off the Great Depression. By 1932, more than a fourth of the nation's workers were unemployed, and industrial production had fallen to barely half the 1929 level. President Herbert Hoover, once the symbol of business prosperity, had become the scapegoat for the depression.

Against this backdrop, the nation turned to Franklin Delano Roosevelt, whose New Deal administration restored confidence in the capitalist economic system. The New Deal also set into motion far-reaching changes in the role of the federal government, notably the emergence of a modern state of significant size. In addition to accepting responsibility for managing the economy, the government now guaranteed a wide range of social and economic benefits for ordinary Americans. During the 1930s, more than a third of the population received direct government assistance from such new federal programs as Social Security, farm loans, relief, and mortgage guarantees. Roosevelt became one of the most popular presidents in United States history and won election an unprecedented four times.

The New Deal represented an important period of political and economic reform, but its programs were hardly revolutionary. Even before the deepening depression, President Hoover had taken the first steps toward involving the federal government more actively in economic life. The New Deal also built on the organizational and bureaucratic structure that had been developed in World War I and refined during the 1920s.

The New Deal's welfare state—that is, the federal government's acceptance of primary responsibility for the individual and collective welfare of the people—was limited in many respects. Many social welfare programs of the New Deal represented contradictory responses to the emergency of the depression. Benefits were small and programs operated haphazardly. The government expanded during the 1930s, but World War II, not the New Deal, gave the United States a massive federal bureaucracy and large budget deficits. And not until the Great Society programs of President Lyndon Johnson in the 1960s did the welfare system reach significant numbers of America's poor. Many of the achievements—and problems—commonly ascribed to the New Deal belong to a later era.

WALL STREET, OCTOBER 1929
When the stock market collapsed, Julius Rosenwald, the chairman of Sears, Roebuck and Company, offered to guarantee the accounts of Sears employees who had bought stocks on margin. Comedian Eddie Cantor jokingly asked for a job as a Sears office boy. (UPI)

Herbert Hoover and the Great Depression

In 1932, the journalist William Allen White wrote an article about the outgoing president entitled "Herbert Hoover—The Last of the Old Presidents, or the First of the New?" Like historians ever since, White concluded that Hoover had been a little of both. Hoover's early efforts to fight the depression are now credited with foreshadowing many New Deal programs, and his reputation among historians has risen steadily through the years. Hoover, who lived until 1964, offered a simple explanation for the improvement in his historical stature. He told Chief Justice Earl Warren of the Supreme Court that he had simply managed "to outlive the bastards."

The Causes of the Depression

The Great Depression began slowly and without much notice. Consumer spending declined after 1927, and housing construction slowed. In 1928 and 1929, inventories piled up and manufacturers began to cut back production and lay off workers. The reduced incomes and buying power reinforced the downturn. By the summer of 1929, the economy was clearly in a recession, although at that point not as severe as the downturn that had begun in 1920.

The economy had tolerated minor recessions before without suffering long periods of excessive unemployment and slack industrial production. But this time was different. By 1933, the United States had sunk into the worst economic collapse in its history, which seemed particularly bitter coming on the heels of the high-income, high-employment boom of the 1920s.

Among the causes of the Great Depression, a flawed stock market played an important, but not dominant, role. By 1929, the market had become the symbol of the nation's prosperity and an icon in American middle-class culture. Financier John J. Raskob captured the "get rich" mentality in a *Ladies Home Journal* article called "Everyone Ought to Be Rich." Invest fifteen dollars a month on sound common stocks, Raskob advised, and the investment will grow to eighty thousand dollars in twenty years. Such inflated expectations drove stock prices up and up in

1928 and 1929. Contrary to popular wisdom, however, not everyone played the stock market. About four million Americans owned stock in 1929; with their families, they represented about 10 percent of the nation's households. A mere 1.5 million had a portfolio large enough to require the services of a stock broker.

As the frenzied stock market speculation continued, investors assumed, incorrectly, that stock prices could rise indefinitely, more rapidly than any concrete measure of industrial progress. A noted economist proclaimed in mid-October 1929 that "Stock prices have reached what looks like a permanently high plateau." Neither the government nor the Federal Reserve System did anything to dampen the speculative fever.

"Black Tuesday"—October 29, 1929—went down in history as the day the bubble burst, but actually the stock market had been sliding since early September. The 1929 recession had already cast doubt on the likelihood that stock prices would continue to rise indefinitely. When small, inexperienced investors suddenly found themselves heavily in debt and began to sell their stocks, others followed suit to protect their investments. Waves of panic selling developed quickly. By November, stock values had fallen from a peak of $87 billion (at least on paper) to $56 billion. The market eventually bottomed out at $18 billion in 1933. The precipitous decline of stock prices became known as the Great Crash.

The stock market crash intensified the course of the Great Depression in several ways. It wiped out the savings of many thousands of Americans and damaged commercial banks that had invested in corporate stocks. Less tangibly, it smashed the optimism of people who had seen the stock market as the crowning symbol of America's limitless economic prosperity. This crisis of confidence prolonged the depression.

However, the stock market crash does not adequately explain either the severity or the length of the Great Depression, especially the deep plunge between 1931 and 1933. Other factors that contributed to the prolonged decline included the legacy of "sick" industries from the 1920s, the growing inequality of wealth, an unstable international financial situation, and the monetary policies of the Federal Reserve System.

Important segments of the economy had not shared equally in the prosperity of the 1920s. Agriculture was in the worst shape; farmers had never recovered from the sharp depression that followed World War I. Farmers faced high fixed costs for equipment and mortgages incurred during the inflationary war years. At the same time, overproduction and surpluses drove prices even lower, causing farmers to default on mortgage payments and risk foreclosure of their farms. In 1929, farmers' yearly income averaged only $223, compared to $870 for other occupations. Because about a fourth of the nation's gainfully employed workers in 1929 were engaged in farming, the difficulties in agriculture weakened the general economic structure.

The economic troubles of certain basic industries also marred the otherwise prosperous 1920s. Many of these problems dated back to World War I or the depression of 1920–1921. The textile industry, for example, had moved steadily into decline after the war. Textile firms abandoned New England for the cheaper labor markets of the South but continued to be hurt by decreasing demand and excess capacity. The railroad industry likewise declined, hit by shrinking passenger revenues, stagnant freight levels, and inefficient management. The railroads also faced stiff new competition from truck transportation on publicly subsidized highways.

Mining and lumbering, which had expanded in response to wartime demands, found themselves with a productive capacity too great for peacetime. Coal mining was especially troubled, battered by overexpansion, technological obsolescence, and a legacy of bitter labor struggles. As with the railroads, coal faced competition from new sources, including hydroelectric power, fuel oil, and natural gas. Herbert Hoover, while secretary of commerce, had plans to help these ailing industries, but the trade associations that he promoted did little to stabilize or revitalize them.

The country's unequal distribution of wealth also contributed to the deepening depression. During the 1920s, the share of national income going to families in the upper- and middle-income brackets increased. The tax policies of Secretary of the Treasury Andrew Mellon contributed to this concentration of wealth by easing personal tax rates, eliminating excess-profits taxation, and expanding deductions that favored

BOULDER DAM
In 1928, Congress passed the Boulder Canyon Project Act, which provided for the construction of a dam on the Colorado River at the Arizona-Nevada border for flood control purposes. The $175 million cost of the dam, now called Hoover Dam, was to be repaid through the sale of electricity from the project's power plant. Under a compromise agreement, the government sold hydroelectric power only at wholesale to specified private and municipal distributors, not to the public. (Historical Pictures Service)

wealthy individuals and corporations. The lowest 40 percent of the population received only 12.5 percent of the aggregate family personal income in 1929, while the top 5 percent got 30 percent. With this unequal base of purchasing power, not enough people could afford the levels of consumer spending necessary to revive the economy after the depression began.

As the Great Depression ground on relentlessly after 1929, it became self-feeding. The longer the economy contracted, the more expectations of continued depression built up, which further inhibited the consumption and investment necessary to stimulate economic recovery. Business investment plummeted 88 percent from 1929 to 1933. Consumers were afraid to spend—even if they had any money. Jobless workers struggled to keep their families from destitution. The economy showed some signs of recovery in the summer of 1931 as many inventories were eliminated and low prices encouraged renewed consumption, but the upturn did not last. The economy plunged again in late fall.

At this point, the chronically depressed agricultural sector exerted pressure on the commercial banking system, further deepening the economic contraction. The nation's banks had already been weakened by the stock market crash. When agricultural prices and incomes fell even more steeply in 1930, farmers went over the

edge into bankruptcy. Bank failures, particularly in the cotton belt, came one after another after the harvest of 1930. By November and December, the defaulting of rural banks on their obligations touched off failures of urban banks. The wave of bank failures drove fearful depositors to withdraw their savings, further worsening the banking crisis.

A change in the nation's monetary policy in 1931 added to the banking problems. During the first phase of the depression, the Federal Reserve System had reacted cautiously. In October 1931, the system took a gravely incorrect step. The New York Reserve Bank significantly increased the discount rate—that is, the interest rate it charged to loan money to member banks. It also sharply curtailed the amount of money it placed in circulation through the purchase of government securities. Through these actions, the Federal Reserve severely limited the ability of the banking system to meet domestic demands for currency and credit. By March 1933, when the economy reached its lowest point, the money supply had fallen by about a third of its August 1929 level.

The main effects of an inadequate money supply were to force prices down and deprive business of investment funds. In the face of such a substantial contraction of the money supply, the American people could have pulled the country out of the depression only by spending more rapidly. But because of falling prices, rising unemployment, and a banking system in crisis, they preferred to save their dollars. And many Americans believed that savings were safer under a mattress than in a bank, which further limited the amount of money in circulation.

The economic problems of the United States soon had an impact on the rest of the world. The international economic system had been out of kilter since World War I. It could function only as long as American banks exported enough capital for European countries to repay their debts and continue to buy American manufactured goods and agricultural products. As the depression worsened, American financiers reduced foreign investments and consumers cut purchases of European goods, making debt repayment even more difficult. European demand for American exports fell drastically. The critical reduction of American capital exports turned the depression into an international event. No other major trading nation, however, was as severely affected as the United States.

A further blow to the international economic system occurred in 1931 when Great Britain abandoned the gold standard. This action deprived the world market of a system for the orderly adjustment of values of international currencies. Forty-one countries had followed Britain's example by 1932. Fear spread in Europe that the United States also would abandon the

gold standard. Consequently, holders of dollars abroad began to demand gold, and gold flowed out of the United States. In an attempt to reverse this flow, the Federal Reserve drove up short-term interest rates in October 1931. This policy successfully attracted gold holders to U.S. investments, thereby saving the gold standard, but at a high cost. Because of the Federal Reserve's contraction of the money supply, the banking system could not meet internal demands for currency.

Herbert Hoover later blamed the international economic situation for the severity of the depression in the United States. He had a point, although domestic factors far outweighed international ones in causing America's protracted collapse. When the depression hit, no single country stepped forward to provide leadership and stability for the world market, as Britain had done prior to World War I. Nations raised tariff barriers and imposed exchange controls to hoard precious gold, dollars, and pounds sterling. Such economic nationalism, by the United States and many other countries, prolonged the depression. The world economy finally showed signs of recovery by 1933, although progress remained uneven.

The Republican Response

President Hoover's reaction to the Great Depression was shaped by the commitment to associationalism that he had exhibited as secretary of commerce. He turned to the business community for help in pulling the nation out of the depression. Hoover asked business to maintain wages voluntarily, keep up production, and work with the government to build confidence in the soundness of the system. Greeting a business delegation in June 1930, the president announced, "Gentlemen, you have come sixty days too late. The Depression is over."

Hoover also used public budgets to encourage recovery. Soon after the stock market crash, he cut taxes and called on the state and local governments to increase capital outlays. In 1930 and the first half of 1931, he increased the federal public works budget. In addition, Hoover eased the international crisis by bringing about, early in the summer of 1931, a moratorium on the payment of Allied debts and reparations. The federal government's efforts to encourage

TABLE 24.1 AMERICAN BANKS AND
BANK FAILURES, 1920–1980

Year	Total Number of Banks	Total Assets	Bank Failures
1920	30,909	$53.1 billion	168
1929	25,568	72.3	659
1931	22,242	70.1	2,294
1933	14,771	51.4	4,004
1934	15,913	55.9	61
1940	15,076	79.7	48
1950	14,676	179.2	5
1960	14,019	282.9	2
1970	14,187	611.3	7
1980	14,870	1543.5	10

SOURCE: *Historical Statistics of the United States: Colonial Times to 1970*, pp. 1019, 1038–1039; *Statistical Abstract of the United States, 1981* (Washington, D.C.: U.S. Government Printing Office, 1981), pp. 510–511.

THE "1932ND PSALM"

Hoover is my Shepherd, I am in want,
He maketh me to lie down on park benches,
He leadeth me by still factories,
He restoreth my doubt in the
Republican Party.
He guided me in the path of the
Unemployed for his party's sake,
Yea, though I walk through the alley of soup
   kitchens,
I am hungry.
I do not fear evil, for thou art against me;
Thy Cabinet and thy Senate, they do discomfort
   me;
Thou didst prepare a reduction in my wages;
In the presence of my creditors thou annointed my
   income with taxes,
So my expense overruneth my income.
Surely poverty and hard times will follow me
All the days of the Republican administration.
And I shall dwell in a rented house forever.
Amen.

Source: E. J. Sullivan, "The 1932nd Psalm." *Seaman's Journal* 46 (October 1932): 259. Quoted in Robert S. McElvaine, *Down & Out in the Great Depression.* Chapel Hill: University of North Carolina Press, 1983. 34.

---

recovery were moderately effective, but the depression continued.

By 1931, more drastic action became necessary. Hoover, however, faced a cruel dilemma that had been set in motion by the Federal Reserve's contraction of the money supply. He could continue budget deficits and thereby encourage recovery through increased government spending. But this course pitted the borrowing needs of the federal government against those of private investors, which would drive up interest rates. Fearing that significantly higher interest rates would choke recovery, Hoover asked Congress in December 1931 for tax increases to raise revenues by a third and balance the budget. The resulting Revenue Act of 1932 represented the largest peacetime tax increase in the nation's history. But higher taxes seriously impeded both consumption and investment. Along with monetary restriction, they contributed to the unique severity of the Great Depression.

The Hoover administration took additional steps to fight the deepening depression. It spent $700 million, an unprecedented sum for the time, on public works. Hoover supported the Glass-Steagall Banking Act of 1932, which made government securities available to back Federal Reserve notes in order to counter credit contractions from gold withdrawals. This step temporarily propped up the ailing banking system.

Hoover remained adamant in his refusal to consider any plan for direct federal relief for unemployed Americans. Throughout his career, he had advocated that private organized charity meet social welfare needs. During World War I, Hoover headed the Commission for Relief of Belgium, a private group that distributed five million tons of food to relieve the suffering of Europe's civilian populations. In 1927, Hoover coordinated the massive rescue and cleanup operation after a devastating Mississippi River flood left 16.5 million acres of land under water in seven states. This effort involved both private charities, including the Red Cross and the Rockefeller Foundation, as well as such government agencies as the U.S. Public Health Service and the National Guard. The success of these and other predominantly private responses to public emergencies confirmed Hoover's belief that private charity, not federal aid, was the "American way." Meanwhile, charities and state and local relief agencies struggled to meet the growing needs of the unemployed.

The centerpiece of Hoover's new initiative to combat the depression was the Reconstruction Finance Corporation (RFC). Modeled on the War Finance Corporation of World War I, and developed in collaboration with the business and banking communities, the RFC represented the first federal institution set up to intervene directly into the economy during peacetime. The RFC provided federal loans to railroads, financial institutions, banks, and insurance companies in an attempt to get the economy moving again. This financial strategy has sometimes been called "pump priming." Money loaned at the top of the economic structure stimulates production, which in turn creates new jobs and increases consumer spending. Benefits thus "trickle down" to the rest of the economy.

The RFC received $500 million, but the agency's cautiousness in lending money limited its impact. In July 1932, Congress doubled this amount and authorized loans to the states totaling $300 million for relief and public works. Once again acting far too cautiously, the RFC lent only $30 million by the end of 1932. Furthermore, it allocated and spent only 20 percent of the $1.5 billion appropriated for public works projects.

The Reconstruction Finance Corporation stands as a watershed in American political history. When voluntary cooperation failed, the president turned to federal action to stimulate the economy. Yet Hoover's break with the past had clear limits. In many ways, his support of the RFC amounted to simply another example of the philosophy of encouraging business confidence. Compared with previous presidents, Hoover responded on an unprecedented scale. Compared to the nation's needs during the Great Depression, his programs were too little and too late.

The 1932 Election

As the depression deepened, hatred of Herbert Hoover became widespread. His declarations that nobody was starving and that hoboes were better fed than ever before seemed cruel and insensitive. His apparent willingness to bail out businesses and banks, but not to feed starving Americans, added to his cold-hearted image. New terms entered the vocabulary, including "Hoovervilles" (shanty towns where people lived in packing crates and other makeshift homes), waving "Hoover flags" (empty pockets turned inside out), and sleeping under "Hoover blankets" (newspapers). Newspaper columnist Russell Baker remembered his aunt's exaggerated recital of Hoover's faults:

> People were starving because of Herbert Hoover. My mother was out of work because of Herbert Hoover. Men were killing themselves because of Herbert Hoover, and their fatherless children were being packed away to orphanages . . . because of Herbert Hoover.

The final straw came in the summer of 1932 with Hoover's handling of the "Bonus Army." A ragtag group of about fifteen thousand unemployed World War I veterans had hitchhiked to Washington to demand that their bonuses, originally scheduled for distribution in 1945, be paid immediately. While they unsuccessfully lobbied

Congress, members of the "Bonus Expeditionary Force" (parodying the wartime American Expeditionary Force) camped out in the capital, a visible reminder of the despair of the unemployed. "We were heroes in 1917, but we're bums now," one veteran remarked bitterly. When the marchers refused to leave their camp, Hoover called out riot troops led by General Douglas MacArthur, assisted by Majors Dwight D. Eisenhower and George S. Patton, to clear the area. More than a hundred bonus marchers were injured in the fight that followed. Most Americans found the spectacle of the U.S. Army firing on U.S. citizens deeply disturbing.

The Bonus Army was not the only sign of unrest in the summer of 1932. Midwestern farmers had watched the price of wheat fall from three dollars a bushel in 1920 to barely thirty cents in 1932. Now they joined together in the Farm Holiday Association under the charismatic leadership of Milo Reno, the sixty-four-year-old former president of the Iowa Farmers' Union. Reno failed in an attempt to organize a farm strike to

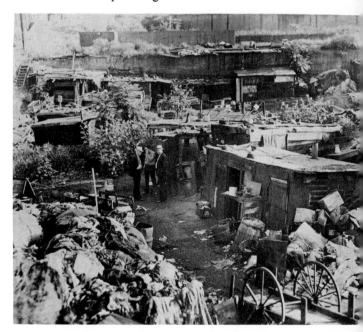

HOOVERVILLES
By 1930, shantytowns had sprung up in most of the nation's cities. In New York City, squatters camped out along the Hudson River railroad tracks, built makeshift homes in Central Park, or lived in the city dump. Such shantytowns were called "Hoovervilles," a pointed reference to the increasingly unpopular president. (Brown Brothers)

keep products out of markets until prices rose. At the same time, groups of unemployed citizens in many cities battled local authorities over inadequate relief. Rent riots and hunger marches occurred frequently. Mayor Anton J. Cermak of Chicago challenged a congressional committee to send either relief or troops.

Despite the unrest among city dwellers and farmers, the nation was not in a revolutionary mood as it approached the 1932 election. Despair and apathy, more than anger, characterized the feelings of most Americans. The Republicans, who could find no credible way to dump an incumbent president, unenthusiastically renominated Herbert Hoover. The Democrats turned to Governor Franklin Delano Roosevelt of New York, who capitalized on that state's record of innovative responses to relief and unemployment to win the nomination.

Franklin Roosevelt's route to the governor-

ship, and from there to the White House, began on a Hudson River estate north of New York City. Born into a wealthy family in 1882, Franklin attended the Groton School, Harvard, and Columbia Law School. Roosevelt gave up his law career in 1910 for a seat in the New York legislature. He served as assistant secretary of the navy in the Wilson administration, which earned him the vice-presidential nomination on the losing Democratic ticket in 1920. He consciously modeled his career on that of his distant cousin, Theodore Roosevelt, whose niece Eleanor he married in 1905.

Franklin Roosevelt's strategy of following his cousin's path to the White House was sidetracked by an attack of polio in 1921, which left him paralyzed from the waist down for the rest of his life. Roosevelt battled back from his infirmity, emerging from the ordeal a stronger, maturer personality. "If you had spent two years in bed trying to wiggle your toe," he later commented, "after that anything would seem easy." Eleanor Roosevelt strongly supported her husband's return to public life, serving as his stand-in during the 1920s. She and Louis Howe, Roosevelt's devoted political aide, masterminded his reentry into Democratic politics. Roosevelt won the New York governorship in 1928 and the Democratic presidential nomination in 1932.

The 1932 campaign foreshadowed little of the New Deal. Roosevelt hinted at new approaches to the depression but stated his goals in vague, unspecific terms. "The country needs and, unless I mistake its temper, the country demands bold, persistent experimentation," he said. Roosevelt won easily, receiving 22.8 million votes to Hoover's 15.7 million. Despite the economic collapse, Americans remained firmly committed to the two-party system. The Socialist party candidate, Norman Thomas, got fewer than a million votes. The Communist party, which had successfully organized hunger marches in major cities, drew only 100,000 votes for its candidate, party leader William Z. Foster.

The 1932 election reflected the American people's desire for a change in leadership. But it also represented a major step toward the forging of the New Deal coalition that would dominate political life for the next four decades. In 1932, Roosevelt won with the support of the Solid South, which returned to the Democratic fold after de-

ROOSEVELT IN WARM SPRINGS
President Franklin D. Roosevelt, shown here in Warm Springs, Georgia, in 1933, was a consummate politician who loved the adulation of a crowd. He began to spend several months a year at Warm Springs in 1924 to rehabilitate his polio-stricken legs. Later, he often went there to escape the pressures of Washington. (UPI)

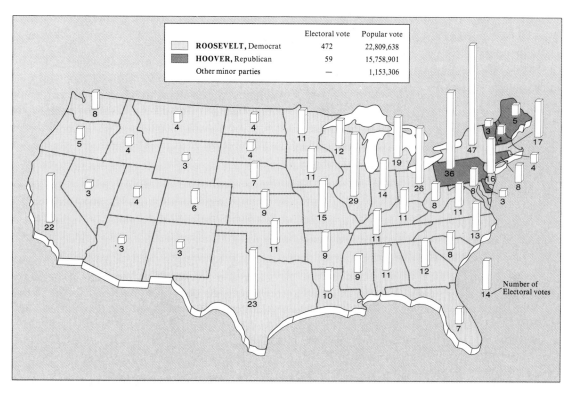

	Electoral vote	Popular vote
ROOSEVELT, Democrat	472	22,809,638
HOOVER, Republican	59	15,758,901
Other minor parties	—	1,153,306

MAP 24.1 THE ELECTION OF 1932

Franklin Roosevelt's convincing election victory over Herbert Hoover in 1932 resulted from realignments in the Democratic party and dissatisfaction with the incumbent president, who had become the scapegoat for the Great Depression. The candidates of the Communist and Socialist parties could not rally voters even during the gravest economic crisis that the American capitalist system had ever faced. Together they received fewer than a million votes of almost 40 million cast.

fections in 1928 because of Al Smith's religion and views on prohibition. Roosevelt also drew substantial support in the West. An increasingly large urban vote continued the trend first noticed in the 1928 election, when the Democrats successfully appealed to recent immigrants and ethnic groups in the nation's cities. However, the voters hardly gave Roosevelt an unlimited mandate to reshape American political and economic institutions. Many people voted against Hoover as much as for Roosevelt.

Having spoken, the voters had to wait until March before Roosevelt could put his new ideas into action. (The long interval between the presidential election and inauguration never occurred again. The passage of the Twentieth Amendment in 1933 moved the inauguration permanently to January.) In the worst winter of the depression, Americans could do little but hope

things would get better. According to the most conservative estimates, from 20 to 25 percent of the work force was unemployed. The percentage stood as high as 50 percent in Cleveland, 60 percent in Akron, and 80 percent in Toledo.

By the winter of 1932–1933, the depression had totally overwhelmed public welfare institutions. Private charity and local public relief, whose expenditures had risen dramatically over earlier levels, still reached only a fraction of the needy. Hunger haunted cities and rural areas alike. When a teacher tried to send a coal miner's daughter home from school because she was weak from hunger, the girl replied, "It won't do any good . . . because this is sister's day to eat." In New York City, hospitals reported ninety-five deaths from starvation. This was the America that Roosevelt inherited when he took the oath of office on March 4, 1933.

The New Deal Takes Over

Franklin Roosevelt's promise of a New Deal for the American people reassured them that hard times could be overcome. "So, first of all, let me assert my firm belief that the only thing we have to fear is fear itself," he boldly proclaimed in his inaugural address. The restoration of hope and confidence was perhaps Roosevelt's greatest contribution during the depression decade of the 1930s. The specific means for ending the depression remained less clear. The New Deal was not a carefully formulated plan. Its ideology contained many contradictions. But it provided a measure of economic security against the worst depression in United States history.

The Hundred Days

Franklin Roosevelt first used the term *New Deal* in his acceptance speech at the Democratic National Convention of 1932, but he hardly realized that he had named his era. Plucked from deep in the speech by the newspaper cartoonist Rollin Kirby, the term came to stand for the Roosevelt administration's response to the depression. The federal government dominated political and economic life so thoroughly during the 1930s that the term *New Deal* is often used as a synonym for the decade itself.

The New Deal represented many things to many people, but one unifying factor was the personality of its master architect, Franklin Roosevelt. As one historian aptly noted, the New Deal was "a very personal enterprise." Roosevelt, a superb politician, crafted his administration's program in response to shifting political and economic conditions, rather than by following a set ideology or plan. He experimented with one idea, and if it did not work, he tried another. Roosevelt used people in the same way. Senator Huey Long of Louisiana complained, "When I talk to him, he says 'Fine! Fine! Fine!' But Joe Robinson [the Senate majority leader] goes to see him the next day and again he says 'Fine! Fine! Fine!' Maybe he says 'Fine!' to everybody." Roosevelt remained unperturbed by criticism that his administration did not follow a consistent ideological course. "I have no expectation of making a hit every time I come to bat," he disarmingly told critics. "What I seek is the highest possible batting average." Roosevelt parlayed this experimental tone into a highly effective political and governmental style.

The first problem that Roosevelt confronted was the banking crisis. On the eve of his inauguration, thirty-eight states had closed their banks and banks operated on a restricted basis in the rest. By 1933, about nine million depositors had lost their savings, a total of $2.5 billion. Senator "Cotton Ed" Smith of South Carolina began carrying his cash in a money belt on the Senate floor rather than entrust it to a bank. On March 6, two days after Roosevelt's inauguration, the president declared a national "bank holiday," a euphemism for closing all the banks. Three days later, Congress passed Roosevelt's proposed banking bill, which permitted banks to reopen beginning on March 13, but only if a Treasury Department inspection showed they had sufficient cash reserves to operate on a sound basis.

THE CCC
The Civilian Conservation Corps (CCC) was one of the most popular New Deal programs. Over ten years, it enrolled 2.75 million young Americans who worked for a dollar a day on such projects as soil conservation, disaster relief, reforestation, and flood control. Because the CCC was limited to men only, critics asked, "Where is the she-she-she?" (Wide World)

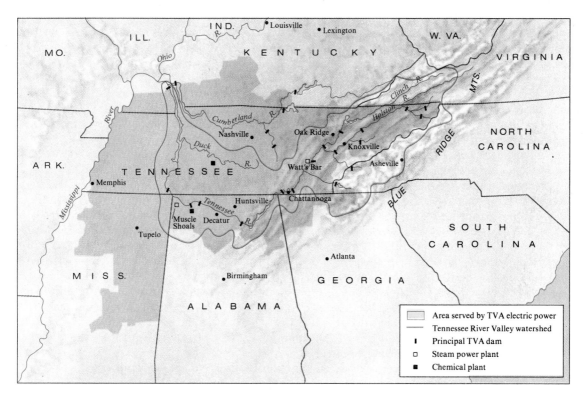

MAP 24.2 THE TENNESSEE VALLEY AUTHORITY
The need for dams to control flooding and erosion in the Tennessee River Basin, a seven-state area
with some of the country's heaviest rainfall, had long been recognized. Early in the New Deal, the
Tennessee Valley Authority won approval to develop the region's resources under public control.
From 1933 to 1952, the TVA built twenty dams and improved five others. The cheap hydroelectric
power generated by the dams brought electricity to more local residents than ever before.

The House approved the plan after only thirty-eight minutes of debate.

The Banking Act, developed in consultation with banking leaders, was a conservative document. Herbert Hoover could have proposed it. The difference was the public's reaction. On the Sunday evening before the banks reopened, Roosevelt made his first "fireside chat" to a radio audience estimated at sixty million. In simple terms, he reassured the people that the banks were now safe—and they believed him. When the banks reopened on Monday morning, deposits exceeded withdrawals. "Capitalism was saved in eight days," observed Raymond Moley, a Columbia University professor who had served as Roosevelt's speechwriter in the 1932 campaign. The banking bill did its job. More than four thousand banks failed in 1933, but only sixty-one closed their doors in 1934.

The Banking Act was the first of fifteen pieces of major legislation enacted by Congress during the opening months of the Roosevelt administration. This legislative session, which came to be called the "Hundred Days," remains one of the most productive ever. Congress created the Home Owners Loan Corporation to refinance home mortgages, and 20 percent of the nation's homeowners took advantage of this opportunity to make their home ownership more secure. The Federal Deposit Insurance Corporation (FDIC) insured bank deposits up to $2,500. The Civilian Conservation Corps (CCC) sent 250,000 young men to live in camps where they performed reforestation and conservation work. The Tennessee Valley Authority (TVA) received legislative approval for its imaginative plan of government-sponsored regional development and public power. The price of electricity in the seven-state Tennessee valley area soon dropped from ten cents a kilowatt hour to three cents. And in a move that lifted public spirits immeasurably, Roosevelt legalized beer in April. Full repeal of prohibition came eight months later, in December 1933.

The Roosevelt administration targeted three areas for immediate attention—curbing agricultural overproduction, stimulating business recovery, and providing for the unemployed. Agriculture received top priority. The Agricultural Adjustment Act (AAA) was developed by Secretary of Agriculture Henry A. Wallace and Assistant Secretary Rexford Tugwell, a Columbia University economist and agricultural expert, in close collaboration with leaders of major farm organizations. A domestic allotment system for seven major commodities (wheat, cotton, corn, hogs, rice, tobacco, and dairy products) gave cash subsidies to farmers in return for cutting production; these benefits were financed by a tax on processing. New Deal planners hoped prices would rise in response to the federally subsidized scarcity.

The AAA stabilized the farm situation, but its benefits were distributed unevenly. The subsi-

dies for reducing production went primarily to large and medium-sized farm owners, who in turn often cut the acreage of their renters and sharecroppers while continuing to farm their own more profitable land. In the South, this inequality of New Deal benefits had a racial component, because many sharecroppers were black and the land owners and government administrators were white.

The New Deal attacked the problem of economic recovery with the National Industrial Recovery Act, which created the National Recovery Administration (NRA). This agency drew on the World War I experience of Bernard Baruch's War Industries Board and extended the trade association thrust of the Coolidge and Hoover administrations. The NRA set up a system of industrial self-government to handle the problems of overproduction, cutthroat competition, and price instability. This objective would be achieved through codes of fair competition, tailored to prevent the specific practices within each industry that had forced prices downward. In effect, these legally enforceable agreements suspended

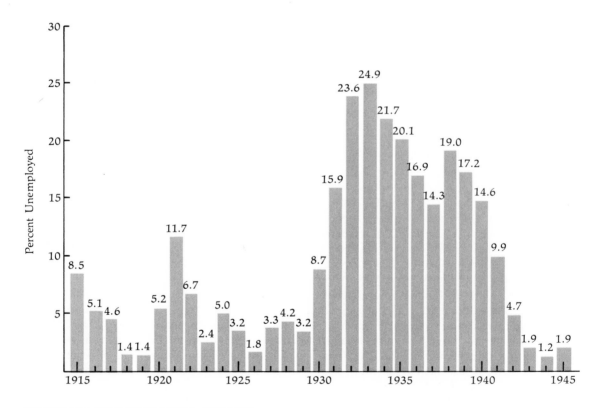

FIGURE 24.1 UNEMPLOYMENT, 1915–1945

the antitrust laws. Each code also contained provisions covering working conditions. For example, the codes established minimum wages and maximum hours and outlawed child labor completely. Under Section 7(a), workers received the right to organize and bargain collectively "through representatives of their own choosing."

General Hugh Johnson, a colorful if somewhat erratic administrator, headed the NRA. He oversaw negotiations for more than six hundred NRA codes, ranging from large industries, such as coal, cotton, and steel, to dog food, costume jewelry, and even burlesque theaters. The code process theoretically included equal input from management, labor, and consumers, but business trade associations basically set the terms. Because large companies dominated the trade associations, the code-drafting process further solidified the power of large businesses at the expense of smaller enterprises. Labor had little input, consumer interests almost none.

The early New Deal also addressed the critical problem of unemployment. The total exhaustion of private and local sources of charity made some form of federal relief essential in this fourth year of the depression. Roosevelt moved reluctantly toward federal responsibility for relief. The Federal Emergency Relief Administration (FERA), set up in May 1933 under the direction of Harry Hopkins, a New York social worker, was a matching federal-state program designed to keep people from starving until other recovery measures had a chance to take hold. Hopkins spent $5 million in his first two hours in office. When told that some of the projects he had just authorized might not be sound in the long run, Hopkins replied, "People don't eat in the long run—they eat every day." During its two-year existence, the FERA spent $1 billion.

Roosevelt always maintained a strong distaste for the dole. Wherever possible, his administration promoted work relief, no matter how makeshift, over cash subsidies. The Public Works Administration (PWA), under Secretary of the Interior Harold L. Ickes, received a $3.3 billion appropriation in 1933 for a major public works program. However, Ickes's cautiousness in initiating projects limited the PWA's effectiveness in spurring recovery or providing jobs. In November 1933, Roosevelt assigned $400 million in PWA funds to a new agency, the Civil Works

Administration (CWA), headed by Harry Hopkins. Within thirty days, the CWA put four million men and women to work repairing bridges, building highways, constructing public buildings, and setting up community projects. CWA workers received fifteen dollars a week. The CWA, regarded as a stopgap measure to get the country through the winter of 1933–1934, lapsed the next spring after spending all its funds.

When an exhausted Congress recessed in June 1933, much had been accomplished. Rarely had a president so dominated a legislative session. A mass of "alphabet agencies," as the New Deal programs came to be known, flowed from Washington. They gave the impression of action, but they had not turned the economy around. A slight economic boom occurred that summer, but the depression stubbornly persisted.

Nevertheless, Americans saw a ray of hope. In April 1933, at the height of the excitement of the Hundred Days, Walt Disney released a cartoon film called *Three Little Pigs*. Echoing FDR's assertion that they had nothing to fear but fear itself, many people hummed the cartoon's theme song, "Who's Afraid of the Big Bad Wolf?" as they started down the road toward renewed confidence.

Consolidating the New Deal

If the measures taken during Franklin Roosevelt's first hundred days had cured the Great Depression, the rest of the New Deal probably would not have occurred. Legislative action now turned to structural reform rather than the emergency recovery measures of 1933. Roosevelt still hoped for a balanced budget; he still abhorred the idea of direct federal relief. However, as a politician aiming to create a coalition capable of winning reelection in 1936, Roosevelt responded to popular demands to do more. He also recognized the need to try additional wide-ranging solutions to the depression.

During Roosevelt's first term, the nation's basic economic institutions got some much-needed reform. In 1934, the stock market came under federal regulation through the establishment of the Securities and Exchange Commission (SEC). The commission had the power to regulate buying stocks on credit, which was called margin buying, and to restrict speculation by people with inside information on corporate plans. The Holding Company Act of 1935 similarly reformed the structures of utility companies.

The banking system came under scrutiny as well. The Banking Act of 1935 represented a significant consolidation of federal control over the nation's banks. The law authorized the president to appoint a new Board of Governors of the Federal Reserve System. This reorganization squarely placed control of interest rates and other money market policies at the federal level rather than with regional banks. By requiring all large state banks to join the Federal Reserve System by 1942 in order to use the federal deposit insurance system, the law further encouraged the centralization of the nation's banking system.

Roosevelt had no special hostility toward the business community. He heartily accepted the capitalist system but realized that modern industrial life required certain structural changes in order to bring the system under more explicit federal control. "To preserve we had to reform," Roosevelt commented succinctly. Even though he styled himself as the savior of capitalism, he provoked strong hostility from many well-to-do Americans. To the wealthy, Roosevelt became simply "That Man," a traitor to his class. Business leaders and conservative Democrats formed the Liberty League in 1934 to organize public opposition to the New Deal.

The New Deal also faced mounting criticism from those who claimed that it had not gone far enough. The chief challenges came from three individuals, each of whom presented an alternative vision of social change. Perhaps the most benign was Francis Townsend, a Long Beach, California, doctor who spoke for the nation's elderly. Americans greatly feared the poverty of old age because so few of them had pension plans. In 1934, Townsend proposed an Old Age Revolving Pension Plan, which would give two hundred dollars a month to citizens above the age of sixty. To receive payment, people would have to retire from their jobs, thereby easing unemployment by opening the positions to others, and spend the money within the month. Townsend clubs soon sprang up throughout the country.

More overtly political challenges to Roosevelt's leadership came from Father Charles

"THE KINGFISH"
Huey Long, the Louisiana governor and senator, still ranks as one of the most controversial figures in American political history. Long inspired one of the most powerful political novels of all time, Robert Penn Warren's *All The King's Men*, which won a Pulitzer Prize in 1946. (UPI)

Coughlin and Senator Huey Long of Louisiana, both of whom attracted large followings. Coughlin, a parish priest in the Detroit suburb of Royal Oak, had turned to the radio in the mid-1920s to enlarge his pastorate. By 1933, about forty million Americans listened to the "Radio Priest." In many Roman Catholic neighborhoods during the summer, Coughlin's sermon could be heard blaring from open windows. He supported the New Deal at first but soon broke with Roosevelt over the president's refusal to support economic measures such as nationalization of the banking system and expansion of the money supply. Coughlin organized the National Union for Social Justice in 1935 to promote his views as an alternative to "Franklin Double-Crossing Roosevelt." As a Catholic priest, and because he had been born in Canada, Coughlin could not run for president, but his rapidly growing constituency became a factor in the 1936 election.

Huey Long represented the most direct political threat to Roosevelt. Flamboyant and outrageous, yet politically shrewd and enormously popular, Long built roads, public works, and schools for his backward state after his election as governor in 1928. He maintained virtual dictatorial control over Louisiana's political machine, even after being elected to the United States Senate in 1930. Long supported Roosevelt in 1932 but made no secret of his own ambitions. In 1934, he published a book called *My First Days in the White House.*

By 1934, Long had broken with the New Deal, arguing that its programs did not go far enough. Like Coughlin, he soon headed his own national movement, which had about four million followers in 1935. His Share-Our-Wealth Society attacked the unequal distribution of wealth in the United States. Long proposed taxing all incomes over $1 million and all inheritances over $5 million, and distributing the money to the rest of the population. Every family would be guaranteed about $2,000 annually, he predicted. Meanwhile, the "Kingfish" (Long's nickname, from a character in the popular radio show "Amos 'n' Andy") criticized what he considered the New Deal's inadequate social welfare programs. His rapid rise in popularity suggested a potentially large volume of public dissatisfaction with the Roosevelt administration. The president's strategists feared that Long might form a third party by combining his forces with those of Coughlin and Townsend, enabling the Republicans to win the 1936 election.

By 1935, Roosevelt had abandoned his hope of building a classless coalition of rich and poor, workers and farmers, and rural and urban dwellers. Pushed from the Left to do more, and bitterly criticized by the Right for what he had already done, the president had no choice but to abandon the middle ground. For both political and ideological reasons, and with an eye fixed firmly on the 1936 election, Roosevelt moved dramatically to the left, thwarting such opponents as Long and Townsend.

Historians use the term *Second New Deal* to describe the outpouring of legislation that followed. Roosevelt's change of direction benefited organized labor first. The rising number of strikes in 1934, about eighteen hundred involving a total of 1.5 million workers, reflected a growth of rank-and-file militancy. Labor demanded permanent legislation that would protect labor's rights to organize and bargain col-

lectively. That year, Senator Robert F. Wagner of New York, one of labor's staunchest supporters in Congress, introduced legislation to replace the ineffective Section 7(a) of the NRA. Only when Congress was on the verge of passing Wagner's bill did Roosevelt reluctantly support the legislation. He signed the National Labor Relations Act, also known as the Wagner Act, on June 5, 1935. The new law, proudly called "labor's Magna Carta," spurred unionization in all sectors of the economy.

The Wagner Act placed the weight of the federal government on labor's side in the struggle to organize. It upheld the right of workers to join unions by outlawing many unfair labor practices, such as engaging in industrial espionage, firing or blacklisting workers because of union activities, and supporting company unions. The act established the nonpartisan National Labor Relations Board (NLRB) to protect workers from employer coercion, and to supervise representation elections and enforce the guarantee of collective bargaining. If a union won a majority of the votes in a secret election, usually conducted by the NLRB, it was entitled to recognition as the sole bargaining agent for all the employees in a factory or other appropriate bargaining unit. The NLRB had the authority to issue cease and desist orders to force employers to comply.

The Social Security Act, signed by President Roosevelt on August 14, 1935, was the second major piece of legislation enacted in this period. The law was a partial response to the political mobilization of the nation's elderly through the Townsend and Long movements. It also represented the prodding of social reformers such as Grace Abbott, head of the Children's Bureau, and Secretary of Labor Frances Perkins, the first woman cabinet member. The Social Security Act provided for old-age assistance through a federal-state pension fund to which both employers and employees contributed. The use of payroll deductions, rather than financing the plan with general tax revenues, was designed to insulate the Social Security program from political attack. The act also provided for a joint federal-state system of unemployment compensation, funded by an unemployment tax on employers.

Having addressed the problems of labor and the elderly, Roosevelt now confronted the needs

ROOSEVELT AND CIVIL RIGHTS
President Roosevelt moved cautiously on civil rights. When blacks voted overwhelmingly Democratic in 1936, however, Roosevelt increasingly took note of their importance to the New Deal coalition. Here he meets with scientist George Washington Carver at the Tuskegee Institute in 1939. (Franklin D. Roosevelt Library)

of the millions of Americans still out of work in the sixth year of the depression. Harry Hopkins, who had run the Federal Emergency Relief Administration from 1933 to 1935, took command of the Works Progress Administration (WPA), the main federal relief agency for the rest of the depression. Whereas the FERA had supplied grants to the states for relief programs, the WPA put relief workers on the federal payroll. Between 1935 and 1943, the WPA employed 8.5 million Americans and spent $10.5 billion. The agency constructed 651,087 miles of roads, 125,110 public buildings, 8,192 parks, 853 airports, and built or repaired 124,087 bridges.

The WPA, though an extravagant operation by the standards of the 1930s (it gave rise to a new word, "boondoggling," and such nicknames as "We putter around" and "We poke along"), never reached more than a third of the nation's unemployed. Its average wage of $55 a month, although well below the government-defined subsistence level of $1,200 a year, enabled workers to eke out a bare living.

Furthermore, the money they spent offered a stimulus to renewed economic production. The government cut back the program severely in 1941 and ended it in 1943. The WPA was no longer needed in the full-employment economy resulting from World War II.

One final measure of the Second New Deal showed Roosevelt's willingness to push reforms considered too controversial earlier in his presidency. Much of the business community had already turned violently against Roosevelt in protest of such federal measures as the NRA, the Social Security Act, and the Wagner Act. In 1935, he antagonized the wealthy further by proposing a tax reform bill that called for federal inheritance and gift taxes, higher personal income tax rates in the top brackets, and increased corporate taxes. Conservatives quickly labeled this legislation an attempt to "soak the rich." Roosevelt was more interested in the political advantage of such a bill, especially defusing some of the popularity of Huey Long's Share-Our-Wealth plan, than in its actual results. The final version of the bill increased tax revenues by only $250 million a year.

As the 1936 election approached, the broad range of New Deal programs brought many new voters into the Democratic coalition. Some had been personally helped by federal programs; others benefited because their interests had found new support in the expanded functions of the government. Roosevelt could now count on a potent urban-based coalition of workers, organized labor, blacks, ethnic groups, Catholics, Jews, liberals, intellectuals, progressive Republicans, and middle-class families concerned about old-age dependence and unemployment. At the same time, the Democrats held on, though somewhat uneasily, to their traditional sources of strength among white southerners.

To run against Roosevelt, the Republicans chose Governor Alfred M. Landon of Kansas, who accepted the general precepts of the New Deal but criticized the inefficiency and expense of many of its programs. The Republicans could not compete with Roosevelt's popularity and his potent New Deal coalition. The expected third-party challenge from the combined Long-Coughlin forces fizzled in the aftermath of Long's assassination by a Baton Rouge doctor in September 1935.

Roosevelt won the 1936 election in one of the biggest landslides in United States history. He received 60.8 percent of the popular vote and carried every state except Maine and Vermont. Landon fought such an uphill battle that columnist Dorothy Thompson quipped, "If Landon had given one more speech, Roosevelt would have carried Canada." The New Deal was at high tide.

Stalemate

"I see one-third of a nation ill-housed, ill-clad, ill-nourished," the president declared in his second inaugural address in January 1937. Roosevelt's frank appraisal suggested that he was considering the further expansion of the welfare state that had begun to form late in his first term. However, retrenchment, controversy, and stalemate, not further reform, marked the second term.

Only two weeks after his inauguration, Roosevelt stunned Congress and the nation by asking for fundamental changes in the structure of the Supreme Court. He believed a grave constitutional crisis called for this drastic judicial reorganization. Simply put, the Supreme Court seemed on the verge of invalidating the entire New Deal. On "Black Monday," May 27, 1935, the Court struck down a farm mortgage act on the grounds that it deprived creditors of property without due process of law. That same day, in the case of *Schecter v. United States*, the Supreme Court unanimously ruled the National Industrial Recovery Act an unconstitutional delegation of legislative power. (The so-called "sick-chicken" case concerned a Brooklyn, New York firm convicted of violating NRA codes by selling diseased poultry.) Roosevelt publicly claimed that the Court's narrow interpretation returned the Constitution to "horse-and-buggy days." In 1936, the Court struck down the Agricultural Adjustment Act, the Guffey-Snyder Coal Conservation Act, and New York's minimum wage law. With the Wagner Act, the TVA, and Social Security coming up on appeal, the whole future of New Deal reform legislation appeared in doubt.

In response to this threat, Roosevelt proposed adding one new justice to the Court for each one over the age of seventy. This scheme, which would have increased the number of justices from nine to fifteen, smacked of political expediency. Roosevelt's opponents accused him of trying to "pack" the Court with justices favorable to the New Deal. The president's proposal was also regarded as an assault on the institution of the Supreme Court and on the principle of separation of powers. The issue became moot when the Supreme Court, in what journalists called "a switch in time that saved nine," upheld several key pieces of New Deal legislation, including Washington state's minimum wage law and the Wagner Act.

Charitably one could say that Roosevelt had lost a skirmish but won the war. Within four years, he reshaped the Supreme Court to suit his liberal philosophy with seven new appointments, including those of Hugo Black, Felix Frankfurter, and William O. Douglas. Yet his handling of the Court issue was a costly blunder at a time when he was vulnerable to the lame-duck syndrome that often afflicts second-term administrations. (No one yet suspected that FDR would break tradition and become the first president to seek a third term.) Throughout his second term, a conservative coalition in Congress, composed mainly of southern Democrats and Republicans from rural areas, blocked or impeded further social legislation. One of the few pieces of reform legislation to win passage was the 1938 Fair Labor Standards Act. This law made permanent the minimum wage and maximum hours provisions and the abolition of child labor first tried in the NRA codes.

The "Roosevelt recession" of 1937–1938 probably dealt the most devastating blow to the president's political standing during his second term. It showed that policymakers still did not understand the impact of their fiscal instruments on the national economy. Until that point, the economy had been making steady progress. The gross national product had grown at a yearly rate of about 10 percent from 1933 to 1937. Industrial output finally reached 1929 levels in 1937, as did real income. Unemployment declined from 25 percent to 14 percent, which meant that almost half the people without a job in 1933 had found one by 1937. Many Americans agreed with Senator James F. Byrnes of South Carolina that "the emergency has passed."

The steady improvement cheered Roosevelt. Reflecting his basic fiscal conservatism, he had never overcome his dislike of large deficits and huge federal expenditures for relief. Accordingly, he slashed the federal budget in 1937. Congress cut the WPA's funding in half between January and August, laying off about 1.5 million WPA workers. Adding to the nation's economic woes, the withholding of $2 billion from workers' paychecks to fund the new Social Security system reduced purchasing power. On another front, the Federal Reserve, fearing inflation, tightened credit. The stock market promptly collapsed, and unemployment soared to 19 percent, leaving more than ten million workers without a job. Roosevelt found himself in the same situation that had confounded Hoover. Having taken credit for the recovery between 1933 and 1937, he now had to take the blame for the recession.

Roosevelt spent his way out of the downturn. Large WPA appropriations and a resumption of public works poured enough money into the economy to snap it out of the recession by early 1938. Roosevelt and his economic advisers were groping toward the general theories being advanced by John Maynard Keynes, a British economist. Keynes proposed that governments use deficit spending to stimulate the economy when private spending proved insufficient. The increase in federal defense spending for World War II, which finally ended the Great Depression, provided the most striking confirmation of Keynesian theory.

By 1938, the New Deal had basically run out of steam. It had no climax; it simply withered away. For six years, Franklin Roosevelt had inspired public confidence that hard times could be overcome. He had pragmatically sought solutions to the depression and found them in Keynesian economics. Roosevelt showed himself to be a superb politician, successfully balancing demands for more government programs with his own assessment of what was politically feasible. His political skill and enormous personal popularity cemented the formation of the Democratic coalition that had started to develop in the 1920s.

Throughout the New Deal, however, Roosevelt always demonstrated clear limits on how far he was willing to go. His instincts were basically conservative, not revolutionary; he saved the capitalist economic system by reforming it. He created new public instruments to make economic life more predictable, initiatives that reinforced the ongoing private efforts to ensure stability in a modern industrial economy. The New Deal has been credited with a major expansion of the governmental role, but mainly the emergency of the depression pushed Roosevelt in that direction. Under normal circumstances, he would have served out his second term and a new president would have been elected in 1940. Roosevelt won election to a third term—and eventually a fourth—only because events in Europe became so serious that a change in leadership seemed dangerous.

The New Deal's Impact on Society

The New Deal was, as one historian put it, "somehow more than the sum of its parts." To understand its impact on society, we must look beyond the new federal programs coming out of Washington and consider broader changes in American political and social life. The New Deal set in motion a major expansion of presidential power and engendered a dramatic growth in the federal bureaucracy. The Roosevelt administration opened unprecedented opportunities for groups such as women, blacks, and labor to play larger roles in public life. It also laid the groundwork for the modern welfare system that shapes American life today.

The Growth of the Presidency and the Federal Bureaucracy

Every president since the 1930s has lived in the shadow of Franklin Roosevelt. Few of his successors have matched his raw political talent or had the opportunities offered by the twin crises of depression and war in which to act "presidentially." By concentrating public attention so dramatically on the presidency and the national state, Roosevelt raised expectations that the federal government could solve major problems in social and economic life. These promises have proven difficult to deliver.

President Roosevelt established unusually close rapport with the American people. Many credited him with the positive changes in their lives, saying "He gave me a job" or "He saved my home." Ordinary citizens felt he was their

ROOSEVELT'S RELATIONS WITH THE PRESS

T.R.B. (Richard Lee Strout), columnist for The New Republic, *recalls Roosevelt's press conferences.*

Roosevelt started off having two press conferences a week. He continued that until the war came; then he had one press conference a week. Altogether, I think he had a thousand press conferences. I was present at practically all of them. One press conference was held in the morning for the afternoon papers, one in the afternoon for the morning papers the next day. We'd gather outside and there'd be anywhere from fifty or more reporters. At big times, 200 reporters might be there. We'd go in and stand around his desk. It was covered with dolls, totems, and knick-knacks. It was like a meeting of a club.

Television has destroyed the press conference as we knew it, destroyed the old freedom, the intimacy, the lack of inhibition, and that jocular familiarity between two antagonists that we had then. We were antagonists, but we liked each other and we laughed and we had a perfect understanding of what each was trying to do and there was a certain degree of affection.

The publishers of papers were generally hostile, but the reporters were won by his personality. We might not have agreed with his politics, but we had a symbiotic relationship. He got everything he could from us and we got everything we could from him. We nearly always got a good story. . . .

People often ask me why Roosevelt's being crippled was concealed from the public: "Why didn't you say so when you wrote a story about him? Why didn't you say he was in a wheelchair? Why didn't you say he was heaved up or heaved down?" We just took it for granted. Everybody knew it. It was common knowledge. . . . That had nothing to do with politics.

Source: Reprinted by permission of the publishers from *The Making of the New Deal: The Insiders Speak* ed. by Katie Louchheim, Cambridge, Mass.: Harvard University Press, © 1983 by the President and Fellows of Harvard College. 13–14.

---

friend. "Mr. Roosevelt is the only man we ever had in the White House who would understand that my boss is a son of a bitch," remarked one worker. Roosevelt's masterful use of the new medium of radio fostered this personal identification. During an early fireside chat (he broadcast sixteen during his first two terms), Roosevelt interrupted his text to ask for a glass of water. After swallowing audibly, he told his listeners, "My friends, it's very hot here in Washington tonight." An average of five thousand to eight thousand letters a week poured into the White House throughout the 1930s. One person had handled public correspondence during the Hoover administration, but it took a staff of fifty under Roosevelt. Further reflecting the new importance of communicating with the public, Roosevelt became the first president to engage a press secretary.

Much of the mail was addressed to Eleanor Roosevelt. While her husband's expansion of the personalized presidency had roots in the administrations of Theodore Roosevelt and Woodrow Wilson, the nation had never seen a First Lady like Eleanor Roosevelt. Franklin and Eleanor's marriage represented one of the most successful political partnerships of all time. He was a pragmatic politician, always aware of what could or could not be done. She was an idealist, a gadfly, always pushing him—and the New Deal—to do more. Eleanor Roosevelt observed in her autobiography,

> He might have been happier with a wife who was completely uncritical. That I was never able to be, and he had to find it in other people. Nevertheless, I think I sometimes acted as a spur, even though the spurring was not always wanted or welcome. I was one of those who served his purposes.

Eleanor Roosevelt underestimated her influence. She served as the conscience of the New Deal.

The First Lady kept up her own career during her husband's four terms. She held press

"*For gosh sakes, here comes Mrs. Roosevelt!*"

A FIRST LADY WITHOUT PRECEDENT
Eleanor Roosevelt's globe-trotting travels provoked
comment from both her family and the press. The famous
New Yorker cartoon shown above reflected the First Lady's
tendency to turn up in odd places. She did indeed soon
go down in a coal mine to visit the miners. (Drawing by
Robert Day; © 1933, 1961 The New Yorker Magazine,
Inc.)

conferences for woman journalists, wrote a
popular syndicated news column called "My
Day," and traveled extensively throughout the
country. Some people wondered why the First
Lady could not be content to stay home at the
White House like a good wife. But most admired
her determination to support the causes she believed in. A Gallup poll in January 1939 showed
that 67 percent approved of Eleanor Roosevelt's
conduct, a higher approval rate than the president's at that time. In 1938, *Life* magazine hailed
her as the greatest American woman alive.

During the Roosevelt years, basic institutional
changes occurred in the office of the presidency.
From the beginning, Roosevelt centralized decision making in the White House and dramatically expanded the role of the executive branch
in initiating policy. In drafting legislation and
setting policy, he still relied on the advice of
his talented cabinet. But he was just as likely to
turn to advisers and administrators scattered
throughout the New Deal bureaucracy. His closest advisers, such aides as Raymond Moley,
Rexford Tugwell, and Adolph Berle, became
known as the "Brain Trust."

Roosevelt's attempts to reorganize the executive branch proved more controversial. In 1937
and 1938, Congress refused to consider a Roosevelt plan that would have consolidated all independent agencies into cabinet-rank departments,
extended the civil service system, and created
the new position of auditor general. The conservative coalition in Congress blocked the reorganization plan, effectively playing on lawmakers'
fears that the president's bid for centralized executive management would dramatically reduce
congressional power. Opponents also linked
Roosevelt's attempt to reorganize the executive
branch with popular fears about fascism and dictatorship. He had to settle for a weak bill in 1939,
allowing him to create the Executive Office of
the President and name six administrative assis-
tants to the White House staff. The White House
also took control of the budget process by moving the Bureau of the Budget to the Executive
Office from its old home in the Treasury Department.

The growth of the office of the presidency
was part of the general expansion of the federal
bureaucracy set in motion by the New Deal's
programs. The number of civilian government
employees, which had reached 579,000 in 1929
under Herbert Hoover, exceeded a million in
1940. This expansion represented an 80 percent
increase in just a decade. The number of federal
employees who worked in Washington grew at
an even faster rate, doubling between 1929 and
1940. Power became centered increasingly in the
nation's capital, not in the states.

Eager young people flocked to Washington to
join the New Deal. Lawyers in their mid-20s
fresh out of Harvard found themselves drafting
major legislation or being called to the White
House for strategy sessions with the president.
Paul Freund, a Harvard Law School professor
who worked in the Reconstruction Finance
Corporation and the Department of Justice, remembered, "It was a glorious time for obscure
people." Many young New Dealers went on
to distinguished careers in government or public
service but recalled that nothing ever matched
the excitement of the early New Deal.

Along with the growth in the federal bureaucracy came greatly expanded federal budgets. In
1930, the Hoover administration spent $3.1 bil-
lion and had a surplus of almost $1 billion. With

the increase in federal programs to fight the depression, federal expenditures grew steadily—$4.8 billion in 1932, $6.5 billion in 1934, and $7.6 billion in 1936. In 1939, the last year before war mobilization affected the federal budget, expenditures hit $9.4 billion. Government spending outstripped receipts throughout this period, producing yearly deficits of about $3 billion. Roosevelt came close to balancing the budget in 1938, but only at the cost of a major recession. The deficit climbed toward $3 billion again as soon as he spent his way out of the so-called Roosevelt recession.

The New Deal has often been associated with the beginnings of big government and bureaucracy. It did spend money and run up deficits at a rate unprecedented for the time. But the real step toward big government spending came during World War II, not the depression. Federal outlays in the 1930s never topped $9.4 billion a year. They routinely surpassed $95 billion in the 1940s. Deficits grew from $4 billion annually during the depression to $50 billion during the war. Although the deficit declined in the postwar era, government expenditures never returned to their pre–World War II levels.

Minorities and the New Deal

The growth of the federal government in the 1930s increased the potential impact that its decisions (and its spending) had on various constituencies. The New Deal considered a broader cast of characters worthy of inclusion in the political process, especially if they were organized into pressure groups. Politicians realized the importance of satisfying the concerns of certain blocs of voters in order to cement their allegiance to the Democratic party. Sympathetic government administrators promoted the interests of groups previously overlooked. As a result, native Americans, women, blacks, and labor received more attention from the federal government and had a higher visibility in public life than ever before.

Native Americans made up one of the nation's most disadvantaged and powerless minorities. Their annual average income in 1934 totaled only forty-eight dollars, and their unemployment rate was three times the national average. Concerned New Deal administrators,

such as Secretary of the Interior Harold Ickes and Commissioner John Collier of the Bureau of Indian Affairs, tried to correct some of these inequalities. The Indian Reorganization Act of 1934 reversed the Dawes Severalty Act of 1887 by promoting more extensive self-government through tribal councils and constitutions. The government also changed the former emphasis on integration into American society by now pledging to pay greater attention to preserving Indian languages, arts, traditions, and other tribal heritages. The economic problems of native Americans were so severe, however, that no practical change in federal policy could have produced dramatic results.

Women as a group also received government attention during the 1930s. In the experimental climate of the New Deal, unprecedented numbers of women accepted positions in the Roosevelt administration. The New Deal included the first woman cabinet member, director of the mint, assistant secretary of the treasury, head of a major WPA division, and judge of the circuit court of appeals. Many of these women were close friends as well as professional colleagues, and they cooperated in an informal network to advance both feminist and reform causes.

Eleanor Roosevelt exemplified the growing prominence of women in public life. Close behind her in importance came Secretary of Labor Frances Perkins and Mary (Molly) Dewson, a social reformer-turned-politician who headed the Women's Division of the Democratic National Committee. By 1936, the Women's Division had organized eighty thousand women at the grassroots level. Dewson pushed an issue-oriented program that educated women about what the New Deal had done for their communities.

Without the vocal support of prominent women such as Eleanor Roosevelt, Molly Dewson, and the rest of the female political network, women's needs during the depression might have been totally overlooked. Grave flaws still marred the treatment of women in New Deal programs. For example, although NRA codes raised wages and improved working conditions for four million workers, a fourth of the codes adopted a lower minimum wage for women than for men performing the same jobs. Women received little help from such New Deal agencies as the Civil Works Administration or Public

ELEANOR ROOSEVELT AND CIVIL RIGHTS
One of Eleanor Roosevelt's greatest contributions was her commitment to civil rights. She developed an especially fruitful working relationship with Mary McLeod Bethune of the National Youth Administration. This photograph shows Bethune and the First Lady at a conference on black youth in 1939. (Franklin D. Roosevelt Library)

Works Administration, whose construction projects were considered unsuitable employment for female workers. Only 7 percent of the CWA workers were women. The Civilian Conservation Corps, which benefited 2.5 million young men, excluded women entirely. The Fair Labor Standards Act and the Social Security Act did not cover major areas of female employment, such as domestic service.

Women fared somewhat better under the Works Progress Administration. At the WPA's peak, 405,000 women were on its rolls. Still, at a time when women accounted for about 23 percent of the labor force, they comprised only between 14 percent and 19 percent of the WPA workers. The Women's and Professional Projects Division of the WPA, headed by Ellen Sullivan Woodward, a Mississippi social worker, created hundreds of programs to put women to work. For the most part, however, progress for women did not come from specific attempts to single

them out as a group. It occurred as part of the broader effort to improve the economic security of all Americans.

Black Americans had a similar experience. They benefited more from the general social and economic programs of the New Deal than from any concerted commitment to promote civil rights. There were striking parallels between the situation of blacks and women. (For black women, who belonged to both groups, race proved more important than gender in determining treatment from the New Deal.) Mary McLeod Bethune, an educator who became head of the Office of Minority Affairs of the National Youth Administration, headed the "black cabinet." This informal network worked for fairer treatment of blacks by New Deal agencies in the way that the women's network advocated feminist causes. Both groups benefited greatly from the support of Eleanor Roosevelt. The First Lady's promotion of equal treatment for blacks in the New Deal ranks as one of her greatest legacies.

The vast majority of the American people did not regard civil rights as a legitimate objective for federal intervention in the 1930s. The New Deal provided little specific aid for blacks, for whom hard times were a permanent feature, not just a product, of the 1930s. Franklin Roosevelt repeatedly refused to support a federal antilynching bill, claiming it would antagonize southern members of Congress whose support he needed for passage of New Deal measures. Many New Deal programs reflected prevailing racist attitudes. CCC camps segregated blacks, and many NRA codes did not protect black workers.

At the same time, blacks received enormous benefits from New Deal relief programs directed toward poor Americans regardless of race or ethnic background. Public works projects channeled funds into black communities. Blacks made up about 18 percent of the WPA's recipients, although only 10 percent of the population. Such agencies as the Resettlement Administration fought for the rights of black tenant farmers in the South. Many blacks reasoned that the tangible aid coming from Washington outweighed the discrimination that marred many New Deal programs.

Help from the WPA and other economic programs, and a belief that the White House—at least Eleanor Roosevelt—realized their plight, caused a dramatic change in blacks' voting behavior. Since the Civil War, blacks had voted Republican, a loyalty resulting from Abraham Lincoln's freeing of the slaves. As late as 1932, black voters in northern cities overwhelmingly supported Republican candidates. Then, in fewer than four years, blacks turned Lincoln's portrait to the wall and substituted that of Franklin Roosevelt. They gave him 71 percent of their votes in 1936. Black voters have remained overwhelmingly Democratic ever since.

The Rise of Organized Labor

During the 1930s, labor became a legitimate arena for federal action and intervention. At the same time, organized labor claimed a place in the national political life of the United States. Its dramatic growth in the 1930s represented one of the most important social and economic changes of the decade.

LABOR STRIFE
Despite the guarantees of the 1935 National Labor Relations Act, the drive for union recognition often provoked confrontations, and even violence, between workers and management, such as this confrontation during the General Motors strike in Flint, Michigan in 1937. (Wide World)

THE SIT-DOWN STRIKE
The sit-down tactic pioneered by the United Auto Workers was soon used by other members of the work force, including the sales clerks at Woolworth's shown above. Sit-down strikes, however, were unpopular with many nonunion members, who saw them as assaults on property rights. The Supreme Court outlawed the practice in 1939. (The Archives of Labor and Urban Affairs, Wayne State University)

Several factors produced the breakthrough for labor. They included the inadequacy of welfare capitalism in the face of the depression, New Deal legislation such as the Wagner Act, the rise of the Congress of Industrial Organizations (CIO), and the growing militancy of rank-and-file workers. By the end of the decade, the number of unionized workers had tripled to almost nine million, covering 23 percent of the nonfarm work force. Union strength grew rapidly in manufacturing, transportation, and mining. Organized labor won not only the battle for union recognition, but also higher wages, seniority systems, and grievance procedures. Labor also greatly expanded its political involvement.

The CIO served as the cutting edge of the union movement. It did so by promoting industrial unionism—that is, it organized all the workers in an industry, both skilled and unskilled, into one union. John L. Lewis, leader of the United Mine Workers and a founder of the CIO, was the leading exponent of industrial unionism. His philosophy put him at odds with

RANK AND FILE MEMBER REMEMBERS EARLY DAYS OF THE CIO

I got in the mills in 1936, and I [was] fortunate to be caught up in a great movement of the people in this country. And that doesn't happen very often in one's lifetime, but it's an experience that I think is important to anyone who has been able to participate in a movement of this kind. . . . It's indeed a very important event in his or her life. Because a movement of the kind that we had in the Steelworkers Union and in the CIO was a movement that moved millions of people, literally, and changed not only the course of the working man in this country, but also the nature of the relationship between the working man and the government and between the working man and the boss, for all time in this country. . . .

I was hired at the Inland Steel Company in 1936. And I remember I was hired at 47 cents an hour, which was the going rate, and at a time when there were no such things as vacations, holidays, overtime, insurance, or any of the so-called fringe benefits everybody talks about today. But the worst thing—the thing that made you most disgusted—was the fact that if you came to work and the boss didn't like the way you looked, you went home; and if he did like the way you looked, you got a promotion. Anything and everything that happened to you was at the whim and will of the fellow who was your boss and your supervisor. . . . When the CIO came in, the people were ready to accept a change. And because they were ready to accept a change, it was not a difficult task to organize the people in the steel mills. Thousands upon thousands of them, in a spontaneous movement, joined the steelworkers' organization at that time. And they did it because conditions in the mill were terrible, and because they had become disgusted with the political set-up in this country and the old tales told by the Republican Party about the free enterprise system in this country in which any man was his own boss, and there was no sense in having an organization, and organizations and unions were anti-American, and so on. All this fell off the backs of the people at that time. They realized that there was going to be a change—both a political and an economic change—in this country, and there was.

Source: John Sargent, interviewed in Alice and Staughton Lynd, eds., *Rank and File: Personal Histories by Working-Class Organizers.* Princeton, N.J.: Princeton University Press, 1973. 105–106.

---

the American Federation of Labor, which favored organizing workers on a craft-by-craft basis. Lewis began to detach himself from the AFL in 1935, and the break became complete by 1938. Although the CIO generated much of the excitement on the labor front during the 1930s, the AFL gained more than a million new workers between 1935 and 1940. The two organizations reunited in 1955.

The CIO scored its first major victory in the automobile industry. On December 31, 1936, General Motors workers in Flint, Michigan, staged a sit-down strike. They vowed to stay at their machines until management agreed to bargain collectively with them. The workers lived in the factories and machine shops for forty-four days before General Motors recognized the United Automobile Workers (UAW). The CIO soon won a second major victory, this time at the United States Steel Corporation. Despite a long history of bitter opposition to unionization (as demonstrated in the 1919 steel strike), "Big Steel" capitulated without a fight and recognized the Steel Workers Organizing Committee (SWOC) on March 2, 1937.

The victory in the steel industry was not complete, however. A group of companies known as "Little Steel" chose not to follow the lead of U.S. Steel in making peace with the CIO. Steelworkers struck the Republic Steel Corporation plant in South Chicago. On the afternoon of May 31, 1937, strikers and their families gathered for a holiday picnic and rally outside the plant gates. Tension mounted, rocks were thrown, and the police fired on the crowd, killing ten protesters. All were shot in the back. A newsreel photographer recorded the scene, but Paramount Pictures suppressed the film of the "Memorial Day Massacre," considering it too inflammatory. The road to recognition for labor, even with New Deal protections, was often still violent.

The 1930s were one of the most active periods of labor solidarity in American history. The sit-down tactic spread rapidly. In March 1937, 167,210 workers staged 170 sit-down strikes. Labor unions called nearly five thousand strikes that year and won favorable terms in 80 percent of them. Rank-and-file militancy, not union leadership, fueled many of labor's breakthroughs.

The CIO attracted new groups to the union movement. Blacks, for example, found the CIO's commitment to racial justice a strong contrast to the AFL's long-established patterns of exclusion and segregation. Woman workers, about eight hundred thousand strong, also found a limited welcome in the CIO. Women participated in major CIO strikes and served as union organizers, especially in textile organizing drives in the South. Blacks and women held few union leadership positions, however.

Women found other ways beside joining a union to participate in the labor movement. The Women's Emergency Brigade, a group of wives, sisters, and girlfriends of striking workers, supplied food and first aid in the Flint sit-down strike against General Motors in 1937. Wearing distinctive red berets and armbands, they picketed, demonstrated, and occasionally resorted to such tactics as breaking windows to counter the tear gas used against the strikers. After the strike, however, UAW leaders politely but firmly told the women to go back home where they belonged.

Labor's new vitality spilled over into political activity. The AFL had always stood aloof from partisan politics, but the CIO quickly allied itself with the Democratic party. Through Labor's Nonpartisan League, the CIO gave $770,000 to Democratic campaigns in 1936. Labor also provided one of the few solid lobbies behind President Roosevelt's plan to reorganize the Supreme Court. In the 1940s, the CIO's Political Action Committee became a permanent and sophisticated contributor to the Democratic war chest.

Despite these breakthroughs, the labor movement never developed into as dominant a force in American life as had seemed possible in the heyday of the late 1930s. Roosevelt never made the growth of the labor movement a high priority. Many workers remained indifferent or even hostile to calls for unionization. Large numbers of middle-class Americans felt alienated by sit-down strikes, which they considered attacks on private property.

The Wagner Act, the New Deal's greatest contribution to labor, guaranteed unions a permanent place in American industrial relations. The effect of New Deal legislation in changing actual working conditions was not revolutionary, however. Collective bargaining, while an important gain, did not redistribute power in American industry; it merely granted labor a measure of legitimacy. Management even found that unions could be useful as a buffer against rank-and-file militancy. In addition, New Deal programs diffused some of the radical spirit prevalent before 1937 by channeling significant social welfare benefits to workers. The labor movement, which had seemed on the verge of even greater breakthroughs when the 1930s ended, entered a period of stalemate and consolidation over the next several decades.

The New Deal Legacy

The New Deal stands as a creative, exciting period of American history. The national government, no longer a distant or insignificant force, now occupied the center of the nation's political and economic activity. For the first time, people experienced the federal government as a concrete part of everyday life through mortgage guarantees, farm subsidies, NRA codes, social insurance, and work relief. The rapidly growing level of federal expenditures had emerged as a central factor in modern economic life. In 1939, a British observer summed up this new orientation: "Just as in 1929 the whole country was 'Wall Street conscious,' now it is 'Washington conscious.'"

While the New Deal took the federal government in new directions, it did so in a pragmatic, nonrevolutionary manner. Neither Franklin Roosevelt nor the American people wanted a fundamental restructuring of American economic or social life. The New Deal basically preserved the existing system of corporate capitalism by

TIME LINE
THE NEW DEAL: TOWARD THE MODERN WELFARE STATE

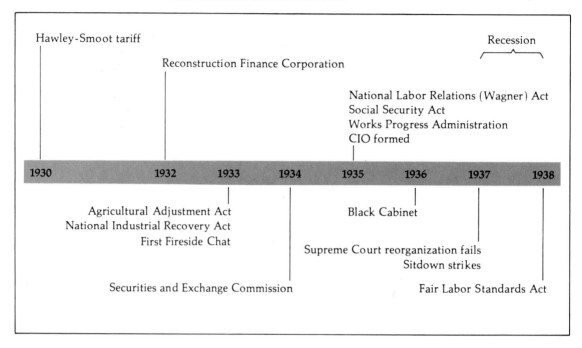

grafting a limited welfare state onto a capitalist foundation. It neither sought nor accomplished a radical redistribution of income. During the 1930s, the poorest 40 percent of the nation's families increased their share of the national income only marginally, from 12.5 percent in 1929 to 13.5 percent in 1941. The share of the top 5 percent of families dropped from 30 percent to 24 percent. Most of the redistributed income went to the middle class, whose share of income rose from 33 percent to 39 percent during the 1930s. These limited changes were as much the result of economic factors as of direct government action.

Despite the conservative thrust of the New Deal, the political and economic history of the 1930s had a wide-reaching impact on the decades that followed. The Roosevelt administration set precedents and made decisions that have shaped American institutions ever since. The New Deal represented the politicization and bureaucratization of modern American life. It brought three major changes—a new federal role in the management of the economy, the founda-

tions of the nation's welfare state, and the solidification of the New Deal coalition.

During the 1930s, the government made a concrete commitment to intervene in the economy when private instruments of power proved insufficient to guarantee economic stability. New legislation regulated the stock market more tightly and reformed the Federal Reserve system by placing more power in the hands of Washington policy makers. It also brought many practices of modern corporate life under federal regulation. The New Deal basically continued the pattern begun during the progressive era of using federal regulation of economic practices to bring order and regularity to modern industrial life.

The modern welfare system began to take shape about 1935 with the passage of the Social Security Act. One of Social Security's most important components was categorical assistance, such as aid to the blind, deaf, and disabled, and to dependent children. These were the so-called "deserving poor," people who could not support themselves through no fault of their own. The categorical assistance programs have grown dramatically since the 1930s. Aid to Dependent Children, which covered only 700,000 youngsters in 1939, by 1974 had become Aid to Families of Dependent Children with 10.8 million Americans on the welfare rolls. Programs that had formed merely a small part of the New Deal gradually grew through the years until they made up most of the American welfare system.

The other component of the emerging welfare system, old age pensions and unemployment compensation, did not amount to welfare at all. These benefits were funded by contributions from employers and employees, not by general revenues. Their greatest drawback was their failure to reach a significant minority of American workers. For example, the Social Security program excluded domestic servants and farm workers entirely for many years. Another problem, especially with unemployment compensation, stemmed from the fact that state governments administered these programs. Benefits varied widely from state to state, with the South consistently providing the lowest amounts. Payments were so low that people could barely get by on Social Security or unemployment compensation without additional resources. The social insurance system also failed to protect the chronically unemployed. After exhausting their unemployment insurance, they were at the mercy of inadequate state and local general relief.

In assessing the foundations of America's welfare state, it is hard to escape the limited nature of the New Deal commitment. The New Deal offered more benefits than American citizens had ever had before, but its safety net had many holes. Franklin Roosevelt never willingly embraced large expenditures for social welfare programs. He stated forcefully in January 1935 that the government "must and shall quit this business of relief." The government operated under the assumption that once the depression had been overcome, full employment and an active economy would take care of welfare needs. Policymakers hoped, although unrealistically, that poverty would simply wither away. It did not do so. When later administrations confronted the persistence of inequality and unemployment in modern industrial society, they grafted welfare programs to the modest jerry-built system left over from the New Deal.

To its credit, the New Deal recognized that poverty was a structural economic problem, not a matter of personal failure. After hard times ended, the federal commitment to economic security for citizens remained. In fact, it grew steadily during the period after World War II. Yet the American welfare system would always be marked by its birth during the crisis atmosphere of the Great Depression. The pressing emergency needs to restore jobs, incomes, and morale precluded the development of a coherent blueprint for the modern welfare state.

Even if the early welfare system set some ill-advised, or perhaps fatal, economic and social precedents, it was brilliant politics. The frenzied activity of the New Deal gave Americans hope and confidence that the nation would pull through the depression. The Democratic party courted the allegiance of citizens who benefited from New Deal programs. Organized labor aligned itself with the administration that had promoted it as a legitimate force in modern industrial life. Blacks voted Democratic in direct relation to the economic benefits that poured into their communities. The unemployed also looked kindly on the Roosevelt administration. According to one of the earliest Gallup polls, 84 percent of those on relief voted the Democratic ticket in 1936.

The Democratic party did not attract only the down and out. Roosevelt's magnetic personality and the dispersal of New Deal benefits to families throughout the social structure brought middle-class voters, many of them first- or second-generation immigrants, into the Democratic fold. The New Deal thus completed the transformation begun in the 1920s toward a party reflecting the interests of ethnic groups, city dwellers, organized labor, blacks, and a broad cross section of the middle class. All these people benefited from and supported the expansion of federal initiatives represented by the New Deal. These voters provided the backbone of the Democratic coalition for decades to come.

$\mathscr{T}$he economic prosperity of the 1920s rested on shaky grounds. After the stock market crash of 1929, the economy entered a downward spiral that did not bottom out until 1932–1933. The Hoover administration authorized the first direct federal intervention into the economy during peacetime in an attempt to win business and public confidence. However, such measures did not end the Great Depression, and the nation turned to Franklin D. Roosevelt and the Democrats in 1932.

Roosevelt's New Deal did not cure the depression, but it restored confidence that hard times could be overcome. Through a variety of legislation that touched the economy, agriculture, labor, and unemployment, the New Deal got the country moving again. Yet it could hardly be called revolutionary. The commitment toward meeting Americans' welfare needs remained limited.

The New Deal led to a dramatic expansion of the federal government. Washington suddenly became a force that touched individual lives. The New Deal also set in motion other changes, including the growth of the presidency and a larger role in public life for blacks, women, and labor. It cemented the reorientation of the Democratic coalition begun in the 1920s. By 1938, however, the New Deal had run out of steam and hard times were far from over. World War II finally broke the depression's grasp.

Suggestions for Further Reading

William E. Leuchtenberg, *Franklin D. Roosevelt and the New Deal* (1963), remains the best concise introduction to the New Deal. Other useful surveys include Robert S. McElvaine, *The Great Depression* (1984); Albert Romasco, *The Politics of Recovery* (1983); and Paul Conkin, *The New Deal* (1967). Arthur M. Schlesinger, Jr., *The Age of Roosevelt* (three volumes, 1957–1960), and Frank Freidel's multivolume biography, *Franklin D. Roosevelt* (four volumes, 1952–1973), examine the era and its leading protagonist in detail.

Hoover and the Great Depression

Historians and economists continue to debate the causes of the Great Depression. See John Kenneth Galbraith, *The Great Crash* (1954); Milton Friedman and Anna Schwartz, *The Great Contraction, 1929–1933* (1965); and Peter Temin, *Did Monetary Forces Cause the Great Depression?* (1976). For general overviews of economic developments, see Charles Kindelberger, *The World in Depression* (1973), and Jim Potter, *The American Economy Between the Wars* (1974). Irving Bernstein, *The Lean Years* (1960), offers a compelling portrait of hard times during the Hoover years.

Hoover's response to the depression is chronicled in Alfred Romasco, *The Poverty of Abundance* (1965), and Jordan Schwartz, *The Interregnum of Despair* (1970). See also David Burner, *Herbert Hoover* (1978), and Joan Hoff Wilson, *Herbert Hoover: Forgotten Progressive* (1975). Eliot Rosen, *Hoover, Roosevelt, and the Brain Trust* (1977), treats the transition between the two administrations, as does Frank Freidel, *Launching the New Deal* (1973). For the 1932 election and the beginnings of the New Deal coalition, see David Burner, *The Politics of Provincialism* (1967); Samuel Lubell, *The Future of American Politics* (1952); and John Allswang, *The New Deal in American Politics* (1978).

The New Deal Response

The New Deal has inspired a voluminous bibliography. Frank Freidel, *Launching the New Deal* (1973) covers the first hundred days in detail. Monographic studies include Bernard Bellush, *The Failure of the NRA* (1975); Thomas K. McCraw, *TVA and the Power Fight* (1970); John Salmond, *The Civilian Conservation Corps* (1967); Susan Kennedy, *The Banking Crisis of 1933* (1973); and Michael Parrish, *Securities Regulation and the New Deal* (1970). Ellis Hawley, *The New Deal and the Problem of Monopoly* (1966), provides a stimulating account of economic policy. Agricultural developments are covered in Van L. Perkins, *Crisis in Agriculture* (1969); Richard S. Kirkendall, *Social Scientists and Farm Politics in the Age of Roosevelt* (1966); David Conrad, *The Forgotten Farmers* (1965); Paul Mertz, *The New Deal and Southern Rural Poverty* (1978); and Sidney Baldwin, *Poverty and Politics: The Rise and Decline of the Farm Security Administration* (1968). Alan Brinkley, *Voices of Protest* (1982), describes the Coughlin and Long movements; see also T. Harry Williams, *Huey Long* (1969). Roy Lubove, *The Struggle for Social Security* (1968), and J. Joseph Huthmacher, *Senator Robert Wagner and the Rise of Urban Liberalism* (1968), cover major initiatives from the Second New Deal.

The second term has drawn far less attention than the 1933–1936 period. James McGregor Burns, *Roosevelt: The Lion and the Fox* (1956), provides an overview. For the Supreme Court fight; see Joseph Alsop and Turner Catledge, *168 Days* (1938), and Leonard Baker, *Back to Back* (1967). The growing opposition to the New Deal is treated in James T. Patterson, *Congressional Conservatism and the New Deal* (1967), and Frank Freidel, *FDR and the South* (1965). See also Richard Polenberg, *Reorganizing Roosevelt's Government* (1966), and Barry Karl, *Executive Reorganization and Reform in the*

New Deal (1963). James T. Patterson, *The New Deal and the States* (1969), examines changing patterns of federalism, while Charles Trout, *Boston: The Great Depression and the New Deal* (1977), examines the impact of the New Deal on one city.

The New Deal's Impact on Society

For minorities and the New Deal, see Harvard Sitkoff, *A New Deal for Blacks* (1978); Raymond Wolters, *Negroes and the Great Depression* (1970); and Nancy J. Weiss, *Farewell to the Party of Lincoln* (1983). Donald Parman, *Navajoes and the New Deal* (1976), summarizes Indian policy. On women and the New Deal, see Susan Ware, *Beyond Suffrage* (1981). Joseph Lash, *Eleanor and Franklin* (1971), provides a comprehensive account of Eleanor Roosevelt's activities, which can be supplemented by her autobiographies, *This Is My Story* (1937) and *This I Remember* (1949). George Martin, *Madam Secretary* (1976), covers the career of Frances Perkins. Also

of interest is Perkins's memoir, *The Roosevelt I Knew* (1946).

Irving Bernstein, *The Turbulent Years* (1970), chronicles the story of the labor movement in compelling detail through 1941. Additional studies include Peter Friedlander, *The Emergence of a UAW Local* (1975); Melvin Dubofsky and Warren Van Tine, *John L. Lewis* (1977); Sidney Fine, *Sit-Down: The General Motors Strike of 1936–1937* (1969); and David Brody, *Workers in Industrial America* (1980).

The creation of the New Deal's welfare system is treated in James T. Patterson, *America's Struggle Against Poverty* (1981), which carries the story through 1980. See also John Garraty, *Unemployment in History* (1978), and Otis Graham, *Towards a Planned Society: From Roosevelt to Nixon* (1976). Katie Louchheim, ed., *The Making of the New Deal: The Insiders Speak* (1983), provides an engaging introduction to some of the men and women who shaped the New Deal.

25

THE SOCIAL FABRIC OF DEPRESSION AMERICA

The 1930s represent a distinct historical unit in the history of the United States. The decade symbolically began with the stock market crash of October 29, 1929, and ended with the bombing of Pearl Harbor by the Japanese on December 7, 1941. More than any other factor, the Great Depression provides the unifying theme for the decade.

Yet not every event of the 1930s can or should be interpreted through a depression-focused lens. For many people, times had always been hard. They did not experience a radical change for the worse during the depression. One historian who studied oral histories collected during the 1930s by the Works Progress Administration (WPA) expressed surprise at how rarely people actually mentioned the depression by name. "The Depression was not the singular event it appears in retrospect," she concluded. "It was one more hardship."

On the other hand, the depression loomed larger in the interviews conducted by the writer Studs Terkel during the 1960s. As the years went by between the hard times and the present, people's recollections of the depression's impact grew. More and more, survivors of the decade told uncomprehending children and grandchildren, "If you only understood how we struggled during the depression."

By interpreting the 1930s solely in terms of the depression, we also run the risk of ignoring important elements of continuity that shaped American institutions in the twentieth century. Family values and gender definitions remained stable. The popular culture of the 1920s survived, and even expanded, during the depression. For example, movies, radio, and mass-circulation magazines played important roles in keeping spirits up while Americans waited for good times to return.

Almost all our impressions of the 1930s are in terms of black and white. Widely distributed photographs taken at the time by government photographers have etched this stark visual image of depression America. Yet conditions were not uniformly grim. The depression was not on everyone's mind twenty-four hours a day. People continued their daily routine of work, family, and leisure. Literature and the arts flourished. The novelist Josephine Herbst noticed "an almost universal liveliness that countervailed universal suffering."

Hard Times

"Mass unemployment is both a statistic and an empty feeling in the stomach," observed a perceptive historian. "To fully comprehend it, you have to both see the figures and feel the emptiness." As the legions of unemployed exceeded a fourth of the nation's work force, many Americans began to lose faith in the Horatio Alger ethic of upward mobility through hard work. Many of the down-and-out blamed themselves for their misfortune.

The Invisible Scar

Some people actually got rich in the Great Depression. Joseph P. Kennedy, the father of the future president, increased his family fortune substantially during the 1930s by buying real estate and stocks that few others could afford. Chicago millionaire W. Clement Stone claimed that any ambitious young person could start at the bottom as he himself had and work to the top by taking advantage of depression-induced opportunities. All the person had to have, said Stone, was what he called PMA (Positive Mental Attitude). Such success stories merely reinforced the intense sense of personal failure among Americans who felt confused and unneeded as they lost jobs, homes, and self-respect.

"You could feel the depression deepen," recalled the writer Caroline Bird, "but you could not look out the window and see it." Many people never saw a bread line or a man selling apples on the street corner. The depression caused a private kind of despair that often simmered behind closed doors. "I've lived in cities for many months broke, without help, too timid to get in bread lines," the writer Meridel LeSueur remembered. "I've known many women to live like this until they simply faint on the street from privations, without saying a word to anyone. A woman will shut herself up in a room until it is taken away from her, and eat a cracker a day and be as quiet as a mouse. . . ."

The victims of the depression were a varied group. The depression did not create poverty; it merely publicized the conditions of the poor. People who had always been poor were joined

THE BREADLINE
Some of the most vivid images from the depression were breadlines and men selling apples on street corners. Women rarely appeared in breadlines, perhaps due to the different standards of "respectability" for men and women. (Franklin D. Roosevelt Library)

by the newly poor. These formerly solid working-class and middle-class families strongly believed in the work ethic and the American dream but suddenly found themselves floundering in a society that no longer had a place for them. They were proud people who felt humiliated by their plight. "What is going to become of us?" asked an Arizona man. "I've lost twelve and a half pounds this last month, just thinking. You can't sleep, you know. You wake up at 2 A.M. and you lie and think."

Hard times were especially distressing for old people, who had struggled all their lives and now faced total destitution in their final years. The loss of savings in bank failures contributed to their plight. In a cartoon from the 1930s, a squirrel asks an old man on a park bench why he had not saved for a rainy day when times were good. "I did," the man replies listlessly. No wonder older Americans responded enthusiastically to Francis Townsend's plan for old-age pensions and cheered the passage of the Social Security Act in 1935. But many still felt bitter. A man from Lincoln, Nebraska wrote to Eleanor Roosevelt in 1934. "Now as we are Old and down and out of no reason of our own," he asked, "would it be asking too much of our Government and the young generation to do by us as we have tried our best to do by them even without complaint."

Children, on the other hand, often escaped the sense of bitterness and failure that gripped their elders. Some youngsters thought it was fun to stand in a soup line. They did not feel ashamed. Yet the experience of hard times matured children quickly. A ten-year-old girl was thinking more about family survival than childhood playthings when she wrote President Roosevelt in 1935. "We have no one to give us a Christmas present," she said, "and if you want to buy a Christmas present please buy us a stove to do our cooking and to make good bread."

Downward mobility was especially hard for middle-class Americans. "Lady," an unemployed Pittsburgh man told FERA investigator Lorena Hickok, "you just can't know what it's like to have to move your family out of the nice house you had in the suburbs, part paid for, down into an apartment, down into another apartment, smaller and in a worse neighborhood, down, down, down, until finally you end up in the slums." Before a laid-off chauffeur started his relief construction job, he spent the day watching how the other men handled their picks and shovels so he could "get the hang of it and not feel so awkward." A wife broke into tears when her husband, formerly a white-collar worker, put on his first pair of overalls to go to work.

The key to surviving the depression was maintaining self-respect. One man spent two years painting his father's house; in fact, he painted it twice. Keeping up appearances, keeping life as close to normal as possible, was an essential strategy. Camaraderie and cooperation helped many families and communities survive because other people found themselves in the same boat. When a truck driver "accidentally" dumped a load of oranges or coal off the back of his truck, he probably was contributing to the welfare of the neighborhood. Hoboes developed an elaborate system of sidewalk chalk marks to tell one another at which back doors they could get a meal, an old coat, or some spare change.

When hard times struck, families coped as best they could. Many appealed directly to Franklin or Eleanor Roosevelt. More than 450,000 letters poured into the White House in the week following the president's inauguration. People believed that the Roosevelts sincerely cared about their lives. "Never before have we had leaders in the White House to whom we felt we could go with our problems," an Alabama woman wrote Eleanor Roosevelt, "for never before have our leaders seemed conscious of the masses. The knowledge that my President is trying to uplift 'the forgotten man' has made me bold to write to you." Sometimes citizens approached the White House with specific requests, such as a loan to pay the electric bill, or one of the First Lady's cast-off coats. More often, they wrote poignant descriptions of situations that had no easy solution.

After savings and credit had been exhausted, many families faced the humiliation of going on relief. Seeking aid from the government offended people's values of self-help or the traditional pattern of reliance on relatives, neighbors, and institutions such as churches in times of need. A young caseworker tearfully remembered her embarrassment when investigating the homes of these proud people:

The father was a railroad man who had lost his job. I was told by my supervisor that I really had to *see* the poverty. If the family needed clothing, I was to investigate how much clothing they had at hand. So I looked into this man's closet . . . he was a tall, gray-haired man, though not terribly old. He let me look into the closet—he was so insulted. . . . He said, "Why are you doing this?" I remember his feeling of humiliation . . . this terrible humiliation. He said, "I really haven't anything to hide, but if you really must look into it. . . ." I could see he was very proud. He was so deeply humiliated. And I was, too. . . .

Despair, apathy, and cynicism were common reactions to such experiences. Here is how some Americans described their plight: "We're about down and out and the only good thing about it that I see is that there's not much farther down we can go." "A man over forty might as well go out and shoot himself." "It's funny. A lot of times I get offered a drink. It seems like people don't want to drink alone. But no one ever offers me a meal. Most of the time when I take a drink it makes me sick. My stomach's too empty." "No work, no hope; just live from one day to the next. Maybe better times are coming. Personally I doubt it." "New Deal? They forgot to cut the deck. That's what we say around here."

Such hardships left deep wounds. Author Caroline Bird called them the "invisible scar." An elderly civil servant told Studs Terkel that she had bought a plot of land outside Washington so that if the depression ever recurred, she would have something to live off. Labor organizer Larry Van Dusen described another common reaction: "The depression left a legacy of fear, but also a desire for acquisition—property, security. I now have twenty times more shirts than I need, because all during that time, shirts were something I never had." Some people concluded that the system was rotten and had to be changed, but most drew a different lesson. Virginia Durr, a white civil rights activist from Alabama, observed, "The great majority reacted by thinking money is the most important thing in the world. Get yours. And get it for your children. Nothing else matters. Not having that stark terror come at you again." For many Americans, "that stark terror" of losing control over their lives summed up the Great Depression.

Blacks and the Depression

Black Americans viewed the despair of the depression differently than most whites did. One black man told Studs Terkel the reaction of a typical black male: "It didn't mean too much to him, the Great American Depression, as you call it. There was no such thing. The best he could be is a janitor or a porter or shoeshine boy. It only became official when it hit the white man." The novelist and poet Maya Angelou recalled the same sentiments from her childhood in Stamps, Arkansas. "The country had been in the throes of the Depression for two years before the Negroes in Stamps knew it," she said. "I think that everyone thought the depression, like everything else, was for the white folks." Writer Langston Hughes expressed it most forcefully: "The depression brought everybody down a peg or two. And the Negroes had but few pegs to fall."

Black Americans felt little of the shame and personal guilt experienced by many whites during the depression. Discrimination and limited opportunities had always been such a large part of their lives that they had no reason to blame themselves for their misfortune. That attitude hardly helped them overcome the staggering obstacles they faced in the 1930s, however.

As late as 1940, more than 75 percent of the nation's black population lived in the South, including nearly all of the black farmers. Only 20 percent of these farmers owned their own land. The rest toiled on the bottom rung of the exploitative southern agricultural system, working as tenant farmers, farm hands, and sharecroppers. They rarely earned more than an average of $200 a year. The yearly earnings of black women cotton pickers in one Louisiana parish averaged only $41.67.

Throughout the 1920s, southern agriculture had suffered from falling prices and overproduction. The depression made an already desperate situation even worse. Such New Deal programs as the Agricultural Adjustment Administration displaced as many as two hundred thousand black tenant farmers from their land. When white owners cut back on production to get their government subsidy checks, they simply let the blacks go and continued to farm their own land. The Resettlement Administration was one of the few New Deal agencies that supported the rights

AN INDIANA LYNCH MOB
The threat of lynching remained a terrifying part of black life in the 1930s, and not just in the South. This picture shows two young blacks who were lynched by an Indiana mob in 1930. Twenty blacks were lynched in the United States that year, twenty-four in 1933, and eighteen in 1935. Appeals by the National Association for the Advancement of Colored People (NAACP) for federal antilynching legislation received little support from President Roosevelt and other politicians. (UPI)

of black sharecroppers, but angry southerners in Congress soon cut its appropriations drastically.

Some black farmers fought back by joining the Southern Tenant Farmers Union (STFU), one of the few southern groups that welcomed both blacks and whites. "It won't do no good for us to divide because there's where the trouble had been all the time," an elderly black farmer reminded the organizing committee. "The same chain that holds you holds my people, too. If we're chained together on the outside we ought to stay chained together in the union."

The STFU, founded in 1934, encountered repression and violent harassment from landowners who had a stake in keeping black and white sharecroppers divided and unorganized. The Southern Tenant Farmers Union could do little to reform an agricultural system so dependent on one crop, cotton. It won only slight improvements in the treatment of tenant farmers by New Deal programs.

The Scottsboro case reflected the harsh social and political discrimination that almost all blacks faced in the South during the 1930s. On March 25, 1931, a freight train pulled into Scottsboro,

Alabama carrying a number of hoboes and transients who had caught a free ride on the rails. Acting on a tip from the conductor, sheriff's deputies arrested nine black men for fighting with some white hoboes.

Suddenly, two white women wearing men's clothing stepped off the boxcar and claimed they had been raped by the nine blacks. The officers accepted without question the accusations of the women, Victoria Price and Ruby Bates, and barely kept an angry white crowd from lynching the men. Within two weeks, juries composed entirely of white males found the nine defendants guilty of rape and sentenced eight of them to death. One defendant, a minor, escaped the death penalty. The U.S. Supreme Court overturned the sentences in 1933 and ordered new trials on the grounds that the defendants had been denied adequate legal counsel.

The youth of the Scottsboro defendants, their rapid trials, and especially their harsh sentences stirred public protest. The case aroused emotions centering on the issues of class, race, gender, and sectional suspicion. The International Labor Defense (ILD), a labor organization loosely affiliated with the Communist party, took over the defense of the so-called "Scottsboro boys." White southerners resented not only the presence of these radical lawyers, but also that all were northerners and Jews. Southerners felt they should be left alone to deal with the episode, as local custom demanded. Some believed they should be congratulated because the accused men had been brought to trial rather than lynched on the spot.

The southern myth of the inviolate honor and chastity of white womanhood also complicated the case. No evidence confirmed that the two women had had sexual intercourse on the train, and their stories contained many inconsistencies and unsupportable claims. Ruby Bates eventually recanted her story and agreed that the Scottsboro boys had been framed by racism. In the South, however, when a white woman claimed to have been raped by a black man, her word was always accepted over that of the accused rapist. As one court observer remarked, Victoria Price "might be a fallen woman, but by God she is a white woman."

The case dragged on through the courts for the next decade. Five of the defendants were convicted and sentenced to long prison terms in trials held in 1936 and 1937. The charges against the other four were dropped in 1937. Four of the convicted men were paroled in 1944. The fifth escaped to Michigan, whose governor refused to return him to Alabama.

The Scottsboro case received wide coverage in black communities of both the North and the South. Coupled with an increase in lynching in the early 1930s, it provided a strong inducement for black Americans to head for northern cities. The lure of the North was offset, however, by the lack of economic opportunities caused by the depression. Consequently, the black exodus of the 1930s totaled only about half of that in the 1920s. About four hundred thousand black men and women left the South during the 1930s. By 1935, eleven northern cities had a black population of more than a hundred thousand. Two of the most popular destinations were Harlem in New York City and the South Side of Chicago.

Harlem presents a case study of what awaited blacks when they journeyed north. Harlem had been New York's first suburb, a neighborhood of wealthy city families in the late nineteenth century. As late as 1900, blacks made up only a small minority of the Harlem population. Then came the great migration from the South set in motion by the social and geographic mobility of World War I. At the same time that blacks moved into Harlem, second-generation Italians and Jews began to move out.

Harlem reached the height of its fame in the 1920s, when it became a mecca for both whites and blacks. Adventurous New Yorkers associated Harlem with the Cotton Club and other glittering jazz palaces catering to white audiences. Meanwhile, black intellectuals founded the literary movement called the Harlem Renaissance, which celebrated racial pride and cultural identity in the midst of white society. Such authors as Alain Locke, Claude McKay, Langston Hughes, Jean Toomer, Jessie Fauset, and Zora Neale Hurston represented the "New Negro" in fiction. These cultural developments had little impact on the masses of black Americans, however.

During the 1920s, the black population of New York City increased by about 115 percent, putting a drastic strain on Harlem's resources. This once prosperous middle-class community was on its way to becoming a slum. The depression made a bad situation worse. Residential segregation kept blacks from moving elsewhere. They paid excessive rents while unscrupulous realtors allowed housing to deteriorate rapidly. Crowded living conditions caused disease and death rates to rise severely; tuberculosis became one of Harlem's leading causes of death. Unemployment there climbed to 50 percent, as whites now clamored for jobs traditionally held by blacks—domestic servants, elevator operators, garbage collectors, and waiters.

In March 1935, Harlem exploded in the nation's only major race riot of the decade. Its residents were angry about the lack of jobs, a slowdown in relief, and pervasive economic exploitation of the black community; the white-owned stores, although dependent entirely on black trade, would not employ blacks. The arrest of a teenage black shoplifter, followed by rumors that he had been severely beaten by white police officers, triggered the riot. False reports of his death increased the panic, and the city mobilized five hundred police officers. Four blacks were killed, and property damage totaled $2 million.

Reflecting the harsh conditions experienced by black Americans in northern cities, black religious and colonization movements gained support during the 1920s and 1930s. In the 1920s, the Universal Negro Improvement Association (UNIA) promoted racial pride and black separatism under the leadership of Jamaican-born Marcus Garvey. Based in Harlem, the UNIA was the first mass movement among the nation's black working class. At its height, it claimed four million followers. Garvey urged blacks to return to Africa because, he said, they would never be treated justly in countries ruled by whites. Amy Jacques Garvey attracted black women by combining her husband's black nationalism with a feminist outlook emphasizing women's contributions to cultural and political life.

The Universal Negro Improvement Association grew rapidly in the early 1920s. It published a newspaper called *Negro World* and opened "liberty halls" for its followers in major northern cities. The UNIA also undertook extensive business ventures as part of its support for black capitalism. The most ambitious project was the Black Star Line, a steamship company to ferry cargo between the West Indies and the United States, and to provide passage to Africa for American blacks. This venture caused the downfall of the UNIA. Financial irregularities in raising money led to mail fraud indictments against Garvey and several of his associates. Garvey was convicted in 1925 and sentenced to five years in prison. President Calvin Coolidge paroled him in 1927, and Garvey was deported to Jamaica. His movement collapsed without his charismatic leadership.

During the 1930s, a black religious leader named Father Divine rose to fame in Harlem. Divine promised his loyal followers a kingdom in heaven that recognized no distinctions of sex, race, color, or economic status. He became noted for establishing shelters and soup kitchens staffed by the Divine Peace Mission. At the height of the Great Depression, Divine provided three thousand free meals a day for Harlem's destitute. Unlike Marcus Garvey, Divine did not bar whites from his movement.

Although the "Divine Deal" competed with the New Deal for the loyalty of many Harlem residents, Father Divine's cult had little impact on political development. In politics, Harlem be- came overwhelmingly Democratic by 1936, a striking confirmation of the shift in black allegiance to the New Deal. In 1920, only 3 percent of Harlem's blacks voted for the Democratic ticket of James M. Cox and Franklin D. Roosevelt. By 1928, 28 percent of them supported Al Smith. The percentage rose to 50.8 percent for Roosevelt in 1932.

The impact of the New Deal programs on economic conditions in Harlem, especially the increased expenditures in the wake of the 1935 riot, raised Roosevelt's support to 81.3 percent in the 1936 election. The president maintained that level of popularity in the black community in 1940. The number of black voters in Harlem rose 78 percent during the 1930s, far outstripping the population increase from migration. Despite the harshness of the depression—or, more likely, because of it—national politics assumed a new relevance for black Americans in northern cities.

Dust Bowl Migrations

Like black Americans, farmers had long experienced depressed economic conditions. That situation merely continued in the 1930s. For farmers on the Great Plains, however, things got worse—much worse. In Oklahoma, Arkansas, and Texas, the decade became known as the "Dirty Thirties" because of the dust storms that blighted the land. A drought that began in 1930 and lasted until 1941 was the worst in the history of the country. Throughout the decade, the three words most often repeated by farmers were "if it rains."

Dust became a part of everyday life. When the clouds of dust rolled in, street lights blinked on in what seemed like nighttime darkness. Dust seeped into houses and, one historian wrote, "blackened the pillow around one's head, the dinner plates on the table, the bread dough on the back of the stove." The dust storms were not confined to the Plains. In May 1934, the wind took dust clouds to Chicago, where the grime fell like dirty snow, dumping the equivalent of four pounds of debris for every person in the city. Several days later, the same clouds blackened the skies and dirtied the streets of Buffalo, Boston, New York and Washington.

Farmers who moved onto the semiarid Great Plains after the 1870s had always risked the rav-

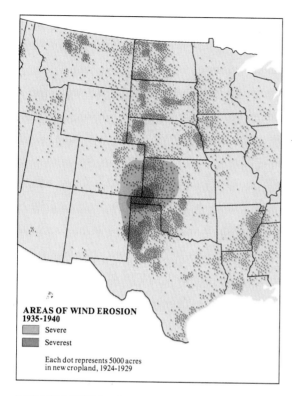

**AREAS OF WIND EROSION
1935-1940**

Severe

Severest

Each dot represents 5000 acres
in new cropland, 1924-1929

MAP 25.1 THE DUST BOWL
A U.S. Weather Bureau scientist called the drought of the
1930s "the worst in the climatological history of the
country." Conditions were especially severe in the
southern plains, where the dramatic increases in farming
on marginal land had already strained production before
the drought struck. Winds whipped the loosened topsoil
into devastating dust storms. One dust-storm blackout in
Amarillo, Texas lasted eleven hours.

ages of drought. Even in wet years, the average
rainfall of twenty inches or less was barely
enough to raise grain crops. But low rainfall
alone did not cause the Dust Bowl, an area of
the Great Plains that included parts of Oklahoma, Texas, New Mexico, Colorado, and Kansas. The aggressive expansion of the farming
frontier beyond its natural limits destroyed the
delicate ecological balance of the plains. After
marginal land had been stripped of its natural
vegetation, nothing remained to hold the soil
when the rains dried up and the winds came.

This ecological disaster caused an exodus
from the land. The term "Okies" (for Oklaho-
mans) came into use to describe the members of
farm families who loaded all their belongings

into a beat-up Ford and headed west along
Route 66 to the promised land of California.
John Steinbeck's classic novel *The Grapes of Wrath*
(1939) immortalized this saga. Its central character, Ma Joad, symbolized the family's attempt to
keep its spirit unbroken in the face of economic
and social disaster.

Families like the Joads abandoned their land
not only because of drought, but also as a result
of economic forces that had changed American
agriculture. Large-scale commercialized farming
was spreading to the plains. The Joads had
farmed with animals. After the bank foreclosed
their mortgage, a gasoline-engine tractor, the
symbol of mechanized farming, plowed under
their crops and pushed down their house.

California had already undergone massive
changes that created a type of agriculture vastly
different from the traditional farming the Joads
left behind. Farming in California was large
scale, intensive, and diversified. In the late nineteenth century, the Imperial Valley had been
arid wasteland; only the introduction of irrigation made farming possible. Growers at first cultivated wheat, but soon switched to fruits and
vegetables. The steady supply of cheap labor
provided by Chinese, Mexicans, Okies, and,
briefly, even Hindustani made such farming economically feasible. Carey McWilliams, whose
Factories in the Field (1939) rivaled *The Grapes of
Wrath* in focusing national attention on migrant
workers, noted that California agriculture was
basically industrial in nature.

> Ownership is represented not by physical
> possession of the land, but by ownership of cor-
> porate stock; farm labor, no longer pastoral in
> character, punches a time clock, works at piece
> or hourly wage rates, and lives in a shack or
> company barracks, and lacks all contact with the
> real owners of the farm factory on which it is
> employed.

Encouraged by handbills promising good jobs
in California, at least 350,000 Okies headed west
during the 1930s. White, native-born Americans
had made up about 20 percent of the migratory
farm labor force before the depression, but their
proportion increased to more than 85 percent by
the late 1930s. Since growers needed only
175,000 workers at the peak of the picking season, many more people wanted a job than could

MIGRANT LABOR IN CALIFORNIA

By the 1930s, about thirty-five thousand Filipinos were working as migrant laborers in California, including these lettuce workers in Salinas. At first, Filipinos were highly desired as migratory workers because they worked long hours for low wages. But they soon began to demand higher wages. In 1934, three thousand Filipino lettuce workers went on strike near Salinas. The strike was brutally broken, and many of the workers were driven from the community. (Library of Congress)

find one. This surplus of labor assured the growers a cheap and usually docile wage force willing to work at any price. That price was incredibly low in the 1930s. The average yearly family income for farm workers in California ranged from $350 to $450, less than a third of the subsistence level.

Thousands of Mexican-American workers in the Southwest also found grim conditions. The 1930 census reported 617,000 Mexican-Americans, but the number had dropped to 377,000 by 1940. A formal deportation policy instituted by the U.S. government caused part of the decline, although many more Mexicans left voluntarily when work ran out or because they feared deportation. The deportation of Mexican-Americans was not simply a response to the arrival of migrants from the Dust Bowl. The largest number of Mexican-American deportations occurred under the Hoover administration, well before the Dust Bowl exodus reached its peak. Many southwestern communities realized that it was cheaper to send the migrant workers back to Mexico than to support them on relief during the winter, when there were no crops to pick. A one-way train ticket cost the equivalent of a week's relief allotment in 1932.

The experience of Mexican-Americans in the 1930s reflected ongoing ambivalence in the United States about whether to encourage or dis-

courage migration across the border. The first *bracero* (day-laborer) program promoting Mexican immigration had been established during World War I to meet the labor shortages caused by mobilization. The importation of cheap Mexican labor continued throughout the 1920s. After the forced exodus in the depression, the tide changed again. Mexican workers found themselves coaxed back when World War II caused another labor shortage. A second bracero program, started in 1942, remained in effect on an informal basis until 1964.

Except for short periods following the two world wars and during the Great Depression, Mexican migration to the United States—both legal and illegal—has increased steadily throughout the twentieth century. The influx of Spanish-speaking migrants with their own distinct culture helped shape the patterns of life in the Southwest.

The experiences of a young Mexican-American in the 1930s named Cesar Chavez influenced him to become a farm union organizer. Chavez was a child of ten when his father lost his farm near Yuma, Arizona, in 1934. The Chavez family became migrant workers in California, joining the army that followed the crops. They experienced continual discrimination, including rejection by many restaurants whose signs proclaimed "White Trade Only." The family never stayed long in one place because Cesar's father became involved in several bitter labor strikes that hit the Imperial Valley in the mid-1930s. All these strikes failed, but they gave young Chavez a heritage of labor organizing that he used in founding a national farm workers' union in 1962.

Family Values

"We didn't go hungry, but we lived lean." That poignant memory sums up the experiences of many American families during the Great Depression. The vast majority were neither very rich nor very poor. For most, the depression did not mean losing millions of dollars in the stock market or leaving an expensive boarding school because their parents could no longer pay the bills. Nor did it mean living in cardboard "Hoovervilles" or going on relief. The husband in a typical family in the 1930s had a job, and his wife was a homemaker. Life was not easy, but it consisted of "making do" rather than stark deprivation.

MEXICAN-AMERICAN POVERTY IN TEXAS

In 1937, Antonia and Pablo Martinez lived in a one-room house in San Antonio, Texas, with his parents and older brother. If either Pablo or Antonia worked in 1937, it was probably in San Antonio's pecan-shelling industry, which depended heavily on the cheap labor of Mexican-Americans. (The San Antonio Light Collection, U. T. Institute of Texan Cultures)

The Family Faces the Great Depression

Sociologists who studied family life during the 1930s found that the depression usually intensified existing trends of behavior. For example, if a family had been stable and cohesive before the depression, it now pulled together to surmount the new obstacles. If, however, a family had shown signs of disintegration, the dislocations of the depression made the situation worse. On the whole, the researchers thought far more families hung together than broke apart.

The depression encouraged a return to traditional values. Church attendance rose slightly. The family unit again became the center of leisure activities, replacing the expensive commercial amusements of the 1920s. Spending the evening at home listening to the radio became a popular pastime, as did reading books borrowed from the public library. People enjoyed such bestsellers as Pearl Buck's *The Good Earth* (1931), Hervey Allen's *Anthony Adverse* (1933), Dale Carnegie's *How to Win Friends and Influence People* (1936), and Margaret Mitchell's *Gone With the Wind* (1936). Columnist Russell Baker recalled another activity that everyone could afford: "Talking was the Great Depression pastime. Unlike the movies, talk was free. . . . "

The depression directly affected demographic trends in the 1930s. The marriage rate fell from 10.14 per thousand persons in 1929 to 7.87 in 1932. Temporary postponements of marriage became permanent in many cases. Elsa Ponselle, a Chicago schoolteacher who later became the principal of one of the city's largest elementary schools, recalled her experience:

> Do you realize how many people in my generation are not married? . . . It wasn't that we didn't have a chance. I was going with someone when the Depression hit. We probably would have gotten married. He was a commercial artist and had been doing very well. . . . Suddenly he was laid off. It hit him like a ton of bricks. And he just disappeared.

The marriage rate rebounded after 1933, but the number of women aged twenty-five to thirty in 1930 who never married was 30 percent higher than in 1925. Since people could not afford the legal expense necessary to dissolve an unhappy marriage, the divorce rate dropped as well. The birthrate was the demographic factor most sensitive to the depression. It had fallen steadily since 1800, but it dropped from 21.3 live births per thousand population in 1930 to 18.4 three years later, a 13 percent decrease. The 1933 level, if maintained, would have led to a population decline.

Economic factors played a dominant role in the falling birthrate. Many people regarded pregnancy as a misfortune because they worried about bringing a child into a world with such limited opportunities. The birthrate rose slightly after 1934 but had reached only 18.8 by the end of the decade. In contrast, the birthrate increased to 25 per thousand population at the height of the baby boom following World War II.

The extensive limitation of births during the Great Depression required access to effective contraception. The production of diaphragms and condoms was one of the few businesses that thrived in the 1930s. Abortion remained illegal, but hard times increased the number of women who visited an abortionist to end an unwanted pregnancy. Such abortions were risky because many abortionists operated under unsanitary conditions that caused illness or death. Between

MARGARET SANGER AND BIRTH CONTROL
Margaret Sanger was probably the twentieth century's most influential birth control reformer. In 1923, she opened the first doctor-staffed birth control clinic in the United States. By 1938, more than three hundred such clinics operated nationwide. Here she testifies before a Senate subcommittee in 1931 in support of a bill to legalize the distribution of birth control information. (UPI)

eight thousand and ten thousand women died each year from botched abortions.

The 1930s marked a significant stage in the long history of the birth control movement in America. A 1936 federal court decision in the case of *United States v. One Package of Japanese Pessaries* struck down all federal bans on the dissemination of contraceptive information. Doctors now had wide discretion in prescribing birth control for married women, which became legal in all the states except Massachusetts and Connecticut. Public support of birth control also increased. A 1936 Gallup poll found that 63 percent of those interviewed favored the teaching and practice of contraception.

Margaret Sanger played a major part in encouraging popular acceptance of birth control in America. She had started her career as a public health nurse in the slums of New York in the 1910s. Anxious immigrant women continually asked Sanger to tell them the "secret" of how to avoid having more babies. When a patient who had been referred to her died from the effects of an illegal abortion, Sanger dedicated her life to birth control. At first, she linked forces with socialist movements aimed at the working class. But by the 1920s, she appealed for support almost entirely to the middle class, which she identified as the key to the movement's success. Sanger also courted the medical profession, pioneering in the establishment of birth control clinics staffed by doctors. In the process, birth control became less a feminist demand and more a medical issue.

Birth control had long been a private decision between individuals. Its public acceptance increased greatly during the 1930s because of the widespread desire to limit family size for economic reasons. In 1942, the American Birth Control League, an organization Sanger had founded in 1921, became Planned Parenthood, an organization that remains very active today.

Women and the Depression

Men and women experienced the Great Depression differently. In many ways, the depression disrupted women's lives less than men's. Millions of men lost their jobs, but few of the nation's twenty-eight million homemakers lost theirs. In fact, women's roles in the home took on greater importance.

ONE WOMAN'S STRUGGLE FOR AN EDUCATION DURING THE DEPRESSION

Frances Ridgway's story of life in rural Michigan speaks for the experiences of many depression-era women.

The Depression caused my family to change their way of living. There were six of us kids and in order to feed us all, my parents traded their town home for an eighty-acre farm. There was no electricity there, no running water, and no flush toilet. And the house was back off the road a half a mile.

But my father thought at least we could eat, living on a farm. And we did, even if it was only beans. My mother would put up 600 or 700 quarts of beans every year.

When I reached twelve years old, I wanted to go to high school; but back in northern Michigan they didn't encourage farm girls to get much of an education. Now, I really insisted that my parents let me go live with this family who paid me two dollars a week to take care of the house and kids.

I did that kind of work for the better part of four years. Some-times I stayed at home, but when I did I'd have to walk almost four miles to get to the place where the school bus stopped.

I'll tell you, I washed and I cleaned and did all the dirty work, you know. Anyway, when I started that first year of high school, I had six dollars saved, and that was enough to buy all my supplies until Christmas. I supplemented my income in another way, by writing all the book reports for the boys on the football team at a nickel apiece. And you know for a nickel you could get a big, thick pad of paper.

During my senior year I got an NRA grant of six dollars a month for helping the teachers correct papers. I thought that was wonderful.

But on the whole, it was hard. I was so very poor. I had one skirt I made out of an old coat in home economics class. And I wore NRA pants. You know, my family got food supplements, and they'd come in sacks that had NRA stamped on them. My mother'd dye them a dark seal brown, but the NRA was still there. My brothers used to always call my NRA pants, "Nuts Running America." I forget . . . I think it meant National Recovery Act.

Anyway, I had no clothes and no money but I finished at the top of my class and I competed for a scholarship and won. It was to Wellesley, a big Eastern college for women. Well, of course, that was out of the question. I didn't even have the money to get there, let alone all the extras I'd need.

But I had a goal for myself. Ever since I was twelve years old there was one major goal in my life . . . one thing . . . and that was to never be poor again. I wasn't especially attractive, and I was poor. I couldn't do anything about the one, but I made up my mind I wasn't always going to be poor.

Source: Frances Ridgway, quoted in Jeane Westin, *Making Do: How Women Survived the '30s.* Chicago: Follett, 1976. 152–153.

The difference in the depression's impact resulted from the traditional gender roles that governed male and female behavior in the 1930s. Men had been trained from childhood to be breadwinners for their families. If they no longer could fulfill this expectation, they considered themselves failures. Women, on the other hand, saw their self-importance increase as they struggled to keep their families afloat. The sociologist Robert Lynd noticed this phenomenon in the follow-up study of Middletown (Muncie, Indiana) published in 1937:

The men, cut adrift from their usual routine, lost much of their sense of time and dawdled helplessly and dully about the streets; while in the homes the women's world remained largely intact and the round of cooking, housecleaning, and mending became if anything more absorbing.

A woman recalled her own experience:

I did what I had to do. I seemed to always find a way to make things work. I think hard times is harder on a man, 'cause a woman will

RURAL ELECTRIFICATION

In 1935, less than one tenth of the nation's 6.8 million farms had electricity. For millions of farm families, this stark fact meant a life of unremitting toil made even harsher by the lack of mechanical aids. Farm families used an average of two hundred gallons of water a day. Any household or barnyard chore that involved water—and most did—meant pumping the water from a distant well and carrying it to the house or barn in a pair of buckets weighing as much as sixty pounds full. If hot water were needed, it had to be heated on a wood stove that required constant tending. Meeting a family's yearly water needs took sixty-three eight-hour days and involved carrying the water a total of 1,750 miles.

The lack of electricity affected farm wives especially hard. A Farm Belt senator recalled "hundreds of thousands of women . . . growing old prematurely; dying before their time." Canning, a necessity because families had no way to store food by refrigeration, kept women over boiling cauldrons of peaches, berries, or vegetables, often in the worst summer heat before the freshly harvested produce spoiled. Washday, traditionally Monday, involved three large zinc washtubs for washing, rinsing, and bleaching. One week's wash consisted of at least four to eight loads, each requiring three washtubs of clean water hauled from the well. Few farm households could afford commercial soap, and so they used lye, which roughened women's hands and did not get ground-in dirt out of soiled clothes too well. If farm women dreaded washday on Monday, they hated ironing on Tuesday even more. Ironing was another all-day job. The iron, a six- or seven-pound wedge of metal, had to be heated on the stove. Because the metal did not retain heat for more than a few minutes, it usually took several irons to do a single shirt. The women in Texas's Hill Country called them "sad irons."

After a day that began in pitch darkness and continued with backbreaking work for twelve hours, evenings brought few comforts. Reading strained the eyes because the only available light came from cumbersome kerosene lamps that provided the equivalent of 25 watts of light at best. Children's eyes might be strong enough to read in the semidarkness, but few older folks could read without squinting. In addition, the absence of electricity meant no radios to provide a bit of amusement or some contact with the world beyond the boundaries of the darkened farmhouse.

Electricity brought relief from

---

do something. Women just seem to know where they can save or where they can help, more than a man. It's just a worry for him, and he feels so terrible when he can't take care of his family.

Women made many contributions to family survival during the depression years. With the national median annual income at $1,160, a typical woman had $20 to $25 a week to feed, clothe, and provide shelter for her family. Deflation had lowered the cost of living so that milk sold for 10 cents a quart, bread 7 cents a loaf, and butter 23 cents a pound. Yet housewives still had to watch every penny. Two friends who often bought hamburger split the two pounds that sold for 25 cents and took turns keeping the extra penny. Eleanor Roosevelt described these women's lives: "It means endless little economies and constant anxiety for fear of some catastrophe such as accident or illness which may completely swamp the family budget." The line between making do and doing without was often thin.

Despite the hard times, Americans managed to maintain a fairly high level of consumption. Continuing the pattern of the 1920s, much of this buying was done by households in the middle-income range, the 50.2 percent of American families with an income of $500 to $1,500 in 1935. Several factors enabled these families to approximate their former standard of living despite the pay cuts or unemployment common in the depression. Deflation lowered the cost of living almost 20 percent between 1929 and 1935. Families also made different choices of how to spend their lower incomes. For example, telephone use and clothing purchases dropped sharply during the depression. People had a harder time giving up cigarettes, movies, radios, and newspapers, once considered luxuries but now regarded as necessities. An automobile proved to be one of the most depression-proof items in the family budget. Sales of new cars

the drudgery and isolation of farm life. A host of farm machines and appliances powered by electricity became available by the 1930s. An electric milking machine saved hours of manual labor, most of it previously done in pitch darkness or by the faint glow of a kerosene lamp before dawn so farmers could conserve the daylight hours for outdoor chores. An electrically powered water pump lightened many farm chores, especially hauling water for family use or the stock. Electric irons, vacuum cleaners, and washing machines lightened women's work in the home. Studies had shown that farmers found so many uses for electricity that they would be good customers. But power companies claimed the cost of running lines to individual farms would be so high that the idea was economically unfeasible. The main reason rural electrification moved so

slowly, however, was that power companies made plenty of money in urban areas and had no incentive to expand into the rural countryside.

In 1935, the New Deal made a federal commitment to bring power to rural America. The Rural Electrification Administration, an independent agency, promoted the formation of nonprofit farm cooperatives to bring electricity to their localities. Local farmers, for a five-dollar down payment each, could form an association to apply for low-interest federal loans to cover the cost of installing power lines for their area. Each household was committed to a monthly minimum usage, usually about three dollars, but the rates came down as usage increased. By 1940, 40 percent of the nation's farms had electricity. The rate reached 90 percent by 1950.

The human impact of rural

electrification was especially poignant. A small child later told his mother, "I didn't realize how dark our house was until we got electric lights." One farm woman remembered, "I just turned on the light and kept looking at Paw. It was the first time I'd ever really seen him after dark." Another family, caught unawares by the timing of the hookup, saw their house from a distance and thought it must be on fire. A rural cooperative held a mock funeral for their kerosene lamps, and schoolteachers noticed that children did better at school when they could do their homework by light. Along with the automobile, electricity probably did more than any other technological innovation to break down the barriers between urban and rural life in twentieth-century America.

"BLUE MONDAY"
Laundry was one of women's hardest household chores. Although this woman did not have to haul water from an outdoor well, she still had to pump it by hand in order to do the wash because her home lacked electricity. She also had to wring out the wet clothes manually, another arduous task. (The Bettmann Archive)

dropped, but gasoline sales stayed stable, suggesting that people turned to used cars or kept their old models longer.

To maintain family lifestyle, housewives often substituted their own labor to provide goods and services they had formerly purchased. These economies financed such budget items as cars and movies, which could not be manufactured at home. Women sewed their own clothes and canned fruits and vegetables. They practiced small economies such as buying day-old bread and heating several dishes in the oven at once to save fuel. Women who previously employed servants began to do all their own housework. In countless ways around the home, women took up the slack, making a contribution whose dollar value would be impossible to calculate. Women generally accepted this new work stoically. "We had no choice," remembered one housewife. "We just did what had to be done one day at a time."

Some families maintained their lifestyle in the 1930s through "deficit living"—that is, using installment payments and credit to stretch their income. This strategy added about 10 percent to a family income under $500, and 2 to 5 percent for a family in the $500 to $1,500 range. By 1936, consumer credit in the United States had increased 20 percent over 1929 levels. A Middletown resident reflected the growing dependence on installment buying as a tactic for family survival. "Most of the families I know are after the same things today that they were after before the Depression," she said, "and they'll get them in the same way—on credit."

Other families kept up their standard of living by sending an additional member of the household into the work force. At the turn of the century, this additional family worker probably would have been a child or young adult. In the 1930s, it was increasingly a married woman. The depression, instead of expelling women from the work force, solidified their place in it. The 1940 census reported almost eleven million women in the work force, a small increase over 1930. By the end of the depression, women made up about a fourth of the labor force, again a small rise from the start of the decade.

Important changes in the backgrounds of working women had occurred by the 1930s. At the turn of the century, the typical woman with a job was young, single, and poor, in most cases a recent immigrant. By the 1930s, more native-born, middle-class, and older women had entered the labor market. Most dramatic was the 50 percent increase in this decade of married women employed outside the home.

Working women, especially married ones, did not have an easy time during the depression. Even if their husband had no job, working wives still had almost total responsibility for housework and child care. They also faced harsh and widespread accusations that they had stolen jobs from men. A 1936 Gallup poll asked whether wives should work when their husbands had a job, and a resounding 82 percent of the people interviewed said no. Many states adopted laws that prohibited the employment of married women; such laws were especially widespread in the field of education. Ironically, the proportion of married female school teachers rose from 17.9 percent in 1930 to 24.6 percent in 1940. From 1932 to 1937, even the federal government would not allow a husband and wife to hold government jobs at the same time.

Norman Cousins, editor of the *Saturday Review of Literature*, offered a quick solution that reflected the resentment women faced when they entered the work force. After calculating that the number of employed women roughly equaled the 1939 unemployment total, he suggested this tongue-in-cheek remedy: "Simply fire the women, who shouldn't be working anyway, and hire the men. Presto! No unemployment. No relief rolls. No depression."

The attempt to make women scapegoats for the depression rested on shaky grounds, both morally and economically. Most women worked because of economic necessity. A sizable minority were the sole support of their families; their husbands had either left home or could not find work. Furthermore, women rarely took jobs away from men, and men had difficulty moving into women's jobs. "Few of the people who oppose married women's employment," observed one feminist in 1940, "seem to realize that a coal miner or steel worker cannot very well fill the jobs of nursemaids, cleaning women, or the factory and clerical jobs now filled by women." Norman Cousins failed to understand that the economy had always been roughly divided between "men's" and "women's" jobs. Custom, rather than law or economics, dictated this practice and made crossovers fairly uncommon.

The division of the work force by gender gave women a small edge during the depression. Many fields with large numbers of female employees, including clerical and sales work, and service and trade occupations, suffered less from economic contraction than did such male areas as steel, mining, and manufacturing. A woman could sometimes find a job even if her husband could not, because women cost less to hire. Women earned from sixty to sixty-three cents for every dollar earned by men. As a result, female unemployment rates, although extremely high, were somewhat lower than men's. This small bonus came at a heavy price, however. The jobs held by women reinforced the traditional stereotypes of female work. Women found themselves even more concentrated in low-paying, no-advancement jobs when the depression ended than when it began.

During the Great Depression, there were few feminist demands for reallocation of power to women either at home or on the job. On an individual basis, women's self-esteem probably rose because of their importance to family survival. Both men and women, however, continued to believe that the two sexes should have fundamentally different roles and responsibilities. The substantial contributions by women in the 1930s actually reinforced their overall identification with the home. The foundation had been laid for the so-called feminine mystique of the 1950s.

Hard Times for Youth

The depression hit the nation's twenty-one million young people especially hard. Unlike children who only dimly glimpsed the sacrifices of life in the 1930s, adolescents knew that "making do" usually meant "doing without." Writer Maxine Davis, who traveled ten thousand miles in 1936 interviewing the nation's youth, described them as "runners, delayed at the gun." She added, "The depression years have left us with a generation robbed of time and opportunity just as the Great War left the world its heritage of a lost generation."

Studies of social mobility confirm that the young men who entered their twenties during the depression era had less successful careers than those before or since. Thoughts of marriage also had to be shelved until at least the prospect of a job came into sight. Lowered expectations became so demoralizing that about 250,000

young people simply took to the road as hoboes and "sisters of the road," the term for female tramps.

Young people who stayed home spent increasing time in school because job prospects appeared so dim. Public schools did not charge tuition, and they provided warmth from the elements, an important consideration in winter. For the first time, most young Americans from fourteen to eighteen went to high school. Less than half the nation's youth attended high school in 1930, but three-fourths of them did in 1940. Changing expectations for boys, who had traditionally dropped out of school at an earlier age than girls in order to work, contributed to this expansion of the high school population.

Although a majority of American teenagers went to high school, college remained the privilege of a distinct minority. With times so rough, the "college of hard knocks" was all most depression-era youths could expect. Yet about 1.2 million young people, or 7.5 percent of the population between eighteen and twenty-four, attended college in the 1930s. Women made up 40 percent of these undergraduates. After 1935, college became a little easier to afford because of the National Youth Administration (NYA), which gave part-time employment to more than 2 million college and high school students. This New Deal agency also provided work for 2.6 million out-of-school youths.

College students were a studious group in the 1930s; financial sacrifices encouraged their seriousness of purpose. The schools never lost their share of men who happily accepted a "gentleman's C" as a grade in a course, or of women who were hunting for a husband. On the other hand, the influence of fraternities and sororities on campus life declined during the depression. Large numbers of students became involved in various political movements. Fueled by disillusionment with World War I, thousands of them took the "Oxford Pledge" never to support a war in which the United States might be involved. In 1936, the Student Strike Against War drew support from several hundred thousand students who cut classes to demonstrate on campuses throughout the country.

Despite the economic sacrifices demanded by the depression, adolescence became increasingly institutionalized in the 1930s. Through high school and college attendance, organized athletics, and extracurricular activities, young people developed their own values and patterns of behavior. Peer culture, rather than parents, influenced their values and tastes. Teenagers throughout the country read the same comics, wore the same style clothes, flocked to the same movies, hung out at corner drugstores, and borrowed the family Ford. The expansion of education at both the secondary and collegiate levels provided one environment for the growth of these new customs.

The rise of the youth culture in twentieth century America had a close link to changes in the family. As the family unit lost many of its economic functions during industrialization, it became an emotional unit; affection and nurture replaced production as its central function. Power in the family became more democratically distributed. Families grew increasingly child conscious; the declining birth rate reflected parents' desire to have fewer children in order to better provide for them. Young people's fashions, fads, and values, closely tied to an ethos of consumption, were increasingly disseminated by such mass media as magazines and movies. Youth culture took its place as another example of the modern secular way of life.

Popular Culture

Popular culture played an important role in pulling the United States through the trauma of the Great Depression. Such diversions as movies and radio programs provided a welcome outlet from the quiet desperation of daily life. The mass culture first recognized in the 1920s flourished in the following decade.

Movies were the most popular entertainment during the 1930s. More than 60 percent of the American people saw at least one movie every week. The films of the depression decade transported moviegoers to a world where hard times appeared only infrequently. Yet these motion pictures offered more than escapism. "Hollywood," observed one film historian about the decade, "directed its enormous powers of persuasion to preserving the basic moral, social and economic tenets of traditional American culture."

Films from the 1930s reflected the values of popular culture at the time. Gangster films were especially popular in the grim early years of the depression. Two of the most successful ones were *Little Caesar* (1930), starring Edward G. Robinson, and *The Public Enemy* (1931), in which

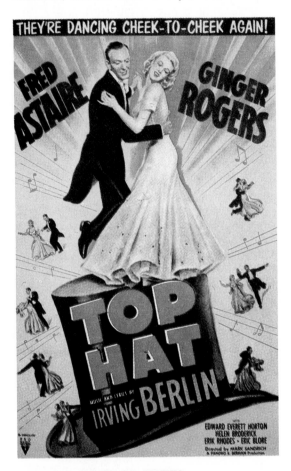

DANCING CHEEK TO CHEEK
During the Great Depression, Americans turned to such cheap recreational activities as listening to the radio and going to the movies. Hollywood film companies produced a number of gala musicals, and one of the most popular attractions of the 1930s was the dance team of Fred Astaire and Ginger Rogers. Astaire and Rogers starred together in ten movies. (The Bettmann Archive)

James Cagney shoved a grapefruit in Mae Clark's face. The extravagant Busby Berkeley musicals that replaced gangster movies in popularity suggest an upswing in the public mood around the time of Franklin Roosevelt's election and inauguration. Three blockbusters, *42nd Street*, *Golddiggers of 1933*, and *Footlight Parade*, appeared in 1933. The 1930s also featured the "screwball comedy"—sophisticated, fast-paced romantic comedies with top stars such as Clark Gable and Claudette Colbert in *It Happened One Night* (1934), John Barrymore and Carole Lombard in *Twentieth Century* (1934), Katharine Hepburn and Cary Grant in *Bringing Up Baby* (1938), and Irene Dunne and Grant in *The Awful Truth* (1938). The Marx brothers kept people laughing with such irreverent classics as *Animal Crackers* (1930) and *Duck Soup* (1933). The bawdy Mae West titillated audiences with such lines as "Why don't you come up and see me some time?" and "I used to be Snow White, but I drifted." Walt Disney produced 198 cartoons during the depression in addition to such feature-length classics as *Snow White and the Seven Dwarfs* (1937) and *Fantasia* (1940).

Movies influenced the consumer culture, even at the height of the depression. One of the decade's top box-office stars was a curly-headed little girl named Shirley Temple, who made twenty-one films by 1941. Soon Shirley Temple dolls, books, and clothes flooded the market. Similarly, sales of peroxide hair rinse skyrocketed in the 1930s because of the popularity of such blond stars as Jean Harlow, Carole Lombard, and Mae West. Undershirt sales fell drastically after Clark Gable, a leading sex symbol of his day, took off his shirt in *It Happened One Night* and revealed his bare chest.

Although movies had the greatest influence on popular values, they competed with newspapers' ability to provide quick coverage of news events. The kidnapping of the twenty-month-old son of Charles and Anne Morrow Lindbergh in 1932 instantly became a major national news story. Seventy-five days later, searchers found the child's body in the woods near the Lindbergh home in New Jersey. "BABY DEAD" ran the headlines, and everyone knew what the two words meant. Other leading news events of the depression years included the birth of the Dionne quintuplets in Canada in 1934; the gunning down of John Dillinger, Public Enemy Number One, by the FBI in 1934; the abdication in 1936 of King Edward VIII of Great Britain so he could marry "the woman I love," an American divorcee named Wallis Warfield Simpson; aviator Amelia Earhart's disappearance on a round-the-world flight in 1937; and the fiery crash of the *Hindenburg*, a German dirigible, at Lakehurst, New Jersey in 1937.

Radio took over an increasingly large place in popular culture during the 1930s. About 13 million households had a radio set in 1930, and 27.5 million owned one in 1939. Listeners tuned in to daytime serials such as "Ma Perkins" and "John's Other Wife." "The Betty Crocker Hour" offered useful household hints. Ventriloquist Edgar Bergen and his impudent dummy, Charlie McCarthy, delighted Sunday night audiences with their comedy routines. Twenty million listeners followed the adventures of the Lone Ranger three times a week.

One of the most famous radio programs in history took place on a Sunday night in October 1938. Actor Orson Welles's "Mercury Theater of the Air" broadcast a modern rendition of *The War of the Worlds* (1898) by the English writer H. G. Wells. Orson Welles used fictional news bulletins interspersed with simulated on-the-spot reports to describe the landing of an imaginary meteor near Princeton, New Jersey which supposedly unleashed death-ray wielding Martian invaders on the unsuspecting countryside. Even though the broadcast included four announcements that the attack was just a dramatization, mass hysteria broke out. The event seemed so realistic that many people fled from their homes. No one doubted the power of radio anymore.

There may have been a deeper reason that people so readily accepted Orson Welles's dramatic production as an actual event. During September 1938, radio programs had been interrupted repeatedly by ominous news bulletins about a possible European war between England and Germany. Even the news on September 30 of the Munich Agreement, which prevented war for another year, did not erase public fears of im-

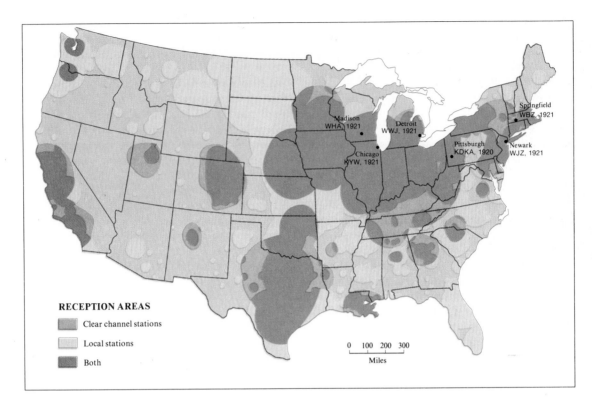

MAP 25.2 THE SPREAD OF RADIO
In 1938, more than twenty-six million American households, or about three-quarters of the population, had a radio. Four national networks dominated the field, broadcasting news and entertainment across the country. Powerful clear-channel stations reached listeners hundreds of miles distant. Independent local stations opened in large and small cities. By the period covered in this map, only a few sparsely populated areas were beyond radio's reach.

minent catastrophe. When Welles staged his monumental hoax a month later, he convinced large numbers of people that the United States had been invaded. Popular culture increasingly reflected America's involvement in the complexities of international political and economic life. Three years later when radios announced that the Japanese had attacked Pearl Harbor, Americans realized this news flash was not a joke.

Culture and Commitment

The depression had a tremendous impact on creative expression in the United States. Few decades have had a greater contrast in their literary themes than the 1920s and 1930s. During the prosperous Twenties, many artists felt so alienated by what they saw as the anti-intellectual and complacent tone of American life that they settled in Europe, especially in France. Ernest Hemingway's *A Farewell to Arms* (1929), which portrayed the disillusionment with World War I, and F. Scott Fitzgerald's *The Great Gatsby* (1925), which questioned the mindless pursuit of material wealth and riches, reflected many writers' disenchantment with American values.

A different tone animated most cultural expression in the depression-plagued Thirties. A collective sense of cooperation and community replaced alienation. As a result of the depression, American artists redefined their relationship to society. Social and economic questions could no longer be ignored, action toward common goals became necessary to surmount the crisis, and world events overshadowed domestic literary concerns. Not all the creative leaders of the 1930s fitted neatly into the pattern of socially relevant art. Yet the critic Malcolm Cowley expressed the spirit of the times when he said in 1939 that never had there been a decade "when literary events followed so closely on the flying coat-tails of social events."

New Deal Culture

Federal One, a WPA project which put unemployed artists, actors, and writers to work, was a unique example of federal patronage of the arts. The depression had dried up traditional sources of private patronage. Like most Americans, creative artists had nowhere to turn except Washington. Such WPA projects never lost sight of their initial purpose—to provide subsistence for needy artists. But their spirit and goals extended far beyond mere relief. New Deal administrators sought to redefine the relationship between artists and the community, so that art no longer would be consumed only by the elite who could afford to pay. "Art for the millions" became a popular New Deal slogan.

The New Deal's call for a fusion of democracy with art drew a talented group of administrators to Washington in the 1930s. Nicholas Sokoloff, conductor of the Cleveland Symphony Orchestra from 1918 to 1933, headed the Federal Music Project, which employed fifteen thousand musi-

cians. Government-sponsored orchestras toured the country, presenting free concerts of classical and popular music. The Music Project, like many other New Deal programs, emphasized American themes as part of the nation's introspective and nationalistic mood during the depression. Composer Aaron Copland wrote his *Billy the Kid* and *Rodeo* suites for the WPA, compositions which specifically incorporated western folk melodies. Musicologist Charles Seeger, and his wife, composer Ruth Crawford Seeger, undertook the extensive project of collecting and cataloguing examples of the American folk tradition.

The Federal Art Project (FAP) employed many of the twentieth century's leading painters, muralists, and sculptors. They received government assistance at a point in their careers when the lack of private patronage would have prevented them from continuing their work. Jackson Pollack, Alice Neel, Willem de Kooning, and Louise Nevelson all received support from the FAP. Under the direction of Holger Cahill, an expert on American folk art, the FAP was best known for sponsoring the murals that decorated public buildings and post offices throughout the country. The FAP commissioned Victor Arnautoff to paint the *City Life* mural for San

RELIEF BLUES
Between 1934 and 1939, an Italian immigrant named O. Louis Guglielmi found work on the Federal Art Project of the WPA, to which he submitted this painting in 1937. Entitled *"Relief Blues,"* it represents the social concern and urban realism prominent in American painting of the 1930s. The starkness of the room and its occupants is intensified by the bright red slippers, the pink rose on the floor, and the red lipstick and nail polish of the woman on the left. (National Museum of American Art, Smithsonian Institution. Transfer from The Museum of Modern Art)

CONSTRUCTION OF A DAM

Social realist painter William Gropper, a cartoonist for *New Masses*, portrayed the contributions of labor in modern industry. His mural of dam construction was commissioned for the Department of the Interior Building in Washington, D.C. The heroic, dynamic style was typical of public art during the depression. (William Gropper. *Construction of a Dam*, Study for the Mural. National Museum of American Art, Smithsonian Institution. Transfer from U.S. Department of Interior, National Park Service)

Francisco's Coit Tower. Huge WPA murals covered the walls and ceilings of terminals at the newly constructed La Guardia airport in New York; later, as artistic tastes changed, most of the murals were painted over. FAP art tended towards socially relevant themes, such as work scenes, family life, and pioneers struggling to tame the land. No one claimed that all the results were great art. As Franklin Roosevelt diplomatically remarked, "Some of it good, some of it not so good, but all of it native, human, eager and alive."

Former journalist Henry Alsberg headed the Federal Writers' Project (FWP), which employed about five thousand writers at its height. Young FWP writers who later achieved fame included Saul Bellow, Ralph Ellison, Arna Bontemps, Margaret Walker, Jack Conroy, Conrad Aiken, Tillie Olsen, and John Cheever. The black folklorist and novelist Zora Neale Hurston finished three novels while on the Florida FWP, among them *Their Eyes Were Watching God* (1937). This story's central character, Janie Crawford, typifies the proud, determined, and beautiful black women who appear in Hurston's fiction. Richard Wright won the 1938 *Story* magazine prize for the best tale by a WPA writer. He used his spare time on the project to complete *Native Son* (1940), the bitter novel about Bigger Thomas, a black man who finds expression in a white-dominated world only through hatred and violence.

The Federal Writers' Project produced more than a thousand publications. It collected oral histories of Americans in many walks of life, including a set of two thousand narratives of former slaves. The 150-volume *Life in America* series included *Baseball in Old Chicago* and *These Are Our Lives*, a set of oral histories from people in North Carolina, Tennessee, and Georgia. Part of the series consisted of ethnic studies, such as *The Italians of New York*, *The Armenians of Massachusetts*, and *The Hopi*.

The most ambitious FWP project was a set of state guidebooks to the United States. Fifty-one state and territorial guides, thirty city guides, and twenty regional guides, including *U.S. One, Maine to Florida*, and *The Oregon Trail*, were published, mostly by commercial presses. These guides combined tourism, folklore, and history, and they reflected the resurgence of interest in everything American. The guides became widely popular, but the choice of subjects occasionally annoyed politicians and state boosters. For example, the 675-page Massachusetts guide gave only fourteen lines to the Boston Tea Party and five to the Boston Massacre, while alloting thirty-one to the Sacco-Vanzetti case.

Anzia Yezierska, a novelist who had won

fame with her 1925 novel *Bread Givers* but then had fallen on hard times, joked about her new job on the Writers' Project: "The Savior of Art! At the bargain price of $23.86 per artist." An unexpected by-product was the camaraderie that creative artists found by working together. Yezierska reveled in this new spirit:

> A new world was being born. A world where artists were no longer outcasts, hangers-on of the rich, but backed by the government, encouraged to produce their best work. . . . Each morning I walked to the Project as light-hearted as if I were going to a party. The huge barracks-like Writers' Hall roared with the laughter and greetings of hundreds of voices. . . .

Of all the federal creative programs, the Federal Theatre Project (FTP) was the most ambitious. American drama thrived in the 1930s, the only time that the United States has had a federally supported national theater. Under the gifted direction of Hallie Flanagan, former head of Vassar College's Experimental Theater, the Theatre Project reached an audience of twenty-five to thirty million in the four years of its existence. Talented directors, playwrights, and actors, including Orson Welles, John Huston, Arthur

Miller, E. G. Marshall, and John Houseman, offered their services.

The Theatre Project's most successful productions included T. S. Eliot's *Murder in the Cathedral*, Mark Blitzstein's *The Cradle Will Rock*, William Shakespeare's *Macbeth* with an all-black cast in a Haitian voodoo setting, and the *Swing Mikado*, a jazz rendition of the Gilbert and Sullivan operetta. Sinclair Lewis's *It Can't Happen Here* opened simultaneously in eighteen cities across the country, including productions in Spanish and Yiddish. Also popular were mini-plays called "living newspapers," among them *Triple A Plowed Under*, about farm problems, and *Power*, concerning public ownership of utilities.

The theater was one of the most politically committed fields of American creative life in the 1930s. However, Congress proved unwilling to appropriate federal funds for its often controversial productions, and the Federal Theatre Project was terminated in 1939. Federal One limped on under federal-state sponsorship until 1943, when wartime priorities dealt it a final blow.

Public support for permanent government patronage of the arts never developed during the 1930s. The arts programs remained tied too closely to their original relief-oriented purpose of

SCOTT'S RUN, WEST VIRGINIA

Ben Shahn was a multi-talented social realism artist—a painter, lithographer, muralist, and photographer. His art always had a point of view. Some of his best-known work was a series of twenty-three paintings in defense of Sacco and Vanzetti. This 1937 tempera painting depicts a railroad depot shut down by a coal miners' strike. (Whitney Museum of American Art, New York)

feeding hungry artists. But while federal support lasted, it fostered an enormous outburst of creativity that made a substantial and lasting contribution to American artistic expression.

The Documentary Impulse

The WPA arts projects were influenced by a broad artistic trend called the "documentary impulse." It attempted to combine social relevance with distinctively American themes, an approach that characterized artistic expression in the 1930s. The documentary impulse, probably the decade's most distinctive genre, influenced practically every aspect of American culture—literature, art, music, film, dance, theater, and radio.

The documentary impulse was the communication of real life, the presentation of actual facts and events in a way that aroused the interest and emotions of its audience. It emphasized observation and narration, but without relying on overembellished prose for impact. A photograph or some other visual image often supplied the emotional force that words could not convey. This technique exalted the ordinary, finding beauty and emotion in subjects not usually considered the province of art. It tried to make you, the audience, experience the subject as though you were actually on the scene.

The documentary impulse influenced every facet of American creative expression in the 1930s. It can be seen in John Steinbeck's fiction, especially *In Dubious Battle* (1935) and *The Grapes of Wrath* (1939), and in Erskine Caldwell's *Tobacco Road* (1932). John Dos Passos's *U.S.A.* trilogy used actual newspaper clippings, dispatches, and headlines throughout its fictional story. The *March of Time* newsreels, which movie audiences saw before the feature film, presented visual images of the world in a pre-television age. The standard opening of radio news broadcasts, "We now take you to . . .", did the same thing. Filmmaker Pare Lorentz commissioned the composer Virgil Thompson to create music that set the mood for such documentary movies as *The Plow that Broke the Plains* (1936) and *The River* (1936). The new photojournalism magazines, including *Life* and *Look*, founded in 1936 and 1937, respectively, reflected this documentary approach. So

did many creative works of the New Deal, from the living newspapers of the Federal Theatre Project to the American Guide series and oral history interviews prepared by the Federal Writers' Project. The New Deal actually institutionalized the documentary impulse. It frequently sent investigators, such as Lorena Hickok and Martha Gellhorn, into the field to report on conditions of people on relief.

The camera was the prime instrument of the documentary impulse. The use of cameras to document social conditions and awaken social consciousness dated back to the probing photography of Jacob Riis and Lewis Hines at the turn of the century. When the nation entered another period of intense social and economic questioning in the 1930s, photographers revived and updated this technique. Such great photographers as Dorothea Lange, Walker Evans, and Margaret

THE POWER OF PHOTOGRAPHY

"Migrant Mother" by Dorothea Lange is perhaps the most famous documentary photograph of the 1930s. Lange spent only ten minutes in the pea picker's camp in California where she captured this image, and did not even get the name of the woman whose despair and resignation she so powerfully recorded. (Library of Congress)

Bourke-White permanently shaped the image of the Great Depression.

Documentary photography became widely popular in *Life, Look,* and in other magazines and books that combined photography with narration. *You Have Seen Their Faces* (1937), by Margaret Bourke-White and Erskine Caldwell, studied southern agriculture, emphasizing the physical and emotional devastation of sharecropper poverty. Dorothea Lange collaborated with the social economist Paul Taylor on several projects about migrant labor conditions. Lange and Taylor produced *An American Exodus: A Record of Human Erosion* (1939), a study of the effects of drought and mechanization on farmers in the Dust Bowl and the South.

The ultimate documentary collaboration between a photographer and a writer remains *Let Us Now Praise Famous Men* (1941), by James Agee and Walker Evans. Agee's rich prose describing the lives of three white tenant farm families in the South—he devoted fifty thousand words simply to an inventory of tenant homes—was framed by Evans's stark photographs of rural life. Through the years, this book has come to epitomize life in the 1930s. Ironically, only about six hundred copies were sold in 1941, the year it was published.

The federal government played a leading part in compiling the photographic record of the 1930s. In 1935, Roy Stryker, a Columbia economics instructor who had been a teaching assistant under brain trust member Rexford Tugwell, took charge of the Historical Section of the Resettlement Administration. He had a mandate to document and photograph the American scene for the government. Stryker gathered a talented group of photographers for this massive task, including Walker Evans, Dorothea Lange, Ben Shahn, Arthur Rothstein, Marion Post Wolcott, and Russell Lee. The government hired these photographers solely for their professional skills. Unlike the Federal Art and Federal Writers' Projects, the Historical Section, which later became part of the Farm Security Administration (FSA), was not established to provide relief for struggling photographers. The collection of FSA photographs ranks as the best visual introduction to life in the United States during the depression decade.

The Popular Front

By the mid-1930s, ominous developments on the international scene resulted in new forms of political action by writers and other intellectuals. Many literary figures participated in the "popular front," a broad leftist movement dedicated to stopping the spread of fascism throughout the world. In this leftward shift, the Communist party played a leading role.

The mid-1930s marked the Communist party's greatest appeal in American society. No longer a small sectarian group, the party had about a hundred thousand members at its peak in 1939. For many recruits, the depression was the main influence that led them to join. Marxism, having predicted the collapse of capitalism, provided an alternative vision of social and economic organization. Communists could be found scattered throughout all walks of life in the 1930s—working-class activists, intellectuals, housewives, union organizers, farmers, blacks, and even a few New Deal administrators. Yet one fact distinguished Communists from other activist groups in political life during the 1930s. American Communists could debate for hours the latest directive from Moscow, but they could never change it. Moscow demanded total loyalty for the party line developed in the Soviet Union.

From 1929 to 1935, the Communist party of the United States conducted activities on several fronts. Communists organized marches of the unemployed, led unionizing drives, and reached out to oppressed groups, such as industrial workers and blacks. The party's support of the defendants in the Scottsboro case represented an attempt to win over blacks in the South as part of its worldwide fight against racism. These recruiting attempts produced little success. Fewer than a thousand blacks joined the Communist party in the early 1930s. "It's bad enough being black, why be red?" was a common reaction. After five years of the gravest depression ever faced by capitalism, the party had fewer than thirty thousand members.

The Communist party had a powerful impact on the collective consciousness of American writers in the 1930s. As a literary historian has observed, however, "It was the times, not the party, that made them radicals." In 1932, fifty-two writers, including Sherwood Anderson, Erskine Caldwell, Malcolm Cowley, John Dos Passos, Theodore Dreiser, Granville Hicks, and Edmund Wilson, pledged their support to William Z. Foster, the party's presidential candidate. While some writers actually joined the Communist party, many others considered themselves only "fellow travelers." They sympathized with the party's objectives, wrote for the *Daily Worker* and other party newspapers, or associated with organizations sponsored by the party. Author Mary McCarthy recalled the fascination that the party held for her and other intellectuals: "For me, the Communist Party was *the* party, and even though I did not join it, I prided myself on knowing that it was the pinnacle."

During the 1930s, many writers wrote so-called proletarian novels, which glorified Marxist themes. The books of such committed communist writers as Michael Gold and Joseph Freeman represented this literary genre at its best, although much of this radical writing was wooden and formalistic. In many novels with proletarian themes, the plot built to a stirring climax where the main character, always a member of the working class, suddenly proclaimed the need for revolutionary change. Many proletarian novels centered on real events. The textile strike in Gastonia, South Carolina, in 1929 inspired six fictional works.

The American Writers' Congress, sponsored by the Communist party in 1935, typified the rapport between the party and major writers and intellectuals. Theodore Dreiser, Josephine Herbst, Langston Hughes, Meridel LeSueur, Nathanael West, Genevieve Taggard, and Richard Wright signed the call for the conference. The participants explored the relationship between revolutionary activism and creative work and discussed the tensions between ideology and art.

The courting of intellectuals was part of an important shift in Communist party tactics in response to the rise of fascism. Adolf Hitler had

AMERICAN COMMUNISTS
The Communist party played an active role in the social and political ferment of the 1930s. Communists organized demonstrations by the unemployed and homeless, participated in strikes and labor-organizing drives, and mobilized public opposition to fascism with the so-called popular front. This 1930 photograph shows that the party took seriously, both ideologically and in social relations, its commitment to ending racism. (Library of Congress)

THE MASSES VERSUS THE MILITIA

Marching! Marching!, *excerpted here, won the 1935 New Masses contest for a novel on an American proletarian theme.*

It's day. For hours we've been coming together, eager to start. . . . We're coming from all directions. Some of us carry banners and slogans. Hey, what's the delay? If we're all here, let's start. . . .

As we near a street corner, a worker bursts into view, running toward us, waving his arms. "MILITIA!" he yells. "They've called out the militia!" . . . The ugly news leaps from mouth to mouth. "Christ's sake!" says a scared voice, "they're going to shoot us. They wont shoot." A woman shrills, "We aint afraid!" just as Matt raises both hands for our attention and yells, "Are we going to let them stop us?" "NO!" we roar. "Let's go!" "Fall in, everybody!" The line reforms, straightens, and we're marching again. We come to the corner and round it. We march steadily to the next corner, turn it, and swing into Broadway. "There they are!" The street seems jammed with them, guns held ready—a dung-colored mass drawn up against us. Bayonets! They've got bayonets! The sun glints on their helmets and flashes steel-bright from the points of their bayonets. "Jesus Christ!" whispers someone. "They're just young kids—strangers! They'll shoot! They dont know what they're doing . . ." thinking *Our boys wouldnt gas and shoot their own fathers and mothers and brothers and sisters . . .* A few of us gasp, flinching the way horses do from the menace of snakes, but we dont stop or slow. We keep marching, but we tighten, looking ahead . . . some of us thinking *Jeez! Bayonets! Machine guns! They got gas masks in those bags around their necks on their chests—gas!* and others *For God's sake, you guys, dont shoot us! Come over to our side. Why should you kill us? We are your brothers.*

For a few seconds we hear only the sound of our own feet, the steady pound of ourselves marching forward. Then suddenly Annie turns and waves a signal to our marshals. Each lifts a hand for a moment while a word is spoken from rank to rank. The signalling hands go down in unison and we're all singing:

"Hold the fort for we are coming;
    Workingmen be strong! . . ."

Source: Clara Weatherwax, *Marching! Marching!* New York: John Day, 1935. 253–256.

---

seized absolute power in Germany the day after Franklin Roosevelt was inaugurated in 1933. Hitler's Nazi regime concentrated all economic and political power in a centralized state. Benito Mussolini had introduced fascism in Italy when he took control of that country in 1922. When Italy invaded Ethiopia in 1935, the League of Nations could not stop the aggression. Hitler began to rearm Germany and prepared to seize the Rhineland, in violation of the Versailles treaty. Fears grew of a world war caused by the advance of fascism.

Fearful of fascist aggression, the Soviet Union attempted to mobilize support in democratic countries. Both in Europe and the United States, communist parties called for a "popular front." The party now welcomed cooperation with any group concerned about the threat of fascism to such areas as civil rights, organized labor, and world peace. Communists sought to ally themselves with liberal political movements throughout the country, adopting the slogan, "Communism is 20th Century Americanism." Despite earlier scorn of the New Deal as reactionary and insincere, the party now supported President Roosevelt and worked for his reelection in 1936. Eleanor Roosevelt, once depicted as a slave of the ruling class, received praise for her humanitarianism. This effort at joining forces with American liberal groups in the mid-1930s represented the height of the party's impact on the United States.

The popular-front strategy became even more urgent with the outbreak of the Spanish Civil War in 1936. Army forces led by Generalissimo Francisco Franco led a rebellion against the elected coalition government. Franco received strong support from the fascist regimes in Germany and Italy. Only the Soviet Union and Mexico backed the Spanish government forces,

TIME LINE
THE SOCIAL FABRIC OF DEPRESSION AMERICA

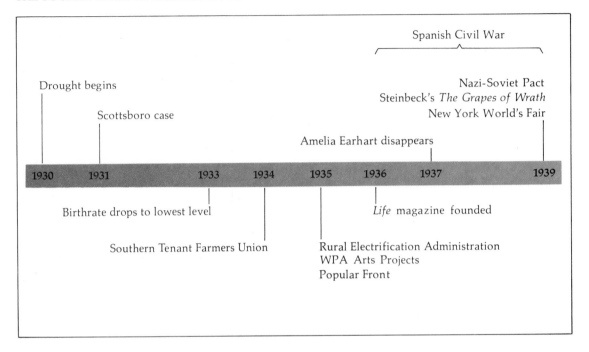

called the Loyalists. The governments of the United States, Great Britain, and France sympathized with the Loyalists but stayed neutral. In the United States, strict neutrality legislation in 1935, 1936, and 1937 forbade arms shipments to either side. Since Franco was receiving substantial military aid from Germany and Italy, the neutrality policy doomed the Loyalists.

Most American activists and intellectuals expressed shock at the policy of nonintervention. The Spanish Civil War became the most vital issue of their generation. "People of my sort," observed writer Malcolm Cowley, "were more deeply stirred by the Spanish Civil War than by any other international event since the World War and the Russian Revolution." Ernest Hemingway immortalized the Spanish conflict in his famous novel *For Whom the Bell Tolls* (1940).

Approximately thirty-two hundred American men and women volunteered to fight on the Loyalist side. Calling themselves the Abraham Lincoln Brigade, they formed part of an international force of soldiers, ambulance drivers, and military personnel who aided the Loyalist cause. Years later, survivors recalled the struggle as the

"good fight." Outnumbered and inadequately supplied, more than half the American volunteers died in the carnage of Spain. By 1939, the Spanish Republic had fallen to Franco's forces.

Although American intellectuals applauded the Soviet Union's active support of the Spanish Loyalists, many literary figures began to feel uncomfortable in leftist circles. The Communists remained suspicious of intellectuals, many of whom were too independent to submit to party discipline. A number of writers found it increasingly difficult to satisfy both their artistic urges and the party's demand for fiction that reflected working-class concerns. Rumors of political repression by the Soviet leader Joseph Stalin also distressed them.

The final blow came in August 1939, when the Soviet Union, eager to avoid war, signed a nonaggression pact with Nazi Germany. Germany thus had a free hand to invade Poland, while the Soviet Union in return shared in the division of that unfortunate country. This harsh act and Stalin's willingness to deal with Hitler came as a bitter blow to many supporters of the popular front. Die-hard communist members loyally accepted the policy change, but others left the party in disgust. The heyday of American Communism ended abruptly.

With the signing of the Nazi-Soviet pact, the world again stood on the brink of war. Now that Germany no longer feared fighting a war on two fronts, the Nazis moved closer to their goal of European—and ultimately world—conquest. Although many Americans considered themselves isolationists—they hoped the United States could remain aloof from European conflicts—they began to realize that the nation faced an even greater enemy than the economic problems that had gripped it for the past decade. Barely twenty years after the war to end all wars, the United States prepared once again to enter another worldwide struggle for the survival of democracy.

---

*T*he Great Depression left an "invisible scar" on people who lived through the 1930s. Those who wanted to work blamed themselves if they could not find a job. The depression did not make as much difference to black Americans, for whom times had always been hard. But things did get worse for farmers in the Midwest, who also had experienced hard times in the 1920s. A drought created the Dust Bowl, forcing many farmers off their land.

Despite the devastating impact of the depression, many aspects of American life and culture continued to conform to traditional patterns. Families pulled together, although women took on expanded roles, and often new jobs, to help support their households. Young people adapted by staying in school longer. Families turned to forms of popular culture, especially movies and radio programs, to take their minds off their troubles.

The collapse of the economy encouraged a reassertion of American values in literature and other forms of culture. This artistic flowering was partly supported by a unique experiment in government patronage of the arts through the WPA. Another feature of cultural expression in the 1930s involved documenting the American experience. Many writers blended artistic concerns with intense political commitment. This activism culminated in the popular front, where liberals and Communists joined together to oppose the spread of fascism, especially in the Spanish Civil War. The brief alliance ended when the Soviet Union signed an agreement with Nazi Germany, bringing the world to the brink of war again.

Suggestions for Further Reading

Hard Times

A wealth of material brings the voices of the 1930s to life. The Federal Writers' Project, *These Are Our Lives* (1939); Tom Terrill and Jerrold Hirsch, eds., *Such as Us: Southern Voices of the Thirties* (1978); and Ann Banks, ed., *First-Person America* (1980), all draw on oral histories collected by the Works Progress Administration during the 1930s. See also Richard Lowitt and Maurine Beasley, eds., *One Third of a Nation: Lorena Hickok Reports the Great Depression* (1981), and Robert S. McElvaine, ed., *Down & Out in the Great Depression* (1983), for first-hand accounts. Evocative secondary sources are Studs Terkel, *Hard Times: An Oral History of the Great Depression* (1970), and Caroline Bird, *The Invisible Scar* (1966).

Developments in the black community during the 1920s and 1930s are covered in Gilbert Osofsky, *Harlem: The Making of a Ghetto* (1966); Nathan Huggins, *Harlem Renaissance* (1971); and Gunnar Myrdal, *An American Dilemma* (1944). David Cronin, *Black Moses* (1962), and Theodore Vincent, *Black Power and the Garvey Movement* (1970), describe Marcus Garvey, and they can be supplemented by Robert Weisbrot, *Father Divine and the Struggle for Racial Equality* (1983). Dan T. Carter, *Scottsboro* (1969), remains the classic depiction of this case. Donald Grubbs, *Cry from Cotton* (1971), tells the story of the Southern Tenant Farmers Union.

Donald Worster, *Dust Bowl* (1979), evokes the plains during the "dirty thirties." The first volume of Robert Caro's biography of Lyndon Johnson, *The Path to Power* (1982), contains a moving portrait of the harshness of farm life before electricity. For more on rural electrification, see D. Clayton Brown, *Electricity for Rural America* (1980), and Marquis Childs, *The Farmer Takes a Hand* (1952). The experiences of Mexican-Americans during the 1930s are treated in Rodolfo Acuna, *Occupied America* (1981); Wayne Cornelius, *Building the Cactus Curtain* (1980); and Mark Reisler, *By the Sweat of Their Brow* (1976).

Family Values

Descriptions of family life in the 1930s include Robert and Helen Lynd, *Middletown in Transition* (1937); Mirra Komarovsky, *The Unemployed Man and His Family* (1940); and Roger Angell, *The Family Encounters the Depression* (1936). Russell Baker's autobiography, *Growing Up* (1982), provides an often humorous description of family life in the 1930s. For more on youth, see Maxine Davis, *The Lost Generation* (1936), and Eileen Eagan, *Class, Culture and the Classroom* (1981). Frederick Lewis Allen, *Since Yesterday* (1939), provides an overview of the popular culture of the 1930s. Specific studies of movies include Robert Sklar, *Movie Made America* (1975); Andrew Bergman, *We're in the Money* (1971); and Molly Haskell, *From Reverence to Rape: The Treatment of Women in the Movies* (1974).

Material on women in the 1930s is found in Susan Ware, *Holding Their Own* (1982); Winifred Wandersee, *Women's Work and Family Values, 1920–1940* (1981); Lois Scharf, *To Work and To Wed* (1980); and Alice Kessler-Harris, *Out to Work* (1982). For the special dimensions of rural women's lives, see Margaret Hagood, *Mothers of the South* (1939). Jeane Westin, *Making Do: How Women Survived the '30s* (1976), is a lively account drawn from interviews. The birth control movement is surveyed in Linda Gordon, *Woman's Body, Woman's Right* (1976), and James Reed, *From Private Vice to Public Virtue* (1978). See also *Margaret Sanger: An Autobiography* (1938).

Culture and Commitment

The various New Deal programs have found their historians in Jerry Mangione, *The Dream and the Deal: The Federal Writers' Project, 1935–1943* (1972); Monty Penkower, *The Federal Writers' Project* (1977); Richard McKinzie, *The New Deal for Artists* (1973); and Jane DeHart Mathews, *The Federal Theater, 1935–1939* (1967). General studies of cultural expression include William Stott, *Documentary Expression and Thirties America* (1973); Richard Pells, *Radical Visions and American Dreams* (1973); and R. Alan Lawson, *The Failure of Independent Liberalism, 1933–1941* (1971). See also Karen Becker Ohrn, *Dorothea Lange and the Documentary Tradition* (1980).

Daniel Aaron, *Writers on the Left* (1961), provides the best overview of literary currents in the decade. For selections from the 1930s, see Harvey Swados, ed., *The American Writer and the Great Depression* (1966). Material on the relationship between intellectuals and the Communist party is in Harvey Klehr, *The Heyday of American Communism* (1984), and Irving Howe and Lewis Coser, *The American Communist Party* (1957). Warren Susman, "The Thirties," in Stanley Coben and Lorman Ratner, eds., *The Development of an American Culture* (1970), contains a provocative analysis of culture and commitment in the 1930s.

THE NEW YORK WORLD'S FAIR OF 1939-1940

On April 30, 1939, two hundred thousand people clogged the turnstiles on opening day of the New York World's Fair. At a cost of $160 million, a marshy dump in Queens called Flushing Meadows, which writer F. Scott Fitzgerald once described as "a valley of ashes," had been transformed into a sparkling 1,216-acre showplace with the theme "Building the World of Tomorrow." Sixty countries, thirty-three states, and major industries and business companies contributed exhibits and pavilions. The fair's backers optimistically predicted it not only would stimulate the local depression-ravaged economy, but also would demonstrate that hard times could be overcome, that democracy could survive the threats of fascism and communism, and that the alienated individual could be reintegrated into modern society. The 1939 World's Fair thus was a cultural document of American values and aspirations at a crucial crossroads between the Great Depression and World War II.

"This is *your* Fair, built for *you*, and dedicated to *you*," the fair's organizers proclaimed. "Here are the materials, ideas and forces at work in our world. . . . You are the builders; we have done our best to persuade you that these tools will result in a better World of Tomorrow; yours is the choice." After grimly struggling for a decade to overcome the hard times brought on by the Great Depression, many Americans were more than ready to embrace this rosy vision of a future of social harmony,

PLATE 1

Cartoonist James Thurber drew this cover for the April 29, 1939 issue of *The New Yorker* magazine to celebrate the official opening of the World's Fair. The fair had so many exhibits that few visitors could see everything in one day. In fact, the average visitor came to the fair 2.3 times. (The Newberry Library, Chicago)

interdependence, and material prosperity.

The principal symbols of the 1939 World's Fair were two huge structures called the Trylon and the Perisphere. The Trylon, a tall, thin pyramid, and the Perisphere, a globe, dominated the landscape, "a dazzling white reminder of a world that somehow science and technology might achieve" (plate 2). The fair's theme was further carried out by exhibits covering seven major facets of modern life—production and distribution, transportation, communications and business systems, food, medicine and public health, science and education, and community interests. The concepts of social harmony and interdependence were reinforced by the fair's physical layout, which radiated like the spokes of a wheel from the Trylon and the Perisphere. (plate 3).

Not only did the two structures serve as focal points of the fair, but the Perisphere also housed one of the most popular theme exhibits, Democracity, a diorama of a planned community in the year 2039. As created by industrial designer Henry Dreyfuss, Democracity consisted of Centerton (the business and cultural hub), Pleasantvilles (residential suburbs), and Millvilles (light industrial areas) (plate 5, on page 798). Greenbelt tracts provided land for recreation and agriculture, and a system of highways linked the various sections. Visitors took a six-minute trip into the future via two rotating balconies. The tour featured a narration by popular newscaster H. V. Kaltenborn synchronized to music by black composer William Grant Still.

The theme exhibits prepared by the fair's organizers were complemented, indeed often overshadowed, by the plazas and pavilions erected by American business. The fair unabashedly dedicated itself to the promotion and celebration of the world's first mass-consumer-based society. Visitors were viewed as po-

PLATE 2
Joseph Binder's prize-winning poster was widely distributed for publicity and advertising. Its prominent featuring of the Trylon and Perisphere was typical of the World's Fair promotional material, as was its crisply stylized lettering and composition. (The Queens Museum. Gift of Carla Binder)

PLATE 3
This stylized map appeared in *The New Yorker*. It helped visitors find exhibits within the fair's seven thematic zones, such as Government, which included the Court of Peace and Lagoon of Nations (upper left); and Transportation (lower left), which housed the General Motors and Ford exhibits. The amusement section (right) was deliberately separated from the rest of the fair by a wide boulevard. (The Newberry Library, Chicago)

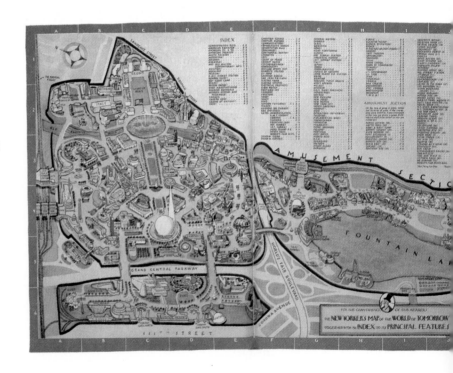

tential customers for the goods and services lavishly displayed by American businesses eager to acquaint consumers with their products. The D. E. Leathers family of Clarendon, Texas, chosen as a "typical American family," received a Ford Super Deluxe Fordor sedan from the Ford Motor Company, and many visitors sported a Heinz pickle pin, one of the souvenirs handed out by the exhibitors. With its emphasis on consumption spread democratically throughout society by a beneficial capitalist system, historian Warren Susman noted, "the Fair became a rather generalized advertisement for something the 1930s had begun to call the American way of life."

The World's Fair offered a stimulating visual experience, especially at night, when light, fire, color, water, and sound created dazzling multi-media displays (plate 7, on page 799). Most of the buildings featured large, blank walls enlivened by colorful murals, sculpture (plate 8, on page 800), and landscaping. Other architectural innovations included "streamlining" (industrial design characterized by rounded contours and smooth surfaces), extensive use of clear plastics such as Lucite and Plexiglas, and fluorescent interior lighting. A final novelty was air conditioning.

The most popular exhibit was the General Motors Futurama, a glimpse of motorized America in 1960. Long lines formed at the entrance of the Futurama, which handled as many as twenty-eight thousand visitors a day. The exhibit simulated a cross-country trip by carrying visitors in moving chairs with individually synchronized commentary throughout the one-third mile tour. The most striking aspect of the scale model was the extensive arterial highway system, where seven-lane superhighways enabled mo-

PLATE 4

The World's Fair featured spectacular "sound and light" shows every night. This view, which looks from the Court of Peace to the Theme Center, shows the vibrancy of the night illumination in a way that resembles the photographs of earth sent by the Apollo spacecraft three decades later. The statue is of George Washington, the 150th anniversary of whose inauguration the fair was also dedicated to commemorate. (Alex Siodmak)

PLATE 5

The Democracity diorama was contained in the Perisphere at the fair's Theme Center. To enter, visitors stepped on an escalator that took them up to one of two balconies revolving in opposite directions. Once the six-minute rotation was complete, visitors exited by way of the Helicline, a 950-foot spiral ramp that encircled the Trylon and Perisphere. (Richard Wurts. Museum of the City of New York)

PLATE 6

The focal point of the Ford exhibit was "The Road of Tomorrow," a spiral, three-tiered ramp on which new model cars circled for more than half a mile over the building and through its Garden Court. The Ford Motor Company frequently used pictures of its World's Fair pavilion in its national advertising (this one ran in *The New Yorker*) as a way of stimulating consumer interest in Ford products. (The Newberry Library, Chicago)

torists to drive at speeds up to a hundred miles an hour through city and countryside alike. This glorification of the private automobile was hardly surprising in an exhibit funded by a major car company. At the end of the tour, visitors exited into an intersection that was an exact replica of the Futurama's final stop. No wonder consumers began to believe that the future was now.

Another popular exhibit was the Westinghouse time capsule (plate 9, on page 801), a container more than seven feet long. Officials of the fair filled it with such items as a Mickey Mouse cup, newsreel footage of Jesse Owens's victory in the hundred-yard dash at the 1936 Olympics in Berlin, a copy of Margaret Mitchell's epic novel *Gone With the Wind*, and the 1938 Sears, Roebuck catalog.

Fair visitors sampled a wide range of exhibits promoting the latest in technological innovations for the home and workplace. The Westinghouse exhibit featured a seven-foot robot named Elektro, and General Electric offered a kitchen with talking appliances. The Consolidated Edison exhibit showed a totally electrified diorama of metropolitan New York, complete with streetlights, moving subways, and busy factories (plate 10). RCA showcased live television transmissions from the fair, the first demonstration of TV's potential for mass communication and entertainment. Every day, American Telephone and Telegraph let 150 persons make a free long-distance phone call (then still something of a novelty) to anywhere in the country while the rest of the crowd listened in.

The amusement zone of the fair offered more traditional entertainment, such as the 250-foot-high parachute jump sponsored by Life Savers. Another popular attraction was Billy Rose's Aqua-

PLATE 7
Gallup pollsters found that the USSR Pavilion was the best liked of the foreign exhibits. With its 79-foot stainless steel figure of a worker with a red star (irreverently nicknamed "Big Joe" or "the Bronx Express Straphanger"), the Soviet Pavilion was the second tallest structure at the fair after the Trylon. (Courtesy Peter M. Warner)

cade, which featured Buster Crabbe, (who played Flash Gordon in the movies), Olympic gold medalists Johnny Weissmuller and Eleanor Holm, and other Hollywood stars performing in a ten-thousand-seat aquatic amphitheater.

Twenty-six million Americans visited the New York World's Fair in 1939, but attendance fell far short of its backers' projections. Many people stayed away because of the seventy-five-cent general admission fee (twenty-five cents for children under fourteen), which was a lot of money at a time when a subway ride in New York cost only a nickel. The Futurama and many of the other most popular exhibits charged an additional admission fee. A family could expect to spend about fourteen dollars for admissions, food, and souvenirs on a day-long trip to the fair. Such entertainment was simply too extravagant for many Americans still struggling to recover from hard times.

In an attempt to recoup its financial losses, the World's Fair was extended for the 1940 season. Reflecting the worsening international situation, the 1940 fair took a more sober theme: "For Peace and Freedom." Attendance rose after the admission fee was dropped to fifty cents (see plate 11, on page 802), but the 1939–1940 fair ended with a $19-million deficit. The fair's temporary structures were razed, and the Trylon and Perisphere were melted down for scrap metal as part of the country's defense mobilization for World War II. The Flushing Meadows site languished until it hosted the 1964–1965 New York World's Fair. By then, the technological progress and material prosperity of postwar America had made even the most futuristic predictions of the 1939 World's Fair looked tame indeed.

PLATE 8
Augusta Savage's sculpture "The Harp" depicts a choir supported by the arm of God. The figure in front holds the opening bars of James Weldon Johnson's "Lift Every Voice and Sing," often referred to as the black national anthem. Savage was the only black artist to receive a commission from the fair's organizers. (Richard Wurts. Museum of the City of New York)

PLATE 9

The Westinghouse Corporation buried this sleek,
futuristic, streamlined time capsule at the Flushing
Meadows site with instructions not to open it for five
thousand years. The capsule included newsreel footage of
such events as veterans at the 75th anniversary of
Gettysburg and Howard Hughes's record-breaking
round-the-world flight in 1938, along with detailed
instructions on how to build a movie projector.
(Westinghouse Historical Collection)

PLATE 10

Commonwealth Edison's "City of Light" diorama filled
an entire city block. In just twelve minutes, an entire city
day passed before the spectators, including a spectacular
thunderstorm that caused the lights in the city to flick on
in response to the darkened skies. Some of the diorama's
model structures, such as the Empire State Building
pictured above, were as tall as three stories. (Walter
Dorwin Teague Associates)

PLATE 11
The National Cash Register building
totalled daily attendance at the fair.
Deeming it too blatant in its
commercialism, fair organizers
banished the cash register to the
Amusement Zone, where it stood
next to the parachute jump ride.
(Alex Siodmak)

PLATE 12
Professional photographer Alex Siodmak poses with
his camera in front of the Helicline. Who knows
how many family scrapbooks are filled with aging
Kodak snapshots of the 1939 World's Fair, legacies
of amateur photographers who attempted to record
what the fair meant to them. (Alex Siodmak)

26

THE WORLD
AT WAR

*W*orld War II ranks with the New Deal as a crucial period of political and economic change. Mobilization pumped money and confidence into the economy, ending the Great Depression. Most Americans at last had money in their pockets. Due to wartime shortages, however, they had little to spend it on. The result was a pent-up demand for a variety of goods and services that extended the wartime prosperity into the postwar period. Despite widespread fears, the depression did not return.

The task of fighting a global war accelerated the growing influence of the federal government on all aspects of American life, one of the themes that has defined the modern era. World War II hastened the concentration of power in the presidency and extended federal intervention in the regulation and management of economic life. Mobilization of the country's vast industrial resources demanded cooperation between top-level business executives and political leaders in Washington. Their joint action solidified the partnership that had been growing since World War I.

Fighting a world war also caused dramatic social changes on the home front. The labor move-ment, fresh from its victories in the late 1930s, strengthened its position. Geographic mobility increased as families followed loved ones entering the armed services or took jobs in defense industries. The war opened new opportunities for women, the "Rosie the Riveters" who filled men's jobs in war plants and other factories. Blacks used the war against Nazi racism as a weapon to challenge notions of white supremacy and discrimination in the United States. They sowed the seeds of the civil rights movement of the 1950s and 1960s.

Perhaps the most far-reaching effect of World War II was America's break with its traditional isolation from international affairs. After the war, the United States accepted a leading role in world diplomacy and a permanent peacetime military establishment. Henry Luce, the publisher of *Life* magazine, confidently predicted the beginning of the "American century" when the war was over. In 1945, the United States stood alone as the only major power to come out of the war physically unscathed and in possession of the secret of the atomic bomb. Those two factors gave force to the predictions of world supremacy.

WARTIME PROSPERITY
War mobilization brought prosperity to many American households. This photograph, taken in 1942, shows the Hall family of Sheffield, Alabama, at ease in their home, part of a defense housing project connected with the TVA. Although the picture's cheerfulness may have been posed, it reflects the new levels of comfort prosperity brought. (Library of Congress)

Internationalism Replaces Isolationism

International developments during the 1930s threatened the fragile world peace that had prevailed since the end of World War I. Fascism took control in Germany and strengthened its hold in Italy, while Japanese militarism grew in the Far East. The League of Nations, set up by the Versailles treaty to resolve potential disputes, proved too weak to deal with those threats to peace. The United States, which had never ratified the treaty or joined the League, followed its own isolationist course. By 1939, however, President Franklin D. Roosevelt was leading the nation toward war.

Depression Diplomacy

Fighting the Great Depression took top priority during Roosevelt's first term, but the president remained deeply interested in foreign affairs. Franklin Roosevelt was an internationalist. He wanted the United States to play a prominent role in a system of worldwide economic and political interdependence that would foster the long-term prosperity necessary for a lasting peace. Conditions in the early 1930s did not encourage such a policy. Only when the United States regained a stable economy at home could it be an effective leader abroad.

In dealing with the international economy, Roosevelt put national interests first. At an economic conference in London in 1933, his message that the United States would not participate in world plans to stabilize currency killed any hope of common action. The president was announcing to the world that he wanted to promote domestic recovery—in this case, keeping control over the value of the dollar—even at the expense of international cooperation.

Political involvement in international affairs remained limited in the early New Deal. One of Roosevelt's few initiatives was formal recognition of the Soviet Union. Mutual distrust had prevailed since the Bolshevik Revolution of 1917 and the U.S. intervention in 1918 and 1919, and the two countries had never formalized diplomatic relations. The lure of trade with the Soviets led to recognition in November 1933.

In general, Roosevelt steered clear of Europe

and Asia during the 1930s and worked to consolidate American influence in the Western Hemisphere. His diplomatic strategy, which combined both political and economic goals, became known as the Good Neighbor Policy. Under the Reciprocal Trade Agreements Act of 1934, the president was empowered to raise or lower tariffs, without congressional approval, in return for reciprocal concessions from other nations. Secretary of State Cordell Hull negotiated a series of agreements, mainly with European and Latin-American countries where the United States already played the leading role in trade. The volume of trade with nations of the Western Hemisphere rose 100 percent in the 1930s.

As a corollary to economic expansion, the United States also voluntarily renounced the use of military force and armed intervention in the Western Hemisphere. At the Pan-American Conference in Montevideo, Uruguay, in December 1933, Hull proclaimed that "No state has the right to intervene in the internal or external affairs of another." The U.S. Congress agreed in 1934 to repeal the Platt Amendment, a relic of the Spanish-American war that had asserted the right of the United States to intervene in Cuba's internal affairs.

During the first two years of the Roosevelt administration, relatively few citizens were concerned about foreign affairs despite the significant international events taking place. In 1933, Adolf Hitler became chancellor of Germany, and the *Reichstag* (legislature) soon gave him dictatorial powers. Hitler took the title of *Fuhrer* (leader) and outlawed all political parties except his own National Socialists, also called Nazis. They were fiercely anti-semitic. The 1935 Nuremberg laws deprived Jews of all citizenship rights and forbade intermarriage between Jews and Gentiles. Hitler announced that he planned to rearm Germany, a violation of the Versailles treaty, and he withdrew German membership in the League of Nations. A Nazi slogan declared ominously, "Today Germany, tomorrow the world."

In the United States, Hitler's rise to power produced no widespread call for collective security or joint international action. On the contrary, it encouraged a dramatic rise in the isolationist sentiment. Reflecting a long-standing determination to stay clear of dangerous foreign entanglements, most American political leaders sought to strengthen democracy at home rather than commit U.S. resources abroad.

In 1934 and 1935, Senator Gerald P. Nye, a North Dakota Republican, conducted a congressional investigation that revived disillusionment with American participation in World War I. Nye initially looked into the profits of munitions makers during World War I. He widened the investigation to examine the influence of economic interests on America's decision to join the war effort in 1917. Nye's committee concluded that profiteers, whom they called "merchants of death," had maneuvered the United States into the war to save their investments.

Most of the Nye committee's charges were dubious, but they added momentum to the growing isolationist movement. In late 1934, President Roosevelt revived a proposal supported by the Republican administrations of Calvin Coolidge and Herbert Hoover for the United States to join the World Court. This proposal amounted to a mild internationalist gesture that had greater symbolic than actual importance. In January 1935, reflecting the rising isolationist sentiment, Congress rejected participation in the World Court.

The Neutrality Act of 1935 had a greater impact. This law was explicitly designed to prevent a recurrence of the events that had pulled the United States into World War I by, in effect, abandoning the country's rights as a neutral nation under international law. The Neutrality Act imposed an embargo on arms trade with countries at war, and declared that American citizens could travel on belligerent ships only at their own risk. Congress expanded the Neutrality Act in 1936 to include loans to belligerents and, in 1937, made it even stricter by adopting a "cash and carry" provision. If a country at war wanted to purchase nonmilitary goods from the United States, it had to pay cash and pick up the supplies in its own ships. Congress intended this restriction to prevent American trading ships from being the targets of attack. Roosevelt did not like the legislation, which gave him no discretion to decide whether some belligerents, such as the Spanish Loyalists, deserved American military support. Because of the rising tide of isolationism, however, he had no choice but to accept the verdict of Congress.

The Storm Clouds Gather

In 1936, Hitler and Mussolini joined forces in the Rome-Berlin Axis, a political and military alliance. That same year, German troops occupied the Rhineland, again violating the Versailles treaty. The Nazis also increased their persecution of Jews. In 1938, Hitler sent his troops into Austria and proclaimed an *Anschluss* (union) between Germany and Austria.

France and Great Britain, as they had been doing since Hitler started on his road of conquest, hoped he would go no further. But the German dictator was already aiming to seize part of Czechoslovakia, the strategic keystone of Europe. War seemed imminent because Czechoslovakia had a firm alliance with France. At the Munich Conference in September 1938, Prime Minister Neville Chamberlain of Britain and Prime Minister Edward Daladier of France capitulated to Hitler. They agreed to let Germany annex the Sudetenland, the German-speaking section of Czechoslovakia, in return for Hitler's pledge that he would seek no more territory.

Despite Chamberlain's announcement that the Munich agreement guaranteed "peace in our time," Hitler overran the rest of Czechoslovakia within six months and threatened to march into Poland. Britain and France realized the folly of their policy of appeasement and prepared to take a stand over Poland. Hitler, meanwhile, had signed his nonaggression pact with the Soviet Union, protecting Germany from having to wage war on two fronts. He attacked Poland on September 1, 1939, and Britain and France declared war on Germany two days later. World War II had begun.

For more than two years after war broke out in Europe, the United States debated its course of action. Most Americans held two contradictory positions. The overwhelming majority supported the Allies. A 1939 poll showed 84 percent wanted an Allied victory, 2 percent supported the Nazis, and 14 percent had no opinion. On the other hand, most Americans also did not want to be drawn into another European war. This strong isolationist sentiment severely limited President Roosevelt's options.

As early as 1936, Roosevelt had foreseen the possibility of U.S. participation in another European war, but he had determined to stay in line with public opinion. During the 1936 campaign, the president made a stirring antiwar statement: "I have seen war . . . I have seen blood running from the wounded. I have seen men coughing out their gassed lungs . . . . I have seen children starving. I have seen the agony of mothers and wives. I hate war." In October 1937, Roosevelt seemed to take a small step away from isolationism. He spoke against "the present reign of terror and international lawlessness" and called on peace-loving nations to oppose such aggression through a "quarantine."

Roosevelt's 1937 statement reflected rhetorical opposition to militarism more than a specific call for collective security. Domestic affairs, including the prevailing isolationism, made it impossible for him to risk a foreign policy confrontation at the beginning of his second term. A Gallup poll at this time showed that two-thirds of the American people believed the United States had made a mistake in entering World War I.

By 1939, Roosevelt had embarked on what *Time* magazine later called his "thousand-step road to war." After hostilities broke out, he made no secret of his sympathies. "This nation will remain a neutral nation," he stated, "but I cannot ask that every American remain neutral in thought as well." The president wanted to supply the Allies with military supplies, an action forbidden by the Neutrality Act's embargo on the sale of arms to warring nations. After a bitter battle in Congress, he won a slight modification of the neutrality laws. The Allies now could buy weapons from the United States, but only on a "cash and carry" basis.

A false calm settled over Europe after the German conquest of Poland in September 1939. This "phony war" lulled many Americans into thinking that their arms supply policy would be enough to defeat Germany in a war of attrition. Hitler soon shattered that complacency. On April 9, 1940, Nazi *Panzer* forces (armored troops) overran Denmark in a few hours. Norway fell to the Nazi *blitzkrieg* (lightning war) soon after, followed by Holland and Belgium. Next, the Germans stormed into France, bypassing the fixed defenses of the Maginot line and quickly defeating the massed English and French troops. By June 1940, only England stood between the United States and Hitler's plans for world domination.

Toward War

In the midst of the Nazi blitzkrieg, the United States prepared for the 1940 election. Would Roosevelt seek an unprecedented third term? He had not designated a successor as head of the Democratic party, and the situation in Europe in the spring of 1940 convinced him to run again. He submitted to a "draft" at the Democratic National Convention. Although the delegates acclaimed Roosevelt's renomination, they balked at his choice of Secretary of Agriculture Henry A. Wallace for vice-president to replace John Nance Garner of Texas, a conservative who had long since broken with the New Deal. The nomination of the liberal Wallace went through only after Eleanor Roosevelt flew to the convention in Chicago and asked the delegates to put politics aside in a national crisis.

The Republicans nominated a political newcomer, Wendell Willkie of Indiana, president of the Commonwealth and Southern Electric Utilities Company. Willkie, a former Democrat, supported many of the New Deal's domestic and international policies and tried to portray himself as a man of the people. This strategy led crusty Secretary of the Interior Harold Ickes to call him "a simple barefoot Wall Street lawyer." The platforms of the two parties differed only slightly. Both pledged aid to the Allies but stopped short of calling for American participation in the war.

Roosevelt may have clinched his election victory when he declared on October 30, 1940, "I have said this before, but I shall say it again and again and again: Your boys are not going to be sent into any foreign wars." Willkie's spirited campaign resulted in an election closer than the ones in 1932 or 1936. But Roosevelt still received 55 percent of the popular vote and won a lopsided victory in the electoral college.

The debate about America's stance toward the European war continued. Journalist William Allen White and the influential Committee to Defend America by Aiding the Allies led the interventionist side. In 1940, such isolationists as Charles Lindbergh, Senator Gerald Nye, and former NRA administrator Hugh Johnson formed the America First Committee, which agitated to keep the nation out of the war. The *Chicago Tribune*, the Hearst newspapers, and other conservative publications gave full support to the isolationist cause, especially in the Midwest.

Despite the efforts of the America First Committee, the United States moved closer to involvement in 1940 and 1941. The number of Americans who believed that a German victory would threaten national security increased from 43 percent in March 1940 to 69 percent after the fall of France. In June 1940, Roosevelt brought two prominent Republicans, Henry Stimson and Frank Knox, into his cabinet as secretary of war and of the navy, respectively, to give a bipartisan character to the war preparations.

During the summer of 1940, the president traded fifty old destroyers to Great Britain for the right to build military bases on British possessions in the Atlantic. This trade circumvented the 1939 neutrality legislation. Roosevelt also began putting the American economy and government on a defense footing by creating the National Defense Advisory Commission and the Council of National Defense in May 1940. In October of that year, Congress instituted the first peacetime draft registration and conscription in American history. When the draft law came up for extension in 1941, it passed by a single vote.

The United States virtually entered the war when Congress passed the Lend-Lease Act in March 1941. This legislation enabled the nation to serve, in Roosevelt's words, as the "arsenal of democracy." Great Britain, already at war for eighteen months and under nightly bombing attacks from the German air force, could no longer afford to pay cash for supplies. Roosevelt decided to "get away from the dollar sign." In a fireside chat to build support for Lend-Lease, Roosevelt used the analogy of lending a neighbor a garden hose to put out a fire: "I don't say to him, . . . 'Neighbor, my garden hose cost me fifteen dollars; you have to pay me fifteen dollars for it.' . . . I don't want fifteen dollars—I want my garden hose back after the fire is over." Under the Lend-Lease Act, the president was empowered to "lease, lend, or otherwise dispose of" arms and other equipment to any country whose defense was vital to the security of the United States.

As in World War I, supplying the Allies brought German attacks on American and Allied ships. By September 1941, Nazi submarines and American vessels were fighting an undeclared naval war in the Atlantic. In October, Congress

PEARL HARBOR
The USS *Shaw* roils in flames and smoke after receiving a direct hit during the Japanese attack on
Pearl Harbor on December 7, 1941. It was early Sunday morning in Hawaii and many American
servicemen were still asleep. More than twenty-four hundred Americans were killed. The Japanese
suffered only light losses. (FPG)

authorized the arming of merchant vessels. Roosevelt still hesitated to ask for a declaration of war against Germany without an actual enemy attack.

The final provocation came from Japan, not Germany. Conflict between Japan and the United States had been building throughout the 1930s. Japanese military advances, including the conquest of Manchuria in 1931 and the occupation of northern China in 1937, upset the balance of political and economic power in the Far East. The United States had long enjoyed the economic benefits of the Open Door trade policy, but Japan now controlled the region's rich raw materials and large markets. Nevertheless, the U.S. government avoided taking a strong stand, even when provoked. The Japanese sank an American gunboat, the *Panay*, in the Yangtze River near Nanking in 1937. The United States allowed Japan to apologize for the incident and pay more than $2 million in damages, and it was quickly forgotten.

Japanese intentions soon became more expansive. In 1940, Japan signed a diplomatic pact with Germany and Italy. In response, Roosevelt imposed an embargo on shipments of scrap metal to Japan. By the fall of 1941, after Japanese troops occupied French Indochina, the United States had effectively cut off trade with Japan, including vital oil shipments. Before its supplies ran down, Japan would either have to decide for war or accept American demands that it cease its expansionist activities in east Asia.

In September 1941, the government of Prime Minister Hideki Tojo began secret preparations for war. By November, American military intelligence had learned that Japan was planning an attack, but the United States did not know where it would come. Military strategists assumed that the Japanese would attack British Malaya, the American-controlled Philippines, or Thailand. In fact, Japan had selected the United States naval base at Pearl Harbor in Hawaii as the target. Early on Sunday morning, December 7, 1941, Japanese bombers attacked Pearl Harbor, killing more than twenty-four hundred Americans. Eight battleships, three cruisers, and three destroyers—practically the entire Pacific fleet—and almost two hundred airplanes were destroyed or heavily damaged.

President Roosevelt went before Congress the next day and, calling December 7 "a date that will live in infamy," asked for a declaration of war against Japan. The Senate unanimously voted for war, and the House concurred by a vote of 388 to 1. The lone dissenter was Jeannette Rankin of Montana, who had also opposed American entry into World War I. Three days later, Germany and Italy declared war on the United States, and the United States in turn declared war on them.

Mobilizing for Victory

Pearl Harbor Day is etched in the memories of several generations of Americans who remember precisely what they were doing when they heard about the Japanese attack. Many felt relief that the period of indecision and waiting had finally ended.

Coordinating the massive shift from civilian to war production, and assembling the necessary work force, taxed the powers of the government agencies set up to do the job. As in World War I, the nation confronted a number of fundamental questions. For example, how much power should the federal government wield over the economy? What benefits should go to workers as opposed to industrialists? What role should politics play in the conduct of the war?

Defense Mobilization

Defense mobilization not only ended the Great Depression, but it caused the economy to more than double during World War II. In 1940, the gross national product stood at $99.7 billion; it reached $211 billion by 1945. After-tax profits of American business companies rose from $6.4 billion in 1940 to $10.8 billion in 1944. In addition, agricultural output increased by one third.

During the war, the federal government spent $186 billion on war production, sometimes as much as $250 million a day. The peak of mobilization occurred in late 1943, when two-thirds of the economy was directly involved in the war effort, as opposed to only one quarter in World War I. The aircraft industry, whose 46,638 workers had produced 5,865 planes in 1939, peaked in 1944 with more than 2.1 million employed and 96,369 planes produced. By 1945, a total of 86,000 tanks, 296,000 airplanes, 15 million rifles and machine guns, 40 billion bullets, 4 million tons of artillery shells, 64,000 landing craft, and 6,500 naval ships had been produced. Mobilization on this gigantic scale energized the economy after years of depression.

The federal bureaucracy also expanded dramatically, growing far more than it had during the eight years of the New Deal. The number of government civilian employees increased from a million to 3.8 million. At the height of wartime hiring, the government gave the civil service exam two or three times daily. The federal budget rose from $9.4 billion in 1939 to $95.2 billion in 1945. The national debt grew sixfold, topping out at $258.6 billion in 1945.

Taxes paid about half the cost of the war, compared with 30 percent in World War I. The Revenue Act of 1942, which President Roosevelt called the "greatest tax bill in American history," set the foundation for the modern tax structure. This law increased corporate income taxes to a maximum of 40 percent and set a flat rate of 90 percent on excess profits. It also expanded the number of people who had to file a return from thirteen million in 1941 to fifty million in 1942. The system of payroll deductions and tax withholding started in 1943. Bond drives and war loans, in which people put their savings at the disposal of the government through the purchase of long-term Treasury bonds, financed the remaining cost of the war. In addition to encouraging patriotism, war bonds withdrew money from circulation and thus helped hold down inflation.

As Woodrow Wilson had done during World War I, Roosevelt turned to business leaders to run the war economy. Defense preparations had been underway since 1940; before Pearl Harbor, 25 percent of the economy was already devoted to war production. In January 1941, Roosevelt established the Office of Production Management under William Knudsen, the president of General Motors. After Pearl Harbor, Roosevelt disbanded that agency and replaced it with the more powerful and comprehensive War Production Board (WPB). Donald Nelson, a former executive of Sears, Roebuck and Company, headed the WPB.

The War Production Board awarded defense contracts, evaluated military and civilian requests for scarce resources, and oversaw the conversion of industries to military production. Many business leaders, with the depression still on their minds, hesitated to invest heavily in plant expansion or new production. Therefore, the government granted generous tax write-offs for plant construction, approved contracts with cost-plus provisions that guaranteed profits, and promised that industries could keep the plants after the war. As Secretary of War Henry Stimson said, "If you . . . go to war . . . in a capitalist country, you have to let business make money out of the process or business won't work."

In the interest of efficiency and production, the WPB found it easier to deal with major corporations than with small businesses. The fifty-six largest corporations received about three-fourths of the war contracts, and the top ten obtained a third. This allocation system, along with the suspension of antitrust prosecution during the war, hastened the concentration of business in large corporate structures. In 1940, the largest hundred companies manufactured 30 percent of the nation's industrial output. Their share grew to 70 percent by the end of the war.

However, Roosevelt remained unsatisfied with the overall mobilization performance. Nelson and the WPB had allowed the armed forces too much control over priorities. There were too many government agencies, often with overlapping jurisdictions and mandates. In late 1942, Roosevelt persuaded Justice James F. Byrnes to resign from the Supreme Court and head the Office of Economic Stabilization and, after 1943, the Office of War Mobilization. Byrnes soon became the second most important person in the administration and finally brought order to production goals for civilian and military needs.

The results were remarkable. Shipbuilding showed the strength of American productive capacity. By 1941, the German navy had sunk about 12 million tons of Allied, mainly United States, shipping in the North Atlantic, crippling transatlantic transport. The speedy production of new transport vessels called Liberty ships became a high priority. An experienced sailor, Roosevelt called these easy-to-build but hardly graceful ships "ugly ducklings." Ugly or not, the United States produced 19 million tons of merchant shipping by 1943, up from a million tons just two years earlier.

The achievements of Henry J. Kaiser, a West Coast shipbuilder, typified the shipyard produc-

tion miracles. In less than a year, by using the mass production techniques of the automobile industry, Kaiser cut the time needed to build a transport ship from three hundred days to seventeen. He motivated workers through high pay and attractive fringe benefits, including one of the country's first prepaid medical programs.

Kaiser's name became synonymous with getting things done fast. Although not all industries could boast such relative freedom from snafus (an acronym coined during the war from the expression *situation normal, all fouled up*), business and government compiled an impressive record. As in World War I, American industrial might contributed significantly to the military victory.

Labor and the War Effort

A huge hole opened in the American work force when more than thirteen million men entered military service. The backlog of depression-era unemployment quickly disappeared, and the United States faced the reverse problem, a critical labor shortage. About seven million new workers took jobs in the nation's defense industries. They included great numbers of women and blacks who found employment opportunities for the first time. Many of these wartime gains did not last, however. The upward occupational mobility of women and blacks in defense industries evaporated when the veterans came home. And organized labor faced increasing public hostility to its demands for a larger role in industrial life.

Government planners "discovered" the nation's women while casting about for workers to fill the jobs vacated by departing servicemen. The recruiting campaign stressed patriotism. One poster urged, "Longing won't bring him back sooner . . . GET A WAR JOB!" Another showed a woman announcing, "I'm proud . . . my husband *wants* me to do my part." To supplement the emotional appeal of getting loved ones back sooner, government recruiters stressed how easy war work would be for women: "Millions of women find war work pleasant and as easy as running a sewing machine, or using a vacuum cleaner." Women would take to riveting machines and drill presses "as easily as to electric cake-mixers and vacuum

"ROSIE THE RIVETER"
War mobilization created an ideological climate supporting larger roles for women in the workplace. Between 1940 and 1945, the female labor force grew by more than 50 percent. Yet many female defense workers, probably including the riveter shown here, lost their jobs when the war ended. (Library of Congress)

cleaners." The artist Norman Rockwell created a popular image of these patriotic women with his "Rosie the Riveter" cover for the *Saturday Evening Post.*

The government directed its propaganda campaign at housewives, and about six million women responded by taking jobs for the first time. In addition, women who already had employment gladly abandoned low-paying "women's" jobs, such as domestic service and clerical work, for higher-paying work in defense factories. Female riveters, welders, blast furnace cleaners, and drill press operators suddenly filled the nation's factories. Women made up 36 percent of the labor force in 1945, compared with 24 percent at the beginning of the war. An overwhelming majority said they wanted to keep their jobs when the war ended.

However, government planners regarded women's war work as temporary; women were just filling in while the men were away. For this reason, employers offered such benefits as day care for children and flexible hours on a limited basis only. Because women maintained responsibility for home care as well as their defense jobs, they had a higher absentee rate than men did.

Often, the only way to get shopping done or take a child to the doctor was to skip work. Women war workers also faced discrimination on the job. In shipyards, women with the most seniority and responsibility earned $6.95 a day, while the top men made as much as $22.

When the servicemen came home and the war plants returned to peacetime operations, men soon displaced the Rosie the Riveters. Many women, however, refused to put on aprons and go back home. Women's participation in the labor force dropped temporarily following the war, but then it rebounded steadily for the rest of the 1940s. After being fired from defense plants, women simply took a cut in pay and returned to the jobs they had traditionally held in restaurants, telephone exchanges, laundries, offices, and domestic service. By 1950, 29.1 percent of the nation's adult women belonged to the labor force, far higher than prewar levels.

Organized labor also seized wartime opportunities made available by the need for skilled workers in the mobilization effort. No dramatic labor changes occurred, but the war confirmed that the industrial breakthroughs of the 1930s had become permanent. By the end of the war, almost fifteen million workers, a third of the nonagricultural labor force, belonged to unions.

Organized labor began the war with a rush of patriotic unity. On December 23, 1941, representatives of major unions made a "no strike" pledge for the duration of the war. This pledge was not binding, however. To maintain industrial peace, in January 1942 President Roosevelt set up the National War Labor Board (NWLB), composed of representatives of labor, management, and the public. The board established wages, hours, and working conditions and had the authority to order government seizure of plants that did not comply. The government took control of forty plants during the war.

The NWLB handled 17,650 disputes affecting twelve million workers. It faced two controversial issues, union membership and wage increases. Union organizers favored either the union shop or the closed shop, but management preferred the open shop. (In a union shop, the employees must belong to a certain union or join it within a specified period. In a closed shop, the employer may hire only members of a union. An open shop employs both union and nonunion workers.) As a compromise, the NWLB imposed

THE SHIPYARD DIARY OF A WOMAN WELDER

Back to work and more welding. I "dis-improved" as rapidly after lunch as I had improved during the morning. One girl stopped to ask, "How you doin'?" and watched me critically. "Here, let me show you, you're holding it too far away." So she took over, but she couldn't maintain the arc at all. She got up disgusted, said, "I can't do it—my hand shakes so since I been sick," and I took over again. But she was right. I held it closer and welded on and on and on. . . .

We were called to another safety lecture—good sound advice on Eye Safety. . . . Only Chile has a higher accident rate than the United States. Last year the shipyard had fairly heavy absenteeism, but this year they hope to build an extra ship on the decrease in absenteeism. He cautioned us about creating hazards by wearing the wrong kind of clothing, and told us not to wear watches or rings. After it was over, Missouri was bothered about her wedding ring. It hadn't been off in fourteen years. She was willing to take it off, but only if necessary.

The lecturer brought up the rumor that arc welding causes sterility among women. He said that this was untrue, and quoted an authoritative source to prove its falsity. . . . Actually, welders had *more* children than other people. "No, thanks," said the first girl; "I don't like that either!" . . .

I, who hate heights, climbed stair after stair after stair till I thought I must be close to the sun. I stopped on the top deck. I, who hate confined spaces, went through narrow corridors, stumbling my way over rubber-coated leads—dozens of them, scores of them, even hundreds of them. I went into a room about four feet by ten where two shipfitters, a shipfitter's helper, a chipper, and I all worked. I welded in the poop deck lying on the floor while another welder spattered sparks from the ceiling and chippers like giant woodpeckers shattered our eardrums. I, who've taken welding, and have sat at a bench welding flat and vertical plates, was told to weld braces along a baseboard below a door opening. On these a heavy steel door was braced while it was hung to a fine degree of accuracy. I welded more braces along the side, and along the top. I did overhead welding, horizontal, flat, vertical. I welded around curved hinges which were placed so close to the side wall that I had to bend my rod in a curve to get it in. I made some good welds and some frightful ones. But now a door in the poop deck of an oil tanker is hanging, four feet by six of solid steel, by *my* welds. Pretty exciting!

Source: Augusta Clawson, *Shipyard Diary of a Woman Welder*. New York: Penguin, 1944, quoted in Rosalyn Baxandall, Linda Gordon, and Susan Reverby, eds., *America's Working Women: A Documentary History, 1600 to the Present*. New York: Random House, 1976. 288–289.

---

the principle of maintenance of membership. Workers did not have to join a union, but those already in a union had to maintain their membership during the life of the contract.

Pressure for wage increases caused a more serious disagreement. In contrast to the deflation that characterized the depression, inflation pushed prices up throughout the war. Because management wanted to keep production (and profits) running smoothly, it expressed willingness to pay the higher wages demanded by workers. Such raises, however, would have conflicted with the public policy of keeping inflation as low as possible. In 1942, the NWLB established the "Little Steel Formula," which granted a 15 percent wage increase to match a similar increase in the cost of living since January 1, 1941. Although the NWLB froze hourly wages in principle, it allowed them to rise another 24 percent by 1945. Actually, incomes rose as much as 70 percent because workers earned overtime pay, which was not covered by wage ceilings. The tremendous increase in worker output during World War II resulted largely from working overtime.

Despite higher wages than anyone had dreamed possible during the depression, many union members felt cheated as they watched corporate profits soar while their wages remained frozen. The high point of dissatisfaction came in 1943. A nationwide railroad strike was narrowly averted. But then John L. Lewis led more than half a million United Mine Workers out on strike to demand higher wages than the Little Steel Formula allowed. Lewis won concessions, but he alienated Congress and became one of the most disliked public figures of the 1940s for defying the government.

Congress countered Lewis's activism by passing the Smith-Connally Labor Act of 1943, which required a thirty-day cooling-off period before a strike and prohibited strikes in defense industries entirely. Nevertheless, about fifteen thousand strikes occurred during the war. This number represented less than a tenth of 1 percent of working hours, but the public perceived the disruptions as far larger. Unionized labor won acceptance during the war years but also faced increasing hostility from other social groups.

Politics in Wartime

At a press conference late in 1943, President Roosevelt playfully announced that "Dr. Win the War" had replaced "Dr. New Deal." The reform agenda of the New Deal had been dormant since 1938. During the 1940s, Roosevelt rarely pressed for further social and economic change, thus placating conservative members of Congress whose support he needed to conduct the war in a bipartisan spirit. With little argument, he agreed to drop several popular New Deal programs. In 1943, the National Youth Administration, the Works Progress Administration, and the Civilian Conservation Corps were dismantled. Severe budget cuts crippled the Farm Security Administration, which had represented the interests of poor farmers. The rapidity with which the government terminated these agencies suggests that they had been a response to the crisis of the depression rather than a commitment to expanding federal programs to promote the general welfare. Such programs as Social Security remained untouched, however.

The war years brought a significant decline in the reform spirit that had flourished in Washington during the 1930s. Unlike World War I, few public figures talked about using the war to bring about social change. Business leaders replaced the reformers and social activists who had staffed New Deal relief agencies in the 1930s. These business executives became known as "dollar-a-year men" because they volunteered for government service while remaining on their corporate payrolls.

Roosevelt had hoped politics could be shelved for the duration of the war, but that proved to be an unreasonable expectation. In the 1942 election, the Republicans picked up seats in both houses of Congress and increased their share of state governorships. These gains reflected the general tendency of the party out of power to improve its position in off-year elections. The Republicans also benefited from a low voter turnout. The decline resulted from dislocations caused by servicemen's going into the armed forces and the difficulty of many voters in meeting residency requirements after moving to new localities.

Roosevelt himself had hardly given up politics for the duration. After concluding that continuation of the war made a fourth term necessary, he went on a mild offensive to attract Democratic voters. In his state of the union address in 1944, the president called for a second Bill of Rights. As the basis of postwar prosperity, he pledged such rights as a job, adequate food and clothing, a decent home, proper medical care, and an education.

The president's sweeping commitment remained largely rhetorical. Congressional support did not exist in 1944 for this vast extension of the welfare state. It was possible, however, to win some of these pledges for a special group of American citizens, the returning veterans. The GI Bill of Rights, passed in 1944, provided education, job training, medical care, pensions, and mortgage loans for men and women who had served in the armed forces during the war.

"I am an old campaigner and I love a good fight," Franklin Roosevelt had said during the 1940 election. He approached the 1944 campaign with the same verve, but the years of the presidency had taken their toll. When Republicans tried to raise the issue of his health, the sixty-two-year-old Roosevelt replied by making several strenuous campaign appearances, including a four-hour, fifty-mile drive in pouring rain through New York City. Concern about presidential succession prompted the Democrats to drop Vice-President Henry Wallace, whose outspoken support for labor, civil rights, and further domestic reform was too extreme for many party leaders. In Wallace's place, they chose Senator Harry S Truman of Missouri. Truman had become known for heading a Senate investigation of government waste and inefficiency in defense contracts during the war.

The Republicans nominated New York Governor Thomas E. Dewey. Dewey, only forty-two years old, had won fame for his fight against organized crime while serving as a U.S. attorney. He accepted the broad outlines of the welfare state and belonged to the internationalist wing of the Republican party. The 1944 election was the closest since 1916. Roosevelt received 53.4 percent of the popular vote. The Democrats lost ground among farmers, but most ethnic groups remained solidly Democratic. Roosevelt got his customary support from the South, augmented by the overwhelming allegiance of servicemen and women, who voted by absentee ballot. His margin of victory came from the cities. In urban areas with more than a hundred thousand people, the president drew 60 percent of the vote.

Roosevelt also received strong support from organized labor. Under the prodding of CIO leaders Sidney Hillman and Philip Murray, labor contributed more than $1.5 million, or about 30 percent of the Democratic party's election funds. The CIO's Political Action Committee conducted door-to-door canvassing drives and voter registration campaigns. This venture into electoral politics reflected a change in labor's priorities to include political action as well as union organizing drives. Organized labor continued to play a significant role in the Democratic party after the war.

The Home Front

In contrast to World War I, there was almost no domestic opposition to the nation's role in World War II. Americans fought for their way of life and for the preservation of democracy against the forces of Nazi and Japanese totalitarianism. People on the home front had a job to do just like the soldiers in uniform. A national mood characterized by unity, determination, and commitment made World War II perhaps America's last truly patriotic war.

At the same time, many Americans remember the war years as much for the return of prosperity as anything else. Not only did unemployment disappear, but per capita income rose from $691 in 1939 to $1,515 in 1945. Despite geograph-

ical dislocations and shortages of various items, about 70 percent of the people on the home front admitted midway in the war that they had personally experienced "no real sacrifices."

"For the Duration"

Although the United States did not suffer the physical devastation that ravaged much of Europe and the Far East, the war affected the lives of those who stayed behind. Families with a loved one anywhere near the front lines wondered every time they saw the Western Union boy on his bicycle whether they might receive the dreaded telegram from the War Department telling them that their son or husband or father would not be coming home. Other Americans put up with far less traumatic experiences. "Don't you know there's a war on?" became the standard reply to almost any request that could not be fulfilled. People calmly accepted the fact that their lives would be different "for the duration."

Many Americans on the home front contributed enthusiastically to the war effort. They took defense jobs, worked on civilian defense committees, performed volunteer work, collected old newspapers and scrap material, donated blood, and served on local rationing or draft boards. All seven war loan drives were over-subscribed. Advertising campaigns displaying the popular "V for Victory" slogan stressed patriotic unity. About twenty million home "victory gardens" produced 40 percent of the vegetables grown in the United States.

Movie attendance soared during the 1940s. Workers on the home front had few other places to spend their first steady income in years. Theaters operated around the clock to accommodate war workers on the swing and night shifts. Many movies featured patriotic themes. In *Since You Went Away* (1943), Claudette Colbert held her family together when her husband went off to war; near the end of the film, she took a job as a welder in a shipyard. In *Casablanca* (1943), Humphrey Bogart and Ingrid Bergman renewed an old love affair against the backdrop of freedom fighters escaping from Nazi persecution in North Africa. At the end, the previously cynical Bogart character joined the fight against fascism.

The war caused much geographical mobility. When men volunteered or were drafted into the

HOME-FRONT PATRIOTISM
The sale of defense bonds and stamps by the government raised money for the war effort and encouraged patriotism. These housewives from the Parent–Teacher Association of Turlock, California, did their part for the U.S. Treasury Department in a booth set up in a local store in 1942. (Library of Congress)

armed services, their families often followed them to their training bases or points of debarkation. The lure of high-paying defense jobs also resulted in migration. About fifteen million Americans changed their residences during the war years, and half of them moved into another state. This movement was not simply an exodus from rural to urban areas, although the pace of urbanization increased. About 5.4 million people left farms, but 2.5 million moved onto them. A million southerners, black and white, went north, but 600,000 migrants moved south. The greatest number of people went west. California, the center of much defense production, gained 1.4 million newcomers.

Migration often strained family cohesion. Harriet Arnow's novel *The Dollmaker* (1954) described a family's wartime uprooting. Gertie Nevels, her husband Clovis, and their children leave eastern Kentucky for Detroit. The family settles in a miserably inadequate housing project filled with other migrants from the rural South.

Clovis gets a job in a defense plant, but his wages barely keep up with the inflated expenses of urban life in wartime. One son flees back home to Kentucky. A daughter, deeply disturbed by the move, distractedly falls beneath the wheels of a train and is killed. Gertie Nevels finds her only solace in woodcarving. But in a final act of desperation, she cuts up the Christ figure she has been whittling so she can make trinkets to sell for money to feed her family.

For most Americans, the dramas of everyday life occurred on a less dramatic scale. The Office of Price Administration and Civilian Supply (OPA) oversaw the home front consumer economy, allocating domestic resources and trying to keep inflation down. By February 1942, retail prices were rising at the rapid rate of 2 percent a month. In April, the OPA froze most prices and rents at their March 1942 level. When loopholes, especially concerning food prices, undermined the effort, Congress passed the Anti-inflation Act, which stabilized wages, prices, and salaries. The Consumer Price Index rose 28.3 percent between 1940 and 1945, but most of the inflation occurred before 1943.

During the war, almost anything that Americans ate, wore, or used was subject to rationing or regulation. Rubber became the first scarce item. The Japanese conquest of Malaya and the Netherlands East Indies cut off 97 percent of America's imports of natural rubber, a serious threat to war production. By late 1944, an entirely new industry devoted to the production of synthetic rubber supplied 762,000 tons a year, most of it for the war effort.

Meanwhile, the government ordered the rationing of tires to conserve rubber, a hard sacrifice for the nation's thirty million drivers. Rubber campaigns recycled such items as old boots, heating bottles, doormats, and tires. Many people put their cars up on blocks for the duration. Bicycle tires were also in short supply. If people walked instead, they risked wearing out their shoes. By 1944, the annual allotment was two pairs per person, barely half the average number purchased before the war.

Gasoline and fuel oil became the next items to be rationed. German attacks on oil tankers crossing the Atlantic from the Middle East had disrupted supplies. Shortages of fuel oil forced schools and restaurants to shorten their hours, and home thermostats to be lowered to 65 degrees. Gasoline rationing, introduced in December 1942, was both a response to depleted gasoline supplies and an attempt to save wear on precious rubber tires. Rationing categories ranged from "nonessential" to "unlimited." An "A" (nonessential) card entitled a motorist to buy four gallons of gasoline a week, the equivalent of about sixty miles of driving. That ration was later cut in half. To discourage additional fuel consumption, Congress imposed a nationwide speed limit of thirty-five miles per hour. Highway death rates dropped dramatically.

People found it harder to cut back on eating than on driving. Many food commodities were in short supply during the war. Sugar quickly disappeared from grocery shelves, and the government soon rationed it at the rate of eight to twelve ounces per person a week. However, the manufacturers of such products as Coca-Cola and Wrigley's chewing gum received unlimited sugar quotas by convincing the government that these items helped the morale of the men and women in the armed forces.

By the midpoint of the war, a complicated system of rationing points and coupons regulated how much meat, butter, and other food Americans could buy. The government limited butter to one pound per person monthly, barely a fourth of the prewar consumption level. The food restrictions resulted in a black market, especially in meat. Most people cooperated with the restrictions, but almost a fourth thought that buying items on the black market was occasionally justified.

Shortages of consumer durables also hit the home front. Following the Great Depression, people finally had enough money to buy refrigerators, cars, and radios. But they found that rubber, copper, steel, and other necessary components had been earmarked for war production. The last Ford rolled off the assembly line in 1942 as automobile plants converted to bomber production. To dampen consumer demands, many companies ran advertisements encouraging delayed gratification. After the war, they told the public, you can buy that new house and fill it with all the appliances that were temporarily unavailable.

But some purchases just could not wait. One of the most highly desired items on the black market was women's stockings. In the 1930s, women had worn silk stockings, but they switched to nylons when the war with Japan cut off imports of silk. Unfortunately, nylon was essential to war production. Thirty-six pairs of nylons equalled one parachute. A besieged hosiery executive jested, "We could figure a way to knit them of grass one day and the next day there would be a priority on grass." Many women began wearing slacks in public, a dramatic fashion change of the 1940s. The strict rationing of food and other items eased in the summer of 1944, when victory appeared on the horizon.

Seeds of Change for Black Americans

"A wind is rising throughout the world of free men everywhere," Eleanor Roosevelt wrote during the war, "and they will not be kept in bondage." This rising wind characterized the experience of black Americans. The war disrupted a number of traditional patterns, both of society in general and of race relations in particular, and many barriers to racial equality tottered or broke down.

The first evidence that the war might encourage greater black activism came in 1941. A. Philip Randolph, head of the Brotherhood of Sleeping Car Porters, a black union, announced a "March on Washington" to protest the exclusion of black workers from defense plants. Of the nation's 100,000 aircraft workers in 1940, only 240 were black, and most of them were janitors. Black leaders demanded that the government require defense contractors to integrate their work forces. Randolph predicted that a hundred thousand black Americans would march in the demonstration at the capital. Roosevelt, though not a strong supporter of civil rights, feared the public embarrassment of such a massive protest. Even more, he feared a disruption of war preparations. The president agreed to meet many of Randolph's demands, and the union leader cancelled the march.

The compromise between Randolph and Roosevelt involved the issuance of an executive order. The government declared it to be the policy of the United States "that there shall be no discrimination in the employment of workers in defense industries or government because of race, creed, color, or national origin." The president established the Fair Employment Practices Committee (FEPC) in the Office of Production Management to enforce that policy.

This federal commitment to guaranteeing black employment rights was unprecedented but still limited in scope. It did not, for example, affect segregation in the armed forces. Moreover, the FEPC, which could not require compliance with its orders, often found that the needs of defense production took precedence over fair employment.

The FEPC received more than eight thousand complaints, of which it resolved about a third. By 1944, blacks made up 8 percent of the defense workers, probably more as a result of the labor shortage than of the FEPC prodding. Nevertheless, they got great satisfaction from the symbolic federal action against discrimination in the work force.

Spurred by the new economic opportunities in defense and factory work, black migration from the South increased dramatically after the temporary lull during the depression. More than a million blacks moved to defense centers in California, Illinois, Ohio, and Pennsylvania. Their need for jobs and housing led to racial conflict in a number of northern cities.

Detroit, the new home of a large number of southern migrants, both black and white, experienced some of the worst racial violence. Many incidents occurred because of competition over scarce housing. Early in 1942, black families encountered resistance and intimidation when they tried to move into the Sojourner Truth housing project in Hamtramck, a Polish community of Detroit. Similar tensions erupted into major violence in 1943, when a race riot in Detroit left thirty-four people dead, twenty-five of them blacks. Racial conflicts broke out in forty-seven cities throughout the country.

Tensions in the cities extended beyond hostility between whites and blacks. The activities of Hispanic youths in Los Angeles polarized that city. These young people organized *pachuco* (youth) gangs that dressed in a distinctive style including broad felt hats, pegged trousers, pocket knives on gold chains, and long greased hair. They became known as "zoot suiters." White hostility toward the Hispanic gangs had been smoldering for some time. In July 1943, rumors that a gang had beaten a sailor set off a four-day riot, during which white servicemen entered Hispanic neighborhoods and attacked zoot suiters. The sailors took special pleasure in slashing the pegged pants of their Hispanic targets. The attacks occurred within full view of white police officers who did nothing to stop the violence.

On the other hand, a new mood of militancy among the nation's minorities appeared during the war years. Black leaders effectively suggested parallels between Germany's treatment of Jews and racial discrimination against blacks in America. Although the full horror of Hitler's extermination of six million Jews in concentration camps did not become widely known until after the war, black leaders capitalized on the revulsion felt by many Americans at Hitler's anti-semitism. Civil rights leaders pledged themselves to a "Double V" campaign—victory over Nazism abroad and victory over racism and inequality at home.

Encouraged by the ideological climate of the war years, black organizations reported a large

A ZOOT SUITER

Zoot suit fashions gained wide popularity among young Americans during the war. In 1943, this well-dressed teenager greased his hair in a ducktail and wore a loosely cut coat with padded shoulders (called "fingertips") that reached mid-thigh, baggy pleated pants cut tight ("pegged") around the ankles, and a long gold watch chain. The easy fit of a zoot suit accommodated the current dance craze, the jitterbug. (UPI)

increase in membership. The National Association for the Advancement of Colored People (NAACP) grew ninefold to 450,000. In 1942, A. Philip Randolph helped found the Congress of Racial Equality (CORE). Unlike the NAACP, which favored lobbying and legal strategies, CORE used more aggressive tactics, including mass demonstrations and sit-ins. In 1944, CORE forced several restaurants in Washington, D.C., to serve blacks. Pickets carried signs that read "Are You for Hitler's Way, or the American Way? Make Up Your Mind."

A heightened awareness of civil rights surfaced in other ways as well. The Swedish sociologist Gunnar Myrdal wrote a monumental study of race relations, *An American Dilemma: The Negro Problem and Modern Democracy* (1944). Other books that focused national attention on black issues included such novels as Richard Wright's *Black Boy* (1945) and Lillian Smith's *Strange Fruit* (1944). In 1944, in the case of *Smith v. Allwright*, the Supreme Court ruled that Texas's all-white primary election, a common device used to disfranchise blacks in southern states, was unconstitutional. Following the Court's decision, Congressman Wright Patman of Texas vowed that blacks would vote in his district "over my dead body." Soon, however, Patman began courting black voters at church picnics and other social events in his successful re-election campaigns. These wartime developments laid the groundwork for the civil rights explosion of the 1950s and 1960s.

Japanese Relocation

Events such as the Detroit race riot of 1943 recalled the widespread racial tensions during World War I. But in most other ways, the home fronts of the two wars differed greatly. In the 1940s, German culture and German-Americans did not come under suspicion; nor did Italian-Americans suffer persecution. Leftists and Communists faced little domestic repression, mainly because the Soviet Union became an ally of the United States after the Pearl Harbor attack. The lack of war hysteria largely reflected the strong patriotic consensus in support of the nation's war aims.

One glaring exception marred the wartime record of tolerance and patriotism: the internment of Japanese-Americans on the West coast. The racial prejudice and hysteria directed at them serve as a reminder of how fragile civil liberties can be in wartime.

At first, the West Coast remained calm after Pearl Harbor. But then, partly reflecting the region's vulnerability to attack, coastal residents began to demand protection against the threat of supposed Japanese spies. The Japanese-Americans, who lived clustered in highly visible communities, were a small, politically impotent minority. California's long history of racial antagonism against both Japanese and Chinese immigrants helps explain why the Japanese, rather than German- or Italian-Americans, were singled out. "A Jap's a Jap," an army general

MAP 26.1 WRA RELOCATION CAMPS
In 1942, the government ordered 112,000 Japanese-Americans living on the West Coast into internment camps in the nation's interior because of their supposed threat to public safety during wartime. The freedom of 150,000 Japanese-Americans in the multi-racial, multi-ethnic society of the U.S. territory of Hawaii was not restricted. In California and other states, they were a highly visible and vulnerable minority.

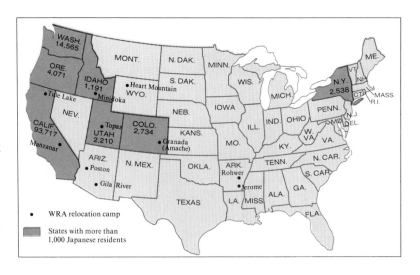

THE INSULT AND INJURY OF INTERNMENT

Peter Ota remembers his family's internment in a relocation camp during World War II.

It was just my sister and myself. I was fifteen, she was twelve. In April, 1942, we were evacuated to Santa Anita. At the time we didn't know where we were going, how long we'd be gone. We didn't know what to take. A toothbrush, toilet supplies, some clothes. Only what you could carry. We left with a caravan.

Santa Anita is a race track. The horse stables were converted into living quarters. My sister and I were fortunate enough to stay in a barracks. The people in the stables had to live with the stench. Everything was communal. We had absolutely no privacy. When you went to the toilet, it was communal. It was very embarrassing for women especially. . . .

We had orders to leave Santa Anita in September of 1942. We had no idea where we were going. Just before we left, my father joined us. . . . I can still picture it to this day: to come in like cattle or sheep being herded in the back of a pickup truck bed. We were near the gate and saw him come in. He saw us. It was a sad, happy moment, because we'd been separated for a year.

He never really expressed what his true inner feelings were. It just amazes me. He was never vindictive about it, never showed any anger. I can't understand that. A man who had worked so hard for what he had and lost it overnight. There is a very strong word in Japanese, *gaman*. It means to persevere. Old people instilled this into the second generation: you persevere. Take what's coming, don't react.

He had been a very outgoing person. Enthusiastic. I was very, very impressed with how he ran things and worked with people. When I saw him at Santa Anita, he was a different person.

We were put on a train, three of us and many trains of others. It was crowded. The shades were drawn. During the ride we were wondering, what are they going to do to us? We Niseis [first-generation Japanese Americans] had enough confidence in our government that it wouldn't do anything drastic. My father had put all his faith in this country. This was his land.

Oh, it took days. We arrived in Amache, Colorado. That was an experience in itself. We were right near the Kansas border. It's a desolate, flat, barren area. The barracks was all there was. There were no trees, no kind of landscaping. It was like a prison camp. Coming from our environment, it was just devastating. . . .

When I think back to my mother and father, what they went through quietly, it's hard to explain. [Cries.] I think of my father without ever coming up with an angry word. After all those years, having worked his whole life to build a dream—an American dream, mind you—having it all taken away, and not one vindictive word. His business was worth more than a hundred thousand. He sold it for five. When he came out of camp, with what little money he had he put a down payment on an apartment building. It was right in the middle of skid row, an old rooming house. . . . He died a very broken man.

Source: Peter Ota, interviewed in Studs Terkel, *"The Good War."* New York: Pantheon, 1984. 29–30, 32–33.

---

stated. "It makes no difference whether he is an American citizen or not."

Mounting fears on the West Coast in early 1942 brought a far-reaching decision from Washington. President Roosevelt approved a War Department plan to intern Japanese-Americans in relocation camps for the duration of the war. In March, Milton Eisenhower, a career civil servant and brother of General Dwight D. Eisenhower, took over the War Relocation Authority, a civilian agency created to carry out the policy. Few public leaders opposed the plan. The Supreme Court upheld its constitutionality as a legitimate exercise of power during wartime in *Hirabayashi v. United States* (1944), ruling that "residents having ethnic affiliations with an invading enemy may be a greater source of danger than those of different ancestry."

The relocation announcement shocked Japanese-Americans, of whom more than two-thirds were native-born American citizens of Japanese ancestry. They comprised the *Nisei* generation, the children of the foreign-born *Issei* generation. The government gave families barely a few days to dispose of their belongings and prepare for relocation. They could take with them only what they could carry. Eager speculators snatched up Japanese real estate for a fraction of its value. Businesses that had been developed over a lifetime had to be liquidated overnight. A Japanese-American piano teacher got only $30 for her treasured piano. Another woman broke every piece of her family's heirloom porcelain rather than accept $17.50 from a secondhand dealer. The government later estimated the total financial loss at $400 million, but Congress appropriated only $38 million to compensate Japanese-Americans after the war.

Relocation took place in two stages. First the government sent the Japanese-Americans to temporary assembly centers, such as the Santa Anita racetrack in Los Angeles, where they lived in stables that horses had occupied a few days earlier. Then they were moved to ten permanent camps away from the coast. These camps, located in California, Arizona, Utah, Colorado, Wyoming, Idaho, and Arkansas, "were in places where nobody had lived before and no one has lived since," one historian commented. Milton Eisenhower had hoped to pattern the relocation camps on the CCC youth camps of the New Deal, but the barbed wire and enforced communal living mocked his hopes. The relocation centers, although sometimes compared to Nazi concentration camps, most closely resembled Indian reservations.

All ten camps were located in hot, dusty climates, and their primitive conditions made family life nearly impossible. Communal bathroom and dining facilities undermined morale even more. The lack of privacy was hardest to bear; only flimsy partitions separated the hastily built rooms. When one baby cried, babies cried up and down the barracks. Eight people often lived in a room that measured only twenty-five by twenty feet. Small families might have strangers assigned to their room. Generational differences between the Issei, who had an average age of fifty-five, and the Nisei, who averaged seventeen years old, added to the tensions. Everyone found boredom a major problem.

Almost every Japanese-American in California, Oregon, and Washington was involuntarily detained for some period during World War II,

a total of approximately 112,000 people. The 15,000 Japanese-Americans who lived outside the West Coast war zone were not affected. Cracks soon appeared in the relocation policy. Japanese-Americans had played important roles in agriculture, and the labor shortage in farming led the government to furlough seasonal agricultural workers as early as 1942. In addition, about forty-three hundred young people who had been in college when the relocation order came were allowed to return to their studies—if they transferred out of the West Coast military zone.

Some young men took advantage of another route out of the camps. Their government, despite imprisoning them, allowed Japanese-Americans to volunteer for military service in Europe. The 442nd Infantry Combat Team, composed entirely of Nisei volunteers, became the most decorated unit in all the armed forces. Its battle and casualty record provided convincing proof of the loyalty of Japanese-Americans.

Most Japanese-Americans accepted relocation. They hoped that by proving their loyalty, they would be accepted again after the war. Many Japanese-Americans of the third generation, called the *Sansei*, some of whom were born in the internment camps, and the fourth generation, the *Yonsei*, do not understand why their elders did not protest more strongly. With each generation, the memory of the wartime deprivation grows dimmer, but nothing can erase this shameful episode from the national conscience.

Victory

The United States gave top priority to fighting Germany, but the battle against the Japanese on the islands of the Pacific was just as difficult. Coordinating the massive military effort strained the Grand Alliance of the United States, Great Britain, and the Soviet Union. In wartime diplomacy lay the seeds of the Cold War that followed victory.

Fighting on Two Fronts

The overall strategy for winning the war resulted from give-and-take discussions among the dominant personalities of the Grand Alliance: Franklin Roosevelt, Prime Minister Winston Churchill of Great Britain, and Joseph Stalin, premier of the Soviet Union. Roosevelt's strong commitment to Britain's survival provided the basis for a strong, if not always smooth, relationship with Churchill. The two men first met at a secret conference aboard a cruiser off the Newfoundland coast in 1941. Stalin, on the other hand, was something of a mystery. He and Roosevelt did not meet until the Teheran Conference in November 1943. Although the United States and Great Britain disagreed on such issues as the postwar fate of colonial empires, the potential for conflict with the Soviet Union was far greater because of the profound differences between their economic and political systems and their opposed visions of the world order of the future. This uncertainty affected both the conduct of the war and the plans for the postwar peace.

The Atlantic Charter, drafted by Roosevelt and Churchill in the summer of 1941, provided the ideological foundation of the Allied cause. It bore similarities to the Fourteen Points proclaimed by Woodrow Wilson in 1918. The Atlantic Charter affirmed the sovereign rights of nations and the freedom of each nation to choose its form of government. The charter called for postwar economic collaboration and guarantees of political stability to ensure freedom from want, fear, and aggression. It condemned territorial gains achieved as the spoils of victory.

The Allied commitment to national self-determination represented the most striking element of continuity with Wilson's Fourteen Points. It became the thorniest problem to confront the three leaders. Roosevelt's hope for self-determination in Eastern Europe conflicted with Stalin's demand for a band of satellite states under Soviet control for protection against invasion from the west. To a lesser degree, the issue caused Roosevelt's disagreement with Churchill over the fate of the British colonial empire after the war. Despite such conflicts, Roosevelt hoped that the Allies could maintain friendly relationships that would survive the war and provide the basis of a constructive postwar system. At the heart of this postwar cooperation would be an international organization, the United Nations, that would serve as a forum to resolve tensions and prevent further aggression.

These long-term goals interacted with the military necessities of fighting a global war. Defeating Germany always occupied top military priority, with Japan relegated to a secondary posi-

tion. One way to wear down the Germans lay in opening a second front on the European continent, preferably in France, as soon as possible. The Russians strongly argued for this strategy, because a second front would draw German troops away from the fighting on Russian soil. Roosevelt assured Stalin informally that such a front would be opened in 1942.

The two-year delay in opening a second front proved to be one of the most damaging blows to the harmony among the three main Allies. The issue came up so many times that Soviet Foreign Minister Vyacheslav Molotov was said to know only four English words, "yes," "no," and "second front." The delay resulted from a combination of military priorities and British opposition. In 1942, the Allies did not have the necessary equipment, especially landing craft, to mount a successful invasion across the English Channel

"Wisht I could stand up an' git some sleep."

WILLIE AND JOE
World War II contributed its share of humor as well as horror. Cartoonist Bill Mauldin won a Pulitzer Prize in 1945 for his drawings, which featured realistic portrayals of the war through the eyes of Willie and Joe, two common soldiers. Here, as grimy, exhausted infantrymen, they huddle on the beachhead at Anzio following the Allied invasion of Italy. (By permission of Bill Mauldin and Wil-Jo Associates, Inc.)

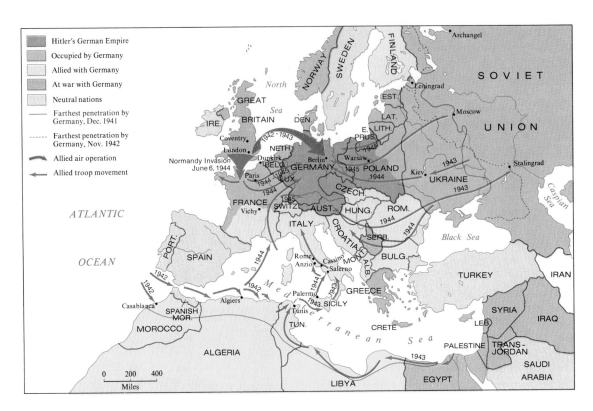

MAP 26.2 EUROPE, 1942–1945
The height of German control came in 1942. The Allies countered first in North Africa in 1942–1943, and then moved onto the European mainland via the Italian peninsula in 1943–1944. In the meantime, the Soviets had begun to push the Germans back from Russian territory. In 1944–1945, Allied activity concentrated in Northern Europe with the successful D-Day invasion in France and the push toward Berlin that ended the war in May 1945.

against the heavily defended French coast. Churchill adamantly opposed launching the invasion, fearing that the Allies would be trapped in a destructive ground war in France as had happened during World War I.

The repeated delays in opening the second front meant that for most of the war, the Soviet Union bore the brunt of the land battle against Germany. The Soviets lost as many as 20 million military and civilian dead during the war, about 8 percent of their people. In contrast, 292,000 Americans were killed and 671,000 wounded in the fighting. These casualties represented less than half of 1 percent of the population. Roosevelt and Churchill's unfulfilled pledges angered Soviet leaders, who were already suspicious about American and British intentions. This mistrust and bitterness carried over into the postwar world.

At first, the military news was so bad that it

threatened to swamp the alliance completely. During the first six months of 1942, the Allies suffered severe defeats everywhere. German armies pushed deeper into Soviet territory and started an offensive in North Africa that menaced the Suez Canal. At sea, German submarines were crippling the transatlantic convoying of American supplies to Europe.

The news from the Pacific was even grimmer. In the wake of Pearl Harbor, Japan had scored quickly with seaborne invasions of Hong Kong, Wake Island, and Guam. Japanese forces conquered much of Burma, Malaya, and the Philippines, as well as the Solomon Islands. Japan achieved this huge expansion of territory in only three months.

A major turning point of the war occurred in the winter of 1942–1943, when the Soviets halted the German advance in the Battle of Stalingrad. Now came the task of pushing the Germans back through eastern Europe. By October 1943, Soviet armies stood on the east bank of the Dnieper River, ready to drive through the Ukraine into Romania. At the same time, the Allies launched a major offensive in North Africa, Churchill's substitute for a second front in France. Between November 1942 and May 1943, Allied troops defeated Germany's crack Afrika Korps led by General Erwin Rommel. From Africa the Allied command planned an invasion of Sicily and the Italian mainland, following Churchill's strategy of attacking Europe through what he called its "soft underbelly." By mid-1943, the fascist regime of Benito Mussolini had fallen. The Allies invaded Italy in the fall of 1943 but encountered such heavy resistance that they did not enter Rome until June 1944.

The long-awaited invasion of France came on D-Day—June 6, 1944. That morning, after an agonizing delay because of bad weather, an armada of Allied troops and equipment moved across the English Channel. The beaches of Nor-

mandy where the Allies landed—Utah, Omaha, Juno, Gold, and Sword—soon became household words in the United States. Under the command of General Dwight D. Eisenhower, more than 1.5 million soldiers landed on the beaches during the next few days. Allied troops liberated Paris in August and drove the Germans out of most of France and Belgium by September.

By the autumn of 1944, the German military situation looked hopeless. All that year, long-range Allied bombers had made daring daylight raids that damaged Nazi military and industrial installations. The massive air campaign killed about 305,000 people and wounded 780,000, showing that civilians no longer remained free from attack.

Despite the Allied assault, the Germans were not ready to give up. In December 1944, German forces in Belgium mounted an attack that started the Battle of the Bulge, named for the dent it made in the Allied defenses. After weeks of heavy fighting in what turned out to be the final

HITTING THE BEACH AT NORMANDY
These American reinforcements landed on the Normandy beach two weeks after D-Day, June 6, 1944. More than a million Allied troops came ashore during the next month. The Allies liberated Paris by August and pushed the retreating Nazi forces back behind the German border by September. (UPI)

German attack of the war, the Allies regained their momentum. Their goal was Berlin. American and British troops led the drive from the west, and Soviet troops advanced on the German capital from the east through Poland. On April 30, in what remained of Berlin, Hitler committed suicide. Germany surrendered on May 8, 1945, which became known as V-E (Victory in Europe) Day.

The United States still faced the task of defeating Japan. Throughout the war, policymakers had balanced their commitment to defeat Germany with the need to fight Japan. Unlike the combat in Europe, which was shared by U.S., British, French, and Russian troops, American forces did almost all the fighting in the Pacific. By early 1945, victory over Japan was in sight.

The tide had begun to turn on April 18, 1942, when Colonel James H. Doolittle led sixteen American bombers on the first air raid on Tokyo. On May 7–8, in the decisive Battle of the Coral Sea near southern New Guinea, American naval forces halted the Japanese offensive that had threatened to engulf Australia. Then, at the island of Midway in June, the Americans inflicted extensive damage on the Japanese fleet. Dive bombers and fighters, launched from the aircraft carriers *Enterprise, Hornet,* and *Yorktown,* provided the margin of victory in both battles.

From that point on, the American military command under General Douglas MacArthur and Admiral Chester W. Nimitz took the offensive in the Pacific. For the next eighteen months, American forces advanced arduously from one island to the next, winning major victories at Tulagi and Guadalcanal in the Solomon Islands and at Tarawa and Makin in the Gilberts. They reached the Marshall Islands in early 1944. In October 1944, MacArthur began the reconquest of the Philippines by winning the Battle of Leyte Gulf, a massive naval encounter. The Japanese lost practically their entire remaining fleet, while the Americans suffered only minimal losses.

The island-hopping campaign in the Pacific moved slowly toward an invasion of Japan. For a successful assault on the Japanese mainland, the Americans needed the islands of Iwo Jima and Okinawa. Airstrips there would put U.S. planes within striking distance of Tokyo. American Marines won the battles for Iwo Jima (February 14–March 20, 1945) and Okinawa (April 1–June 10) in some of the fiercest fighting of the war. At Iwo Jima, the Marines sustained more than twenty thousand casualties, including six thousand dead; at Okinawa, the toll reached thirteen thousand dead and nearly forty thousand wounded.

By mid-1945, Japan's land troops, naval ships, and air force had suffered devastating losses. American bombing of the mainland had killed about 330,000 civilians and crippled the Japanese economy. In a last-ditch effort to stem the tide, Japanese pilots began *kamikaze* (suicide) missions, crashing their planes into American ships. This desperate action suggested that Japan would not soon surrender despite its overwhelming losses.

A NEW TYPE OF NAVAL WARFARE
The battles of Coral Sea and Midway in 1942 marked a revolution in naval warfare. For the first time, major sea battles were waged—and decided—primarily by planes launched from aircraft carriers. American planes such as these dive bombers sank four carriers during the Battle of Midway. (Frank Scherschel, *Life* Magazine © 1942 Time, Inc.)

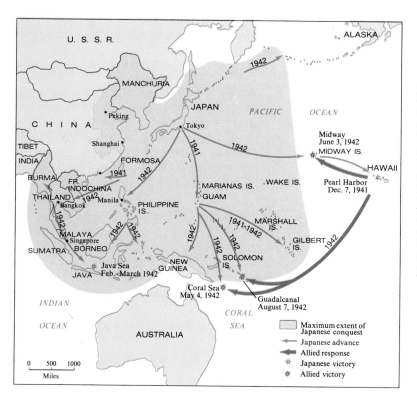

MAP 26.3 WAR IN THE PACIFIC: THE EXTENT OF JAPANESE CONTROL, 1942–1943
After the attack on Pearl Harbor in December 1941, the Japanese rapidly extended their domination in the Pacific, both on land and at sea. The Japanese flag soon flew as far east as the Marshall and Gilbert Islands and as far south as the Solomon Islands and parts of New Guinea. Japan also controlled the Philippines, much of Southeast Asia, and parts of China, including Hong Kong. This great territorial expansion occurred in just three months.

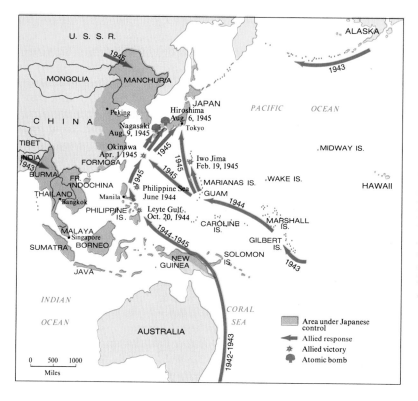

MAP 26.4 WAR IN THE PACIFIC: THE ALLIED RESPONSE, 1944–1945
The American counterattack began in mid-1942, when the Battle of the Coral Sea stopped further Japanese expansion to the south. Allied forces retook the islands in the Central Pacific in 1943 and 1944, and the Philippines in early 1945. The capture of Iwo Jima and Okinawa put U.S. bombers in position to attack the Japanese mainland. Instead of a land invasion, with the tremendous potential loss of American lives, the United States chose to end the war quickly by dropping atomic bombs on Hiroshima and Nagasaki in August 1945.

The American Fighting Force

During World War II, the armed forces of the United States numbered more than 15 million men and women. The army enlisted the most—about 10.5 million—but almost 4 million served in the Navy, 600,000 in the Marines, and 240,000 in the Coast Guard. Although stationed in deserts, jungles, and tropical rain forests, American service personnel faced no more risk from disease than they would have at home. Medical advances cut the death rate in battle in half from the World War I level, thanks to new drugs such as penicillin and sulfa.

Draft boards registered about 31 million men between the ages of eighteen and forty-four. The draft age was lowered from twenty to eighteen in 1942. The government gave physical examinations to about a sixth of the male population prior to induction for military service. More than half the men failed to meet the minimum physical standards, which required a height of 5 feet; weight of 105 pounds; correctable vision; at least half the number of natural teeth; and no flat feet, hernia, or venereal disease. Defective teeth and eyes, traceable largely to inadequate dental and medical care, caused the greatest number of rejections.

War correspondents, including Ernie Pyle and John Hersey, reported on the GIs (short for "government issue") for readers back in the United States. "The American soldier," wrote Pyle, "is a born housewife. . . . I'll bet there's not another army in the world that makes itself a 'home away from home' as quickly as ours does." (Pyle was killed in a foxhole by a Japanese bullet during the battle for Iwo Jima.) Cartoonist Bill Mauldin created two scruffy infantrymen named Willie and Joe for the armed services newspaper *Stars and Stripes*. "Do retreatin' blisters hurt as much as advancin' blisters?" Willie asked Joe during the Italian campaign. "Joe," said Willie in another drawing, "yesterday ya saved my life an' I swore I'd pay ya back. Here's my last pair of clean socks." Such books as *A Bell for Adano* (1944) by John Hersey, *Mister Roberts* (1946) by Thomas Heggen, and *The Naked and the Dead* (1948) by Norman Mailer immortalized the war in fiction. James Jones's *From Here to Eternity* (1951) described army life in Hawaii just before the Japanese attacked Pearl Harbor.

War reporters often portrayed the GIs as ordinary boys doing their patriotic duty. John Hersey described a bunch of Marines in Guadalcanal:

> When you looked into the eyes of those boys, you did not feel sorry for the Japs: you felt sorry for the boys. The uniforms, the bravado . . . were just camouflage. . . . They were just American boys. They did not want that valley or any part of its jungle. They were ex-grocery boys, ex-highway laborers, ex-bank clerks, ex-schoolboys, boys with a clean record . . . not killers.

But, of course, soldiers were trained to kill. Another Marine who had fought at Guadalcanal painted a different picture of war than John Hersey, calling it a matter of simple survival: "The only way you could get it over with was to kill them off before they killed you. The war I knew was totally savage."

Another popular theme was the ethnic and racial diversity of the American forces. A film critic noted that almost every war movie featured "one Negro, one Jew, a Southern boy, and a sprinkling of second-generation Italians, Irish, Scandinavians and Poles." *Time* reported that the men who liberated France sounded like "the roster of an All-American eleven." Soldiers with names such as Czeklauski, Pucilowski, Hakenstod, Gemmill, Christensen, and Dreiscus fought side by side with old-stock Americans named Thacker, Walsh, Eaton, and Tyler.

Most reporters ignored the class distinctions and racial discrimination prevalent in the armed forces, much of it directed against the approximately seven hundred thousand blacks in uniform. Blacks served in all branches of the armed forces, but they were assigned the most menial duties; a great number served as messmen on navy ships, for example. The army segregated black and white blood banks, a practice without genetic or scientific merit. Race riots broke out on several military bases. The NAACP and other civil rights groups chided the government with such reminders as, "A Jim Crow army cannot fight for a free world," but the military remained rigidly segregated.

About 350,000 American women, both black and white, enlisted in the armed services and achieved permanent status in the military establishment. There were about 140,000 WACS (Women's Army Corps), 100,000 WAVES

WOMEN AVIATORS
WASPs like this flyer piloted every type of military aircraft, from the huge B-29 bombers to sleeker fighter craft. Barred from combat duty, women pilots mainly ferried planes and supplies for the Army Air Force throughout the United States and Canada. The treatment of WASPs reflected the sexism and racism of the armed forces: women's monthly pay was $70 less than comparable men's pay, and the program remained all white. Because women pilots never achieved full military status, they were ineligible for military and veterans' benefits when the war ended. (U.S. Air Force)

(Women Appointed for Volunteer Emergency Service in the Navy), 23,000 members of the Marine Corps Women's Reserve, and 13,000 SPARS in the Coast Guard. (The word SPAR comes from *Semper Paratus*, the Coast Guard motto, and *Always Ready*, the English translation.) In addition, about 1,000 WASPs (Women's Airforce Service Pilots) flew sixty million miles ferrying planes and supplies in noncombat areas. A third of the nation's registered nurses volunteered for military duty. About 60,000 served in the army, and 14,000 in the navy.

As with blacks, the armed forces limited the type of duty allowed for women. They barred women from combat, although nurses and medical personnel often served in battle, sometimes risking capture. Many jobs assigned to women in military service reflected stereotypes of women's roles in civilian life—office work, communications, and health care. The pin-up pictures widely distributed to the troops—Betty Grable in a bathing suit, Rita Hayworth in a flimsy nightgown, and, for the black soldiers, the tempestuous singer Lena Horne—were probably closer to the average GI's view of women than was a WAC in uniform.

By the spring of 1944, about a million soldiers had finished their military duty, which averaged

sixteen months, and were returning home. The war had been a dirty, bloody job, not an idealistic fight. Visions of marriage, a house in the suburbs, and a new car sustained many soldiers through its horror and tedium. By 1947, veterans and their families made up a fourth of the American population.

Wartime Diplomacy and the Onset of the Atomic Age

Throughout the war, the three leaders of the Grand Alliance met to discuss the progress of the fighting and to plan the postwar peace. In January 1943, Roosevelt and Churchill met in Casablanca, Morocco; Stalin declined to attend because the Soviet Union's battle against the Germans had reached a crucial point. In November 1943, Roosevelt finally met Stalin for the first time at a conference in Teheran, Iran. Roosevelt expressed confidence that the personal rapport he developed with Stalin would aid postwar harmony among the superpowers.

At Teheran, Roosevelt and Churchill agreed to Stalin's demand for a second front within six months. In return, Stalin promised to join the fight against Japan after the war in Europe ended. Churchill and Roosevelt also agreed to Stalin's demand to redraw Poland's borders to give the Soviet Union more territory. The three men disagreed sharply, however, about the governments that should control the rest of Poland and the neighboring eastern European states. Their failure to resolve these territorial questions in 1943 affected the postwar peace significantly. By the time of the next Big Three conference early in 1945, Soviet troops occupied most of Eastern Europe.

The three leaders held their last, and by far most controversial, wartime conference in February 1945 at Yalta, a Black Sea resort. Victory in Europe was in sight, but no agreement had been reached on the shape of the peace to come. Roosevelt was concerned about maintaining Allied unity after the war. Stalin had become increasingly inflexible on the issue of Eastern Europe, arguing that he needed friendly governments there to provide a buffer for Soviet national security. Roosevelt acknowledged the legitimacy of this demand, but he also hoped for democratically elected regimes in Poland and the neighboring countries.

The compromise reached at Yalta was open to multiple interpretations. Admiral William D. Leahy, Roosevelt's chief military aide, described the agreement as "so elastic that the Russians can stretch it all the way from Yalta to Washington without technically breaking it." As early as 1943, Roosevelt had implied that Stalin could have a free hand in Eastern Europe, but he had neglected to inform the American public of his promises. At Yalta, Roosevelt and Churchill agreed in principle to the idea of a Soviet sphere of influence in Eastern Europe, but they left its actual dimensions deliberately vague. In return, Stalin pledged to hold "free and unfettered elections" at an unspecified time. These elections never took place.

The Yalta conference also proceeded with plans to divide Germany into four zones, to be controlled by the United States, Great Britain, France, and the Soviet Union. Berlin, which lay in the middle of the Soviet zone, would also be partitioned among the four powers. The issue of German reparations remained unsettled.

The Big Three did agree on an international organization to prevent future wars and aggression. Roosevelt, determined to avoid Woodrow Wilson's mistakes, had already cultivated congressional support for American participation in a postwar organization. Realizing that such an

THE LIVING DEAD

When Allied troops advanced into Germany in the spring of 1945, they came face to face with what had long been rumored— concentration camps, Adolf Hitler's "final solution of the Jewish question." The Nazis liquidated six million Jews, plus about as many Poles, Gypsies, and Magyars, in death camps such as Buchenwald, shown here; Dachau; Bergen-Bilsen; and the extermination center at Auschwitz, Poland. (Margaret Bourke-White, *Life* Magazine © 1945 Time, Inc.)

TIME LINE
THE WORLD AT WAR

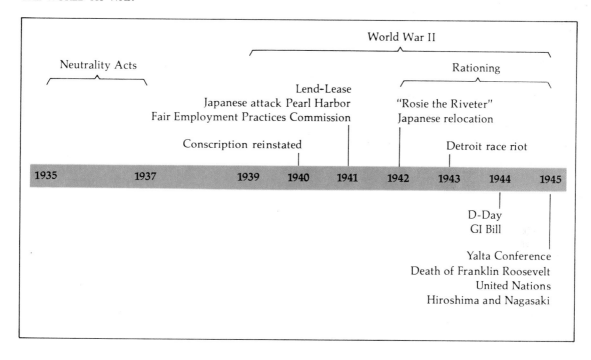

organization would be impotent without Soviet participation, he also courted Soviet support for it.

British, American, and Soviet representatives had met at Dumbarton Oaks, an estate in Washington, D.C., in September 1944 to begin planning the structure of the organization. At Yalta, the Big Three agreed that the Security Council of the United Nations should consist of five major powers—the United States, Britain, France, China, and the Soviet Union—plus six elected nations on a rotating basis. They also decided that the permanent members of the Security Council should have veto power over decisions of the United Nations General Assembly, in which all nations would be represented. Roosevelt, Churchill, and Stalin announced that the United Nations would convene in San Francisco on April 25, 1945.

Roosevelt returned to the United States in February, visibly exhausted from his fourteen-thousand-mile trip. When he reported to Congress on the Yalta agreements, he made an unusual acknowledgment of his physical infirmity. Referring to the heavy steel leg braces he always wore, he asked Congress to excuse him

if he gave his speech sitting down. Roosevelt by now was a very sick man, suffering from heart failure and hypertension. On April 12, 1945, during a short visit to his vacation home in Warm Springs, Georgia, the president suffered a cerebral hemorrhage and died. He was only sixty-three years old. Many Americans could not imagine any leader other than Franklin Roosevelt in the White House. Those who reached adulthood in the 1930s and 1940s had never known another president.

V-E Day came less than a month after Roosevelt's death and Harry Truman's ascent to the presidency. The war in the Pacific ended after the United States dropped an atomic bomb on two Japanese cities, Hiroshima on August 6, and Nagasaki on August 9. The awesome new weapons killed a hundred thousand people at Hiroshima and sixty thousand at Nagasaki. Tens of thousands more Japanese died slowly of radiation poisoning. Japan surrendered on September 2, 1945, which President Truman designated as V-J (Victory over Japan) Day. World War II had ended, but the atomic age of insecurity had just begun.

The development of the atomic bomb was

closely linked to wartime military strategy. In December 1938, German scientists had discovered that the nuclei of atoms could be split into even smaller parts, a process called fission. With materials prepared from uranium, a chain reaction of nuclear fission would release tremendous amounts of energy. American scientists, many of them refugees from Nazi Germany and fascist Italy, produced the first controlled chain reaction on December 2, 1942, at the University of Chicago.

Scientists soon began working frantically to harness such nuclear reactions for military purposes. Their goal was the development of an atomic bomb for use against Germany or, later, Japan. The secret research, called the Manhattan Project, cost $2 billion, involved the construction of thirty-seven installations in nineteen states, and employed 120,000 people, including most of the country's top physicists.

President Roosevelt followed the bomb's progress closely. He and his planners had a dual purpose for rushing the project. They wanted to use the bomb to end the war without the dreadful number of American casualties that had been predicted for an invasion of Japan. At the same time, policymakers hoped that the sole possession of such a powerful weapon by the United States would make the Soviet Union more flexible in international affairs after the war ended. Ironically, instead of lessening tensions, the atomic bomb propelled the United States and the Soviet Union into a deadly arms race conducted in an atmosphere of fear and mistrust.

Until the last moment, the scientists did not know if the atomic bomb would work. On July 16, 1945, near Alamogordo, New Mexico, they watched in wonder as the test bomb exploded into a huge mushroom cloud. President Truman received news of the successful detonation in Potsdam, near Berlin, where he was about to meet with Churchill and Stalin. Truman, who had not even known about the bomb before he became president, was ecstatic about the potential of the new weapon. He ordered the use of atomic weapons against Japanese cities and, following the destruction of Hiroshima, exclaimed to aides, "This is the greatest thing in history."

Others were not so sure. J. Robert Oppenheimer, one of the leading scientists in the Manhattan Project, watched the test on that early July morning in the New Mexico desert. Overwhelmed by its frightening power, he recalled the words from the *Bhagavad Gita*, the Hindu bible: "I am become Death, Destroyer of Worlds."

The international situation deteriorated rapidly throughout the 1930s, and the world was again at war by 1939. Although strong isolationist sentiment opposed American participation, President Roosevelt began mobilizing public opinion for U.S. intervention. The Japanese attack on Pearl Harbor on December 7, 1941, brought the nation into World War II.

Defense mobilization ended the Great Depression. As had happened during World War I, mobilization led to a dramatic expansion of the federal bureaucracy. On the home front, the war resulted in rationing and shortages of many items. Geographical mobility increased as labor shortages opened job opportunities for women, blacks, and Mexican-Americans. The ideological climate of fighting Nazism aided the cause of civil rights. However, Japanese-Americans on the West Coast suffered a devastating denial of civil liberties when the government moved them into internment camps in the nation's interior.

World War II was a global war, consisting of massive military campaigns in both Europe and the Pacific. The war news was bleak at first, but by 1943 the Allies had started to move toward victory. At the same time, Roosevelt attempted to maintain harmony among the United States, Great Britain, and the Soviet Union. Many of the problems that plagued the postwar world resulted from disagreements in wartime diplomacy.

Of all the major powers that fought in World War II, only the United States emerged physically unharmed. And at the end of the war, only the United States had the powerful new weapon, the atomic bomb.

Suggestions for Further Reading

John Morton Blum, *V Was For Victory* (1976), offers a good introduction to American politics and culture during the war years. Also useful are Richard Polenberg, *War and Society* (1972); Geoffrey Perrett, *Days of Sadness, Years of Triumph* (1973); and Richard Lingeman, *Don't You Know There's A War On?* (1970).

Internationalism Replaces Isolationism

Depression and wartime diplomacy are effectively covered in Robert Dallek, *Franklin D. Roosevelt and American Foreign Policy, 1932–1945* (1979). For more on American policy between the wars, see Lloyd Gardner, *Economic Aspects of New Deal Diplomacy* (1964), and Selig Adler, *The Uncertain Giant* (1966). William L. Langer and S. Everett Gleason provide a detailed chronology of American entry in *The Challenge to Isolation, 1937–1940* (1952) and *The Undeclared War, 1940–1941* (1953); see also Robert Divine, *The Reluctant Belligerent* (1965). Selig Adler, *The Isolationist Impulse* (1957); Manfred Jonas, *Isolationism in America* (1966); and Wayne S. Cole, *Charles A. Lindbergh and the Battle Against American Intervention in World War II* (1974), discuss American public opinion. Warren T. Kimball, *The Most Unsordid Act* (1969), describes the Lend-Lease controversy of 1939–1941. Roberta Wohlstetter, *Pearl Harbor* (1962), and Herbert Feis, *The Road to Pearl Harbor* (1950), describe the final chain of events that led to American entry.

Mobilizing for Victory

George Flynn, *The Mess in Washington* (1979); Bruce Catton, *War Lords of Washington* (1946); Donald Nelson, *Arsenal of Democracy* (1946); and Gerald T. White, *Billions for Defense* (1980), discuss America's economic mobilization. Alan Winkler, *The Politics of Propaganda* (1978), covers the Office of War Information. On labor's role during war, see Joel Seidman, *American Labor From Defense to Reconversion* (1953); Nelson Lichtenstein, *Labor's War at Home: The CIO in World War II* (1982); Howell Harris, *The Right to Manage* (1982); and Paul Koistinen, *The Hammer and the Sword: Labor, the Military, and Industrial Mobilization, 1920–1945* (1979). James C. Foster, *The Union Politic* (1975), details the CIO's political involvement. For more on politics in wartime, see James McGregor Burns, *Roosevelt: The Soldier of Freedom* (1970).

Women's roles in wartime are covered by Susan Hartmann, *The Home Front and Beyond* (1982); Karen Anderson, *Wartime Women* (1980); Leila J. Rupp, *Mobilizing Women for War* (1978); and William Chafe, *The American Woman* (1972).

The Home Front

Additional material on America's home-front experience can be gleaned from Richard Polenberg, ed., *The War at Home* (1968), and Lester Chandler, *Inflation in the United States, 1940–1948* (1951). Alan Clive, *State of War* (1979), provides a case study of Michigan during World War II. The experience of black Americans is treated by A. Russell Buchanan, *Black Americans in World War II* (1977); Neil Wynn, *The Afro-American and the Second World War* (1975); and Louis Ruchames, *Race, Jobs, and Politics* (1953). August Meier and Elliott Rudwick, *CORE* (1973), describes the founding of this important civil rights organization. Richard Dalfiume, *Desegregation of the U.S. Armed Forces* (1969), covers black soldiers in the military. Two compelling accounts of Japanese relocation are Audre Girdner and Anne Loftus, *The Great Betrayal* (1969), and Roger Daniels, *Concentration Camps, USA* (1972).

Victory

Extensive material chronicles the American military experience during World War II. Albert R. Buchanan, *The United States and World War II* (two volumes, 1962), and Russell F. Weigley, *The American Way of War* (1973), provide overviews. Cornelius Ryan, *The Last Battle* (1966), and John Toland, *The Last Hundred Days* (1966), describe the end of the fighting in Europe. For the Far East, see John Toland, *Rising Sun: The Decline and Fall of the Japanese Empire* (1970); William Manchester, *American Caesar* (1979) on General Douglas MacArthur; and Barbara Tuchman, *Stilwell and the American Experience in China* (1971).

American diplomacy and the strategy of the Grand Alliance are surveyed in Dallek, *Franklin D. Roosevelt and American Foreign Policy*; William McNeill, *America, Britain, and Russia, 1941–1946* (1953); and Gaddis Smith, *American Diplomacy during the Second World War* (1965). The relationship between the wartime conferences and the onset of the Cold War are treated by Walter LaFeber, *America, Russia, and the Cold War* (1976); John L. Gaddis, *The United States and the Origins of the Cold War* (1972); and Herbert Feis, *Between War and Peace* (1960). Martin Sherwin, *A World Destroyed* (1975), provides a compelling account of the development of the atomic bomb; it can be supplemented by Gar Alperovitz, *Atomic Diplomacy* (1965), and Gregg Herken, *The Winning Weapon* (1980).

27

AFFLUENCE AND ITS CONTRADICTIONS

*B*y 1945, four years of war-induced prosperity had made the American people the richest in the world. Over the next two decades, the gross national product more than tripled, and Americans became even more affluent. Industrial workers in the largest smokestack industries found their unions accepted at last, and their wages rose and fringe benefits expanded. Employees of the successful large corporations—New York accountants, Georgia factory managers, Chicago engineers, San Francisco advertising executives, Dallas office managers—saw their incomes increase as well. Soon they were able to move their families into new houses in the suburbs, where they joined the doctors, lawyers, bankers, and brokers who serviced the growing metropolitan areas.

At the heart of this postwar prosperity lay the involvement of the federal government in national economic life; by the mid-1950s, federal expenditures accounted for a fifth of the gross national product. Another component of postwar prosperity was the "baby boom"—the dramatic rise in the nation's birthrate—which heightened demand for goods and services by the expanding middle class. Increased federal outlays for defense and domestic programs, combined with galloping consumer spending, seemed to promise a continually rising standard of living.

Meanwhile, the nation's economy underwent sweeping structural and technological changes. Agriculture declined as an occupation, white-collar employment rose, and women entered the labor force in unprecedented numbers. Bureaucracies grew larger and corporations more diversified. Such changes often proved disruptive to individual American workers—the farmers who were forced off their land, the alienated assembly-line workers, the bored clerical workers who watched the clock from 9 to 5, and the middle-level managers who tried desperately to fit into impersonal corporate bureaucracies. The bountiful advantages of affluence were tempered by unsettling changes in the lives of ordinary Americans.

Postwar society was also characterized by the growing concentration of population in metropolitan areas. Urbanization, one of the most momentous changes of the nineteenth and early twentieth centuries, had slowed to a trickle during the Great Depression. After 1940, urban migration accelerated once again, with the new arrivals settling not just in cities but in their surrounding suburbs. Poor migrants from rural areas, Puerto Rico, and Mexico, lured by dreams of better jobs and housing, moved into the central cities. The more affluent migrants moved to suburban housing developments on the surrounding fringe. State and local governments struggled to cope with both kinds of growth.

Between 1945 and the mid-1960s, affluence and abundance permeated most—but not all—aspects of American society. In certain areas, those themes of the immediate postwar period continued to characterize American social and economic life through the 1970s. At the same time, underlying contradictions tempered the complacency that went with being the richest nation in the world. These lurking problems in the economic, social, and political spheres eventually surfaced, setting the tone for American life from the 1960s to the present.

Technology and Economic Change

After 1945, technological change transformed one sector of the American economy after another. In agriculture, large-scale agribusiness replaced the old family farm. Industry increasingly

relied on automation, and the nation became a society of white-collar clerks rather than producers of goods. Meanwhile, business corporations diversified both domestically and internationally. Accompanying these structural changes was the steady performance of the American economy. The country's gross national product grew from $213 billion in 1945 to more than $500 billion in 1960; by 1970, the GNP approached $1 trillion. Much of this growth was fueled by increased federal spending, especially for defense.

The Economic Record

The impact of war mobilization laid the foundations for postwar economic developments. The United States enjoyed overwhelming political and economic advantages at the end of World War II. Unlike the Soviet Union, which had lost more than 20 million citizens, or Western Europe and Japan, whose landscapes and economies had been devastated by the fighting, the United States emerged physically unscathed from the war. In fact, the U.S. economy was in far stronger shape in 1945 than when the war began. Consumers had accumulated wartime

CONSUMER CULTURE
This 1962 painting by Tom Wesselman mocks the consumer culture that it so lavishly illustrates with a table well stocked with brand-name goods. Realistic painting in the 1960s took on an air of cynicism, especially as practiced by artists such as Andy Warhol. Wesselman's *Still Life* treats the most ordinary objects of American life as icons, hinting at the new power of consumerism in popular culture. (*Still Life No. 24.* The Nelson-Atkins Museum of Art, Kansas City, Mo. Gift of the Guild of the Friends of Art)

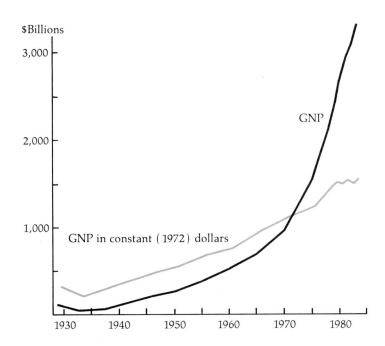

FIGURE 27.1 GROSS
NATIONAL PRODUCT,
1929–1983

savings of $140 billion, which created a strong market for the consumer goods that had been unavailable during the war. The federal government eased conversion to a peacetime economy by allowing businesses to buy factories built for the war effort at a fraction of their cost. In addition, business quickly applied the scientific and technological innovations developed for war production, such as plastics and synthetic fibers, to the production of consumer goods.

To working Americans, the steady growth of the gross national product meant a 25 percent rise in real income between 1946 and 1959. Most Americans rightly felt they had more money to spend than ever before. In 1940, 43 percent of American families owned their homes; by 1960, 62 percent did. But while the standard of living was rising, there was no redistribution of income. The percentage of income received by each segment of the population was substantially the same as it had been in 1939 and in 1910. Americans were living better, but the concentration of income remained unchanged—the top tenth still earned more than the bottom half.

One reason ordinary Americans felt better off was that inflation finally had been brought under control by the 1950s, a boon to both investors and individuals on fixed incomes. Inflation had skyrocketed during the immediate postwar

reconversion period; it averaged 7 percent per year in the 1940s. By contrast, inflation slowed to 2 to 3 percent annually during the 1950s. It stayed low until 1965, when the increased military spending for the Vietnam War set off an inflationary spiral that pushed inflation rates to the 7 to 10 percent range for the next fifteen years. The dramatic rise in world oil prices after 1973 further fueled inflation.

Despite high rates of economic growth, a rise in real income, and low inflation, there was an unevenness to the postwar economy that qualified the rosy picture of economic success and affluence. The economy was plagued by periodic recessions accompanied by high unemployment. At the height of the 1948–1949 recession, unemployment hit 8 percent, although it soon fell to 3 percent with the partial mobilization for the Korean War. Twice when the Eisenhower administration cut defense spending (at the end of the Korean War in 1953 and again in 1957–1958), recessions set in. In the severe 1957 recession, unemployment exceeded 8 percent. Even in nonrecessionary years, the unemployment rate ranged from 4.1 to 5.5 percent, meaning that between 2.7 and 3.7 million workers could not find work. The unemployment rate for nonwhite men averaged 10.6 percent between 1955 and 1959, more than double the rate for white males. During the early 1960s, the general unemployment rate ranged from 5 to 6 percent.

These persistent levels of high unemployment show that not all Americans shared in the general prosperity. The permanently unemployed, the aged, female-headed households, and nonwhites all found themselves at a significant disadvantage. Economist John Kenneth Galbraith, whose book *The Affluent Society* (1958) surveyed the modern economic structure, admitted that the poor were only an "afterthought" in the minds of economists and politicians, who assumed that poverty was well on its way to extinction. Yet, as he noted, more than one family out of thirteen in the 1950s had a cash income of less than a thousand dollars. Not until the publication of Michael Harrington's forceful *The Other America* (1962) did most middle- and upper-class Americans begin to wake up to the fact that between 40 and 50 million Americans—a fourth of the population—were poor.

The Agricultural Revolution

In the major postwar transformations that the economic system underwent, no sector changed more dramatically than agriculture. The number of American farmers had grown until 1910, and even in 1935 nearly a third of all gainfully employed Americans were farmers or farm workers. As late as the end of World War II, a fourth of the American work force consisted of farmers. During the next twenty-five years, however, 25 million people left rural America; by 1969, only 5 percent of the population lived on farms. A federal task force on rural development called this shift "one of the largest migrations of people in recorded history," rivaling European immigration to the New World and America's westward expansion.

This farm-to-city migration was the result of two interrelated trends—a technological revolution in agriculture that reduced the need for labor, and the steady decline of the small, often subsistence, family farm. These agricultural developments in turn dovetailed with the growing metropolitanization of American life.

New technology brought an astonishing increase in agricultural productivity after 1945. Before the war, the typical American farm had been a small, modestly equipped family enter-

prise where horses and mules outnumbered tractors. In 1935, an hour of labor produced about 2½ pounds of cotton, 2 bushels of wheat, just over 1 bushel of corn, 33 pounds of milk, or 3 chickens. In the next two decades, the massive application of new technology—such as harvesting machines, better seed, and improved chemical fertilizers and pesticides—revolutionized farming. By 1978, a single hour's labor produced 50 pounds of cotton, 11 bushels of wheat, 25 bushels of corn, 250 pounds of milk, or 100 chickens. This improved output often had unforeseen consequences. While chemicals such as DDT were initially hailed as miracles of modern science, the publication of Rachel Carson's book *Silent Spring* in 1962 forced consumers and government officials to confront the hazards such pesticides posed to human life.

Mechanization also enabled a farmer to manage a larger farm. Between 1940 and 1980, the average size of an American farm grew two and a half times, from 180 acres to 450. Such

IMPROVED FARM MACHINERY
This machine could plant multiple rows of corn or soybeans while dispensing fertilizer and insecticide. The rising cost of farm machinery was one of the factors that threatened the survival of small family farms. In the late 1940s, a tractor cost a maximum of about $1,500. By the mid-1970s, it cost between $20,000 and $30,000, with some models approaching $100,000. (USDA, Soil Conservation Service)

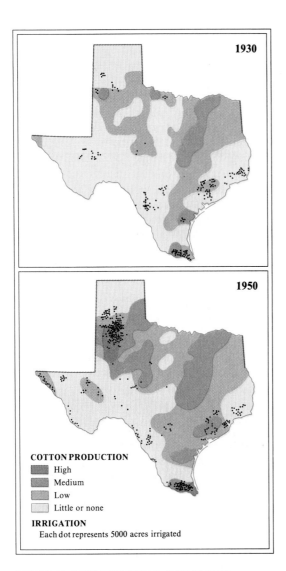

MAP 27.1 AGRICULTURAL ADVANCES
IN TEXAS
In Texas, as elsewhere, the major changes in cotton
production after 1930 included government price
supports begun by the New Deal; greater reliance on
chemicals and pesticides; and the growing use of
machinery. Irrigation was largely responsible for
increased production in arid regions of southeastern and
northern Texas.

large-scale agriculture required major capital investments, beginning with investment in increasingly expensive land. Between 1940 and
1955, the cost of fuel and repairs for farm machines quadrupled, the cost of fertilizer quadrupled, and total operating costs tripled. Family
farms often lacked the capital to compete with

the large, technologically advanced farm units.
In 1948, the 10 percent of American farms with
the most acreage produced 24 percent of the total farm output. By 1974, their share had more
than doubled to 55 percent.

The technological revolution transformed the
lives of many of those who remained on the
land. American farmers had long sought to produce the crops that would bring the greatest return in the market, but they had often hedged
their bets by producing a diversified array of
crops for sale as well as for home consumption.
As long as they had relied on horses and mules,
farmers had also enjoyed considerable self-suffi-
ciency in terms of energy and fertilizer.

All this now came to an end. Each farmer began to specialize in the one or two crops that
yielded the highest return on investment. Land
formerly devoted to oats and hay to feed farm
animals was now planted for corn, soybeans, or
other cash crops. The farmer relied on outside
industrial sources for fertilizer, feed, seed, and
pesticides and for the energy needed to run the
expanding array of gasoline-powered equipment. Farm families increasingly purchased consumer goods from commercial sources, rather
than producing them at home.

After 1940, American farmers lost their intimate connection with the land. They now managed specialized organizations—small factories
that poured industrial materials into the land
and extracted raw products for immediate sale.
Farming had become a business enterprise,

TABLE 27.1 TRENDS IN AMERICAN FARMING,
1935–1980

	Number of farms (thousands)	Farm population (thousands)	Percent of total population
1935	6,814	32,161	25.3%
1940	6,350	30,547	23.1
1945	5,967	24,420	17.5
1950	5,648	23,048	15.2
1956*	4,514	18,712	11.1
1960	3,963	15,635	8.7
1965	3,356	12,363	6.4
1970	2,949	9,712	4.7
1975	2,521	8,864	4.2
1980	2,428	6,051	2.7

*Data unavailable for 1955.
Source: Gilbert Fite, American Farmers (Bloomington: Indiana University Press, 1981). 101.

closely tied to other business enterprises. These ties made farmers, like other businesspeople, increasingly dependent on national and international market conditions, on scientific and technological developments, and on federal economic and farm policies.

The fuller integration of farmers into the national economy, and the diminishing number of Americans who made farming their occupation, greatly reduced the differences between rural and urban life. Farmers, once a major force in political life, no longer wielded much clout in electoral politics except in the United States Senate, where a bloc of farm states still affected national policy. At the same time, the introduction of electricity and labor-saving machinery on the farm lessened the harshness of farm life. Measurable farm income, which ranged from only 40 to 60 percent of the national average between the 1930s and 1950s, rose above 80 percent—and briefly to 110 percent—in the 1970s. As farm income rose and farming came to resemble other occupations, those who remained on the farm increasingly shared the experiences, views, and aspirations of other Americans.

White-Collar World

A revolution in American industry paralleled the revolution in agriculture. Well into the 1940s, the United States had been a nation of goods producers. By 1956, however, a majority of Americans were white-collar workers. The sociologist C. Wright Mills captured the new white-collar world in this riveting image: "What must be grasped is the picture of society as a great salesroom, an enormous file, an incorporated brain, a new universe of management and manipulation." In many ways, this shift of American workers into commerce, government, services, and the professions was as significant a watershed as the closing of the frontier in 1890. Soon panelists on the popular TV quiz show "What's My Line?" learned to ask their mystery guests this question: "Do you deal in services?"

Numbers suggest the dimension of the shift. In 1940, two-thirds of all workers held blue-collar jobs that required them to use physical strength and skills to make products. From 1947 to 1957, the number of factory workers dropped 4 percent, while the ranks of clerical workers rose 23 percent and those of salaried middle-class work-

THE RISING WHITE-COLLAR WORK FORCE
These salespeople at Macy's department store in New York, photographed in 1956, represented the increase in service and retail jobs that characterized the postwar economy. Sales jobs, although not paying high salaries, were considered respectable for women, partly because the flexible hours allowed female workers to combine employment with their family roles. (Eliot Elisofon, *Life* Magazine © 1956 Time, Inc.)

ers jumped 61 percent. A new middle class was created by America's transformation from a society of producers to one of white-collar workers. The new middle class consisted of corporate managers, salaried professionals (such as teachers, professors, and researchers), salespeople, and office workers. They earned a salary, which distinguished them from self-employed entrepreneurs and from service and blue-collar workers who earned an hourly wage. These new members of the middle class had taken advantage of the great expansion of high school and college education after the 1920s, and the explosion of universities after 1945, to make themselves much better educated than their elders. Their new skills enabled them to advance more quickly, and at a younger age, than previous generations. Such advancement usually led them through the giant corporate structures—big business, government agencies, universities, and other bureaucratic organizations—that came to dominate the twentieth century.

The upper level of new middle class had little time to identify with any particular residential community. Atlas Van Lines estimated in the 1950s that corporate managers moved an average of fourteen times—once every two and a half years—during their careers. Perpetually mobile IBM managers joked that the company's initials stood for "I've Been Moved."

Switching jobs, or even careers, necessitated such personality traits as adaptability and the ability to get along in a variety of situations. Corporate managers worked hard, sometimes with the assistance of the resident corporate psychologist, to be "well adjusted." Their philosophy was "Evade, don't confront." Sociologist David Riesman contrasted the stern, formal, "inner-directed" small business and professional types of earlier years with the new managers of the postwar world. He concluded that members of the new middle class were "other-directed," more concerned about their relations with their immediate associates than about adherence to fundamental principles. Sociologist William Whyte painted a more somber picture of these "organization men" as "the ones of our middle class who have left home spiritually as well as physically to take the vows of organization life."

The new middle class accepted a strong role for the federal government in modern economic life. The managers of large corporations and their professional neighbors had shed the small entrepreneur's traditional opposition to government regulation. Many of the new middle class voted Democratic. They had seen their families hurt by the Great Depression and felt that the New Deal and wartime changes had given them opportunities far superior to those available to their parents. "As the poor and underprivileged prospered and climbed they remained loyal to the Democratic party," journalist Samuel Lubell concluded in 1952. "The new middle class . . . seems as Democratic by custom as the older middle class elements are instinctively Republican."

The Changing World of Work

The new hierarchy of work confused old patterns of status and class. In the late nineteenth century, an office job as a secretary was a prized

FIGURE 27.2 LABOR UNION STRENGTH, 1900–1985

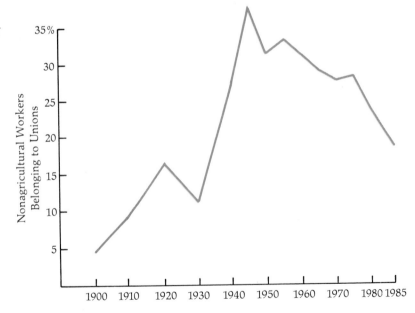

AUTOWORKER IN LORDSTOWN, OHIO

They use time, stopwatches. They say, It takes so many seconds or hundreds of seconds to walk from here to there. We know it takes so many seconds to shoot a screw. We know the gun turns so fast, the screw's so long, the hole's so deep. Our argument has always been: That's mechanical; that's not human.

The workers said, We perspire, we sweat, we have hangovers, we have upset stomachs, we have feelings and emotions, and we're not about to be placed in a category of a machine. When you talk about that watch, you talk about it for a minute. We talk about a lifetime. We're gonna do what's normal and we're gonna tell you what's normal. We'll negotiate from there. We're not gonna start on a watch-time basis that has no feelings.

When they took the unimates on, we were building sixty [Vegas] an hour. When we came back to work, with the unimates, we were building a hundred cars an hour. A unimate is a welding robot. It looks just like a praying mantis. It goes from spot to spot to spot. It releases that thing and it jumps back into position, ready for the next car. They go by them about 110 an hour. They never tire, they never sweat, they never complain, they never miss work. Of course, they don't buy cars. I guess General Motors doesn't understand that argument.

Source: Gary Bryner, interviewed in Studs Terkel, *Working.* New York: Pantheon, 1974, 190–191.

---

position for a working woman, a badge of upward social mobility and respectability, as well as an opportunity for increased pay. By the 1950s, the jobs of office workers were not too different from those of factory operatives—narrow, repetitive, and lacking in control and autonomy. Confounding the old formula that work with your brain counted for more than work with your hands, many unionized factory operatives had higher incomes than those in service or professional occupations such as teaching and social work.

The changing structural composition of the work force and the shifting nature of work itself posed challenges for the labor movement in the postwar world. Labor unions reached the peak of their strength immediately after the war. By 1955, the schisms of the 1930s had healed enough that Walter P. Reuther of the United Automobile Workers could lead the CIO back into an alliance with the AFL. This merger created a single organization, the AFL-CIO, that represented more than 90 percent of the nation's 17.5 million union members. George Meany, a New York building-trade unionist, headed this organization from 1955 to 1979.

New priorities shaped labor-management relations after World War II. Postwar inflation and changing patterns of consumption produced demands for higher incomes. Wage increases brought many workers real incomes that were secure, predictable, and steadily rising. In exchange, union leaders promised labor peace and stability—that is, fewer strikes. In 1950, General Motors and the United Automobile Workers signed a contract containing two key provisions. An escalator clause provided that wages would be adjusted to reflect changes in the cost of living, and a productivity clause guaranteed that wages would rise as productivity in the industry increased. In 1955, autoworkers won a guaranteed annual wage.

These contracts shared a common tendency to emphasize union members' status as consumers rather than workers. George Meany accepted the thrust of government-subsidized business prosperity; his goal was to ensure that labor got its share. Workers paid for these improved wages not only by limiting the number and duration of strikes, but also by putting aside their traditional claims for control over the pace of work. In return for higher wages and fringe benefits, workers allowed technologically minded managers to exert increasing control over their lives on the job.

But labor still had to fight for legitimacy in postwar society. The most virulent antilabor attack came in 1947, when Congress passed the Taft-Hartley Act. This law outlawed the closed shop and restricted the political power of unions by prohibiting the use of union dues for political activity. It allowed the president to declare a

60-day cooling-off period in strikes with national impact. Unions especially disliked Section 14b of the act, which allowed states to pass "right to work" laws to prohibit the union shop. Taft-Hartley chipped away at some of the protections guaranteed by the 1935 National Labor Relations Act and showed that the New Deal labor reforms remained controversial a decade after their passage.

The displacement of American jobs by expansion abroad posed another problem for labor leaders and workers alike. Between 1957 and 1967, General Electric built sixty-one plants overseas. Its rationale was simple: why pay workers in its Ashland, Massachusetts plant $3.40 an hour when workers in Singapore would be glad to do the work at 30 cents an hour? By the 1960s and 1970s, plant closings and relocations had become rampant, costing the United States close to a million jobs between 1966 and 1971, according to an AFL-CIO estimate. General Instruments transferred TV-tuner production from New England to Portuguese and Taiwanese factories, and over three thousand jobs at home were lost. Zenith radio laid off more than seven thousand American workers when it relocated production to Taiwan.

Unions found it difficult to develop a consistent response to the foreign threat. Labor was at a distinct disadvantage because large industrial corporations had international mobility; they could take their operations anywhere. Union workers, though, could not follow jobs out of the country. Even moving to different parts of the United States to follow work, as when companies left the Northeast for the South or West, was difficult. Switching occupations entirely was harder still, especially for older workers. "People are not fungible," observed one study of the global corporation. "The man who assembles radios cannot easily become a computer programmer or a packaged-food salesman."

The labor movement also faced displacement of union workers by automation. Mechanization had long threatened skilled workers, but, by the 1950s, new technology affected the jobs of unskilled factory operatives as well. By 1977, four hundred thousand workers in the steel industry produced twice as much steel as six hundred thousand had in 1947. Similar patterns held in the automobile industry, which had pioneered the assembly line. In 1952, Ford Motor Company introduced automatic drilling machines at a Cleveland engine plant, enabling 41 workers to do a job that formerly employed 117. By the 1970s, automatic machines equipped with sensors not only determined whether engine blocks had been produced in accordance with specifications, but also corrected the defects.

When labor leader Walter Reuther inspected one of these automated engine plants, a Ford manager kidded him: "Well, you won't be able to collect dues from all these automated machines." "You know," Reuther replied, "that is not what is bothering me. What is bothering me is, how are you going to sell cars to all of these machines?" Reuther's reply was right on the mark. Without workers earning sufficient income to continue buying consumer goods, the American economy would falter.

These structural changes affected the labor movement in the postwar period. During the momentous 1930s and 1940s, unions had organized heavy industries such as mining, manufacturing, construction, and transportation, but these sectors were no longer growing. The labor movement had to look elsewhere for new recruits, such as the less skilled, often black or Hispanic, workers in the lower-paying service and agricultural sectors or the millions of secretaries and file clerks in the nation's offices. The union movement needed to expand its industrial midwestern base into southern and western states, areas of rapid economic growth that were traditionally antiunion. Organized labor also had to woo younger workers who now saw unions as part of management, rather than as advocates of the rank and file. Finally, it had to branch out to organize white-collar employees in such previously untapped professions as teaching, nursing, and municipal services.

Organized labor met some, but not all, of these new challenges. By the mid-1950s, the labor movement had stalled. The unionized percentage of the nonagricultural work force peaked at 35.5 percent in 1946 and held level until 1954. Then union membership began a steady decline—31.4 percent in 1960, 27.3 percent in 1970, 23 percent in 1980, and 18.8 percent in 1984. This erosion of the labor movement stood in stark contrast to labor's vitality at the end of the New Deal.

Corporations in an Unpredictable World

Successful corporate managers adopted four strategies to cope with risk and uncertainty in the postwar economic world. They tapped federal money for research and development, diversified their range of products, expanded their multinational operations, and sought to improve their ability to plan. In the struggle to survive and expand in the changing postwar economy, giant corporations had a distinct advantage. In 1968, the five hundred largest corporations controlled 64 percent of all industrial sales in the United States. By 1973, the annual sales of General Motors were greater than the gross national products of Switzerland, Pakistan, or South Africa.

The pattern of business-government partnership that had been accelerated by World War II continued to characterize modern corporate life in the postwar period. According to the National Science Foundation, federal money underwrote 90 percent of the cost of research on aviation and space, 65 percent on electricity and electronics, 42 percent on scientific instruments, 24 percent on automobiles, and 20 percent on chemicals. With the government footing part of the bill, corporations transformed new ideas into useful products faster than ever before. After the Pentagon backed IBM's investment of $5 billion in integrated circuits in the 1960s, the new devices, crucial to the computer revolution, were in commercial production within three years.

Diversification was the most important corporate strategy of the postwar era. The classic corporation of the early twentieth century had produced a single line of products. After World War II, the most successful managers developed new product lines and moved into new markets. Because the largest corporations could afford research laboratories, they diversified more easily. CBS, for example, hired the Hungarian inventor Peter Goldmark, who developed color television during the 1940s, long-playing records in the 1950s, and a video recording system in the 1960s. As head of CBS Laboratories, Goldmark patented more than a hundred new devices.

Postwar managers also diversified through mergers, acquiring other firms to make it easier to invest in expanding new markets. The nation's third great merger wave (the first two had taken place during the 1890s and the 1920s) climaxed during the 1960s. International Telephone and Telegraph became a diversified conglomerate corporation by acquiring Continental Baking, Sheraton Hotels, Avis Rent-a-Car, Levitt and Sons home builders, and Hartford Fire Insurance. Ling-Temco-Vought, another conglomerate, simultaneously produced steel, built ships, developed real estate, and brought cattle to market. In 1947, the largest two hundred corporations accounted for 30 percent of all value added by manufacturing. By 1972, the largest two hundred, now heavily diversified, accounted for 43 percent of this sum.

Expansion into foreign markets also helped managers build giant corporations. International strategies enabled American business to enter new areas when domestic markets became saturated or when American recessions cut into sales. By the 1970s, such corporations as Gillette, IBM, Mobil, and Coca-Cola earned more than half their profits abroad. ITT had a worldwide payroll of 425,000 workers in seventy countries.

In their effort to direct large organizations through the uncertainties of the postwar economy, managers placed increasing emphasis on a fourth master strategy, planning. Always anxious to know how much they could sell and when a competing product might take over their markets, corporate planners tried to take economic, technological, and social trends into account as they weighed and balanced corporate investments. Top executives were increasingly recruited for their business-school training, their ability to manage information, and their skill in corporate planning, marketing, and investment. As a result, corporate managers found themselves working more closely with their counterparts in other corporations, large banks, investment firms, economic research organizations, and the federal government.

The predominant thrust of modern corporate life after 1945 was consolidation of economic and financial resources in oligopolies, where a few large producers controlled the national and, increasingly, the world market. In 1970, the top four U.S. firms produced 91 percent of all motor vehicles; the top four in tires produced 72 percent, in cigarettes 84 percent, and in detergents

70 percent. In 1970, the four largest banks held 16 percent of the nation's banking assets; the top fifty banks held 48 percent.

A case study of the beer industry illustrates this growing concentration of economic power. Beer has always been a highly profitable, high-volume business. At the end of World War II, the United States had about 450 breweries. Each produced a distinctive-tasting brand of beer, due to variations in the local water and differences in brewing techniques. New York City alone had more than a dozen beers, many of which were brewed by family-run businesses.

In the early 1950s, this pattern of competing products and regional diversity changed dramatically. Large corporations went after the national market that had been created in part by advertising on network television. National companies such as Anheuser-Busch developed a beer that could be manufactured anywhere in the country, no matter what the local water was like. They then used modern marketing techniques to push this homogenized product.

Soon the national brands were driving out local competition. Whereas the seven leading beers in 1946 had accounted for barely 20 percent of national sales, by 1970 the ten largest breweries had captured 70 percent of the beer market. In 1960, the number of breweries had dropped to 170; by 1970, it was down to 70. American consumers could find the beer advertised on their favorite television programs at local supermarkets, but they were choosing among a much smaller selection of beers with much blander taste. In beer, as in many other consumer industries, oligopolistic concentration and a national consumer market cut the variety of products—and thus the diversity of American life.

Cities and Suburbs

In the postwar years, Americans lived predominantly in metropolitan areas, largely because available jobs and housing were concentrated there. Economic activity in the twenty-five largest metropolitan areas picked up considerably after 1945. This growth did not occur in the central cities, which lost 300,000 jobs, but in the surrounding suburban areas, which gained an astounding 4 million jobs. By the late 1960s, suburbs surpassed cities in the number of manufacturing jobs they offered. Only in white-collar office work did inner-city employment rise.

These patterns of employment and economic growth reinforced the growing gap between city dwellers and their suburban neighbors. Metropolitan areas developed a striking pattern of residential segregation that persists to this day. Poorer people, many of them nonwhites, clustered in the decaying inner cities, while the more prosperous middle class flocked to the suburbs.

Metropolitan Life

As early as 1880, demographers had noticed the appearance of sprawling metropolitan areas centered around one or more large cities and including scattered suburbs and satellite towns. That year, the U.S. Census identified twenty-five such regions, ranging in size from New York–Brooklyn–Newark, with 6,500,000 people, to Portland, Oregon, with 215,000. In 1920, the Census Bureau announced that urban population had surpassed rural for the first time, a major turning point in the modern era. By then, a dozen metropolitan areas—located on the Atlantic Coast, near the Great Lakes or the Ohio River, or in California—had at least a million people each. Pilots flying along the East Coast at night began to notice that they could no longer distinguish one city from the next; a continuous strand of light stretched from Newport News, Virginia, past New York, and up to Boston. After World War II, metropolitan regions became the dominant form of American settlement. They had two-thirds of the people in 1960, and three-fourths by 1980.

The growth of new metropolitan areas was most striking in the South and West, where large portions of the population had traditionally been rural and impoverished. Miami, strengthened by the capital and expertise of thousands of refugees from Fidel Castro's revolution in Cuba in 1959, developed into an important center for the management of trade with Latin America. Texas cities grew as the petrochemical industry expanded rapidly after 1945; the oil and gas industries, together with the banks and law firms that served them, concentrated in Hous-

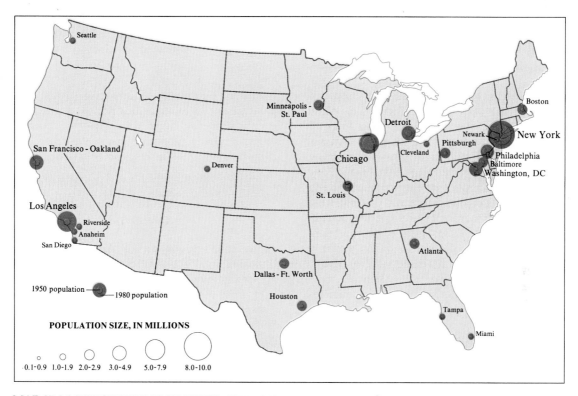

MAP 27.2 METROPOLITAN GROWTH, 1950–1980

A metropolitan area is generally defined as a central city which, in combination with its surrounding territory, forms an integrated economic and social unit. The U.S. Census Bureau introduced the "Standard Metropolitan Statistical Area" in 1950, but later changes in the definition of what comprises an SMSA make it difficult to generalize from the 1950 figures. This map compares the population of central cities in 1950 with population figures for the more broadly defined metropolitan areas in 1980 to illustrate the extent and geographic distribution of metropolitan growth in the postwar period.

ton. Other expanding cities included Atlanta, Baton Rouge, Long Beach, Mobile, and Phoenix. By the 1970s, boosters were heralding the booming metropolitan economies of the "Sun Belt." Overall, the South and West grew twice as fast as the Northeast between 1940 and 1970.

California provided the most dramatic example of this new growth. Acting as a magnet that pulled people from all parts of the country, California absorbed 2.6 million people in the 1940s and added 3.1 million more in the 1950s. Much of this growth was spurred by expansion of defense industries, such as aircraft and electronics. By 1970, California had about a tenth of the entire U.S. population. Reflecting this growth, California was allotted twenty-five electoral votes in 1940 but forty-five in 1970; by contrast, New York's declined from forty-seven to forty-one in the same period. The only state that rivaled this

phenomenal growth was Florida, which added 3.5 million people, many of them older or retired Americans, between 1940 and 1970. State growth of another kind was represented by the admission of Alaska and Hawaii to the union in 1959.

During the postwar era, professional sports mirrored the new patterns of geographical and sectional growth, heralding a broader definition of a "big-league city." In 1958, baseball's Brooklyn Dodgers moved to Los Angeles and the New York Giants went to San Francisco. Teams in other professional sports also followed the sprawling metropolitan population. The New England Patriots played football in Foxboro, Massachusetts, halfway between Boston and Providence; the Detroit Lions moved to Pontiac, Michigan; and the Los Angeles Rams played in suburban Orange County.

While the older metropolitan areas in the

Northeast grew less rapidly than the new Sunbelt centers, they experienced fundamental changes in their economies. Boston and nearby Lowell, Lawrence, and Salem, Massachusetts, lost most of their textile and manufacturing jobs, but high-technology industries that produced Polaroid instant cameras and Digital and Wang computers gave new life to the New England economy. Several high-tech companies moved into rehabilitated mill buildings, with whirring disk drives replacing clanking textile looms. New York City lost many of its garment-making and printing jobs, but outlying areas profited from the relocation of corporate headquarters to suburbs such as White Plains, New York, and Stamford, Connecticut. Grumman and Northrup developed an important airplane and weapons-manufacturing industry on Long Island.

Their similar appearances and economies gave metropolitan regions less sharply defined social and economic profiles than had prevailed in the late nineteenth and early twentieth centuries. In 1940, the average person in the three wealthiest regions of the country—the Far West, the Middle Atlantic states, and New England—had 95 percent more income than the average American in the three poorest sections—the South Atlantic, the Southwest, and the South Central states. In 1960, incomes in the wealthiest sections were 50 percent higher than those in the poorest sections; in 1980, they were only 20 percent higher. The advent of metropolitan economies and the dramatic decline in subsistence farming caused by the agricultural revolution enabled people in the southern and mountain states to have incomes similar to those earned elsewhere in the nation. The migration of poor blacks and whites out of rural areas such as Appalachia into northern cities provided a further equalizer by relocating rural poverty to urban areas. Regional economic inequalities that had persisted since Reconstruction finally began to disappear.

Urban Neighborhoods, Urban Poverty

"The world's image of Los Angeles," wrote a British critic, "is of an endless plan endlessly gridded with endless streets, peppered endlessly with ticky-tacky houses clustered in indistinguishable neighborhoods, slashed across by endless freeways that have destroyed any community spirit that may once have existed." This view, widely held, was somewhat unfair. It ignored the rich diversity of social life in Los Angeles—and every other metropolitan area. The differentiation of neighborhoods reflected cultural preferences and economic and racial pressures.

Migration from other parts of the country and from abroad added to the growth and ethnic diversity of the nation's urban population. The War Brides Act of 1946 and the Displaced Per-

SUBURBAN SPRAWL
This new housing development, built in Los Angeles in 1965, symbolized the dramatic growth that characterized many Sun Belt cities during the postwar period. In 1940, Los Angeles was the nation's fifth largest city with a population of 1.5 million. By the early 1980s, 3 million people lived in Los Angeles, and 7.5 million in its metropolitan area. Los Angeles passed Chicago, which had been number two (hence its nickname, "the Second City"), since 1900. (© Bruce Davidson, Magnum)

sons Act of 1948 permitted large numbers of people from southern and eastern Europe and from Asia to enter the United States. The Immigration Act of 1965 abolished the national quota system imposed in 1924 and set a new annual limit of 290,000 immigrants—170,000 from the Eastern Hemisphere, 120,000 from the Western. Husbands, wives, and children of U.S. citizens were exempt from these quotas, as were specially identified groups of refugees from Cuba and Indochina. Altogether, about 350,000 immigrants entered the United States each year during the 1960s. More than 400,000 came yearly during the 1970s. Most of these new arrivals ended up in the nation's metropolitan areas.

Chicanos (Mexican-Americans) represented one of the largest waves of postwar migrants, swelling populations in southwestern cities. Whereas most Mexican-Americans had lived in rural areas before World War II, 80 percent lived in cities by 1960, making them more urbanized than the general population. Southwestern cities with a high proportion of Chicano citizens included Los Angeles, Long Beach, El Paso, and Phoenix. Large numbers of Mexican-Americans also settled in Chicago, Detroit, Kansas City, and Denver. By the 1970s, five million Mexican-Americans lived in the United States legally (along with perhaps two million illegal aliens), making them one of the nation's largest ethnic groups and a growing force in American political and cultural life.

Another major group of Hispanic migrants came from the American-controlled territory of Puerto Rico. Residents of this island had been American citizens since 1917, but before World War I fewer than two thousand had migrated to the mainland. Migration increased dramatically after World War II, as Puerto Ricans were lured by the promise of better economic opportunities and social services. The inauguration of cheap, direct air service between San Juan and New York City made Puerto Ricans this country's first group to immigrate by air, not boat.

Most of the Puerto Rican migrants went to New York, where they settled first in East ("Spanish") Harlem and then in other areas throughout the city's five boroughs. This massive influx, which grew from 70,000 in 1940 to 613,000 just twenty years later, transformed the ethnic composition of the city. More Puerto Ri-

cans now lived in New York City than in San Juan. They faced conditions common to all recent immigrants—crowded and deteriorating housing, segregation, unemployment or restriction to menial jobs, poor schools, and the problems of a bilingual existence.

Black Americans were the other major group of migrants to the postwar cities. Blacks had been leaving the South since Reconstruction, but 77 percent of the black population still lived there as late as 1940, predominantly in rural areas. By 1960, a majority of blacks lived in the North; by 1970, four-fifths of the northern blacks were urban dwellers. Black Americans thus incurred the double dislocation of moving from South to North, and from a rural to an urban environment, all within a generation or two. (These dislocations applied to Puerto Ricans and Mexican-Americans as well.) Like all other migrants, blacks responded to both "push" and "pull" factors. On the one hand, they were pushed out of the South when the agricultural revolution and mechanized farming ended the traditional southern dependence on sharecropping and tenant farming. On the other hand, they responded to the pull of a better life, economically and socially, in northern cities.

The nation's cities saw their nonwhite populations swell at the same time that whites flocked to the suburbs. From 1950 to 1960, the nation's twelve largest central cities lost 3.6 million whites while gaining 4.5 million nonwhites. During the 1950s, the nonwhite population of Washington, D.C., rose from 35 to 55 percent of the total, and Chicago's from 14 to 24 percent. The pattern continued in the 1960s as New York's black and Hispanic population grew from 14 to 21 percent of the total, Los Angeles's from 13.5 to 18 percent, and Detroit's from 29 to 44 percent.

By the time that blacks, Mexican-Americans, and Puerto Ricans moved into the inner cities in the 1940s and 1950s, urban America was in dire shape. Housing continued to be a crucial problem. One common response to the problem of deteriorating inner-city housing in the 1950s was urban renewal—that is, razing blighted urban neighborhoods and replacing them with modern, supposedly better buildings. Urban renewal often produced grim high-rise housing projects that destroyed feelings of neighborhood pride

CLAUDE BROWN TALKS ABOUT BLACK MIGRATION

I want to talk about the first Northern urban generation of Negroes. I want to talk about the experiences of a misplaced generation, of a misplaced people in an extremely complex, confused society. . . . The characters are sons and daughters of former Southern sharecroppers. These were the poorest people of the South, who poured into New York City during the decade following the Great Depression. These migrants were told that unlimited opportunities for prosperity existed in New York and that there was no "color problem" there. They were told that Negroes lived in houses with bathrooms, electricity, running water, and indoor toilets. To them, this was the "promised land" that Mammy had been singing about in the cotton fields for many years.

Going to New York was good-bye to the cotton fields, good-bye to "Massa Charlie," good-bye to the chain gang, and, most of all, good-bye to those sunup-to-sun-down working hours. One no longer had to wait to get to heaven to lay his burden down; burdens could be laid down in New York.

So, they came, from all parts of the South, like all the black chillun o' God following the sound of Gabriel's horn on that long-overdue Judgment Day. The Georgians came as soon as they were able to pick train fare off the peach trees. They came from South Carolina where the cotton stalks were bare. The North Carolinians came with tobacco tar beneath their fingernails.

They felt as the Pilgrims must have felt when they were coming to America. But these descendants of Ham must have been twice as happy as the Pilgrims, because they had been catching twice the hell. Even while planning the trip, they sang spirituals such as "Jesus Take My Hand" and "I'm On My Way" and chanted, "Hallelujah, I'm on my way to the promised land!"

It seems that Cousin Willie, in his lying haste, had neglected to tell the folks down home about one of the most important aspects of the promised land: it was a slum ghetto. There was a tremendous difference in the way life was lived up North. There were too many people full of hate and bitterness crowded into a dirty, stinky, uncared-for closet-size section of a great city.

Before the soreness of the cotton fields had left Mama's back, her knees were getting sore from scrubbing "Goldberg's" floor. Nevertheless, she was better off; she had gone from the fire into the frying pan.

The children of these disillusioned colored pioneers inherited the total lot of their parents—the disappointments, the anger. To add to their misery, they had little hope of deliverance. For where does one run to when he's already in the promised land?

Source: Claude Brown, *Manchild in the Promised Land.* New York: Macmillan & Co., 1965. vii–viii.

---

and created a combat zone for street crime. Local residents were rarely consulted about whether they wanted their neighborhoods "renewed." Complained one resident of an East Harlem housing project:

> Nobody cared what we wanted when they built this place. They threw our houses down and pushed us there and pushed our friends somewhere else. We don't have a place around here to get a cup of coffee or a newspaper even, or borrow fifty cents. Nobody cared what we need. But the big men come and look at that grass and say, "Isn't it wonderful! Now the poor have everything!"

Between 1949 and 1961, urban renewal projects demolished almost 150,000 buildings and displaced 500,000 people. By 1967, the number of razed structures topped 400,000, and 1.4 million urban dwellers had been forced to relocate.

Urban renewal projects often benefited the wealthy at the expense of the poor. Many downtown "revitalization" projects supplanted established ethnic neighborhoods with expensive rental housing or shiny office buildings where suburban commuters worked. Boston's West End, a flourishing, if poor, Italian community, was razed by a private developer between 1958 and 1960 to build Charles River Park, an apartment complex whose rents were far too steep for the old-time residents. West Enders were forced into less desirable parts of the city, cut off from the vitality of their former neighborhood.

Despite such urban "gentrification," the cities were increasingly becoming a place of last resort for the nation's poor. Unlike earlier immigrants, for whom cities were gateways to social and economic betterment, inner-city residents in the postwar period faced diminishing hopes for improvement. Lured by the promise of plentiful jobs, migrants found that many of these supposed opportunities had relocated to the suburban fringe. Steady employment was thus out of reach for those who needed it most.

That the poor were increasingly trapped in the cities was due largely to racism. Migrants to the city, especially blacks, faced racial hostility and institutional barriers to mobility. Blacks were barred by explicit covenants and informal practices from moving into better neighborhoods. A 1968 federal commission, set up to investigate the race riots that rocked northern cities in the 1960s, concluded ominously that there were "two increasingly separate Americas"—a white society located in suburbs and peripheral areas, and an inner city made up of blacks, Mexican-Americans, and other disadvantaged groups. This widespread metropolitan segregation remains one of the most striking and disturbing aspects of modern urban life.

THE BLIGHT OF URBAN RENEWAL
The West End area of Boston is shown as it looked in 1960, after an urban renewal program had cleared the land. Of the thriving community where seven thousand people had lived just eighteen months earlier, only Saint Joseph's Catholic Church still stood (far right). Within two years, the site was covered with twenty-four hundred units of luxury housing, whose rents far exceeded what the former residents could afford. (Herbert Gans. Reprinted from *The Urban Villagers,* Updated and Expanded edition, Free Press 1982)

The Growth of Suburbia

As late as 1945, many cities had pastures and working farms on their outskirts. Just five or ten years later, these cities were surrounded by tract housing and shopping centers. Between 1950 and 1960, the population of fourteen of the nation's fifteen largest cities shrank, while the suburbs surrounding these cities grew dramatically. New York, despite the influx of Puerto Rican migrants, lost 2 percent of its population in the 1950s, but its suburbs grew by 58 percent. The population of Nassau County, on Long Island, grew from just over 400,000 people in 1940 to 1.3 million twenty years later. The population of Orange County, outside Los Angeles, doubled in the 1940s and then tripled from that level in the 1950s. Other areas that underwent rapid growth included San Mateo County, south of San Francisco; Cook and DuPage counties, north and west of Chicago; and Prince Georges County in Maryland, outside Washington, D.C. By 1960, more people lived in suburbs than in cities.

What spurred this dramatic suburban growth? Automobiles and highways played a crucial role. Suburbanites needed cars to get to work or to take children to school and piano lessons. About 90 percent of suburban families owned cars, and 20 percent had more than one. Whereas twenty-five million cars had been registered in 1945, the number rose to fifty-one million in 1955 and ninety million in 1970.

The car culture that first emerged in the 1920s expanded dramatically during the 1950s, with cars becoming personal metaphors for status and success. With gas cheap, no one cared about fuel efficiency, and cars became heavier and more stylized; the fins of a Chevrolet added two feet to the chassis. One of the most popular cars was the 1957 "Chevy," of which 1.5 million were manufactured. The Chevy came in sixteen solid and fifteen two-tone colors and cost between $1,885 and $2,757.

More cars required more highways, which were funded largely by the federal government. In 1947, the government authorized the construction of 37,000 miles of highway. In 1956, it increased its commitment by another 42,500 miles in the greatest civil engineering project of world history. The new roads would be at least four lanes wide and would link the entire country in an integrated interstate system. (The national highway network was also promoted to speed civilian evacuation in the event of nuclear attack.) Gas taxes and user fees for commercial vehicles provided the necessary funds. Federal expenditures for highway construction rose correspondingly from $429 million in 1950 to $4.6 billion in 1970.

The interstate system of the 1960s changed both the cities and the countryside. It rerouted traffic through rural areas, bypassing old main roads like Route 1 and Route 66 and creating new communities of gas stations, fast-food outlets, and motels at anonymous cloverleaf exchanges. In urban areas, new highways cut wide swaths through urban neighborhoods, forcing relocation and readjustment. Cities were soon plagued by the problems that cars brought to

IMAGES OF AFFLUENCE
Two dominant and interrelated themes of postwar consumer culture were advertising and automobiles. By 1960, annual advertising expenditures topped $10 billion, mainly for consumer goods such as tobacco, legal drugs and alcohol, home furnishings, and automobiles.
(© Elliott Erwitt, Magnum)

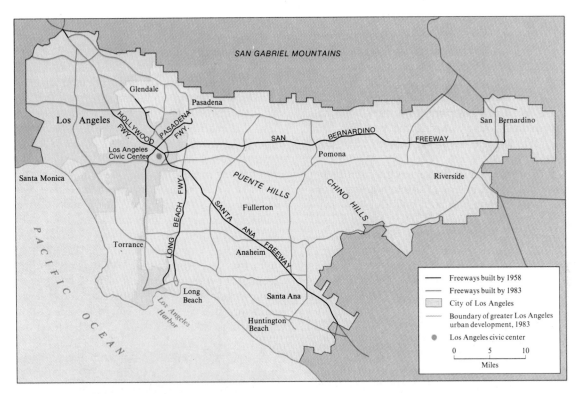

MAP 27.3 THE LOS ANGELES FREEWAY SYSTEM

Los Angeles epitomizes a metropolitan area dominated by the automobile. The city's famous freeway system consists of 650 miles of high-speed expressways (only the major arteries are shown on this map). In the 1920s and 1930s, Los Angeles had one of the nation's best public transportation systems. By the 1960s, however, automobiles accounted for 95 percent of the travel within the city.

modern life—air pollution from exhausts and traffic jams at rush hours. Critics now complained about "autosclerosis," a hardening of the urban arteries.

Highway construction had far-reaching effects on patterns of consumption and shopping. Instead of taking a train into the city to shop or walking to a corner grocery store, people now hopped into their cars and drove to suburban shopping malls and supermarkets. Although the first mall had appeared in the 1920s, there were only eight in 1945. The number mushroomed to almost four thousand by 1960. Contractors who built the shopping centers knew that suburbanites soon would arrive. "People have path-habits like ants," one builder noted.

The federally constructed highways threatened the demise of mass transit. Los Angeles, a city now largely dependent on freeways, had a viable mass transit system as late as the 1940s. On Long Island, master builder Robert Moses planned an extensive expressway system and deliberately omitted the option of adding a mass transit system along its right of way, thereby condemning Long Island to reliance on only cars and freeways. The Highway Trust Fund set up in 1956 specifically prohibited use of its collected fees to promote urban mass transit. By 1960, two-thirds of all Americans drove to work each day.

Another spur to suburban development was the availability of mortgage money from the Federal Housing Administration and the Veterans Administration. Before World War II, banks usually demanded a 50 percent down payment for homeowner's loans and granted no more than ten years to pay back the balance. After the war, the FHA required only a 5 to 10 percent down payment and gave homeowners up to thirty years to pay back mortgages at the modest rate of 2 to 3 percent. The Veterans' Administration was even more lenient, requiring only a token one-dollar down payment from those who had served their country during the war. By 1955, these two agencies wrote 41 percent of all non-farm mortgages.

In the end, people flocked to the suburbs because they followed the available housing. Very little new housing had been built during the depression or war years, and when World War II veterans wanted to establish households and families, they faced a critical housing shortage. The 1950s witnessed a dramatic surge in construction. By 1960, a fourth of all housing in the country had been built during the preceding decade.

The suburban housing market was revolutionized by a Long Island building contractor named Arthur Levitt and Sons, which cut costs and sped production by applying mass-production techniques to home construction. In 1947, Levitt's basic four-room house, complete with kitchen appliances and an attic that could be finished on weekends into two additional bed-

rooms, was priced at less than ten thousand dollars. Levitt did not need to advertise; word of mouth brought more customers than the firm could handle.

Levitt built planned communities in New York, New Jersey, and Pennsylvania. The developments contained few old people and even fewer unmarried adults. Even the trees were young. Owners had to agree to cut their lawns once a week between April and November and not to hang out the laundry on weekends. When residents complained that the streets and the houses were so similar that they could not find their way home, the developer added more variety in style and site placement. A sociologist who studied a Levittown community by living in it for two years concluded, ''Whatever its imperfections, Levittown is a good place to live.'' Soon other developers were snapping up cheap farmland surrounding urban areas, further hastening the exodus from both the farm and the central city.

These suburban developments were almost exclusively for whites. Levittown homeowners had to sign a covenant with this restrictive clause, ''No dwelling shall be used or occupied by members of other than the Caucasian Race,'' although ''the employment and maintenance of

A NATION OF JOINERS
Suburban life was relentlessly organized. Although some suburban organizations, such as churches and PTAs, attracted both men and women, many were limited to one sex. In Fullerton, California, in 1959, men would have joined the male-only Kiwanis, Lions, or Elks, while women would have belonged to the Business and Professional Women or other women's clubs. (© Eve Arnold, Magnum)

other than Caucasian domestic servants" was permitted. Not until 1960 did Levitt sell houses directly to blacks. Even then, the company carefully screened black families and made sure that no two black families lived next door to each other.

While suburbia was often portrayed as a homogeneous, even bland, environment, there were strong cultural and class variations among the suburbs. Older, wealthy suburbs already occupied the most pleasant locations, including the hills of northwest Atlanta, the gracious lakes of Minneapolis, the spectacular hills north and west of Los Angeles, Chicago's North Shore, and the heights well to the east of Cleveland's industrial Cuyahoga Flats. When the less affluent firefighter, plasterer, machine-tool maker, or sales clerk moved to the suburbs, he or she was far more likely to move to a modest Levittown than to an upper-class suburb such as Winnetka, Illinois; Scarsdale, New York; or Shaker Heights, Ohio. Blacks shut out of white suburbs established their own communities, such as Lincoln Heights, outside Cincinnati; Robbins, on the edge of Chicago; and Kinloch, near St. Louis. In well-equipped living quarters at bargain prices, even working-class and black families could share in the ultimate postwar suburban dream "to give every kid an opportunity to grow up with grass stains on his pants."

State and Local Government

The task of governing cities and suburbs fell to state and local governments. The average citizen lived under multiple layers of government—local, county, state, and federal—but local governments often had the greatest impact on people's daily lives. They collected taxes, ran the schools, supplied fire and police protection, picked up the trash, and cleaned the streets. State governments licensed the services of workers ranging from beauticians to lawyers, enforced building and health codes, and protected workers through child-labor laws and workers' compensation.

Like the federal government, state and local governments experienced rapid growth in the postwar period. In fact, their expenditures and payrolls increased much faster than the nondefense activities of the federal government during

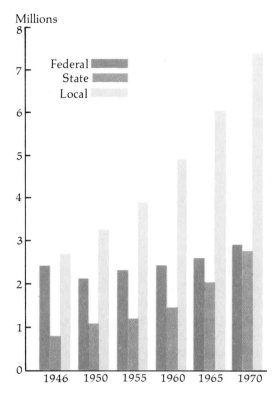

FIGURE 27.3 FEDERAL, STATE, AND LOCAL EMPLOYEES, 1946–1970

this time. State and local expenditures totaled $18 billion in 1949; by 1979, they had risen to more than $300 billion, accounting for two-thirds of total government spending on domestic programs. Employment by local governments grew from 3.2 million in 1950 to 7.4 million in 1970. (The number of federal government employees rose from 2.1 million to 2.8 million in the same period.) By the 1970s, roughly one of six Americans worked for some government bureaucracy.

State and local revenues came primarily from taxation. In 1954, state and local governments relied on property and sales taxes for almost half their revenues. In the following two decades, dependence on property and sales taxes declined somewhat, while state and city income taxes doubled. Federal aid, which supplied 8.5 percent of local and state budgets in 1954, accounted for 19.9 percent by 1976.

State and local governments spent more money on education than on any other item.

Expenditures for education in 1974–1975 took up 39.1 percent of states' budgets and 45 percent of local budgets. Funding covered not only primary and secondary schools; 80 percent of college students attended publicly supported institutions. Although education remains primarily a state and local affair, the federal government has increased its contribution to education since the 1960s through direct aid to educational institutions and programs such as guaranteed student loans and work-study. The rest of the state and local budget covers welfare and social services (the second largest category), highways, health and hospitals, and other services.

Central cities and their surrounding suburban areas often have grossly unequal resources to meet local needs. Since the property tax still provides a sizable part of local budgets, a wealthy community such as Grosse Pointe in suburban Detroit can far more easily provide funds for first-rate schools, clean streets, public recreational facilities, and police and fire protection than can Detroit, whose tax base shrank as businesses and wealthy citizens relocated in the suburbs. While many of the problems of urban life—sewage, traffic, pollution, and police and fire protection—are shared by the cities and their surrounding areas, existing forms of government do not readily allow for cooperation. Political fragmentation is the rule. There are more than a thousand governmental units in the Chicago area, and fourteen hundred in the New York City region. Suburban communities remain reluctant to surrender their fiscal independence, to say nothing of the tradition of local self-rule, to the huge cities with their myriad social and economic problems.

Many urban planners turned their gaze to federal funding to equalize the disparity between the inner cities and the surrounding suburban rim. A national urban policy, they argued, could supply the funding to deal with problems on a metropolitan-area-wide scale. Indeed, the general expansion of federal functions in the 1960s did produce greater attention to the cities—the creation of the Department of Housing and Urban Development (HUD), the Model Cities program, and such antipoverty programs as VISTA and Head Start. These programs, however, hardly dented the massive problems facing urban areas. The needs of the cities have remained a low priority on the national agenda.

The Affluent Society

In 1955, the United States, which accounted for only six percent of the world's population, produced and consumed more than a third of the planet's goods and services. The steady performance of the economy allowed a level of affluence for a wider segment of society than anyone would have dreamed possible during the dark days of the depression. Many members of the new middle class, as well as working-class people who could afford this lifestyle, settled in the sprawling suburban developments that proliferated in the postwar period. The suburbs offered an opportunity to live the child-centered existence that was the hallmark of family culture after World War II.

Consumer Culture

In some respects, the postwar consumer culture seemed like a return to the 1920s—an overabundance of new gadgets and appliances, the expansion of consumer credit and advertising, more leisure time, the growing importance of the automobile, and the development of new types of mass media. Yet there was a difference. The postwar economy was far better balanced than that of the 1920s; no depressed agricultural sector detracted from the prosperity and no Great Depression lurked on the horizon. Furthermore, by the 1950s the American economy was more geared toward the production of consumer goods than thirty years earlier. Consumption had become integral to middle-class culture. Due to rising incomes, even blue-collar families now had discretionary income to spend on consumer goods.

As in the 1920s, though, the postwar prosperity was helped along by a dramatic increase in consumer credit, which enabled families to stretch their incomes. Between 1946 and 1958, short-term consumer credit rose from $8.4 billion to almost $45 billion. A hefty portion of this increase involved financing for the purchase of automobiles on the installment plan. The Diners Club credit card, introduced in 1950 and followed by the American Express card and Bank Americard in 1959, was initially geared toward the business traveler. But by the 1960s and 1970s, the ubiquitous plastic credit cards had revolutionized personal and family finances.

BUY NOW, PAY LATER
Most advertising was geared to American women, who were urged to find fulfillment in buying
things for their homes. Companies like General Electric made the process easier by offering credit
terms for the purchase of vacuum cleaners and other appliances. (FPG)

One symbolic casualty of the consumer credit phenomenon was the pawnshop, which no longer found much call for its services.

Along with expanded consumer credit came a spurt in advertising. In 1951, businesses spent more on advertising ($6.5 billion) than taxpayers did on primary and secondary education ($5 billion); by 1960, advertising expenditures topped $10 billion. To assure continued growth in sales of consumer commodities, advertising sought to "create the wants it seeks to satisfy," as John Kenneth Galbraith put it. Businesses also relied on the idea of planned obsolescence—that is, frequent style changes and minor improvements to make consumers trade in old products for newer, fancier models.

Advertising promoted a variety of new consumer appliances to fill the suburban home. Production of some of these appliances had been halted by wartime priorities; others were new to the postwar market. In 1946, automatic washing machines replaced the old machines that re-

quired wringing out clothes by hand. Electric dryers came on the market that same year. In 1955, 1.2 million dryers were sold, twice the 1953 total, and commercial laundries across the country went out of business as more American homemakers chose to do their own laundry. Another new item on the market was the home freezer, which enabled families to eat seasonal foods, such as fruits and vegetables, all year. The availability of home freezers in turn encouraged the frozen-food industry, which grew dramatically in the 1960s and 1970s, as people spent less time cooking for themselves.

While washing machines, freezers, and refrigerators lightened housekeeping chores, other gadgets offered more frivolous benefits. Blenders, first patented in 1922, originally came in two speeds, on and off. The 1950s brought high and low, and then intermediate speeds. "It was crazy," admitted one executive, "the more buttons, the better they sold. We got as high as sixteen, and the things still couldn't do much more than whip cream." Due in part to the purchases of electrical gadgets for the home, consumer use of electricity doubled during the 1950s.

Consumers had more time to spend money than ever before. In the 1920s, workers toiled six days a week, and few employers offered paid vacations. By the 1960s, the average worker put in a five-day week, with eight paid holidays each year (double the 1946 standard) plus a paid two-week vacation. In 1950, Americans devoted a seventh of the gross national product to spending on leisure and entertainment. One growth area in the 1950s was the travel industry. Americans traveled both domestically (encouraging the dramatic growth in motel chains, roadside restaurants, and fast-food eateries) and internationally, aided by the strong U.S. dollar abroad and the introduction of jet air travel in 1958.

One of the most widespread leisure activities was watching television. TV's leap to cultural prominence was swift and overpowering. In 1947, there were only ten broadcasting stations in the entire country, and a meager 7,000 sets were manufactured. Just three years later, Americans had purchased 7.3 million TV sets. By 1955, 66 percent of all American families had at least one television set; by 1970, 96 percent. More Americans owned a TV set than a refrigerator.

Television transformed American life, fostering a mass national culture in a way similar to, but far more completely than, radio's effect in the 1920s. Television promoted homogeneity, encouraged consumption through its incessant commercials, and reduced regional and ethnic differences by its national network programming. By assuming such a central role in American popular culture, television supplanted radio, whose stars quickly made the transition to the "tube," and movies, which had enjoyed cultural predominance from the 1920s through the 1940s. Movie attendance plummeted throughout the postwar period.

Television also encouraged the consumerism and advertising that had characterized mass culture since the 1920s. New items entered the home. For example, 1954 brought the introduction of the frozen TV dinner of turkey, peas, and mashed potatoes. Now a family could eat a meal in front of the television without having to talk. *TV Guide* became the most successful new periodical of the 1950s. Television even affected city services. In 1954, the Toledo water commissioner

"FATHER KNOWS BEST"
The television program "Father Knows Best" made its debut in 1953. Its title reflected the patriarchal basis of family life at the time. One historian described the character of Robert Anderson, played by Robert Young, as having "no politics, no opinions, and no connections with the world about him"—in short, a perfect organization man of the 1950s. (UPI)

wondered why water consumption rose dramatically during certain three-minute periods. The answer? All across Toledo, TV watchers flushed their toilets during commercials.

What Americans saw on television, besides the omnipresent commercials, was a world that reflected the complacent self-image of American society that prevailed until the political and social upheavals of the 1960s—a predominantly white, Anglo-Saxon world of nuclear families, suburban homes, and middle-class life. The popular show "Father Knows Best," starring Robert Young and Jane Wyatt, typified this norm. We never knew what Father actually did, except that he left home each morning wearing a suit and carrying a briefcase. Mother was a full-time housewife, parent to three children, and personification of all the negative stereotypes about women. For example, she drove badly and was hopelessly emotional. While the new medium did offer some serious programming, notably live theater and documentaries, Federal Communications Commissioner Newton Minow concluded in 1963 that television was "a vast wasteland."

Women—Back to the Home

"The suburban housewife was the dream image of the young American woman," feminist Betty Friedan has said of the 1950s. "She was healthy, beautiful, educated, concerned only about her husband, her children, and her home." Friedan herself gave up a psychology fellowship and a career as a journalist to marry, move to the suburbs, and raise three children. "Determined that I find the feminine fulfillment that eluded my mother . . . I lived the life of a suburban housewife that was everyone's dream at the time," she said.

The 1950s were characterized by a pervasive, indeed pernicious, insistence that women's proper place was in the home. There was nothing new about such emphasis on domesticity. What Betty Friedan tagged the "feminine mystique" of the 1950s—that "the highest value and the only commitment for women is the fulfillment of their own femininity"—bore remarkable similarities to the nineteenth-century's cult of true womanhood. But women's lives had changed dramatically since the nineteenth century, due to increased access to education and jobs and the greater availability of consumer goods and services. It was much harder to convince women to stay in their homes in the 1950s than it had been in the 1850s.

The updated version of the cult of domesticity drew on new elements of twentieth-century science and culture, even Freudian psychology, to give it more force. It claimed that feminism was a neurosis and that women who sought careers were sexually maladjusted. And reflecting the consumer culture, the feminine mystique insisted that women's primary role was to buy appliances and other consumer goods for her home and family. The mass media, such as women's magazines and advertisements, pushed this message relentlessly. "Love is said in many ways," ran an ad for toilet paper. "It's giving and accepting. It's protecting and selecting . . . knowing what's safest for those you love. Their bathroom tissue is Scott Tissue always." Another ad played on the housewife's insecurity by asking, "Can a woman ever feel right cooking on a dirty range?"

The dislocations of the war years made both men and women yearn for a return to traditional family values. A popular 1945 song was "Gotta Make Up for Lost Time." The average age of marriage for women dropped to twenty, and a third of all young women in 1951 were married by the time they reached nineteen. This generation approached life with an optimism and confidence notably absent from the depression generation of the 1930s. The GI Bill and other federal programs aided their quest for unprecedented levels of material security.

The most dramatic result of this family- and consumer-oriented life-style was the postwar "baby boom." After a century and a half of declining family size, the birthrate suddenly shot up. In contrast to the Great Depression, when the birthrate had dropped to a low point of 18.4 per 1,000 population, the annual rate peaked at 25.3 per 1,000 by 1957. (The American rate approached that of the developing nation of India.) Families now had an average of almost four children. Caring for such large households further encouraged women to define themselves as full-time mothers.

Suburbia was child-centered. When asked why they had moved to the suburbs, most new

HOME LIFE IN THE 1950s: THE IDEAL
This photograph reflects an idealized picture of family life
in the 1950s. Taken in Long Island in 1958, it suggests the
theme of "togetherness," a word coined by *McCall's*
magazine in 1954. Many popular magazines promoted
the notion of an idyllic home life for women who made a
full-time career of home-making, regardless of family size.
(© Eve Arnold, Magnum)

homeowners gave the same answer: "We did it
for the children." Scarred by the depression,
parents eagerly sought the wider opportunities
that suburban living offered the next generation.
Children's lives were relentlessly organized.
Their mothers put them in play groups at the
age of three, the Little League or dancing lessons
at eight, and tennis lessons at twelve. Parents
flocked to the PTA, cheered the high school
football team, and applauded the school play.

For their child rearing, parents increasingly
relied on the advice of experts, notably Dr. Benjamin Spock, whose best-selling book *Baby and
Child Care* sold a million copies a year after its
publication in 1946. Dr. Spock urged mothers to
abandon the rigid feeding and baby-care schedules of an earlier generation. New mothers
found Spock's common-sense approach liberating, but it did not totally soothe their insecurities. If they wanted to work outside the home,
they felt guilty about neglecting their family. If
mothers were too protective of their children,

they might hamper their adjustment to a normal
adult life. Dr. Spock could only recommend that
mothers be constantly available to respond to
their children's needs.

In large part because of the baby boom, the
American population rose dramatically in the
postwar period: from 140 million in 1945 to 179
million in 1960, and 203 million in 1970. After the
baby boom produced between 20 and 30 million
more Americans than had been expected, demographers predicted that the population would
reach 300 million by the end of the century.
When the boom tapered off in the mid-1960s
and the birthrate entered a period of steady decline, demographers revised their predictions
and estimated a population of 250–260 million
for the year 2000.

In addition to the rising birthrate and immigration, the declining death rate contributed to
the population growth. Life expectancy at birth
had improved steadily over the first half of the
twentieth century, from forty-seven years in
1900 to sixty-three years in 1940. Continued improvements in diet, public health, and surgical
practices lengthened the life span. So did "mira-
cle drugs," such as penicillin, introduced in 1943;
streptomycin in 1945; cortisone in 1946; and ter-
ramycin in 1949. When Dr. Jonas Salk perfected
a polio vaccine in 1954, he became a national
hero. Life expectancy at birth continued to increase—to seventy years by 1960 and seventy-
four years by 1980.

The baby boom had a broader impact on
American society than simply reinforcing
women's domestic roles and confounding demographers' predictions. The consumer needs of
all those babies fueled the economy as families
bought food, diapers, toys, and clothing for their
expanding broods. When the children got a little
older, manufacturers discovered a vital teenage
market for stereos, records, clothes, and cars.
Family spending on consumer goods joined federal expenditures on national security as the basis for the unparalleled prosperity and economic
growth that characterized American society
through the 1960s.

The baby boom also encouraged a major expansion of the nation's educational system. The
new middle class, America's first college-
educated generation, placed a high value on
education. To make schools into showplace

community centers, suburbanites approved 90 percent of the proposed school bond issues during the 1950s. By 1970, school expenditures accounted for 7.2 percent of the gross national product, double the 1950 level.

The effects of the baby boom are still felt. In the 1950s, children provided plenty of patients for doctors and dentists, students for teachers, and customers for tricycles and swings—and, later, stereos and cars. In the 1960s, the baby-boom generation participated in a broad expansion of higher education, especially at the college level. Not coincidentally, it also contributed to the ranks of student protesters in the late 1960s. By the 1970s, when the baby boom generation entered the workplace, it had to compete for a limited number of jobs in what had become a stagnant economy. In the 1980s, the delayed marriages and later childbearing of the career-oriented baby boomers temporarily caused the birthrate to rise again.

An awareness that the baby boomers were voting finally seeped into politics. At least one major Democratic presidential candidate of the 1980s, Senator Gary Hart of Colorado, specifically addressed his campaign of new ideas to the young people who were the products of the 1950s and 1960s. More successful was his Republican opponent, Ronald Reagan, who nostalgically promised to restore the social conditions of the 1950s and early 1960s, when the baby boomers were growing up. The decisions made by couples in the immediate postwar period to have large families will continue to ripple through American social and economic life for decades to come.

The Great Contradiction—Women at Work

Although women's domestic roles were glorified in the 1950s, a contradictory pattern also emerged—a dramatic rise in the number and kind of women who worked for pay outside the home. Economist Eli Ginzberg later called this trend "the single most outstanding phenomenon of our century."

When World War II ended, women war workers wanted to hold on to their high-paying, skilled jobs, but they stepped aside for returning veterans. Women felt betrayed, however, when,

HOME LIFE: ONE REALITY
This young mother in New Rochelle, a suburb of New York City, was photographed in 1955. Her frenzied situation hints at why twenty-four thousand American women responded to a 1960 *Redbook* magazine article entitled "Why Young Mothers Feel Trapped." (© Elliott Erwitt, Magnum)

after all the veterans had been placed in jobs, plants began to hire and train new young male workers, rather than call the experienced women back to their old positions. Their inability to keep or regain skilled jobs did not send these women back to the home, however. They simply returned to jobs that women traditionally had held. By 1960, there were twice as many women at work as in 1940.

The increase in the number of working women was paralleled by another change of equally significant proportions—the dramatic rise in the number of older, married, middle-class women who took jobs. At the turn of the century, the average female worker was a young recent immigrant who worked only until she married. By mid-century, the average woman worker was in her forties, was married, and had children in school. In 1940, only 15 percent of all wives worked. This percentage doubled by 1960, hit 40 percent by 1970, and passed 50 percent by 1980. Woman workers were not just part-time

TIME LINE
AFFLUENCE AND ITS CONTRADICTIONS

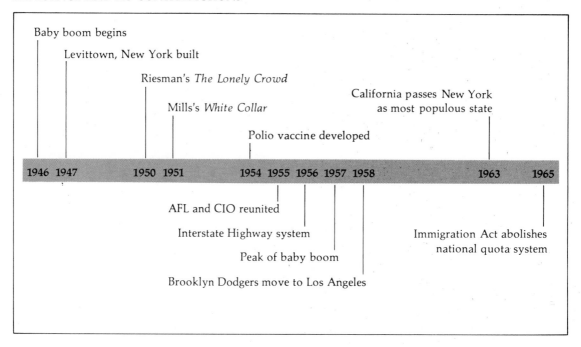

employees; 50 percent of them worked full-time in 1950, and the proportion rose to 70 percent by 1975.

Why did women enter the paid labor force? Many worked to supplement their family income. For many families, postwar inflation and changing consumption habits required two incomes. The wages that many men earned even in the prosperous 1950s and 1960s could not pay for all the necessities of new middle-class life—cars, houses, vacations, and college for the children. The structural needs of the economy were an equally significant factor; there was a demand for workers in fields traditionally filled by women. The shortage was especially acute in clerical work, a predominantly female field that expanded as rapidly as any other white-collar sector in the economy. Teachers to staff the nation's burgeoning school systems were also in demand. Lower-paying jobs went to women in growing sectors such as restaurant and hotel work, hospitals, and beauty care—jobs that critical observers accurately called the "pink-collar ghetto."

Occupational segmentation remained a fun-

damental characteristic of women's work in the postwar period. More than 80 percent of all working women held jobs in stereotypical "women's work," as salespersons, health-care technicians, waitresses, flight attendants, domestic servants, receptionists, telephone operators, and secretaries. In 1960, women represented only 3.5 percent of all lawyers and 6.1 percent of all physicians, but 97 percent of the nurses, 85 percent of the librarians, and 57 percent of the social workers. Along with women's jobs went women's pay, which averaged 63.9 percent of men's in 1955 and dropped to 60 percent in 1963. By the 1970s, a woman earned only 59 cents for every dollar earned by a man.

How could the society of the 1950s so steadfastly uphold the domestic ideal while an increasing number of wives and mothers took jobs? In many ways, the dramatic increase was kept invisible by the women themselves, who, fearing public disapproval of their decisions, usually interpreted their work in very individual terms: "I took a job to put Susie through college, but I still believe a woman's place is at home." The absence of an active feminist movement in the 1940s and 1950s meant that few public figures or organizations paid attention to this major demographic and social shift. Finally, when women took on jobs outside the home, they invariably maintained full responsibility for child care and household management, which allowed families and society to avoid the full implications of women's new roles. As one overburdened woman noted, she now had "two full-time jobs instead of just one—underpaid clerical worker and unpaid housekeeper."

While the American Dream became a reality after 1945 for more citizens than had ever seemed possible, not everyone shared equally in this postwar prosperity. Many people—dis-

placed mill workers and coal miners, destitute old people, female-headed households, blacks and Hispanics—watched the affluent society from the outside and wondered why they were not permitted to share in its bounty. These contrasts between the lure of the city for the poor and minorities and the reality of its segregated existence, between affluence and "the other America," between a heightened emphasis on domesticity and widening opportunities for women, would spawn protest and change in the turbulent 1960s. Amid the booming prosperity of the late 1940s and 1950s, however, these fundamental social and economic contradictions were barely noticed.

---

*P*ostwar affluence rested on several foundations. The most important was federal intervention in the economy, especially in the form of defense spending to maintain permanent mobilization. Spending for consumer goods also fueled the prosperity, playing an especially important role in the reconversion to a peacetime economy. Technological change stimulated increased productivity, notably in agriculture and industry.

Much of the economic activity in the postwar period concentrated in the growing metropolitan areas, especially in their expanding suburbs. Metropolitan areas exhibited a striking dichotomy as poor migrants settled in the inner city while the more affluent took their families to the suburbs. For the new middle class, the postwar

period brought a higher standard of living and access to an array of new consumer goods. Blacks, Puerto Ricans, and Chicanos rarely shared in this affluence, however.

The structural changes transforming the American economy had a strong impact on individual Americans. White-collar workers now outnumbered blue-collar employees, and more women joined the work force. The labor movement could not maintain its momentum from the 1930s. Many of the smoldering contradictions of the postwar period—an unequally shared affluence, institutionalized racism that limited opportunities for nonwhite Americans, and tensions in women's lives—soon surfaced in the social-protest movements of the 1960s.

Suggestions for Further Reading

Technology and Economic Change

W. Elliot Brownlee, *Dynamics of Ascent* (1979), covers the postwar period more extensively than most surveys of economic history. For an even more detailed picture, see Harold G. Vatter, *The U.S. Economy in the 1950s* (1963). Herman P. Miller, *Rich Man, Poor Man* (1971), and Gabriel Kolko, *Wealth and Power in America* (1962), discuss inequality in income distribution. Michael Harrington, *The Other America* (1962), documents the persistence of poverty. John Kenneth Galbraith's lively books, *American Capitalism* (1952), *The Affluent Society* (1958), and *The New Industrial State* (1967), shaped

much of the public discussion of the economy in the period. Robert L. Heilbroner, *The Limits of American Capitalism* (1965), is equally readable and more critical.

John L. Shover, *First Majority-Last Minority* (1976), analyzes the transformation of rural life in America. It can be supplemented by Willard W. Cochrane and Mary E. Ryan, *American Farm Policy, 1948–1973* (1976), and Gilbert C. Fite, *American Farmers: The New Minority* (1981).

David Brody, *Workers in Industrial America* (1980); David Montgomery, *Workers' Control in America* (1979); and James R. Green, *The World of the Worker* (1980), provide stimulating overviews of labor in the twentieth century. On the impact of technology and automation, see Elting E. Morison, *From Know-How to Nowhere* (1974), and David F. Noble, *Forces of Production: A Social History of Industrial Automation* (1984). Harry Braverman, *Labor and Monopoly Capital* (1974), looks at the degradation of work from a Marxist perspective. Studs Terkel's superb oral history, *Working* (1974), lets people from all walks of life talk about what they do and how they feel about it.

The most influential study of the new middle class is still David Reisman, with Nathan Glazer and Ruel Denney, *The Lonely Crowd* (1950). William H. Whyte, *The Organization Man* (1956), provides a similar perspective. See also the work of C. Wright Mills, especially *White Collar* (1951) and *The Power Elite* (1956). Samuel Lubbell describes middle-class voting patterns in *The Future of American Politics* (1956) and *Revolt of the Moderates* (1956).

Alfred D. Chandler, *The Visible Hand* (1977), is the definitive history of American corporate structure and strategy. Myra Wilkin, *The Maturing of Multinational Enterprise* (1974), and Richard J. Barnet and Ronald E. Muller, *Global Reach* (1974), describe American business abroad. See also Robert Sobel, *The Age of Giant Corporations* (1972).

Cities and Suburbs

There is extensive literature on the growth of urban areas and their surrounding suburbs. Zane L. Miller, *The Urbanization of Modern America* (1973), and Blake McKelvey, *The Emergence of Metropolitan America, 1915–1966* (1968), provide comprehensive overviews; Sam Bass Warner, Jr., *The Urban Wilderness* (1972), is more interpretive. Herbert J. Gans, *The Urban Villagers* (1962), tells the story of an Italian community in Boston displaced by urban renewal. Jane Jacobs, *The Death and Life of Great American Cities* (1961), is an opinionated look at urban problems. Stephen Thernstrom, *The Other Bostonians* (1973), suggests why blacks in urban areas did not find upward social mobility. Robert A. Caro, *The Power Broker* (1974), provides a case study of the impact of highways on the landscape of metropolitan New York City through the career of Robert Moses.

Jon C. Teaford, *City and Suburb: The Political Fragmentation of Metropolitan America, 1850–1970* (1979), surveys the impact of suburban growth on American life. Standard texts on suburbia include Robert C. Wood, *Suburbia: Its People and their Politics* (1959), and William M. Dobriner, *Class in Suburbia* (1963). Michael N. Danielson, *The Politics of Exclusion* (1976), describes how blacks were kept out of suburbia. Zane Miller, *Suburb* (1981), is a case study of Forest Park, Ohio. Herbert Gans, *The Levittowners* (1967), describes the two years he spent as a participant-observer in that New Jersey community. Bennett M. Berger, *Working-Class Suburb* (1960), and Scott Donaldson, *The Suburban Myth* (1969), question the homogeneity of the suburban experience.

The Affluent Society

An excellent introduction to postwar society that stresses the consumer culture is William E. Leuchtenberg, *A Troubled Feast* (1979). Other useful overviews highlighting social and economic developments are Godfrey Hodgson, *America In Our Time* (1976); Carl Degler, *Affluence and Anxiety* (1968); Geoffrey Perrett, *A Dream of Greatness* (1979); James Gilbert, *Another Chance* (second edition, 1986); and David Potter, *People of Plenty* (1954). See also Douglas T. Miller and Marion Nowak, *The Fifties: The Way We Really Were* (1977), and Jeffrey Hart, *When the Going was Good! American Life in the Fifties* (1982).

Eric Barnouw, *The Image Empire* (1970), chronicles the impact of television. Other treatments of the mass media include Marshall McLuhan, *Understanding Media* (1964); Frank Mankiewicz and Joel Swerdlow, *Remote Control: Television and the Manipulation of American Life* (1978); and Edward J. Epstein, *News from Nowhere* (1973). Robert Sklar, *Movie-Made America* (1975), shows how movies reacted to the threat from television. Vance Packard's influential *The Hidden Persuaders* (1957) unmasks the advertising industry.

Richard Easterlin, *American Baby Boom in Historical Perspective* (1962) and *Birth and Future: The Impact of Numbers on Personal Welfare* (1980), analyze the demographic changes, as does Landon Y. Jones, *Great Expectations: America and the Baby Boom Generation* (1980). Developments in medicine are treated in James Bordley and A. McGehee Harvery, *Two Centuries of American Medicine* (1976).

Betty Friedan, *The Feminine Mystique* (1963), provides a witty perspective on the lives of educated suburban women, which should be contrasted with Mirra Komarovsky, *Blue Collar Marriage* (1962). William H. Chafe, *The American Woman* (1972), and Carl Degler, *At Odds* (1980), survey women's public and private roles; Alice Kessler-Harris, *Out to Work* (1982), concentrates on women at work. For an interpretive overview of women in the 1950s, see Eugenia Kaledin, *Mothers and More* (1984).

28

THE POLITICS OF POST-NEW DEAL AMERICA

*T*he New Deal and World War II made the federal government the single most important force in American life. In 1929, the government employed fewer than six hundred thousand people, spent $3.1 billion, and comprised about 3 percent of the total national economic activity. By 1953, the government spent $75 billion a year, employed more than 2.5 million people (4 percent of the civilian work force), and accounted for 17 percent of the gross national product. During the 1960s, federal budgets surpassed $150 billion, making up 20 to 25 percent of the GNP. Outlays for national defense caused most of this growth in the federal budget, but increased federal responsibilities for social welfare programs also played a role. These structural changes in the scope of federal activity underlay postwar political developments.

The major debate within the political system from 1945 to 1968 concerned the purposes that this vastly expanded federal power ought to serve. With the memory of the Great Depression still fresh, many citizens wanted the government to use its power to ensure economic stability and growth. At the same time, such groups as blacks and labor unions wanted the federal government to intervene actively to improve social and political conditions. Other citizens, however, opposed

any extension of federal power, especially in sensitive areas such as civil rights.

Other unresolved questions animated postwar politics. Could the New Deal coalition of labor unions, black voters, urban dwellers, and ethnic groups survive and regroup after the death of its charismatic leader, Franklin D. Roosevelt? What new goals would it set? The postwar years saw a widening of the New Deal agenda to encompass topics not addressed in the 1930s, most notably civil rights. Little of this platform was translated into legislation in the 1940s and 1950s, but it came to fruition during the Democratic 1960s. The Democratic coalition was inherently unstable, however, torn among its diverse constituencies and their conflicting priorities for the exercise of federal power. The impact of the "new politics" on national elections after 1960, which focused attention on candidates rather than on traditional party structures, also weakened the New Deal coalition. After the 1960s, it struggled to maintain its predominance in the political system.

In the 1950s and 1960s, some of the most dramatic decisions affecting people's daily experiences came from the Supreme Court. Unlike the New Deal years, when the Supreme Court played an obstructionist role, during the postwar period the Supreme Court often acted as a catalyst for sweeping social change. The court decisions of this period arguably had as great an impact on American society as anything proposed by the president or Congress. So much of this judicial dynamism was linked to Earl Warren, the Chief Justice from 1953 to 1969, that the Supreme Court of these years is often referred to as the Warren Court.

These postwar political developments occurred against a backdrop of dramatic new responsibilities in foreign affairs. The United States and the Soviet Union were locked in an intense ideological confrontation, called the cold war, throughout most of the postwar period. The desire of American leaders to stop the worldwide spread of communism led to vastly increased defense spending, the forging of permanent diplomatic and military alliances with other nations, and the deployment of U.S. military forces in Korea and Vietnam. Insecurities about the nation's new role abroad fueled fears of communist infiltration and internal subversion at home, a reflection of the blurring of the lines between international and domestic events that characterized the postwar period.

As commander-in-chief of the world's most powerful military apparatus and manager of an ever-growing federal bureaucracy, the president became the most important policymaker in the political system. Franklin Roosevelt's enormously successful four terms in office had heightened expectations for presidential leadership. Increasingly, many citizens looked to Washington for solutions to national and local problems. The four presidents who followed Roosevelt—Harry S Truman, Dwight D. Eisenhower, John F. Kennedy, and Lyndon B. Johnson—all grappled with the responsibilities and challenges of this new presidential power.

Harry Truman and the Fair Deal

When Harry Truman was summoned to the White House on April 12, 1945, after learning of Roosevelt's death, he asked the president's widow, "Is there anything I can do for you?" Eleanor Roosevelt responded with another question, "Is there anything we can do for you? For you are the one in trouble now." Truman, not content to be a caretaker president for a Roosevelt fifth term, wanted to be a strong president in his own right. He kept the fractious New Deal coalition alive by proposing new federal programs to advance the interests of the varied groups that comprised it. His "Fair Deal" shaped the Democratic party's agenda for the next twenty years.

The Man from Missouri

Many observers asked, "Who the hell is Harry Truman?" when Franklin Roosevelt chose him as his running mate in the 1944 presidential campaign. Widely regarded as a political lightweight, Truman had been an unsuccessful small-town haberdasher in Missouri before rising through state and national politics, partly due to his connections with Tom Pendergast's Democratic machine in Kansas City. His Senate investigations into waste and inefficiency in the war mobilization effort won him a spot on the 1944 ticket.

Truman brought a complex character to the presidency. Alternately humble and cocky, thick-skinned and easily outraged, he had none of Roosevelt's patrician ease. Yet he handled affairs with an assurance and crisp dispatch that has endeared him to later generations. "If you can't stand the heat, stay out of the kitchen," he liked to say of presidential responsibility. Two mottoes graced his desk. One was "The buck stops here"; the other was a remark by fellow Missourian Mark Twain, "Always do right. This will gratify some people and astonish the rest."

When Harry Truman took over the presidency, Americans welcomed him with an initial approval rate of 87 percent, according to Gallup polls. Within a year, his popularity had dropped to 32 percent and new phrases such as "To err is Truman" had entered the political language. What had happened? New to the presidency, Truman had to oversee the complex conversion of a war economy to a peacetime one. At the same time, he had to grapple with deteriorating relations with the Soviet Union. When the economy suffered and the cold war worsened, Americans blamed their president.

The main problem was inflation. While consumers sought the end of wartime restrictions and price rationing, Truman feared economic chaos if all controls were lifted immediately. In the summer of 1945, he eased industrial controls but retained the wartime Office of Price Administration. When the OPA was disbanded in 1946, prices soared. That year saw an annual inflation rate of 18.2 percent. The persistence of shortages of food and products also irritated consumers.

The rapidly rising cost of living prompted demands for higher wages by the nation's workers. By 1945, the number of union members had swelled to more than 14 million—two-thirds of all workers in the mining, manufacturing, construction, and transportation industries. The labor movement had held the line on wages during the war but now was angered as corporate profits doubled while real wages declined due to inflation and the end of wartime overtime pay. Determined to make up for their war-induced sacrifices, workers mounted strikes in major sectors of the economy, crippling the automobile, steel, and coal industries. By the end of 1946, 5 million workers had idled factories and mines for a total of 107,476,000 work days.

HELEN GAHAGAN DOUGLAS
Representative Helen Gahagan Douglas of California, a former Broadway and film star, illustrated a 1947 speech supporting the reestablishment of price controls by bringing a market basket of food to a press conference. Douglas served in Congress from 1944 until 1950, when she was defeated in a bid for the Senate by Representative Richard M. Nixon. (Western History Collections, University of Oklahoma Library)

Truman never doubted his proper course of action. It was the president's job to ensure domestic tranquillity and economic stability, even if it meant alienating organized labor, an important component of the Democratic coalition. "If you think I'm going to sit here and let you tie up this whole country, you're crazy as hell," Truman told leaders of a nationwide railroad strike in the spring of 1946. Truman seized the nation's railroad system and asked Congress for power to draft striking workers into the army, a move that infuriated labor. The president also took a tough stand against labor leader John L. Lewis and the striking United Mine Workers by seizing control of the mines that spring. Such actions won Truman support from Americans fed up with labor disruptions, but he incurred the enmity of organized labor.

These domestic upheavals did not bode well for the Democrats at the polls. In the 1946 elections, Republicans capitalized on popular dissatisfaction with the myriad reconversion problems with the simple slogan "Had enough?" The Republicans gained control of both houses of Congress for the first time since 1928. Truman and the Democrats seemed thoroughly repudiated.

Unity had returned to the Democratic coalition by the time of the 1948 presidential election, however. The most dramatic reversal came from labor. The Republican Congress elected in 1946 was determined to undo the New Deal's social welfare measures, and it singled out labor legislation as a special target. In 1947, Congress passed the Taft-Hartley Act, a direct challenge to several provisions of the 1935 National Labor Relations Act. Truman issued a ringing veto of the Taft-Hartley bill in June 1947, calling it "bad for labor, bad for management, and bad for the country." Congress easily overrode Truman's veto, but his action brought labor back into the Democratic fold.

The 1948 Election

Most observers believed that Truman faced an impossible task in the presidential campaign of 1948. The Republicans were united and well led. They maintained the loyal support of most middle- and upper-income Protestants outside the South, and many farmers and skilled workers. Eager to attract votes from traditional Democratic

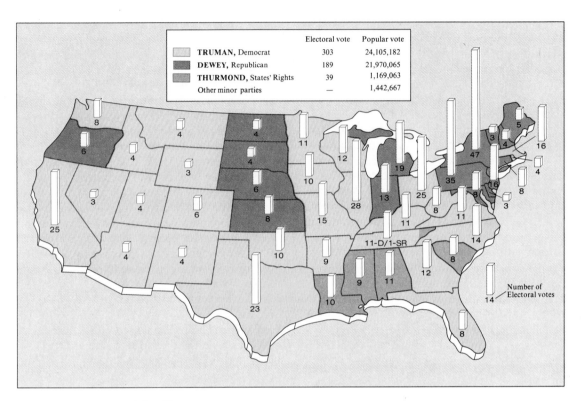

	Electoral vote	Popular vote
TRUMAN, Democrat	303	24,105,182
DEWEY, Republican	189	21,970,065
THURMOND, States' Rights	39	1,169,063
Other minor parties	—	1,442,667

MAP 28.1 ELECTION OF 1948
Political adviser Clark Clifford planned Truman's successful electoral strategy in 1948, arguing that the president should concentrate his campaign in urban areas where the Democrats had their greatest strength. In an election marked by low turnout, Truman held onto enough support from the Roosevelt coalition of blacks, union members, and farmers to defeat Dewey by more than two million votes.

constituencies, they rejected their own conservative favorite, Senator Robert A. Taft of Ohio, in favor of a moderate, Governor Thomas E. Dewey of New York. A renowned prosecuting attorney, Dewey had demonstrated his attractiveness as a national candidate in his 1944 campaign against Roosevelt. To increase their appeal in the West, the Republicans nominated Earl Warren, governor of California, for vice-president. Their brief platform promised to continue most New Deal reforms. Dewey was so certain of victory that he acted, as one journalist observed, "like a man who has already been elected and is merely marking time, waiting to take office."

Truman, in contrast, led a party in severe disarray. Both the left and right wings of the Democratic party split off and nominated their own candidates. Henry A. Wallace, a former New Dealer whom Truman had fired as secretary of commerce in 1946 over disagreements on foreign policy, chose to run as the candidate of the new Progressive party. Wallace advocated increased government intervention in the economy and more power for labor unions. Most controversially, he called for greater cooperation with the Soviet Union, saying in 1946, "The tougher we get, the tougher the Russians will get."

Southern Democrats also bolted the party. At the Democratic national convention, leaders such as Mayor Hubert H. Humphrey of Minneapolis and gubernatorial candidate Adlai E. Stevenson of Illinois had pushed through a strongly prolabor, procivil rights platform, which called for the repeal of Taft-Hartley, the establishment of a permanent Fair Employment Practices Commission, and federal antilynching and antipoll tax legislation. The civil rights plank was too much for the southerners. They had grudgingly supported Roosevelt's and Truman's internationalist foreign policy and a greater role for the government in the economy, but they would not tolerate federal interference in race relations. Three days after the convention, southern Democrats met in Birmingham, Alabama to set up the States' Rights, or Dixiecrat, party. They nominated Governor J. Strom Thurmond of South Carolina for president.

In spite of the fractured Democratic coalition and confident Republican opposition, Truman fought back with one of the most effective presidential campaigns ever waged. He dramatically called Congress back into summer session to give the Republicans a chance to enact their platform into law. When, predictably, they failed to do so, he launched a strenuous cross-country speaking tour, hitting out at the "do-nothing Republican Congress." He also hammered away at the Republicans' support for the antilabor Taft-Hartley Act and their opposition to full-parity price supports for farmers. Truman struck just the right chord. At his rallies enthusiastic listeners took up the cry, "Give 'em hell, Harry!"

TRUMAN TRIUMPHANT
In one of the most famous photographs in American political history, Harry S Truman gloats over an inaccurate headline in the *Chicago Tribune*. Pollsters had predicted an overwhelming victory for Thomas E. Dewey. Their primitive polling techniques, however, did not reflect the dramatic shift in support for Truman during the last days of the campaign. (Saint Louis Globe Democrat)

Truman won a remarkable victory, receiving 49.6 percent of the vote to Dewey's 45.1 percent. Strom Thurmond and the Dixiecrats carried four southern states. Henry Wallace failed to carry a single state. Truman basically owed his election to the ongoing vitality of the Democratic coalition. As *The New Republic* observed, "Harry Truman won this election because Franklin Roosevelt had worked so well." Truman retained the support of organized labor and Jewish and Catholic voters in the big cities; the allegiance of northern black voters to the Democratic party offset the southern losses to the Dixiecrats. (The discovery that the Democrats could capture the presidency without the Solid South paved the way for later civil rights legislation.) Most important, Truman appealed effectively to people like himself who hailed from the farms, towns, and small cities in the nation's heartland. He had grasped something the pollsters had missed: "Everybody's against me but the people."

Truman's Fair Deal

On September 6, 1945, just four days after Japan surrendered to end World War II, Truman staked his claim to domestic leadership with a call for expanded federal responsibilities that he named the Fair Deal. Against a backdrop of abundance, rather than the austerity that had shaped the New Deal, Truman phrased his proposals in terms of the rights of individual citizens—the right to a "useful and remunerative" job, stable prices, protection from monopoly, good housing, "adequate medical care," "protection from the economic fears of old age," and a "good education." Soon Truman added support for civil rights as well.

Despite a generally hostile Congress, the Truman administration accomplished much of this agenda. The minimum wage was raised from forty cents an hour to seventy-five; the Social Security system was extended to cover ten million new workers and its benefits raised by 75 percent. The National Housing Act of 1949 declared as public policy "the goal of a decent home and a suitable living environment for every American family" and called for the construction of 810,000 units of low-income housing.

With the Employment Act of 1946, the federal government also began to develop tools to pursue a coherent economic policy. The legislation formally integrated Keynesian ideas into American economic policy, proposing federal fiscal planning on a permanent basis, not just in times of crisis such as the Great Depression. Beside supporting the use of government spending to spur economic growth, the Employment Act envisioned the use of tax policy as a tool for managing the economy—cut taxes to spur economic growth; raise taxes to slow inflation. Yet the act failed to establish clear economic priorities, such as the proper weight between the commitment to full employment and the need for a balanced budget. And the new three-member Council of Economic Advisers, appointed by the president and directly responsible to the White House, played only an advisory role. On balance, however, the Employment Act of 1946 marked an important turning point toward federal responsibility for the performance of the economy.

The Truman administration also made civil rights a national political issue for the first time. Several factors explained this shift. Black expectations had been raised by wartime opportunities. In addition, Truman realized that black voters played an increasingly large role in the Democratic party as they migrated from the South, where they were effectively disenfranchised, to northern cities. Finally, Truman was sensitive to the world's view of the American government's treatment of blacks, especially since the Soviet Union often compared segregation of southern blacks with the Nazis' treatment of the Jews.

Truman's civil rights proposals included a federal anti-lynching law, federal protection of voting rights (such as an end to poll taxes), and a permanent federal agency to guarantee equal employment opportunities. A filibuster by southern conservatives effectively blocked such legislation in Congress, but Truman found other means to advance the cause of civil rights. By executive order, he began the process of desegregating the armed forces. He ordered the Justice Department to prepare *amicus curiae* (friend of the court) briefs in Supreme Court cases such as *Shelley v. Kraemer* (1948), which struck down as unconstitutional restrictive covenants designed to enforce residential segregation. He appointed a National Civil Rights Commission, whose recommendations called for an expanded federal role in civil rights that foreshadowed much of the legislation of the 1960s.

Despite such accomplishments, the Democratic coalition in the 1940s was not strong enough to overcome the opposition of various interest groups on several key items on the Fair Deal agenda. The American Medical Association squashed the movement for national health insurance by denouncing it as the first step toward "socialized medicine." Catholics successfully opposed any aid-to-education proposal that omitted subsidies for parochial schools. Filibusters by southern senators prevented congressional action on civil rights. Farmers refused to join labor in supporting the outright repeal of Taft-Hartley. While the Fair Deal forestalled any wholesale attacks on the New Deal, with the exception of the revisions to the National Labor Relations Act contained in Taft-Hartley, the Truman administration could not mobilize popular and congressional support for enlarged federal responsibilities in the economic and social spheres.

Two further factors limited the Fair Deal's chances for legislative success. One was the outbreak of the Korean War in 1950. The United States sent troops to repel an attack on South Korea by North Korean Communists, draining both money and energy away from domestic reform. The other was the nation's growing fear of internal subversion. The anticommunist crusade was just one manifestation of the increasing preoccupation with the cold war that was seeping into all facets of American life. Truman's own administration played a major role in fueling these domestic tensions.

The Great Fear

The deterioration of relations with the Soviet Union after 1945 and the onset of the cold war underlay the domestic repression that gripped the country in the late 1940s and early 1950s. Americans often call this phenomenon "McCarthyism," after Senator Joseph R. McCarthy of Wisconsin, the decade's most vocal anticommunist. But this "great fear" was actually much broader than the work of just one man. The obsessive concern over internal subversion reflected a deep-seated American insecurity spawned by worsening cold war tensions. Few Communists were actually found in positions of power; far more Americans became innocent victims of the false accusations and innuendoes that flourished in the postwar climate of fear.

In the 1930s, liberals and Communists had cooperated in a "popular front" against fascism. By the mid-1940s, however, deteriorating relations with the Soviet Union made that totalitarian state seem as large a threat to the American way of life as fascism had been a decade earlier. Some postwar liberals, notably Henry Wallace and his followers in the Progressive party, continued to seek cooperation with the Soviet Union and were not disturbed by the presence of communist activists in their political movement. Yet many other liberals, best represented by the Americans for Democratic Action, founded in 1947, broke from the popular front by including a strident anticommunist plank in their political agenda.

Similarly, Communists had been active in the labor-organizing drives of the 1930s, and their contributions were welcomed, if not openly acknowledged. By the late 1940s, however, the labor movement reversed itself and suddenly purged Communists from its membership. CIO president Phillip Murray denounced communist sympathizers as "skulking cowards . . . apostles of hate." Unions that refused to oust their left-wing leaders, such as the United Electrical, Radio and Machine Workers of America, were expelled from the CIO.

The federal government also undertook its own antisubversion campaign. In 1947, President Truman outraged many supporters by ordering a comprehensive investigation into the loyalty of all federal employees. More than six million individuals were subjected to security checks, and fourteen thousand underwent intensive FBI investigation. Two thousand resigned, although not a single case of espionage was found.

The case of Dorothy Bailey, a forty-one-year-old graduate of Bryn Mawr College and the University of Minnesota, typified the abuses of the federal program. A fourteen-year veteran of the U.S. Employment Service, Bailey lost her job because an unidentified informer claimed she was a Communist and associated with known Communists. Brought before the District of Columbia regional loyalty board, she denied the charge. No evidence against her was introduced and no

witnesses testified to support the charges, but she lost her job anyway.

Soon many state and local governments, colleges and universities, and private institutions and businesses undertook their own antisubversion campaigns. All 11,000 faculty members at the University of California were required to take a loyalty oath; UCLA alone fired 157 who refused to do so. In Hollywood, ex-FBI agents circulated a blacklist of actors, directors, and writers whose names had been mentioned in congressional investigations or whose associations and friends had been described as dubious. Industry executives denied the existence of any such list, but for ten years, hundreds of people were shut out of work in the entertainment industry. The Weavers, a popular group of folk singers, were blacklisted after 1954, and politically active actors such as Zero Mostel and John Garfield had difficulty finding work. One day Jean Muir headlined the popular radio show "The Aldrich Family"; the next she was out of a job, fired, the network said, not because she was a Communist but because gossip about her had made her too "controversial."

The House Committee on Un-American Activities (HUAC) played an especially active role in fanning the anticommunist hysteria. HUAC had been ferreting out supposed Communists in government since its 1938 investigation into the New Deal's Federal Theatre Project. In 1947, HUAC intensified its crusade by holding widely publicized hearings on communist infiltration in the film industry. For example, HUAC members objected to the 1944 film *Song of Russia*—made while the United States was still allied with the Soviet Union—because the director had shown Communists smiling. Novelist Ayn Rand, called as an expert witness, explained, "It is one of the stock propaganda tricks of the Communists to show these people smiling." When asked if no one in the Soviet Union ever smiled, Rand replied, "If they do, it is privately and accidentally. Certainly, it is not social. They don't smile in approval of their system." A group of writers and directors, soon dubbed the "Hollywood Ten," went to jail for contempt of Congress when they cited the First Amendment rather than testify about their past associations.

HUAC next took up, with a vengeance, the case of Alger Hiss, a former New Deal State

PETE SEEGER TESTIFIES BEFORE THE HOUSE COMMITTEE ON UN-AMERICAN ACTIVITIES (1955)

Seeger, a folksinger, songwriter, and member of the Weavers, was one of many performers and artists called to testify before HUAC.

Mr. Tavenner: When and where were you born, Mr. Seeger?

Mr. Seeger: I was born in New York in 1919.

Mr. Tavenner: What is your profession or occupation?

Mr. Seeger: Well, I have worked at many things, and my main profession is a student of American folklore, and I make my living as a banjo picker—sort of damning, in some people's opinion. . . .

Mr. Tavenner: You said that you would tell us about the songs. Did you participate in a program at Wingdale Lodge in the State of New York, which is a summer camp for adults and children, on the weekend of July Fourth of this year? [Witness consulted with counsel.]

Mr. Seeger: Again, I say I will be glad to tell what songs I have ever sung, because singing is my business.

Mr. Tavenner: I am going to ask you.

Mr. Seeger: But I decline to say who has ever listened to them, who has written them, or other people who have sung them.

Mr. Tavenner: Did you sing this song, to which we have referred, "Now Is the Time," at Wingdale Lodge on the weekend of July Fourth?

Mr. Seeger: I don't know any song by that name, and I know a song with a similar name. It is called " Wasn't That a Time." Is that the song?

Chairman Walter: Did you sing that song?

Mr. Seeger: I can sing it. I don't know how well I can do it without my banjo.

Chairman Walter: I said, Did you sing it on that occasion?

Mr. Seeger: I have sung that song. I am not going to go into where I have sung it. I have sung it many places. . . .

Chairman Walter: I direct you to answer the question. Did you sing this particular song on the Fourth of July at Wingdale Lodge in New York?

Mr. Seeger: I have already given you my answer to that question, and all questions such as that. I feel that is improper to ask about my associations and opinions. I have said that I would be voluntarily glad to tell you any song, or what I have done in my life.

Chairman Walter: I think it is my duty to inform you that we don't accept this answer and the others, and I give you an opportunity now to answer these questions, particularly the last one.

Mr. Seeger: Sir, my answer is always the same.

Source: Eric Bentley, ed., *Thirty Years of Treason: Excerpts from Hearings before the House Committee on Un-American Activities, 1938–1968.* New York: Viking, 1971. 686, 690.

Department official who had accompanied Franklin Roosevelt to Yalta. The case against Hiss rested on the 1948 testimony of former Communist Whittaker Chambers, a senior editor at *Time.* Chambers claimed that Hiss had passed him classified documents in the 1930s as part of his duties as a member of a secret communist cell in the government. Congressman Richard M. Nixon of California orchestrated the HUAC investigation of Hiss, which culminated in the dramatic release of the so-called Pumpkin Papers, microfilm that Chambers had hidden in a pumpkin patch on his Maryland farm. (This supposedly incriminating cache, when declassified, contained only Navy Department documents on life rafts and fire extinguishers.) Since the statute of limitations on espionage had expired by 1949, Hiss was charged instead with perjury for denying Chambers's charges before HUAC. The first trial resulted in a hung jury; the second found Hiss guilty of perjury in early 1950.

The hysteria soon became worse. In 1946, Senator Joseph McCarthy, a Marine Corps veteran, had won election in the 1946 Republican landslide with the slogan "Wisconsin Needs a

Tail Gunner in the Senate." In late 1949, McCarthy discovered that an anticommunist attack on a liberal Madison, Wisconsin newspaper brought him favorable attention. In a February 1950 speech in Wheeling, West Virginia, he launched what one columnist later called his string of "multiple untruths" by declaring, "I have here in my hand a list of the names of 205 men that were known to the Secretary of State as being members of the Communist Party and who nevertheless are still working and shaping the policy of the State Department." McCarthy never revealed the names on his list, later changing the number to 81, then to 57.

McCarthy's political genius was his ability to make his name synonymous with the issue of subversives in government. Politicians who attacked him exposed themselves to charges of being soft on communism, the kiss of death in the postwar political climate. McCarthy's supporters at first were more visible than his detractors; such Democratic congressmen as John F. Kennedy of Massachusetts thought "McCarthy may have something." But President Truman called McCarthy's charges "slander, lies, character assassination," although he could do nothing to curb them. Even when Republican Dwight D.

THE MCCARTHY ERA
Senator Joseph R. McCarthy of Wisconsin became famous in the early 1950s when he charged that Communists held many positions in the government. This photograph shows McCarthy and his two chief aides on the Senate Committee on Government Operations, Roy Cohn (left) and G. David Schine (right). (© Eve Arnold, Magnum)

NIXON AND THE HISS CASE
As a member of the House Un-American Activities Committee, Richard Nixon (far right) parlayed his aggressive questioning of Alger Hiss, a former State Department official, into a national political reputation. In his memoirs called *Six Crises* (1962), Nixon devoted the first chapter to the Hiss case. (UPI)

Eisenhower was elected president in 1952, he did not publicly challenge his party's most outspoken senator.

The momentum of international events allowed McCarthy to retain credibility, despite his failure to identify a single Communist in government. Alger Hiss was convicted in 1950. The Korean War broke out soon after, embroiling the United States in a frustrating fight against communism in a faraway land. And in a sensational but isolated case, Julius and Ethel Rosenberg were accused in 1951 of passing atomic secrets to the Soviet Union. They were convicted, and were executed in 1953.

In 1954, McCarthy finally overreached himself by launching an investigation into possible subversion in the U.S. Army. The lengthy televised hearings brought McCarthy's smear tactics and leering innuendoes into the nation's living rooms, and support for him declined. Later that year, the Senate voted 67 to 22 to censure McCarthy. He died three years later at the age of forty-eight, his name forever attached to a period of political repression of which he was only the most flagrant manifestation.

Modern Republicanism

The Republican party found it difficult to rival the New Deal coalition. The party's greatest strength lay in the largely Protestant and rural states of the Midwest. Since only a third of the nation's registered voters were Republicans, however, the party had to find a candidate who could attract Democrats and independents. Republican leaders quickly realized that General Dwight D. Eisenhower would be just such a candidate. His election in 1952 did not carry with it a stable Republican majority to replace the prevailing Democratic coalition, but it led the party back to national power and slowed the expansion of the federal government.

The Soldier Turned Politician

Dwight Eisenhower's status as a war hero was his greatest political asset. Born in 1890 and raised in Abilene, Kansas, he graduated from the United States Military Academy at West Point in 1915. General Douglas MacArthur chose him as his aide in the early 1930s, and Eisenhower rose dramatically through the ranks. After Pearl Harbor, he came to Washington under the sponsorship of a second mentor, General George C. Marshall. By 1944, Eisenhower was Supreme Commander of Allied Forces in Europe, where he directed the D-Day invasion of France. To hundreds of thousands of soldiers, and to the millions who followed the war on newsreels, he was simply "Ike," the best known and best liked of the nation's military leaders.

By 1952, Eisenhower had placed himself in a superb position for a presidential campaign. As a professional military man, he could insist that he stood "above politics." While in the army, in fact, he had never voted because he felt that such political activity would represent an intrusion of the military into civilian affairs. Many Democrats had hoped to make him their candidate for president in 1948, and again in 1952. Eisenhower did want the office, but as a Republican.

When conservative candidate Senator Robert A. Taft of Ohio did well in the early primaries, Eisenhower resigned his military position to campaign. He quickly proved an effective politician. He defeated Taft in primaries in New Hampshire, Pennsylvania, and New Jersey and took delegates away from Taft in a tough fight at the Republican National Convention. Eisenhower then asked Senator Richard M. Nixon of California to be his running mate. Young, tirelessly partisan, and with a strong anticommunist record from his crusade against Alger Hiss, Nixon brought an aggressive campaign style, as well as ideological and regional balance, to the ticket.

The Democrats never seriously considered renominating Harry Truman, who by 1952 was a thoroughly discredited leader. During the last two years of his presidency, his public approval rating had never risen above 32 percent and at one point had plunged to 23 percent. Lack of popular enthusiasm for the Korean War dealt the severest blow to Truman's support, but a series of widely publicized scandals involving federal officials in bribery, kickback, and influence-peddling schemes caused voters to complain about the "mess in Washington." With a certain relief, the Democrats turned to Governor Adlai E. Stevenson of Illinois, who enjoyed the support of respected liberals such as Eleanor Roosevelt and of organized labor. To appease southern voters, the Democratic convention nominated Senator John A. Sparkman of Alabama for vice-president.

Throughout the 1952 campaign, Stevenson advocated New Deal–Fair Deal policies with an almost literary wit and eloquence, but Eisenhower's artfully unpretentious speeches proved more effective with the voters. Eager to get maximum support from a broad electorate, Eisenhower played down specific questions of policy. Instead, he attacked the Democrats with the "K_1C_2" formula—"Korea, Communism, and Corruption." In a campaign pledge that clinched the election, he vowed to go to Korea to end the stalemated war if elected. Stevenson lamely quipped, "If elected, I shall go to the White House."

The only slip in the Republican campaign was the revelation that wealthy Californians had set up a secret "slush fund" for Richard Nixon. While Eisenhower contemplated dropping Nixon from the ticket, the vice-presidential candidate adroitly used television to appeal directly for voters' sympathy. He had not misused campaign funds, he asserted. Whereas Truman appointees had accepted mink coats from contractors—a reference to a widely reported case involving a loan examiner for the Reconstruction Finance Corporation—his wife wore only a "Republican cloth coat." Nixon did admit accepting one gift, a puppy his young daughters had named Checkers. That gift he would not give back, he declared earnestly. Nixon's televised pathos turned an embarrassing incident into an advantage. He effectively bypassed traditional Republican leaders by winning support from the general public to keep him on the ticket. The "Checkers speech" showed how the mass media—notably the new medium of television—were fundamentally changing the political process.

The Republican campaign paid off handsomely, with Eisenhower winning 55 percent of the popular vote. He carried all the northern and western states and won majorities in four southern states. Although Eisenhower won a great personal victory, Republican candidates for Congress ran far behind him. They won control of the House of Representatives by a slender margin of four seats; in 1954, Democrats regained control of both houses, an advantage they held for the rest of the Eisenhower years. When the enormously popular Eisenhower won an easy

reelection over Adlai Stevenson in 1956, he became the only president to win election while his party lost control of both houses of Congress.

The "Hidden-Hand" Presidency

Seeking a middle ground between liberalism and conservatism, Eisenhower offered "modern Republicanism" as an alternative to the Democrats' New Deal and Fair Deal. He did his best to set a quieter national mood, to slow down the pace of public life. As columnist Richard L. Strout observed in *The New Republic*, "The less he does the more they love him. Here is a man who doesn't rock the boat." Even Democratic challenger Adlai Stevenson agreed that "it is time for catching our breath." The nation's voters put it more simply in a popular slogan: "I Like Ike."

Yet Eisenhower was no stooge as president. Several historians have characterized his style of leadership as the "hidden-hand presidency." They point to Eisenhower's deft behind-the-scenes maneuvering while maintaining a public demeanor of a benign leader who did not concern himself with partisan questions. They also cite the president's skillful handling of the press. When his press secretary, James Hagerty, asked what he would say at a press conference about

PRESIDENT IKE
Arthur Krock of *The New York Times* characterized President Dwight D. Eisenhower's news conferences as events "in which numbers and genders collide, participles hang helplessly and syntax is lost forever." Eisenhower's vagueness and confusion in public contrasted with his more decisive and effective style behind the scenes. (UPI)

a tricky foreign policy issue, Eisenhower replied, "Don't worry, Jim. If that question comes up, I'll just confuse them." He proved just as adept in personnel situations. In a characteristic move, Eisenhower recognized the outspoken anticommunism of Clare Booth Luce, an author, playwright, and former Republican member of Congress from Connecticut, by making her the nation's second woman ambassador. At the same time, by sending Luce to Italy, he removed her strident opinions from the Washington scene.

Eisenhower's presidential style deliberately avoided confrontation. He refused to speak out publicly, for example, against Senator Joseph McCarthy. Likewise, he displayed little leadership in the emerging area of civil rights. Inadvertently, though, he contributed to the advance of the black cause. In September 1953, he named Governor Earl Warren of California as chief justice of the Supreme Court. Warren's quiet persuasion convinced the Court to rule unanimously in *Brown v. Board of Education of Topeka* (1954) that racial segregation in the public schools was unconstitutional. Eisenhower remained disturbed by the decision, asserting, "I don't believe you can change the hearts of men with laws or decisions." Nonetheless, in 1957 he sent federal troops to enforce the integration of Central High School in Little Rock, Arkansas. Congress also passed the Civil Rights Act of 1957, a weak bill most notable for being the first national civil rights legislation passed since Reconstruction.

Eisenhower presided over other cautious increases in federal activity. When the Soviet Union launched the first satellite (called *Sputnik,* or "earth traveler") into space in 1957, Eisenhower supported a U.S. space program to catch up with the Russians. Arguing that the cold war required more scientists and experts on foreign affairs, he persuaded Congress to appropriate additional money for college and university scholarships, as well as increased support for research and development in universities and industry. He also yielded to demands of interest groups for increased federal outlays on veterans' benefits, unemployment compensation, housing, and Social Security. The minimum wage was raised from seventy-five cents an hour to a dollar. The creation of the new Department of Health, Education, and Welfare (HEW) con-

firmed the federal commitment to welfare programs. When HEW head Oveta Culp Hobby, the second woman to hold a cabinet position, suggested that it would be "socialized medicine" for the government to offer free distribution of the new Salk polio vaccine, she was forced from office by the adverse public reaction.

Under the Eisenhower administration, the government undertook new commitments on a more massive scale. It sponsored the construction of the Saint Lawrence Seaway to link the Great Lakes with the Atlantic Ocean. In a move that drastically altered the American landscape and favored the trend toward privately owned automobiles rather than mass transit, the Federal Highway Act of 1956 authorized $26 billion over a ten-year period for the construction of a nationally integrated highway system. Projects such as the Saint Lawrence Seaway and interstate highways were the largest public works programs to date, surpassing anything the New Deal had undertaken.

Dwight Eisenhower realized that the vast federal budget, which reached almost 23 percent of the gross national product by the late 1950s, gave the government a major responsibility for the overall health of the nation's economy. The president made the fight against inflation, not full employment, his top economic priority. Eisenhower and his advisers believed their policies would encourage business confidence and lead to prosperity, but the economy grew only at the modest rate of 2.9 percent per year between 1953 and 1960—too slowly to absorb all those who sought work. Furthermore, Eisenhower's drive for a balanced budget and stable prices contributed to the recessions of 1953–1954, 1957–1958, and 1960–1961.

Modern Republicanism, it turned out, resisted the unchecked expansion of federal power but did not cut it back in any tangible fashion. The responsibilities now accepted by the federal government—which included social welfare programs inherited from the New Deal, a commitment to managing the economy, and increased defense expenditures necessitated by the United States' larger role abroad—negated any return to the limited Republican government that had prevailed in the 1920s. When Eisenhower retired from public life in 1961, the government had become an even greater presence in everyday life than when he took office.

The New Politics and the 1960 Campaign

The crucial question for the Republicans in 1960 was whether they could maintain their hold on the presidency without popular Dwight D. Eisenhower. The Twenty-Second Amendment now limited a president to two terms. A Republican-controlled Congress had passed the measure in 1951 to prevent another long-term presidency such as Franklin Roosevelt's. Ironically, it precluded another Eisenhower term.

The Republicans turned without opposition to Vice-President Richard M. Nixon, who like a good junior executive had patiently served Eisenhower, gaining experience and waiting for his turn at the top. Nixon campaigned for an updated version of Eisenhower's policies, carefully staking out a position between the Republican conservative wing, now led by Senator Barry M. Goldwater of Arizona, and the moderate wing represented by Governor Nelson A. Rockefeller of New York. Nixon was hampered, however, by the occasionally lukewarm support he received from Eisenhower. Asked whether Nixon had helped make any major policy decisions in his administration, Eisenhower replied, "If you give me a week I might think of one."

After two unsuccessful tries with Adlai Stevenson as their candidate, the Democrats turned to Senator John Fitzgerald Kennedy of Massachusetts, who beat out Hubert Humphrey and Lyndon Johnson for the nomination. An alumnus of Harvard and a World War II hero, Kennedy had inherited his love of politics from his grandfathers, both of whom had been colorful Boston politicians. His wealthy father, Joseph P. Kennedy, had headed the Securities and Exchange Commission and served as ambassador to Great Britain under Roosevelt. First elected to Congress in 1946, John Kennedy moved to the Senate in 1952. Ambitious, hard-driving, and deeply aware of style, he made full use of his many advantages to become, as novelist Norman Mailer put it, "our leading man." Besides his youth—he was only forty-three—Kennedy's greatest disadvantage was his Catholicism.

The 1960 campaign marked the introduction to the national scene of political practices called the "new politics." Originally developed in California in the late 1940s and early 1950s, this political style was well suited to a state that was growing so fast that it did not have entrenched political machines or active party organizations. California covered such a huge territory that candidates had to rely on billboard and newspaper advertising, radio spots, and television ads rather than personal contact with voters to win statewide office. The state also lacked the strong union tradition that influenced politics in other parts of the country.

Charisma, style, and personality, rather than issues and platforms, were the hallmarks of the new politics. The media were the key to the new approach, and politicians paid special attention to the ability of television to reach individual voters. (By 1960, 88 percent of the nation's households owned at least one TV set.) Professional media consultants now advised candidates on their proper image, and professional pollsters

THE NEW POLITICS COMES TO NEW HAMPSHIRE

John Fitzgerald Kennedy, the first Catholic ever elected president, was also the first Democratic presidential nominee from New England in over one hundred years. Here the Massachusetts senator campaigns in neighboring New Hampshire, whose primary he won handily in February 1960. (Hank Walker. *Life* Magazine © 1960 Time, Inc.)

not only told candidates whether they were leading their opponents, but also what ideas to stress in order to get elected.

The spread of the new politics contributed to a decline in the role of traditional political party organizations at the national level. The new politics targeted its appeal to enthusiastic amateurs outside the traditional party organization, rather than to the ward bosses, state committee officials, and party machines that once delivered the votes on election day. By using the media, campaigns could bypass the party structures to touch, if only with a thirty-second commercial, the ordinary citizen.

Running such campaigns took money, however, and the required funds often far exceeded those available through the traditional party coffers. Once candidates began to seek campaign funds from other sources (wealthy donors, mass mailings, or, by the 1970s, from political action committees set up by corporations, labor unions, or special interest groups to channel contributions to candidates), the influence of political parties diminished even further. In addition, party loyalty declined as growing numbers of voters identified themselves as independents, a major shift from patterns of political behavior in the nineteenth and early twentieth centuries. The combination of these factors made it increasingly difficult to maintain the New Deal coalition.

John Kennedy was a perfect candidate to take the new politics to the national level in 1960, and his campaign altered the nature of American presidential contests. His family's wealth and the contributions he raised from sources outside traditional party donors paid for this expensive campaign. Thanks both to his media advisers

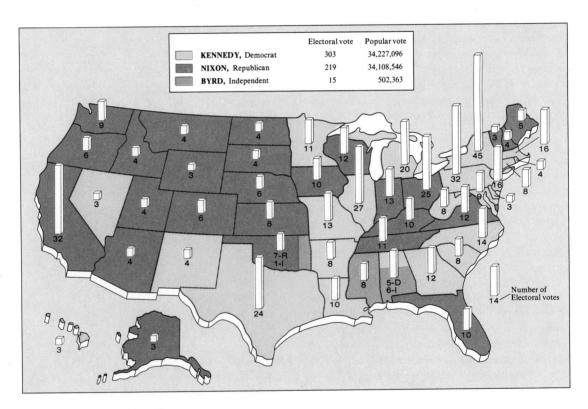

	Electoral vote	Popular vote
KENNEDY, Democrat	303	34,227,096
NIXON, Republican	219	34,108,546
BYRD, Independent	15	502,363

MAP 28.2 ELECTION OF 1960
The election of 1960 produced the closest popular vote since 1884. Kennedy won twelve states, including Illinois, by less than 2 percent of the two-party vote tally, and lost six others, including California, to Nixon by a similarly small margin. Kennedy won 303 electoral votes, the same number that President Truman had received in 1948, but his margin of victory was far slimmer, showing how the electoral college vote can be misleading as an indicator of popular support.

and to his personality, he projected a superb television image. His mastery of this method enabled him to appeal directly to the voters, rather than through the Democratic party.

Another innovation of the 1960 campaign was a series of four televised debates between the two major candidates. These debates further confirmed the new dominance of mass media in political life. Nixon, a far less photogenic personality than Kennedy and at an added disadvantage because he was recovering from a minor illness, looked sallow and unshaven under the intense studio lights. Kennedy, by contrast, looked vigorous, cool, and self-confident on the TV screen, and he dispelled voters' doubts that he was not as well prepared for the presidency as the former vice-president. Confirming that appearances swayed political perceptions, voters who listened to the first debate on the radio concluded that Nixon had won, whereas TV viewers judged in Kennedy's favor.

Despite the ground Kennedy picked up in the debates, he won only the narrowest of victories, receiving 49.7 percent of the popular vote to Nixon's 49.5 percent. Kennedy had successfully appealed to the diverse elements of the Democratic coalition, attracting large proportions of Catholic voters and blacks and strengthening his party's appeal to the middle class. Yet only 120,000 votes out of a total of 69 million cast separated the two candidates, and the shift of a few thousand votes in key states such as Illinois would have reversed the election results. Although Kennedy had campaigned on a promise to get America moving again, the electoral results hardly gave him a popular mandate for sweeping change.

The Politics of Expectation

During the 1960s, Americans placed new demands on the federal government. John F. Kennedy's brilliant articulation of the aspirations of many Americans, enhanced by his youth and self-confidence, enabled him to reconstitute the Democratic coalition. Kennedy's shocking assassination in November 1963, and the extraordinary energy of his successor, Lyndon Baines Johnson, then set in motion a remarkable expansion of federal power. In 1964, big-city Catholics,

the middle class, and many southern whites joined organized labor and blacks in one of the largest and most diverse political coalitions ever assembled in the United States.

For a brief period in 1965–1966, this coalition held together. Under Johnson's leadership, the Democrats enacted nearly all of the legislative program Harry Truman had outlined in 1946. By making the federal government far more powerful than ever before, the new legislation encouraged the constituents of the Democratic coalition to redouble their demands. By 1968, this dramatic expansion of federal power had raised unanticipated problems for the coalition.

Kennedy's Thousand Days

The administration of John Fitzgerald Kennedy began amid great promise. "Let the word go forth from this time and place," he orated in his inaugural address, "to friend and foe alike, that the torch has been passed to a new generation of Americans, tempered by war, disciplined by a hard and bitter peace, proud of our ancient heritage." Unlike his predecessor, Kennedy believed the federal government ought to be strong, visible, and active and that the president should set the tone for such leadership. In foreign policy, he remained a resolute cold warrior. At home, his "New Frontier" would be built on patriotism and service. "Ask not what your country can do for you," he insisted at his inauguration. "Ask what you can do for your country."

Kennedy's dramatic emphasis on the importance of the federal government attracted unusually bright and ambitious people to his administration. Robert S. McNamara, former president of the Ford Motor Company, introduced "systems analysis" techniques to the Department of Defense. Republican banker C. Douglas Dillon brought the corporate managers' desire for expanded markets and stable economic growth to the Department of the Treasury. The president's younger brother Robert took over the Department of Justice as attorney general, and his brother-in-law Sargent Shriver headed the popular Peace Corps. A host of "honorary Kennedys," trusted advisers and academics from leading universities, flocked to Washington to join the New Frontier.

Kennedy expected his appointees to move

quickly. "The deadline for everything is the day before yesterday," exclaimed one cabinet member. House Speaker Sam Rayburn was skeptical about this vigorous approach to government. Kennedy's people "might be every bit as intelligent as you say," he told his old friend Lyndon Johnson, "but I'd feel a whole lot better about them if just one of them had run for sheriff once."

The expansive vision of presidential leadership that Kennedy and his advisers brought to the White House stood in stark contrast to their rather meager legislative accomplishments. Kennedy was hampered by his lack of a popular mandate, which left him with a tiny Democratic majority of two in the Senate and twenty-two in the House. A conservative coalition of southern Democrats and western and midwestern Republicans effectively stalled most liberal initiatives.

One domestic program that did win both popular and congressional support was increased funding for space exploration. In 1958, seven astronauts had been chosen for America's Mercury space program. On May 5, 1961, just three months after Kennedy took office, Alan Shepard became the first American launched into space; on February 2, 1962, John Glenn became the first American to orbit the earth. (Soviet cosmonaut Yuri Gagarin held the distinction of being the first person in space with his 108-hour flight in April 1961.) At the height of American fascination with space in 1961, Kennedy proposed that "this nation should commit itself to achieving the goal, before this decade is out, of landing a man on the moon and returning him safely to earth." To accomplish this mission, achieved in July 1969, he supported the creation of a massive new federal agency, the National Aeronautics and Space Administration (NASA).

The Peace Corps was the New Frontier program that most captured the public imagination. The idea, Kennedy explained on March 1, 1961, was to create "a pool of trained American men and women" to be sent "overseas by the United States government or through private organizations and institutions to help foreign countries meet their urgent needs for skilled manpower." Thousands of idealistic Americans, most of them recent college graduates, responded to the call, agreeing to devote two or more years to such tasks as teaching English to Philippine schoolchildren and helping African villagers obtain adequate supplies of water. As Kennedy aide Arthur M. Schlesinger, Jr., explained, the Peace Corps embodied Kennedy's desire "to replace protocol-minded, striped-pants officials by reform-minded missionaries of democracy who mixed with the people, spoke the native dialects, ate the food, and involved themselves in local struggles against ignorance and want."

Kennedy's most striking domestic achievement was his successful use of modern economics to shape fiscal policy. Initially Kennedy had shared the belief of many conservative business leaders that the federal government could best contribute to economic growth by reducing the national debt and maintaining a balanced bud-

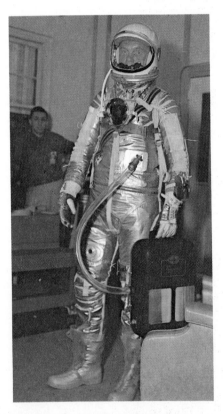

THE AMERICAN SPACE PROGRAM
Marine Lieutenant Colonel John Glenn, shown preparing for his historic 1962 flight, became the first American to orbit the earth. The space program had cold war overtones as the United States tried to catch up and surpass early successes of the Soviet Union, including beating the Russians to the moon. (FPG)

get. However, at the urging of Walter Heller, chairman of the Council of Economic Advisers, Kennedy decided on a different course to stimulate the economy. Rather than increase federal spending to accomplish this result, he proposed a dramatic cut in the taxes paid by businesses and the public. A tax cut, he argued, would leave more money in the hands of taxpayers, enabling them to increase their investments and purchases, and thus bring about economic growth by creating more wealth and jobs. For a time, federal expenditures would exceed federal income, but after a year or two, the expanding economy would raise taxpayers' incomes, leading in turn to higher tax revenues.

Congress predictably balked at this unorthodox proposal. But Lyndon Johnson pressed for it after Kennedy's assassination and signed it into law in February 1964. The Kennedy-Johnson tax cut of 1964 marked the first purposeful use of the federal budget—fiscal policy—to encourage steady economic growth. Although economic expansion started before the effects of the tax cut could be felt, Kennedy and his economic advisers got credit for it anyway. The gross national product grew at a rate of 5 percent during the 1960s, nearly twice the rate achieved during the Eisenhower administration. Much of this growth, however, was fueled by massive defense expenditures for the escalating Vietnam War.

Kennedy's interest in stimulating economic growth did not include a corresponding commitment to spending for domestic needs. John Kenneth Galbraith, his most liberal economic adviser, had argued that it would be better to stimulate the economy by expanding social programs than by cutting taxes: What is the advantage, Galbraith asked, "in having a few more dollars to spend if the air is too dirty to breathe, the water is too polluted to drink, the commuters are losing out in the struggle to get in and out of cities, the streets are filthy, and the schools are so bad that the young, perhaps wisely, stay away"? Kennedy rejected such advice, advocating increased spending only for weapons and space, and sent Galbraith off as ambassador to India.

The president did not entirely ignore the legislative agenda Franklin Roosevelt and Harry Truman had set for the Democratic party. He proposed federal aid to elementary and secondary schools, federal investment in mass transportation, medical insurance for the elderly funded through Social Security, and wilderness preservation. But he failed to define any of these proposals in terms satisfactory to a majority in Congress and all were defeated.

Dissension within the Democratic coalition was particularly evident in the case of aid to education. Most northern Democrats favored such aid, but they disagreed about important details. Blacks and civil rights advocates insisted that federal school aid go only to desegregated schools, while Catholics insisted that federal assistance be extended to parochial systems. After great effort, Kennedy persuaded black leaders to accept a school aid plan that ignored existing segregation, but he told southern whites that federal aid would not be guaranteed to segregated schools in the future. Because Kennedy was himself a Catholic, however, he feared angering Protestants if he proposed a bill that permitted aid to parochial schools. In the absence of a bill acceptable to all these groups, the education proposal died in committee.

Kennedy failed to provide decisive leadership in other domestic fields. He ignored women's issues and appointed fewer women to federal positions than Eisenhower or Truman had. Most tellingly, he never made civil rights a top priority. He believed he would need the votes of southern whites to win reelection in 1964, and he sought to hold them in the Democratic coalition by delaying the civil rights reforms he had promised during the 1960 campaign. He doubted such measures would pass in any case. "There is no sense in raising hell," he insisted, "and then in not being successful."

Some of the most controversial decisions of the early 1960s, however, came not from the Kennedy administration, but from the Supreme Court under the leadership of Chief Justice Earl Warren. This activist Supreme Court came to represent for many Americans an intrusive federal presence they had not sought and did not want. In *Gideon v. Wainright* (1963), *Escobedo v. Illinois* (1964), and *Miranda v. Arizona* (1966), the Supreme Court greatly expanded the rights of suspects accused of crimes. Tackling the issue of reapportionment in *Baker v. Carr* (1962) and *Reynolds v. Sims* (1964), the Court put forth the

THE WARREN COURT
This photograph of the Supreme Court was taken in 1965, with Chief Justice Earl Warren in the middle of the front row. Until President Ronald Reagan named Sandra Day O'Connor to the Court in 1981, all pictures of the nation's highest court showed nine solemn robed men. (© Fred Ward, Black Star)

doctrine of "one person, one vote," which substantially increased the representation of urban areas, with their concentration of black and Hispanic residents, at the expense of rural regions. Perhaps the most controversial decision of all was *Engel v. Vitale* (1962), which outlawed prayer in public schools as a violation of the First Amendment's injunction that "Congress shall make no law respecting an establishment of religion." President Kennedy, like President Eisenhower before him, could only pledge to uphold the law of the land, even when he disagreed with the scope of judicial activism.

By late 1963, Kennedy had realized little of his promise. He had expanded the government through his space and arms programs, his intervention in the economy, and his successful effort to attract able people to federal service. While partisans later claimed he planned to expand antipoverty, health, and education programs; commit federal resources to civil rights; withdraw American troops from Vietnam; and reduce tensions with the Soviet Union, we will never know what he might have accomplished.

On November 22, 1963, Kennedy went to Texas, a state he needed to win in order to be reelected in 1964. As he rode in an open car past the Texas School Book Depository in Dallas, he was shot and killed by an assassin's bullet. Before Air Force One left Dallas to take the presi-

dent's body back to Washington, a grim-faced Vice-President Lyndon Johnson was sworn in as president. Kennedy's stunned widow, Jacqueline, still wearing a bloodstained pink suit, looked on.

By 1 P.M. Dallas time, just thirty minutes after the shooting, 68 percent of the adults in the United States, about seventy-five million people, knew that Kennedy had been shot. By late afternoon, the proportion had risen to 99.8 percent, showing how within a few hours, the mass media could connect practically every person in the nation. As on Pearl Harbor Day in 1941, people never forgot what they were doing when they first heard Kennedy had been shot. The shock that greeted the assassination reflected the personal identification that ordinary Americans felt with the occupant of the White House, a situation quite different from the last assassination of an American president, that of William McKinley in 1901.

Americans suspended normal activities for four days as they sought reassurance in ceremonies of grief and continuity. All three major television networks canceled their commercial programs, and an estimated audience of 100 million Americans collectively mourned the slain president. They saw 250,000 people pay their last respects as Kennedy's body lay in state in the Capitol rotunda; they watched as his coffin was drawn up Pennsylvania Avenue on a horse-drawn caisson, led by a riderless horse with reversed boots in the stirrups; they admired the dignified bearing of Jacqueline Kennedy as she and her two young children walked behind the casket; and they joined the procession past a million mourners to the burial place in Arlington National Cemetery on a hill overlooking the city of Washington. These shared televison images bound the American people together at a time of national grief.

Kennedy's buoyant youth, the trauma of his assassination, and the collective sense that Americans had been robbed of a promising leader contributed to a powerful Kennedy mystique. This mythologizing process had begun even before his tragic death. In June 1963, about 59 percent of the people surveyed claimed to have voted for Kennedy, and after the assassination, this figure rose to 65 percent. British journalist Godfrey Hodgson called it "a posthumous landslide."

The Kennedy assassination also set off a national wave of self-examination. Americans debated whether the murder of the president had been an isolated act or the symbol of a deep tragic flaw in the democratic system. (The argument that there was something wrong with the nation gained credence two days after the assassination, when Kennedy's accused killer, Lee Harvey Oswald, a twenty-four-year-old loner who had spent three years in the Soviet Union, was himself gunned down by Jack Ruby, a Dallas nightclub owner, on live network television.) Chief Justice Earl Warren warned ominously about "forces of hatred and malevolence" that made such acts possible, and newspapers and magazines asked, "What sort of nation are we?" Later in the 1960s, many Americans overwhelmed by the social conflict of that decade looked back on November 22, 1963, as the day when things began to come apart.

Johnson and the Great Society

Without offering any radical or sweeping programs, John Kennedy fostered an atmosphere conducive to challenging the status quo, a climate that has been called the "politics of expectation." President Lyndon Johnson, through his astonishing energy and genius for compromise,

translated these unformed strivings for change into a concrete program.

Born in the central Texas hill country in 1908, Johnson had served in Washington since 1932 as congressional aide, New Deal administrator, congressman, senator, senate majority leader, and finally vice-president. He had far more legislative experience than any modern president, and he used his talent to great effect. A man of singular force, he often got his way by using what one journalist called the "Johnson treatment." Approaching unsuspecting colleagues, he moved "in close, his face a scant millimeter from his target, his eyes widening and narrowing, his eyebrows rising and falling. From his pockets poured clippings, memos, statistics. Mimicry, humor, and the genius of analogy made the Treatment an almost hypnotic experience." Johnson invariably left his targets overwhelmed and bruised—and willing to go along.

Johnson seized the initiative almost as soon as Kennedy's assassination thrust him into the presidency. He called for rapid passage of New

THE "JOHNSON TREATMENT"
Lyndon B. Johnson, a shrewd and adroit politician, learned many of his legislative skills while serving as Majority Leader of the Senate from 1953 to 1960. Here, in characteristic LBJ style, he zeroes in on Senator Theodore Francis Green of Rhode Island. After succeeding John Kennedy in the White House, Johnson remarked, "They say Jack Kennedy had style, but I'm the one who's got the bills passed." (George Tames, *The New York Times*)

CAMPAIGNING FOR GOLDWATER
Lyndon B. Johnson's election to the presidency in 1964 was made easier when the Republicans nominated Senator Barry Goldwater of Arizona as their candidate. Goldwater rallied conservatives behind the motto, "In your heart you know he's right." Democrats effectively played on fears that Goldwater might support the use of nuclear weapons by countering, "In your heart you know he might." (© Declan Haun)

Frontier proposals, especially the tax cut and civil rights legislation, as a memorial to the slain president. Dramatically reminding Congress that he himself, a Texan, had supported civil rights, he made it difficult for any southerner to oppose the issue. "I urge you again, as I did in 1957 and again in 1960," he told Congress, "to enact a civil rights law so that we can move forward to eliminate from this nation every trace of discrimination and oppression that is based upon race or color."

By June, black pressure and Johnson's sure-handed tactics had their impact. Breaking a southern filibuster, the Senate approved the most far-reaching civil rights legislation since Reconstruction. The 1964 Civil Rights Act guaranteed equal access to public accommodations and schools and prohibited discrimination by employers and unions. It granted new powers to the U.S. attorney general to enforce these guarantees and established the Equal Employment Opportunity Commission to prevent job discrimination by race, religion, national origin, or sex.

If 1964 was a year of liberal triumph in Congress, it was a year of conservative retrenchment within the Republican party. The Republican nominee for president in 1964 was Senator Barry Goldwater of Arizona. Goldwater, who was determined to offer "a choice, not an echo," campaigned against the expansion of federal power in such areas as the economy and civil rights. Goldwater's crisp speeches rejected efforts to build a moderate coalition. "Extremism in the defense of liberty is no vice," he stated. "Moderation in the pursuit of justice is no virtue."

President Johnson easily won his party's nomination. Reaffirming his commitment to the liberal Democratic agenda, but putting some distance between himself and the Kennedy administration, Johnson passed over Robert F. Kennedy for vice-president in favor of Senator Hubert H. Humphrey of Minnesota, who in 1948 had introduced the controversial civil rights plank that split the party. An attempt by an avowed segregationist, Governor George C. Wallace of Alabama, to exploit a white backlash against civil rights showed early momentum but then fizzled. The Johnson-Humphrey ticket won by one of the largest margins in history, receiving 61.1 percent of the popular vote. It even surpassed the 1936 landslide of that great coalition builder, Franklin D. Roosevelt, Johnson's political idol and mentor. Johnson's sweeping victory brought with it Democratic gains in Congress and state legislatures.

Lyndon Johnson held an expansive view of presidential leadership. Eager to make his own mark on American history and only too aware that the liberal majority in Congress was likely to be short-lived, Johnson pressed for prompt legislation to achieve his "Great Society." "Hurry boys, hurry," he urged his staff. "Get that legislation up to the Hill and out. Eighteen months from now ol' Landslide Lyndon will be Lame-Duck Lyndon." As he forcefully put it, "There are some administrations that do and some that don't. This one is gonna do."

The Eighty-ninth Congress enacted more social-reform measures than any session since Roosevelt's first term, offering something for every important element of the Democratic coalition. Responding to growing black demands, Johnson increased federal support for civil rights. The Voting Rights Act of 1965 authorized the attorney general to send federal examiners to the South to register voters. In 1963, only a fourth of all southern blacks were registered to vote; when Johnson left office in 1969, their ranks had swelled to two-thirds.

Johnson also found a way to break the congressional deadlock on aid to education. The Elementary and Secondary Education Act of 1965 authorized $1 billion in federal funds to benefit impoverished children attending Catholic schools, rather than aiding the schools themselves. With his flair for the dramatic, Johnson signed the education bill in the one-room Texas schoolhouse he had attended as a child.

The Eighty-ninth Congress also gave Johnson the votes to enact the federal health insurance legislation first proposed by President Truman. Realizing it could no longer block federal health insurance in its entirety, the American Medical Association proposed that federal funds be used to pay doctors as well as hospitals. The resulting compromise was an expansive new program that included both Medicare, a plan for the elderly funded from an increment to Social Security payroll taxes, and Medicaid, a health plan for welfare recipients paid for by general tax revenues. By 1975, the cost of Medicare reached $18 billion. Medicaid grew more slowly at first, but by the mid-1970s it covered twenty-four million people and cost $14 billion annually. Few policymakers had anticipated that Medicare and Medicaid costs would spiral so dramatically.

The middle class benefited from Democratic programs as much as the poor did. Federal urban renewal and home mortgage assistance aided those who could afford to live in single-family homes or in modern apartments. Medicare assistance went to every elderly person covered by Social Security, regardless of need. Much of the federal aid to education benefited the children of the middle class. Johnson successfully pressed for expansion of the national park system, for legislation to improve the quality of the air and water, for increased land-use planning, and, at the insistence of his wife, Lady Bird Johnson, for the Highway Beautification Act of 1965. That year also saw the creation of the National Endowment for the Arts to support the performing and creative arts, and the National Endowment for the Humanities, which encouraged efforts to understand and interpret the nation's cultural and historical heritage.

Although Johnson's programs offered something for every constituency in the Democratic coalition, he always insisted that the top priority of his Great Society was "an end to poverty in our time." The problem of poverty was very real. As political activist Michael Harrington had pointed out in his book *The Other America: Poverty in the United States* (1962), the poor were everywhere, but their poverty was curiously invisible in affluent America. Poor people made up about a fourth of the American population; three-fourths of the poor were white. The poor in the United States were isolated farmers and miners in Appalachia, country folk recently uprooted from the land, blacks mired in urban ghettos, Hispanics in migrant labor camps and urban barrios, native Americans on reservations, women trying against all odds to raise families on their own, and the abandoned and destitute elderly. Modern American technology had "made a longer, healthier, better life possible," Harrington observed, yet it left the poor "on the fringe, on the margin": "They watch the movies and read the magazines of affluent America, and these teach them that they are internal exiles."

New Deal social welfare programs had failed to reach these people. Since unemployment insurance ran out after a few months, it did nothing to protect against extended joblessness. Social Security and other social-insurance programs provided benefits to workers who paid for them through special taxes; such measures did not cover farm workers, hospital janitors and orderlies, laundry workers, or women who cared for their children at home or cleaned other people's houses. Social welfare programs such as Old Age Assistance, Aid to Dependent Children, and Aid to the Blind carried strict restrictions regarding eligibility.

The Office of Economic Opportunity (OEO), established by the omnibus Economic Opportunity Act of 1964, became the Great Society's showcase in the "War on Poverty." OEO programs were so numerous and diverse that they recalled the alphabet agencies of the New Deal. Sargent Shriver, who left the Peace Corps to head the new agency, admitted, "It's like we

MICHAEL HARRINGTON DESCRIBES "THE OTHER AMERICA" (1962)

There are perennial reasons that make the other America an invisible land.

Poverty is often off the beaten track. It always has been. The ordinary tourist never left the main highway, and today he rides interstate turnpikes. He does not go into the valleys of Pennsylvania where the towns look like movie sets of Wales in the thirties. He does not see the company houses in rows, the rutted roads (the poor always have bad roads whether they live in the city, in towns, or on farms), and everything is black and dirty. And even if he were to pass through such a place by accident, the tourist would not meet the unemployed men in the bar or the women coming home from a runaway sweatshop. . . .

These are the normal and obvious causes of the invisibility of the poor. They operated a generation ago; they will be functioning a generation hence. It is more important to understand that the very development of American society is creating a new kind of blindness about poverty. The poor are increasingly slipping out of the very experience and consciousness of the nation. . . .

Clothes make the poor invisible too: America has the best-dressed poverty the world has ever known. For a variety of reasons, the benefits of mass production have been spread much more evenly in this area than in many others. It is much easier in the United States to be decently dressed than it is to be decently housed, fed, or doctored. Even people with terribly depressed incomes can look prosperous. . . .

And finally, the poor are politically invisible. It is one of the cruelest ironies of social life in advanced countries that the dispossessed at the bottom of society are unable to speak for themselves. The people of the other America do not, by far and large, belong to unions, to fraternal organizations, or to political parties. They are without lobbies of their own; they put forward no legislative program. As a group, they are atomized. They have no face; they have no voice. . . .

These, then, are the strangest poor in the history of mankind.

They exist within the most powerful and richest society the world has ever known. Their misery has continued while the majority of the nation talked of itself as being "affluent" and worried about neuroses in the suburbs. In this way tens of millions of human beings became invisible. They dropped out of sight and out of mind; they were without their own political voice.

Yet this need not be. The means are at hand to fulfill the age-old dream: poverty can now be abolished. How long shall we ignore this underdeveloped nation in our midst? How long shall we look the other way while our fellow human beings suffer? How long?

Source: Michael Harrington, *The Other America: Poverty in the United States.* New York: Macmillan, 1962. 11–13, 170.

---

went down to Cape Kennedy [the NASA space center in Florida] and launched a half dozen rockets at once."

The War on Poverty produced some of the most significant and controversial measures of the Johnson administration. Head Start provided free nursery schools designed to prepare disadvantaged preschoolers for kindergarten. The Job Corps and the Neighborhood Youth Corps trained young people. Upward Bound gave low-income teenagers the skills and motivation to plan for college. The Appalachian Regional Development Act, the Metropolitan Area Redevelopment Act, and the Demonstration Cities Act were intended, like foreign aid, to spur development of impoverished areas. Volunteers in Service to America (VISTA), modeled on the Peace Corps, provided technical assistance to the rural poor. The Community Action Program encouraged the poor to organize to demand "maximum feasible participation" in the decisions that affected them. Community Action organizers worked closely with the two thousand lawyers employed by the Legal Services Program to provide the poor with free access to the legal system.

The OEO quickly drew criticism, however. VISTA and Community Action Program agents had encouraged poor people to mount militant demands for public services long withheld by unresponsive local governments controlled by middle- or upper-class politicians. Community organizers on the government payroll in Syracuse, New York, for example, formed tenants' rights groups to protest conditions in public housing, conducted voter registration drives to unseat unpopular elected representatives, and even used public funds to bail out activists arrested for protesting at local welfare offices. Legal Services lawyers challenged welfare and housing administrations in class-action suits. Needless to say, such activism upset entrenched political elites. Such mayors as Sam Yorty in Los Angeles and Richard J. Daley in Chicago vociferously resisted OEO guidelines for including poor people in program planning and administration.

The Great Society also tried to reduce poverty by expanding long-established social insurance and welfare programs. It broadened Social Security to include waitresses, cleaning people, farm workers, and hospital employees. Benefits for the elderly were raised, extended to include Medicare, and (in 1972) indexed to rise with inflation. Social welfare expenditures also increased rapidly, especially for Aid to Families with Dependent Children (AFDC). Housing programs provided $3 billion worth of public housing and rent subsidies annually by 1974. The Food Stamp program, begun in 1964 largely to stabilize farm prices, grew into a major program of assistance to low-income families.

In the end, however, the War on Poverty did little to reduce poverty or redistribute wealth. Using a definition of poverty as half the median family income, the poverty line in 1963 was set at three thousand dollars. That year, 20 percent of the population lived below the poverty line. In 1976, the median family income had risen to fifteen thousand dollars, but 20 percent of the nation still received less than half that amount. Technological change and economic growth had raised everyone's material standard of living so that the poor were better off in an absolute

sense. Relatively, however, they remained as far behind the middle class as ever. In effect, the War on Poverty and related welfare efforts simply provided the nation's poor with about the share of income they had always received.

The ambiguous accomplishments of the Great Society suggest the difficulties of promoting fundamental political and economic change through federal initiatives. Its record also reveals contradictions inherent in the New Deal coalition. These contradictions had been lurking in political life ever since Franklin Roosevelt and Harry Truman began to expand the impact of the

BUTTER, NOT GUNS
This placard graphically protested that the Vietnam War diverted money from government social and economic programs aimed at aiding the nation's poor. Many Americans shared this view, and antiwar demonstrations spread across the United States. The protesters included students on hundreds of college campuses. (© Michael Abramson, Gamma-Liaison)

TIME LINE
THE POLITICS OF POST-NEW DEAL AMERICA

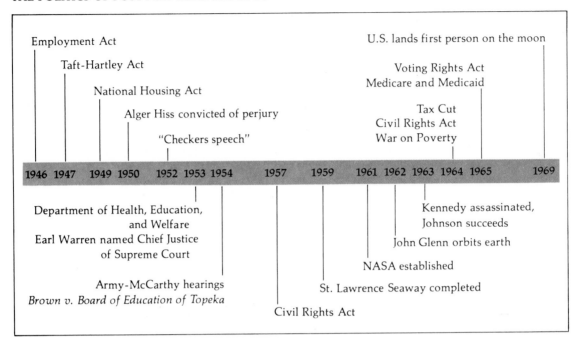

federal government on American society. John Kennedy and Lyndon Johnson had brought an extraordinarily diverse set of groups into the New Deal coalition—middle-class and poor; white, black, and Hispanic; Protestant and Catholic; urban and rural. As the functions and responsibilities of the government grew, so did demands for further action from this widening cast of politically organized constituencies. Yet the demands of certain groups—such as the cry of blacks for civil rights and of the urban poor for increased political power—conflicted with the interests of other Democratic supporters, such as white southerners and northern political bosses eager to maintain the status quo. In the end, the New Deal coalition, which had fostered a vast and powerful federal government, could not sustain a consensus over the purposes that such a government ought to serve.

The Great Society was not just a victim of the factionalism of the Democratic coalition. It was also, in the haunting phrase of civil rights leader Martin Luther King, Jr., "shot down on the battle-fields of Vietnam." In 1966, the government spent $22 billion on the Vietnam War and only $1.2 billion on the War on Poverty. Nearly two hundred thousand American soldiers were fighting in Vietnam by the end of 1965, four hundred thousand by the end of 1966, and half a million a year later. After 1966, as Lyndon Johnson turned his full attention to the escalating war, the domestic programs of the Great Society fell by the wayside.

Johnson never admitted to the American people the extent of the nation's growing involvement in Vietnam; nor did he confront the true cost of ending poverty through legislative activism. At a time of nearly full employment, his failure to press for a tax increase to cover the expanded budget commitments at home and abroad led to a growing deficit and accompanying high inflation. Johnson's attempt to carry out simultaneously, in historian Garry Wills's apt phrase, a "welfare" and "warfare" state provoked by 1968 a profound crisis from which the Democratic coalition has yet completely to recover.

The growth of the federal government dominated the postwar period. The major concern in postwar politics was the purposes that this expanded federal power should serve. The concentration of power in Washington also led to a corresponding growth in the responsibilities of the president, whom citizens now invested with rising expectations of leadership. John F. Kennedy especially stimulated this "politics of expectation."

The Democratic party set much of the legislative agenda for the postwar period, expanding the reforms first introduced by Franklin Roosevelt in the 1930s. Harry Truman's Fair Deal won only limited legislative victories but added civil rights to the national political agenda. The Republican administration of Dwight Eisenhower did not seek to roll back the New Deal and, in fact, presided over cautious increases in federal power. Lyndon Johnson, building on the wave of public emotion after Kennedy's assassination, significantly expanded the welfare state with his Great Society.

In political party organization, the two decades after 1945 were dominated by the Democratic coalition first assembled during the New Deal—labor, blacks, urban dwellers, ethnic groups, and a large section of the middle class who had benefited from New Deal programs. Between 1952 and 1960, despite the personal popularity of President Eisenhower, the Republicans were unable to establish a majority to overtake the vital New Deal coalition. By the late 1960s, however, the consensus of the Democratic party was threatened by controversy over social programs at home and the escalating Vietnam war abroad.

Suggestions for Further Reading

Three lively books provide excellent introductions to the politics of the postwar period: William Manchester, *The Glory and the Dream: A Narrative History of America, 1932–1972* (1973); Godfrey Hodgson, *America in Our Time* (1976); and William E. Leuchtenberg, *A Troubled Feast: American Society Since 1945* (1979).

Harry Truman and the Fair Deal

Harry S Truman's *Memoirs* (1955–1962) tell his story in characteristically pointed language; see also Merle Miller's oral history, *Plain Speaking* (1980). Eric F. Goldman, *The Crucial Decade and After—America, 1945–1960* (1961), offers an account of the period. The best description of Truman's presidency is Alonzo L. Hamby, *Beyond the New Deal: Harry S. Truman and American Liberalism* (1973). See also Richard J. Donovan, *Conflict and Crisis* (1977). Critical perspectives are presented in Barton J. Bernstein, ed., *Politics and Policies of the Truman Administration* (1970). Arthur M. Schlesinger, Jr., states the case for Fair Deal liberalism in *The Vital Center* (1949).

The story of the Democratic coalition can be traced in Samuel Lubbell, *The Future of American Politics* (1965); V. O. Key, *Politics, Parties, and Pressure Groups* (1964); Angus Campbell, ed., *Elections in the Political Order* (1967); and Everett C. Ladd and Charles Hadley, *Transformations of the American Party System* (1978). The 1948 campaign is described in Irwin Ross, *The Loneliest Campaign* (1968), and Jules Abels, *Out of the Jaws of Victory* (1959). The best account of Henry Wallace's challenge to Truman is Norman D. Markowitz, *The Rise and Fall of the People's Century: Henry A. Wallace and American Liberalism* (1973). Joseph P. Lash, *Eleanor: The Years Alone* (1972), describes the former First Lady's continuing work for liberal causes. James T. Patterson, *Mr. Republican: A Biography of Robert A. Taft* (1972), is the best account of Truman's chief Republican critic.

Stephen K. Bailey's model *Congress Makes a Law* (1957) covers the battle over the Employment Act of 1946. Other aspects of the Truman administration are treated by Arthur F. McClure, *The Truman Administration and the Problems of Postwar Labor* (1969); Allen J. Matusow, *Farm Policies and Politics in the Truman Years* (1967); and Susan Hartmann, *Truman and the 80th Congress* (1971).

The literature on McCarthyism is voluminous and intense. David Caute, *The Great Fear* (1978), provides a vivid introduction, which can be supplemented by Victor Navasky, *Naming Names* (1980), and Athan G. Theodaris, *Spying on Americans* (1978). Two biographies are Thomas C. Reeves, *The Life and Times of Joe McCarthy* (1982), and David Oshinsky, *A Conspiracy So Immense* (1983); but Richard Rovere's *Senator Joseph McCarthy* (1959) still commands attention. Michael P. Rogin, *The Intellectuals and McCarthy* (1967), analyzes McCarthy's base of support, while Robert Griffith, *The Politics of Fear* (1970), and Richard Fried, *Men Against McCarthy* (1976), look at the politics involved.

Allen Weinstein, *Perjury: The Hiss-Chambers Case* (1978), covers the still-debated Alger Hiss case. Walter and Miriam Schneir, *Invitation to an Inquest* (1965), and Ronald Radosh and Joyce Milton, *The Rosenberg File*

(1983), cover the Rosenberg case. Lillian Hellman offers her biting memoir of the period in *Scoundrel Time* (1976). Eric Bentley, ed., *Thirty Years of Treason* (1971), collects excerpts from testimony before the House Committee on Un-American Activities.

Modern Republicanism

Two standard overviews of the Eisenhower administration, Herbert S. Parmet, *Eisenhower and the American Crusades* (1972), and Charles C. Alexander, *Holding The Line* (1975), can be supplemented by Fred I. Greenstein, *The Hidden-Hand Presidency* (1982), and Stephen Ambrose, *Eisenhower the President* (1984). Blanche Wiesen Cook, *The Declassified Eisenhower* (1984), contrasts the covert activities of the administration with its public image. For scientific developments, consult James R. Killian, Jr., *Sputnik, Scientists, and Eisenhower* (1976). Richard M. Nixon, *Six Crises* (1962), offers the perspective of the vice-president.

For the Supreme Court, useful surveys include Archibald Cox, *The Warren Court* (1968); Alexander Bickel, *The Supreme Court and the Idea of Progress* (1970); and Philip B. Kurland, *Politics, the Constitution, and the Warren Court* (1970). Anthony Lewis, *Gideon's Trumpet* (1964), narrates one of the era's most famous cases.

The Politics of Expectation

The best histories of politics in the 1960s are Allen J. Matusow, *The Unraveling of America: A History of Liberalism in the 1960s* (1984); Jim F. Heath, *Decade of Disillusion: The Kennedy-Johnson Years* (1975); and James L. Sundquist, *Politics and Policy: The Eisenhower, Kennedy, and Johnson Years* (1968).

The indispensible account of the 1960 presidential campaign is Theodore H. White, *The Making of the President—1960* (1961). Arthur M. Schlesinger, Jr., *A Thousand Days* (1965), and Theodore Sorenson, *Kennedy* (1965), offer uncritical, but highly readable accounts of the New Frontier. See also Roger Hilsman, another Kennedy aide, *To Move a Nation* (1967). Critical views appear in David Halberstam, *The Best and the Brightest* (1972); Henry Fairlie, *The Kennedy Promise: The Politics of Expectation* (1973); and Gary Wills, *The Ken-*

nedy Imprisonment (1980). The best account of President Kennedy's assassination is William Manchester's overwritten *The Death of the President* (1967); Anthony Summer's *Conspiracy* (1980) provides a careful review of the ongoing controversy.

Lyndon Johnson's own account of his presidency is *The Vantage Point* (1971). Doris Kearns, *Lyndon Johnson and the American Dream* (1976), and Merle Miller, *Lyndon: An Oral Biography* (1980), are based on extensive conversations with Johnson. Rowland Evans and Robert D. Novak offer a vigorous portrait in *Lyndon B. Johnson: The Exercise of Power* (1966), and Robert A. Caro provides a critical interpretation of Johnson's early career in *The Path to Power* (1982). Eric F. Goldman, *The Tragedy of Lyndon Johnson* (1969), and George E. Reedy, *The Twilight of the Presidency* (1975), are sympathetic but critical views from former aides. For the 1964 election, see Theodore H. White, *The Making of the President—1964* (1965). Barry M. Goldwater presented his ideas in *The Conscience of a Conservative* (1960), which can be supplemented by Phyllis Schlafly, *A Choice Not an Echo* (1964).

Michael Harrington called attention to poverty in *The Other America* (1962). Other accounts of poverty include Harry M. Caudill, *Night Comes to the Cumberlands* (1963); J. Wayne Flynt, *Dixie's Forgotten People* (1979); and Susan Estabrook Kennedy, *If All We Did Was to Weep at Home* (1979). Sar A. Levitan describes the war on poverty in *The Great Society's Poor Law* (1969) and, with Robert Taggart, argues that it was quite effective in *The Promise of Greatness* (1976). Charles R. Morris, *A Time of Passion* (1984), offers thoughtful reflections from a former antipoverty administrator. Daniel P. Moynihan criticizes the community action programs in *Maximum Feasible Understanding* (1969). Other critical discussions of antipoverty programs include John Donovan, *The Politics of Poverty* (1973); Peter Marris and Martin Rein, *Dilemmas of Social Reform* (1973); and Richard Cloward and Frances Fox Piven, *Poor People's Movements* (1978). Marvin E. Gettleman and David Mermelstein, eds., *The Great Society Reader* (1965), criticize the prevailing assumptions behind many Johnson initiatives.

29

PERMANENT MOBILIZATION AND THE COLD WAR

*W*orld War II brought about a revolution in American foreign policy, ending two centuries of isolation from world diplomatic affairs. Before the war, the United States had no formal alliances, no troops stationed on foreign soil, and only a small defense budget. After 1945, the United States willingly sought a lasting, indeed dominant, role in international affairs. A state of permanent mobilization has characterized American society ever since, whether or not the United States has been formally at war. By the late 1960s, the military budget exceeded $80 billion annually, more than 1.5 million military personnel were stationed in a hundred foreign countries, and the United States had entered into defense treaties with forty-eight other nations.

American postwar foreign policy combined both old and new concerns. In keeping with the ideals enunciated by Woodrow Wilson during World War I, the United States continued to promote the peaceful expansion of its capitalist economic system throughout the world. It also maintained support for political democracy, national self-determination, and the breakup of colonial empires. Yet new policy directions rivaled, and finally overshadowed, those economic and

political considerations. The most striking aspect of postwar American foreign policy was strident ideological confrontation with the Soviet Union, accompanied by military and diplomatic efforts to contain the spread of communism. The desire to maintain military parity with the Soviets, and the corresponding Soviet push to match American strength, set in motion the arms race that dominated the postwar period.

The dramatic shift in American foreign policy after 1945 had important domestic repercussions. Permanent mobilization required higher defense expenditures and a military draft. Every neighborhood seemed to have at least one son in military service. It fostered the creation of a powerful military establishment that linked the armed services with scientific and corporate communities in the cause of national security. Finally, permanent mobilization led to a revolution in American government, as the executive branch assumed an almost uncheckable authority over the conduct of foreign affairs. In keeping with the centralization of American life and culture throughout the twentieth century, decisions made in Washington, and in other capitals across the world, now had an impact on ordinary lives.

The Origins of the Cold War

The defeat of Germany and Japan did not bring stability to the world. Within a year of the end of World War II, the United States was engaged in a global ideological struggle with the Soviet Union that historians call the cold war. The U.S. government developed a cold war mentality, characterized by a fear of communist expansion and a tendency to interpret all revolutionary activity as part of a monolithic communist movement controlled by Moscow. The Soviet Union, in turn, viewed American economic and political initiatives throughout the world as a threat to its security. Cold war assumptions still fundamentally shape American and Soviet diplomatic and military priorities today.

Descent into Cold War

Franklin Roosevelt had hoped that the establishment of the United Nations would provide a forum to resolve postwar conflicts and promote freedom throughout a stable, peaceful world. Unlike the disagreements that had doomed American participation in the League of Nations after World War I, the Senate ratified the United Nations by a margin of 80 to 2 in July 1945. Roosevelt had died that April, and the United Nations became in part a memorial to his hopes for postwar peace and cooperation. One of the United Nations' most tireless supporters—and a member of the U.S. delegation from 1946 to 1953—was the president's widow, Eleanor Roosevelt.

The planning for the United Nations was done at the Dumbarton Oaks Conference in Washington in 1943–1944, the Yalta conference in early 1945, and in San Francisco later that spring. It reflected President Roosevelt's aspirations for international cooperation and collective security—that is, the maintenance of the security of all member nations by common action. Yet elements of the United Nations charter explicitly continued traditional patterns of international relations. While the General Assembly granted one vote to each member nation, the Security Council functioned strictly along the lines of traditional big-power diplomacy. The United States, Great Britain, France, the Soviet Union, and China each had veto power over any Security Council action. Because any superpower could veto Security Council sanctions leveled against its own aggression or that of its allies, the United Nations was fundamentally hampered in its quest for collective security. Yet since neither the Soviet Union nor the United

ELEANOR ROOSEVELT, U.N. REPRESENTATIVE
Eleanor Roosevelt won over her fellow members of the United Nations delegation by doing her homework and standing firm on her convictions. Republican John Foster Dulles admitted to her, "I feel I must tell you that when you were appointed I thought it terrible and now I think your work here has been fine!" Eleanor Roosevelt was proudest of her role in drafting the 1948 Universal Declaration of Human Rights. Here she entertains delegates from UNESCO at her home in Hyde Park, New York. (FPG)

States was willing to entrust its national security totally to an international organization, the veto was a necessary condition to induce all the superpowers to participate.

Although Roosevelt heartily supported the United Nations, he also believed it was essential for the United States to continue good relations with the only other power whose strength realistically rivaled that of the United States in 1945, the Soviet Union. Yet events in the immediate postwar period, especially the sensitive issue of Soviet domination of Eastern Europe, proved far too controversial to be settled amicably between the two great powers. Within twenty-four hours of taking over the presidency, Harry Truman questioned whether the United States could cooperate with its former wartime ally. "We must stand up to the Russians," he stated privately. America and Russia's descent into cold war had begun, and the United Nations could do nothing to stop it.

Why did the Grand Alliance fall into disarray so quickly in the immediate postwar period? Profound disagreements marred American and Russian priorities for the postwar world. The Soviet Union, embittered by the German invasion and the loss of twenty million Soviet civilians during the war, put its own security needs first. The United States wanted to continue Wilsonian policies of encouraging national self-determination throughout the world. The administration was also responsive to the political realities of the large Polish-American community in the United States, a voting block that was staunchly opposed to Soviet control of Eastern Europe. In addition to the disagreements about self-determination, American and Soviet leaders disagreed over whether the world market should operate under capitalist or state-controlled systems. Soviet control of Eastern European economies, and American fears that such domination would reach throughout the emerging Third World, threatened American plans for free-market principles and international trade in the postwar world.

Other deep-seated causes added to the climate of suspicion between the United States and the Soviet Union. Soviet leaders had not forgotten that President Wilson had dispatched American troops onto Russian soil in 1918 and 1919 to undermine the fledgling Bolshevik regime. They remembered their exclusion from the Versailles conference. The initiation of diplomatic relations in 1933 did little to break the ice. Wartime pressures only heightened the level of distrust, even though the two powers fought on the same side. Especially damaging was Roosevelt's and Churchill's repeated delay in implementing their promise to open a second front in Europe to relieve the Soviets of the brunt of fighting the Germans.

The immediate aftermath of the war did nothing to ease tensions. Soviet leaders were especially angered by Truman's reaction to events in Eastern Europe. As the Soviet army drove the Germans out of Russia and back through Romania, Bulgaria, and Hungary, Soviet-sponsored, procommunist provisional governments were established in those countries. At the Yalta conference, both American and British diplomats, including President Roosevelt, had in effect agreed to recognize this Soviet "sphere of influence" in the region along its borders, even though it conflicted with America's traditional commitment to national self-determination. But as soon as the war ended, Truman backed away from the Yalta pledges. The new president berated Soviet Foreign Minister V. M. Molotov for imposing a Soviet-controlled government on Poland. Molotov had never "been talked to like that in my life," he told Truman. "Then keep your agreements!" Truman retorted.

American officials feared that Stalin was not just establishing a buffer zone to protect the Soviet Union from invasion from the West, but was embarking on a plan for worldwide domination. Republican Senator Arthur Vandenberg of Michigan rose in the Senate to ask, "What is Russia up to now? We ask it in Manchuria. We ask it in Eastern Europe and the Dardanelles. We ask it in Italy. . . . We ask it in Iran. . . ." One of the few leaders to urge a more conciliatory approach was Secretary of Commerce Henry A. Wallace, who warned that Truman's pronouncements ignored the Soviet Union's "dire economic needs and disturbed sense of security." When Wallace continued to question Truman's emerging hard line toward the Soviets, the president removed him from office.

Far more in line with Truman's attitudes were those of Winston Churchill, whom Truman invited to Fulton, Missouri, in March 1946 for a major foreign policy address. The former British prime minister had always opposed Soviet ambitions in Europe. Now, out of power and eager to regain a forum for his views, he warned ominously about the "expansive tendencies" of the Soviet Union: "From Stettin in the Baltic to Trieste in the Adriatic, an iron curtain has descended across the Continent." If the West hoped to preserve peace and freedom in the face of the Soviet challenge, Churchill declared, it must remember that "there is nothing they admire so much as strength, and there is nothing for which they have less respect than for military weakness." Churchill's widely publicized "iron curtain speech" helped convince many Americans that the Soviet Union posed a dangerous threat to national security.

The Containment Policy

By 1946, these new perceptions of the Soviet Union led American diplomats to conclude that it was futile to bargain with the Russians. Instead, they turned to containment, a strategy designed to limit Soviet and communist expansion. In one version or another, containment has defined the foreign policy of every subsequent administration, both Democratic and Republican.

George F. Kennan, an intense, scholarly diplomat who had devoted his entire career to the study of Russia, provided the rationale for containment. From his post at the U.S. embassy in Moscow, Kennan sent his superiors in Washington an eight-thousand-word cable in February 1946. At the "bottom of the Kremlin's neurotic view of world affairs," Kennan asserted, was "the traditional and instinctive Russian sense of insecurity." The Soviet Union saw the world as irrevocably divided into socialist and capitalist camps, and the "basic Soviet instinct" held "that there can be no compromise with rival power and the constructive work can start only when Communist power is dominant." Kennan concluded, "Impervious to logic of reason, [the Soviet Union] is highly sensitive to logic of force. For this reason it can easily withdraw—and usually does—when strong resistance is encountered at any point."

Kennan's analysis impressed George C. Marshall, who was about to cap his distinguished military and diplomatic career by becoming secretary of state. Marshall brought Kennan to Washington, and, working closely with President Truman, they developed the containment policy. As Kennan argued in 1947, the Soviets moved "inexorably along the prescribed path, like a persistent toy automobile wound up and headed in a given direction, stopping only when it meets unanswerable force." It was necessary, therefore, to pursue a policy of "firm containment, designed to confront the Russians with unalterable counterforce at every point where they show signs of encroaching upon the interests of a peaceful and stable world." Such a policy left little room for such international organizations as the United Nations.

The first test of containment came in Greece in 1947. Local communist-inspired guerrillas, whom American advisers mistakenly believed were controlled by Moscow, had fought for control of Greece since the end of 1944. By 1946, they were engaged in a full-scale civil war against anticommunist forces aided by Great Britain. Early in 1947, the British informed Truman that they could no longer afford to assist the Greek anticommunists. "If Greece was lost," Truman feared, Stalin "would then direct the communist parties of Italy and France to grab for power" and thus threaten to bring the industrially developed regions of Western Europe into the Soviet sphere.

To counter this perceived menace, the president announced what became known as the Truman Doctrine. In order to win acceptance for an unprecedented change in the U.S. stance toward the rest of the world, the president followed the advice of Senator Vandenberg "to scare the hell out of the country." Not just Greece, but freedom itself, was at issue, Truman declared. He painted a picture of a world deeply polarized between two competing ways of life, one "based upon the will of the majority," the other based "upon the will of a minority forcibly imposed upon the majority." It was clear where American loyalties lay:

It must be the policy of the United States to support free peoples who are resisting attempted subjugation by armed minorities or outside pressures. . . . The free peoples of the world look to us for support in maintaining their

Α ΤΟΥ ΑΜΕΡΙΚΑΝΙΚΟΥ ΣΧΕΔΙΟΥ ΜΑΡΣΑΛΛ
ΔΙΑ ΤΗΝ ΕΛΛΑΔΑ
ΡΤΙΟΝ ΑΥΤΟ ΜΕΤΑΦΕΡΕΤΑΙ ΔΙΑ ΤΗΣ ΣΙΔΗΡΟΔΡΟΜΙΚΗΣ
ΙΣ ΑΘΗΝΩΝ — ΘΕΣΣΑΛΟΝΙΚΗΣ ΤΩΝ ΣΕΚ ΜΗΚΟΥΣ
ΙΟΜΕΤΡΩΝ. ΤΩΡΑ ΑΙ ΔΥΟ ΜΕΓΑΛΕΙΤΕΡΑΙ ΠΟΛΕΙΣ ΤΗΣ
ΟΣ ΣΥΝΔΕΟΝΤΑΙ ΚΑΙ ΠΑΛΙΝ ΣΙΔΗΡΟΔΡΟΜΙΚΩΣ ΔΙΑ
Ν ΦΟΡΑΝ ΑΠΟ ΤΟ 1944

MERICAN MARSHALL PLAN GOODS
FOR GREECE
FREIGHT IS BEING TRANSPORTED OVER THE
MILE ATHENS-SALONIKA RAILROAD LINE OF
RR. GREECE'S TWO LARGEST CITIES ARE NOW
D BY RAIL FOR THE FIRST TIME SINCE
1944

THE MARSHALL PLAN
Many people in European cities lived on subsistence diets after World War II. "The patient is sinking while the doctors deliberate," Secretary of State George C. Marshall declared after traveling to Europe and the Soviet Union to survey the war's devastation. In 1948, Congress established the Marshall Plan to help European nations cooperate in economic recovery. At first, humanitarian and military aid were equally important components of American assistance to war-torn Europe, but from the 1950s on, the United States tended to emphasize military assistance. (Wide World)

freedoms. If we falter in our leadership, we may endanger the peace of the world—and we shall surely endanger the welfare of our own Nation.

The Truman Doctrine represented an important step in the shift of foreign policy formulation from Congress to the executive branch. Despite the breadth and open-endedness of this military and political commitment, Congress quickly approved Truman's request for $400 million in aid to Greece and Turkey in a bipartisan show of support. This appropriation reversed the postwar policy of sharp cuts in foreign spending.

One of the few voices raised against the containment doctrine was that of Walter Lippmann, one of the nation's most respected journalists. In 1947, Lippmann criticized containment as a "strategic monstrosity" that threatened to require unlimited defense expenditures and involve the United States unnecessarily in disputes throughout the world. "The Eurasian continent is a big place," Lippmann noted drily, "and the military power of the United States has certain limitations." Containment could be implemented "only by recruiting, subsidizing, and supporting a heterogeneous array of satellites, clients, dependents, and puppets." American efforts to make "Jeffersonian Democrats" out of Asian peasants would prove futile and costly, he asserted. Although conflicts in China, Korea, and Vietnam later demonstrated the validity of Lippmann's critique, it had little impact on public opinion at the time.

A few weeks after Congress approved aid to Greece, Secretary of State Marshall proposed a plan to provide economic as well as military aid to Europe. In Truman's words, the Marshall Plan was "the other half of the walnut." By bolstering the free-world economy, Marshall and Truman believed, the United States could forestall the economic dislocation thought to give rise to communism. European economies had not recovered from the war, and the cold, hard winter of 1946–1947 brought even worse privation. Crowds of gaunt, haggard people had begun to heed communist-led attacks on the governments of Italy and France. Speaking at the Harvard University commencement in June 1947, Marshall urged the nations of Europe to work out a comprehensive recovery program and then ask the United States for aid. "Any government willing to assist in the task of reconstruction," he promised, "will find full cooperation on the part of the United States."

Congress overwhelmingly approved funds for the Marshall Plan. Over the next four years the United States contributed nearly $13 billion to a highly successful recovery effort. Western European industrial production increased 64 percent, and such revived economic activity opened new areas for American trade. U.S. policymakers saw this economic revitalization as creating a hospitable climate for democratic developments in the region, a further wedge against Soviet encroachment.

The Marshall Plan did not specifically exclude Eastern Europe or the Soviet Union, but it did require that all participating nations exchange economic information and work toward the mutual elimination of tariffs and other trade barriers. Soviet leaders denounced these conditions and forbade their new satellites to participate. In February 1948, a pro-Soviet coup prevented Czechoslovakia from participating in the Marshall Plan. Later that year, when Stalin's agents failed to unseat Yugoslavia's tough, resourceful

leader, Marshal Tito, Stalin expelled Yugoslavia from the Soviet bloc.

Germany, which was jointly administered by the Soviet Union, the United States, France, and Great Britain, continued to be a bone of contention. Especially troublesome was the fate of Berlin, the capital, which lay deep within the Soviet zone of occupation. The Soviet Union had installed a communist regime in East Berlin and demanded control over the entire city, including the sectors of West Berlin governed by the Western allies. The allies refused, and when Western nations took steps to revive the Berlin economy in the spring of 1948, the Soviet Union imposed a blockade on all highway, rail, and river traffic to West Berlin. Truman replied with an airlift. For nearly a year, American and British pilots, who had been dropping bombs on Berlin only four years earlier, flew in 2.5 million tons of food and fuel, nearly a ton for each Berlin citizen. By late 1949, Stalin lifted the blockade, which by then had made West Berlin a symbol of resistance to communism.

The Berlin airlift and the crises in Czechoslovakia and Yugoslavia led to a dramatic turning

MAP 29.1 COLD WAR EUROPE
The core of the American alliance system with Western Europe was the North Atlantic Treaty Organization (NATO), established in 1949. Twelve nations signed the original pact, whose central article read: "The parties agree that an armed attack against one or more of them in Europe or North America shall be considered an attack against them all." The U.S. Senate ratified the treaty by a vote of eighty-two to thirteen.

point in U.S. diplomatic history. In 1949, for the first time since the American Revolution, the United States bound itself to Western Europe by a formal military alliance. Arguing that it was necessary to meet the Soviet threat with "an inclusive security system," Truman orchestrated the creation of the North Atlantic Treaty Organization (NATO). On April 4, 1949, the United States, Britain, France, Italy, Belgium, The Netherlands, Luxembourg, Denmark, Norway, Portugal, Iceland, and Canada agreed that "an armed attack against one or more of them in Europe or North America shall be considered an attack against them all." In May 1949, these nations also agreed to the creation of the Federal Republic of Germany (West Germany). All assumed that it would join NATO, which it did in 1955.

Distressed by the aggressive American effort to promote a new economic and political order in Western Europe, the Soviet Union tightened its grip on Eastern Europe. It created a separate government for East Germany, which now became the German Democratic Republic. The Soviets also sponsored an economic association called COMECON (1949) and a military alliance for Eastern Europe, the Warsaw Pact (1955). The postwar division of Europe was nearly complete.

Containment Militarized

September 1949 brought another shock to U.S. policymakers. American military intelligence detected a sudden rise in radioactivity, proof that the Soviet Union had set off an atomic bomb. The United States' atomic monopoly, which some military and political advisers had argued would last for decades, had ended in less than four years. The nation had lost a major bargaining chip with which to confront the Russians. To many Americans, the world looked even more threatening now that the Soviets had the bomb.

The end of American atomic supremacy forced a major reassessment of the nation's foreign policy. To devise a new blueprint for diplomatic and military priorities, Truman turned to the National Security Council (NSC), an advisory body charged with assisting the president to set defense and military priorities. The NSC formed part of the unified military establishment set up by the National Security Act of 1947,

which created a single Department of Defense to replace the previous Departments of War and the Navy. The newly established Joint Chiefs of Staff coordinated army, navy, and air force policy. And a new Central Intelligence Agency (CIA) gathered and analyzed military intelligence. These bureaucratic structures were a concrete reminder of permanent mobilization.

In April 1950, the National Security Council delivered its report to President Truman. This document, known as NSC-68, reflected the bleak assumptions that American policymakers held about the Soviet Union. In their view, the Soviet Union aimed for world domination:

> The Kremlin is inescapably militant because it possesses and is possessed by a world-wide revolutionary movement, because it is the inheritor of Russian imperialism, and because it is a totalitarian dictatorship. . . . It is quite clear from Soviet theory and practice that the Kremlin seeks to bring the free world under its dominion by the methods of the cold war.

Since Moscow possessed tremendous military power that enabled the Soviet Union to "back up infiltration with intimidation," policymakers predicted an "indefinite period of tension and danger."

NSC-68 made several specific recommendations. It favored further development of the hydrogen bomb, an advanced weapon that was a thousand times more destructive than the atomic bombs that had destroyed Hiroshima and Nagasaki. (The United States exploded its first hydrogen bomb in late 1952, and the Soviet Union followed suit in 1953.) It supported increases in American conventional forces and a strong system of Western alliances. Most important, it called for an increase in taxes to finance "a bold and massive program of rebuilding the West's defensive potential to surpass that of the Soviet world." NSC-68 suggested that the administration mobilize an American consensus on the need for "sacrifice" and "unity" that would justify defense budgets totaling up to 20 percent of the gross national product, four times their level at the time.

The need for increased defense spending was directly linked to the end of atomic supremacy. The United States had been relying too heavily on atomic deterrence at the expense of its conventional military arsenal. Now that the nation's atomic monopoly had been broken, a general buildup of the American military arsenal was needed. The Korean War, which began just two months after NSC-68 was completed, provided the impetus necessary to put this new policy into practice. Before 1950, the military budget stood at $13.5 billion. In just six months, Truman more than tripled it to nearly $50 billion.

The Cold War in Asia

American cold war ideology was developed primarily to prevent Soviet expansion beyond its sphere of influence in Eastern Europe. As the mutual suspicion between the United States and the Soviet Union hardened, cold war containment doctrines formed the basis of the American stance toward Asia as well. American policymakers soon found, however, that it was much more difficult to apply the containment doctrine to Asia than to Europe, where China, rather than the Soviet Union, was the dominant force.

The "Fall" of China

A civil war had been raging in China since the 1930s. Communist forces led by Mao Zedong (Mao Tse-tung) and Zhou Enlai (Chou En-lai) contended for power with conservative nationalist forces under Jiang Jieshi (Chiang Kai-shek). Jiang had strong connections with the Chinese business community and with the western world. His wealthy wife had been educated at Wellesley College in Massachusetts. In contrast, Mao was the son of struggling peasants. He was a tough, uncompromising leader, indifferent to personal comfort and absolutely dedicated to revolution. Mao inspired loyalty in his associates and won the devotion of China's overtaxed, land-hungry peasants. By the mid-1940s, Mao's forces were gaining the upper hand.

The Truman administration, somewhat reluctantly, stuck with its nationalist allies until the bitter end. Betwen 1945 and 1949, the United States provided more than $2 billion to Jiang's forces, to no avail. In 1947, General Albert Wedemeyer, who had tried to work with Jiang, reported to President Truman that "until drastic political and economic reforms" were undertaken by the "corrupt, reactionary, and ineffi-

cient Chinese National government, United States aid cannot accomplish its purpose." By 1949, nearly half the nationalist troops had defected, and Jiang's regime had been forced off the Chinese mainland and onto the island of Formosa (Taiwan). Wedemeyer attributed Jiang's defeat to "lack of spirit," not lack of equipment. "In my judgment," he said, "they could have defended the Yangtze with broomsticks if they had had the will to do it." Assistant Secretary of State Dean Acheson agreed, declaring that "China lost itself."

Many Americans, however, viewed Mao's success as a defeat for the United States. A pronationalist "China lobby," supported by such Republicans as Senators Karl Mundt of South Dakota and William S. Knowland of California, protested that the State Department was responsible for the "loss of China." Publisher Henry R. Luce, born in China to missionary parents, spread these accusations through his magazines, including *Time* and *Life*. Bowing to pressure from the China lobby, most of the State Department's experts on the Far East were forced to resign during the McCarthy period for supposedly having been too sympathetic to the Chinese Communists. The United States refused to recognize the new communist state, instead giving recognition to the nationalists ensconced on Taiwan. For almost twenty years afterward, American administrations acted as if mainland China, the world's most populous country, did not exist.

The Korean War

Although Truman acknowledged that communist success in China raised urgent questions for American foreign policy, he recognized the limits of American power in Asia. In December 1949, his new secretary of state, Dean Acheson, clarified American policy. The United States, he said, would help Asian nations realize their own aspirations but would consider itself bound to protect only a "defensive perimeter" that ran from the Aleutian Islands in Alaska to Japan, the Ryukyus (a chain of small islands that stretch from Japan to Taiwan), and the Philippines. If an attack occurred outside this perimeter—on Korea, Taiwan, or Southeast Asia, for example—"the initial reliance must be on the people attacked to resolve it and then upon . . . the United Nations."

A test of this new policy came quickly, but events unfolded quite contrary to Acheson's pronouncement. On June 25, 1950, North Korean troops launched a surprise attack across the thirty-eighth parallel, the line at which the United States and the Soviet Union had partitioned Korea in 1945. North Korean leader Kim Il Sung may have expected Truman to ignore this armed challenge to the U.S.–supported government of Syngman Rhee in South Korea. If so, he was badly mistaken. The president immediately ordered General Douglas MacArthur in Japan to send American troops to help Rhee, and asked the U.N. Security Council to authorize a "police action" against the invaders. Since the Soviet Union was temporarily boycotting the Security Council to protest the exclusion of the

People's Republic of China from the U.N., it could not veto Truman's request, and the United Nations voted to send a peacekeeping force.

The outbreak of the Korean War further tipped the balance of foreign policy formulation from Congress to the president. When Republican Senator Robert A. Taft of Ohio objected that the president should have obtained congressional approval before committing American troops to Korea, Truman boldly insisted that he already had all the power he needed as commander-in-chief of the armed forces and as executor of the treaty binding the United States to the United Nations.

The rapidly assembled United Nations army in Korea remained overwhelmingly American. On September 15, 1950, U.N. commander Douglas MacArthur launched a brilliant amphibious attack at Inchon, far behind the lines of the North Korean invasion, which had cut deeply into the south. Within two weeks, the U.N. forces controlled Seoul, the South Korean capital, and almost all the territory up to the thirty-eighth parallel.

Stimulated by this success, General MacArthur sought authority to lead his forces across the thirty-eighth parallel into North Korea itself. Truman's initial plan had been to restore the 1945 border; now he agreed to the broader goal of creating "a unified, independent and democratic Korea." The Chinese government in Beijing (Peking) warned repeatedly that such a move would provoke its retaliation. American officials failed to take these warnings seriously. In late 1950, MacArthur drove rapidly northward, confident that he would reach the Chinese border at the Yalu River by Christmas. Just after Thanksgiving, however, a massive Chinese counterattack forced a retreat. By January 1951, communist troops had reoccupied Seoul. "They really fooled us when it comes right down to it, didn't they?" a senator later asked Secretary of State Acheson. "Yes, sir," he replied. Two months later, the American forces and their allies counterattacked, regained Seoul, and pushed back to the thirty-eighth parallel. Then a stalemate set in.

Truman and his advisers in Washington decided to work for a negotiated peace. They did not wish to tie down large numbers of U.S. troops in a remote corner of Asia, far from what they considered more strategically important

MAP 29.2 THE KOREAN WAR
The first months of the Korean War featured dramatic shifts in control up and down the six-hundred-mile peninsula. By September 1950, North Korean troops had overrun most of the territory below the thirty-eighth parallel. Then General Douglas MacArthur's amphibious landing at Inchon routed the North Koreans and enabled United Nations forces to push north almost to the Chinese border. The UN troops were forced to retreat to the thirty-eighth parallel, however, and the war became a stalemate for the next three years.

trouble spots in Europe and the Middle East. The Soviet Union, not China, remained the focus of their cold war strategy. If the Korean War became a general war with China, insisted General Omar N. Bradley, chairman of the Joint Chiefs of Staff, it would be "the wrong war, in the wrong place, with the wrong enemy."

MacArthur disagreed. Headstrong, arrogant, and brilliant, he fervently believed the nation's future opportunities lay in Asia, not in Europe. Disregarding Truman's instructions, MacArthur traveled to Taiwan and urged the nationalists to join in an attack on communist China. He pleaded for American use of the atomic bomb against targets in China. In an inflammatory letter to the House Minority Leader, Republican Joseph J. Martin of Massachusetts, he denounced the Korean stalemate. "We must win," MacArthur declared. "There is no substitute for victory."

Martin released MacArthur's letter on April 6,

MacARTHUR'S RETURN FROM KOREA
General Douglas MacArthur received a tumultuous welcome in San Francisco in 1951, the first time the popular general had set foot on the American mainland in fourteen years. The public outcry over President Harry Truman's dismissal of MacArthur for insubordination reflected frustration with the stalemated Korean War. (© Wayne Miller, Magnum)

1951, as part of a concerted Republican campaign to challenge President Truman's conduct of the war. The strategy backfired. On April 11, Truman relieved MacArthur of his command in Korea and Japan, accusing him of insubordination. "MacArthur left me no choice," Truman later insisted. "Even the Joint Chiefs of Staff came to the conclusion that civilian control of the military was at stake. . . . I didn't let it stay at stake very long."

Truman's decision was highly unpopular. According to a Gallup poll, 69 percent of the American people supported MacArthur rather than Truman. The general returned to tumultuous receptions in San Francisco, Chicago, and New York. In Washington, he delivered an impassioned address to a joint Congressional session that ended with a line from an old West Point ballad, "Old soldiers never die, they just fade away." But when the shouting died down, Truman had the last word. Failing to get the Republican presidential nomination in 1952, MacArthur did indeed fade away from public view.

The war dragged on for more than two years after MacArthur's dismissal. The armistice ultimately negotiated in July 1953 left Korea divided very near the thirty-eighth parallel. North Korea remained firmly allied with the Soviet Union; South Korea signed a mutual defense treaty with the United States in 1954, tying itself to the American sphere of influence in the Pacific. During the next thirty years, American and Japanese investments helped South Korea rapidly expand its economy.

The Korean War had only a limited domestic impact on the United States. The government did not control the economy to the extent it had during World War II. Limited mobilization stimulated the economy and reduced unemployment, contributing to the general prosperity that characterized the 1950s.

Few soldiers felt the patriotic fervor that had characterized service during World War II. Struggling against subzero cold and snow, the men grew to hate the endless fighting and "those damned hills of Korea." One griped, "You march up them but there's always the sinking feeling you are going to have to march right back down." A corporal from Chicago asserted, "I'll fight for my country, but I'm damned if I see why I'm fighting for this hellhole." When an Oregon newspaper prominently

THE KOREAN WAR
The American GI's who fought in Korea were often younger brothers of the men who had served in
World War II. Fighting in Korea was grim duty; it lacked the patriotic fervor that had characterized
service in the 1940s. The most popular expression of weary GI's in Korea was the fatalistic, "Well,
that's the way the ball bounces." (UPI)

ran the same news dispatch from Korea two days in a row, not a single reader called the repetition to its attention.

Conditions did improve for black soldiers during the Korean War. Although President Truman had signed an executive order desegregating the armed forces in 1948, little progress had been made before the war began. During the rapid mobilization, demands for efficiency (such as processing draftees) outweighed customary mores (such as keeping black and white draftees separate), thus speeding up the integration process. The generally successful experience of an integrated armed services during the Korean War hastened the emergence of the civil rights movement later in the 1950s.

The Korean War cost the United States 34,000 dead, 103,000 wounded, and $54 billion in military expenditures. It showed the nation's willingness to take concrete steps to stop communist aggression, no matter how remote from its shores, and it reminded Americans that containment required a heavy, ongoing commitment. In contrast to the triumphs on World War II battlefields, however, the protracted stalemate proved frustrating. "If we are so powerful," many asked, "why can't we win?" When an ar-

mistice was finally signed in 1953, few public celebrations took place. Similar frustration surrounding a limited war to stop the spread of communism in Asia surfaced little more than a decade later over American intervention in Vietnam.

Extending Containment

Although Dwight D. Eisenhower promised to take a new look at American defense policy when elected president in 1952, his two terms continued the nation's commitment to containment. His secretary of state, John Foster Dulles, accused the Russians of looking "upon anybody who is not for them as against them," but the same could have been said of the United States. Despite the Eisenhower administration's attempt to hold down the defense budget, the 1950s saw the growth of what Eisenhower himself labelled the "military-industrial complex." At the same time, the new Republican leaders faced a challenge that had also plagued previous Democratic administrations—to develop a consistent policy toward the new nations created by the breakup of imperialism in the wake of World War II.

Alliances and Arms

Dwight Eisenhower had earned a reputation for excellent judgment in military and diplomatic affairs while serving as the commander of NATO military forces in Europe in 1951–1952. As president, he worked closely with Secretary of State Dulles to define the administration's foreign policy. Dulles, an experienced international lawyer and diplomat, was an outspoken critic of "atheistic communism." Rather than just limiting further Soviet expansion, he argued, the United States ought to promote the "liberation" of the "captive nations" of Eastern Europe.

At the beginning of the Eisenhower administration, the Soviet Union briefly appeared more interested in better relations with the West. Joseph Stalin died in March 1953, and his duties were assumed by Georgi Malenkov, who adopted a more conciliatory tone toward the West. After an intraparty struggle that lasted until 1956, Nikita S. Khrushchev solidified his position as Stalin's successor. He soon startled communists thoughout the world by denouncing Stalin as "a distrustful man, sickly and suspicious," and detailing publicly for the first time Stalin's "crimes" and "tortures" of the 1930s and 1940s. Khrushchev likewise surprised Westerners by calling for "peaceful coexistence" between communist and capitalist societies. He also seemed more willing to tolerate different approaches to communism, such as that developed by Yugoslavia's previously ostracized leader Marshal Tito. When Polish leader Wladislaw Gomulka, who had once been jailed in a Stalinist purge, insisted that his nation's communists be allowed to work out Poland's problems in their own way, Khrushchev agreed.

On the other hand, Khrushchev made certain that Russia's Eastern European satellites did not deviate too far from the Soviet path. When a nationalist revolt erupted in Hungary in 1956, Soviet tanks rapidly moved into Budapest. Demonstrating their willingness to use massive force to retain control in Eastern Europe, the Soviets crushed the revolt and installed a puppet regime. Despite Dulles's rhetoric, the United States responded only by loosening immigration quotas for Hungarian refugees.

The Soviet repression of the Hungarian revolt confirmed that American policymakers had few, if any, options to "roll back" Soviet power in Eastern Europe short of going to war with the USSR. An alternative strategy, already in force, sought to limit communist expansion through a permanent alliance structure. Truman, Marshall, and Acheson had established key military alliances in Europe and Asia. Dulles added new agreements with nations that bordered on the Soviet Union and China—the Baghdad Pact (1953), with Great Britain and nations on the Soviet Union's Middle Eastern flank (Turkey, Iran, Iraq, and Pakistan); bilateral defense treaties with South Korea and the nationalist Chinese regime on Taiwan (1954); and the creation of the Southeast Asia Treaty Organization (SEATO) in 1954. The secretary of state regarded the establishment of these overtly anticommunist alliances as an imperative. "Neutrality," Dulles maintained, was not only "obsolete" but "immoral."

Firm in the righteousness of his cause, Dulles did not shrink from covert interventions against governments that were, in his opinion, too closely aligned with communism. For such tasks, he used the Central Intelligence Agency, which was headed by his brother, Allen Dulles. During the Eisenhower administration, the CIA moved beyond its original mandate of intelligence gathering to active—if secret—involvement in the internal affairs of countries where such covert action suited American objectives.

In the 1950s, the CIA successfully directed the overthrow of several foreign governments. When Iran's nationalist premier, Mohammed Mossadegh, seized British oil properties in 1953, CIA agents helped the young shah, Mohammed Reza Pahlevi, depose him. Using both economic leverage and a repressive secret police, the shah soon solidified his power within Iran. In 1954, the CIA supported a coup in Guatemala against popularly elected Jacobo Arbenz Guzman, who had expropriated 250,000 acres held by the American-owned United Fruit Company and accepted arms from the communist government of East Germany. The CIA also tried, unsuccessfully, to overthrow Achmed Sukarno of Indonesia in 1958 and Fidel Castro of Cuba in 1961. Eisenhower specifically approved these efforts. "Our traditional ideas of international sportsmanship," he wrote privately in 1955, "are scarcely applicable in the morass in which the world now flounders."

Although Eisenhower strongly opposed communism, he hoped to keep the cost of containment at a manageable level. To encourage the nation's allies to bear some of the responsibility for maintaining large armed forces, his administration increased the flow of American military aid. Truman had emphasized foreign economic assistance; the United States sent more than $22 billion abroad between 1946 and 1952, more than twice the amount spent on military aid. Eisenhower reversed the priorities. He reduced economic aid to $18 billion between 1953 and 1961, while increasing military aid to more than $19 billion.

Eisenhower and Dulles also devised the policy of "massive retaliation" or "brinksmanship."

TESTING AN ATOMIC BOMB
Throughout the 1950s, the Atomic Energy Commission conducted above-ground atomic tests, including this one at Camp Desert Rock in Nevada in 1957. Thousands of soldiers were exposed to fallout during the tests. The AEC, ignoring or suppressing medical evidence to the contrary, mounted an extensive public relations campaign to convince local residents that the tests did not endanger their health. (U.S. Army)

They believed the United States could economize by developing an effective nuclear deterrent rather than relying solely on expensive conventional armed forces. Nuclear weapons delivered "more bang for the buck." If the nation's major foreign enemy were a worldwide communist movement led by Moscow, they reasoned, the United States did not need to keep a large number of soldiers under arms, because atomic weapons could threaten the Soviet Union directly and force it to back down. To this end, the Eisenhower administration expanded its commitment to develop the hydrogen bomb, which the United States tested in the atmosphere between 1954 and 1958. The administration also supported research to develop the long-range bombing capabilities of the Strategic Air Command. To improve U.S. defenses against an air attack from the Soviet Union, the administration installed the Distant Early Warning (DEW) line of radar stations in Alaska and Canada in 1958.

These efforts did little to improve the nation's security, as the Soviets matched the United States weapon for weapon in an escalating arms race. The Soviet Union carried out its own atmospheric tests of hydrogen bombs between 1953 and 1958 and developed a fleet of long-range bombers. It won the race to build an intercontinental ballistic missile (ICBM) and beat the United States into space with the *Sputnik* space probe of October 1957. The United States successfully launched its own ICBM in 1958 and by 1960 had deployed Polaris nuclear submarines carrying atomic-tipped missiles within striking distance of Soviet targets. Soviet leaders raced to produce equivalent weapons.

While the Soviet Union viewed the Eisenhower-Dulles policies of anticommunist alliances and massive deterrence as inherently hostile, Eisenhower continued to work toward a negotiated arms limitation agreement. Although preliminary discussions with Soviet leaders between 1955 and 1957 had not yielded the "open skies" mutual arms inspection treaty he had wanted, they did produce plans for a summit meeting with Khrushchev in May 1960. Then, on May 5, an American spy plane was shot down over Soviet territory. Rejecting the opportunity to deny personal knowledge of the flight, Eisenhower replied that he had authorized this and many other secret flights by high-flying U-2 reconnaisance aircraft over the Soviet Union. Eisenhower's last chance to negotiate an arms agreement evaporated.

The Emerging Third World

Though preoccupied with the Soviet Union throughout the postwar period, American policymakers faced another challenge: developing a coherent policy toward the new nations that were rapidly emerging from the disintegrating European empires in Africa and Asia. At the outset of World War II, there had been five geopolitical blocs—the Western Hemisphere, in which the United States was preeminent; the European continent, split between Britain and Germany; the center of the Eurasian land mass, dominated by the Soviet Union; the Pacific Basin and Southeast Asia, controlled by Japan, China, or Western imperialist powers; and Africa and the Middle East, also under Western European influence. When the war ended, the latter two areas came up for grabs.

Nationalism, socialism, and religious fanaticism had already inspired powerful anticolonial movements before World War II; such forces intensified and spread, especially in the Middle East, Africa, and the Far East, during the 1940s and 1950s. The end to colonial empires fulfilled a goal the United States had sought in vain after World War I, and the nation in general welcomed the independence of the new states. At the same time, both the Truman and Eisenhower administrations were so caught up in cold war polarities that they often failed to recognize that indigenous nationalist or socialist movements in these emerging nations had their own goals and were not always under the strict control either of local communists or the Soviet Union. This failure to appreciate the complexity of local conditions limited the effectiveness of American policy toward the emerging Third World.

The Middle East presented the most serious challenges in the 1950s. Egypt had gained independence from Britain in 1952. When Gamal Abdel Nasser came to power in 1954, he pledged to lead not just Egypt but the entire Middle East out of its dependent, colonial relationship through a form of pan-Arab socialism. Nasser

obtained arms and promises of economic assistance from the Soviet Union in return for Egyptian cotton. When the Soviets offered to finance a dam on the Nile River at Aswan, Secretary of State Dulles countered with an offer of American assistance. Nasser refused to distance himself from the Russians, however, and in July 1956, Dulles abruptly withdrew the U.S. offer.

Retaliating against the withdrawal of American financial aid, Nasser nationalized the Suez Canal, over which Britain had retained administrative authority. Nasser said he would use the tolls from the canal to build the dam himself. After several months of fruitless negotiation, Britain and France, in alliance with Israel (which had become an independent state in 1948), responded by retaking the canal by force. When Eisenhower and the United Nations condemned this action, they reluctantly pulled back. Egypt was left more angry and defensive than ever—but it controlled the canal. In the end, these events increased, rather than decreased, Soviet influence in the Third World and produced dissension among the leading members of the Western European alliance.

In early 1957, still preoccupied with East-West conflict, the president persuaded Congress to approve the "Eisenhower Doctrine." This policy stated that American forces would assist any Middle Eastern nation "requiring such aid, against overt armed aggression from any nation controlled by International Communism." Invoking the doctrine, Eisenhower sent the U.S. Sixth Fleet to the Mediterranean Sea to aid King Hussein of Jordan in 1957. A year later, Eisenhower landed eight thousand troops to back up a pro-United States government in Lebanon.

The attention that the Eisenhower administration paid to developments in the Middle East in the 1950s confirmed that American policymakers no longer believed that containment of Soviet power in Eastern Europe was enough to guarantee American national security. Now the United States had to be concerned about communism globally, especially in emerging Third World countries. The case of the small country of Vietnam, which won its independence from France in 1954, would show that localized communist wars for national liberation could be just as troubling for American foreign policy as the threat of worldwide Soviet domination.

GRAVE IMPLICATIONS OF THE MILITARY-INDUSTRIAL COMPLEX

From President Eisenhower's Farewell Address (January 17, 1961).

. . . A vital element in keeping the peace is our Military Establishment. Our arms must be mighty, ready for instant action, so that no potential aggressor may be tempted to risk his own destruction.

Our military establishment today bears little relation to that known by any of my predecessors in peacetime, or indeed by the fighting men of World War II and Korea.

Until the latest of our world conflicts, the United States had no armaments industry. American makers of plowshares could, with time and as required, make swords as well. But now we can no longer risk emergency improvisation of national defense; we have been compelled to create a permanent armaments industry of vast proportions. Added to this, 3½ million men and women are directly engaged in the Defense Establishment. We annually spend on military security more than the net income of all United States corporations.

This conjunction of an immense Military Establishment and a large arms industry is new in the American experience. The total influence—economic, political, even spiritual—is felt in every city, every statehouse, every office of the Federal Government. We recognize the imperative need for this development. Yet we must not fail to comprehend its grave implications. Our toil, resources, and livelihood are all involved; so is the very structure of our society.

In the councils of government we must guard against the acquisition of unwarranted influence whether sought or unsought, by the military-industrial complex. The potential for the disastrous rise of misplaced power exists and will persist.

We must never let the weight of this combination endanger our liberties or democratic processes. We should take nothing for granted. Only an alert and knowledgeable citizenry can compel the proper meshing of the huge industrial and military machinery of defense with our peaceful methods and goals so that security and liberty may prosper together.

Source: Public Papers of the Presidents: Eisenhower, 1960–1961. Washington, D.C., 1961. 1038–1040.

The Military-Industrial Complex

When Eisenhower left office in January 1961, he warned the nation of a "military-industrial complex" that already employed 3.5 million Americans and whose concentrated power posed a threat to democratic processes and liberties.

Eisenhower's farewell address showed that he well understood the major transformations in economic and political structures that the cold war had forced on American life. The military-industrial complex that Eisenhower identified had its immediate roots in the business-government partnership of World War II. It entered a second stage in the late 1940s and 1950s, when cold war mobilization and the Korean War led to a major expansion of the military establishment. Defense-related industries and the scientists and engineers they employed entered into a long-term

THE U-2 INCIDENT
Pilot Gary Powers was flying an American U-2 reconnaissance plane, similar to this aircraft, over the Soviet Union in 1960 when the Russians shot him down. The plane's surveillance equipment was so sophisticated that enlargements of photographs showed newspaper headlines from ten miles up. (Wide World)

relationship with the federal government in the name of national security. The Defense Department became practically a state within the state, with its headquarters at the sprawling Pentagon in Arlington, Virginia. In 1968, the Pentagon alone contracted for more than $44 billion of goods and services.

Certain companies did so much of their business with the government that they became almost exclusive clients of the Defense Department. By the mid-1960s, Boeing and General Dynamics received 65 percent of their income from military contracts, Raytheon 60 percent, Lockheed 81 percent, and Republic Aviation 100 percent. Furthermore, the Pentagon tended to award contracts to the largest firms. In 1967, the hundred largest corporations got 65 percent of the government contracts, while the top ten alone received more than 30 percent.

The growth of this military-industrial establishment reflected a dramatic shift in national priorities. As late as 1950, less than a third of the federal budget went to the military. By 1969, the percentage had grown to 56 percent. In dollar amounts, the defense budget grew from $13 billion in 1950 to $47 billion in 1961 and $80 billion in 1972. At the same time, military spending took up a greater percentage of national income as measured by the gross national product. Between 1900 and 1930, except for the two years that the United States fought in World War I, the

country spent less than 1 percent of its GNP for military purposes. In the 1930s, defense absorbed only 1.3 percent of the GNP. By the 1960s, the United States regularly devoted close to 10 percent of its GNP to military spending.

The expansion of the military-industrial complex had a direct and ongoing impact on the American people. In 1973, for example, the average New York City resident paid $642 in taxes to support the Pentagon. Channeling money into national security limited the resources available for domestic social needs. Critics of military spending added up the trade-offs—the cost of a subway system for Washington, D.C., equaled the cost of a nuclear aircraft carrier and support ships; the deficit of the Philadelphia school system in 1971 amounted to the cost of a single B-1 bomber; and sixty-six units of low-income housing matched the cost of one Huey helicopter.

The defense buildup also meant jobs, however, and lots of them. In 1966, 17 percent of California's workers were employed in jobs directly generated by defense contracts. In 1971, the Pentagon itself employed 3.8 million workers, with an additional 2.2 million in defense-related private employment. Taking into account the multiplier effect, which measures the indirect benefits of such employment (the additional jobs created to serve and support the defense workers), perhaps as many as one worker in seven owed his or her job to the defense establish-

FIGURE 29.1 NATIONAL DEFENSE AS A PROPORTION OF TOTAL FEDERAL SPENDING, 1940–1970

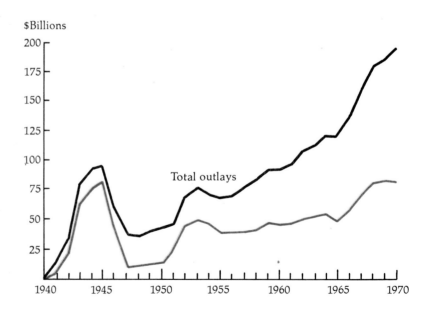

ment. This dependence of individual jobs on heavy defense spending graphically illustrates how the growth of a vast bureaucratic national state, especially one committed to worldwide military responsibilities, affected ordinary lives in the postwar period.

The Limits of Containment

In his inaugural address in January 1961, John F. Kennedy boldly declared that "we shall pay any price, bear any burden, meet any hardship, support any friend, oppose any foe to assure the survival and success of liberty." But in more reflective moods, the young president acknowledged that the United States was "neither omnipotent nor omniscient . . . there cannot be an American solution to every problem." Yet a strongly anticommunist thrust more often than not prevailed with Kennedy, as it did with his successor, Lyndon B. Johnson. The Vietnam War illustrated the limitations of this approach.

Activism Abroad

During the 1960 presidential campaign, Kennedy charged that the Eisenhower administration had permitted the Soviet Union to develop superior nuclear capabilities. Once in office, he found that no such "missile gap" existed. The new president quickly concluded, however, that Eisenhower's strategy of massive retaliation had emphasized nuclear weapons at the expense of conventional military strength. In his first defense message to Congress, Kennedy insisted that the nation develop a diverse arsenal, with weapons "to deter all wars, general or unlimited, nuclear or conventional, large or small." What the United States needed, Kennedy maintained, was the ability to mount a "flexible response," one precisely calibrated to meet actual situations that arose.

Congress quickly acceded to Kennedy's military requests. It boosted the number of combat-ready army divisions from eleven to sixteen and authorized the construction of ten Polaris submarines and other warships. It intensified the training of special military units—Kennedy suggested the name "Green Berets"—capable of employing "counterinsurgency" tactics against

THE PEACE CORPS
In some areas of the world, Peace Corps volunteers, such as this agricultural expert in Dahomey, were known as "Kennedy's children." One idealistic volunteer wrote, "Should it come to it, I had rather give my life trying to help someone than to have to give my life looking down a gun barrel at them." (U.S. Peace Corps)

procommunist guerrillas in the new Third World nations. Overall, Kennedy presided over a major expansion of the military-industrial complex as part of his campaign pledge to get the nation moving again. By 1964, the Kennedy administration had tripled the destructive power of the U.S. nuclear arsenal.

Kennedy also won congressional support for his expanded program of economic aid to foreign countries, of which the Peace Corps was the most popular component. The new Agency for International Development coordinated foreign aid for the Third World, and the Food for Peace program distributed surplus agricultural products to developing nations. In 1961, the president proposed "a ten-year plan for the Americas" called the Alliance for Progress, a partnership between the United States and the

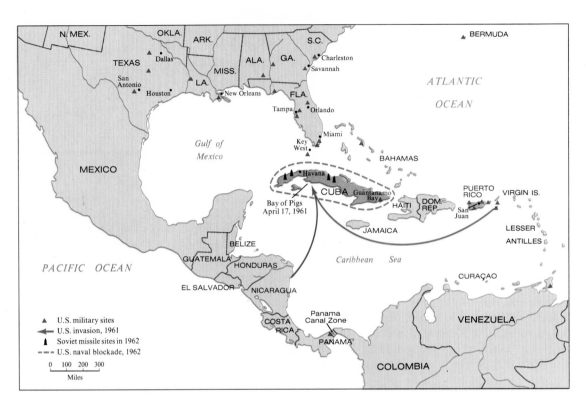

MAP 29.3 THE UNITED STATES AND CUBA, 1961–1962

With Fidel Castro's takeover in Cuba in 1959, American policymakers were confronted with a visible communist stronghold only ninety miles from Florida. In 1961, the United States tried unsuccessfully to overthrow Castro's regime with an invasion launched from Nicaragua. In 1962, a major confrontation with the Soviet Union occurred over Russian missile sites in Cuba. The Soviets removed the missiles after President Kennedy ordered a naval blockade of the island.

republics of Latin America designed to reduce the appeal of communism in that region. Kennedy aides promoted economic growth to stave off the working-class revolution that policymakers feared would result from an unstable economic system. The $100 billion plan was received with cautious optimism south of the border.

An expanded, flexible military and diplomatic force required strong centralized management. Taking the institutional changes of the 1947 National Security Act a step further, Kennedy enhanced the authority of the National Security Council by moving its chief directly into the White House. Reflecting his activist approach to presidential leadership, Kennedy often turned for advice to a small circle of personal aides rather than relying primarily on formal Pentagon

and State Department channels. Such a shift further concentrated foreign policy initiation at the White House.

The nation's strengthened military arsenal and streamlined defense establishment, however, failed to bring Kennedy the universal diplomatic success he had anticipated. Just as Kennedy took office in January 1961, Soviet Premier Nikita Khrushchev publicly described conflicts in Vietnam, Cuba, and elsewhere as "wars of national liberation" that were worthy of Soviet support. Kennedy took Khrushchev's words as a challenge, especially as they applied to Cuba.

Ever since Cuba had won its independence in the Spanish-American War, it had been economically and politically reliant on its powerful neighbor to the north. By 1956, American companies owned 80 percent of Cuba's utilities, 90 percent of its mining operations, and 40 percent of its sugar plantations. On New Year's Day in 1959, Fidel Castro overthrew the unpopular dictatorship of Fulgencio Batista and called for a revolution to reshape Cuban society. American diplomats grew concerned at these social changes, as well as Castro's growing friendliness with the Soviet Union. In early 1961, Kennedy authorized plans originally drawn up by the Eisenhower administration for an invasion by two thousand exiled Cubans to foment an anti-Castro uprising.

The invaders had been trained by the Central Intelligence Agency, but they were ill prepared for their task. After landing at the Bay of Pigs, the hapless forces were crushed by Castro's troops before they could even establish a beachhead. Symptomatic of the inept CIA planning, pilots in Nicaragua who were supposed to provide air cover for the landing forces forgot to set their watches ahead to Cuban time and arrived at the beach an hour too soon. The anticipated rebellion never occurred. The Bay of Pigs fiasco of April 1961 blighted the new administration with an embarrassing failure and cast doubts on Kennedy's activist approach to international affairs.

Although Kennedy devoted much of his attention to developments in the Western Hemisphere, he never lost his preoccupation with the Soviet Union. In June 1961, he met with Khrushchev in Vienna, an encounter that produced only a frank exchange of disagreements. Just days after this meeting, Khrushchev heightened international tensions by deploying soldiers to sever East Berlin from the western sector of the city. In mid-August, the Russians erected the Berlin wall, which still divides the historic German capital, to stop the exodus of East German citizens to the West. Kennedy later visited the Berlin wall, where he invoked the solidarity of the free world by declaring "Ich bin ein Berliner" ("I am a Berliner").

For thirteen days in October 1962, the United States and the Soviet Union came close to war. The Russians had stepped up their aid to the Castro regime after the Bay of Pigs invasion of the previous year. In mid-October, American U-2 aircraft photographed Soviet missile bases under construction in Cuba, complete with missiles that, when assembled, would be able to reach U.S. targets as far as 2,200 miles away. With Cuba just 90 miles from the Florida coast, the threat was too close to ignore.

Kennedy publicly confronted the Soviet Union over their actions. The United States, he declared in a somber televised address, would use its newly enlarged navy to blockade Soviet shipping to Cuba until the missiles were removed. Both the United States and the Soviet Union went on full military alert. On the following Sunday, after one of the most harrowing weeks of the nuclear age, Kennedy and Khrushchev reached an agreement and the Russians removed their missiles from Cuba. To allow Khrushchev to save face, the United States dismantled some outdated missiles in Turkey. "We're eyeball to eyeball," Secretary of State Dean Rusk observed, "and I think the other fellow just blinked."

The cold war tensions raised by the Berlin and Cuban missile crises heightened public support for Kennedy's proposed nationwide system of civil defense shelters. Defense analyst Herman Kahn's popular book, On Thermonuclear War (1960), had argued that, with careful civil defense planning, America would only lose between twenty and thirty million people in a nuclear attack. Influenced by Kahn's dark optimism, Kennedy encouraged individual families to build their own backyard bomb shelters. That city dwellers and poor people might not have backyards, or the income to build such shelters, escaped the attention of most policymakers.

This "do-it-yourself" approach to nuclear survival soon got out of control. Several Nevada communities claimed they were ready to shoot invading Californians who sought shelter over the state border. A Catholic priest published an article entitled "Ethics at the Shelter Doorway," which argued, "I doubt that any Catholic moralist would condemn the man who used available violence to repel panicky aggressors plying crowbars at the shelter door." The resulting public furor showed how disturbing "shelter ethics" really were.

After 1963, the backyard fallout shelter craze simply evaporated, as did plans for a comprehensive national shelter program. As the bombs grew larger, the chances of surviving an all-out nuclear attack in a backyard bomb shelter grew more dim. With intercontinental missiles capable

A HOME BOMB SHELTER
The manufacturer of this 1955 "Kiddie Kokoon" claimed that the home bomb shelter would provide three to five days of protection from a hydrogen bomb attack. Studies later showed that children who went through air raid drills at home or in school during the 1950s and early 1960s experienced frequent nightmares, many of which centered on the terror of their own death in a nuclear attack. (Library of Congress)

of reaching their targets a scant thirty minutes after launch, plans for evacuating thousands or millions of people from metropolitan areas seemed exercises in moving them from one place of death to another. Some Americans questioned what kind of a world would await them when they cautiously emerged after weeks or months underground.

Sobered by the Cuban missile crisis and the threat of nuclear annihilation, Kennedy began to seek ways to reduce cold war tensions. In a notable speech at American University in June 1963, he stressed the need to "make the world safe for diversity." Russians and Americans alike, he observed, "inhabit this small planet. We all breathe the same air. We all cherish our children's future. And we are all mortal." Soviet leaders, also chastened by the confrontation over Cuba, were now willing to talk. The two nations agreed to ban the testing of nuclear weapons in the air or in the seas. The test-ban treaty was ratified by the Senate in the fall of 1963.

Kennedy's desire to work out a pattern of peaceful coexistence with the Soviet Union, like Eisenhower's before him, reflected a strand of foreign policy that came to be called "détente." Détente was a different approach from cold war containment. Instead of challenging the Soviet Union, militarily or otherwise, at every corner of the globe, détente accepted the Soviets as an adversary with whom the United States could negotiate and bargain. Coexistence rather than confrontation, and common interests rather than polarities, distinguished détente from the cold war approach of the 1940s and 1950s. But no matter how often American leaders talked about opening channels of communication with the Russians, the obsession with the Soviet military threat to American national security never completely disappeared from U.S. policy. Nor did the Soviet Union moderate its obsession with the threat of the United States to its own security. Throughout the postwar period, both parties have maintained the cold war tensions.

The Vietnam War

Vietnam, which challenged American administrations from Harry Truman's to Richard Nixon's, became a test case of America's cold war policy. Lyndon Johnson echoed the reasoning that justified U.S. involvement in Vietnam in the name of containment:

> In the forties and fifties we took our stand in Europe to protect the freedom of those threatened by aggression. . . . Now, the center of attention has shifted to another part of the world where aggression is on the march and the enslavement of free men is its goal. . . . If we allow the Communists to win in Vietnam, it will become easier and more appetizing for them to take over other countries in other parts of the world. We will have to fight again some place else—at what cost no one knows. That is why it is vitally important to every American family that we stop the Communists in South Vietnam.

The needs and desires of the Vietnamese people hardly entered into this formulation.

The roots of U.S. involvement in Vietnam lay in the instability produced by the decolonization of Southeast Asia after World War II. In Vietnam during the 1940s, a nationalist movement known as the Viet Minh—led by French-educated communist Ho Chi Minh and military strategist Vo Nguyen Giap—demanded independence from France. The French refused to consider the Viet Minh request. Vietnam, the French argued, was "the pillar of the defense of the West in Southeast Asia. . . . If this pillar falls, Singapore, Malaysia, and India will soon fall prey to Mao Tse-tung."

President Truman found such reasoning persuasive. He also wanted to maintain good relations with France, whose support was crucial to the successful operation of the new NATO alliance. Early in 1950, the United States recognized the French-supported government of Bao Dai in Vietnam and began sending supplies to French troops there, a policy maintained by the Eisenhower administration. Meanwhile, Ho Chi Minh and his communist forces stepped up their fight against the French colonial administration. By 1954 the United States had sent more than $2 billion worth of military supplies to the French in Vietnam, paying nearly 80 percent of the cost of continuing the war.

Despite these joint French-U.S. efforts, Viet Minh forces gained strength in northern Vietnam. By the spring of 1954, they had trapped a large French force at the isolated administrative fortress of Dienbienphu. France asked the United States for direct military intervention. Eisenhower refused, and Dienbienphu fell in May 1954, after a fifty-six-day siege.

This dramatic turn of events sent the major parties to the negotiating table. The 1954 Geneva Accords temporarily partitioned Vietnam at the seventeenth parallel, committed France to withdraw its forces from north of that line within ten months, and forbade both North and South Vietnam from entering into any military alliance with an outside power. A final declaration provided that the two partitioned sectors would hold free elections in July 1956 to choose a unified government for the entire nation. The United States was never a party to the agreement. Before the scheduled elections could be held, a pro-western government headed by Ngo Dinh Diem took power in South Vietnam. Diem refused to allow the national elections to take place, mainly because he realized that the popular candidate Ho Chi Minh would easily win in both the north and south. Diem quickly consolidated his power in the south, including a rigged election in which Diem's ballots were printed on red paper, a Vietnamese symbol of good luck, while his opponent's were green, which stood for misfortune.

The Geneva Accords proved only an interlude between two wars, one to rid the country of French colonial control and a second to reunify Vietnam. By January 1955, the United States had replaced France as the dominant power in South Vietnam. American policymakers now asserted that a noncommunist South Vietnam was vital to the security interests of the United States and they charted U.S. policy accordingly. Between 1955 and 1961, the Eisenhower administration sent Diem an average of $200 million a year in aid, mostly military. In addition, approximately 675 American military advisers were stationed in Saigon, the capitol of South Vietnam.

Inheriting the Vietnam situation from the previous administration, President Kennedy initially sought to bolster the faltering regime of Ngo Dinh Diem, whom Vice-President Lyndon

AN IMMINENT COUP IN SOUTH VIETNAM, 1963

U.S. Ambassador Henry Cabot Lodge was the last American official to speak with South Vietnamese President Ngo Dinh Diem before his assassination.

Diem: Some units have made a rebellion and I want to know what is the attitude of the U.S.?

Lodge: I do not feel well enough informed to be able to tell you. I have heard the shooting, but am not acquainted with all the facts. Also it is 4:30 A.M. in Washington and the U.S. Government cannot possibly have a view.

Diem: But you must have some general ideas. After all, I am a Chief of State. I have tried to do my duty. I want to do now what duty and good sense require. I believe in duty above all.

Lodge: You have certainly done your duty. As I told you only this morning, I admire your courage and your great contributions to your country. No one can take away from you the credit for all you have done. Now I am worried about your physical safety. I have a report that those in charge of the current activity offer you and your brother safe conduct out of the country if you resign. Had you heard this?

Diem: No. (And then after a pause) You have my telephone number.

Lodge: Yes. If I can do anything for your physical safety, please call me.

Diem: I am trying to re-establish order.

Source: The Pentagon Papers. New York: Bantam, 1971. 232.

Johnson was fond of calling the "George Washington of South Vietnam." Eager to instruct Diem's soldiers in counterinsurgency techniques, Kennedy increased the number of American military advisers to more than fifteen thousand by November 1963. He also sent in economic development specialists to work with Vietnamese peasants to increase agricultural production. Kennedy refused, however, to send American combat troops to assist the South Vietnamese. "In the final analysis," he told a journalist just before his assassination, "it is their war."

The American aid did little good. Diem's political inexperience, combined with his Catholicism in a predominantly Buddhist country, made it impossible for him to create a stable, popular government. He enjoyed much more support from his faraway American backers than he did in his native land. The National Liberation Front (NLF, or Viet Cong), North Vietnam's revolutionary front in the south, made consistent headway against the unpopular Diem regime. These guerrillas blended easily into the local South Vietnamese population. As the situation deteriorated, Diem consistently misled his American allies about South Vietnamese military and social progress.

Matters came to a head in late 1963. Militant Buddhists staged a dramatic series of demonstrations against Diem, including several self-immolations that were recorded by American television crews. Kennedy decided that Diem had to be removed. Ambassador Henry Cabot Lodge, Jr., let it be known in Saigon that the United States would support a military coup that had "a good chance of succeeding." In the fall of 1963, Diem was driven from office and assassinated.

Kennedy's advisers had given little thought to what would follow Diem's ouster. Before they could formulate any plans, Kennedy himself was assassinated and Lyndon Johnson took his place as president. Johnson saw his mission in clearcut terms. "I am not going to lose Vietnam," he stated emphatically within weeks of becoming president. "I am not going to be the President who saw Southeast Asia go the way China went." A new phase in the Americanization of the war began.

During the 1964 presidential campaign, Johnson declared, "We are not going to send American boys nine or ten thousand miles away from home to do what Asian boys ought to be doing for themselves." Yet plans were already under way for a major escalation of the United States effort, the only way, policymakers agreed, that the South Vietnamese government could prevent a communist takeover. The escalation, which was accomplished during the first several months of 1965, took two forms: the initiation of direct U.S. bombing attacks against North Vietnam and the deployment of American ground troops.

Before escalation could proceed, however, the administration had to have at least tacit congressional support for stepping up the war. Presidential adviser Walt Rostow was one of the first to point out that bombing North Vietnam would

MAP 29.4 THE VIETNAM WAR, 1954–1975
The Vietnam War was a guerrilla war. Fighting was marked by skirmishes and inconclusive encounters rather than decisive battles and major offensives. North Vietnamese supporters of the National Liberation Front filtered into South Vietnam along the Ho Chi Minh trail, which wound through Laos and Cambodia. In the south, the guerrillas followed the formula for revolution promoted by the Chinese leader Mao Zedong and blended into the local population "like fish in the water."

probably require some form of congressional declaration of war. Originally, Johnson had wanted to wait until after the 1964 election to place this potentially controversial request before Congress, but events gave him the opportunity to win such authorization earlier.

During the summer of 1964, American naval forces had supported several South Vietnamese amphibious attacks on the North Vietnamese coast. The North Vietnamese resisted such attacks, and in August, President Johnson told the nation that North Vietnamese torpedo boats had fired on American destroyers in international waters in the Gulf of Tonkin. Johnson asked Congress to authorize him "to take all necessary measures to promote the maintenance of peace and security in Southeast Asia" and to "prevent further aggression." The Gulf of Tonkin resolution passed 88 to 2 in the Senate and 416 to 0 in the House. Only Senators Wayne Morse of Oregon and Ernest Gruening of Alaska opposed the resolution as a "predated declaration of war" that further increased the president's ability to carry out foreign policy without consulting Congress.

Many questions were later raised about the resolution. A draft resolution had been ready for several months awaiting just such an incident. The evidence of a North Vietnamese attack was sketchy at best. As the president admitted soon afterward, "For all I know, our navy was shooting at whales out there." But this trumped-up attack got Johnson what he wanted—the only formal approval of American intervention in Vietnam ever voted by Congress. In Johnson's typically colorful language, he privately compared the resolution to "Grandma's nightshirt—it covered everything."

With congressional support assured and the 1964 election safely won, the Johnson administration began the fateful moves toward total Americanization of the Vietnam War. National security adviser McGeorge Bundy argued that the United States should retaliate against attacks on South Vietnamese military units by bombing a carefully selected set of targets in North Vietnam. Such bombing raids, Bundy reasoned, would cripple the North Vietnamese economy and force the communists to the bargaining table. A special target was the Ho Chi Minh trail, an elaborate network of paths, bridges, and shelters that snaked from North Vietnam through

FRIENDS OR FOES?
U.S. Marines often entered South Vietnamese hamlets to search for suspected Vietcong sympathizers and destroy the bunkers where they hid, a process that could inflict heavy damage on the village and sometimes led to civilian deaths. One soldier noted that such behavior hardly won over the local peasantry: "Their homes had been wrecked, their chickens killed, their rice confiscated—and if they weren't pro-Vietcong before we got there, they sure as hell were by the time we left." (© P. J. Griffiths, Magnum)

Cambodia and Laos into South Vietnam. Some twenty thousand North Vietnamese soldiers moved southward along this route each month by 1967, as well as the military hardware and other resources necessary to supply them. Between 1965 and 1968, Operation Rolling Thunder, which got its name from an old Protestant hymn, dropped a million tons of bombs on North Vietnam, eight hundred tons a day for three and a half years. From 1965 to 1973, the United States dropped three times as many bombs on North Vietnam, a country roughly the size of Texas, as had fallen on Europe, Asia, and Africa during World War II.

Much to the amazement of American advisers, the bombing had no effect on the ability of the North Vietnamese to wage war. The flow of troops and supplies to the south continued un-abated. Instead of destroying enemy morale and bringing the North Vietnamese to the bargaining table, the bombing rekindled North Vietnam's nationalism and intensified its will to fight. American leaders should have learned a lesson from World War II, when extensive bombing of Germany in 1944–1945 had failed to cripple Nazi industrial production and had actually boosted enemy morale. Since North Vietnam had little industry to destroy, the impact of similar bombing on an agricultural society would predictably be even less. The bombing continued nevertheless.

The other major escalation of the American commitment in 1965 was the assignment of American ground troops to combat duty in South Vietnam. Even with the help of numerous American advisers and millions of dollars of supplies, South Vietnamese troops were no longer able to resist the Viet Cong. The first U.S. Marines waded ashore at Da Nang on March 8, 1965, ostensibly to protect the large American air base there. Soon they were patrolling the countryside and skirmishing with the enemy. The American people were not told that a major change in policy had occurred.

During the next three years, the number of U.S. troops in Vietnam grew dramatically. The war increasingly became an American struggle, fought for American aims. More than 75,000 soldiers were fighting there by June 1965, and 190,000 by the end of that year. By 1966, almost 400,000 American soldiers were stationed in Vietnam, 500,000 by 1967, and 540,000 in 1968. In early 1968, the commander of the U.S. forces in Vietnam, General William Westmoreland, asked for 206,000 additional troops, a request that was never fulfilled. Westmoreland's escalating demands confirmed a prediction made by presidential adviser George Ball in 1961. Ball had warned President Kennedy that if American ground toops were committed to Vietnam, there would be 300,000 there within five years. Kennedy had laughed and said, "George, you're cra-

zier than hell." But as Kennedy observed before his death, requests for troops were like having a drink: "The effect wears off, and you have to take another."

The massive commitment of troops and supplies after 1965 brought the United States and South Vietnam no closer to victory. Taking to the extreme Johnson's call "to leave the footprints of America in Vietnam," extensive defoliation and military bombardment destroyed the beautiful country and made it difficult for peasants to practice the agriculture that provided the economic and cultural base of Vietnamese society. After one devastating but not unusual engagement, the commanding U.S. officer claimed, using the logic of the times, "It became necessary to destroy the town in order to save it." Meanwhile, American soldiers and dollars flowed into Saigon and other cities, distorting the local economy and setting off wild, unmanageable inflation.

Why did the American presence in Vietnam have so little effect? The determination of the North Vietnamese and their South Vietnamese sympathizers was a major factor. In the 1940s, Ho Chi Minh had told his French imperialist

JUNGLE WARFARE IN VIETNAM
The horror of losing a buddy in war is plain in the faces of these marines as they try to drag a comrade to safety under fire. Almost two-thirds of the American soldiers who died in action in Vietnam were twenty-one years old or younger. (© Robert Ellison, Black Star)

TIME LINE
PERMANENT MOBILIZATION AND THE COLD WAR

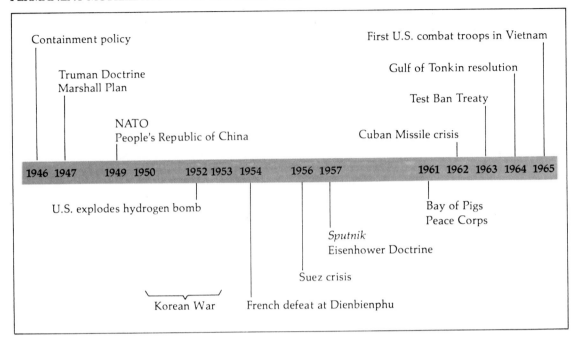

foes, "You can kill ten of my men for every one I kill of yours, but even at those odds, you will lose and I will win." That same strategy held true against the Americans. The Viet Cong were prepared to accept limitless casualties and to fight for as many years as necessary. (Four million Vietnamese on both sides were either killed or wounded in the war, approximately 10 percent of the population.) North Vietnamese strategists astutely realized that the war did not have to be won on the battlefield. They accurately predicted that the United States would be unable to wage an extended war of attrition because American public opinion would eventually limit U.S. participation.

The kind of guerrilla fighting that characterized the Vietnam War also favored the Viet Cong rather than the American ground troops. There were no fronts or actual battles, just skirmishes. A former Marine captain recalled:

> You never knew who was the enemy and who was the friend. They all looked alike. They all dressed alike. They were all Vietnamese. Some of them were Vietcong. Here's a woman of twenty-two or twenty-three. She is pregnant, and she tells an interrogator that her husband works in Danang and isn't a Vietcong. But she watches your men walk down a trail and get killed or wounded by a booby trap. She knows the booby trap is there, but she doesn't warn them. Maybe she planted it herself.

He concluded graphically, "It wasn't like the San Francisco Forty-Niners on one side of the field and the Cincinnati Bengals on the other. The enemy was all around you."

The success of the fighting was measured not in territory gained, but in gruesome "body counts"—the number of enemy soldiers killed. Such casualty figures were sometimes deliberately inflated. As a twenty-four-year old Special Forces captain recalled, "I went out and killed one VC and liberated a prisoner. Next day the major called me in and told me that I'd killed fourteen VC and liberated six prisoners. You want to see the medal?" The pressure of waging war under these conditions drove many soldiers, whose average age was only nineteen, to seek escape with cheap and readily available drugs.

By 1967, despite the glowing reports that were fed to the American public, many administration officials had privately reached more pessimistic conclusions. Pentagon analysts estimated that the North Vietnamese, with only marginal assistance from other communist powers, could keep sending two hundred thousand guerrillas a year into South Vietnam indefinitely. Despite such a prognosis, President Johnson continued to insist that an American victory in Vietnam was vital to U.S. national security and prestige. "If we are driven from the field in Vietnam," he asserted, "then no nation can ever again have the same confidence in American protection." Journalists soon commented that the Johnson administration suffered from a "credibility gap."

Domestic events also forced Johnson and his advisers to reassess their policy. In 1966, the federal deficit stood at $9.8 billion. The deficit jumped to $23 billion in 1967, with the Vietnam War costing the taxpayers $27 billion that year. (The total cost of the war from 1965 to 1973 has been estimated at $120 billion.) Although the war was consuming only 3 percent of the gross national product, compared with 48 percent for World War II and 12 percent for the Korean War, Johnson could no longer hide the enormous expense of the war from the American people. But only in the summer of 1967 did

he ask for a 10 percent surcharge on individual and corporate income, which Congress delayed approving until 1968. By then the inflationary spiral that plagued the American economy throughout the 1970s was already out of control. In addition to the economic dislocations, domestic dissent over the war escalated as the 1968 presidential election neared. Such internal pressures confirmed Ho Chi Minh's prediction that a democratic society could not fight a protracted war of attrition halfway around the world. Time was on North Vietnam's side.

The struggle in Vietnam reflected problems characteristic of every new nation in the post-colonial world—nationalist ambitions, religious and cultural conflicts, economic needs, and political turmoil. In reality, Vietnam was too small to play a significant part in the international balance of power. North Vietnamese communism was intensely regional and nationalistic. Yet the Kennedy and Johnson administrations, and their predecessors, allowed their perception of a worldwide communist threat to control their actions in Vietnam. By 1968, what Lyndon Johnson had once referred to as "a raggedy-ass little fourth-rate country" had brought the world's most powerful military giant to its knees. As in the Korean conflict, the American people were learning that fighting communism was a complicated task.

𝒯he end of World War II brought a dramatic shift in American foreign policy, as the United States broke from its isolationist tradition to seek a permanent role in world affairs. The predominant characteristic of this new policy was the cold war with the Soviet Union. Containment originally emerged in response to Soviet pressure on Eastern Europe, but that doctrine was expanded by succeeding administrations to include resistance to communism wherever it appeared. The Korean and Vietnam wars were two outgrowths of the containment doctrine. A cold war mentality shaped U.S. foreign policy throughout the post-World War II era.

Fighting a worldwide battle against communism had strong domestic repercussions. The new importance of foreign affairs enhanced the power of the president. Permanent mobilization concentrated power in the Pentagon and led to the creation of a military-industrial complex dependent on production for war. Growing defense expenditures took up an ever-larger part of the gross national product. Besides paying for defense through taxes and growing deficits, American citizens now lived in a world where fear of nuclear attack became part of daily life and small foreign wars were a constant possibility.

Suggestions for Further Reading

The Origins of the Cold War

The two best overviews are Walter LaFeber, *America, Russia, and the Cold War*, 3rd edition (1976), which takes the story to 1975; and John L. Gaddis, *The United States and the Origins of the Cold War* (1972), which covers the 1940s. Two other excellent studies are Daniel Yergin, *Shattered Peace* (1977), which focuses on the rise of the national security state; and Lloyd Gardner, *Architects of Illusion* (1970), which surveys the policy makers. See also Stephen Ambrose, *Rise to Globalism*, 2nd edition (1980); John W. Spanier, *American Foreign Policy Since World War II*, rev. ed. (1973); and Richard J. Barnet, *The Roots of War* (1972). For perspectives quite critical of American aims, see Joyce and Gabriel Kolko, *The Limits of Power* (1970) and Robert J. Maddox, *The New Left and the Origins of the Cold War* (1977). Martin J. Sherwin, *A World Destroyed* (1975) and Gar Alperowitz, *Atomic Diplomacy* (1965) cover the impact of atomic weapons on policy formulation. Useful for assessing the links between foreign and domestic policy are Robert A. Divine, *Foreign Policy and U.S. Presidential Elections, 1940–1960*, 2 vols. (1974) and Richard Freeland, *The Truman Doctrine and the Origins of McCarthyism* (1972).

The period can also be viewed through individual policy makers. Indispensible are George F. Kennan, *American Diplomacy, 1900–1950* (1952) and *Memoirs, 1925–1950* (1967); and Dean Acheson's modestly titled *Present at the Creation* (1970). Walter Lippmann, *The Cold War* (1947) can be supplemented by Ronald Steel's fine biography, *Walter Lippmann and the American Century* (1980). Adam Ulam presents the Soviet point of view in *The Rivals: America and Russia Since World War II* (1971).

The Cold War in Asia

Akira Iriye, *The Cold War in Asia* (1974) is the best starting point. See also Tang Tsou, *America's Failure in China, 1941–1950* (1963); Kenneth Shewmaker, *Americans and the Chinese Communists* (1971); and Michael Shaller, *The United States and China in the 20th Century* (1979). E. J. Kahn, Jr., *The China Hands* (1975) and Ross Y. Kuen, *The China Lobby in American Politics* (1974) cover the domestic repercussions.

David Rees, *Korea: The Limited War* (1964) is a good introduction, which can be supplemented by Allen S. Whiting, *China Crosses the Yalu* (1960) and Frank Baldwin, ed., *Without Parallel* (1975). Ronald J. Caridi, *The Korean War and American Politics* (1969) covers the Republican response. William Manchester, *American Caesar* (1979) offers an engrossing biography of Douglas MacArthur.

Extending Containment

In addition to LaFeber, *America, Russia, and the Cold War*, the 1950s are well treated in Robert Divine, *Eisenhower and the Cold War* (1981); Ronald Steel, *Pax Americana* (1967); and Blanche Wiesen Cook, *The Declassified Eisenhower* (1981). An excellent book on the CIA is Victor Marchetti and John D. Marks, *The CIA and the Cult of Intelligence* (1974). For developments linking economics, corporations, and the defense industry, see Mira Wilkins, *The Maturing of Multinational Enterprise* (1974); Richard Barnet and Ronald Muller, *Global Reach* (1974); and Paul Hammond, *Organizing for Defense* (1971). On specific policy situations, see Robert Divine, *Blowing in the Wind: The Nuclear Test Ban Debate, 1954–1960* (1978); Robert Stookey, *America and the Arab States* (1975); John Snetsinger, *Truman, the Jewish Role and the Creation of Israel* (1974); and Hugh Thomas, *Suez* (1967). Of interest given his later career are Henry Kissinger, *Nuclear Weapons and Foreign Policy* (1957) and *The Necessity of Choice* (1961).

The Limits of Containment

Godfrey Hodgson, *America in Our Time* (1976) treats the entire postwar period, but the heart of its powerful analysis covers the 1960s. Richard Walton, *Cold War and Counterrevolution* (1972) surveys the foreign policy of the Kennedy administration. Robert Kennedy, *Thirteen Days* (1969) provides a participant's account of the Cuban missile crisis. Richard Barnet, *Intervention and Revolution* (1968) provides the best introduction to United States relations with the Third World. See also John L. S. Girling, *America and the Third World* (1980) and Samuel Baily, *The United States and the Development of South America, 1945–1975* (1977).

Two superb books introduce the Vietnamese conflict and the American role in it: Frances Fitzgerald, *Fire in the Lake* (1972) and Stanley Karnow, *Vietnam: A History* (1983). George Herring, *America's Longest War* (1980) and Alexander Kendrick, *The Wound Within: America in the Vietnam Years, 1945–1974* (1974) also provide overviews. A fascinating source to digest is *The Pentagon Papers* (1971). David Halberstam, *The Best and the Brightest* (1972) gives a deft, and deadly, portrait of the leaders who got the United States into Vietnam. Guenter Lewy offers a controversial defense of the commitment in *America in Vietnam* (1978). James C. Thompson, *Rolling Thunder* (1980) and John Galloway, *The Gulf of Tonkin Resolution* (1970) cover specific topics. Gloria Emerson, *Winners and Losers* (1976) and Michael Herr, *Dispatches* (1977) convey what the war meant to the soldiers who fought it.

THE PHOTOGRAPHIC EYE

Photographs play such an important part in modern life that we rarely stop to think about what they are, what they stand for, or how pervasive they are. How could modern societies exist without photographs on student and employee ID cards, drivers' licenses, and police mug shots? How would consumers decide what to buy without the alluring photographs that accompany modern advertising? How could families keep track of their vacations—and their histories—without albums and shoeboxes full of old photographs? How would people know what their political leaders looked like? We

have a much clearer image of such figures as Abraham Lincoln and Eleanor Roosevelt, of whom abundant photographs exist, than of George Washington and Abigail Adams, who lived before the photographic process was developed. No wonder the writer James Agee proclaimed the camera "the central instrument of our time."

Photography is a product of the forces of technological and economic change that industrialization set in motion. The earliest photographs were called *daguerreotypes* (plate 1), after the French inventor Louis J. M. Daguerre, who in 1839 patented the

process of transferring an image of light onto a polished mirror surface. By the 1860s, daguerreotypes had been made obsolete by new techniques that allowed multiple copies to be produced from a single negative and printed on paper, rather than glass. In the 1880s, the long exposure time that had been required to record a photographic image was dramatically reduced, enabling the camera to record moving objects. At about the same time, the halftone printing process was developed. This innovation permitted photographs to be reproduced widely in newspapers and magazines. By the

PLATE 1
It was hard work having a daguerreotype taken in the mid-nineteenth century. Subjects had to sit still for nearly thirty seconds while trying to maintain a fairly natural expression (no wonder smiles were rare). In this daguerreotype, Mrs. Kiah Sewall and four of her five children did fine, but the baby moved. (Maine Historical Society)

PLATE 2
In the 1890s, American consumers
could buy a Kodak "Brownie" for
$25, which included processing.
"You press the button, we do the
rest" was the Kodak slogan.
Such photographs were called
"snapshots," a term hunters used to
describe shooting from the hip
without taking careful aim.
(International Museum of
Photography at George Eastman
House)

PLATE 3
Edward S. Curtis devoted his life to
photographing "the vanishing race"
of the American Indian. Between
1907 and 1930, he published twenty
volumes entitled *The North American
Indian,* including this 1925
photogravure of *Francisca Chiwiwi-
Islete.* (The Art Institute of Chicago.
Gift of Mr. and Mrs. Gaylord
Donnelly.)

1890s, the introduction of flexible rolls of film and gelatine dry plates made photography faster and more convenient. In 1895, a small portable camera called the "Brownie" took photography into homes across the nation (plate 2).

From the outset, photography was linked to family culture. Before the Civil War, the cost of having a picture taken had fallen to less than fifty cents, bringing photographs within the range of ordinary Americans. Photo albums began to appear in parlors alongside the family Bible. In an increasingly mobile and transient society, photographs represented direct and tangible ties with friends and relatives who were absent or dead. Photos mailed to loved ones in distant communities provided a way to keep in touch as family members migrated west. Photographs thus helped maintain family and community cohesion at a time of explosive social and economic change. They still perform this function today.

Photographs have many other purposes as well, and early photographers realized the vast potential of their new medium. For example, photographers in the mid-nineteenth century quickly began to document significant events in American history. Mathew Brady and his associates took about seven thousand photographs of the Civil War; the impact of these pictures was heightened by the novelty of the medium. Later in the century, photographers recorded such milestones as the final link in the first transcontinental railroad and the opening of the Oklahoma frontier to white settlers. Evocative images by W. H. Jackson and Edward S. Curtis documented the vanishing way of life of the Plains Indians (plate 3). Photographs of little-known but spectacularly beautiful places, such as the Yellowstone area and

Yosemite Valley, hastened the creation of the National Park System.

Photography proved especially well suited to awakening the American conscience during the progressive era at the turn of the twentieth century. Although photographs give the illusion of objectivity, they are never neutral; they always present a point of view. One of the first reformers to use photographs to promote social change was Jacob Riis, a Danish immigrant. Riis's book *How the Other Half Lives* (1890), which featured dramatic photographs of the plight of the nation's urban poor, helped pioneer the modern field of photojournalism. Two decades later, Lewis Hine produced what he called "human documents" or "photo-interpretations" on topics such as child labor (plate 4) and immigration, including a series on new arrivals at Ellis Island. In the 1920s, Hine focused on the world of work, including a breathtaking series on the construction of the Empire State Building (plate 5). "If I could tell the story in words," he said, "I wouldn't have to lug a camera." Hine's socially committed photography strongly influenced the documentary photographers who

PLATE 4

Between 1908 and 1921, Lewis Hine took more than five thousand photographs for the National Child Labor Committee. This picture captures a group of breaker boys at the entrance to a Pennsylvania coal shaft in 1910. Breaker boys separated useless slate by hand from the miners' yield of coal. (International Museum of Photography at George Eastman House)

PLATE 5

To capture pictures of the construction of the Empire State Building in New York City, Lewis Hine followed workers up exposed girders, out onto the mooring mast (pictured here), and even had himself suspended in a crane to photograph the final rivet at the top of the 102-story building, then the tallest in the world. Hine published these photographs in *Men at Work* (1932). (International Museum of Photography at George Eastman House)

917

roamed the country for the Farm Security Administration during the Great Depression. Today, many photographers who cover stories for leading news magazines carry on this tradition.

Although the camera has been used extensively to document the human condition, it also has been an instrument of individual expression, an example of the artist's spiritual and creative control over a machine. Alfred Stieglitz, whose journal *Camera Work* provided a forum for the developing art of photography between 1902 and 1917, epitomized the serious art photographer in European and American culture. The artist Pablo Picasso com-

mented admiringly about Stieglitz's photograph *The Steerage* (plate 6), "This is exactly what I have been trying to say in paint."

During the 1920s and 1930s, photography underwent something of a flowering and became a prevalent part of American life and culture. Such photographers as Paul Strand, Berenice Abbott, Edward Weston, Imogen Cunningham, Ansel Adams, and Margaret Bourke-White rose to prominence. Although each of these artists dealt with different types of subject matter—Abbott became known for her images of New York skyscrapers, Cunningham for her photographs of flowers, Adams for his dramatic shots

of the American West (plate 7), Bourke-White for her industrial scenes—they all emphasized precise focus, sharp lighting, clarity of subject, and high-quality prints. Their realistic "straight" photography, as it was known, tried to bring out the beauty and significance in the details of everyday life and to focus the viewer's eye on commonplace objects and scenes. Among the many outstanding photographers who furthered their careers with work for the WPA, Walker Evans showed a special appreciation for the humor and the individuality of rural Americans (plate 8).

At the same time, mass-circulation illustrated magazines be-

PLATE 6
Alfred Stieglitz was promenading along the first-class deck of the luxury liner *Kaiser Wilhelm II* when he spotted a scene with artistic possibilities. He rushed back to his cabin for his Graflex camera, and snapped *The Steerage* (1907). Stieglitz considered this his finest picture. (The Art Institute of Chicago. Alfred Stieglitz Collection)

PLATE 7

For Ansel Adams, "a great photograph" has to be "a full expression of what one feels about what is being photographed in the deepest sense and is, thereby, a true expression of what one feels about life in its entirety." *Moonrise, Hernandez, New Mexico* (1941) speaks for Ansel Adams's deep affinity for the American West. (The Art Institute of Chicago. Peabody Purchase Fund)

PLATE 8

In the photographs of Walker Evans, one critic observed, "even the inanimate things, bureau drawers, pots, tires, bricks, signs, seem waiting in their own patient dignity, posing for the picture." This 1936 photograph is a visual inventory of these people's daily lives. (*Roadside Stand near Birmingham, 1936.* The Art Institute of Chicago. Gift of Mrs. James Ward Thorne)

gan to bring new photographs into American homes every week. The most celebrated of these magazines was *Life*, which premiered in 1936. Its first cover featured one of Bourke-White's striking photos of the construction of Fort Peck Dam in Montana (plate 9). As never before, editors relied on pictures to tell news stories.

Pictures were also used for entertainment and escapism. Motion pictures opened a different avenue for photographic expertise and gave people new celebrities to admire—the movie stars. Even "serious" photographers saw movie stars as fascinating subjects. Edward Steichen's early portrait of Greta Garbo (plate 10) is but one example.

By the 1940s, photography had become not only a recog-nized art, but also one of the dominant elements of American mass communication. Its importance was marked by the establishment of a photography department at the Museum of Modern Art in New York City in 1940 and the formation of the International Museum of Photography in Rochester, New York in 1949.

Since World War II, American photography has evolved in different directions. Human interest photography, exemplified by the highly influential "Family of Man" exhibit that Edward Steichen organized at the Museum of Modern Art in 1955, used photographs as metaphors for the human condition. Other photographers gravitated toward subjects on the fringes of society. At the hands of artists such as Diane Arbus and Robert Frank, even supposedly "normal" people and scenes seem freakish or bizarre. Arbus's work (plate 11) suggests that something was amiss in the affluent society of the late 1960s and early 1970s. But, unlike the documentary photography of a few decades earlier, it offers no solutions or calls for reform. The problems that Arbus brought to light in her quirky, often disturbing images could not be corrected by progressive legislation; they ran deeper, suggesting something of a spiritual void at the heart of American society. Robert Frank's photographs, generally more somber, showed Americans as a people who had lost their identity to a massive impersonal society. Their work found great acceptance during the soul-

PLATE 9
In late 1936, publisher Henry Luce assigned Margaret Bourke-White to photograph a series of New Deal dams under construction in the Columbia River Basin for the brand new *Life* magazine. Many of the country's best photojournalists worked for *Life* over the next four decades. (*Life* Magazine © 1936 Time, Inc.)

LIFE

NOVEMBER 23, 1936   10 CENTS

PLATE 11

Diane Arbus was drawn to unconventional subjects, such as transvestites, nudists, carnival freaks, and dwarfs. Most of her subjects look directly into the camera, which makes them look even stranger. The 79-year-old King and 72-year-old Queen that Arbus photographed at a senior citizens' dance in 1970 had never met before. Their names had been picked out of a hat. (© 1970 Estate of Diane Arbus)

PLATE 10

Great photographs have "magic," said Edward Steichen, and his 1928 portrait of actress Greta Garbo certainly does. The movie-going public was fascinated by glamorous stars like Garbo. Monthly fan magazines such as *Photoplay* and *Modern Screen* featured photographs to satisfy the public's insatiable appetite for news about the opulent off-screen lives of Hollywood stars. (International Museum of Photography at George Eastman House. Reprinted with the permission of Joanna T. Steichen)

searching, self-critical years of the Vietnam War and the civil rights movement.

As Americans grappled with difficult social issues in the late 1960s, technological progress brought further advances in photography. One of the most memorable news photos of the twentieth century showed astronauts walking on the moon for the first time, on July 20, 1969. By the 1980s, the two *Voyager* spacecraft were sending back full-color images of Jupiter, Saturn, and Uranus. Photography, which had always recorded scientific phenomena closer to home, was now expanding our knowledge of other worlds.

The capacity for knowledge was also broadened immeasurably by the advent of television, a medium that relied on a special form of camera. Television was developed shortly before World War II, but it did not begin to reach into millions of American homes until the postwar years. The number of photographic images that TV brought to Americans every day became almost limitless.

By the late 1970s and early 1980s, the national storehouse of visual material had grown so vast and powerful that many artists felt no need to create new images. Instead, they began to appropriate existing images and superimpose captions that simulated advertising slogans or newspaper headlines with comments on American society. Barbara Kruger, one of the leading figures in this movement, placed the word "Perfect" over a young woman's clasped hands (plate 12) and the phrase "Your manias become science" over an atomic cloud. In this way, she commented on issues ranging from the role of women to the threat of nuclear war.

"The images that have virtually unlimited authority in modern society are mainly photographic images," observed critic Susan Sontag in her 1977 discussion of the aesthetic and moral questions raised by modern photography. Berenice Abbott made a similar claim, stating that "the *picture* has almost replaced the *word* as a means of communication." Although such assertions are open to debate, visual images have become an omnipresent fact of American life. As new visual innovations are developed, such as the computer graphics and music videos of the 1980s, photography in all its forms will come to play an even greater role in American society.

PLATE 12
Barbara Kruger's work is both political and feminist. "Is this headless presence the incarnation of 1950s good girl-ness," asked one critic, "or a vignetted image of prayer as [a] ladder to spiritual perfection?" What stands out most in this 1980 photograph is the absolute authority of the word "PERFECT." (*Perfect* [© D. James Dee])

922

30

THE STRUGGLE FOR EQUALITY AND DIVERSITY

The 1960s are often portrayed as a time of social protest and upheaval, a time when things fell apart. Yet this era of questioning and confrontation was not confined to a single decade. From the early 1950s through the mid-1970s, new issues and movements crowded the national agenda. The demand for civil rights gained momentum in the 1950s with early victories against segregation in the South. The youth rebellion and resurgent feminism were also rooted in the supposedly complacent 1950s, and the women's movement made its greatest impact on society in the 1970s.

Why did these demands for political and social change occur when they did? Demographic and cultural shifts were partly responsible. The black exodus from the South made civil rights a national, not a sectional, issue. The baby-boom generation swelled the enrollments of the nation's universities, providing recruits for student protest in the the 1960s. Changes in women's lives, notably their increased access to education and greater participation in the work force, helped spark the revival of feminism.

The civil rights movement was the first protest movement to develop, and the tactics it pioneered—legislative and judicial challenges, nonviolent protests, and mobilization of public opinion—were later adopted by other groups to press their demands. But although legal and political victories raised awareness and expectations, they did not address the underlying structural causes that limited each protesting group's full participation in American society. The next stage—the quest for social and economic equality—proved far more problematic. It was easier to pass a law banning segregated seating on buses in the South than to tackle problems of unemployment, deteriorating housing, and pervasive racism in the nation's cities. It was simpler to pass legislation that guaranteed women equal pay on the job than to change attitudes that still gave women full responsibility for household management and child care even when they worked full-time outside the home.

Even at the height of the protest movements, the people demanding changes in American society were always outnumbered by those who preferred the status quo. The strength of this dominant majority culture was the main reason why the ambitious agendas for social change proposed in this period were never fully realized. Yet these movements for equality and diversity had an impact on American culture. "What started as an identity crisis for Negroes turned out to be an identity crisis for the nation," observed one participant. By the 1970s, society had had its "consciousness raised" (a phrase from the women's movement) about a host of issues and problems that had not been topics of national concern in the immediate postwar period.

The Civil Rights Movement

The postwar transformation of southern agriculture underlay the emergence of the civil rights movement. New Deal agricultural policies and the development of synthetic fibers such as rayon and Dacron after World War II caused cotton acreage in the South to decline from forty-three million acres in 1929 to fewer than fifteen million in 1959. In addition, the postwar mechanization of farming reduced the need for farm labor. As a result, the southern farm population fell from 16.2 million in 1930 to 5.9 million in 1960. This displacement affected both white and black farmers, and both landowners and sharecroppers. Some of the migrants settled in southern cities, where they obtained industrial jobs; many of the rest headed to northern cities, including 3 million blacks, between 1940 and 1960. By 1970, a majority of blacks lived outside the South, mainly in the nation's metropolitan areas. Since northern blacks could vote (unlike their predominantly disenfranchised brethren in the South), this circumstance ensured that civil rights would eventually become a political issue.

The civil rights movement was enormously successful in its early days. By the 1960s, black Americans had won most of the political and legal rights that whites enjoyed. These breakthroughs were especially dramatic in the South, where segregation, the legalized system of separation of the races that had existed since the turn of the century, was dismantled. Between 1963 and 1965, the focus of the movement shifted from the South to the rest of the nation, where problems such as urban poverty and patterns of discrimination in jobs and housing proved harder to eradicate than segregation in the South. Impatience with the lack of progress led to splits in the civil rights movement, rioting in major northern cities, and a growing white backlash. As the civil rights movement struggled to maintain its momentum, other groups, such as Hispanics and native Americans, took up the cry of equal rights on their own behalf.

The Fight for Legal Equality

In August 1955, G. H. Mehta, India's ambassador to the United States, walked into a restaurant at the Houston airport. To his indignant surprise, Mehta was told he could not be served

INTEGRATION IN LITTLE ROCK
Angry crowds taunted the nine black students who tried to register in 1957 at previously all-white Central High School in Little Rock, Arkansas with chants such as "Two-four-six-eight, we ain't gonna integrate." The court-ordered integration proceeded only after President Eisenhower reluctantly mobilized the Arkansas National Guard. (Wide World)

because he had taken a seat in the "whites only" section. This incident, a keen embarrassment to the U.S. government, occurred because a comprehensive system of state and local laws mandated the separation of the races throughout the South.

In most southern states, it was illegal for whites and blacks to eat in the same rooms in restaurants or luncheonettes, use the same waiting rooms or toilet facilities at bus or train stations, or ride in the same taxis. Even drinking fountains were labeled "White" and "Colored." All forms of public transportation were rigidly segregated, either by custom or law. On buses, for example, if whites had filled all the front seats, blacks were obliged to give up seats in the back until every white had a place.

Since the 1930s, black Americans had a growing arsenal of weapons with which to challenge segregation. The federal government had increasingly paid attention to the problems of blacks. It established the Fair Employment Practices Commission in 1941 and, on President Truman's executive order in 1948, desegregated the armed forces. There was some social progress, too. In 1947, Jackie Robinson broke the color barrier in major league baseball. However, Robinson could not always stay in the same hotels or eat in the same restaurants as his teammates on the Brooklyn Dodgers.

Blacks got further ammunition in their fight against discrimination from the Supreme Court. Since the 1940s, the National Association for the Advancement of Colored People (NAACP) had litigated a series of test cases challenging segregation. These suits began to bear fruit in 1944, when the Court declared that blacks could not be denied the right to vote in party primaries. In 1946, it ruled that states could not require segregated seating on interstate buses, and two years later it struck down restrictive residential covenants that forbade the sale of real estate to members of disfavored racial groups.

A major leap forward occurred in 1954. In the case of *Brown v. Board of Education of Topeka*, the Supreme Court ruled that segregated schools violated the Fourteenth Amendment to the Constitution. The decision thus explicitly reversed the doctrine set forth in *Plessy v. Ferguson* (1896) that "separate but equal" facilities did not violate the civil rights of blacks. Speaking for a unanimous court, Chief Justice Earl Warren ruled:

To separate Negro children solely because of their race generates a feeling of inferiority as to their status in the community that may affect their hearts and minds in a way never to be undone. . . . We conclude that in the field of public education the doctrine of "separate but equal" has no place. Separate educational facilities are inherently unequal.

Blacks reacted joyfully. Black parents believed segregation would end immediately and that their children would soon attend integrated—and superior—schools. Black Americans were especially proud that black lawyer Thurgood Marshall, representing the NAACP, had been instrumental in using the white legal system to win such a stunning judicial victory. White reaction, especially in the South, was almost uniformly hostile. President Dwight Eisenhower refused to comment publicly about the decision, other than to acknowledge that it was now the law of the land. In private, he complained that his appointment of Chief Justice Earl Warren was "the biggest damfool mistake I ever made."

Brown v. Board of Education was one of the most far-reaching decisions ever handed down by the Supreme Court. Following its precedent, over the next several years the Supreme Court ruled against segregation in parks, public beaches, golf courses, all forms of interstate and intrastate transportation, and public housing. Yet progress in desegregating schools was frustratingly slow. The Court had declared only that integration should proceed "with all deliberate speed." As many critics later noted, the deliberation was far more evident than the speed. By 1960, less than 1 percent of southern black children attended desegregated schools. Significant school integration did not occur until the 1970s.

The *Brown* decision was so far in advance of prevailing cultural attitudes that it worked as an agent for social change. It forced the federal government to enter, albeit reluctantly, on the side of desegregation. In September 1957, when nine black children tried to enroll at Central High School in Little Rock, Arkansas, Governor Orval Faubus called out the national guard to bar them, despite a court order to the contrary. Every night, national television carried pictures of a white crowd taunting the poised but obviously terrified black students with such chants as "Go back to the jungle." Eisenhower nationalized the Arkansas guard so that integration could proceed. As happened time and again, white extremism provoked a far more sympathetic response from the federal government than would otherwise have occurred.

The magnitude of resistance to school integration deeply discouraged black and sympathetic white southerners who had hoped that the system of Jim Crow segregation would topple in the wake of the *Brown* decision. The realization that more action would be needed fueled the second major stage of the early civil rights movement—nonviolent protest. A spirit of activism had been growing among members of the black community since the 1930s, but the *Brown* decision had a catalytic effect on black aspirations. It encouraged them to think that change was possible.

On December 1, 1955, Rosa Parks, a church leader and member of the NAACP in Montgomery, Alabama, refused to give up her seat on a city bus to a white man. She was promptly arrested and charged with violating a local segregation ordinance. "I felt it was just something I had to do," Parks stated simply. Black activist Eldridge Cleaver put her act of resistance in a broader context: "Somewhere in the universe a gear in the machinery had shifted."

As Montgomery's black community met to discuss the proper response, it turned to the Reverend Martin Luther King, Jr., who had just accepted the post of pastor at Montgomery's Dexter Street Baptist Church. The son of a prominent black minister in Atlanta, King had earned a Ph.D. in theology at Boston University. King embraced the teachings of Mahatma Gandhi, who had organized the brilliant campaigns of noncooperation and passive resistance that ultimately helped India to win its independence from British rule in 1947. Drawing on Gandhian principles, King proposed a massive nonviolent protest to boycott Montgomery's municipal bus system.

For the next 381 days, a united black community formed carpools or walked to work. "My feets is tired, but my soul is rested," said one black woman. Added another, "I'm not walking for myself. I'm walking for my children and my grandchildren." The bus company neared bankruptcy, and downtown stores complained about loss of business. When a federal court ruled that bus segregation was illegal, the city of Montgomery finally complied.

THE ARREST OF ROSA PARKS
Rosa Parks, a forty-two-year-old department store seamstress, is fingerprinted by a Montgomery, Alabama, police officer after being arrested in 1955 for refusing to give her seat on a bus to a white man. The black community organized a 381-day boycott of the Montgomery bus system and eventually won its demand for unsegregated public transportation. (Wide World)

The Montgomery bus boycott catapulted King into national prominence. In 1957, he joined with the Reverend Ralph Abernathy and other members of the southern black clergy to found the Southern Christian Leadership Conference (SCLC), based in Atlanta. Activist organizations such as the SCLC supplanted the NAACP as the main spurs for racial justice.

The next phase of the movement began in Greensboro, North Carolina, on February 1, 1960. Four black college students from North Carolina Agricultural and Technical College—Ezell Blair, Jr., Franklin McCain, Joseph McNeill, and David Richmond—decided to "sit in" at the "whites only" counter of a local Woolworth store. When Blair asked for a cup of coffee, "The waitress looked at me as if I were from outer space." Over the next few days, they were joined by other black students and a few white supporters. The sit-in tactic spread quickly. Within six months, not only the lunch counter in Greensboro but many others throughout the South had been desegregated. By the end of 1960, about 50,000 people had participated in sit-ins or other demonstrations, and 3,600 had gone to jail. The Student Non-Violent Coordinating Committee (SNCC, pronounced "snick"), an off-shoot of the SCLC, coordinated the student sit-ins.

The momentum next switched to the Congress of Racial Equality (CORE), an interracial group founded in 1942. In 1961, CORE organized a "freedom ride" on interstate buses from Washington, D.C., to New Orleans. Black and white freedom riders planned to challenge the segregation of waiting rooms, toilets, and restaurants throughout the deep South. When they got to Anniston, Alabama, club-wielding Ku Klux Klansmen stopped the bus, stoned it, and set it on fire. The freedom riders escaped only moments before the bus exploded. When other riders were beaten mercilessly in Birmingham, Governor John Patterson refused to step in, saying "I cannot guarantee protection for this bunch of rabble rousers."

Such incidents of white extremism were televised on the nightly news, shocking many citizens. Attorney General Robert Kennedy now intervened to protect the freedom riders. Soon the Interstate Commerce Commission ordered the desegregation of all interstate vehicles and terminals. CORE learned the lesson that nonviolent protest could succeed if it provoked vicious white resistance and generated lots of publicity. Only then, it sometimes appeared, would federal authorities act.

The nonviolent phase of the civil rights movement climaxed in August 1963 with a massive March on Washington. Supported by a broad coalition of black organizations, as well as the Protestant National Council of Churches, the National Conference of Catholics for Interracial Justice, the American Jewish Congress, and the AFL-CIO Industrial Union Department, the March on Washington brought more than 250,000 orderly black and white demonstrators—the largest protest assembled up to that time—to the Lincoln Memorial. Martin Luther King, Jr., capped this event with a memorable speech:

I have a dream that one day on the red hills of Georgia sons of former slaves and the sons of former slaveholders will be able to sit down together at the table of brotherhood. I have a dream that one day even the state of Mississippi, a state sweltering with the heat of injustice . . . will be transformed into an oasis of freedom and justice. I have a dream that my four little

THE FREEDOM RIDERS
Black and white volunteers watch anxiously as they pull into the Montgomery, Alabama, bus station in 1961, while a hostile white crowd gathers outside. Civil rights leader James L. Farmer recalled their determination: "On the bus I noticed . . . boys writing notes and putting them in their pockets, and girls putting them in their brassieres . . . They were writing names and addresses of next of kin. They really had not expected to live beyond that trip. . . ." (© Bruce Davidson, Magnum)

children will one day live in a nation where they will not be judged by the color of their skin but by the content of their character.

He ended with this invocation, "Free at last, free at last, thank God almighty, we are free at last."

King's eloquent speech, and the spectacle of blacks and whites marching solemnly together, did more than any other event to make black protest acceptable to white Americans. The March on Washington epitomized the liberal faith that blacks and whites could work together peacefully to promote racial harmony. It also confirmed King's position, at least in the eyes of the white community, as the leading speaker for the black cause. King's stature rose even higher when he won the Nobel Peace Prize in 1964.

Ironically, as King gained appeal among whites, he lost support in the fragmenting civil rights movement. Students who had risked physical assault to sit in at lunch counters and drugstores were impatient with the gradualism of their elders. Freedom riders who had spent months in harsh southern jails found little relevance in King's commitment to brotherhood and nonviolent change. Activists who had seen fellow workers gunned down by white racists shared the bitterness of one CORE member who said, "I'm sick and tired of going to the funerals of black men who have been murdered by white men." By 1963, the legalistic, nonviolent approach was giving way to demands for immediate action of a more far-reaching nature.

The Federal Response

The accelerating momentum of the civil rights movement had profound implications for the federal government. President Kennedy realized that blacks had helped elect him, but he had dallied on civil rights for fear of alienating conservative white southern supporters in Congress. Events in 1963 pushed the Kennedy administration to take a stronger stand. In Birmingham, Alabama, Martin Luther King, Jr., and the Reverend Fred Shuttlesworth called for demonstrations to protest conditions in what King called "the most segregated city in the United States." In April, thousands of black demonstrators marched toward Birmingham's downtown department stores to picket. They were met by Eugene ("Bull") Connor, the city's commissioner of public safety, who used snarling dogs, electric cattle prods, and high-pressure fire hoses to break up the crowd; the fire hoses were so strong that they ripped bark from trees and tore bricks from buildings. Television cameras captured the entire scene. "The civil rights movement should thank God for Bull Connor," Kennedy noted. "He's helped it as much as Abraham Lincoln."

President Kennedy, realizing he could no longer straddle the issue, now determined to step up the federal role in civil rights. He went on television in June 1963, to promise major civil rights legislation. Kennedy extemporized at the end of his speech:

> We are confronted primarily with a moral issue. It is as old as the scriptures and is as clear as the American Constitution. If an American, because his skin is dark, cannot eat in a restaurant open to the public, if he cannot send his children to the best public school available, if he cannot vote for the public officials who represent him, if, in short, he cannot enjoy the full and free life which all of us want, then who among us would be content to have the color of his skin changed and stand in his place?

For some, Kennedy's speech came too late. That same night, Medgar Evers, a prominent NAACP activist, was shot in the back and killed in Jackson, Mississippi. Kennedy submitted a strong bill to Congress, but even with the killing of Evers, the March on Washington, and the bombing in September of a Birmingham church that killed four black girls, the measure stalled. Two months later, Kennedy was assassinated.

Lyndon Johnson promptly turned passage of civil rights legislation into a memorial to his slain predecessor. The Civil Rights Act, passed in June 1964, was a landmark in the history of American race relations and one of the greatest achievements of the 1960s. Title VII of the act—which outlawed discrimination in public accommodations or employment based on race, religion, national origin, or sex—was its keystone. In addition, the law gave opponents of segregation two powerful new weapons. They could now ask the attorney general to withhold federal funds from any state program, including education, that was not desegregated. They also could appeal discrimination in public accommo-

FANNIE LOU HAMER REGISTERS TO VOTE IN MISSISSIPPI

So then that was in 1962 when the civil rights workers came into this country. Now I didn't know anything about voter registration or nothin' like that, 'cause people had never been told that they could register to vote. . . . So they had a rally. I had gone to church that Sunday, and the minister announced that they were gon' have a mass meeting that Monday night. Well, I didn't know what a mass meeting was, and I was just curious to go to a mass meeting. So I did . . . and they was talkin' about how blacks had a right to register and how they had a right to *vote*. . . . Just listenin' at 'em, I could just see myself votin' people outa office that I know was wrong and didn't do nothin' to help the poor. I said, you know, that's sumpin' I really wanna be involved in, and finally at the end of that rally, I had made up my mind that I was gonna come out there when they said you could

go down that Friday [August 31, 1962] to try to register. . . .

He [the registrar] brought a big old book out there, and he gave me the sixteenth section of the Constitution of Mississippi, and that was dealing with de facto laws, and I didn't know nothin' about no de facto laws, didn't know nothin' about any of 'em. I could copy it like it was in the book . . . but after I got through copying it, he told me to give a reasonable interpretation and tell the meaning of that section that I had copied. Well, I flunked out. . . .

Monday, the fourth of December, I went back to Indianola to the circuit clerk's office and I told him who I was and I was there to take that literacy test again.

I said, "Now, you cain't have me fired 'cause I'm already fired, and I won't have to move now, because I'm not livin' in no white man's house." I said, "I'll be here every thirty days until I become a

registered voter."

I passed that second test, but it made us become like criminals. We would have to have our lights out before dark. It was cars passing that house all times of the night, driving real slow with guns, and pickups with white mens in it, and they'd pass that house just as slow as they could pass it . . . three guns lined up in the back. . . . Pap couldn't get nothin' to do. . . .

So I started teachin' citizenship class, and I became the supervisor of the citizenship class in this county. So I moved around the county to do citizenship education and later on I become a field secretary for SNCC. . . .

Source: Interview with Fannie Lou Hamer reprinted by permission of the Putnam Publishing Group from *My Soul Is Rested* by Howell Raines. Copyright © 1977 by Howell Raines. 249–250, 252.

---

dations or employment to the Equal Employment Opportunity Commission, which was set up to enforce Title VII.

Despite the enactment of federal civil rights legislation, intense resistance to voting rights for blacks continued in the South, where barely a quarter of blacks were on the voting lists in the early 1960s. SNCC and CORE conducted voter registration drives in 1962–1963, but their workers faced pressure and outright violence for encouraging blacks to register. Reprisals also extended to individual blacks who dared to register.

Black organizations and churches mounted a major registration drive in the summer of 1964. They recruited several thousand volunteers, many from the nation's campuses, to join in

"Freedom Summer." Violence struck quickly when three volunteers—James Chaney, a CORE volunteer from Mississippi; Andrew Goodman, a student from New York; and Michael Schwerner, a New York social worker—disappeared from Philadelphia, Mississippi, in June 1964. An investigation was mounted, and Rita Schwerner, Michael's wife, noted, "We all know that this search . . . is because Andrew Goodman and my husband are white. If only Chaney was involved, nothing would have been done." When their bodies were found several weeks later, Goodman and Schwerner had been killed by a single bullet each, while Chaney had been brutally beaten with a chain and then shot several times. Members of the Ku Klux Klan committed the crime, it was later revealed. Fifteen civil rights workers were murdered in the South during Freedom Summer. Only sixteen hundred black voters were registered.

The case for federal action grew stronger in 1965. In February of that year, sheriff's deputies in Marion, Alabama, killed Jimmy Lee Jackson, a black voting-rights advocate, during a voter registration march. Angry black leaders called for a massive protest march from nearby Selma to the state capital, Montgomery, fifty-four miles away. Sheriff's deputies and a mounted posse attacked as soon as the marchers left Selma. The assault took place in broad daylight and was filmed for national television. To add to the nation's shock, Viola Liuzzo, a white woman married to a Detroit union official, was shot and killed by the Ku Klux Klan while ferrying protesters back and forth at the Selma demonstrations. Liuzzo's death and other acts of violence in Selma assured passage of federal voting rights legislation.

The Voting Rights Act of 1965 banned the literacy tests that most southern states had used to prevent blacks from registering to vote. It also placed the entire registration and voting process under direct federal control by authorizing government examiners to register voters in counties where less than 50 percent of the minority residents were on the voting lists. Together with the adoption in 1964 of the Twenty-fourth Amendment to the Constitution, which outlawed the poll tax, the Voting Rights Act made it possible for millions of blacks to register and vote for the first time. Congress extended the Voting Rights Act in 1970, 1975, and 1982.

By the 1970s, the proportion of eligible blacks who were registered in Selma, Alabama, had risen from 2 percent to 60 percent. During the same period, the number of black voters registered in Mississippi rose from twenty-two thousand to three hundred thousand, two-thirds of the black voting-age population there. Nationwide, 20 percent of all blacks were registered in 1960, 39 percent in 1964, and 62 percent in 1971.

Black voters had considerable impact. They triggered the end of the domination of the South by a lily-white Democratic party. In 1965, the former states of the Confederacy had only seventy-two black elected officials; fifteen years later, there were about three thousand. Atlanta and Birmingham had black mayors, Houston had a black chief of police, and candidates who were once ardent segregationists began to court the black vote. By the 1970s, black voters had become an established part of southern politics.

Hartman Turnbow, a black Mississippi farmer who had risked his life to register to vote in a SNCC-sponsored drive during the Freedom Summer of 1964, summed up the momentous changes that had occurred in that decade:

> Anybody had a jus told me 'fore it happened that conditions would make this much change between the white and the black in Holmes County here where I live, why I'da just said, "You're lyin'. It won't happen." I just wouldn't have believed it. I didn't dream of it. I didn't see no way. But it got to workin' just like the citizen-

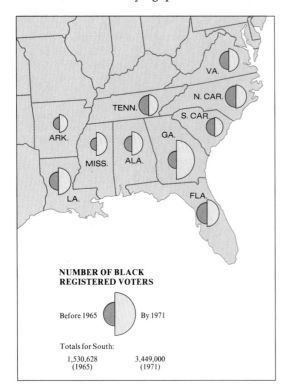

NUMBER OF BLACK
REGISTERED VOTERS

Before 1965   By 1971

Totals for South:
1,530,628   3,449,000
  (1965)   (1971)

MAP 30.1 BLACK VOTER REGISTRATION IN THE SOUTH
After the passage of the Voting Rights Act of 1965, black registration in the South increased dramatically. These circles are divided to show the number of blacks registered before 1965 (left) and by 1971 (right). States in the deep South, including Mississippi and Georgia, showed the biggest rises.

ship class teacher told us—that if we redish to vote and just stick with it. He says it's gon' be some difficults. He told us that when we started. We was looking for it. He said we gon' have difficults, gon' have troubles, folks gon' lose their homes, folks gon' lose their lives, people gon' lose all their money, and just like he said, all of that happened. He didn't miss it. He hit it ka-dap on the head, and it's workin' now. It won't never go back where it was.

From Civil Rights to Black Power

Blacks throughout the country, not just in the South, had been energized by the *Brown* decision and federal civil rights legislation. Newly raised expectations led to more demands. Now that the system of legalized segregation had fallen in the South, black leaders concentrated on a more difficult goal—eliminating the institutional, economic, and social structures that made blacks second-class citizens. The civil rights movement now moved from attacking de jure segregation (that is, enforced by law) to de facto segregation (enforced by custom).

Although less flagrant than in the South, northern discrimination was real and pervasive, especially regarding education, housing, and employment opportunities. Although the *Brown* decision outlawed separate but equal schools, it did nothing to change conditions in educational systems where schools were predominantly all-black or all-white because of patterns of residential segregation. In the 1960s, for example, 90 percent of Chicago's black students attended all-black schools. Not until 1973 did federal judges begin to order the desegregation of schools in the North as they had in the South two decades earlier.

As the civil rights movement escalated its demands, it found itself deeply polarized along generational lines. While their elders held back, younger blacks were eager for confrontation and ever faster change. They insisted that they be called blacks or Afro-Americans, not Negroes, a term they judged demeaning because of its historic association with slavery and discrimination.

By the mid-1960s, many young activists even questioned the goal of assimilation into white society itself. Black separatism dated back to the nineteenth century; the Marcus Garvey move-

MARTIN LUTHER KING, JR.
The Reverend Martin Luther King, Jr. (1929–1968) pictured here at a 1957 Prayer Pilgrimage for Freedom in Washington, D.C., was the most eloquent advocate of the black cause in the 1950s and 1960s. By the mid 1960s, his policy of nonviolence was under attack by young black activists. (© Bob Henrique, Magnum).

ment in the 1920s represented its most vibrant twentieth-century appearance to date. In the 1960s, new impetus came from the Nation of Islam, or Black Muslim movement, led by Elijah Muhammad. The Black Muslim ideology was extremely hostile not only to whites but also to traditional civil rights organizations. Forcefully rejecting integration in favor of black nationalism, it stressed black pride, unity, and self-help. Malcolm X, who caustically referred to Martin Luther King's 1963 march as "the farce on Washington," emerged as one of the Black Muslims' most charismatic figures. His autobiography, published after he was gunned down in 1965 by a rival Muslim faction, became one of the decade's most influential books.

The Black Muslims' demand for cultural and political independence appealed to the young veterans of SNCC and CORE. Abandoning the

MALCOLM X ON THE "FARCE ON WASHINGTON"

Not long ago, the black man in America was fed a dose of another form of the weakening, lulling and deluding effects of so-called "integration." It was that "Farce on Washington," I call it. . . .

The morning of the March, any rickety carloads of angry, dusty, sweating small-town Negroes would have gotten lost among the chartered jet planes, railroad cars, and air-conditioned buses. What originally was planned to be an angry riptide one English newspaper aptly described now as "the gentle flood."

Talk about "integrated"! It was like salt and pepper. And, by now, there wasn't a single logistics aspect uncontrolled.

The marchers had been instructed to bring no signs—signs were provided. They had been told to sing one song: "We Shall Overcome." They had been told *how* to arrive, *when*, *where* to arrive, *where* to assemble, when to *start* marching, the *route* to march. First-aid stations were strategically located—even where to *faint*!

Yes, I was there. I observed that circus. Who ever heard of angry revolutionists all harmonizing "We Shall Overcome . . . Suum Day . . ." while tripping and swaying along arm-in-arm with the very people they were supposed to be angrily revolting against? Who ever heard of angry revolutionists swinging their bare feet together with their oppressor in lily-pad park pools, with gospels and guitars and "I Have A Dream" speeches?. . . .

Hollywood couldn't have topped it.

In a subsequent press poll, not one Congressman or Senator with a previous record of opposition to civil rights said he had changed his views. What did anyone expect? How was a one-day "integrated" picnic going to counter-influence these representatives of prejudice rooted deep in the psyche of the American white man for four hundred years?

The very fact that millions, black and white, believed in this monumental farce is another example of how much this country goes in for the surface glossing over, the escape ruse, surfaces, instead of truly dealing with its deep-rooted problems.

What that March on Washington did do was lull Negroes for a while. But inevitably, the black masses started realizing they had been smoothly hoaxed again by the white man. And, inevitably, the black man's anger rekindled, deeper than ever, and there began bursting out in different cities the "long, hot summer" of 1964, unprecedented racial crises.

Source: Malcolm X (with Alex Haley), *The Autobiography of Malcolm X.* New York: Random House, 1965. 278, 280—281.

---

earlier faith in interracial cooperation, SNCC's Stokely Carmichael coined a new militant slogan, "black power," in 1966. "The only way we gonna stop them white men from whupping us is to take over," he declared. "We been saying freedom for six years and we ain't got nothing. What we gonna start saying is Black Power!" Carmichael's successor at SNCC, H. Rap Brown, was even more rebellious, saying, "America won't come around, so we're going to burn America down" and "Violence is as American as cherry pie." Huey Newton, leader of the militant Black Panthers in California, provocatively insisted that blacks follow the admonition of China's communist leader Mao Zedong that "political power comes through the barrel of a gun."

The black power ideology had important implications for the civil rights movement. Such militancy was confrontational and potentially violent; it rejected Martin Luther King's teachings, especially the goal of integration into white society. There was no longer a question of fine-tuning the system, because the whole system had to be changed. As author James Baldwin asked, "Do I really *want* to be integrated into a burning house?" Within several years of Martin Luther King's "I have a dream" speech, certain elements in the civil rights movement had moved from cooperation with whites to separatism, from nonviolence to armed self-defense, from working within the system to preparing for revolution.

As a result of this growing militancy, most

black organizations went through major identity crises in 1965. By the next year, for all intents and purposes, whites had been kicked out of the civil rights movement. CORE's decision to bar whites from leadership positions symbolized this shift. Whites were told they could not understand what it meant to be black; many whites themselves felt guilty about their own complicity in the institutionalized racism that blacks had experienced.

The new black assertiveness alarmed many other white Americans, however. They had been willing to go along with the moderate reforms of the 1950s and early 1960s, but they balked when blacks started demanding immediate access to higher-paying jobs, better housing in previously white neighborhoods, integrated schools, and increased political power. In 1964, only 34 percent of all whites thought blacks were demanding too much change; by 1966, 84 percent thought so.

More than any other cause, the riots in northern cities between 1964 and 1968 undermined white support for the civil rights movement. Why did the nation's cities explode in violence? The rapid growth of segregated metropolitan areas during the postwar period provided the backdrop. Migration from the country to the city made many black people, especially young adults, painfully aware of their exclusion from the dominant consumer culture. Moreover, they

were angry at white landlords who owned the substandard housing they were forced to live in; at white shopkeepers who made their money from black trade but would not hire black clerks or salespeople; and at all-white unions—especially the building trades—that controlled access to skilled neighborhood jobs. Stimulated by television coverage of southern blacks who banded together to challenge whites and who got results, young urban blacks expressed their grievances with their own brand of "direct action." Their parents and adult neighbors often supported them in spirit. By 1968, riots had occurred in at least seventy-five cities.

The first of the "long hot summers" took place in 1964, when a police shooting of a black criminal suspect in Harlem led to a week of looting and rioting there. The underlying causes, as in many of the later riots, were white control and exploitation of business and real estate in the black community, high black unemployment and poverty, and the volatile issue of police brutality.

Racial turmoil worsened the following summer. A riot in the Watts section of Los Angeles, where 60 percent of the population was on relief, left thirty-four blacks dead and produced the frightening refrain "Burn, baby, burn." Ironically, Watts erupted just five days after President Johnson had hailed passage of the Voting Rights Act of 1965 as the next great step toward racial

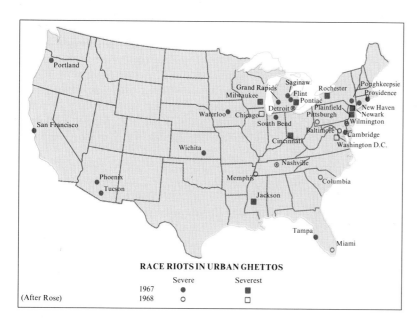

RACE RIOTS IN URBAN GHETTOS

	Severe	Severest
1967	●	■
1968	○	□

(After Rose)

MAP 30.2 RACIAL UNREST IN AMERICA'S CITIES, 1967–1968
The urban riots of 1967 occurred in scattered large urban areas throughout the United States, including the South and West. In 1968, by contrast, rioting broke out only east of the Mississippi River. Major rioting usually did not occur in the same city in two consecutive years.

THE WATTS RIOT
The nation's worst racial disturbance since the Detroit race riot of 1943 began in the Watts section of Los Angeles on August 11, 1965. An altercation broke out when white police officers stopped two blacks for a minor traffic violation. Thirty-four persons died in the Watts riot. (© Michael Alexander, Black Star)

equality. For many young urban blacks, however, the gains of the civil rights movement were often irrelevant to the poverty and economic exploitation that pervaded their daily lives. An exchange between Martin Luther King and a twenty-year-old unemployed black rioter in the smoldering ruins of Watts captured this frustration. "We won!" shouted the young man. How can we have won, King countered, when so many people died, homes were destroyed, and the community lay in ruins? "We won because we made the whole world pay attention to us," the rioter replied. "We made them come."

The riots of 1967 were the most serious of all. Rioting began early in several southern cities, built up in June, and engulfed twenty-two cities in July and August. Large-scale disturbances hit Toledo, Ohio; Grand Rapids, Michigan; Plainfield, New Jersey; and Milwaukee, Wisconsin. Violent riots in Newark and Detroit produced widespread destruction and loss of life. Forty-three people were killed in Detroit alone, and at least a fourth of the city was burned, with $50 million worth of property destroyed. Mayor Jerome Cavanaugh of Detroit compared the devastated city to war-ravaged Berlin in 1945. As

was true of most of the riots, the arson and looting was directed at white-owned property, but little physical violence took place against white people. Almost all the reported sniping turned out to involve wild shooting by the police.

The assassination of Martin Luther King in Memphis on April 4, 1968, by James Earl Ray, a white ex-convict whose motive was unknown, set off a final cataclysm of urban rioting. Major violence broke out in more than forty cities. In Washington, national guardsmen with machine guns protected the Capitol, which was framed against fires from the neighboring ghettoes. In Chicago, where rioting and looting engulfed most of the city's West Side, Mayor Richard J. Daley ordered police to "shoot to kill" suspected snipers.

With King's assassination, the civil rights movement lost the one black leader who still had the capacity to stir the conscience of white America. At the time of his death, he was only thirty-nine years old. During the last years of his life, King had moved toward a more comprehensive view of the structural problems of poverty and racism that blacks faced in contemporary America. In 1967, he confronted the issue of residential segregation in a losing battle for open housing in Chicago. He came out forcefully against the Vietnam War. In 1968, he was planning a poor people's campaign to raise issues of economic injustice and inequality. He had gone to Memphis the day he was shot to support a strike by predominantly black sanitation workers. His premature death robbed the country of a forceful leader in the next stage of the battle.

The 1950s and 1960s brought permanent, indeed revolutionary, changes in American race relations. Jim Crow segregation was overturned in less than a decade, and the passage of significant federal legislation ensured black Americans their basic civil rights. Yet by the time of King's death in 1968, race relations had become polarized. Candidates such as Governor George C. Wallace of Alabama exploited a white backlash against black activism that was by no means confined to the South. By the 1970s, black Americans were too diverse and too divided, both economically and politically, to mount a unified drive for jobs and improved education. Like all Americans, they found that American society provided highly unequal rewards.

The Spreading Demand for Equal Rights

The civil rights movement influenced other groups, such as Hispanics and native Americans, to organize to press their claims. Until 1960, few Hispanic-Americans had participated in politics. Poverty, uncertain legal status, and language barriers kept them politically silent. This situation began to change when the Mexican American Political Association (MAPA) mobilized Hispanics to vote for John F. Kennedy in 1960, providing an important margin of victory in closely contested states such as Texas, New Mexico, and Illinois. In return, several Hispanic-American leaders received prominent appointments in Washington, and federal authorities paid increased attention to their demands.

Younger Hispanics quickly grew impatient with the MAPA, however. More radical and more inclined to celebrate their group's cultural achievements and traditions, the younger leaders pursued increasingly diverse goals. The *barrios*—crowded, neglected slums in Los Angeles

and other California cities—produced the militant Brown Berets, who modeled themselves on Huey Newton's Black Panthers. In 1969, a new term, "Chicano," was coined to replace "Mexican-American." This revolution in consciousness also produced a political party, La Raza Unida ("the united race"), to promote Hispanic interests and candidates in public life.

The founding of La Raza Unida was just one manifestation of a heightened interest in politics and political mobilization. AFL-CIO unions worked to increase Hispanic participation in elections. The civil rights legislation of the 1960s also stimulated Hispanics to get into politics. This strategy paid off with the election of Henry Cisneros as mayor of San Antonio in 1981; Toney Anaya as governor of New Mexico and Louis Montano as mayor of Sante Fe in 1982; and Federico Peña as mayor of Denver in 1983, where Hispanics comprised only 18 percent of the population.

Chicano strategists also pushed for economic objectives. Working in the fields around Delano, California, labor leader Cesar Chavez (shown on page 936) organized the United Farm Workers, the first successful union to represent migrant workers. A 1966 grape pickers' strike and a nationwide boycott of table grapes brought Chavez and his union national publicity. Quietly advocating his cause, Chavez won the support of the AFL-CIO and Senator Robert F. Kennedy of New York. Chavez soon was receiving almost as much media attention as Martin Luther King, Jr.

Puerto Ricans, the second largest component of the nation's Hispanic population, were divided politically. The dream of independence fueled a nationalist movement that occasionally turned to violence; in 1950, a band of nationalist Puerto Rican terrorists made an unsuccessful assassination attempt on President Truman. Most Puerto Ricans, however, favored the militant pursuit of equality and opportunity within the United States. New York City's Herman Badillo, the first Puerto Rican to sit in the U.S. House of Representatives, symbolized their growing political presence.

Cuban refugees comprised the third large group of Hispanics. Nearly half a million people fled Cuba in the wake of Fidel Castro's ascent to power in 1959, creating a refugee community so large and vigorous that it turned Miami into a

CESAR CHAVEZ
Mexican-American labor leader Cesar Chavez addresses a rally in Guadalupe, California. Chavez won national attention in 1965 during a strike of migrant farm workers, most of them Mexican-Americans, against California grape growers. Drawing on tactics from the civil rights movement, Chavez called for nonviolent action and effectively mobilized support from white liberals. (FPG)

cosmopolitan, bilingual city almost overnight. Although Miami's new Cubans prospered economically, at first they remained dedicated to the overthrow of Castro and their return to Cuba. As the Castro regime consolidated its position, thus foreclosing prospects of returning home, Cuban-Americans increased their political activity in the United States. They differed from most other Hispanic voters in being predominantly middle class, violently anticommunist, and generally conservative.

American Indians also found a model in the civil rights movement. Like blacks and Hispanics, they proposed a new name for themselves—native Americans—and organized dramatic protests and demonstrations to build support for their cause. Native Americans, who numbered nearly 1.5 million by 1980, had much to protest. Their unemployment rate, 40 percent in the 1970s, exceeded that of blacks. They suffered the worst poverty, the most inadequate housing, the highest disease rates, and the least access to education of any group in the United States.

Like other groups in American society, native Americans organized pressure groups to win better treatment. As early as World War II, the National Council of American Indians had lobbied for improvement in Indians' lives. The late 1960s saw the founding of far more radical groups, such as the American Indian Movement (AIM), which drew its strength from the third of the Indian population who lived in the "red ghettoes" in cities throughout the West.

AIM consciously modeled itself on the activist black power movement, and for a few years the tactics of AIM and similar groups attracted considerable public attention. In November 1969, AIM seized the deserted federal penitentiary on Alcatraz Island in San Francisco Bay, offering the government twenty-four dollars worth of trinkets to pay for it. (This was what the white settlers had paid the Indians for Manhattan Island in 1626.) The Indian occupation of Alcatraz lasted until the summer of 1971. In November 1972, a thousand protesters occupied the headquarters of the Bureau of Indian Affairs in Washington, D.C., inflicting $2 million of damage on government records and property. In February 1973, AIM members began a seventy-one day occupation of the town of Wounded Knee, South Dakota, the site of the army massacre of Sioux Indians in 1890. They were protesting the light sentences given a group of white men convicted of killing a Sioux in 1972. The protesters took eleven hostages and occupied several buildings to dramatize their cause. But when a gun battle left one protester dead and another wounded, the siege collapsed.

Such militant confrontations, designed largely to capture the interest of the media, did not always increase public support. Therefore, native Americans also used other methods to advance their cause. Such books as *Custer Died for Your Sins* (1969), by Vine Deloria, Jr., a Sioux; N. Scott Momaday's Pulitzer Prize–winning novel *House Made of Dawn* (1968); and Dee Brown's best-selling *Bury My Heart at Wounded Knee* (1971) increased white empathy for Indian concerns. Potentially the most far-reaching tactic was the initiation of lawsuits to reclaim Indian lands illegally taken in violation of federal laws and treaties. Such suits, pitting the Indian claimants against citizens in states from Maine to Alaska who were currently living on the land, produced economic gains for native Americans and represented a growing public awareness of the injustices they had suffered.

Civil rights, which began as a demand for the rights of black people, also spurred other groups to claim justice and equality. Poor people, led by George Wiley and the National Welfare Rights Organization, organized in the 1960s to demand a larger voice in welfare policy. Calling welfare a right, not a privilege, welfare activists used such tactics as sit-ins at government offices to win better treatment and higher benefits. Homosexual men and women also banded together to protest legal and social restrictions based on sexual preference. The gay liberation movement started with the 1969 "Stonewall riot" in New York City, where patrons of a gay bar in Greenwich Village fought back against police harassment. This assertion of gay pride would probably not have occurred without the example of the civil rights movement. Such increased political activism represents one of the most important legacies of the black demand for equality.

The Challenge of Youth

"There is everywhere protest, revaluation, attack on the Establishment," asserted social critic Paul Goodman at the end of the 1960s. Novelist Norman Mailer agreed. "We're in a time that's divorced from the past," he said. "There's utterly no tradition anymore." The black drive for equality had touched off the challenge to established institutions. Now American youth joined in, mounting colorful and sometimes shocking challenges to authority and traditional social values. Shifts in youth rebellion followed with such bewildering frequency that one anthropologist concluded, "We seem to be producing a new generation every three or four years."

Student Activism

The 1960s witnessed the first active student movement since the 1930s. The idealism of John Kennedy and the New Frontier raised students' expectations of what they and their society could accomplish. The civil rights movement exposed white youths to the brutality of race relations in the South and taught college students new tactics—marches, sit-ins, and mass confrontations—to use in protests. In addition, the escalation of the Vietnam War in 1965 offered a compelling political cause to rally around.

The depression-scarred generation of the 1930s had been unable to afford higher education, but its children flocked to colleges and universities in the postwar period. In 1940, when only 15 percent of all college-age youth attended college, graduating was a major sign of upward social mobility for members of most ethnic groups and other minorities. By 1960, the year of John Kennedy's election, 40 percent of the college-age population was in college, and by 1963, the year of his assassination, the proportion had reached almost 50 percent.

During the 1950s most students reflected the practical career-oriented values of their society. Business administration was the most popular course of study, and students took little part in politics. Some social critics suggested that students had responded to the repressive atmosphere of McCarthyism by becoming a "silent generation." Yet many young people felt dissatisfied even in the 1950s. A vague awareness of poverty, the black struggle for civil rights and equality, and the looming threat of nuclear war caused some young people to question the materialism of the world. J. D. Salinger's novel *Catcher in the Rye* (1951) became a best-seller because readers identified with Holden Caulfield's quiet revulsion at the thoughtless hypocrisy of his family, neighbors, and schoolmates.

Student dissatisfaction began to coalesce in the early 1960s. In June 1962, forty students from Big Ten and Ivy League universities met at a United Auto Workers conference center in Port Huron, Michigan, to found the Students for a Democratic Society (SDS). Their manifesto, written by Tom Hayden, a University of Michigan student, drew heavily on the writing of C. Wright Mills, a radical Columbia sociologist. It expressed hostility toward bureaucracy, rejected cold war ideology, emphasized community participatory politics, and designated students as the major force for change in society. SDS consciously modeled itself on the activist style pioneered by SNCC, adopting the name "New Left" to distinguish itself from the "Old Left" Communists of the 1930s.

The Free Speech Movement (FSM) at the University of California at Berkeley in 1964 was the first expression of a new student aggressiveness. The university administration announced that political activity would no longer be allowed along a strip of land at the Telegraph Avenue entrance to the campus, where student groups had traditionally distributed leaflets and recruited volunteers. In response, all the major organizations on campus, ranging from SNCC to the conservative Youth for Goldwater, formed a coalition to protest what they considered an abridgment of free speech. They organized a sit-in at the main administration building and won revocation of the ban on political solicitation on campus.

The Free Speech Movement owed a strong debt to the civil rights movement. Berkeley had sent more volunteers to Freedom Summer in Mississippi in 1964 than any other campus, and the students had been radicalized by the experience. Free Speech leader Mario Savio spoke for many of them:

> Last summer I went to Mississippi to join the struggle there for civil rights. This fall I am engaged in another phase of the same struggle, this time in Berkeley. The two battlefields may seem quite different to some observers, but this is not the case. The same rights are at stake in both places—the right to participate as citizens in a democratic society and to struggle against the same enemy. In Mississippi an autocratic and powerful minority rules, through organized violence, to suppress the vast, virtually powerless majority. In California, the privileged minority manipulates the university bureaucracy to suppress the students' political expression.

On a deeper level, Berkeley students had challenged the university because it had grown too big, too impersonal, and too insulated from the major social questions of the day. The largest universities, like the largest corporations, had grown the fastest in the postwar era. Only two campuses had as many as twenty thousand students in 1940. By 1969, thirty-nine had grown at least that large. Many students objected that they were treated as impersonally as a computer punch card. "I am a student," one slogan ran, "Please do not fold, spindle, or mutilate." Emboldened by the Berkeley experience, students at institutions across the country found reasons to protest everything from dress codes to course requirements, tenure decisions, and academic grading systems.

Many students also increasingly felt a deep moral outrage against the Vietnam War. In March 1965, several months after the Berkeley confrontation, President Lyndon Johnson began the major escalation that committed American ground troops to fight in Vietnam. In response, faculty members and student activists at the University of Michigan organized a "teach-in" against the war, where, in marathon sessions, they debated the political, diplomatic, and moral facets of U.S. involvement in Vietnam. This type of forum quickly spread to other universities. Groups such as the Students for a Democratic Society, which at first had focused on grass-roots organizing in the nation's cities, turned their full attention to protesting the Vietnam War. A strong spur to activism was the abolition in January 1966 of automatic student deferments from the draft. Now male students faced conscription to fight in a war many of them considered morally repugnant.

Soon students realized that universities themselves were deeply implicated in the Vietnam War. In certain cases, 60 percent of a university's research budget might come from government contracts, especially from the Defense Department; faculty members might be working on nuclear weapons or counterinsurgency strategies. Students organized to block campus recruitment by the army, the CIA, and the Dow Chemical Company, a special target because it produced the napalm used to burn Vietnamese villages and the chemical called Agent Orange, which defoliated South Vietnam's forests. Students demanded that the Reserve Officer Training Corps (ROTC) be removed from campus because, they argued, the university should not train students for war. Protests against ROTC on campus were central to the major confrontations between students and administrators at Columbia in 1968 and Harvard in 1969. As the president of Hunter College in New York City observed in 1968, "Yesterday's ivory tower has become today's foxhole."

Students also protested the universities' complicity in the problems of the ghettoes that surrounded many urban campuses. Columbia, for example, was a major property owner in Harlem, and university expansion impinged on the surrounding neighborhood. At issue in 1968 was a proposed gymnasium near the Columbia campus. Chanting "Gym Crow Must Go," students tore down the fence at the construction site and took over several Columbia buildings, including the office of President Grayson Kirk. (Photographs of protesters sampling Kirk's cigars and sherry did little to build public support.) At Berkeley, students and administrators clashed in 1969 over a parcel of vacant land near campus that a coalition of students and residents had turned into a "People's Park." When the university asserted its rights to the land, a violent confrontation broke out and an onlooker was killed. At both Columbia and Berkeley, and on other campuses as well, the administration's decision to use city police officers to break up the demonstrations radicalized far more students than had originally supported the protest. In many cases, such turmoil brought academic life to a halt.

Along with challenges to university power and policies, mass demonstrations against the war consumed much of the energy of the student movement in the late 1960s. In November 1969, at least 250,000 people marched on Washington to call for a moratorium against the Vietnam War. The final spurt of student unrest occurred in the spring of 1970. When President Richard M. Nixon ordered an American-backed invasion of Cambodia, student leaders organized a national student strike in protest. Tempers ran especially high at Kent State University outside Cleveland. At a noontime rally on May 4, 1970, panicky National Guardsmen fired into a crowd of students, killing four and wounding eleven. Only two of those killed, Jeffrey Miller and Alison Krause, had been involved in the demonstration; William Shroeder and Sandra Scheur were passing by on their way to class. While campuses were still in shock, word came that two black students had been killed at Jackson State College in Mississippi. More than 450 colleges closed down on strike, and 80 percent of all American college campuses experienced some kind of protest.

In June 1970, a Gallup poll reported that campus unrest was the main issue troubling Americans. But after 1970, the universities basically stayed calm. Students had effectively challenged many aspects of university control over their lives, but their broader attack on American society had been less successful. They returned to the classroom, somewhat cynical, burned out, and no longer ready to change the world.

THE KENT STATE KILLINGS
The shooting by National Guardsmen of four students at Kent State University in Ohio on May 4, 1970, set off campus demonstrations and protests throughout the country. The protesters shown here carry a placard memorializing the slain students, as well as the two black students killed soon after at Jackson State College in Mississippi. The president of Columbia University called May 1970 "the most disastrous month . . . in the history of American higher education."
(© Michael Abramson, Black Star)

The Rise of the Counterculture

Together with student activism and protest, new forms of cultural expression emerged among the nation's young. In an amazingly short period of time, youth's clothing and hair styles changed radically. At Berkeley's 1964 Free Speech demonstrations, young men wore coats and ties, women skirts and sweaters. By the time of the antiwar protests, just three or four years later, youth defiantly dressed in a "unisex" fashion that featured ragged blue jeans, tie-dyed T-shirts, beads, and other adornments. Long, unkempt hair symbolized this cultural revolt. The uncomprehending older generation often had a simple response: "Get a haircut."

The forerunners of the "hippies" of the 1960s were members of the Beat Generation of the preceding decade. Given the post-McCarthy climate of conformity, rebellion in the 1950s was far more likely to take artistic than political forms. "Beats" such as poet Allen Ginsberg and writer Jack Kerouac pioneered in articulating the personal alienation that was at the base of much of the rebelliousness of the 1960s. Kerouac's *On the Road* (1957) became the bible of the Beat Generation. Beats popularized beards for men, black tights for women, and sandals for both sexes. They experimented with drugs, and helped revive interest in folk music.

Roots of the cultural rebellion also lay in the active teen culture, which had been developing since the 1920s but flourished in the consumer-oriented 1950s. In 1956, advertisers projected an adolescent market of $9 billion for items including transistor radios (first introduced in 1952), clothes, cars, and records. Such movies as *The Wild One* (1954), starring Marlon Brando, and *Rebel Without a Cause* (1955), featuring James Dean, Natalie Wood, and Sal Mineo, catered to the teen audience. "What are you rebelling against?" a waitress asks Brando in *The Wild One*. "Whattaya got?" he replies.

What really defined the emerging youth generation was its music. Rock and roll sprang forth in the mid-1950s. It developed from white country and western music, black rhythm and blues, and other sources. Elvis Presley became one of the first to popularize this new type of music, and his hit singles "Hound Dog" and "Heartbreak Hotel" sold more than ten million copies in 1956. Adults were appalled. A noted psychiatrist called rock and roll "a communicable disease" and "a cannibalistic and tribalistic kind of music." When Presley appeared on the "Ed Sullivan Show," television cameras showed the teen idol only from the waist up, censoring his skin-tight pants and gyrating pelvis. Young people got the message anyway.

Throughout the 1960s, as English journalist Godfrey Hodgson noted, "popular music coincided uncannily with changing political moods." Folk singer Pete Seeger, free at last from the McCarthy-era blacklist, set the tone for the era's political idealism with such songs as "Where Have All the Flowers Gone?" and Woody Guthrie's "This Land Is Your Land." In 1963, the year of the Birmingham demonstrations and President Kennedy's assassination, Bob Dylan's "Blowin' in the Wind" reflected the impatience of people whose liberalism was turning sour. When folk singers Peter, Paul, and Mary recorded a more melodious version of this song, it sold three hundred thousand copies in two weeks.

Early in 1964, the Beatles, a British band that had honed its sound in the dives of Liverpool, England, and Hamburg, West Germany, burst onto the American scene. Like Elvis Presley eight years earlier, they thrust their way into the national consciousness by a series of appearances on the "Ed Sullivan Show." The Beatles' music, by turns lyrical and driving, was phenomenally successful, spawning a commercial and cultural phenomenon called Beatlemania. The harsher, angrier music of other British groups, notably the Rolling Stones, found a broad audience shortly afterward.

Drugs had almost as important a part as rock music in the youth culture of the 1960s. Drugs were hardly new to the American scene; many jazz musicians in the 1920s and 1930s had used heroin and cocaine to stimulate their creativity, and the Beats had experimented with mind-altering drugs in San Francisco. In the 1960s, however, widespread recreational use of drugs occurred outside artistic and jazz circles.

Marijuana was the preferred drug among college students, but stronger drugs also gained popularity. Lysergic acid diethylamide, popularly known as LSD or "acid," was one of the most potent. First discovered in a Swiss pharmaceutical laboratory in 1938, the hallucinogenic LSD was popularized in California by writer Ken Kesey and his Merry Pranksters, who conducted "acid tests" (public "happenings" where tabs of LSD were distributed) in 1965 and 1966. San Francisco bands such as the Grateful Dead and the Jefferson Airplane, guitarist Jimi Hendrix, and Britain's Pink Floyd developed a style of music known as "acid rock." Even the Beatles, whose early songs had simply stated "I Want to Hold Your Hand" and "Please Please Me," now recorded tunes like "Lucy in the Sky with Diamonds," whose "tangerine trees and marmalade skies" celebrated the new drug-induced consciousness.

For a brief time, adherents of the counterculture—so named because it challenged so many established mores—believed that a new age was dawning, along the lines of the "age of Aquarius" trumpeted in the 1968 Broadway rock musical *Hair*. In 1967, the "world's first Human Be-In" was held at Golden Gate Park in San Francisco. Allen Ginsberg "purified" the site with a Buddhist ritual, political activists embraced "drug freaks," and LSD pioneer Timothy Leary, a former Harvard psychology instructor, urged the twenty thousand people who had gathered to "turn on to the scene, tune in to what is happening, and drop out."

"Tune in, turn on, drop out" and "Make love not war" became catchwords for youthful alien-

ation. By the summer of 1967, San Francisco's Haight-Ashbury, New York's East Village, and similar hippie neighborhoods in other large cities were crowded with young people, as well as swarms of reporters and busloads of tourists who gawked at the so-called flower children. The faith in instant love and peace quickly began to turn sour, however, as dropouts, drifters, and teenage runaways tried to cope with bad drug trips, venereal disease, loneliness, and violence. In 1967, seventeen murders and more than a hundred rapes were reported in Haight-Ashbury alone.

While hippie neighborhoods declined, the appeal of rock music and drugs continued to spread. In August 1969, four hundred thousand young people journeyed to Bethel, New York, to attend the Woodstock Music Festival. Despite torrential rain, people "got high" on music, drugs, and sex. They were treated to one of the finest assemblages of performers ever gathered in one place—Crosby, Stills, Nash, and Young; Santana; Joan Baez; the Who; Sly and the Family Stone; Grace Slick and the Jefferson Airplane; Jimi Hendrix; and others. The successful festival gave its name to the "Woodstock generation" of the late 1960s.

By 1970, the youth culture had revolutionized life-styles and cultural expression. Even as political activism and rebellion waned, their spirit was absorbed and marketed by the consumer

FLOWER CHILDREN
Yale law professor Charles A. Reich celebrated the new freedom of youth in his best-selling book *The Greening of America* (1970). Reich described a new consciousness that had "emerged out of the wasteland of the Corporate State, like flowers pushing up through the concrete pavement. Whatever it touches it beautifies and renews: a freeway entrance is festooned with happy hitchhikers, the sidewalk is decorated with street people, the humorless steps of an official building are given warmth by a group of musicians. And every barrier falls before it." (© Paul Fusco, Magnum)

ANARCHISM
AT THE MOVIES
The movie *Bonnie and Clyde*
(1967), starring Faye Dunaway
and Warren Beatty, became a
cultural phenomenon because its
anarchism, antiheroism, and
violence seemed in keeping with
the mood of the 1960s. Based
loosely on the story of Clyde
Barrow and Bonnie Parker,
famous bank robbers of the 1930s,
the movie builds sympathy for
these appealing criminals, only to
end with their being slain by law
enforcement officials.
(MOMA/Film Stills Archive)

culture. The crowds at Woodstock and other rock festivals revealed the size of the youth market, and corporate entrepreneurs rushed to cash in on it. Advertisers renamed youth the "Pepsi generation." By 1969 rock accounted for two-thirds of the sales of large record companies. The market for expensive stereo systems rose correspondingly.

Forms of alternative expression from the 1960s soon filtered into the dominant culture. *The Village Voice* and *Rolling Stone* outgrew their beginnings as underground publications and became respected pillars of American journalism. Symbols of cultural defiance were co-opted and homogenized by the mass culture. The ragged "bell bottom" blue jeans of the 1960s became the expensive designer jeans of the 1970s. The unkempt hair and beards of male hippies emboldened many middle-aged corporate executives to sport a moustache or allow their hair to cover their ears. The "Afro" hairstyle, once worn only by radical black activists, was now favored by blacks and whites of both sexes who let their hair go natural. Women's fashion picked up the theme of personal liberation with the miniskirt, an innovation that had arrived from England in the mid-1960s.

Popular acceptance of the miniskirt was linked to the new public attitudes about sexuality that characterized the 1960s. As late as 1953, a movie called *The Moon Is Blue* was denied a seal of approval by Hollywood's Production Code Administration because it used words such as "seduce" and "virgin." United Artists released the film anyway. New permissive values soon became commonplace, as expressions that previously had been heard only in locker rooms now entered everyday conversations. By 1968, the film industry devised an "X" rating for films that featured nudity, sex, and explicit language.

Public portrayal and discussion of sexuality changed far more than actual sexual behavior, which had already undergone startling transformations over the course of the twentieth century. In 1948, the book *Sexual Behavior in the Human Male*, by biologist Alfred C. Kinsey, had revealed that 85 percent of all American men claimed to have had intercourse before marriage, that half conducted extramarital affairs, and that 10 percent engaged in homosexual activity for at least part of their adult lives. In 1953, Kinsey's *Sexual Behavior in the Human Female* reported that 62 percent of women masturbated, that half had premarital sexual relations, and that a fourth engaged in extramarital affairs. In 1966, William H. Masters and Virginia E. Johnson published *Human Sexual Response,* the product of their detailed, direct laboratory observations of the physiology of arousal and intercourse in men and women. The book became a national best-seller.

The "sexual revolution" of the 1960s eroded some of the inequalities and inhibitions between the sexes. The new availability of contraceptives such as the birth-control pill, first marketed in 1960, and the intrauterine device (IUD) gave women greater control over their reproductive systems. But women still ran more risks, both with their reputations and their bodies, from sexual activity than men did. The new permissive atmosphere of the 1960s and widespread availability of contraception did not necessarily liberate women. Helen Gurley Brown's *Sex and the Single Girl* (1962) promoted swinging sexual freedom for single women at the same time it emphasized emotional and material dependence on men by telling women that their main goal in life should be to snare a husband. As *Ms.* magazine noted pointedly in 1972, "The Sexual Revolution and the Women's Movement are at polar opposites. Women have been liberated only from the right to say 'no'."

The Revival of Feminism

Feminism was a dead issue in 1960. The government had enacted no legislation specifically targeted for women since the Nineteenth Amendment gave them the right to vote in 1920. Such words as "sexism" and "Ms." had not been coined. There were no rape crisis centers or battered women's shelters. Not a single university offered a course in women's studies, and women's sports programs were nonexistent. At least ten thousand women a year lost their lives in illegal back-alley abortions.

All that changed during the next fifteen years. The women's movement rivaled the civil rights movement in the success it achieved in a short period of time. By the mid-1970s, however, feminism had provoked a backlash, and its progress had stalled.

Women's Changing Lives

Social movements do not just spring up when leaders announce a set of demands. Each movement must have a constituency ready to be mobilized. The success of the civil rights movement was linked in part to the massive migration of blacks out of the South, which made race relations a national problem. Student activism had roots in the expansion of collegiate and university enrollments due to the baby boom. Preconditions for feminism lay in the changing social and demographic bases of women's lives.

In 1900, the average woman married by the age of twenty-two and then bore between three and four children, with her last child arriving when she was thirty-two. She had a life expectancy of sixty-two to sixty-six years, and so she could expect to devote most of her adult life to child-rearing By the 1960s and 1970s, women still married at twenty-two, but the birth rate had dropped dramatically, especially since the immediate postwar period. From a peak of 25.3 births per thousand women in 1957, it dropped to 18.0 in 1970 and 15.7 in 1981. Women typically had one or two children, rather than the three or four common at the beginning of the century. Since a woman who survived to age twenty now had a life expectancy of nearly eighty years, she had approximately forty years of adulthood during which she would not be involved primarily in raising children. The dramatic rise in women's participation in the labor force during the postwar years partly reflected this demographic shift.

Women's lives were undergoing other changes as well. More women went to college, and their percentage of the total student body grew. This pattern reversed a decline in the immediate postwar period when the GI Bill gave men a temporary advantage in access to higher education. Many college women had also dropped out of school to marry and raise families at the height of the emphasis on domesticity. By 1960, however, the percentage of women students had climbed to 35 percent, and by 1970 to 41 percent. Women students made up the majority by the 1980s.

Another factor reshaping women's lives was the increase in marital instability represented by rising divorce rates. In 1900, eight per hundred

JOANIE CAUCUS, MODERN WOMAN

The character of Joanie Caucus in Garry Trudeau's popular comic strip, *Doonesbury*, provided a running commentary on women's changing lives in the 1960s and 1970s. Caucus, a former housewife, ran away from her husband and family to a commune and then tried to raise the consciousness of children at the day care center where she worked. Here she applies to law school. After graduation, she became a legislative aid to a female member of Congress, remarried, and had a child in her forties. (DOONESBURY, By Garry Trudeau. Copyright, 1974, G. B. Trudeau. Reprinted with permission of Universal Press Syndicate. All rights reserved.)

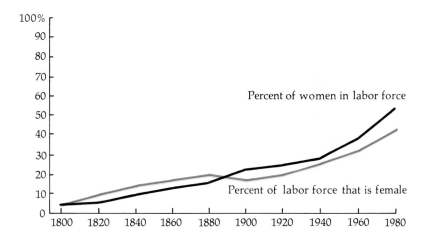

FIGURE 30.1 WOMEN AND THE LABOR FORCE, 1800–1980

married couples divorced. This ratio rose slowly through the 1950s and then shot up in the 1960s. By 1965, the divorce rate reached twenty-seven per hundred marriages. By the 1980s, according to census projections, fifty-two marriages per hundred would end in divorce. Women could no longer assume that their marriage would be the most important event of their lives or that it would last until "death do us part."

A corollary to the rise in marital instability was a growth in female-headed households living in poverty. In economic terms, women did not survive divorce as well as men did. Only about a tenth of all divorced women received alimony payments for their own support; about half got child-support payments, which were notoriously hard to enforce. In addition, the segmentation of the work force generally relegated women to low-paying service jobs, so they earned considerably less than men. By 1980, nearly a fifth of all children were being raised by a single mother. Two-thirds of the female-headed households depended on welfare payments, especially from Aid to Families with Dependent Children (AFDC).

These demographic changes have led to a convergence in the patterns of black and white women's lives. Black women have always had a high participation rate in the work force because of their need to contribute to family income. They have also traditionally headed more households on their own. A similar rise in employment and female-headed households has now occurred among white women. Both races have

also seen a dramatic rise in the birth rate of unmarried teenagers, a pattern first observed in the black community in the 1960s. In 1979, more than half the births to black women were to unmarried females.

Black and white women increasingly hold similar jobs, thanks to civil rights agitation that opened white-collar and service jobs to black women. As a result, the pay differential between black and white women has shrunk. While nonwhite women earned only 38 percent of white women's median wages before World War II, they earned 88 percent by 1977. In 1980, however, white and nonwhite women still earned less on the average ($11,703 and $10,915, respectively) than black men ($13,875) and considerably less than white men ($19,720).

As a result of these changes, the traditional view that women will spend their lives at home as wives and mothers has been dramatically undercut. To be female in America now often includes work and marriage, childrearing and a career, or life in a female-headed household. These changing social realities helped foster the revival of feminism in the 1960s.

Two Paths to Feminism

During the 1960s, two independent movements renewed the national interest in women's concerns. The women's rights branch of the new feminism, symbolized by the National Organization for Women (NOW), consisted of older professional women who sought political change by

BARBAROUS RITUALS

Woman Is:

• Kicking strongly in your mother's womb, upon which she is told, "It must be a boy, if it's so active!"

• Being tagged with a *pink* beaded bracelet thirty seconds after you are born, and wrapped in *pink* blankets five minutes thereafter.

• Being confined to the Doll Corner in nursery school when you are really fascinated by Tinker Toys.

• Wanting to wear overalls instead of "frocks."

• Learning to detest the words "dainty" and "cute."

• Being labeled a tomboy when all you wanted to do was climb that tree to look out and see a distance.

• Learning to sit with your legs crossed, even when your feet can't touch the floor yet.

• Hating boys—because they're allowed to do things you want to do but are forbidden to—and being told hating boys is a phase.

• Learning that something you do is "naughty," but when your brother does the same thing, it's "spunky." . . .

• Seeing grownups chuckle when you say you want to be an engineer or doctor when you grow up—and learning to say you want to be a mommy or a nurse, instead.

• Liking math or history a lot and getting hints that boys are turned off by smart girls.

• Finding that almost all jobs open to you pay less for harder work than to men. . . .

• Learning to be *very tactful* if you have men working "under you." More likely, learning to always be working under men.

• Coming home from work—and starting *in* to work: unpack the groceries, fix supper, wash up the dishes, rinse out some laundry, etc., etc. . . .

• Being widowed, or divorced, and trying to get a "good" job—at your age.

• Getting older, getting lonelier, getting ready to die—and knowing it wouldn't have had to be this way, after all.

Source: "Barbarous Rituals," in Robin Morgan, ed., *Sisterhood is Powerful.* New York: Random House, 1970, 179–181, 184, 186–188.

---

working through the system. The women's liberation branch, on the other hand, attracted primarily younger women—recent college graduates who had been active in civil rights, the New Left, and the antiwar movement. These women had a much more radical vision of feminism, one that concentrated on the oppression produced by traditional family and gender roles. They were often quite hostile to men, their separatism mirroring that of black-power advocates. Unlike the traditional women's rights organizations, which were dues-paying, hierarchical groups, the women's liberation movement was looser and mass based, often without any coordination.

Several events set the stage for the development of the women's rights movement. In 1961, President Kennedy established a Presidential Commission on the Status of Women, an attempt to counter criticism about his administration's poor record on women's issues. Eleanor Roosevelt served as honorary head of the commission. The group's report, issued in 1963, documented the employment and educational discrimination faced by women, but its impact extended beyond its rather conservative recommendations. The presidential commission, and the state commissions that were its offshoots, set up a rudimentary network of women in public life who were concerned about feminist issues.

Another event that increased sympathy for feminism was the publication of Betty Friedan's witty *The Feminine Mystique* in 1963. This book, a pointed indictment of the trap of women's suburban domesticity, grew out of Friedan's own experiences as a housewife in the 1950s. Friedan called it "the problem that has no name":

As she made the beds, shopped for groceries, matched slipcover material, ate peanut butter sandwiches with her children, chauffeured Cub Scouts and Brownies, lay beside her husband at night—she was afraid to ask even of herself the silent question—"Is this all?"

Women responded enthusiastically to her story, especially the white, college-educated middle-class women whose backgrounds resembled the author's. The book sold three million copies, and many more women read excerpts of it in major women's magazines. While *The Feminine Mystique* did not cause the revival of feminism, it became a central text of the new movement, introducing many women to the powerful ideas of modern feminism.

In 1963–1964, the focus shifted toward legislative change. In 1963, on the recommendation of the Presidential Commission on the Status of Women, Congress passed the Equal Pay Act, which directed that men and women be paid the same wages for doing the same job. An event of more far-reaching importance was the passage of the Civil Rights Act of 1964, which had as great an impact on women as it did on blacks and other minorities. The key provision, Title VII, barred discrimination in employment on the basis of race, color, religion, national origin, or sex. The category of sex was added by conservative Representative Howard Smith of Virginia, not out of concern for women's equality—he called it "my little amendment"—but to make the civil rights bill so controversial as to kill it completely. His strategy backfired. Title VII remains a powerful legal tool in the fight against sex discrimination.

Dissatisfaction with the Equal Employment Opportunity Commission's slow implementation of Title VII led to the founding of the National Organization for Women in 1966. This group modeled itself after such black groups as the NAACP: NOW aimed to be a civil rights organization for women. "The purpose of NOW," its statement of purpose declared, "is to take action to bring women into full participation in the mainstream of American society now, exercising all the privileges and responsibilities thereof in truly equal partnership with men." Betty Friedan served as NOW's first president, and its membership grew from a thousand in 1967 to fifteen thousand in 1971. Men made up a fourth of NOW's early membership, and it still ranks as the largest feminist organization in the United States.

Women's liberationists came to feminism by a different path. White women had made up about half the students who went to the South with SNCC in the 1964 Freedom Summer voter-registration project. While in Mississippi, they received conflicting messages. College women developed self-confidence and organizational skills through participation in the project, and they found role models in the black women and older southern white women who had become involved in civil rights through church activities. At the same time, women volunteers were automatically expected to do all the cleaning and cooking at the Freedom Houses where SNCC volunteers lived. "We didn't come down here to work as a maid this summer," one complained, "we came down to work in the field of civil rights."

Given the intensity of their commitment to civil rights, and the lack of a feminist movement as yet to give ideological context to their concerns, Freedom Summer volunteers only tentatively raised their concerns as women. When they did, they compared women's position with that of blacks. "Assumptions of male superiority are as widespread and deeply rooted and every much as crippling to the woman as the assumptions of white superiority are to the Negro," they argued. Such attempts to raise feminist issues were laughed off by both black and white men in the movement. Stokely Carmichael made one of the most pointed retorts: "The only position for women in SNCC is prone."

Black power militancy made white women, like white men, feel less welcome in the civil rights movement after 1966; but when women transferred their energies to student antiwar groups, they found the male-dominated New Left to be just as unsupportive. Once again, women were expected to take notes at meetings, serve coffee, and clean up afterwards, while men did all the intellectual work and monopolized the public-speaking roles. As the New Left focused increasingly on draft resistance as a strategy to oppose the war, women found themselves treated mainly as sex objects. "Girls say yes to guys who say no," went a popular slogan. When women tried to raise feminist issues at conventions, they were shouted off the platform with such jeers as "Move on, little girl, we have more important issues to talk about here than women's liberation." The "little girl" who received this taunt was Shulamith Firestone, whose *The Dialectic of Sex* (1971) was an early bible of the women's movement.

By 1967–1968, groups of radical women

realized that they needed their own movement. The contradictions between the commitment of the New Left to egalitarianism and women's actual treatment by male leaders became so striking that women felt they had no other choice. This process occurred independently in five or six cities. The women's liberation movement went public in 1968 when it staged a protest at the Miss America pageant. The demonstration included a "freedom trash can," into which women were encouraged to throw such symbols of female oppression as false eyelashes, hair curlers, brassieres, and girdles. The media quickly labeled the radical feminists "bra burners." The derisive name stuck, although no brassieres were actually burned.

A technique of more lasting impact was "consciousness raising," group sessions in which women shared common experiences about growing up female. The linkage of women's personal lives with wider societal oppression, summed up by the slogan "The personal is political," was a hallmark of the early radical feminists. As Shulamith Firestone recalled, "Three months of this sort of thing is enough to make a feminist of any woman."

In 1969–1970, the media "discovered" feminism. Media attention brought women's issues to a much broader audience than could ever have been reached by either NOW or the women's liberation collectives. Before 1969, most feminists heard about the movement through word of mouth. After that, the media brought in new converts who broke down the barriers between the two branches of the movement. Feminism's capacity to build a mass base of support was demonstrated on August 26, 1970, when thousands of women throughout the country marched to celebrate the fiftieth anniversary of the Nineteenth Amendment.

Another reason for the blurring of distinctions between women's rights and women's liberation was a growing convergence of interests. Radical women had learned by the early 1970s that some feminist goals could best be accomplished in the political sphere, such as lobbying for child care, equal pay, or abortion reform. In turn, the more traditional political activists developed a much

RUNNING FOR WOMEN'S RIGHTS

Feminists Billie Jean King, (left), Bella Abzug, (with hat), and Betty Friedan, (far right), join runners who carried a torch from Seneca Falls, New York, site of the first women's rights convention in 1848, to Houston for the 1977 National Women's Conference. Funded by Congress in honor of International Women's Year, the conference brought together two thousand delegates and twenty thousand observers who adopted a National Plan of Action for women's rights. (© 1978 Diana Mara Henry)

broader view of women's oppression, including tentative support for divisive issues like lesbian rights and abortion. By 1970, feminists began to think of themselves as part of a broad, growing, and increasingly influential social movement. "It's not a movement," said journalist Sally Kempton, "it's a state of mind." The title of Robin Morgan's best-selling book of that year, *Sisterhood is Powerful*, similarly reflected feminist optimism.

The High Tide of Feminism

Significant progress in the battle for women's equality occurred during the early 1970s. The media had made new terms such as "sexism" and "male chauvinism" part of the national vocabulary. Many colleges across the country started women's studies programs. Former all-male bastions, including Yale, Princeton, and the U.S. Military Academy, admitted woman undergraduates for the first time. *Ms.* magazine was founded in 1972 by Gloria Steinem and other journalists. The proportion of women in graduate and professional schools rose, and more and more women won election to public office. Bella Abzug, Elizabeth Holtzman, Shirley Chisholm, Patricia Schroeder, and Geraldine Ferraro served in Congress; Ella Grasso won election as Connecticut's governor in 1974, and Dixie Lee Ray as Washington's in 1976.

The women's movement achieved passage of significant federal legislation. The Equal Credit Opportunity Act of 1974 prohibited banks and other lenders from discriminating on the basis of sex. Congress authorized child-care deductions for working parents and higher employment benefits for married female federal employees. In many cases, the federal policy on civil rights was simply extended to include women as well as men. Title IX of the Educational Amendments Act of 1972 broadened the coverage of the 1964 Civil Rights Act to include educational institutions; it prohibited colleges and universities that received federal funds from discriminating on the basis of sex. Until a Supreme Court decision undermined it in 1984, Title IX was especially effective in increasing women's access to participation in sports.

The Supreme Court also made several rulings that gave women more control over their repro-

WOMEN IN SPORTS
Tennis star Chris Evert Lloyd shows her joy upon winning her fifth U.S. Open title in 1980. Lloyd symbolized the new opportunities for women in professional sports during the 1970s. Due in large part to Title IX, girls' participation in varsity athletics at the high school level increased 560 percent between 1971 and 1976. (Walter Iooss, Jr./*Sports Illustrated*)

ductive lives. In 1965, the case of *Griswold v. Connecticut* overturned state laws against the sale of contraceptive devices to married women; in 1972, *Baird v. Eisenstadt* extended this protection to single women. In 1973, *Roe v. Wade* struck down Texas and Georgia statutes that allowed abortions only if the mother's life was in danger. According to this controversial decision, states could no longer outlaw abortions during the first trimester, or three months, of pregnancy. The court's reasoning did not address feminist demands for women's control over their bodies. Rather, the justices interpreted abortion as a medical issue, basing their decision on the confidentiality of the doctor-patient relationship. *Roe v. Wade* cemented the liberalization of state abortion laws that began in New York in 1970.

In the 1970s, the women's movement increasingly united around the proposed Equal Rights Amendment to the Constitution (ERA), which stated, "Equality of Rights under the Law shall not be denied or abridged by the United States or any State on the basis of sex." The ERA, first introduced in 1923 by the National Woman's Party, was dusted off by modern feminists after languishing in Congress for almost fifty years. In 1970, the measure passed the House but died in the Senate. In the 1971–1972 session, it passed both houses and was submitted to the states for ratification. Thirty-four states quickly passed the ERA in 1972–1974. Then the momentum stopped. Only Indiana ratified after that point, leaving the amendment three states short of the

necessary three-fourths majority. Most of the states that refused to ratify the ERA were in the South; Illinois also held out, despite spirited campaigns there by ERA supporters. Congress extended the deadline for ratification until June 30, 1982, but the Equal Rights Amendment still fell short.

The fate of the ERA suggested that, by the mid-1970s, much of the momentum of the women's movement had slowed or even stopped. Although 63 percent of women told the Harris poll in 1975 that they favored "efforts to strengthen and change women's status in society," a growing minority of men and women expressed concern over what seemed to be revolutionary changes in women's roles. A new conservatism began to influence political and social life by the mid-1970s, spearheaded by the Moral Majority and other organizations whose mem-

MAP 30.3 STATES RATIFYING THE EQUAL RIGHTS AMENDMENT
The Equal Rights Amendment to the U.S. Constitution quickly won support among the states in 1972 and 1973, but then it stalled. ERAmerica, a coalition of women's groups formed in 1976, lobbied extensively, particularly in Florida, North Carolina, and Illinois, but failed to sway the conservative legislatures in those states. Later efforts to revive the ERA also were unsuccessful.

TIME LINE
THE STRUGGLE FOR EQUALITY AND DIVERSITY

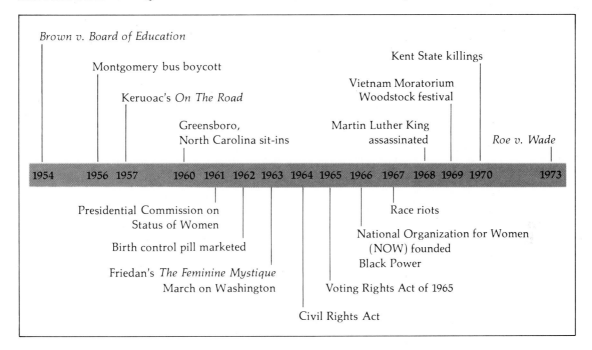

Brown v. Board of Education

Montgomery bus boycott

Keruoac's *On The Road*

Greensboro,
North Carolina sit-ins

Kent State killings

Vietnam Moratorium
Woodstock festival

Martin Luther King
assassinated

Roe v. Wade

| 1954 | 1956 | 1957 | 1960 | 1961 | 1962 | 1963 | 1964 | 1965 | 1966 | 1967 | 1968 | 1969 | 1970 | 1973 |

Presidential Commission on
Status of Women

Birth control pill marketed

Friedan's *The Feminine Mystique*
March on Washington

Civil Rights Act

Voting Rights Act of 1965

National Organization for Women
(NOW) founded
Black Power

Race riots

bers belonged largely to fundamentalist religious groups. Especially disturbing to these conservatives were changes in attitudes that seemed to denigrate women who chose to stay home as full-time housewives.

Phyllis Schlafly, long active in conservative causes—she had written *A Choice, Not an Echo*, a best-seller extolling Barry Goldwater in 1963—led the antifeminist backlash. Despite her law degree and active career while raising five children, Schlafly spoke out in behalf of traditional women's roles. She often opened her speeches by saying, "I'd like to thank my husband for letting me be here tonight." She told audiences, "A man's first significant purchase is a diamond for his bride, and the major financial investment of his life is a home for her to live in." Schlafly's Eagle Forum effectively lobbied against the ERA, which it claimed would create an unnatural "unisex society," cause women to be drafted, legalize homosexual marriages, and eliminate separate toilets for men and women. (All these charges are false and have no basis in the language of the amendment.) Anti-ERA lobbyists showed up at state houses with home-baked

bread and apple pies, symbols of their traditional domestic roles. Schlafly's message that women had more to lose than to gain from passage of the ERA found favor among both men and women deeply troubled by the rapid pace of social change.

Like the civil rights movement before it, the women's movement also found that choices were harder, and causes less clear-cut, as the 1970s progressed. The Affirmative Action program, consisting of guidelines instituted by the Labor Department in 1970 to ensure nondiscriminatory hiring through quotas and preferential treatment to blacks and women, was far more controversial than Title VII. "Comparable worth," the doctrine that people with jobs involving similar levels of skill or responsibility, such as secretaries and maintenance workers, should be paid the same wages, was much trickier than the concept of equal pay for equal work.

The legalization of abortion proved so controversial that it sparked a powerful "right to life" movement. Foes of abortion, placing higher value on the rights of the unborn fetus than on the right of the mother to choose whether to terminate her pregnancy, attempted to circumvent and overturn the *Roe v. Wade* decision. In 1976, Representative Henry Hyde of Illinois drafted legislation to deny Medicaid funds to pay for abortions for poor women. The Supreme Court upheld the Hyde amendment in *Harris v. McRae* in 1980.

Although feminism had been forced on the defensive by the mid-1970s, women's lives showed no signs of returning to the values of 1950 or even of 1970. Pervasive changes were here to stay. So, too, were the victories won by blacks, Hispanics, and native Americans, incomplete though they may have been. American society had been permanently altered by this twenty-year struggle for equality.

---

*B*etween 1954 and 1975, social movements challenged the American status quo. The civil rights movement triggered the process, and its attacks on legalized segregation in the South expanded into challenges to institutionalized racism throughout the country. The tactics and ideology developed in the civil rights movement encouraged other groups, including Hispanics, native Americans, poor people, and women, to demand equality as well. Young people also protested, challenging the policies of their universities and American participation in the Vietnam War.

All the protest movements had their roots in structural and demographic changes and shifting cultural values. Black migration from the South because of the transformation of agriculture made civil rights a national, not just a sectional, problem. The postwar baby boom led to a rapid expansion of higher education. More women took jobs outside the home, faced rising divorce rates, and acquired better access to education.

The protest movements followed a similar progression. At first, efforts centered on the political or judicial front. Early successes led to heightened expectations, but the next stage—changing people's attitudes and winning social and economic justice—proved more difficult. The civil rights and women's movements each produced a backlash from those who thought change had gone far enough, but not before lasting alterations had been made in American society.

Suggestions for Further Reading

Godfrey Hodgson, *America in Our Time* (1976), offers the best overview of the entire postwar period. Three strong surveys of the 1960s are Allen J. Matusow, *The Unraveling of America* (1984); William L. O'Neill, *Coming Apart* (1971); and Milton Viorst, *Fire in the Streets* (1979). For additional general material on the period, see Ronald Berman, *America in the Sixties* (1972); Todd Gitlin, *The Whole World Is Watching* (1981); and Peter Joseph's oral history of the decade, *Good Times* (1973).

The Civil Rights Movement

Harvard Sitkoff, *The Struggle for Black Equality* (1981), surveys the period from 1954 to 1980. Richard Kluger, *Simple Justice* (1975), analyzes the Brown decision and its context, while Anthony Lewis, *Portrait of a Decade* (1964), covers southern reaction to the decision. J. Har-

vie Wilkinson III continues the story of the Supreme Court and integration through the 1970s in *From Brown to Bakke* (1979).

Histories of the major civil rights organizations include Clayborne Carson's study of SNCC, *In Struggle* (1981), and August Meier and Elliot Rudwick, *CORE* (1973). Mary Aickin Rothschild, *A Case of Black and White* (1982), describes northern volunteers during the "Freedom Summer." Victor Navasky, *Kennedy Justice* (1971), is extremely critical of President Kennedy's civil rights record; Carl Brauer, *John F. Kennedy and the Second Reconstruction* (1977), provides a more sympathetic view. William Chafe, *Civilities and Civil Rights* (1980), is a superb case study of the impact of civil rights on Greensboro, North Carolina, from the 1950s through the 1970s.

Major texts of the civil rights movement include Stokely Carmichael and Charles Hamilton, *Black Power* (1967); James Baldwin, *The Fire Next Time* (1963); Eldridge Cleaver, *Soul on Ice* (1968); and Malcolm X, with Alex Haley, *The Autobiography of Malcolm X* (1965). Anne Moody, *Coming of Age in Mississippi* (1968), is a moving autobiography; Howell Raines, *My Soul is Rested* (1977), is a fine oral history. Joanne Grant, *Black Protest* (1968), and August Meier and Elliott Rudwick, *Black Protest in the Sixties* (1970), are good anthologies. Martin Luther King tells his story in *Stride Toward Freedom* (1958) and *Why We Can't Wait* (1964). Biographies of King include David Lewis, *King* (1970), and Stephen Oates, *Let the Trumpet Sound* (1982).

Report of the National Advisory Commission on Civil Disorders (1968) analyzes the decade's major race riots. See also Joe R. Feagin and Harlan Hahn, *Ghetto Revolts* (1973), and Robert Fogelson, *Violence as Protest* (1971). Robert Conot, *Rivers of Blood, Years of Darkness* (1968), studies the Watts riot.

Stan Steiner, *La Raza* (1970), and Matt Meier and Feliciano Rivera, *The Chicanos* (1972), document the growing Hispanic political activity. Vine De Loria, Jr., *Behind the Trail of Broken Treaties* (1974) and *Custer Died for Your Sins* (1969), convey the new Indian assertiveness. See also Stan Steiner, *The New Indians* (1968); Helen Hertzberg, *The Search for an American Indian Identity* (1971); and Wilcomb Washburn, *Red Man's Land, White Man's Law* (1971).

The Challenge of Youth

The student activism of the 1960s drew its share of scholarly chroniclers. See Kenneth Keniston, *The Uncommitted* (1965) and *Young Radicals* (1969); Daniel Bell and Irving Kristol, *Confrontation* (1969); Nathan Glazer, *Remembering the Answers* (1970); and Philip Slater, *The Pursuit of Loneliness* (1970). On student revolt, see Seymour Lipset and Sheldon Wolin, eds., *The Berkeley Student Revolt* (1965), and Jerry Avorn, *Up Against the Ivy Wall* (1968). John P. Diggins, *The American Left in the Twentieth Century* (1973), and Irwin Unger, *The Movement: A History of the American New Left* (1974), provide general background; Kirkpatrick Sale, *SDS* (1973), covers one important organization. Lawrence Baskir and William A. Straus, *The Draft, The War, and the Vietnam Generation* (1978), assess who was drafted and why.

Morris Dickstein, *Gates of Eden* (1977), is an excellent account of cultural developments in the 1960s. The standard texts of the counterculture are Theodore Roszak, *The Making of a Counter Culture* (1969), and Charles Reich, *The Greening of America* (1970). Joyce Maynard,

Looking Back (1973), provides a "chronicle of growing up old" in the 1960s. Gerald Howard, ed., *The Sixties* (1982), is a good anthology of the decade's art, politics, and culture. Philip Norman, *Shout! The Beatles in Their Generation* (1981), covers developments in popular music. Joan Didion *Slouching Toward Bethlehem* (1968) and *The White Album* (1979), explore some of the darker sides of the hippie phenomenon.

For background on the Beat Generation of the 1950s, start with Ann Charters, *Kerouac* (1973); Dennis McNally, *Desolate Angel* (1979); and Jane Kramer, *Allen Ginsberg in America* (1969). John Tytell, *Naked Angels* (1976), covers the lives and literature of the Beat Generation. Tom Wolfe's *Electric Kool-Aid Acid Test* (1965) describes the antics of Beat survivors Ken Kesey and his Merry Pranksters in the 1960s.

The Revival of Feminism

Jo Freeman, *The Politics of Women's Liberation* (1975); Barbara Deckard, *The Women's Movement* (1975); and Judith Hole and Ellen Levine, *The Rebirth of Feminism* (1971), chronicle the revival of feminism in the 1960s and 1970s. Gayle Graham Yates, *What Women Want* (1975), concentrates on the movement's ideology, while William Chafe, *Women and Equality* (1977), draws interesting comparisons between feminism and civil rights. Sara Evans, *Personal Politics* (1979), traces the roots of feminism in the civil rights movement and the New Left. Material on the changing demographic aspects of women's lives is found in Alice Kessler-Harris, *Out to Work* (1982); Carl Degler, *At Odds* (1980); and Valerie Kincaid Oppenheimer, *The Female Labor Force in the United States* (1970). Ethel Klein, *Gender Politics* (1984), specifically links demographic change with the revival of feminism. Phyllis Schlafly, *The Power of the Positive Woman* (1978), and Andrea Dworkin, *Right Wing Women* (1983), present the ideas of antifeminist women that gained force in the 1970s.

Betty Friedan, *The Feminine Mystique* (1963), is still powerful. For Friedan's evolving views, see *It Changed My Life* (1976) and *The Second Stage* (1982). Texts of the early women's movement include Robin Morgan, ed., *Sisterhood Is Powerful* (1970); Shulamith Firestone, *The Dialectic of Sex* (1970); Kate Millett, *Sexual Politics* (1970); Germaine Greer, *The Female Eunuch* (1972); and Susan Brownmiller, *Against Our Will* (1975). Sara Ruddick and Pamela Daniels, eds., *Working It Out* (1977), collects the struggles of twenty-three women to find personal and professional fulfillment during a period of rapid change in women's expectations.

31

A PROUD BUT TROUBLED PEOPLE

At the end of the 1960s, the United States was torn by internal strife and controversy. Much of the domestic unrest stemmed from the Vietnam War. The growing crisis in confidence was increased by an unprecedented scandal at the highest level of the government, culminating in the resignation of President Richard M. Nixon in 1974.

During the decade after Nixon's resignation, the United States faced new challenges in national life. In politics, the New Deal coalition struggled, with less and less success, to maintain a Democratic majority. In the economic sphere, Americans found themselves in a period of declining productivity, limited growth, and runaway inflation, much of it caused by the dramatic rise in imported oil prices that hit like a shock wave after 1973. Inflation abated in the 1980s, but the nation faced an annual federal deficit that approached $200 billion. In foreign policy, following the end of the war in Vietnam, the United States struggled to deal with new challenges such as instability in the Middle East and crises of political authority in Central America. Relations with the Soviet Union remained tense, as both superpowers engaged in an escalating nuclear arms race that threatened the fragile international peace.

While the outlines of economic, political, and international developments are clear, it is harder to generalize about the American people since 1968. The American experience has always been substantially defined not by sameness or consensus, but by elements of difference and diversity—whether by class, race, ethnicity, region, gender, or age. Demographic and social diversity is perhaps the most striking aspect of the American population on the eve of the twenty-first century.

A Time of Troubles

In many ways, the years 1963–1968 had been distinct. The civil rights movement spurred the nation to debate the political issues of the day in terms of morality, justice, fairness, and equality. After 1968, a new set of priorities began to emerge. There was less talk about poverty and civil rights, and more about inflation and law and order. Richard Nixon, who won election as president in 1968 and again in 1972, capitalized on this shifting mood.

1968, a Year of Shocks

The year 1968 ranks as one of the most traumatic in United States history. In Vietnam, it began with the Tet offensive, named for the Vietnamese New Year, on January 31, when a surprise Viet Cong attack struck major installations throughout South Vietnam, including the U.S.

embassy in Saigon. Although the attack was repulsed, the Viet Cong strength mocked American claims that the enemy was being defeated. President Johnson's political stock fell accordingly. Senator Eugene J. McCarthy of Minnesota had already entered the Democratic primaries as an antiwar candidate; in the aftermath of the Tet offensive, he received a stunning 42.2 percent of the vote in the New Hampshire primary in early March. Sensing the vulnerability of the incumbent president, Senator Robert F. Kennedy of New York entered the race several days later. Johnson saw the handwriting on the wall and announced on March 31 that he would not seek reelection. Using the occasion to announce a halt in the bombing of North Vietnam, Johnson vowed to devote his remaining months in office to the search for peace in Vietnam.

Just five days after Johnson's dramatic withdrawal, Martin Luther King, Jr., was assassinated in Memphis, provoking urban riots across the country that left forty-three persons dead. Soon after, a major student confrontation erupted at Columbia University, ending only when police violently removed protesters from the administration buildings they had occupied. Student unrest seemed likely to become a worldwide phenomenon in May, when a massive strike by students and labor unions toppled the French government. Then came the final tragedy. As Robert Kennedy celebrated his victory over Eugene McCarthy in the California primary on June 5, 1968, he was assassinated by Sirhan Sirhan, a young Palestinian who opposed Kennedy's pro-Israel stand. Once again, the nation went through the ritual of burying a Kennedy. A New Yorker captured the mounting sense of frustration and impotence by saying, "I won't vote. Every good man we get they kill."

Disorder and confusion continued to haunt the Democratic party, which was still reeling from Johnson's withdrawal when Kennedy was assassinated. McCarthy proceeded listlessly through the rest of his campaign. Senator George S. McGovern of South Dakota entered the Democratic race in an effort to keep the Kennedy forces together. Meanwhile, Vice-President Hubert H. Humphrey lined up pledges from more traditional Democratic supporters—unions, urban political machines, and state organizations. With Humphrey's growing success, the

ROBERT F. KENNEDY
Bobby Kennedy inspired strong passions during his 1968 campaign. Followers often tore off his cufflinks as they tried to touch him or shake his hand. Kennedy's assassination in June 1968, coming just two months after Martin Luther King, Jr.'s murder, shocked the nation. (© Steve Shapiro, Black Star)

Democrats suddenly found themselves on the verge of nominating not an antiwar candidate but a public figure closely associated with Johnson's war policies. The stage was set for the Democratic National Convention in Chicago in August.

The Democrats had experienced disastrous conventions in the past, as in the 103-ballot-long meeting in 1924, but the 1968 convention hit a new low. Most of the drama occurred not in the convention amphitheater but in the streets of Chicago. On the night that the candidates were nominated, a battle broke out between the Chicago police and antiwar demonstrators. In what the official report later described as a "police riot," the police dispersed protesters with mace, tear gas, and clubs. While the protesters chanted "The whole world is watching!", the television networks ran film of the riot in the midst of their coverage of the nominating speeches. In one memorable exchange, Senator Abraham Ribicoff of Connecticut interrupted his nominating speech for Senator McGovern to interject, "With George McGovern we wouldn't have Gestapo tactics on the streets of Chicago." The cameras panned to Richard J. Daley, Chicago's old-line Democratic mayor, livid with rage and mouthing obscenities.

Television coverage of the riots was hardly excessive—it consisted of thirty-two minutes on CBS and less than fourteen minutes on NBC—but it cemented an impression of the Democrats as the party of disorder. The Democrats dispiritedly gave the nomination to Hubert Humphrey, who chose Senator Edmund S. Muskie of Maine as his running mate. The convention approved a moderate, proadministration platform.

The Chicago convention reinforced a growing backlash in favor of proponents of "law and order," the catch phrase of the next several years.

Many Americans were fed up with protest and dissent. Governor George C. Wallace of Alabama, a third-party candidate, skillfully exploited the public's growing hostility and anger by making student protests and black riots his campaign issues. He also spoke out against school desegregation and busing. Early polls showed that Wallace would receive as much as 20 percent of the vote, possibly sufficient to deadlock the electoral college and send the election to the House of Representatives.

Richard Nixon, even more than George Wallace, tapped the growing conservative mood of the electorate. After his unsuccessful presidential campaign in 1960 and his failure to be elected governor of California in 1962, Nixon had engineered an amazing political comeback. In 1968 he easily beat back challenges from three governors—Ronald Reagan of California, George

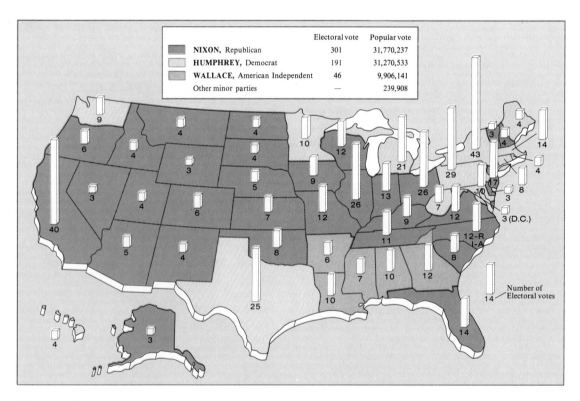

	Electoral vote	Popular vote
NIXON, Republican	301	31,770,237
HUMPHREY, Democrat	191	31,270,533
WALLACE, American Independent	46	9,906,141
Other minor parties	—	239,908

MAP 31.1 Election of 1968

As late as mid-September, third-party candidate George C. Wallace of Alabama had the support of 21 percent of the voters polled, threatening to send the election into the House of Representatives. In the election, however, Wallace received only 13.5 percent of the popular vote, winning five states and showing that the South was no longer solidly Democratic. Republican Richard M. Nixon defeated Hubert H. Humphrey with only 43.4 percent of the popular vote.

Romney of Michigan, and Nelson Rockefeller of New York—to win the Republican nomination. In his campaign, Nixon pledged to represent the "quiet voice" of the "great majority of Americans, the forgotten Americans, the nonshouters, the nondemonstrators." He declared that "The first civil right of every American is to be free from domestic violence."

The election was much closer than might have been expected, considering the Democratic debacle in Chicago. Humphrey rallied in the last weeks of the campaign by disassociating himself from Johnson's war policies. Nixon countered by declaring that he had a "secret plan" to end the war. Nixon received 43.4 percent of the vote and defeated Humphrey by a scant 510,000 votes out of 73 million cast. Wallace finished with 13.5 percent of the popular vote, becoming the most successful third-party candidate since Progressive Robert M. LaFollette in 1924. Nixon's "southern strategy," his carefully crafted inroad into the once solidly Democratic South, gave him an important margin of victory. Yet Nixon owed his election more to the split in the still-potent Democratic coalition than to the emergence of a new Republican majority.

The 1968 election suggested a new mood in the electorate that dominated much of the 1970s. Nixon appealed to what came to be known as the "silent majority," the average voter who was "unblack, unpoor, and unyoung." According to Ben J. Wattenberg and Richard Scammon in their influential book *The Real Majority* (1970), the typical American was not a political science student at Yale but a forty-seven-year-old machinist's wife from Dayton, Ohio:

> To know that the lady in Dayton is afraid to walk the streets alone at night, to know that she has a mixed view about blacks and civil rights because before moving to the suburbs she lived in a neighborhood that became all black, to know that her brother-in-law is a policeman, to know that she does not have the money to move if her new neighborhood deteriorates, to know that she is deeply distressed that her son is going to a community junior college where LSD was found on campus—to know all this is the beginning of contemporary political wisdom.

The images of the first half of 1968 were violent—assassinations, riots, student unrest, and black power. The mood by the time of the election had changed—law and order, distrust of student radicals, and fear of blacks. Nixon's election reflected just one manifestation of a fundamental shift in the political climate. The student protester, the black militant, and the welfare mother were out; the machinist's wife from Dayton was in.

The War at Home

Vietnam, which had long been Lyndon Johnson's war, soon became Richard Nixon's. Fifteen thousand Americans lost their lives in Vietnam during Nixon's presidency. Yet Nixon operated within political parameters that differed fundamentally from Johnson's. Realizing that the public would no longer stand for major sacrifices to win the war in Southeast Asia, Nixon searched for a way out of the Vietnam problem. He dramatically reduced American troop involvement in the ground fighting. When Nixon took office, more than 543,000 American soldiers were serving in Vietnam; by the end of 1970, the number had fallen to 334,000, and two years later it was down to 24,200. American casualties, and the political liabilities they generated, fell correspondingly. At the same time, however, Nixon escalated the American involvement by ordering a massive increase in the bombing raids over North Vietnam and neighboring countries. This expansion of the air war was deliberately downplayed, even hidden from the American public.

Television had much to do with shaping American attitudes toward the war. Vietnam was television's first big war; it brought the fighting directly into the nation's living rooms. The escalation in Vietnam coincided with several trends in news broadcasting, notably the expansion of the nightly network newscast from fifteen minutes to half an hour in 1963. By 1967, CBS and NBC were spending $5 million a year to cover the war from their expanded Saigon bureaus. This investment guaranteed that Vietnam appeared on the news every night. Reporters soon learned that combat footage—what they called "shooting bloody"—had a better chance of airing than reports about pacification or political developments. Every night, the newscasts showed American soldiers steadily advancing in the countryside, while reported body counts suggested staggering Viet Cong losses against minimal U.S. casualties.

The Tet offensive in January 1968 destroyed this complacent picture. Suddenly, television brought home new images—the American embassy in Saigon under siege, with a pistol-wielding staff member peering warily from a window; and the Saigon police chief placing a pistol to the head of a Viet Cong suspect and executing him on the street. About twenty million viewers watched the latter scene, a symbol of the brutality of the war and the corruption and injustice that characterized the regime of Nguyen Van Thieu, the president of South Vietnam from 1967 to 1975.

The Tet offensive set in motion a major shift in American public opinion about the war. Before Tet, a Gallup poll found that 56 percent of the people considered themselves "hawks" (supporters of the war), while only 28 percent identified themselves as "doves" (opponents); women and blacks consistently opposed the war more than did white males. By April 1968, doves outnumbered hawks by 42 to 41 percent. This turnaround did not mean that a majority now supported the peace movement. Many who called themselves doves had concluded that the war was unwinnable and that America ought to cut its losses and get out. They opposed the war on pragmatic, rather than moral, grounds.

At first, Nixon and National Security Adviser Henry Kissinger, a former Harvard government professor, seemed to be extricating the nation from the mire of Vietnam. A new plan called Vietnamization delegated most of the ground fighting to South Vietnamese troops. Vietnamization was a slow process, however, and American policymakers began to consider expanding the war in an attempt to strengthen the faltering South Vietnamese government. In March 1969, Nixon ordered secret bombing raids of neutral Cambodia, through which the North Vietnamese transported supplies and reinforcements. To keep Congress ignorant about these sorties, accurate information about the raids was fed into one Defense Department computer, while fabricated data omitting the Cambodia targets were fed into another computer. The faulty projections from the second computer were made available to Congress. The secret war against Cambodia culminated in an April 30, 1970, "incursion" by American ground forces to destroy enemy troop havens in that neutral country. The Cambodia invasion triggered the campus rioting that led to the Kent State killings. No matter how much the United States escalated its activity, however, the North Vietnamese fought on.

Like Lyndon Johnson, who by 1968 had become so unpopular that his appearance caused protests everywhere except on military bases, Richard Nixon seemed to inspire conflict. Determined to discredit his critics, he denounced student demonstrators as "bums" and stated,

A TELEVISED WAR
This harrowing scene from Saigon during the Tet offensive in 1968 was broadcast on U.S. network news. The NBC bureau chief described the film in a terse telex message: "A VC OFFICER WAS CAPTURED. THE TROOPS BEAT HIM. THEY BRING HIM TO [Brigadier General Nguyen Ngoc] LOAN WHO IS HEAD OF SOUTH VIETNAMESE NATIONAL POLICE. LOAN PULLS OUT HIS PISTOL, FIRES AT THE HEAD OF THE VC, THE VC FALLS, ZOOM ON HIS HEAD, BLOOD SPRAYING OUT. IF HE HAS IT ALL ITS STARTLING STUFF." (Wide World)

VIETNAM VETERAN REMEMBERS

I had been shot. The war had finally caught up with my body. I felt good inside. Finally the war was with me and I had been shot by the enemy. I was getting out of the war and I was going to be a hero. I kept firing my rifle into the tree line and boldly, with my new wound, moved closer to the village, daring them to hit me again. For a moment I felt like running back to the rear with my new million-dollar wound but I decided to keep fighting in the open. A great surge of strength went through me as I yelled for the other men to come out from the trees and join me. I was limping now and the foot was beginning to hurt so much, I finally lay down in almost a kneeling position, still firing into the village, still unable to see anyone. I seemed to be the only one left firing a rifle. Someone came up from behind me, took off my boot and began to bandage my foot. The whole thing was incredibly stupid, we were sitting ducks, but he bandaged my foot and then he took off back into the tree line.

For a few seconds it was silent. I lay down prone and waited for the next bullet to hit me. It was only a matter of time, I thought. I wasn't retreating, I wasn't going back, I was lying right there and blasting everything I had into the pagoda. The rifle was full of sand and it was jamming. I had to pull the bolt back now each time trying to get a round into the chamber. It was impossible and I started to get up and a loud crack went off next to my right ear as a thirty-caliber slug tore through my right shoulder, blasted through my lung, and smashed my spinal cord to pieces.

I felt that everything from my chest down was completely gone. I waited to die. I threw my hand back and felt my legs still there. I couldn't feel them but they were still there. I was still alive. And for some reason I started believing, I started believing I might not die, I might make it out of there and live and feel and go back home again. I could hardly breathe and was taking short little sucks with the one lung I had left. The blood was rolling off my flak jacket from the hole in my shoulder and I couldn't feel the pain in my foot anymore, I couldn't even feel my body. I was frightened to death. I didn't think about praying, all I could feel was cheated.

All I could feel was the worthlessness of dying right here in this place at this moment for nothing.

Source: Ron Kovic, *Born on the Fourth of July.* New York: McGraw Hill, 1976. 221–222.

"North Vietnam cannot defeat or humiliate the United States. Only Americans can do that." Vice-President Spiro T. Agnew followed suit, attacking dissidents as "ideological eunuchs" and "nattering nabobs of negativism," the press as a "tiny and closed fraternity," and Senate opponents of the war as "pampered prodigies." Nixon staunchly insisted that he would not be swayed by the mounting popular protests against the war. When 250,000 protesters marched on Washington in November 1969, the president watched football games on television while barricaded in the White House.

By 1970 dissatisfaction with the war had reached a broader spectrum of American society. Even American troops in Vietnam showed mounting opposition to their mission. They fought on, but many sewed peace symbols on their uniforms. A number of overbearing junior officers were "fragged"—that is, killed or wounded by a fragmentation grenade thrown by their own soldiers. A group called Vietnam Veterans Against the War expressed their profound opposition to the war by turning in their combat medals at mass demonstrations at the U.S. Capitol.

At the same time that Nixon stepped up the bombing raids against North Vietnam, he laid the groundwork for détente with the Soviet Union and China, the two leading communist superpowers. Influenced by the strategy of Henry Kissinger to use China to balance the USSR, Nixon moved away from unconditional support for the nationalist Chinese government on Taiwan. In February 1972, Nixon, long an anticommunist crusader, made a dramatic trip to the People's Republic of China, where he visited the Great Wall and toasted Chinese leaders in

Beijing. (Formal diplomatic relations would be established in 1979.) That May, Nixon made a similar trip to Moscow to sign SALT I, the strategic arms limitations treaty between the United States and the Soviet Union. The two trips were orchestrated to enhance Nixon's presidential stature and to give him considerable television publicity in an election year.

The Democrats would have had a difficult time countering Nixon's public relations coup under any circumstances, but disarray within the party in 1972 made their task even harder. In the aftermath of the 1968 national convention, the party had changed its way of selecting delegates and candidates. The Democrats now pledged to include "minority groups, young people and women in reasonable relationship to their presence in the population." The ratification of the Twenty-Sixth Amendment in 1971, which lowered the national voting age to eighteen, reinforced the impact of this procedural change. Another innovation was the candidate primary, which allowed voters to elect convention delegates directly, rather than have them chosen at party caucuses.

George McGovern reaped the greatest benefit from the new Democratic guidelines. By 1972, the South Dakota senator stood at the head of an army of antiwar activists who blitzed the precinct-level caucuses and won delegate commitments far beyond his voter support. In the past, an alliance of party bosses and union leaders would almost certainly have rejected an upstart candidate like McGovern in favor of a more traditional Democrat such as Hubert Humphrey or Edmund Muskie. But few party leaders qualified as delegates to the nominating convention under the 1972 rules. Typical of the new Democratic look, black leader Jesse Jackson replaced Mayor Richard Daley of Chicago as the head of the Illinois delegation.

McGovern's campaign became an unrelieved disaster. Surprised to learn that his running mate, Senator Thomas F. Eagleton of Missouri, had undergone electro-shock therapy for nervous depression, McGovern first offered him "1,000 percent" support, but then abruptly insisted that he leave the ticket. Sargent Shriver, a brother-in-law of John and Robert Kennedy, was prevailed upon to join the ticket at the last minute. McGovern was far too liberal for many traditional Democrats, who rejected his ill-defined proposals for welfare reform, did not rally around his antiwar stance, and ignored his charges that the Nixon administration had corruptly abused its power.

Nixon took full advantage of McGovern's weaknesses. Although the president had failed to end the war in Vietnam, his Vietnamization policy had reduced weekly American combat deaths from three hundred in 1968 to almost none in 1972. Just a few days before the election, Henry Kissinger returned from negotiations with the North Vietnamese in Paris and announced, somewhat disingenuously, that "peace is at hand."

Nixon won handily. He received nearly 61 percent of the popular vote and carried every state except Massachusetts and the District of Columbia. The threat of a conservative third-party challenge had been removed the previous May, when George Wallace was shot and paralyzed from the waist down by an assailant in a suburban Maryland shopping mall. McGovern's vote demonstrated large cracks in the traditional Democratic coalition; he received only 18 percent of the southern white Protestant vote and 38 percent of the big-city Catholic vote. Only blacks, Jews, and low-income voters remained loyal to the Democratic cause. Yet Nixon failed to kindle strong Republican loyalties in the electorate. Only 55.7 percent of the voters bothered to go to the polls.

In the aftermath of his landslide victory, Nixon moved to end American involvement in Vietnam. Seeking to break the stalemated negotiations, he initiated the "Christmas bombings." From December 17 to December 30, American planes subjected North Vietnamese civilian and military targets to the most destructive bombing of the entire war. Then, on January 27, 1973, a ceasefire was signed; it differed little from the proposal of the previous October. The Paris Peace Accords promised neither peace nor honor. Basically, they mandated the unilateral withdrawal of American troops in exchange for the return of American prisoners of war held in North Vietnam. For most Americans, that amount of face saving was enough.

The public outpouring of emotion that greeted the six hundred returning prisoners contrasted sharply with public indifference to ordinary Vietnam veterans, who in the following years experienced higher than average divorce, suicide, and unemployment rates, as well as recurring physical and psychological problems called the "post-Vietnam syndrome." For many Vietnam veterans, the war never ended.

The signing of the 1973 Peace Accords did little to resolve the civil war that had raged in Vietnam for almost three decades. Without massive U.S. military and economic aid, and with the continued presence of North Vietnamese soldiers in the south, it was only a matter of time before the South Vietnamese government of General Nguyen Van Thieu fell to the more popular North Vietnamese forces. The inevitable occurred in April 1975, when a North Vietnamese invasion reunited the country. American television viewers watched in horror as desperate South Vietnamese officials and soldiers fought with American embassy personnel for space on the last helicopters that flew out of Saigon before the Viet Cong took over the city, soon renamed Ho Chi Minh City. Strife still engulfs Vietnam and its neighbors Laos, Cambodia, and Thailand. The epitaph that journalist David Halberstam coined for American participation in the war applies to Southeast Asia itself: "No light at the end of the tunnel, only greater darkness."

Watergate

Watergate, the great constitutional crisis of the early 1970s, saw a president manage to avoid impeachment only by resigning from office. Its roots lay in Richard Nixon's secretive style of governing—Henry Kissinger once said Nixon was "the first victim of his own unharmonious nature"—and in his obsession with opposition to the Vietnam War at home. Many of the incidents of secrecy, mistrust, and illegality that Americans later lumped together as "Watergate" grew out of the protest era that preceded them.

The new administration began to stretch the boundaries of the law in the guise of national security just four months into Nixon's first term. In the spring of 1969, the *New York Times* broke the story that the United States had been secretly bombing Cambodia. In retaliation, the White House arranged for the FBI to wiretap illegally—that is, without judicial warrants—several low-level staffers on the National Security Coun-

cil, as well as five newspeople, to investigate the source of the leaks. The source was never found.

The next event to trigger White House paranoia was the leaking of the "Pentagon Papers" to the *New York Times* in June 1971 by Daniel Ellsberg, a former Defense Department analyst who had grown disillusioned with the war. The Pentagon Papers, a classified Defense Department document commissioned in the wake of the Tet offensive, contained so much damaging information about American blunders and misjudgments in the conduct of the war that Defense Secretary Robert S. McNamara had commented in 1968, "You know, they could hang people for what is in there." The Nixon administration unsuccessfully attempted to block publication of the Pentagon Papers, further increasing Ellsberg's stature as a hero to the antiwar movement. In an effort to discredit Ellsberg, White House underlings burglarized his psychiatrist's office to look for damaging information. This attempt also failed.

The Ellsberg break-in was part of a broad response by the administration to the supposed threats presented by domestic dissent to national security. In 1970, White House aide Tom Huston, a former army intelligence officer, drew up an extensive plan for secret domestic counterintelligence—such as opening mail, tapping phones, and arranging break-ins—that would involve the FBI, CIA, and Justice Department. President Nixon approved the scheme, only to have it blocked by FBI Director J. Edgar Hoover, who refused to cooperate with other government agencies in activities he interpreted as being exclusively within the scope of the FBI. The White House then established a clandestine group of its own. It was headed by G. Gordon Liddy and Howard Hunt and known as the "plumbers" (because they were supposed to plug "leaks" of government information). Other dubious tactics included the use of government agencies such as the Internal Revenue Service to harass opponents of the administration named on an "enemies list" drawn up by aide John Dean.

These secret and questionable activities, supposedly conducted in the name of national security, led to the Watergate scandal. On the evening of June 17, 1972, five men carrying cameras and wiretapping equipment broke into the headquarters of the Democratic National Committee at the Watergate apartment complex in Washington. An alert security guard foiled the break-in, and the burglars were arrested; two other accomplices were apprehended soon after. Two of the accused men had worked as security consultants in the White House; a third held a responsible position on the Committee to Re-Elect the President (CREEP); the remaining four were all from Miami, where they had been involved in CIA-linked anti-Castro activities. Nixon's press secretary, Ronald Ziegler, dismissed the break-in as a "caper," a "third-rate burglary attempt." Nixon himself stated "categorically" that "no one in the White House staff, no one in this administration, presently employed, was involved in this bizarre incident." The cover-up had begun.

On June 23, 1972, six days after the break-in, the president ordered top aide H. R. Haldeman to instruct the CIA to tell the FBI not to probe too deeply into connections between the White House and the burglars. Although Nixon cited the supposed threat to national security, he really feared that the Watergate burglary would lead to an investigation of the dubious fundraising methods and political sabotage—or "dirty tricks"—used by his reelection committee.

The Watergate burglars were convicted and sent to jail. White House counsel John Dean had sought to buy their silence with $400,000 in hush money and hints of presidential pardons. But prodded by the presiding judge, John Sirica, several of the convicted burglars began to talk. A Senate committee launched an investigation. Two reporters on the *Washington Post*, Carl Bernstein and Bob Woodward, kept the story alive. Dean started to get nervous, and in March 1973 he warned Nixon, referring to the cover-up, that "there is a cancer within, close to the presidency, that is growing." On April 30, Nixon accepted the resignations of Haldeman and chief domestic adviser John Ehrlichman. He also fired Dean. In light of mounting evidence that linked the scandal directly to the Oval Office, press secretary Ziegler declared all previous statements on Watergate "inoperative."

In May, a Senate committee chaired by Senator Sam Ervin of North Carolina heard John Dean implicate President Nixon in the cover-up. The most startling revelation came from aide Alexander Butterfield, who revealed that Nixon had a secret taping system in the White House. "I was hoping you fellows wouldn't ask me about that," Butterfield sheepishly told the committee. Until the tapes, it had been Dean's word against Nixon's; now it might be possible to find out what had actually transpired. The president steadfastly "stonewalled," refusing to release the tapes in the name of executive privilege and national security. When a lower federal court held that he had to give selected tapes to a special prosecutor, Nixon released heavily edited tapes and transcripts whose most frequent phrase seemed to be "expletive deleted." Senate Republican leader Hugh Scott called these edited transcripts "deplorable, disgusting, shabby, immoral." Further damaging Nixon's credibility

NIXON LEAVES THE PRESIDENCY
President Richard M. Nixon frequently posed with his arms outstretched, flashing a "V for Victory" sign. He maintained this stance even on August 9, 1974, as he boarded a helicopter en route to his home in San Clemente, California, minutes after turning over the presidency to Gerald R. Ford. (© Roland Freeman, Magnum)

was a suspicious eighteen-minute gap in the tape of a crucial meeting between Nixon, Haldeman, and Ehrlichman on June 20, 1972, three days after the break-in.

With the evidence becoming increasingly damning, the Watergate affair moved into its final phase in the summer of 1974. The House of Representatives convened impeachment hearings, and on July 30, seven Republicans joined the Democratic majority to vote three articles of impeachment—obstruction of justice, abuse of power, and acting in a way subversive of the Constitution—against Richard Nixon. Two days later, the Supreme Court ruled unanimously that Nixon's claim of executive privilege was insufficient to justify his refusal to turn over the tapes. On August 5, Nixon released the unexpurgated tapes, which contained shocking evidence that he had ordered the cover-up as early as six days after the break-in. In effect, he had been lying to the American people ever since. Senator Barry Goldwater gravely informed the president that Nixon would find no more than fifteen senators willing to defend him. On August 9, 1974, Nixon became the first president to resign from office.

The transfer of power to Vice-President Gerald Ford went remarkably smoothly. (In 1973, Ford had replaced Spiro Agnew, who had resigned after being indicted for allegedly accepting kickbacks on construction contracts while governor of Maryland.) In the wake of the assassinations of John Kennedy, Robert Kennedy, and Martin Luther King, as well as the first resignation of an incumbent vice-president, the idea of substituting leaders no longer seemed quite so unusual to many citizens. The public had greater difficulty a month later in accepting President Ford's "full, free, and absolute" pardon of Nixon on the grounds of sparing the country the agony of rehashing Watergate.

In response to the abuses of the Nixon administration, Congress adopted several reforms to contain the power of what historian Arthur M. Schlesinger, Jr., called "the imperial presidency." The War Powers Act of 1973 required the president to report any use of military force—such as had occurred in Korea, Vietnam, and Cambodia—to Congress within forty-eight hours and directed that hostilities must cease within sixty days unless Congress declared war. The 1974 Congressional Budget and Impoundment Control Act restricted the president's au-

thority to impound federal funds. The Fair Campaign Practices Act of 1974 limited campaign contributions and demanded stricter accounting of campaign expenditures. A strengthened Freedom of Information Act in 1974 gave citizens greater access to the files that the federal government had amassed on them.

In the aftermath of Watergate, twenty-five members of the Nixon administration went to prison, including Nixon's closest advisers, H. R. Haldeman, John Ehrlichman, and Attorney General John Mitchell. Richard Nixon retired to his estate in San Clemente, California. He refused to admit guilt for what had happened, conceding only that Watergate represented an error of judgment.

Lowered Expectations and New Challenges

During the decade after Watergate, some Americans began to suspect that the undisputed world preeminence of the United States since World War II was coming to an end. American economic power in the world market declined as the nation struggled with spiraling inflation, stagnant growth at home, and greater dependence on economic developments abroad. In the wake of Watergate, many citizens became cynical about the federal government and about politicians in general. A sense of growing impotence in foreign policy, foreshadowed by the ambiguities of American involvement in Vietnam, erupted in incidents such as the Iranian hostage crisis of 1979–1981 and the hijacking of a TWA jet by Shiite Muslim terrorists in Lebanon in 1985. In response to disturbing developments on the economic, political, and international fronts, many Americans grappled with the unwelcome idea that perhaps the United States no longer ranked as the world's most powerful country.

Economics, the Environment, and Energy

The American economy at the end of World War II was stronger than that of any other nation. Through the mid-1960s, it achieved a record of steady growth and expansion without inflation or high unemployment. But then the economic picture became clouded. The United States faced

THE COMPUTER REVOLUTION

The first modern computers—that is, information-processing machines capable of storing and manipulating data according to specified programs—appeared in the 1940s. During World War II, engineers and mathematicians at the University of Pennsylvania developed a general-purpose, programmable electronic calculator called ENIAC (Electronic Numerator, Integrator, Analyzer and Computer), which could add five thousand ten-digit decimal numbers in one second. It stood eight feet tall, measured eighty feet long, and weighed thirty tons; it used eighteen thousand vacuum tubes for computations. When it performed complex mathematical computations, one scientist noted, ENIAC sounded "like a roomful of ladies knitting." Although ENIAC lacked a central memory and could not store a program, it was the bridge to the modern computer revolution.

By 1947, six computers were under construction, including UNIVAC (Universal Automatic Computer), the first commercial computer system. The word UN-IVAC was synonymous with computer to the general public in the 1950s. UNIVAC was basically a data-processing system that could be tailored to individual customers' needs. In 1951, the U.S. Census Bureau bought the first UNIVAC. Soon CBS-TV signed on, using a UNIVAC to predict the outcome of the 1952 presidential election. At 9 P.M., with only 7 percent of the votes counted, UNIVAC predicted that Dwight D. Eisenhower would sweep the election with 43 states and 438 electoral votes. CBS programmers and network executives, who had expected a closer election, got jittery and altered the program to produce more conservative findings. When the final tally gave 442 electoral votes to Eisenhower, only four votes off the original projection, commentator Edward R. Murrow confessed, "The trouble with machines is people."

Computers are essentially collections of switches, and programs tell the computer which switches to turn on and off. The puzzle that early computer scientists had to solve was how to increase the speed while lowering the cost of this basic operation. Machines like UNIVAC comprised the first generation of computers, which were characterized by their bulky size, dependence on vacuum tubes for computation power, and the use of punch cards for writing programs and analyzing data. Programming such a computer was a laborious process that could take several days because programmers manually had to set thousands of switches in the On or Off position. The fragile vacuum tubes were the weakest part of early computers; the failure of just a few tubes could shut down the entire system. Furthermore, vacuum tubes gave off enormous amounts of heat, necessitating noisy and cumbersome air-conditioning units wherever computers operated. Relay switches were also temperamental. After a critical signal relay stopped one early program, scientists finally located the problem—a dead moth trapped in the apparatus, the origin of the term "debugging."

The 1947 invention of the

increasing competition in the world economy, often from West Germany and Japan, which had rebuilt their industrial systems after the war. As a result, American goods were in less demand worldwide. In 1971, the United States had its first balance of trade deficit in almost eighty years. By the 1970s, the U.S. dollar was no longer the strongest currency on the world market. The combination of high prices and low demand stagnated production and produced a condition that came to be called "stagflation." As one Democratic politician defined it, stagflation meant "that all the things that should go up—the stock market, corporate profits, real spend-able income, productivity—go down, and all the things that should go down—unemployment, prices, interest rates—go up." These economic conditions set the tone for much of the 1970s.

One of the most destabilizing influences on the economy of the 1970s was the cost of energy, especially the price of imported oil. The United States consumed almost a third of the world's annual output of petroleum, although it had only 6 percent of the world population. Gasoline fueled American businesses and automobiles; industries that depended on petroleum, ranging from the automobile industry to those that produced such petrochemical by-products as plas-

transistor, a development that revolutionized computers and also the whole field of electronics, made possible the second generation of computers. Transistors had the electrical properties of vacuum tubes, but they did not generate heat, burn out, or consume vast quantities of energy. They also were inexpensive to manufacture; a transistor is a semiconductor, and the most plentiful semiconductor is silicon (refined sand). The invention of integrated circuits (IC) in 1958, and greater sophistication in miniaturization, meant that the number of transistors which could be crammed on a silicon chip increased dramatically, with a corresponding increase in computational power. The first 256-bit Random Access Memory (RAM) chip appeared in 1968, soon followed by a 1,024-bit, or 1 K, RAM. By 1971, integrated circuits could contain the entire central processing unit (CPU) of a computer on a single chip called a microprocessor, about the size of the letter "O" on this page. By the mid-1970s, a one-dollar chip provided as much processing power as a computer that had cost a hundred thousand dollars just fifteen years earlier.

Although the microprocessor demonstrated that the technological capability existed to make small computers suitable for home use, industry leaders such as IBM saw no future in such models. Why would anyone want a computer at home? As a result, electronic hobbyists and computer "hackers" led the way in developing the personal computer. In 1974, the magazine *Radio Electronics* published an article on how to build your own computer. In 1975, *Popular Electronics* featured the new Altair 8800 computer, the first personal computer on the market. Its manufacturer, Micro Instrumentation and Telemetry Systems (MITS) in Albuquerque, New Mexico, was swamped with four hundred orders in one afternoon for the $395 kit ($650 assembled). The Altair 8800 had no software. Users had to write their own programs, entering them bit by bit through the toggle switches on the front. The machine had only 256 bytes of memory, too few to do much with the Altair except play with it, which computer hackers happily did.

The big breakthrough came from the upstart Apple Computer Company, the brainchild of Stephen Wozniak and Steven Jobs, two California computer hackers barely in their twenties. After perfecting a machine, they hired a designer who gave their computer a warm beige color and sleek plastic case. A rainbow-colored logo and an imaginative advertising campaign introduced the Apple II to the public in 1977 at a price of $1,195. Apple's annual sales soared from $775,000 in 1977 to almost $1 billion by 1983.

Since the early 1980s, however, the computer industry has entered a period of retrenchment and uncertainty. Industry leaders realized that the market for computers—and the software, games, and other accessories to go with them—was not nearly as huge as it had seemed in the heady days of Apple's early success.

---

tics and nylon, were crucial to the economic structure. The nation's global economic superiority had depended largely on the availability of cheap and abundant energy.

Political and economic developments in the Middle East after 1973 destroyed American complacency regarding energy resources. Oil-rich countries, a group comprised mostly of Arab states, had banded together into an organization called OPEC (Organization of Petroleum Exporting Countries), which began to flex its economic muscle by deliberately raising the price of oil. Between 1973 and 1975 the price of a barrel of oil quadrupled from three to twelve dollars. Because the United States depended heavily on cheap Middle Eastern oil, this price rise, which continued for the rest of the decade, set off a furious inflationary spiral.

Especially disruptive was the OPEC-instituted oil embargo in 1973–1974 in the wake of an Arab-Israeli war. In October 1973, Egyptian and Syrian forces had invaded Israel. They scored stunning military success, partly because Israelis were observing Yom Kippur, the holiest day in Judaism. At first, American policymakers had held back their support of Israel for fear of jeopardizing relations with the oil-producing countries. But the initial attack had been so

NO GAS
During the energy crisis of 1973–1974, American motorists faced widespread gasoline shortages for the first time since World War II. Although gas was not rationed, gas stations were closed on Sundays, air travel was cut by 10 percent, and a national speed limit of fifty-five miles an hour was imposed. (© Dennis Brack, Black Star)

cheap gasoline. Soon the domestic auto industry was in a recession, as Americans bought cheaper, more fuel-efficient foreign cars.

The energy crisis of the 1970s interacted with an environmental movement that had been building since the late 1960s. Early issues that galvanized public opinion included oil spills, such as one in January 1969 off the coast of Santa Barbara, California; the environmental impact of such projects as the Alaska pipeline, and a proposed airport in the Florida Everglades; and the harmful effects of pollution and smog, much of it produced by auto emissions. The environmental movement registered some early successes—enactment of the Clean Air Act and Water Quality Improvement Act in 1970 and the establishment of the Environmental Protection Agency and the Occupational Safety and Health Administration that same year. In 1971, Congress dropped plans to develop supersonic air transport partly because of environmental concerns.

devastating that the United States reversed its stand and sent enough supplies and military equipment to enable the Israelis to regain most of their lost territory. A ceasefire soon ended the fighting, but the international repercussions were just beginning. In retaliation against the United States, Western Europe, and Japan, which had aided Israel in the Yom Kippur War, OPEC halted all exports.

The United States scrambled to meet its domestic energy needs. The resulting gas shortage forced Americans to curtail their driving or spend long hours in line at the pumps. When they looked for more fuel-efficient cars, the automobile industry had nothing to offer but the "gas guzzlers" that had been built to run on

THREE MILE ISLAND
On March 30, 1979, the Three Mile Island nuclear power plant near Harrisburg, Pennsylvania, came close to suffering a dangerous meltdown of its central core reactor. The accident, caused in part by the failure of safety systems and by human error, helped undermine American faith in nuclear technology, as did the Soviet nuclear disaster at Chernobyl in May 1986. (© Robert Moyer, Black Star).

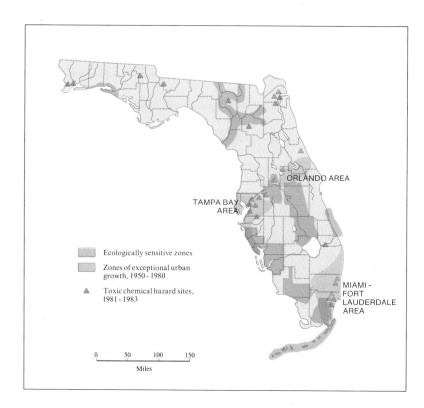

MAP 31.2 ENVIRONMENT IN CRISIS: FLORIDA

Florida is one of the nation's fastest-growing states. Its population increased from 2.8 million in 1950 to 10.6 million in 1983 because of the state's popularity as a retirement center and the growth of its black and Hispanic populations. This predominantly urban growth threatens Florida's delicate ecological balance—its coastlines and swamps, and the Everglades—as well as its production of citrus fruits and vegetables. Sites of toxic chemical wastes also pose ecological dangers.

The environmental movement also raised public awareness of the dangers inherent in the chemicals and petrochemical by-products that had become integral to American consumer goods, including foods, in the postwar period. In 1969, the Agriculture Department banned the use of the pesticide DDT, which, among its many disruptions to the food chain, weakened the shells of birds' eggs. Later in the 1970s, concern shifted to the medical consequences of careless dumping of toxic wastes, by-products of industrial processes. At Love Canal, near Niagara Falls, New York, a housing development had been built over an underground burial site of chemical wastes. Residents noticed that trees turned black and sparks escaped from the pavement; an even graver cause for concern was the abnormally high rate of miscarriages and birth defects reported by Love Canal families. Soon horror stories appeared about other poorly maintained waste-disposal sites across the country. "We just don't know how many potential Love Canals there are," admitted one federal official. "There are ticking time bombs all over."

Another environmental issue, nuclear power, also produced citizen action. In response to the energy crisis, some politicians and business corporations promoted nuclear power as the solution to America's energy needs. By January 1974, forty-two nuclear power plants were in operation and more than a hundred more had been ordered. Their construction often provoked local protest from citizens concerned about their environmental impact. At a reactor construction site in Seabrook, New Hampshire, the "Clamshell Alliance" staged protests reminiscent of the antiwar demonstrations of the previous decade.

Long-standing public fears about nuclear safety seemed to be confirmed in March 1979. At Three Mile Island, outside Harrisburg, Pennsylvania, a nuclear plant came critically close to a meltdown of its central core reactor, which would have released dangerous levels of radioactive material into the environment. A hundred thousand residents were evacuated as a precaution. The problem was brought under control without a major catastrophe, but a member of the panel that investigated the accident admitted, "We were damn lucky."

Three Mile Island made Americans reassess

the future of nuclear power. Once billed as the solution to all energy needs, the cost overruns, faulty construction, and potential dangers of many nuclear power plants raised grave doubts about their viability. The energy shortage had no easy answer.

Post-Watergate Politics—Failed Leadership

Richard Nixon had hoped to end his two terms as president in 1976 with a triumphant celebration of the nation's two hundredth birthday. But by the time of the bicentennial, Nixon had been forced out of office and many Americans had grown cynical about the political process as a result of Vietnam and Watergate. "Don't vote. It only encourages them," read one bumper sticker during the 1976 presidential campaign. "The lesser of two evils is still evil" another proclaimed.

Gerald Ford, the former congressman from Michigan who had become vice-president after Spiro Agnew's resignation, never established his own legitimacy as president during the two years he held the office. His pardon of Nixon a month after becoming president hurt his credibility as a political leader. Distrust toward politicians spilled onto his choice for vice-president, Nelson A. Rockefeller, the former governor of New York, whose extensive family financial holdings were subjected to lengthy and acrimonious Senate hearings before he finally won confirmation.

Ford's biggest problem as president was the economy, reeling with inflation set in motion by spending for the Vietnam War and worsened by the OPEC price rises. The 1974 inflation rate soared to almost 12 percent. In an attempt to curtail runaway prices, the Federal Reserve tightened the money supply and drove up interest rates. In 1975, the economy entered the deepest downturn since the Great Depression. The government refused to increase spending or cut taxes as the economy contracted. Production declined more than 10 percent, and unemployment afflicted nearly 9 percent of the work force. The 1975 recession temporarily returned the inflation rate to less than 5 percent, but it soon rose again.

In foreign policy, Ford found little scope for presidential leadership. He maintained the continuity of Nixon's initiatives toward détente by asking Henry Kissinger to stay on as secretary of state. Ford kept arms control alive by meeting with Soviet leaders at Vladivostok to begin hammering out details of a hoped-for SALT II (Strategic Arms Limitation) agreement, but little concrete progress occurred. Ford and Kissinger followed Nixon's policy of increasing American support for the shah of Iran, failing to notice that the shah's policy of rapid modernization was provoking bitter opposition among Iran's faithful followers of Islam. The fall of Saigon to the North Vietnamese in 1975 reminded Americans of the failure of the Vietnam policy.

After the paranoia and abuses of the Nixon era, Ford's candor and honesty were a breath of fresh air in political life. But he failed to convince the nation that he had the strength to take charge in times of mounting economic and international problems. "Gerald Ford is an awfully nice man who isn't up to the presidency," *The New Republic* concluded. Governor Ronald Reagan of California almost wrested the 1976 Republican presidential nomination away from him, but Ford staved off this conservative challenge. However, he dumped liberal Vice-President Nelson Rockefeller in favor of hardline conservative Senator Robert J. Dole of Kansas.

Only in the skewed political atmosphere of post-Watergate America could the Democrats have chosen their nominee, James E. Carter, Jr., a former entrepreneur in agricultural commodities (chiefly peanuts) from Plains, Georgia, whose sole political experience had been as governor of that state. "Jimmy Who?" the media scoffed at first, but they soon changed their tune as Carter won delegates in key primaries that gave his candidacy both momentum and credibility. Carter played up his role as a Washington outsider; he pledged to restore morality to government, telling voters, "I will never lie to you." In one of the blandest campaigns in some years, both candidates avoided issues and controversy. Carter and his running mate, Senator Walter F. Mondale of Minnesota—whom Carter picked for his ties to traditional Democratic constituencies such as labor, liberals, blacks, and big-city machines—won the election with 50 percent of the popular vote to Ford's 48 percent.

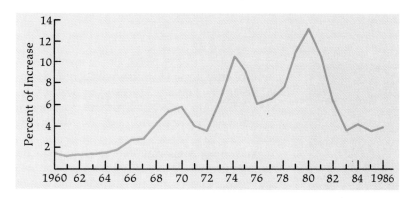

FIGURE 31.1 INCREASE IN
THE CONSUMER PRICE
INDEX, 1960–1986

Jimmy Carter immediately tried to set a different tone for his administration. On Inauguration Day, he renounced formal wear in favor of a business suit; instead of riding in a limousine, he and his wife, Rosalynn, walked from the Capitol to the White House. Throughout his term, he relied heavily on symbolic gestures—dressing in an informal cardigan sweater for fireside chats to the nation, carrying his own luggage on and off planes, holding town meetings, and staying in the homes of ordinary citizens. Carter's homespun approach soon wore thin as people wondered what substance lay beneath the symbols.

Carter failed to develop an effective style of domestic leadership. His campaign as an outsider had distanced him from traditional sources of power in Washington, and he did little to heal this breach. Shying away from established Democratic leaders, he turned to a group of advisers and friends who had worked with him in Georgia, none of whom had national experience. When his budget director, Bert Lance, was questioned about financial irregularities at his Atlanta bank, the case undercut Carter's pledges to restore integrity and morality in government.

The nemesis of inflation presented the main domestic challenge for the Carter administration. When he took office, the nation was just coming out of the severe 1975 recession. To speed recovery, Carter called for increased spending and lower taxes. When that action provoked renewed inflation, he reversed himself, calling for spending cuts and a delay in the tax reductions. This zigzag fiscal policy did little to build either business or consumer confidence. Unemployment hovered between 6 and 7 percent, and inflation rose from 6.5 percent in 1977 to 12.4

percent in 1980, reaching the level of so-called double-digit inflation. As the Federal Reserve raised rates to counter inflation, interest rates briefly topped 20 percent in 1980, a historic high. A deep recession in 1982 broke the inflationary spiral.

Jimmy Carter had greater success in foreign policy, but even there his efforts often failed to produce the results he had hoped for. A commitment to human rights represented Carter's new direction in foreign affairs. He criticized the suppression of dissent in the Soviet Union—especially as it affected the right of Jewish citizens to emigrate—and withdrew economic and military aid from Argentina, Uruguay, Ethiopia, and other noncommunist countries that violated human rights. He also established an Office of Human Rights within the State Department.

President Carter scored a stunning success in the Middle East, a complex arena of international instability. Relations between Egypt and Israel had remained tense since the 1973 Yom Kippur War. In November 1975, Israel's prime minister, Menachem Begin, moved to break the ice by inviting Egyptian president Anwar Sadat to Israel to discuss the possibility of peace. Sadat came, but the talks stalled. Carter broke the stalemate in 1978 by inviting Begin and Sadat for further negotiations at Camp David, the presidential retreat in the Maryland mountains. Two weeks of discussions and Carter's promise of significant foreign aid persuaded Sadat and Begin to agree on a "framework for peace."

In Latin America, Carter's most important contribution was resolution of the dispute over control of the Panama Canal. Carter negotiated two treaties that acknowledged Panamanian

CARTER AND SADAT
President Jimmy Carter's greatest foreign policy
achievement was the personal diplomacy he exerted to
persuade Prime Minister Menachem Begin of Israel and
President Anwar Sadat of Egypt to sign a peace treaty in
1979. Carter, shown here with Sadat, met with the two
leaders both separately and together at Camp David.
(© J. P. Owen, Black Star)

sovereignty over the canal and increased Panama's canal toll revenue. In return, the United
States retained the right to send its ships through
the canal in case of war, even though the canal
itself was declared neutral territory. Despite a conservative outcry that the United States had
given away more than it got, the Senate approved
the treaty.

The most serious foreign problem of the Carter administration occurred in Iran. Early in
1979, a revolution led by a charismatic Muslim
zealot, the Ayatollah Ruhollah Khomeini, seized
power and drove the shah into exile. The United
States lost a strong and secure ally in the Middle
East, and American access to Iran's large oil reserves was jeopardized. Retaliating against a
controversial decision to admit the deposed shah
into the United States for medical treatment,
Muslim students under Khomeini's direction
seized the U.S. embassy in Teheran on November 4, 1979, taking fifty-three American hostages.
American television showed humiliating pictures
of blindfolded hostages at the hands of their
Muslim captors, who demanded that the shah
be returned to Iran for trial and punishment.
The hostages spent 444 days in captivity, win-

ning release at precisely the moment when
Jimmy Carter turned over the presidency to Ronald Reagan on January 20, 1981. The hostages returned home to an ecstatic patriotic welcome, a
reflection of American frustration over their long
ordeal.

While most Americans continued to maintain
patriotically that "We're Number One," the hostage crisis in Iran came to symbolize the loss of
the United States' power to control world affairs.
In many ways, this decline in influence resulted
from the unusual predominance the nation enjoyed after World War II. The return to economic
and political power of Japan and Western Europe, the control of vital oil resources by Middle
Eastern countries, and the industrialization of
part of the Third World had widened the cast
of international actors. Whether future administrations can forge a new U.S. policy to fit a
multipolar world remains to be seen. Many
Americans, however, resisted accepting anything less than the economic and political supremacy of the postwar years.

Social Trends

A new television program heralded the impend-
ing change in social mood between the 1960s
and 1970s. "All in the Family," starring Carroll
O'Connor as Archie Bunker and Jean Stapleton
as his long-suffering wife, Edith, premiered in
1969 and soon became one of the most successful television shows of all time. Mirroring the
concerns of the "silent majority" that had elected
Richard Nixon the previous year, Archie Bunker
railed against the social and cultural changes of
the 1960s—women's liberation, welfare mothers,
busing, and sexual permissiveness. The bum-
bling openness with which he expressed his
prejudices, and the smooth way that his family
neutralized his bigotry, brought the major social
issues of the day to prime-time television.

Archie Bunker's conservative rantings against
the social changes of the 1960s reflected the shifting national mood. No issue became more disruptive in the 1970s than that of forced busing of
children to achieve school integration. Although
the Supreme Court had called for desegregation
"with all deliberate speed" in 1954, little had
happened before 1970. In the 1970s, however,
the courts and the Justice Department pushed

for more action, first in the South, which complied, and then increasingly in northern cities, where deeply ingrained patterns of residential segregation produced all-black schools. The flight of white families to the suburbs made urban school systems even more racially imbalanced.

In 1971, the Supreme Court upheld a federal judge's order requiring the Charlotte, North Carolina, school system to use busing to achieve integration—that is, to transport students from their neighborhood schools in order to integrate the citywide school system. Although the Supreme Court in 1974 rejected the idea that suburban schools and city schools had to be combined to achieve racial balance, it made clear that northern cities would have to use busing within city boundaries to integrate their classrooms. These court decisions provoked controversy and violence; buses that transported black students to previously all-white schools were firebombed in Denver and in Pontiac, Michigan.

Some of the worst violence occurred in Boston in 1974–1975. The strongly Irish Catholic working-class neighborhood of South Boston responded to the arrival of black students from Roxbury with mob scenes reminiscent of Little Rock in 1957. Only armed riot police kept South

Boston High School open. Many white parents in Boston, and in other cities threatened by court-ordered busing, transferred their children to private schools, increasing the racial imbalance that busing was intended to solve. By the late 1970s, however, the federal courts had backed away from their earlier insistence on busing to achieve racial balance, and local communities redoubled their efforts to preserve neighborhood schools.

Almost as divisive as busing was the implementation of affirmative action quotas to achieve racial and sexual balance. Quota systems were used in such areas as college admissions and employment. Whites, especially white males, soon raised the cry of "reverse discrimination," claiming they had been passed over in favor of less qualified minorities or women. In 1978, a white man named Allen Bakke sued the University of California Medical School at Davis, claiming it had rejected him while admitting minority candidates with lower qualifications. The Supreme Court ruling in *Bakke v. University of California* was inconclusive. By a 5 to 4 margin, the Court proclaimed the illegality of absolute quotas and ordered Bakke admitted to the medical school. At the same time, also by a 5 to 4 margin, it upheld the principle of affirmative action

AN ANTI-BUSING CONFRONTATION IN BOSTON
Tensions over court-ordered busing still ran high in Boston in 1976. When a black lawyer tried to cross the City Hall plaza during an antibusing demonstration, he became another victim of Boston's climate of racial hate and violence. This photograph by Stanley Forman for the *Boston Herald American,* showing protesters trying to impale the man with a flagstaff, won a Pulitzer Prize. (© Stanley Forman—Pulitzer Prize, 1976)

by ruling that racial factors could be considered in making hiring or admission decisions.

Most people, however, regarded the *Bakke* decision as a setback to the growing demands for economic and racial equality that had concerned the nation throughout the 1960s. The public outcries of the 1970s against forced busing and affirmative action formed part of a broader backlash against the social changes of the previous decade. Reflecting new conservatism in the social order, many citizens no longer supported the use of federal power or the political system to encourage further change. One target was feminism. The powerful antiabortion "right to life" movement and the stalled progress of the Equal Rights Amendment suggested the impact of this conservatism.

The mood of the 1970s also featured a retreat from idealism and a growing emphasis on personal fulfillment and enjoyment. It now became fashionable to admit to wanting to make money and be successful. (The 1980s coined the term "yuppies"—standing for "young urban professionals"—to denote these upwardly mobile achievers.) This widespread obsession with lifestyles and personal consumption led journalist Tom Wolfe to label the 1970s the "Me Decade" in an influential 1976 magazine article. In 1978, historian Christopher Lasch derisively called the new orientation the "culture of narcissism" in a widely read book of that title.

Much of the energy of personal liberation went into the fitness craze. Thousands of Americans began riding a ten-speed bicycle or working out on a Nautilus machine in a gym. Jim Fixx's *Complete Book of Running* (1977) spurred the jogging boom. In their fashionable Nike or Adidas running shoes, people tried to keep fit by completing their requisite miles per day. Marathons, once the province of an elite group of long-distance runners, became mass events, with thousands lining up to run the 26.2 mile course.

Americans also sought personal fulfillment through a variety of religious and communal movements that had sprung up in the late 1960s and early 1970s. Some joined encounter sessions—nicknamed "T-groups," for "sensitivity training"—in which they tried to "get in touch with their feelings." Many husbands and wives attended marriage-renewal conferences. Others turned to est (Erhard Seminars Training), Transcendental Meditation (TM), yoga, Zen, Hare

Krishna, and Gestalt in a quest for the self. Some parents whose children had joined the Church of Scientology or the Unification Church of the Reverend Sun Myung Moon—whose followers were called "Moonies"—claimed the young people had been brainwashed to give up all their worldly possessions and adopt a rigidly communal life. When hundreds of American followers of the Reverend Jim Jones, a messianic cult leader, ritualistically drank fruit punch laced with cyanide at the "People's Temple" in Guyana in 1978, their mass suicide revealed the excesses of such cults.

The interest in religious cults and aids to inner awareness such as Zen and Transcendental Meditation were part of a major religious revival during the 1970s. Although *Time* magazine had posed the question "Is God Dead?" in a famous 1966 cover, religion in America had been undergoing a revival since the 1950s. Much of this new religious fervor occurred in evangelical Christian denominations, led by such preachers as Billy Graham who learned to use the media to spread the gospel. By the 1970s, seventy million Americans, almost a third of the population, claimed to be "born-again" Christians who had established a direct personal relationship with Jesus Christ. President Jimmy Carter proudly pro-

THE NEW RIGHT
In the 1970s and 1980s, the New Right actively mobilized conservative voters. Two of the movement's most vocal leaders, the Reverend Jerry Falwell and antifeminist crusader Phyllis Schlafly, are shown here at an antiabortion rally in Washington, D.C. (© David Burnett, Contact Press Images)

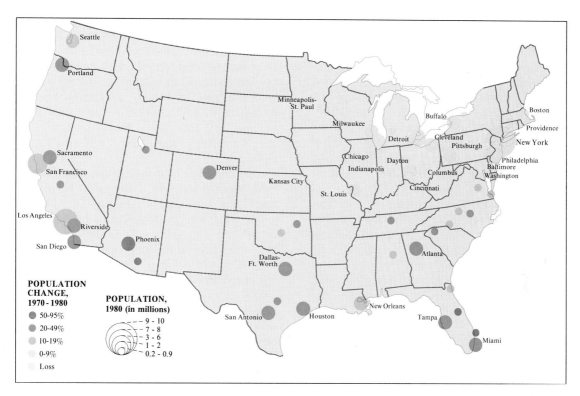

MAP 31.3 THE GROWTH OF THE SUN BELT
While older industrial cities, including New York, Chicago, Philadelphia, and Detroit, lost people in
the 1970s, cities in the Sun Belt added to their populations. Between 1970 and 1980, older Sun Belt
cities such as Dallas and Los Angeles recorded modest gains—6.8 percent and 4.9 percent,
respectively. But booming metropolises registered large increases, among them San Jose, 36.1 percent;
Phoenix, 33.7 percent; Houston, 26.1 percent; and San Diego, 24.7 percent.

claimed his born-again status, as did singers Pat
Boone and Johnny Cash, former Watergate con-
victs Jeb Magruder and Charles Colson, and
black power activist Eldridge Cleaver.

The religious enthusiasm represented by the
evangelical Christians affected national life in
concrete ways. Many evangelical groups set up
their own school systems, newspapers, and
broadcasting networks. The new religious fervor
soon entered public life, as leaders such as the
Reverend Jerry Falwell, who founded the Moral
Majority in 1979, tried to inject their opinions on
such sensitive issues as abortion, busing, school
prayer, and censorship into political discourse.
Yet leaders like Falwell and antifeminist crusader
Phyllis Schlafly expressed their ideas with an
absolutism and fanaticism that offended other
people. "The Moral Majority is neither," read a
popular bumper sticker. Nevertheless, the evan-

gelical religious revival and the new conservatism brought the country to the threshold of the
1980s.

Demographic Diversity

A statistical portrait of the United States in the
1970s and 1980s shows that Americans are living
longer, having fewer children, divorcing more
often, congregating in metropolitan areas, and
enjoying better access to education. Most of
these shifts had begun to emerge by the 1920s
and 1930s, but they accelerated rapidly during
the postwar years. These demographic characteristics supply many of the defining features of
modern American life.

The 1980 census counted 226,504,825 Americans, an 11.5 percent increase over 1970 and
more than twofold jump from the 106 million

counted in 1920. The United States has increasingly become an urbanized society. By 1980, three-quarters of the population lived in urban areas (towns of more than 2,500 inhabitants). Since 1950, however, the rate of urbanization has slowed. Urban population increased only 0.1 percent between 1970 and 1980. The fastest-growing cities and metropolitan areas lay in the West, Southwest, and South. During the 1970s, Los Angeles grew 4 percent while older eastern and midwestern cities such as New York and Chicago declined 11 percent.

Major demographic changes in American lives took place during the post-1945 period. The most important trends, all interrelated to some degree, were the increase in the number of women who worked, a decline in the birth rate, the spread of family arrangements other than the traditional nuclear family, an increase in the number of elderly Americans, and broader access to education.

Perhaps the most dramatic social and economic change of the postwar period was the increase in the number of women working outside the home. In 1920, barely a fifth of all women belonged to the labor force; by 1980, more than half did; by the 1990s the figure is projected to reach 75 percent. The largest growth in the number of women who worked—especially married women—occurred during the postwar period. This transformation of women's roles set off a ripple effect throughout the social and economic structure.

The birth rate ranked as one of the demographic indicators most sensitive to social and economic influences. The birth rate in 1980 was only a fourth of what it had been in 1800, barely half of the rate in 1920. The later age at first marriage—22.1 years for women in 1980, 24.6 for men, both up two years from the 1950s—further reinforced the trend toward smaller families.

The declining birthrate affected both the size and the composition of the nation's households. In 1920, the average household consisted of 4.34 persons. By 1960, even during the postwar baby boom, it had shrunk to 3.3. Just twenty years later, the average household had only 2.75 people. Nor did this average household necessarily fit the traditional stereotype of family life—a gainfully employed father, a housemaker mother, and two children. According to the Labor Department, by the late 1970s only 7 percent of the nation's families matched that pattern. The number of unrelated adults living together became so prevalent that the Census Bureau invented a term to describe these new arrangements, POSSLQ ("persons of the opposite sex sharing living quarters"). A popular refrain the next Valentine's Day asked, "Will you be my POSS-L-Q?"

The growing diversity in the nation's households represented one of the most striking demographic developments of the 1970s. Although the nuclear family survived, many Americans chose alternative arrangements for part or all of their lives. The number of people living alone increased 60 percent in the 1970s; single people comprised almost a fourth of the nation's households, putting pressure on the nation's available housing and creating new markets for such consumer services as fast food. Many elderly people, because of increased benefits offered by Social Security, Medicare, and pension and disability funds, maintained their own households well into old age rather than depend on their children. Homosexual men and women set up households of their own.

The rise of single-parent households presented another variation on the traditional family structure. This new life-style resulted from the congruence of several demographic and social trends—women's ability to support themselves through paid employment, the increase in births to unwed mothers, and the rise in the divorce rate. By 1980, almost a fourth of all children under seventeen (17.3 percent of white children, 57.8 percent of black youngsters) lived with one parent—the mother in the overwhelming majority of cases. The percentage of households headed by women grew from 10.2 percent in 1970 to 17.5 percent in 1980. Since the average income of families headed by women amounted to less than half the national average, the preponderance of these households increased the feminization of poverty.

Marital instability, especially the dramatic increase in the divorce rate, contributed heavily to the rise of single-parent households. In 1920, only 1.6 divorces were recorded per one thousand persons; by 1980, the figure had jumped to

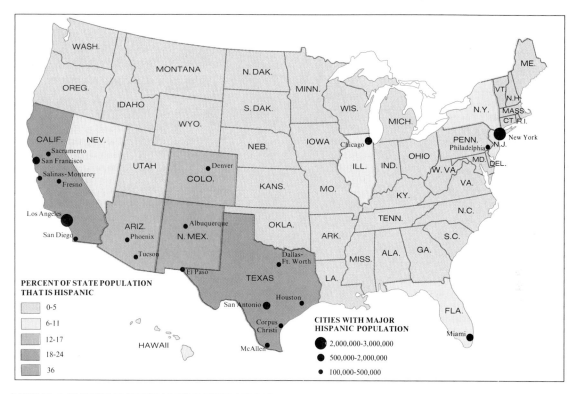

MAP 31.4 AMERICAN HISPANIC POPULATION, 1980

The Hispanic population of the United States is concentrated in California, New York, Texas, Florida, and Illinois, mainly in the major urban areas of those states. In eighteen states, including New Mexico, Arizona, Colorado, California, and Texas, the number of Hispanics exceeds the black population.

5.2. The rate rose most steeply between 1965 and 1975 and then moderated somewhat. Of all the marriages recorded in 1977, however, almost half seemed doomed to end in divorce. Divorce became so common that one commentator called it "almost a necessary initiation into adult relations." A divorce no longer carried the stigma it did in 1962, when it badly damaged the career of Governor Nelson Rockefeller of New York. Americans elected their first divorced president, Ronald Reagan, in 1980.

One of the demographic changes with the most far-reaching consequences was the increasing proportion of people over the age of sixty-five. During the 1970s, this segment of the population grew 20 percent because of the declining birth rate among young people and an increased life expectancy for older Americans. In 1960, for every 100 children under the age of five, there were 81 Americans over sixty-five; by 1980, there were 156. Life expectancy at birth rose from only 54.1 years in 1920 to 73.6 years by 1980. (Women's life expectancy remained consistently several years longer than men's, contributing to an unbalanced ratio between elderly men and women.) Because of the longer life spans, social scientists divided the elderly into two groups— "young old" (ages 65 to 75) and "old old" (75 and up).

In 1981, almost thirty-six million older Americans—approximately 92.5 percent of all those over sixty-five years old—received Social Security payments. The increase in access to Social Security, Medicare, and disability payments meant that workers could retire earlier. In 1980, 28 percent of all men between fifty-eight and sixty-four were not in the labor force, up from 13 percent in 1960. As a result of these cumulative demographic changes, a smaller pool of working Americans underwrote the retirement of a growing population of nonworkers.

Another defining characteristic of the modern age was increased access to education, especially after 1940. Among those aged twenty-five to twenty-nine in 1980, 85.7 percent had completed high school, a jump from 38.1 percent in 1940; in this same age group, the percentage who finished college rose from 5.9 percent in 1940 to 24.3 percent in 1980. Black college enrollment grew more than 250 percent as a result of the civil rights struggle. By the 1980s, however, skyrocketing tuition costs and cutbacks in federal student aid put higher education beyond the reach of even many middle-class families. Still,

Americans generally continued to view a college degree as a step toward personal and professional advancement.

The Reagan Revolution

The post-1968 period had witnessed the slow but steady decline of the New Deal Democratic coalition that dominated politics from Franklin Roosevelt's time to the late 1960s. Although Watergate gave the Democrats a temporary respite, Jimmy Carter's lackluster presidency failed to revitalize the faltering coalition. By the 1980s, the Democratic party no longer had the ability to control the national political system or to set the agenda of significant domestic and foreign issues.

At the same time that the Democrats were

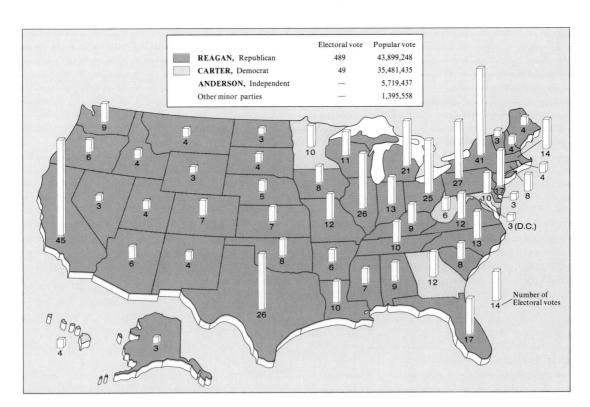

MAP 31.5 ELECTION OF 1980
Ronald Reagan defeated President Jimmy Carter convincingly in the 1980 election, carrying all but five states and the District of Columbia. Even more impressive was that the Republicans won control of the Senate for the first time since 1952 and made gains in the House of Representatives as well. At the age of sixty-nine, Reagan became the oldest person ever elected president.

losing their grip on the electorate, the Republican party was undergoing changes that pointed toward a future of electoral success. The core of the Republican party remained the affluent, upper-middle-class white Protestant voter. But new groups gravitated to the Republicans—southern whites disaffected by big government and civil rights; members of affluent ethnic groups, especially Catholics, who had moved to the suburbs; and young voters who identified themselves as conservatives. Since voting participation is consistently linked to income level, the Republicans benefited from a higher turnout at the polls by their more affluent supporters than did the Democrats, whose party bases lay in the sectors of society (especially the poor and blacks) that were less likely to vote.

Several other factors also sparked the Republican resurgence of the 1980s. Since Republicans had traditionally been the party of the well-to-do and the business community, they had access to financial resources that far outstripped those of the Democrats, whose main support came from the labor movement. This financial superiority enabled the Republicans to excel in direct mailing, fund-raising, and the sophisticated use of television in appealing to voters in the 1970s and 1980s. An additional factor energizing the Republican party was the rise of the New Right, whose social agenda included opposition to abortion, school busing, the Equal Rights Amendment, and the outlawing of prayer in schools. As a southerner and a devout evangelical protestant, Jimmy Carter captured much of this vote in 1976, but by 1980 the New Right was more comfortably ensconced in the Republican party, where its conservative social values formed the basis of the Republican platform. Ronald Reagan parlayed this base of support into a convincing electoral victory in 1980, roundly defeating Carter and Representative John B. Anderson of Illinois, an independent third-party candidate.

Soon after his inauguration, Ronald Reagan seized the chance to redefine the nation's priorities. Ever since Franklin Roosevelt's New Deal, the government had pursued a generally activist approach to social welfare on the assumption that social problems could best be handled by expanding federal action. The election of Ronald

PRESIDENT REAGAN
Ronald Reagan, a former actor, has proved especially adept at mobilizing public support for his policies. Congresswoman Patricia Schroeder of Colorado nicknamed Reagan's administration the "Teflon presidency" because of the tendency for bad news to slip off and leave Reagan's popularity and image unscathed. (© Dennis Brack, Black Star)

Reagan ended this almost fifty-year cycle of activism. "Government is not the solution to our problem," he declared. "Government is the problem." General economic prosperity would better serve the national welfare than government intrusion; freedom, not equality, would be the watchword.

Reagan first moved to reshape the nation's fiscal and tax policies. During his 1980 campaign, he had professed allegiance to the controversial theory of supply-side economics. Instead of increasing demand, Reagan and the supply-siders argued, the government should increase the supply of goods and services offered by the private sector. It could do this by reducing taxes, both for individuals and for businesses, and by balancing the budget. Fewer government regulations, in areas such as pollution control and affirmative action, would enable businesses to expand more productively. A revived economy would eventually yield higher tax revenues, even at lower tax rates.

Reagan won enactment of his economic

A FIRST FOR THE NATION
Geraldine Ferraro, a three-term congresswoman from
New York City, was chosen by Walter F. Mondale to be
his running mate against President Reagan in 1984.
Despite her presence on the ticket, a majority of women
voters supported Reagan. (© Dennis Brack, Black Star)

policy, often called "Reaganomics," from the
Republican-dominated Congress. The 1981 tax
bill was the first since the 1930s that did not produce at least a modest redistribution of income toward those at the lower end of the economic scale.
On the contrary, it favored the wealthy. Deep
cuts in the federal budget, especially for domestic programs, accompanied the tax cut. From
1980 to 1982, according to the Congressional
Budget Office, domestic spending on human resources fell by $101 billion. While congressional
resistance kept some of the more popular social
programs intact, more than half of Reagan's proposed cuts were enacted. The Reagan administration claimed that a "safety net" of welfare
programs would protect the truly needy, but the
net proved inadequate. The Census Bureau reported in 1982 that more than a sixth of all
Americans lived below the poverty line, the
highest proportion since 1965 and a 13 percent
rise over 1980.

The only area of the budget that escaped cuts
was the military, which benefited from Reagan's
commitment to beef up the defense establishment through a five-year, $1.7 trillion military
budget. The allocation of the federal budget
changed accordingly. Military spending in fiscal
1984 comprised 26.8 percent of the budget, up
from 22.6 percent in 1981. Meanwhile, spending
on nonmilitary domestic programs fell from 67.5
percent to 59.5 percent. The rest of the budget
paid the interest on the burgeoning federal debt,
which by 1985 approached $2 trillion.

FIGURE 31.2 THE ESCALATING
FEDERAL DEBT, 1939–1984

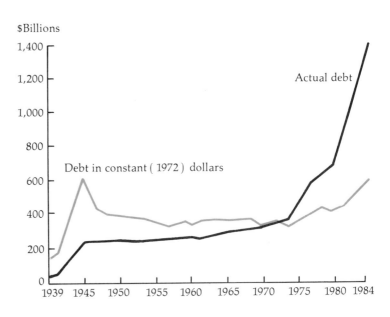

REMEMBERING VIETNAM
When soldiers came home from Vietnam, they received no general homecoming or welcome, no outpouring of support and respect as heroic defenders of freedom abroad. Many returning veterans simply slipped quietly back into the lives they had left behind, with their wounds—both physical and psychic—unhealed. The dedication of the Vietnam Memorial in Washington, D.C., in 1982 marked the beginning of a process of reconciliation that is still going on. (© Peter Marlow, Magnum)

The 1982 recession challenged Reaganomics. Unemployment hit 10.7 percent, its highest level since the depression; black and female workers suffered the most. Due to the severe cutbacks in welfare programs, only 45 percent of those who lost their jobs received unemployment compensation, compared with 75 percent at the height of the harsh 1975 recession. The 1982 recession brought the inflation rate down from its high of 12.4 percent in 1980 to 4 percent. (The decline in worldwide energy costs aided the fight against inflation as well.) The tax cuts enacted in 1981 stimulated spending to bring the economy out of the recession. But politicians and economists still debate whether the economic recovery that began after 1982 resulted from Reagan's supply-side theories.

In one area—deregulation, or removing governmental controls on various facets of economic life—Reagan continued a trend begun during the Carter administration, but with several important differences. Carter focused mainly on regulatory agencies that had been created during the late nineteenth and early twentieth centuries. By the 1970s, he and others argued, such restrictions no longer served their original purposes but instead restricted competition and raised consumer costs. To rectify this situation, Carter had supported the gradual decontrol of oil and natural gas prices as a spur to domestic production and as a way to encourage conservation during the energy crisis. His administration also oversaw the deregulation of the airline, trucking, and railroad industries, as well as approving the phase-out of deposit interest ceiling rates in 1980.

President Reagan chose different targets for his deregulation efforts. His administration focused especially on agencies created during the 1970s, including the Environmental Protection Agency, the Occupational Safety and Health Administration, and the Consumer Product Safety Commission. It moved to abolish or lessen the impact of government regulations in areas such as the environment, the workplace, health care, and consumer protection, claiming that such regulations were not only inefficient but had impeded productivity because of the high cost of compliance. In addition, the Reagan administration used budget and staff cuts to make

THE AFTERMATH OF NUCLEAR WAR

Defense expenditures under Ronald Reagan brought little security from the fear of nuclear war. Jonathan Schell's The Fate of the Earth *(1982) argued that the only guarantee for surviving a nuclear attack was to prevent it from happening.*

Let us consider, for example, some of the possible ways in which a person in a targeted country might die. He might be incinerated by the fireball or the thermal pulse. He might be lethally irradiated by the initial nuclear radiation. He might be crushed to death or hurled to his death by the blast wave or its debris. He might be lethally irradiated by the local fallout. He might be burned to death in a firestorm. He might be injured by one or another of these effects and then die of his wounds before he was able to make his way out of the devastated zone in which he found himself. He might die of starvation, because the economy had collapsed and no food was being grown or delivered, or because existing local crops had been killed by radiation, or because the local ecosystem had been ruined, or because the ecosphere of the earth as a whole was collapsing. He might die of cold, for lack of heat and clothing, or of exposure, for lack of shelter. He might be killed by people seeking food or shelter that he had obtained. He might die of an illness spread in an epidemic. He might be killed by exposure to the sun if he stayed outside too long following serious ozone depletion. Or he might be killed by any combination of these perils. But while there is almost no end to the ways to die in and after a holocaust, each person has only one life to lose: someone who has been killed by the thermal pulse can't be killed again in an epidemic. Therefore, anyone who wishes to describe a holocaust is always at risk of depicting scenes of devastation that in reality would never take place, because the people in them would already have been killed off in some earlier scene of devastation. . . .

In trying to describe possible consequences of a nuclear holocaust, I have mentioned the limitless complexity of its effects on human society and on the ecosphere—a complexity that sometimes seems to be as great as that of life itself. But if these effects should lead to human extinction, then all the complexity will give way to the utmost simplicity—the simplicity of nothingness. We—the human race—shall cease to be.

Source: Jonathan Schell, *The Fate of the Earth.* New York: Knopf, 1982. 24, 95–96.

---

enforcement of existing regulations more difficult. Reagan further lessened the impact of formerly activist regulatory agencies on economic life by choosing appointees who shared his conservative outlook.

In foreign affairs, Reagan did not break as dramatically from postwar traditions as he had in domestic social policy. He argued that national security would be ensured by a stronger American military presence, coupled with cautious but direct action in the world's trouble spots. Reagan's plan to bring peace to the Middle East never got off the ground and was further complicated by the Israeli invasion of Lebanon in 1982. He sent a contingent of U.S. Marines to Lebanon to keep the peace, but 241 American troops were killed in a car bomb explosion in their Beirut barracks in October 1983. The Reagan administration stoutly proclaimed its intention to halt the spread of subversive communism in Central America. The United States supported a repressive right-wing regime in El Salvador in its fight against leftists, sent extensive military and financial aid to the pro-U.S. "contras" who challenged the communist Sandinista government in Nicaragua, and invaded the tiny Caribbean island of Grenada in 1983 to eliminate a Cuban-supported communist regime thought to threaten the other island states of the region. In 1985, Reagan met with the new leader of the Soviet Union, Mikhail S. Gorbachev, in the first summit meeting between the leaders of the world's two most powerful countries since 1979.

After a string of administrations that ended in discord (Johnson and Vietnam), disgrace (Nixon and Watergate), or frustration (Carter and Iran), many Americans responded warmly to Reagan's revival of the presidency as a tool of national leadership. Reagan restored such confidence in the economy and the presidency that when he asked voters during the 1984 campaign, "Are you better off than you were four years ago?", they answered affirmatively and gave him a landslide victory.

The 1984 Democratic challenger, Walter Mondale, symbolized the New Deal coalition. A protégé of Hubert Humphrey, he had strong ties to unions, blacks, and party leaders. He appealed to many women voters with his groundbreaking selection of Representative Geraldine Ferraro of New York as his running mate. But when the 1984 election thus pitted a popular incumbent Republican president against a New Deal liberal,

the contest was not even close. Reagan received 59 percent of the popular vote, carrying the entire country except Minnesota, Mondale's home state, and the District of Columbia. Reagan did especially well among young (eighteen- to twenty-one-year-old) voters, receiving 62 percent of their support.

Reagan's enormous personal popularity recalled Dwight Eisenhower's appeal in the 1950s and gave the Republicans their greatest strength since the 1920s. However, other Republican candidates in 1984 did not run nearly as well as the president, which allowed the Democrats to maintain control of the House and pick up two seats in the Senate.

The unanswered question clouding all

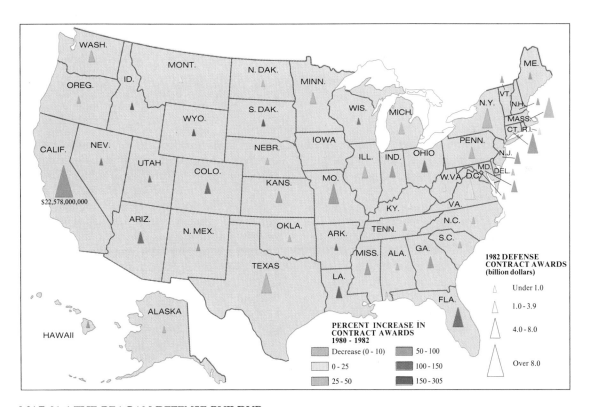

MAP 31.6 THE REAGAN DEFENSE BUILDUP
President Carter began to increase defense spending after its decline in the mid-1970s, but Ronald Reagan increased the buildup dramatically. California continued to be the top recipient of defense dollars. Its $22.5 billion share in 1982 was almost triple the amount received by New York and Texas. High-tech centers such as Connecticut, Massachusetts, and Virginia, as well as states with major defense installations (such as Alaska and Arizona), received defense contracts out of proportion to their population.

TIME LINE
A PROUD BUT TROUBLED PEOPLE

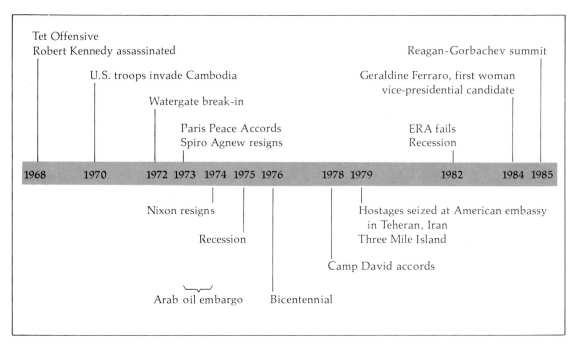

projections for the future was the impact of the increasing federal deficit on politics, government, and the economy. Despite his pledge to balance the budget by 1984, Reagan presided over the largest deficit in American history. From just over $50 billion when he took office in 1981, the deficit rose to an estimated $200 billion annually in 1984. In response, Congress passed the Gramm-Rudman Balanced Budget and Emergency Deficit Reduction Control Act of 1985, which required a balanced budget by 1991. As long as the deficit remained high, budget cutting, not problem solving, would probably assume top priority for the federal government as it approached the twenty-first century.

Despite cries by Ronald Reagan and others for a drastic cut in federal power, such attempts to turn back the clock of history are certain to fail. Perhaps the most far-reaching development of the twentieth century has been the growth of a new bureaucratic order comprised of large-scale national institutions that dominate both public policy and private enterprise. The federal government now plays the predominant role in the nation's economic life, contributing a major share of the nation's gross national product and controlling the growth of the private sector through tax and monetary policies. Although Reagan has changed the priorities of the national government and has attempted to curb its expansion, he has failed to reduce its size or scope. The America of the 1980s and beyond will remain dominated by the modern bureaucratic state.

The year 1968 saw an unprecedented level of domestic unrest, including the assassinations of Martin Luther King, Jr. and Robert F. Kennedy. Richard Nixon was elected president by promising to restore quieter times. However, the nation continued to debate the value of the American involvement in Vietnam, which did not end until the signing of the Paris Peace Accords in January 1973. Meanwhile, the Nixon administration took part in a series of illegal and questionable acts in connection with the president's campaign for reelection in 1972. The resulting Watergate scandal led to Nixon's resignation in 1974.

During the decade after 1974 the United States struggled with economic problems including high inflation, skyrocketing energy costs, and a diminished position in world trade. Many citizens became cynical about national leadership in the wake of Watergate. A new, more conservative social mood limited further progress of the civil rights and women's movements; this mood injected values drawn from evangelical religion into political life. Ronald Reagan capitalized on the changing atmosphere in 1980 by promising a smaller role for the government, a stronger commitment to traditional values, and an end to the burgeoning federal deficit. The one area of the federal budget that continued to grow unabated was defense.

The United States had changed immeasurably from the society it had been in 1900. Longer life spans, a declining birth rate, changing women's roles, greater access to education, and a new diversity in family and living patterns characterized the population. Giant economic and governmental structures further defined the distinctive character of modern American life. On the eve of the twenty-first century, the United States had demonstrably become a modern, post-industrial society.

Suggestions for Further Reading

A Time of Troubles

Two entirely different introductions to the 1968 campaign are provided in Norman Mailer, *Miami and the Siege of Chicago* (1968), and Lewis Chester, Godfrey Hodgson, and Bruce Page, *An American Melodrama* (1970), an account by three British journalists. Kevin Phillips, *The Emerging Republican Majority* (1969), and Richard Scammon and Ben J. Wattenberg, *The Real Majority* (1970), describe the voters whom Richard Nixon tried to reach. See also David Broder, *The Party's Over* (1972); Samuel Lubbell, *The Hidden Crisis in American Politics* (1975), and Frederick G. Dutton, *Changing Sources of Power* (1971). Theodore H. White, *The Making of the President—1972* (1973), covers the Nixon-McGovern contest.

Jonathan Schell, *The Time of Illusion* (1976), offers an insightful discussion of the Nixon administration. It can be supplemented by William Safire, *Before the Fall* (1975); Leonard Silk, *Nixonomics* (1972); and Rowland Evans and Robert Novak, *Nixon in the White House* (1971). Gary Wills, *Nixon Agonistes* (1971), provides a psychological portrait.

Stanley Karnow, *Vietnam: A History* (1983), carries the story through the fall of Saigon in 1975. Tad Szulc, *The Illusion of Peace* (1978), is a general study of the foreign policy of the Nixon administration, while William Shawcross, *Sideshow: Kissinger, Nixon, and the Destruction of Cambodia* (1979), is strongly critical of one aspect. Robert Jay Lifton, *Home from the War* (1973); Paul Starr, *The Discarded Army* (1973); and Lawrence Baskir and William A. Strauss, *Chance and Circumstance* (1978), discuss the problems of returning Vietnam veterans. Ron Kovic, *Born on the Fourth of July* (1976), is a moving personal memoir.

Jonathan Schell's *The Time of Illusion* (1982) links concern over antiwar protest with the Watergate scandal. Anthony Lukas, *Nightmare: The Underside of the Nixon Years* (1976), and Theodore H. White, *Breach of Faith* (1975), are comprehensive accounts. Also of interest are the two books by the *Washington Post* journalists who broke the story, Carl Bernstein and Bob Woodward, *All the President's Men* (1974) and *The Final Days* (1976). John Dean, *Blind Ambition* (1976), is the best account by a participant; see also H. R. Haldeman, *The Ends of Power* (1978), and Richard M. Nixon, *RN: The Memoirs of Richard Nixon* (1978). Richard M. Cohen and Jules Witcover, *A Heartbeat Away* (1974), describes Spiro Agnew's fall from power. Arthur M. Schlesinger, Jr., *The Imperial Presidency* (1973), analyzes changes in the institution that provided a backdrop for the Watergate affair.

Lowered Expectations and New Challenges

Peter Carroll, *It Seemed Like Nothing Happened* (1982), provides a historian's view of the 1970s. General introductions to economic developments of the decade are in Richard J. Barnet and Ronald E. Muller, *Global Reach* (1974); Richard J. Barnet, *The Lean Years* (1980); Robert

Calleo, *The Imperious Economy* (1982); and Gardner Means et al., *The Roots of Inflation* (1975). John M. Blair, *The Control of Oil* (1976), and J. C. Hurewitz, ed., *Oil, the Arab-Israeli Dispute, and the Industrial World* (1976), treat OPEC developments. Barry Commoner, *The Closing Circle* (1971) and *The Poverty of Power* (1976), and Robert Heilbroner, *An Inquiry into the Human Prospect* (1974), cogently assess the origins of the energy crisis and the prospects for the future. See also Lester C. Thurow, *The Zero-Sum Society* (1980), and Robert Stobaugh and Daniel Yergin, *Energy Future* (1980). Influential books in shaping public awareness of ecology included Paul R. Ehrlich, *The Population Bomb* (1968); E. F. Schumacher, *Small Is Beautiful* (1973); Frances Moore Lappe, *Diet for a Small Planet* (1971); and Philip Slater, *Earthwalk* (1974). On the prospects of nuclear annihilation, see Jonathan Schell's powerful *The Fate of the Earth* (1982).

Much of the material on post-Watergate politics has been provided by journalists rather than historians. Richard Reeves, *A Ford, Not a Lincoln* (1975); J. F. ter Horst, *Gerald Ford and the Future of the Presidency* (1974); and John Osborne, *White House Watch: The Ford Years* (1977), cover the Ford presidency. Jules Witcover, *Marathon* (1977), describes the pursuit of the presidency in 1976, while Theodore H. White, *America in Search of Itself* (1982), looks more broadly at the period between 1954 and 1980. Portraits of the Carter presidency, generally unfavorable, are found in Robert Shogan, *Promises to Keep* (1977); Haynes Johnson, *In the Absense of Power* (1980); and Clark Mollenhoff, *The President Who Failed* (1980). James Wooten, *Dasher* (1978), and Betty Glad, *Jimmy Carter: From Plains to the White House* (1980), are competent biographies. See also Jimmy Carter's own campaign manifesto, *Why Not the Best?* (1975). James Fallow, *National Defense* (1981), is an incisive overview of defense developments.

Carroll's *It Seemed Like Nothing Happened* provides a good introduction to the social trends of the 1970s. Stanley Aronowitz, *False Promises* (1973); Richard Krickus, *Pursuing the American Dream* (1976); and Michael Novak, *The Rise of the Unmeltable Ethnics* (1977), describe the concerns of the white ethnic middle-class. Richard P. Adler, *All in the Family* (1979), is an anthol-ogy of the controversy surrounding Archie Bunker. Nathan Glazer, *Affirmative Discrimination: Ethnic Inequality and Public Policy* (1975); Thomas Sowell, *Race and Economics* (1975); and Allan P. Sindler, *Bakke, Defunis, and Minority Admissions* (1978), treat the controversial topic of affirmative action.

Tom Wolfe gave the decade its name in "The Me Decade and the Third Great Awakening," *New York Magazine* (August 23, 1976). Influential books included Christopher Lasch, *The Culture of Narcissism: American Life in an Age of Diminishing Expectations* (1978), and Gail Sheehy, *Passages* (1976). Alan Crawford, *Thunder on the Right* (1980), surveys the new conservatism, as does Peter Steinfels, *The Neo-Conservatives* (1979). John Woodridge, *The Evangelicals* (1975), and Marshall Frady, *Billy Graham* (1979), analyze the rise of evangelical religion; James Reston, Jr., *Our Father Who Art in Hell* (1981), tells the story of Reverend Jim Jones and the Guyana tragedy. Carol Felsenthal's biography of Phyllis Schlafly, *The Sweetheart of the Silent Majority* (1981), shows how the Moral Majority identified feminism as a target.

John L. Palmer and Isabel Sawhill, eds., *The Reagan Record* (1984), offers a comprehensive assessment of Reagan's first term in office. Thomas Byrne Edsall, *The New Politics of Inequality* (1984), analyzes the shift in politics and government from the activism of the Democratic years to the new priorities of the 1970s and 1980s. George Gilder, *Wealth and Poverty* (1981), represents the economic views held by many in the Reagan administration. On Reagan himself, see Bill Boyarsky, *Ronald Reagan: His Life and Rise to the Presidency* (1981).

Two books show that statistics can be fun to read: Andrew Hacker, *U/S: A Statistical Portrait* (1983), and Victor Fuchs, *How We Live* (1983). For material on the changing demographic and social base of the American family, see Christopher Lasch, *Haven in a Heartless World* (1977); Mary Jo Bane, *Here to Stay: American Families in the 20th Century* (1976), and Jane Howard, *Families* (1978). Columnist Ellen Goodman comments on changing American life-styles in *Close to Home* (1979). Betty Friedan, *The Second Stage* (1982), proposes a new phase of feminism that looks back to family values.

Declaration of Independence in Congress, July 4, 1776

*THE UNANIMOUS DECLARATION
OF THE THIRTEEN
UNITED STATES OF AMERICA*

When, in the course of human events, it becomes necessary for one people to dissolve the political bonds which have connected them with another, and to assume, among the powers of the earth, the separate and equal station to which the laws of nature and of nature's God entitle them, a decent respect to the opinions of mankind requires that they should declare the causes which impel them to the separation.

We hold these truths to be self-evident: That all men are created equal; that they are endowed by their Creator with certain unalienable rights; that among these are life, liberty, and the pursuit of happiness; that, to secure these rights, governments are instituted among men, deriving their just powers from the consent of the governed; that whenever any form of government becomes destructive of these ends, it is the right of the people to alter or to abolish it, and to institute new government, laying its foundation on such principles, and organizing its powers in such form, as to them shall seem most likely to effect their safety and happiness. Prudence, indeed, will dictate that governments long established should not be changed for light and transient causes; and accordingly all experience hath shown that mankind are more disposed to suffer, while evils are sufferable, than to right themselves by abolishing the forms to which they are accustomed. But when a long train of abuses and usurpations, pursuing invariably the same object, evinces a design to reduce them under absolute despotism, it is their right, it is their duty, to throw off such government, and to provide new guards for their future security. Such has been the patient sufferance of these colonies; and such is now the necessity which constrains them to alter their former systems of government. The history of the present King of Great Britain is a history of repeated injuries and usurpations, all having in direct object the establishment of an absolute tyranny over these states. To prove this, let facts be submitted to a candid world.

He has refused his assent to laws, the most wholesome and necessary for the public good.

He has forbidden his governors to pass laws of immediate and pressing importance, unless suspended in their operation till his assent should be obtained; and, when so suspended, he has utterly neglected to attend to them.

He has refused to pass other laws for the accommodation of large districts of people, unless those people would relinquish the right of representation in the legislature, a right inestimable to them, and formidable to tyrants only.

He has called together legislative bodies at places unusual, uncomfortable, and distant from the depository of their public records, for the sole purpose of fatiguing them into compliance with his measures.

He has dissolved representative houses repeatedly, for opposing, with manly firmness, his invasions on the rights of the people.

He has refused for a long time, after such dissolutions, to cause others to be elected; whereby the legislative powers, incapable of annihilation, have returned to the people at large for their exercise; the state remaining, in the mean time, exposed to all the dangers of invasions from without and convulsions within.

He has endeavored to prevent the population of these states; for that purpose obstructing the laws for naturalization of foreigners; refusing to pass others to encourage their migration hither, and raising the conditions of new appropriations of lands.

He has obstructed the administration of justice, by refusing his assent to laws for establishing judiciary powers.

He has made judges dependent on his will alone, for the tenure of their offices, and the amount and payment of their salaries.

He has erected a multitude of new offices, and sent hither swarms of officers to harass our people and eat out their substance.

He has kept among us, in times of peace, standing armies, without the consent of our legislatures.

He has affected to render the military independent of, and superior to, the civil power.

He has combined with others to subject us to a jurisdiction foreign to our constitution, and unacknowledged by our laws, giving his assent to their acts of pretended legislation:

For quartering large bodies of armed troops among us;

For protecting them, by a mock trial, from punishment for any murders which they should commit on the inhabitants of these states;

For cutting off our trade with all parts of the world;

For imposing taxes on us without our consent;

I

For depriving us, in many cases, of the benefits of trial by jury;

For transporting us beyond seas, to be tried for pretended offenses;

For abolishing the free system of English laws in a neighboring province, establishing therein an arbitrary government, and enlarging its boundaries, so as to render it at once an example and fit instrument for introducing the same absolute rule into these colonies;

For taking away our charters, abolishing our most valuable laws, and altering fundamentally the forms of our governments.

For suspending our own legislatures, and declaring themselves invested with power to legislate for us in all cases whatsoever.

He has abdicated government here, by declaring us out of his protection and waging war against us.

He has plundered our seas, ravaged our coasts, burned our towns, and destroyed the lives of our people.

He is at this time transporting large armies of foreign mercenaries to complete the works of death, desolation, and tyranny already begun with circumstances of cruelty and perfidy scarcely paralleled in the most barbarous ages, and totally unworthy the head of a civilized nation.

He has constrained our fellow-citizens, taken captive on the high seas, to bear arms against their country, to become the executioners of their friends and brethren, or to fall themselves by their hands.

He has excited domestic insurrection among us, and has endeavored to bring on the inhabitants of our frontiers the merciless Indian savages, whose known rule of warfare is an undistinguished destruction of all ages, sexes, and conditions.

In every stage of these oppressions we have petitioned for redress in the most humble terms; our repeated petitions have been answered only by repeated injury. A prince, whose character is thus marked by every act which may define a tyrant, is unfit to be the ruler of a free people.

Nor have we been wanting in our attentions to our British brethren. We have warned them, from time to time, of attempts by their legislature to extend an unwarrantable jurisdiction over us. We have reminded them of the circumstances of our emigration and settlement here. We have appealed to their native justice and magnanimity; and we have conjured them, by the ties of our common kindred, to disavow these usurpations, which would inevitably interrupt our connections and correspondence. They, too, have been deaf to the voice of justice and of consanguinity. We must, therefore, acquiesce in the necessity which denounces our separation, and hold them, as we hold the rest of mankind, enemies in war, in peace friends.

We, therefore, the representatives of the United States of America, in General Congress assembled, appealing to the Supreme Judge of the world for the rectitude of our intentions, do, in the name and by the authority of the good people of these colonies, solemnly publish and declare, that these United Colonies are, and of right ought to be, FREE AND INDEPENDENT STATES; that they are absolved from all allegiance to the British crown, and that all political connection between them and the state of Great Britain is, and ought to be, totally dissolved; and that, as free and independent states, they have full power to levy war, conclude peace, contract alliances, establish commerce, and do all other acts and things which independent states may of right do. And for the support of this declaration, with a firm reliance on the protection of Divine Providence, we mutually pledge to each other our lives, our fortunes, and our sacred honor.

JOHN HANCOCK

BUTTON GWINNETT
LYMAN HALL
GEO. WALTON
WM. HOOPER
JOSEPH HEWES
JOHN PENN
EDWARD RUTLEDGE
THOS. HEYWARD, JUNR.
THOMAS LYNCH, JUNR.
ARTHUR MIDDLETON
SAMUEL CHASE
WM. PACA
THOS. STONE
CHARLES CARROLL OF CARROLLTON
GEORGE WYTHE
RICHARD HENRY LEE
TH. JEFFERSON
BENJ. HARRISON

THOS. NELSON, JR.
FRANCIS LIGHTFOOT LEE
CARTER BRAXTON
ROBT. MORRIS
BENJAMIN RUSH
BENJA. FRANKLIN
JOHN MORTON
GEO. CLYMER
JAS. SMITH
GEO. TAYLOR
JAMES WILSON
GEO. ROSS
CAESAR RODNEY
GEO. READ
THO. M'KEAN
WM. FLOYD
PHIL. LIVINGSTON
FRANS. LEWIS
LEWIS MORRIS

RICHD. STOCKTON
JNO. WITHERSPOON
FRAS. HOPKINSON
JOHN HART
ABRA. CLARK
JOSIAH BARTLETT
WM. WHIPPLE
SAML. ADAMS
JOHN ADAMS
ROBT. TREAT PAINE
ELBRIDGE GERRY
STEP. HOPKINS
WILLIAM ELLERY
ROGER SHERMAN
SAM'EL. HUNTINGTON
WM. WILLIAMS
OLIVER WOLCOTT
MATTHEW THORNTON

Constitution of the United States of America

PREAMBLE

We the people of the United States, in order to form a more perfect union, establish justice, insure domestic tranquility, provide for the common defense, promote the general welfare, and secure the blessings of liberty to ourselves and our posterity, do ordain and establish this Constitution for the United States of America.

ARTICLE I

Section 1 All legislative powers herein granted shall be vested in a Congress of the United States, which shall consist of a Senate and a House of Representatives.

Section 2 The House of Representatives shall be composed of members chosen every second year by the people of the several States, and the electors in each State shall have the qualifications requisite for electors of the most numerous branch of the State Legislature.

No person shall be a Representative who shall not have attained to the age of twenty-five years, and been seven years a citizen of the United States, and who shall not, when elected, be an inhabitant of that State in which he shall be chosen.

Representatives and direct taxes shall be apportioned among the several States which may be included within this Union, according to their respective numbers, *which shall be determined by adding to the whole number of free persons, including those bound to service for a term of years and excluding Indians not taxed, three-fifths of all other persons.* The actual enumeration shall be made within three years after the first meeting of the Congress of the United States, and within every subsequent term of ten years, in such manner as they shall by law direct. The number of Representatives shall not exceed one for every thirty thousand, but

Note: The Constitution became effective March 4, 1789. Provisions in italic have been changed by constitutional amendment.

each State shall have at least one Representative; *and until such enumeration shall be made, the State of New Hampshire shall be entitled to choose three, Massachusetts eight, Rhode Island and Providence Plantations one, Connecticut five, New York six, New Jersey four, Pennsylvania eight, Delaware one, Maryland six, Virginia ten, North Carolina five, South Carolina five, and Georgia three.*

When vacancies happen in the representation from any State, the Executive authority thereof shall issue writs of election to fill such vacancies.

The House of Representatives shall choose their Speaker and other officers; and shall have the sole power of impeachment.

Section 3 The Senate of the United States shall be composed of two Senators from each State, *chosen by the legislature thereof,* for six years; and each Senator shall have one vote.

Immediately after they shall be assembled in consequence of the first election, they shall be divided as equally as may be into three classes. The seats of the Senators of the first class shall be vacated at the expiration of the second year, of the second class at the expiration of the fourth year, and of the third class at the expiration of the sixth year, so that one-third may be chosen every second year; *and if vacancies happen by resignation or otherwise, during the recess of the legislature of any State, the Executive thereof may make temporary appointments until the next meeting of the legislature, which shall then fill such vacancies.*

No person shall be a Senator who shall not have attained to the age of thirty years, and been nine years a citizen of the United States, and who shall not, when elected, be an inhabitant of that State for which he shall be chosen.

The Vice-President of the United States shall be President of the Senate, but shall have no vote, unless they be equally divided.

The Senate shall choose their other officers, and also a President *pro tempore,* in the absence of the Vice-President, or when he shall exercise the office of President of the United States.

The Senate shall have the sole power to try all impeachments. When sitting for that purpose, they shall be on oath or affirmation. When the President of the

United States is tried, the Chief Justice shall preside; and no person shall be convicted without the concurrence of two-thirds of the members present.

Judgment in cases of impeachment shall not extend further than to removal from the office, and disqualification to hold and enjoy any office of honor, trust or profit under the United States: but the party convicted shall nevertheless be liable and subject to indictment, trial, judgment and punishment, according to law.

Section 4 The times, places and manner of holding elections for Senators and Representatives shall be prescribed in each State by the legislature thereof; but the Congress may at any time by law make or alter such regulations, except as to the places of choosing Senators.

The Congress shall assemble at least once in every year, and such meeting *shall be on the first Monday in December, unless they shall by law appoint a different day.*

Section 5 Each house shall be the judge of the elections, returns and qualifications of its own members, and a majority of each shall constitute a quorum to do business; but a smaller number may adjourn from day to day, and may be authorized to compel the attendance of absent members, in such manner, and under such penalties, as each house may provide.

Each house may determine the rules of its proceedings, punish its members for disorderly behavior, and with the concurrence of two-thirds, expel a member.

Each house shall keep a journal of its proceedings, and from time to time publish the same, excepting such parts as may in their judgment require secrecy; and the yeas and nays of the members of either house on any question shall, at the desire of one-fifth of those present, be entered on the journal.

Neither house, during the session of Congress, shall, without the consent of the other, adjourn for more than three days, nor to any other place than that in which the two houses shall be sitting.

Section 6 The Senators and Representatives shall receive a compensation for their services, to be ascertained by law and paid out of the treasury of the United States. They shall in all cases except treason, felony and breach of the peace be privileged from arrest during their attendance at the session of their respective houses, and in going to and returning from the same; and for any speech or debate in either house, they shall not be questioned in any other place.

No Senator or Representative shall, during the time for which he was elected, be appointed to any civil office under the authority of the United States, which shall have been created, or the emoluments whereof shall have been increased, during such time; and no person holding any office under the United States shall be a member of either house during his continuance in office.

Section 7 All bills for raising revenue shall originate in the House of Representatives; but the Senate may propose or concur with amendments as on other bills.

Every bill which shall have passed the House of Representatives and the Senate, shall, before it becomes a law, be presented to the President of the United States; if he approve he shall sign it, but if not he shall return it with objections to that house in which it originated, who shall enter the objections at large on their journal, and proceed to reconsider it. If after such reconsideration two-thirds of that house shall agree to pass the bill, it shall be sent, together with the objections, to the other house, by which it shall likewise be reconsidered, and, if approved by two-thirds of that house, it shall become a law. But in all such cases the votes of both houses shall be determined by yeas and nays, and the names of the persons voting for and against the bill shall be entered on the journal of each house respectively. If any bill shall not be returned by the President within ten days (Sundays excepted) after it shall have been presented to him, the same shall be a law, in like manner as if he had signed it, unless the Congress by their adjournment prevent its return, in which case it shall not be a law.

Every order, resolution, or vote to which the concurrence of the Senate and House of Representatives may be necessary (except on a question of adjournment) shall be presented to the President of the United States; and before the same shall take effect, shall be approved by him, or being disapproved by him, shall be repassed by two-thirds of the Senate and House of Representatives, according to the rules and limitations prescribed in the case of a bill.

Section 8 The Congress shall have power:

To lay and collect taxes, duties, imposts, and excises, to pay the debts and provide for the common defense and general welfare of the United States; but all duties, imposts and excises shall be uniform throughout the United States;

To borrow money on the credit of the United States;

To regulate commerce with foreign nations, and among the several States, and with the Indian tribes;

To establish an uniform rule of naturalization, and uniform laws on the subject of bankruptcies throughout the United States;

To coin money, regulate the value thereof, and of foreign coin, and fix the standard of weights and measures;

To provide for the punishment of counterfeiting the securities and current coin of the United States;

To establish post offices and post roads;

To promote the progress of science and useful arts by securing for limited times to authors and inventors the exclusive right to their respective writings and discoveries;

To constitute tribunals inferior to the Supreme Court;

To define and punish piracies and felonies committed on the high seas and offenses against the law of nations;

To declare war, grant letters of marque and reprisal, and make rules concerning captures on land and water;

To raise and support armies, but no appropriation of money to that use shall be for a longer term than two years;

To provide and maintain a navy;

To make rules for the government and regulation of the land and naval forces;

To provide for calling forth the militia to execute the laws of the Union, suppress insurrections, and repel invasions;

To provide for organizing, arming, and disciplining the militia, and for governing such part of them as may be employed in the service of the United States, reserving to the States respectively the appointment of the officers, and the authority of training the militia according to the discipline prescribed by Congress;

To exercise exclusive legislation in all cases whatsoever, over such district (not exceeding ten miles square) as may, by cession of particular States, and the acceptance of Congress, become the seat of government of the United States, and to exercise like authority over all places purchased by the consent of the legislature of the State, in which the same shall be, for erection of forts, magazines, arsenals, dockyards, and other needful buildings;—and

To make all laws which shall be necessary and proper for carrying into execution the foregoing powers; and all other powers vested by this Constitution in the government of the United States, or in any department or officer thereof.

Section 9 *The migration or importation of such persons as any of the States now existing shall think proper to admit shall not be prohibited by the Congress prior to the year 1808; but a tax or duty may be imposed on such importation, not exceeding $10 for each person.*

The privilege of the writ of habeas corpus shall not be suspended, unless when in cases of rebellion or invasion the public safety may require it.

No bill of attainder or ex post facto law shall be passed.

No capitation or other direct tax shall be laid, unless in proportion to the census or enumeration herein before directed to be taken.

No tax or duty shall be laid on articles exported from any State.

No preference shall be given by any regulation of commerce or revenue to the ports of one State over those of another; nor shall vessels bound to, or from, one State be obliged to enter, clear, or pay duties in another.

No money shall be drawn from the treasury, but in consequence of appropriations made by law; and a regular statement and account of the receipts and expenditures of all public money shall be published from time to time.

No title of nobility shall be granted by the United States: and no person holding any office of profit or trust under them, shall, without the consent of the Congress, accept of any present, emolument, office, or title, of any kind whatever, from any king, prince, or foreign state.

Section 10 No State shall enter into any treaty, alliance, or confederation; grant letters of marque and reprisal; coin money; emit bills of credit; make anything but gold and silver coin a tender in payment of debts; pass any bill of attainder, ex post facto law, or law impairing the obligation of contracts, or grant any title of nobility.

No States shall, without the consent of Congress, lay any imposts or duties on imports or exports, except what may be absolutely necessary for executing its inspection laws: and the net produce of all duties and imposts, laid by any State on imports or exports, shall be for the use of the treasury of the United States; and all such laws shall be subject to the revision and control of the Congress.

No State shall, without the consent of Congress, lay any duty of tonnage, keep troops or ships of war in time of peace, enter into any agreement or compact with another State, or with a foreign power, or engage in war, unless actually invaded, or in such imminent danger as will not admit of delay.

ARTICLE II

Section 1 The executive power shall be vested in a President of the United States of America. He shall hold his office during the term of four years, and, together with the Vice-President, chosen for the same term, be elected as follows:

Each State shall appoint, in such manner as the legislature thereof may direct, a number of electors, equal to the whole number of Senators and Representatives to which the State may be entitled in the Congress; but no Senator or Representative, or person holding an office of trust or profit under the United States, shall be appointed an elector.

The electors shall meet in their respective States, and vote by ballot for two persons, of whom one at least shall not be an inhabitant of the same State with themselves. And they shall make a list of all the persons voted for, and of the number of votes for each; which list they shall sign and certify, and transmit sealed to the seat of government of the United States, directed to the President of the Senate. The President of the Senate shall, in the presence of the Senate and House of Representatives, open all the certificates, and the votes shall then be counted. The person having the greatest number of votes shall be the President, if such number be a majority of the whole number of electors appointed; and if there be more than one who have such majority, and have an equal number of votes, then the House of Representatives shall immediately choose by ballot one of them for President; and if no person have a majority, then from the five highest on the list said house shall in like manner choose the President. But in choosing the President the votes shall be taken by States, the representation from each State having one vote; a quorum for this purpose shall consist of a member or members from two-thirds of the States, and a majority of all the States shall be necessary to a choice. In every case, after the choice of the President, the person having the greatest number of votes of the electors shall be the Vice-President. But if there should remain two or more who have equal votes, the Senate shall choose from them by ballot the Vice-President.

The Congress may determine the time of choosing the electors and the day on which they shall give their votes; which day shall be the same throughout the United States.

No person except a natural-born citizen, *or a citizen of the United States at the time of the adoption of this constitution,* shall be eligible to the office of President; neither shall any person be eligible to that office who shall not have attained to the age of thirty-five years, and been fourteen years a resident within the United States.

In case of the removal of the President from office or of his death, resignation, or inability to discharge the powers and duties of the said office, the same shall devolve on the Vice-President, and the Congress may by law provide for the case of removal, death, resignation, or inability, both of the President and Vice-President, declaring what officer shall then act as President, and such officer shall act accordingly, until the disability be removed, or a President shall be elected.

The President shall, at stated times, receive for his services a compensation, which shall neither be increased nor diminished during the period for which he shall have been elected, and he shall not receive within that period any other emolument from the United States, or any of them.

Before he enter on the execution of his office, he shall take the following oath or affirmation:—"I do solemnly swear (or affirm) that I will faithfully execute the office of the President of the United States, and will to the best of my ability preserve, protect and defend the Constitution of the United States."

Section 2   The President shall be commander in chief of the army and navy of the United States, and of the militia of the several States, when called into the actual service of the United States; he may require the opinion, in writing, of the principal officer in each of the executive departments, upon any subject relating to the duties of their respective offices, and he shall have power to grant reprieves and pardons for offenses against the United States, except in cases of impeachment.

He shall have power, by and with the advice and consent of the Senate, to make treaties, provided two-thirds of the Senators present concur; and he shall nominate, and by and with the advice and consent of the Senate, shall appoint ambassadors, other public ministers and consuls, judges of the Supreme Court, and all other officers of the United States, whose appointments are not herein otherwise provided for, and which shall be established by law; but Congress may by law vest the appointment of such inferior officers, as they think proper, in the President alone, in the courts of law, or in the heads of departments.

The President shall have power to fill up all vacancies that may happen during the recess of the Senate, by granting commissions which shall expire at the end of their next session.

Section 3   He shall from time to time give to the Congress information of the state of the Union, and recommend to their consideration such measures as he shall judge necessary and expedient; he may, on extraordinary occasions, convene both houses, or either of them, and in case of disagreement between them, with respect to the time of adjournment, he may adjourn them to such time as he shall think proper; he shall receive ambassadors and other public ministers; he shall take care that the laws be faithfully executed, and shall commission all the officers of the United States.

Section 4   The President, Vice-President and all civil officers of the United States shall be removed from office on impeachment for, and on conviction of, treason, bribery, or other high crimes and misdemeanors.

ARTICLE III

Section 1   The judicial power of the United States shall be vested in one Supreme Court, and in such inferior courts as the Congress may from time to time ordain and establish. The judges, both of the Supreme and inferior courts, shall hold their offices during good behavior, and shall, at stated times, receive for their services a compensation which shall not be diminished during their continuance in office.

Section 2 The judicial power shall extend to all cases, in law and equity, arising under this Constitution, the laws of the United States, and treaties made, or which shall be made, under their authority—to all cases affecting ambassadors, other public ministers and consuls;—to all cases of admiralty and maritime jurisdiction;—to controversies to which the United States shall be a party;—to controversies between two or more States;—*between a State and citizens of another State*;—between citizens of different States;—between citizens of the same State claiming lands under grants of different States, and between a State, or the citizens thereof, and foreign states, citizens or subjects.

In all cases affecting ambassadors, other public ministers and consuls, and those in which a State shall be party, the Supreme Court shall have original jurisdiction. In all the other cases before mentioned, the Supreme Court shall have appellate jurisdiction, both as to law and fact, with such exceptions, and under such regulations, as the Congress shall make.

The trial of all crimes, except in cases of impeachment, shall be by jury; and such trial shall be held in the State where said crimes shall have been committed; but when not committed within any State, the trial shall be at such place or places as the Congress may by law have directed.

Section 3 Treason against the United States shall consist only in levying war against them, or in adhering to their enemies, giving them aid and comfort. No person shall be convicted of treason unless on the testimony of two witnesses to the same overt act, or on confession in open court.

The Congress shall have power to declare the punishment of treason, but no attainder of treason shall work corruption of blood, or forfeiture except during the life of the person attainted.

ARTICLE IV

Section 1 Full faith and credit shall be given in each State to the public acts, records, and judicial proceedings of every other State. And the Congress may by general laws prescribe the manner in which such acts, records, and proceedings shall be proved, and the effect thereof.

Section 2 The citizens of each State shall be entitled to all privileges and immunities of citizens in the several states.

A person charged in any State with treason, felony, or other crime, who shall flee from justice, and be found in another State, shall on demand of the executive authority of the State from which he fled, be delivered up, to be removed to the State having jurisdiction of the crime.

No person held to service or labor in one State, under the laws thereof, escaping into another, shall, in consequence of any law or regulation therein, be discharged from such service or labor, but shall be delivered up on claim of the party to whom such service or labor may be due.

Section 3 New States may be admitted by the Congress into this Union; but no new State shall be formed or erected within the jurisdiction of any other State; nor any State be formed by the junction of two or more States, or parts of States, without the consent of the legislatures of the States concerned as well as of the Congress.

The Congress shall have power to dispose of and make all needful rules and regulations respecting the territory or other property belonging to the United States; and nothing in this Constitution shall be so construed as to prejudice any claims of the United States, or any particular State.

Section 4 The United States shall guarantee to every State in this Union a republican form of government, and shall protect each of them against invasion; and on application of the legislature, or of the executive (when the legislature cannot be convened), against domestic violence.

ARTICLE V

The Congress, whenever two-thirds of both houses shall deem it necessary, shall propose amendments to this Constitution, or, on the application of the legislatures of two-thirds of the several States, shall call a convention for proposing amendments, which, in either case, shall be valid to all intents and purposes, as part of this Constitution, when ratified by the legislatures of three-fourths of the several States, or by conventions in three-fourths thereof, as the one or the other mode of ratification may be proposed by the Congress; provided *that no amendments which may be made prior to the year one thousand eight hundred and eight shall in any manner affect the first and fourth classes in the ninth section of the first article; and* that no State, without its consent, shall be deprived of its equal suffrage in the Senate.

ARTICLE VI

All debts contracted and engagements entered into, before the adoption of this Constitution, shall be as valid against the United States under this Constitution, as under the Confederation.

This Constitution, and the laws of the United States which shall be made in pursuance thereof; and all treaties made, or which shall be made, under the authority of the United States, shall be the supreme law of the land; and the judges in every State shall be bound thereby, anything in the Constitution or laws of any State to the contrary notwithstanding.

The Senators and Representatives before mentioned, and the members of the several State legislatures, and all executive and judicial officers, both of the United States and of the several States, shall be bound by oath or affirmation to support this Constitution; but no religious test shall ever be required as a qualification to any office or public trust under the United States.

ARTICLE VII

The ratification of the conventions of nine States shall be sufficient for the establishment of this Constitution between the States so ratifying the same.

Done in Convention by the unanimous consent of the States present, the seventeenth day of September in the year of our Lord one thousand seven hundred and eighty-seven and of the Independence of the United States of America the twelfth. In witness whereof we have hereunto subscribed our names.

GEORGE WASHINGTON
President and Deputy from Virginia

New Hampshire
JOHN LANGDON
NICHOLAS GILMAN

Massachusetts
NATHANIEL GORHAM
RUFUS KING

Connecticut
WILLIAM S. JOHNSON
ROGER SHERMAN

New York
ALEXANDER HAMILTON

New Jersey
WILLIAM LIVINGSTON
DAVID BREARLEY
WILLIAM PATERSON
JONATHAN DAYTON

Pennsylvania
BENJAMIN FRANKLIN
THOMAS MIFFLIN
ROBERT MORRIS
GEORGE CLYMER
THOMAS FITZSIMONS
JARED INGERSOLL
JAMES WILSON
GOUVERNEUR MORRIS

Delaware
GEORGE READ
GUNNING BEDFORD, JR.
JOHN DICKINSON
RICHARD BASSETT
JACOB BROOM

Maryland
JAMES MCHENRY
DANIEL OF ST. THOMAS JENIFER
DANIEL CARROLL

Virginia
JOHN BLAIR
JAMES MADISON, JR.

North Carolina
WILLIAM BLOUNT
RICHARD DOBBS SPAIGHT
HU WILLIAMSON

South Carolina
J. RUTLEDGE
CHARLES C. PINCKNEY
PIERCE BUTLER

Georgia
WILLIAM FEW
ABRAHAM BALDWIN

Amendments to the Constitution

AMENDMENT I [1791]

Congress shall make no law respecting an establishment of religion, or prohibiting the free exercise thereof; or abridging the freedom of speech, or of the press; or the right of the people peaceably to assemble, and to petition the government for a redress of grievances.

AMENDMENT II [1791]

A well-regulated militia being necessary to the security of a free State, the right of the people to keep and bear arms shall not be infringed.

AMENDMENT III [1791]

No soldier shall, in time of peace, be quartered in any house without the consent of the owner, nor in time of war, but in a manner to be prescribed by law.

AMENDMENT IV [1791]

The right of the people to be secure in their persons, houses, papers, and effects, against unreasonable searches and seizures, shall not be violated, and no warrants shall issue but upon probable cause, supported by oath or affirmation, and particularly describing the place to be searched, and the persons or things to be seized.

AMENDMENT V [1791]

No person shall be held to answer for a capital or otherwise infamous crime, unless on a presentment or indictment of a grand jury, except in cases arising in the land or naval forces, or in the militia, when in actual service in time of war or public danger; nor shall any person be subject for the same offense to be twice put in jeopardy of life or limb; nor shall be compelled in any criminal case to be a witness against himself, nor be deprived of life, liberty, or property, without due process of law; nor shall private property be taken for public use without just compensation.

AMENDMENT VI [1791]

In all criminal prosecutions, the accused shall enjoy the right to a speedy and public trial, by an impartial jury of the State and district wherein the crime shall have been committed, which district shall have been previously ascertained by law, and to be informed of the nature and cause of the accusation; to be confronted with the witnesses against him; to have compulsory process for obtaining witnesses in his favor, and to have the assistance of counsel for his defense.

AMENDMENT VII [1791]

In suits at common law, where the value in controversy shall exceed twenty dollars, the right of trial by jury shall be preserved, and no fact tried by a jury shall be otherwise reexamined in any court of the United States, than according to the rules of the common law.

AMENDMENT VIII [1791]

Excessive bail shall not be required, nor excessive fines imposed, nor cruel and unusual punishments inflicted.

AMENDMENT IX [1791]

The enumeration in the Constitution, of certain rights, shall not be construed to deny or disparage others retained by the people.

AMENDMENT X [1791]

The powers not delegated to the United States by the Constitution, nor prohibited by it to the States, are reserved to the States respectively, or to the people.

Note: The first ten Amendments are known as the Bill of Rights.

AMENDMENT XI [1798]

The judicial power of the United States shall not be construed to extend to any suit in law or equity, commenced or prosecuted against one of the United States by citizens of another State, or by citizens or subjects of any foreign state.

AMENDMENT XII [1804]

The electors shall meet in their respective States, and vote by ballot for President and Vice-President, one of whom, at least, shall not be an inhabitant of the same State with themselves; they shall name in their ballots the person voted for as President, and in distinct ballots the person voted for as Vice-President, and they shall make distinct lists of all persons voted for as President, and of all persons voted for as Vice-President, and of the number of votes for each, which lists they shall sign and certify, and transmit sealed to the seat of government of the United States, directed to the President of the Senate;—the President of the Senate shall, in the presence of the Senate and House of Representatives, open all the certificates and the votes shall then be counted;—the person having the greatest number of votes for President shall be the President, if such number be a majority of the whole number of electors appointed; and if no person have such majority, then from the persons having the highest numbers not exceeding three on the list of those voted for as President, the House of Representatives shall choose immediately, by ballot, the President. But in choosing the President, the votes shall be taken by States, the representation from each State having one vote; a quorum for this purpose shall consist of a member or members from two-thirds of the States, and a majority of all the States shall be necessary to a choice. And if the House of Representatives shall not choose a President whenever the right of choice shall devolve upon them, before *the fourth day of March* next following, then the Vice-President shall act as President, as in the case of the death or other constitutional disability of the President.

The person having the greatest number of votes as Vice-President shall be the Vice-President, if such number be a majority of the whole number of electors appointed; and if no person have a majority, then from the two highest numbers on the list the Senate shall choose the Vice-President; a quorum for the purpose shall consist of two-thirds of the whole number of Senators, and a majority of the whole number shall be necessary to a choice. But no person constitutionally ineligible to the office of President shall be eligible to that of Vice-President of the United States.

AMENDMENT XIII [1865]

Section 1 Neither slavery nor involuntary servitude, except as a punishment for crime whereof the party shall have been duly convicted, shall exist within the United States, or any place subject to their jurisdiction.

Section 2 Congress shall have power to enforce this article by appropriate legislation.

AMENDMENT XIV [1868]

Section 1 All persons born or naturalized in the United States, and subject to the jurisdiction thereof, are citizens of the United States and of the State wherein they reside. No State shall make or enforce any law which shall abridge the privileges or immunities of citizens of the United States; nor shall any State deprive any person of life, liberty, or property, without due process of law; nor deny to any person within its jurisdiction the equal protection of the laws.

Section 2 Representatives shall be apportioned among the several States according to their respective numbers, counting the whole number of persons in each State, excluding Indians not taxed. But when the right to vote at any election for the choice of Electors for President and Vice-President of the United States, Representatives in Congress, the executive and judicial officers of a State, or the members of the legislature thereof, is denied to any of the male inhabitants of such State, being twenty-one years of age and citizens of the United States, or in any way abridged, except for participation in rebellion, or other crime, the basis of representation therein shall be reduced in the proportion which the number of such male citizens shall bear to the whole number of male citizens twenty-one years of age in such State.

Section 3 No person shall be a Senator or Representative in Congress, or Elector of President and Vice-President, or hold any office, civil or military, under the United States, or under any State, who, having previously taken an oath, as a member of Congress, or as an officer of the United States, or as a member of any State legislature, or as an executive or judicial officer of any State, to support the Constitution of the United States, shall have engaged in insurrection or rebellion against the same, or given aid or comfort to the enemies thereof. Congress may by a vote of two-thirds of each house, remove such disability.

Section 4 The validity of the public debt of the United States, authorized by law, including debts incurred for payment of pensions and bounties for services in suppressing insurrection or rebellion, shall not be questioned. But neither the United States nor any State shall assume or pay any debt or obligation incurred in aid of insurrection or rebellion against the United States, or any claim for the loss of emancipation of any slave; but all such debts, obligations, and claims shall be held illegal and void.

Section 5   The Congress shall have power to enforce, by appropriate legislation, the provisions of this article.

AMENDMENT XV [1870]

Section 1   The right of citizens of the United States to vote shall not be denied or abridged by the United States or by any State on account of race, color, or previous condition of servitude.

Section 2   The Congress shall have power to enforce this article by appropriate legislation.

AMENDMENT XVI [1913]

The Congress shall have power to lay and collect taxes on incomes, from whatever source derived, without apportionment among the several States, and without regard to any census or enumeraion.

AMENDMENT XVII [1913]

Section 1   The Senate of the United States shall be composed of two Senators from each State, elected by the people thereof, for six years; and each Senator shall have one vote. The electors in each State shall have the qualifications requisite for electors of [voters for] the most numerous branch of the State legislatures.

Section 2   When vacancies happen in the representation of any State in the Senate, the executive authority of such State shall issue writs of election to fill such vacancies: Provided that the legislature of any State may empower the executive thereof to make temporary appointments until the people fill the vacancies by election as the legislature may direct.

Section 3   This amendment shall not be so construed as to affect the election or term of any Senator chosen before it becomes valid as part of the Constitution.

AMENDMENT XVIII [1919]

Section 1   After one year from the ratification of this article the manufacture, sale, or transportation of intoxicating liquors within, the importation thereof into, or the exportation thereof from the United States and all territory subject to the jurisdiction thereof, for beverage purposes, is hereby prohibited.

Section 2   The Congress and the several States shall have concurrent power to enforce this article by appropriate legislation.

Section 3   This article shall be inoperative unless it shall have been ratified as an amendment to the Constitution by the legislatures of the several States, as provided by the Constitution, within seven years from the date of the submission thereof to the States by the Congress.

AMENDMENT XIX [1920]

Section 1   The right of citizens of the United States to vote shall not be denied or abridged by the United States or by any State on account of sex.

Section 2   The Congress shall have power to enforce this article by appropriate legislation.

AMENDMENT XX [1933]

Section 1   The terms of the President and Vice-President shall end at noon on the 20th day of January, and the terms of Senators and Representatives at noon on the 3d day of January, of the years in which such terms would have ended if this article had not been ratified; and the terms of their successors shall then begin.

Section 2   The Congress shall assemble at least once in every year, and such meeting shall begin at noon on the 3d day of January, unless they shall by law appoint a different day.

Section 3   If, at the time fixed for the beginning of the term of the President, the President-elect shall have died, the Vice-President-elect shall become President. If a President shall not have been chosen before the time fixed for the beginning of his term, or if the President-elect shall have failed to qualify, then the President-elect shall act as President until a President shall have qualified; and the Congress may by law provide for the case wherein neither a President-elect nor a Vice-President-elect shall have qualified, declaring who shall then act as President, or the manner in which one who is to act shall be selected, and such persons shall act accordingly until a President or Vice-President shall have qualified.

Section 4 The Congress may by law provide for the case of the death of any of the persons from whom the House of Representatives may choose a President whenever the right of choice shall have devolved upon them, and for the case of the death of any of the persons from whom the Senate may choose a Vice-President whenever the right of choice shall have devolved upon them.

Section 5 Sections 1 and 2 shall take effect on the 15th day of October following the ratification of this article.

Section 6 This article shall be inoperative unless it shall have been ratified as an amendment to the Constitution by the legislatures of three-fourths of the several States within seven years from the date of its submission.

AMENDMENT XXI [1933]

Section 1 The eighteenth article of amendment to the Constitution of the United States is hereby repealed.

Section 2 The transportation or importation into any State, Territory, or Possession of the United States for delivery or use therein of intoxicating liquors, in violation of the laws thereof, is hereby prohibited.

Section 3 This article shall be inoperative unless it shall have been ratified as an amendment to the Constitution by conventions in the several States, as provided in the Constitution, within seven years from the date of submission thereof to the States by the Congress.

AMENDMENT XXII [1951]

Section 1 No person shall be elected to the office of President more than twice, and no person who has held the office of President, or acted as President, for more than two years of a term to which some other person was elected President shall be elected to the office of President more than once. But this article shall not apply to any person holding the office of President when this article was proposed by the Congress, and shall not prevent any person who may be holding the office of President, or acting as President, during the term within which this article becomes operative from holding the office of President or acting as President during the remainder of such term.

Section 2 This article shall be inoperative unless it shall have been ratified as an amendment to the Constitution by the legislatures of three-fourths of the several States within seven years from the date of its submission to the States by the Congress.

AMENDMENT XXIII [1961]

Section 1 The District constituting the seat of Government of the United States shall appoint in such manner as the Congress may direct:

A number of electors of President and Vice-President equal to the whole number of Senators and Representatives in Congress to which the District would be entitled if it were a State, but in no event more than the least populous State; they shall be in addition to those appointed by the States, but they shall be considered for the purposes of the election of President and Vice-President, to be electors appointed by a State; and they shall meet in the District and perform such duties as provided by the twelfth article of amendment.

Section 2 The Congress shall have the power to enforce this article by appropriate legislation.

AMENDMENT XXIV [1964]

Section 1 The right of citizens of the United States to vote in any primary or other election for President or Vice-President, for electors for President or Vice-President, or for Senator or Representative in Congress, shall not be denied or abridged by the United States or any State by reason of failure to pay any poll tax or other tax.

Section 2 The Congress shall have the power to enforce this article by appropriate legislation.

AMENDMENT XXV [1967]

Section 1 In case of the removal of the President from office or of his death or resignation, the Vice-President shall become President.

Section 2 Whenever there is a vacancy in the office of the Vice-President, the President shall nominate a Vice-President who shall take office upon confirmation by a majority vote of both houses of Congress.

Section 3 Whenever the President transmits to the President pro tempore of the Senate and the Speaker of the House of Representatives his written declaration that he is unable to discharge the powers and duties of his office, and until he transmits to them a written declaration to the contrary, such powers and duties shall be discharged by the Vice-President as Acting President.

Section 4   Whenever the Vice-President and a majority of either the principal officers of the executive departments or of such other body as Congress may by law provide, transmit to the President pro tempore of the Senate and the Speaker of the House of Representatives their written declaration that the President is unable to discharge the powers and duties of his office, the Vice-President shall immediately assume the powers and duties of the office as Acting President.

Thereafter, when the President transmits to the President pro tempore of the Senate and the Speaker of the House of Representatives his written declaration that no inability exists, he shall resume the powers and duties of his office unless the Vice-President and a majority of either the principal officers of the executive departments[s] or of such other body as Congress may by law provide, transmit within four days to the President pro tempore of the Senate and the Speaker of the House of Representatives their written declaration that

the President is unable to discharge the powers and duties of his office. Thereupon Congress shall decide the issue, assembling within forty-eight hours for that purpose if not in session. If the Congress, within twenty-one days after receipt of the latter written declaration, or, if Congress is not in session, within twenty-one days after Congress is required to assemble, determines by two-thirds vote of both Houses that the President is unable to discharge the powers and duties of his office, the Vice-President shall continue to discharge the same as Acting President; otherwise, the President shall resume the powers and duties of his office.

AMENDMENT XXVI [1971]

Section 1   The right of citizens of the United States, who are eighteen years of age or older, to vote shall not be denied or abridged by the United States or by any State on account of age.

Section 2   The Congress shall have power to enforce this article by appropriate legislation.

Presidential Elections

Year	Candidates	Parties	Percent of Popular Vote	Electoral Vote	Percent Voter Participation
1789	GEORGE WASHINGTON	No party designations	*	69	
	John Adams†			34	
	Other candidates			35	
1792	GEORGE WASHINGTON	No party designations		132	
	John Adams			77	
	George Clinton			50	
	Other candidates			5	
1796	JOHN ADAMS	Federalist		71	
	Thomas Jefferson	Democratic-Republican		68	
	Thomas Pinckney	Federalist		59	
	Aaron Burr	Democratic-Republican		30	
	Other candidates			48	
1800	THOMAS JEFFERSON	Democratic-Republican		73	
	Aaron Burr	Democratic-Republican		73	
	John Adams	Federalist		65	
	Charles C. Pinckney	Federalist		64	
	John Jay	Federalist		1	
1804	THOMAS JEFFERSON	Democratic-Republican		162	
	Charles C. Pinckney	Federalist		14	
1808	JAMES MADISON	Democratic-Republican		122	
	Charles C. Pinckney	Federalist		47	
	George Clinton	Democratic-Republican		6	
1812	JAMES MADISON	Democratic-Republican		128	
	DeWitt Clinton	Federalist		89	
1816	JAMES MONROE	Democratic-Republican		183	
	Rufus King	Federalist		34	
1820	JAMES MONROE	Democratic-Republican		231	
	John Quincy Adams	Independent Republican		1	
1824	JOHN QUINCY ADAMS	Democratic-Republican	30.5	84	26.9
	Andrew Jackson	Democratic-Republican	43.1	99	
	Henry Clay	Democratic-Republican	13.2	37	
	William H. Crawford	Democratic-Republican	13.1	41	

*Prior to 1824, most presidential electors were chosen by state legislators rather than by popular vote.
†Before the Twelfth Amendment was passed in 1804, the electoral college voted for two presidential candidates; the runner-up became the vice-president.

Year	Candidates	Parties	Percent of Popular Vote	Electoral Vote	Percent Voter Participation
1828	ANDREW JACKSON	Democratic	56.0	178	57.6
	John Quincy Adams	National Republican	44.0	83	
1832	ANDREW JACKSON	Democratic	54.5	219	55.4
	Henry Clay	National Republican	37.5	49	
	William Wirt	Anti-Masonic	8.0	7	
	John Floyd	Democratic	‡	11	
1836	MARTIN VAN BUREN	Democratic	50.9	170	57.8
	William H. Harrison	Whig		73	
	Hugh L. White	Whig	49.1	26	
	Daniel Webster	Whig		14	
	W. P. Mangum	Whig		11	
1840	WILLIAM H. HARRISON	Whig	53.1	234	80.2
	Martin Van Buren	Democratic	46.9	60	
1844	JAMES K. POLK	Democratic	49.6	170	78.9
	Henry Clay	Whig	48.1	105	
	James G. Birney	Liberty	2.3		
1848	ZACHARY TAYLOR	Whig	47.4	163	72.7
	Lewis Cass	Democratic	42.5	127	
	Martin Van Buren	Free Soil	10.1		
1852	FRANKLIN PIERCE	Democratic	50.9	254	69.6
	Winfield Scott	Whig	44.1	42	
	John P. Hale	Free Soil	5.0		
1856	JAMES BUCHANAN	Democratic	45.3	174	78.9
	John C. Frémont	Republican	33.1	114	
	Millard Fillmore	American	21.6	8	
1860	ABRAHAM LINCOLN	Republican	39.8	180	81.2
	Stephen A. Douglas	Democratic	29.5	12	
	John C. Breckinridge	Democratic	18.1	72	
	John Bell	Constitutional Union	12.6	39	
1864	ABRAHAM LINCOLN	Republican	55.0	212	73.8
	George B. McClellan	Democratic	45.0	21	
1868	ULYSSES S. GRANT	Republican	52.7	214	78.1
	Horatio Seymour	Democratic	47.3	80	
1872	ULYSSES S. GRANT	Republican	55.6	286	71.3
	Horace Greeley	Democratic	43.9		
1876	RUTHERFORD B. HAYES	Republican	48.0	185	81.8
	Samuel J. Tilden	Democratic	51.0	184	
1880	JAMES A. GARFIELD	Republican	48.5	214	79.4
	Winfield S. Hancock	Democratic	48.1	155	
	James B. Weaver	Greenback-Labor	3.4		
1884	GROVER CLEVELAND	Democratic	48.5	219	77.5
	James G. Blaine	Republican	48.2	182	
1888	BENJAMIN HARRISON	Republican	47.9	233	79.3
	Grover Cleveland	Democratic	48.6	168	

‡Candidates receiving less than 2.5 percent of the popular vote have been omitted. Hence the percentage of popular vote may not total 100 percent.

Year	Candidates	Parties	Percent of Popular Vote	Electoral Vote	Percent Voter Participation
1892	GROVER CLEVELAND	Democratic	46.1	277	74.7
	Benjamin Harrison	Republican	43.0	145	
	James B. Weaver	People's	8.5	22	
1896	WILLIAM McKINLEY	Republican	51.1	271	79.3
	William J. Bryan	Democratic	47.7	176	
1900	WILLIAM McKINLEY	Republican	51.7	292	73.2
	William J. Bryan	Democratic; Populist	45.5	155	
1904	THEODORE ROOSEVELT	Republican	57.4	336	65.2
	Alton B. Parker	Democratic	37.6	140	
	Eugene V. Debs	Socialist	3.0		
1908	WILLIAM H. TAFT	Republican	51.6	321	65.4
	William J. Bryan	Democratic	43.1	162	
	Eugene V. Debs	Socialist	2.8		
1912	WOODROW WILSON	Democratic	41.9	435	58.8
	Theodore Roosevelt	Progressive	27.4	88	
	William H. Taft	Republican	23.2	8	
	Eugene V. Debs	Socialist	6.0		
1916	WOODROW WILSON	Democratic	49.4	277	61.6
	Charles E. Hughes	Republican	46.2	254	
	A. L. Benson	Socialist	3.2		
1920	WARREN G. HARDING	Republican	60.4	404	49.2
	James M. Cox	Democratic	34.2	127	
	Eugene V. Debs	Socialist	3.4		
1924	CALVIN COOLIDGE	Republican	54.0	382	48.9
	John W. Davis	Democratic	28.8	136	
	Robert M. LaFollette	Progressive	16.6	13	
1928	HERBERT C. HOOVER	Republican	58.2	444	56.9
	Alfred E. Smith	Democratic	40.9	87	
1932	FRANKLIN D. ROOSEVELT	Democratic	57.4	472	56.9
	Herbert C. Hoover	Republican	39.7	59	
1936	FRANKLIN D. ROOSEVELT	Democratic	60.8	523	61.0
	Alfred M. Landon	Republican	36.5	8	
1940	FRANKLIN D. ROOSEVELT	Democratic	54.8	449	62.5
	Wendell L. Willkie	Republican	44.8	82	
1944	FRANKLIN D. ROOSEVELT	Democratic	53.5	432	55.9
	Thomas E. Dewey	Republican	46.0	99	
1948	HARRY S TRUMAN	Democratic	49.6	303	53.0
	Thomas E. Dewey	Republican	45.1	189	
1952	DWIGHT D. EISENHOWER	Republican	55.1	442	63.3
	Adlai E. Stevenson	Democratic	44.4	89	
1956	DWIGHT D. EISENHOWER	Republican	57.6	457	60.6
	Adlai E. Stevenson	Democratic	42.1	73	
1960	JOHN F. KENNEDY	Democratic	49.7	303	64.0
	Richard M. Nixon	Republican	49.5	219	
1964	LYNDON B. JOHNSON	Democratic	61.1	486	61.7
	Barry M. Goldwater	Republican	38.5	52	

Year	Candidates	Parties	Percent of Popular Vote	Electoral Vote	Percent Voter Participation
1968	RICHARD M. NIXON	Republican	43.4	301	60.6
	Hubert H. Humphrey	Democratic	42.7	191	
	George C. Wallace	American Independent	13.5	46	
1972	RICHARD M. NIXON	Republican	60.7	520	55.5
	George S. McGovern	Democratic	37.5	17	
1976	JIMMY CARTER	Democratic	50.1	297	54.3
	Gerald R. Ford	Republican	48.0	240	
1980	RONALD REAGAN	Republican	50.7	489	53.0
	Jimmy Carter	Democratic	41.0	49	
	John B. Anderson	Independent	6.6	0	
1984	RONALD REAGAN	Republican	58.4	525	52.9
	Walter F. Mondale	Democratic	41.6	13	

Admission of States into the Union

State	Date of Admission	State	Date of Admission
1. Delaware	December 7, 1787	26. Michigan	January 26, 1837
2. Pennsylvania	December 12, 1787	27. Florida	March 3, 1845
3. New Jersey	December 18, 1787	28. Texas	December 29, 1845
4. Georgia	January 2, 1788	29. Iowa	December 28, 1846
5. Connecticut	January 9, 1788	30. Wisconsin	May 29, 1848
6. Massachusetts	February 6, 1788	31. California	September 9, 1850
7. Maryland	April 28, 1788	32. Minnesota	May 11, 1858
8. South Carolina	May 23, 1788	33. Oregon	February 14, 1859
9. New Hampshire	June 21, 1788	34. Kansas	January 29, 1861
10. Virginia	June 25, 1788	35. West Virginia	June 20, 1863
11. New York	July 26, 1788	36. Nevada	October 31, 1864
12. North Carolina	November 21, 1789	37. Nebraska	March 1, 1867
13. Rhode Island	May 29, 1790	38. Colorado	August 1, 1876
14. Vermont	March 4, 1791	39. North Dakota	November 2, 1889
15. Kentucky	June 1, 1792	40. South Dakota	November 2, 1889
16. Tennessee	June 1, 1796	41. Montana	November 8, 1889
17. Ohio	March 1, 1803	42. Washington	November 11, 1889
18. Louisiana	April 30, 1812	43. Idaho	July 3, 1890
19. Indiana	December 11, 1816	44. Wyoming	July 10, 1890
20. Mississippi	December 10, 1817	45. Utah	January 4, 1896
21. Illinois	December 3, 1818	46. Oklahoma	November 16, 1907
22. Alabama	December 14, 1819	47. New Mexico	January 6, 1912
23. Maine	March 15, 1820	48. Arizona	February 14, 1912
24. Missouri	August 10, 1821	49. Alaska	January 3, 1959
25. Arkansas	June 15, 1836	50. Hawaii	August 21, 1959

Supreme Court Justices

Name	Terms of Service	Appointed by	Name	Terms of Service	Appointed by
John Jay*, N.Y.	1789–1795	Washington	Joseph P. Bradley, N.J.	1870–1892	Grant
James Wilson, Pa.	1789–1798	Washington	Ward Hunt, N.Y.	1873–1882	Grant
John Rutledge, S.C.	1790–1791	Washington	**Morrison R. Waite,** Ohio	1874–1888	Grant
William Cushing, Mass.	1790–1810	Washington	John M. Harlan, Ky.	1877–1911	Hayes
John Blair, Va.	1790–1796	Washington	William B. Woods, Ga.	1881–1887	Hayes
James Iredell, N.C.	1790–1799	Washington	Stanley Matthews, Ohio	1881–1889	Garfield
Thomas Johnson, Md.	1792–1793	Washington	Horace Gray, Mass.	1882–1902	Arthur
William Paterson, N.J.	1793–1806	Washington	Samuel Blatchford, N.Y.	1882–1893	Arthur
John Rutledge, S.C.	1795	Washington	Lucius Q. C. Lamar, Miss.	1888–1893	Cleveland
Samuel Chase, Md.	1796–1811	Washington	**Melville W. Fuller,** Ill.	1888–1910	Cleveland
Oliver Ellsworth, Conn.	1796–1800	Washington	David J. Brewer, Kan.	1890–1910	B. Harrison
Bushrod Washington, Va.	1799–1829	J. Adams	Henry B. Brown, Mich.	1891–1906	B. Harrison
Alfred Moore, N.C.	1800–1804	J. Adams	George Shiras, Jr., Pa.	1892–1903	B. Harrison
John Marshall, Va.	1801–1835	J. Adams	Howell E. Jackson, Tenn.	1893–1895	B. Harrison
William Johnson, S.C.	1804–1834	Jefferson	Edward D. White, La.	1894–1910	Cleveland
Brockholst Livingston, N.Y.	1807–1823	Jefferson	Rufus W. Peckham, N.Y.	1896–1909	Cleveland
Thomas Todd, Ky.	1807–1826	Jefferson	Joseph McKenna, Cal.	1898–1925	McKinley
Gabriel Duvall, Md.	1811–1835	Madison	Oliver W. Holmes, Mass.	1902–1932	T. Roosevelt
Joseph Story, Mass.	1812–1845	Madison	William R. Day, Ohio	1903–1922	T. Roosevelt
Smith Thompson, N.Y.	1823–1843	Monroe	William H. Moody, Mass.	1906–1910	T. Roosevelt
Robert Trimble, Ky.	1826–1828	J. Q. Adams	Horace H. Lurton, Tenn.	1910–1914	Taft
John McLean, Ohio	1830–1861	Jackson	Charles E. Hughes, N.Y.	1910–1916	Taft
Henry Baldwin, Pa.	1830–1844	Jackson	Willis Van Devanter, Wy	1911–1937	Taft
James M. Wayne, Ga.	1835–1867	Jackson	Joseph R. Lamar, Ga.	1911–1916	Taft
Roger B. Taney, Md.	1836–1864	Jackson	**Edward D. White,** La.	1910–1921	Taft
Philip P. Barbour, Va.	1836–1841	Jackson	Mahlon Pitney, N.J.	1912–1922	Taft
John Cartron, Tenn.	1837–1865	Van Buren	James C. McReynolds, Tenn.	1914–1941	Wilson
John McKinley, Ala.	1838–1852	Van Buren	Louis D. Brandeis, Mass.	1916–1939	Wilson
Peter V. Daniel, Va.	1842–1860	Van Buren	John H. Clarke, Ohio	1916–1922	Wilson
Samuel Nelson, N.Y.	1845–1872	Tyler	**William H. Taft,** Conn.	1921–1930	Harding
Levi Woodbury, N.H.	1845–1851	Polk	George Sutherland, Utah	1922–1938	Harding
Robert C. Grier, Pa.	1846–1870	Polk	Pierce Butler, Minn.	1923–1939	Harding
Benjamin R. Curtis, Mass.	1851–1857	Fillmore	Edward T. Sanford, Tenn.	1923–1930	Harding
John A. Campbell, Ala.	1853–1861	Pierce	Harlan F. Stone, N.Y.	1925–1941	Coolidge
Nathan Clifford, Me.	1858–1881	Buchanan	**Charles E. Hughes,** N.Y.	1930–1941	Hoover
Noah H. Swayne, Ohio	1862–1881	Lincoln	Owen J. Roberts, Penn.	1930–1945	Hoover
Samuel F. Miller, Iowa	1862–1890	Lincoln	Benjamin N. Cardozo, N.Y.	1932–1938	Hoover
David Davis, Ill.	1862–1877	Lincoln	Hugo L. Black, Ala.	1937–1971	F. Roosevelt
Stephen J. Field, Cal.	1863–1897	Lincoln	Stanley F. Reed, Ky.	1938–1957	F. Roosevelt
Salmon P. Chase, Ohio	1864–1873	Lincoln	Felix Frankfurter, Mass.	1939–1962	F. Roosevelt
William Strong, Pa.	1870–1880	Grant	William O. Douglas, Conn.	1939–1975	F. Roosevelt

*Chief Justices in bold type

Name	Terms of Service	Appointed by	Name	Terms of Service	Appointed by
Frank Murphy, Mich.	1940–1949	F. Roosevelt	Charles E. Whittaker, Mo.	1957–1962	Eisenhower
Harlan F. Stone, N.Y.	1941–1946	F. Roosevelt	Potter Stewart, Ohio	1958–1981	Eisenhower
James F. Byrnes, S.C.	1941–1942	F. Roosevelt	Byron R. White, Colo.	1962–	Kennedy
Robert H. Jackson, N.Y.	1941–1954	F. Roosevelt	Arthur J. Goldberg, Ill.	1962–1965	Kennedy
Wiley B. Rutledge, Iowa	1943–1949	F. Roosevelt	Abe Fortas, Tenn.	1965–1970	Johnson
Harold H. Burton, Ohio	1945–1958	Truman	Thurgood Marshall, Md.	1967–	Johnson
Frederick M. Vinson, Ky.	1946–1953	Truman	**Warren E. Burger,** Va.	1969–	Nixon
Tom C. Clark, Texas	1949–1967	Truman	Harry A. Blackmun, Minn.	1970–	Nixon
Sherman Minton, Ind.	1949–1956	Truman	Lewis F. Powell, Jr., Va.	1971–	Nixon
Earl Warren, Cal.	1953–1969	Eisenhower	William H. Rehnquist, Ariz.	1971–	Nixon
John Marshall Harlan, N.Y.	1955–1971	Eisenhower	John Paul Stevens, Ill.	1975–	Ford
William J. Brennan, Jr., N.J.	1956–	Eisenhower	Sandra Day O'Connor, Ariz.	1981–	Reagan

A Demographic Profile of the American People

	Life Expectancy from Birth		Average Age at First Marriage		Number of Children Under 5 (per 1,000 Women Aged 20–44)	Percent of Women in Paid Employment	Percent of Paid Workers Who Are Female
Year	White	Black	Male	Female			
Industrializing America							
1820					1,295	6.2%	·7.3%
1830					1,145	6.4	7.4
1840					1,085	8.4	9.6
1850					923	10.1	10.8
1860					929	9.7	10.2
1870					839	13.7	14.8
1880					822	14.7	15.2
1890			26.1	22.0	716	18.2	17.0
1900	47.6	33.0	25.9	21.9	688	21.2	18.1
1910	50.3	35.6	25.1	21.6	643	24.8	20.0
Modern America							
1920	54.9	45.3	24.6	21.2	604	23.9%	20.4%
1930	61.4	48.1	24.3	21.3	511	24.4	21.9
1940	64.2	53.1	24.3	21.5	429	25.4	24.6
1950	69.1	60.8	22.8	20.3	589	29.1·	27.8
1960	70.6	63.6	22.8	20.3	737	34.8	32.3
1970	71.7	65.3	22.5	20.6	530	42.6	36.7
1980	74.4	69.8	23.6	21.8	440	51.1	42.6

SOURCE: *Historical Statistics of the United States, Colonial Times to 1970 (1975).*

American Population

Year	Population	Percent Increase	Year	Population	Percent Increase
Preindustrial America			**Industrializing America**		
1610	350	—	1820	9,638,453	33.1
1620	2,300	557.1	1830	12,866,020	33.5
1630	4,600	100.0	1840	17,069,453	32.7
1640	26,600	478.3	1850	23,191,876	35.9
1650	50,400	90.8	1860	31,443,321	35.6
1660	75,100	49.0	1870	39,818,449	26.6
1670	111,900	49.0	1880	50,155,783	26.0
1680	151,500	35.4	1890	62,947,714	25.5
1690	210,400	38.9	1900	75,994,575	20.7
1700	250,900	19.2	1910	91,972,266	21.0
1710	331,700	32.2			
1720	466,200	40.5			
1730	629,400	35.0	**Modern America**		
1740	905,600	43.9	1920	105,710,620	14.9
1750	1,170,800	29.3	1930	122,775,046	16.1
1760	1,593,600	36.1	1940	131,669,275	7.2
1770	2,148,100	34.8	1950	150,697,361	14.5
1780	2,780,400	29.4	1960	179,323,175	19.0
1790	3,929,214	41.3	1970	203,235,298	13.3
1800	5,308,483	35.1	1980	226,545,805	11.5
1810	7,239,881	36.4	1985	237,839,000	—*

*Percent increase is not calculated until the next census in 1990.
SOURCE: *Historical Statistics of the United States, Colonial Times to 1970* (1975).

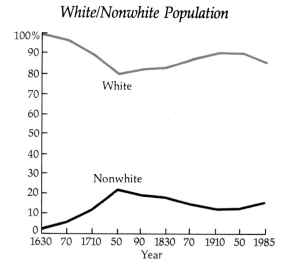

White/Nonwhite Population

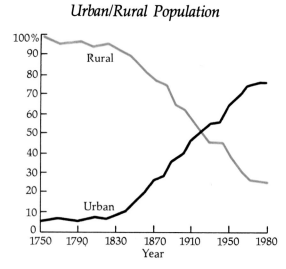

Urban/Rural Population

Foreign Origins of the American People

Immigration by Decade

Year	Industrializing America Number	Percent of Total Population	Year	Modern America Number	Percent of Total Population
1820–1830	151,824	1.6	1921–1930	4,107,209	3.9
1831–1840	599,125	4.6	1931–1940	528,431	0.4
1841–1850	1,713,251	10.0	1941–1950	1,035,039	0.7
1851–1860	2,598,214	11.2	1951–1960	2,515,479	1.6
1861–1870	2,314,824	7.4	1961–1970	3,321,677	1.8
1871–1880	2,812,191	7.1	1971–1980	4,493,000	2.2
1881–1890	5,246,613	10.5	Total	16,000,835	
1891–1900	3,687,546	5.8			
1901–1910	8,795,386	11.6			
1911–1920	5,735,811	6.2			
Total	33,654,785			**1820–1980 Grand total 49,655,620**	

SOURCE: U.S. Bureau of the Census, *Historical Statistics of the United States, Colonial Times to 1970* (1975), Part I, pp. 105–106; U.S. Bureau of the Census, *Statistical Abstract of the United States, 1984* (1983), p. 88.

Regional Origins of Immigrants

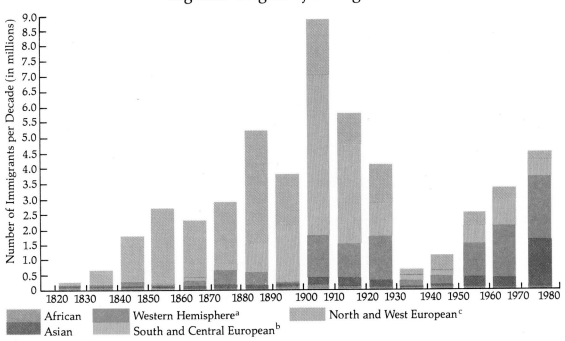

African — Western Hemisphere[a] — North and West European[c]
Asian — South and Central European[b]

[a]Canada and all countries in South America and Central America.
[b]Italy, Spain, Portugal, Greece, Germany (Austria included, 1938–1945), Poland, Czechoslovakia (since 1920), Yugoslavia (since 1920), Hungary (since 1861), Austria (since 1861, except 1938–1945), U.S.S.R. (excludes Asian U.S.S.R. between 1931 and 1963), Latvia, Estonia, Lithuania, Finland, Romania, Bulgaria, Turkey (in Europe), and other European countries not classified elsewhere.
[c]Great Britain, Ireland, Norway, Sweden, Denmark, Iceland, Netherlands, Belgium, Luxembourg, Switzerland, France.
SOURCE: Stephan Thernstrom, ed., *Harvard Encyclopedia of American Ethnic Groups* (1980), p. 480; and U.S. Bureau of the Census, *Statistical Abstract of the United States, 1984* (1983), p. 9.

The Aging of the U.S. Population

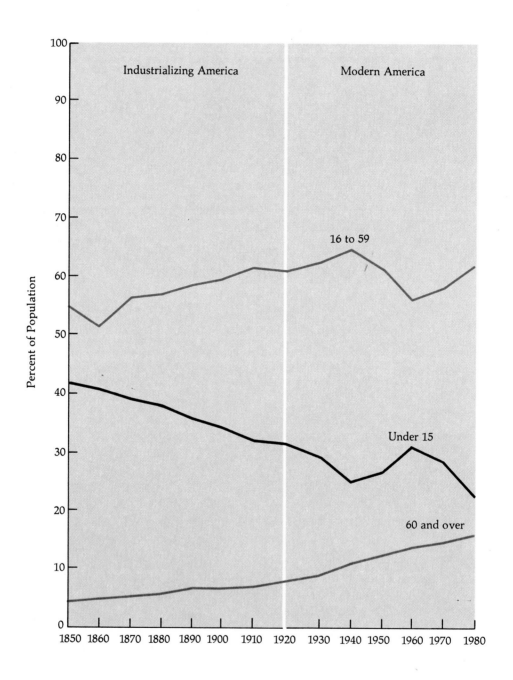

The Labor Force

(thousands of workers)

Year	Agriculture	Mining	Manufacturing	Construction	Trade	Other Services	Total
1810	1,956	11	75	—	—	—	2,330
1840	3,594	32	500	290	350	894	5,660
1850	4,520	102	1,200	410	530	1,488	8,250
1860	5,880	176	1,530	520	890	2,114	11,110
1870	6,790	180	2,470	780	1,310	1,400	12,930
1880	8,920	280	3,290	900	1,930	2,050	17,390
1890	9,960	440	4,390	1,510	2,960	4,060	23,320
1900	11,680	637	5,895	1,665	3,970	5,223	29,070
1910	11,770	1,068	8,332	1,949	5,320	9,041	37,480
1920	10,790	1,180	11,190	1,233	5,845	11,372	41,610
1930	10,560	1,009	9,884	1,988	8,122	17,767	48,830
1940	9,575	925	11,309	1,876	9,328	23,277	56,290
1950	7,870	901	15,648	3,029	12,152	25,870	65,470
1960	5,970	709	17,145	3,640	14,051	37,918	74,060
1970	3,419	664	19,741	4,261	15,234	36,431	79,750

SOURCE: Stanley Lebergott, "Labor Force and Employment, 1800–1960," *Output, Employment, and Productivity in the United States After 1800* (New York: National Bureau of Economic Research, 1966): 118–119. U.S. Bureau of Economic Analysis, *Long-Term Economic Growth, 1860–1970* (Washington, D.C., 1973): 260–263.

Changing Labor Patterns

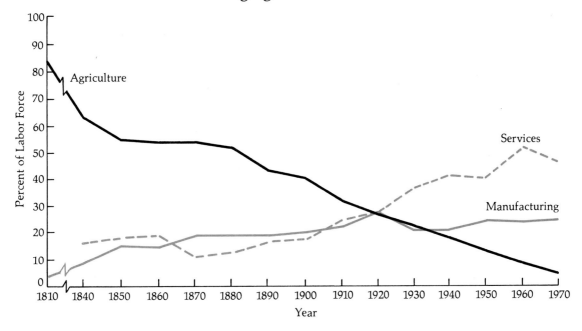

The Growth of the Federal Government

The Federal Government, 1900–1980

EMPLOYEES (millions)				RECEIPTS AND OUTLAYS ($ millions)		
Year	Civilian	Military		Year	Receipts	Outlays
1900	0.23	0.12		1900	567	521
1910	0.38	0.13		1910	676	694
1920	0.65	0.34		1920	6,649	6,358
1930	0.61	0.25		1930	4,058	3,320
1940	1.04	0.45		1940	6,900	9,600
1950	1.96	1.46		1950	40,900	43,100
1960	2.38	2.47		1960	92,500	92,200
1970	2.98	3.06		1970	193,700	196,600
1980	2.87	2.05		1980	520,100	579,600

SOURCE: *Statistical Profile of the United States, 1900–1980.*

Total Federal Debt 1900–1990

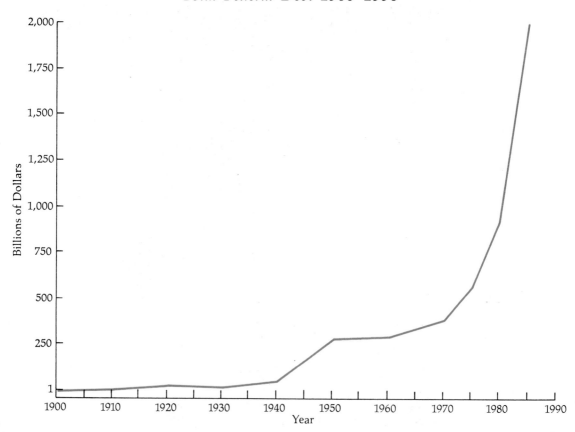

INDEX

Page references to illustrations, maps, and their captions appear in *italics*.

About the Authors

JAMES A. HENRETTA is Priscilla Alden Burke Professor of American History at the University of Maryland, College Park. He received his undergraduate education at Swarthmore College and his Ph.D. from Harvard University. Henretta has taught at the University of Sussex, England; Princeton University; UCLA; Boston University; and, as a Fulbright lecturer, in Australia at the University of New England. His publications include *The Evolution of American Society, 1700–1815: An Interdisciplinary Analysis; "Salutary Neglect": Colonial Administration Under the Duke of Newcastle;* and important articles in early American and social history. His present research is in the fields of legal and political history, on a project entitled *Law and the Creation of the Liberal State in America, 1770–1860.*

W. ELLIOT BROWNLEE is Professor of History and Chair of the Department of History at the University of California, Santa Barbara. He is a graduate of Harvard University, received his Ph.D. from the University of Wisconsin, and specializes in U.S. economic history. He has been awarded fellowships by the Haynes Foundation and the Charles Warren Center, Harvard University. He has been a visiting professor at Princeton University. His published works include *Progressivism and Economic Growth: The Wisconsin Income Tax, 1911–1929; Women in the American Economy: A Documentary History, 1675 to 1929; The Essentials of American History* (with R. N. Current, T. H. Williams, and F. Freidel; and *Dynamics of Ascent: A History of the American Economy.* He is currently at work on a history of taxation, *Taxation and Social Choice in America.*

DAVID BRODY is Professor of History at the University of California, Davis. He has taught overseas at the University of Warwick in England, at Moscow State University in the Soviet Union, and at Sydney University in Australia. He is the author of *Steelworkers in America, Labor in Crisis,* and, most recently, *Workers in Industrial America: Essays on the 20th Century Struggle.* He also serves on the editorial board of *Labor History,* as an editor for a series in American working-class history for the University of Illinois Press, and as a chief historical consultant for a series of television dramas about the history of American workers.

SUSAN WARE specializes in twentieth century U.S. history and the history of American women. She received her undergraduate degree from Wellesley College and her Ph.D. from Harvard University. Ware is the author of *Beyond Suffrage: Women in the New Deal; Holding Their Own: American Women in the 1930s,* and the forthcoming *Partner and I: The Public and Private Worlds of Molly Dewson.* She is Assistant Professor in the Department of History at New York University. Previously affiliated with Harvard University, the University of New Hampshire, and Tufts University, she has received grants from the Radcliffe Research Scholars Program and the American Council of Learned Societies. Her current projects include a women's history anthology from 1880 to the present and a collective biography of six prominent women in twentieth century American life.

A Note on the Type

The text of this book was set in 10½/12 Palatino using a film version of the face designed by Hermann Zapf, which was first released in 1950 by Germany's Stempel Foundry. The face is named after Giovanni Battista Palatino, a famous penman of the sixteenth century. In its calligraphic quality, Palatino is reminiscent of the Italian Renaissance type designs, yet with its wide, open letters and unique proportions it still retains a modern feel. Palatino is considered one of the most important typefaces from one of Europe's most influential type designers.

Interior design by Lucy Lesiak Design, Chicago.

Composition by P&M Typesetting, Inc., Waterbury, Connecticut.

Printed and bound by W. A. Krueger Company, New Berlin, Wisconsin.